成都风物诗记

（中英文版）

POETIC CHRONICLES OF CHENGDU: TIMES AND LEGACY

(CHINESE-ENGLISH VERSION)

何大江　著
Written by He Dajiang

黄　文　杨　彤　译
Translated by Huang Wen & Yang Tong

中国财经出版传媒集团
中国财政经济出版社
·北 京·

图书在版编目（CIP）数据

成都风物诗记：汉、英 / 何大江著；黄文，杨彤译. -- 北京：中国财政经济出版社，2025.7. --（“向古人学生活·中国传统文化中的美学”系列丛书）.

ISBN 978-7-5223-3919-1

Ⅰ. K297.11

中国国家版本馆CIP数据核字第2025UQ1447号

责任编辑：潘　飞　　　　责任校对：胡永立

策划编辑：潘　飞　　　　责任印制：史大鹏

成都风物诗记（中英文版）

CHENGDU FENGWU SHIJI（ZHONGYINGWENBAN）

中国财政经济出版社 出版

URL：http：//www.cfeph.cn

E-mail：cfeph@cfeph.cn

社址：北京市海淀区阜成路甲28号　邮政编码：100142

营销中心电话：010-88191522

天猫网店：中国财政经济出版社旗舰店

网址：https：//zgczjjcbs.tmall.com

涿州汇美亿浓印刷有限公司印刷　各地新华书店经销

成品尺寸：170mm×240mm　16开　33.5印张　368 000字

2025年7月第1版　2025年7月河北第1次印刷

定价：128.00元

ISBN 978-7-5223-3919-1

（图书出现印装问题，本社负责调换，电话：010-88190548）

本社图书质量投诉电话：010-88190744

打击盗版举报热线：010-88191661　QQ：2242791300

前言
PREFACE

历史的诗意

我对地方史的兴趣自清末、民国老照片始，从而大量接触关于成都民俗、历史的文献。沉浸于史料之中，我开始感受到，那些文物与古迹，那些纸上的一行行字，其实承载着前人的情绪与欲望，充满挣扎、博弈与选择，以及随之而来的被称作命运的那种东西。而历史之所以让人感觉像一件泛白的长衫，多半由于我们只把目光聚焦在长时段结构或所谓趋势上，而忽视了对于个体感受的关注。

观察历史，时常需要广角镜与显微镜并用。这本书里，我选择了二十件文物或古迹，由切片深入肌理，再于纵与横两个维度上展开视线，以管窥豹，从一粒沙观察整个世界。比如在第一卷，通过石笋、青铜大立人、三星堆金杖、望丛祠、武担山等文物

The Poetics of History

My interest in local history began with old photographs from the late Qing Dynasty and the Republican era, which led me to explore a wealth of literature on Chengdu's folklore and historical narratives. Immersed in these historical materials, I gradually sensed that cultural relics, ancient sites, and even the faint lines of text on yellowed pages hold within them the emotions and desires of those who came before us—struggles, negotiations, choices, and the mysterious force of what we call "fate". History often feels like a faded long robe, not because it lacks color, but because we tend to focus only on grand structures or so-called "trends" across epochs, while the immediacy of individual lives dissolves into silence.

To observe history, one must often employ both a wide-angle lens and a microscope. In this book, I have selected twenty cultural relics or historical sites, dissecting their intricate textures to reveal hidden narratives before expanding my perspective both vertically and horizontally—glimpsing the whole through the part, observing the world through a grain of sand. For instance, in Volume One, artifacts and sites such as the Stone Stalagmites, the Bronze Giant

或古迹，实际上串起了古蜀国起源、发展、消亡的整个过程。

在数年的写作时间里，除了埋首于故纸堆，推敲、辨析、苦思；也行走于田野乡间，在历史洪流的遗迹上跟时空对话。然而，并非仅仅要完成一部风物记，我是想要写出繁华与落寞，写出王朝的宿命、人与人相通的悲欢，以及于文明的景行行止。

古诗如药引。每一篇都选择了一首诗歌放在文首。这不仅因为诗可以补史之阙，不仅因为“以诗证史”是治学方法之一，更因为以诗之飘逸，或能为沉甸甸的历史抹上一笔轻灵的色彩。

我的两位大学同窗黄文、杨彤，将书译成了英文，希望让不同文化背景下的读者也能感受到这片土地所蕴含的历史的诗意。

何大江

2025年3月23日

Standing Figure, the Gold Scepter of Sanxingdui, the Wang Cong Shrine, and Wudan Mountain collectively trace the entire trajectory of the ancient Shu Kingdom: its origins, development, and eventual decline.

Over the years I spent writing, I buried myself in ancient texts, scrutinizing, analyzing, and pondering—meanwhile, I also wandered through fields and countryside, engaging in a dialogue with time and space amidst the remnants of history's vast currents. Yet, my goal was not merely to compile a record of cultural artifacts. I sought to capture the interplay of splendor and desolation, to write about the fated cycles of dynasties, the shared joys and sorrows of humanity, and the timeless homage to civilization's grandeur.

Each chapter of this book begins with a poem, like a catalyst that awakens history's essence. This approach stems not only from poetry's power to mend gaps in historical records, nor merely because "using poetry to illuminate history" is a recognized scholarly method, but more profoundly because poetry, with its ethereal grace, lends a delicate brushstroke to the weighty canvas of history.

Two of my university classmates, Mr. Huang Wen and Mr. Yang Tong, have translated this book into English—an endeavor to illuminate the poetic resonance of this land's layered history for readers navigating diverse cultural horizons.

He Dajiang

March 23, 2025

目录
CONTENTS

第一卷

Volume 1

石笋
Stone Stalagmites

两株细长的柱状石，一南一北立在唐代碧鸡坊石笋街的街口。北边那株5米出头，直径近1米；南边那株高约4米，直径1.2米。这两株石笋，像科幻电影中的BDO（巨大沉默物体）一样，带给杜甫巨大的震撼。

Two slender pillar-like stones, one sitting to the south and the other to the north, stand at the intersection of Shisun Street, Biji Neighborhood in the Tang Dynasty. The northern stalagmite is over 5 meters tall with a diameter of nearly 1 meter, while the southern one is about 4 meters tall with a diameter of 1.2 meters. These two stone stalagmites, like BDOs（Big Dumb Objects）from science fiction movies, bring immense shock to Du Fu, the poet.

石笋：由此门潜入古蜀秘境
Stone stalagmites: the Entry into the Secret Realm of Ancient Shu

石笋行

唐·杜甫

君不见益州城西门，
陌上石笋双高蹲。
古来相传是海眼，
苔藓蚀尽波涛痕。

An Ode to Stalagmites

Du Fu, Tang Dynasty

By the western gate of Chengdu City they stand,
Tall stalagmites, like guardians in these land.
Legends whisper, they plug up the sea's eyes,
Now weathered and worn, with moss as

雨多往往得瑟瑟，
此事恍惚难明论。
恐是昔时卿相墓，
立石为表今仍存。
惜哉俗态好蒙蔽，
亦如小臣媚至尊。
政化错迕失大体，
坐看倾危受厚恩。
嗟尔石笋擅虚名，
后来未识犹骏奔。
安得壮士掷天外，
使人不疑见本根。

disguise.

In the rain beads shimmer, a misty claim,
Bluish and green, giving way to scepticism.
Perhaps tombs of nobles, voices from the past,
Marked by these stones, a reminder that will last.
Oh, how the commoners are easily deceived,
Seeking favor, as courtiers, in a court depraved.
Mismanagement and mistakes, leading the state astray,
Witnessing impending danger, yet they still sway.
Oh, these stone stalagmites, usurping a hollow name,
Obscure to later comers, scrambling and vying for favoritism.
If only a brave soul could hurl it to the ether,
Unveiling the true essence, erasing all leisure.

在一个号称“未来已来”的时代，设想一下：走在成都闹市街头，突然迎头碰上一根巨大的石柱，它就像溶洞里的石笋。你还必须得抬头仰望，它有两层楼那么高。近处还有一根，略矮，但是更粗壮。因为完全被青苔覆盖，两根石柱倒比喀斯特溶洞里的石笋更像笋子，如果剥开青苔，还能看到地质纪年的痕迹。就叫它们石笋肯定没错，其实它们倒更像是《阿凡达》里哈利路亚山变成的微缩景观。

石笋是细长的柱状石，两株一南一北立在唐代的石笋街街口。北边那株更高，5米出头，直径约95

In an era proclaimed as “the future has arrived”, imagine this: Walking through the bustling streets of Chengdu, suddenly you bump into a gigantic stone pillar, reminiscent of a stalagmite in a cave. You have to tilt your head back to gaze upon its towering presence, reaching heights of two stories. Nearby, there is another pillar, slightly shorter but more robust. Covered entirely in moss, these two pillars resemble bamboo shoots even more than stalagmites in a karst cave. If the moss were peeled away, you could perhaps glimpse geological imprints of ages past. Let’s call them stone stalagmites, though they resemble miniaturized landscapes transformed from the Hallelujah Mountains in *Avatar*.

These two slender columnar stones stand guarding the entrance of the Shisun (stalagmite) Street with the taller one to the north, reaching over 5 meters in height with a diameter of about 95 centimeters, and the other to the south, standing around 4.1 meters tall with a diameter of about 1.2 meters, appearing slightly shorter and stouter.

厘米；南边那株高近4.1米，直径约1.2米，显得要矮胖一些。

不过，从腰围来看，很可能南边的石笋更高。变短是在西汉末年。那时，王莽搞得天下大乱，蜀郡太守公孙述据险割据，中原大地上赤眉、绿林蜂起。乱世之中，南边的那株石笋没能完好保存。

闹市里的巨大沉默物体，就是一个异类，它以令人震慑的尺寸、不言的姿态，显示出与周边的繁华、喧嚣和庸常的格格不入。

在科幻电影《2001年太空漫游》里有这样一个镜头，两个猿类族群争夺水源，其中的一方已学会了使用工具，它们用棒骨击倒敌手，取得胜利后兴奋地将骨头抛向空中，待其落下时，在荧幕上幻化为一般白色的宇宙飞船。猿类突然进化，将自己从普通动物之列拔升为万物之灵，源于一块黑色方碑的点化，而那块黑方碑正是BDO，是高等级文明对于地球生物的昭示。

石笋街街头的两根石笋，也是这样的巨大沉默物体。大，即是力量；沉默，则让力量翻倍——是不是会带来一种强烈的陌生感，让你惊异、不安、惶恐，却又对它携带的讯息充满好奇？

在一千多年以前，大诗人杜甫就曾经有过类似的感受。

However, judging from their girths, it is quite possible that the southern stalagmite is actually taller. It became shorter towards the end of the Western Han Dynasty (202 BC-8 AD). During that time, Wang Mang brought great turmoil to the realm, while Gongsun Shu, the prefect of Shu Commandery, established his stronghold in the midst of chaos, with Red Eyebrows and Green Woodsmen rising in rebellion across the Central Plains. In this era of disorder, the southern stalagmite could not be well-preserved.

The Big Dumb Objects in the bustling city are truly an anomaly, and with their awe-inspiring size and quiet demeanor, they show how out of place they are with the bustle, noise, and mediocrity of their surroundings.

In the science fiction film *2001: A Space Odyssey*, there is a scene where two groups of primates are fighting over a water source. One group has already learned to use tools and manages to defeat their opponents by wielding bones as weapons. After their victory, in a moment of excitement, one of the primates throws the bone into the air, and as it descends, it transforms into a white spaceship on the screen. The primates' sudden evolution, elevating themselves from the ranks of ordinary animals to sentient beings, is all triggered by the enigmatic black monolith known as the BDO. It serves as a message from an advanced civilization to the life forms on Earth, ushering in a new level of understanding and potential.

The two stone stalagmites' sizes signify power, while their silence amplifies that power. They can evoke a strong sense of unfamiliarity, leaving you amazed, uneasy, and even fearful. Yet, at the same time, curiosity fills you regarding the messages they might carry.

Even before more than one thousand years, the great poet Du Fu had experienced such a similar feeling.

当诗人初遇BDO

杜甫挈妇将雏入蜀投友，是在760年。

五年前，“安史之乱”爆发，踏上逃难之路的杜甫，接连经历了落入叛军之手、骨肉流离又重逢、因谏言下狱贬官、关中大饥荒等磨难。

被叛军囚于长安时，他写下了一生中罕见的情诗：“今夜鄜州月，闺中只独看。遥怜小儿女，未解忆长安……”

逃难途中，又以让人心碎的句子记录了难民的惨痛流离：“二十一家同入蜀，惟残一人出骆谷。自说二女啮臂时，回头却向秦云哭。”

When the Poet First Encountered the BDO

Du Fu, accompanied by his wife and children, sought refuge in Sichuan to join his friends in the year 760.

Five years ago, the devastating “An Lushan Rebellion” had erupted. Du Fu, embarking on a journey to escape the chaos, experienced a series of tribulations, including falling into the hands of rebel forces, being separated from his family, reuniting with them, imprisonment and demotion due to his admonitions, and enduring the severe famine in Guanzhong, Shaanxi.

While imprisoned in Chang’an by the rebel forces, Du Fu penned a rare love poem that expressed his longing for his family:

But tonight, it’s just you and the moon,
Sharing a silent bond, a connection that’s strewn.
Yearning for our kids, my heart filled with ache,
Unyielding memories of Chang’an I long to take.

During his journey of displacement, Du Fu also captured the heart-wrenching plight of refugees in a poignant verse:

Twenty-one families entered Shu, their fate entwined,
But only one person emerged from the treacherous Luogu Valley they left behind.
He tells the tale of his two daughters, nibbling the arms for recognition in the future,
Then turning round to look for the clouds of hometown,
Wailing and hugging each other.

经历离乱之痛的杜甫，对成都的一切都充满好奇 冉玉杰 摄
Experiencing great pain in times of tribulations, Du Fu was filled with curiosity about everything in Chengdu. (Photographer: Ran Yujie)

前往成都的一路上，迥异于关中的蜀地风物，无疑治愈了诗人心灵的破碎。杜甫惊奇地发现，此处树木竟然历寒冬不凋；而成都，则俨然是一座并不逊色于长安的大都会。

盛唐时的成都，里坊密布，市廛繁盛，民康物阜。成都城里共计一百二十坊，留名者十五，如书台坊、金马坊、碧鸡坊、文翁坊、小蛮坊；街道则有赤里街、石笋街、扬子巷、煮胶巷等。

杜甫栖居的草堂，在碧鸡坊石笋街以西。他时常跨过杨柳飘拂的石桥，沿着梅香四溢的江边小道，从西门进城。一路上，无人相识，难免生出大隐于市的轻松感。到了金容坊，再顺着通衢大道走上几百步，就会看到那两株耸峭的石笋了。

那时的成都远离战乱，勾栏瓦肆遍布，酒楼茶坊林立，无处不展现着世界级大都市的风采。这座城修筑于公元前311年，从华夏文明、中原王朝的视角来看，它是战国时期秦国蜀郡的郡治；而在那之前，则是古蜀国的都城，属于另外一种形态迥异的文明——古蜀文明。

杜甫在一头撞见石笋的时候，成都城里的盛世子民正忙着享受红尘一等一的繁华，对数千年前曾经在此开

As Du Fu made his way to Chengdu, the landscapes of Shu, so contrasting from the desolation of the Guanzhong region, undoubtedly healed the shattered state of his soul. To his astonishment, he discovered that the trees here remained evergreen despite the harsh winter, and that Chengdu, with its splendor, was an abuzz metropolis no less magnificent than Chang’an.

Chengdu at the glorious age of Tang Dynasty was characterized by its peaceful people, abundant produce, and stable societies; it was filled with numerous neighborhoods and bustling markets, containing a total of 120 neighborhoods with fifteen particularly renowned ones, such as Shutai, Jinma, Biji, Wenweng, and Xiaoman. The streets were equally distinguished, including the famous Chili Street, Shisun Street, Yangzi Lane, Zhujiao Lane, and so on.

Du Fu resided in his thatched cottage located west of Shisun Street in Biji Neighborhood. He often crossed the stone bridge adorned with swaying willows, followed the riverbank path filled with the fragrance of plum blossoms, and entered the city through the West Gate. Along the way, no one came up to greet him and express their admiration because they didn’t recognize him, and he inevitably felt a sense of relief that he was living as a hermit in the lively place. Upon reaching Jinrong Neighborhood and continuing along the main road for a few hundred steps, he would definitely see the two towering stone pillars.

Chengdu at that time was far from the turmoil of war. Its streets were adorned with elegant pavilions housing varieties of entertainment programs, restaurants and tea-houses, etc., showcasing the grandeur of a world-class metropolis. This city was established in 311 BC, serving as the capital of Shu Commandery in the state of Qin during the Warring States period. From the perspective of orthodox Chinese civilization and the Central Plains dynasties,

辟鸿蒙、创建文明的古蜀先民并没有什么兴趣。提起蚕丛、柏灌、鱼凫、杜宇和开明等"古蜀五祖"，只是觉得缥缈恍惚。他们的态度是，说不清楚的事就不说，想不清楚的事就不去想。如果确实避不开，那么就在已知的理论框架中，去抓起一件熟悉的工具来解释。

街头那两株巨大的石笋，正是被如此阐释的。唐代的成都人，认为那两件巨大沉默物体是填镇海眼之物，其下连通大海。是的，这就是"宝塔镇河妖"。

唐代人当然没听说过"巨大沉默物体"或BDO这样的外来语。

"语言的界限就是我们的世界的界限。"维特根斯坦的名言坐实了事物的名与实之间的关系。但语言其实只代表认知的清晰程度，存在着语言无法表达的事实也是一个事实，否则便不会有"欲辩已忘言"的说法。

杜甫虽然没有创造出BDO这样的词汇，但他的确拓展了认知的边界。同是生活在成都，杜甫并不满足于"海眼"这种唾手可得的结论。对于这两株震撼过他心灵的石笋，诗人以超越时代的洞察力加以判断：它们是古蜀国留下的遗迹。

《石笋行》共八句，一半的篇幅

it was the ancient capital of the former Shu Kingdom, representing the ancient Shu civilization with a distinct form.

When Du Fu stumbled upon the towering stone pillars, the prosperous citizens of Chengdu were busy enjoying the splendors of the mortal world. They had little interest in their ancient Shu ancestors who had once pioneered and created civilization out of the primordial world thousands of years ago. The mention of the "Five Ancestors of Ancient Shu"—Cancong, Boguan, Yufu, Duyu, and Kaiming — seemed vague and ethereal to them. Their attitude was to avoid discussing things they couldn't explain and not dwell on matters they couldn't comprehend. If unavoidable, they would rely on familiar tools within their known theoretical framework.

The two massive towering stone pillars on the streets are precisely interpreted in this manner. The people of Chengdu during the Tang Dynasty believed that these silent objects served as guardians to block the eye of the sea, preventing the sea from rising up and pouring into the city. Yes, this is what they compared to erecting a pagoda by the riverside to subdue the demons in the river.

Of course, the people of the Tang Dynasty were not familiar with terms like "Big Dumb Object" or BDO from foreign languages.

Wittgenstein's famous quote, "The limits of my language mean the limits of my world", reaffirms the relationship between the names and realities of things. However, language merely represents the clarity of our cognition, and the existence of facts beyond the scope of language is itself a fact. Otherwise, sayings like "When the desire to argue appears, my words are forgotten" would not exist.

Although Du Fu did not create terms like BDO, he did indeed expand the boundaries of cognition. Living in Chengdu, Du Fu was not satisfied with

在写石笋，又用“立石为表”揭示了真相，剩下的四句则是在抒发感慨。杜甫感叹芸芸众生无知无识，不加思考地听信传言，进而联想到君王受佞臣蒙蔽，以致施政错谬、社稷倾覆。

几乎所有事都可以联想到国家大事、朝堂之上，是一种打有杜甫标签的情怀。屡经患难的杜甫，虽然已弃绝辅佐君王、经世济民之想，却改不了“处江湖之远则忧其君”的儒者底色。尽管如此，对于诗中突然而至的愤怒，我依然难以理解：百姓愚昧，可也不是石笋的错啊，有必要如此震怒吗？为什么突然就破口大骂呢，要跟两根没有知觉的石笋较劲。诗尾还说要将石笋掷向天外，放现在可算破坏文物了。

难道真的是他的性格问题吗？如《旧唐书》所言：“甫性褊躁，无器度。”《新唐书》则说：“（严武）最厚杜甫，然欲杀甫数矣。”剑南节度使严武对杜甫最好，还资助他建了草堂，然而几次想杀他，不知他是如何把好朋友得罪得这么厉害的。

友人在为本书做翻译，而我在读到《石笋行》的英文时，突然福至心灵，发现以前竟然根本没有读懂它的后半截。原来，杜甫是在以石笋喻

easily attainable conclusions like the “sea eye”. In regards to the two towering stone pillars that profoundly touched his soul, the poet used his timeless insight to judge that they were relics left behind by the ancient Shu Kingdom.

Half of *An Ode to Stalagmites* is dedicated to describing the stone spires, and it uses “marked by these stones” to reveal the truth. The remaining four lines express the poet’s deep emotions. Du Fu laments the ignorance and unawareness of countless people, who heedlessly believe rumors without critical thought. This leads him to contemplate how the emperor can be misled by sycophants, resulting in misguided governance and endangering the state.

Almost everything can be related to national affairs and court politics, which is a sentiment distinctly associated with Du Fu’s name. Having experienced numerous hardships, Du Fu, although he had abandoned his aspirations to assist the emperor and govern the people, could not change his Confucian essence of “worrying for the emperor even when far from the court.” Yet, I still struggle to understand the sudden anger in this poem: why blame the stalagmites for the ignorance of the common people? Is it necessary to vent such fury against two insentient rocks? And at the end, he even threatens to hurl the two stalagmites into the outer heavens, which today would be considered vandalism of cultural relics.

Could it really be a problem with his personality? As the *Old Book of Tang* describes, “Du Fu had a narrow and irritable disposition, lacking magnanimity.” The *New Book of Tang* goes further, stating, “Yan Wu, despite his fondness for Du Fu, has considered killing him several times.” Yan Wu, the military governor of Jiannan, was Du Fu’s staunch supporter, even funding the construction of his thatched cottage. Yet, there were moments when he contemplated ending Du Fu’s life. It is puzzling how Du Fu managed to offend such

人，还不仅仅是某一类人，而是可以落实到具体某一人——按照历代注诗者的说法，其人便是唐肃宗时的权宦李辅国。李辅国早年曾是高力士的仆役，后入侍太子李亨。安史之乱时，在马嵬驿，李辅国向太子建议杀杨国忠。公元756年，太子登基，是为唐肃宗。公元758年，李辅国任元帅府行军司马，掌握禁军，一时权倾朝野，连宰相、节度使这样的高官都要争相讨好他。

此时，再来读《石笋行》便会有新发现。"嗟尔石笋擅虚名，后来未识犹骏奔。"这一句非常有画面感，"骏"通"逡"，有来来往往之意。一群人不识石笋真面相，而往来奔走，聚集于其下——这哪里说的是愚民与石笋，分明说的就是一群趋炎附势之徒奔走于李辅国门前。

这是一个简单的比喻，本体是权贵，喻体是石笋。"安得壮士掷天外"，想扔的也并不是石笋，而是祸国殃民之人。

杜甫虽然是我最喜爱的诗人，但平心而论，这个比喻并不高明，联想十分生硬。抛开艺术性不论，从这首诗倒真可以看出杜甫的性格——能够拿刀威胁唐玄宗、能够捕杀唐肃宗张皇后的李辅国，他偏偏要写诗去痛

a good friend so severely.

When my friend is working on translating this book, and as I read the English version of *An Ode to Stalagmites*, I had a sudden realization that I had never truly understood the latter half of the poem before. It turns out that Du Fu was using the stalagmites as a metaphor for people—not just a general type of people, but a specific individual. According to commentators over the centuries, this person is none other than Li Fuguo, an influential eunuch during Emperor Suzong's reign. Li Fuguo was initially a servant of Gao Lishi and later served the crown prince Li Heng. During the An Lushan Rebellion, at Mawei Courier Station, Li Fuguo suggested to the crown prince to kill Yang Guozhong, the chancellor of Emperor Xuanzong. In 756 AD, the crown prince ascended the throne as Emperor Suzong. In 758 AD, Li Fuguo was appointed as the Marshal's Office Supervisor, commanding the imperial guards. His power was immense, and even high officials like the prime ministers and the military governors vied for his favor.

With this context, reading *An Ode to Stalagmites* offers new insights. The line "嗟尔石笋擅虚名，后来未识犹骏奔" becomes very vivid. The character "骏" (jun) is read as "逡" (qun), meaning to come and go. A crowd of people fails to recognize the true nature of the stalagmites, bustling around beneath them—this clearly refers not to ignorant commoners and the stalagmites, but to a group of sycophants flocking to curry favor with Li Fuguo.

This is a simple metaphor where the actual subject is the powerful official, and the metaphorical object is the stalagmites. The line "安得壮士掷天外" means it's not the stalagmites he wants to throw away, but those who bring calamity to the nation and its people.

Although Du Fu is my favorite poet, to be fair, this metaphor lacks subtlety and the connection

骂。此时，我就相信《新唐书》中记载的剑南节度使严武欲杀好友杜甫一事的真实性了。

feels somewhat forced. Putting aside the artistic merit, this poem does reveal something about Du Fu's character—writing a poem to fiercely criticize Li Fuguo, a man who dared to threaten Emperor Xuanzong with a knife and was capable of killing Empress Zhang of Emperor Suzong. At this point, I'm inclined to believe in the authenticity of the account in the *New Book of Tang* where Yan Wu, the military governor of Jiannan, contemplated killing his close friend Du Fu.

雨后瑟瑟

青苔掩盖着沧海桑田的痕迹，两株石笋如天外飞峰一般神秘。而在石笋身边，还时常有些奇异之事发生，不由得让蜀人浮想联翩。

盛夏季节，大雨滂沱之后，石笋旁会出现一地的瑟瑟。今人第一次听说瑟瑟，多是来自白居易那句“半江瑟瑟半江红”。瑟瑟，一般解释为“青绿色”，但这只是其延伸意义。瑟瑟是个外来词，本指来自波斯的珠宝，后来也指珠宝的色泽。

雨后出现在石笋之旁的珠子很小，以青黄色居多，上面还有小孔，可以用线串起来。石笋的神秘之处还不止于此。

有时，雨后会发生地陷，石笋近旁平地陡现大洞。洞中有积水，居然还很清亮。拿来竹竿往下戳，探不到

Se se, Bluish-green Beads, Appear After the Rain

Moss conceals the traces of the changing tides, while the two stone pillars stand mysteriously like peaks from beyond the heavens. Strange occurrences often happened near the stone pillars, leading the people of Shu to let their imaginations run wild.

During the peak of summer, after a heavy downpour, the ground next to the stone pillars would be covered in "Se se" . The first time people heard of this word is most often from Bai Juyi's phrase "The river was half Se se (a deep turquoise colour) and half a red." Se se is commonly interpreted as "bluish-green", but this is just its extended meaning. It is a loanword that originally referred to Persian jewelry, and later also to the colour of the jewellery.

The beads that appear next to the stone pillars after the rain are very small, mostly in shades of greenish-yellow, with tiny holes on them for stringing with thread.

Sometimes, after the rain, there would be land subsidence near the stone pillars, abrupt cavities appearing on the flat ground. These cavities would hold clear and bright water. Even when probed with bamboo poles, the bottom couldn't be reached.

底。好奇心重的人，又找来绳子绑了石头往下扔，依然深不可测。到了北宋的嘉祐年间，一辆牛车经过时，石笋旁突然地陷，把车困在了里面。

古代的成都人，就了解地下水的存在了，但地理知识还不够完善，认为泉眼、井眼都直通大海——至于井水、泉水为何不咸，似乎没有深想。于是就说此处是海眼，石笋是镇海眼之物，要是一拔了，海水就要从里面汩汩冒出来，整个成都城都要被淹没。

海眼传说，实则是水神崇拜留下的心理遗迹。上古时代，低洼卑湿之地常年受到水害的侵袭，人们便想象出兴风作浪的水怪，更用真材实料的石柱、石笋以及耗费人力的石塔、石井，来镇压意识里的虚构之物。所谓“宝塔镇河妖”，其实镇的更是心中妄念。

成都早年的确水患频繁，水神崇拜已沉潜入蜀民的集体无意识之中。芸芸众生满足于“海眼”一说，但作为知识分子中的翘楚，杜甫是不相信的，他在考据历史文献之后，在《石笋行》一诗里提出了自己的见解。

杜甫认为，石笋下面是古蜀权贵的墓室，而高耸地面的巨大石笋，则是墓地的标识——石表。而雨后出现

Curious individuals then tied stones to ropes and dropped them down, yet the depth remained unfathomable. During the Jia You era of the Northern Song Dynasty, a day came when an oxcart was passing by the stalagmite, the ground suddenly sank, trapping the cart inside.

The ancient people of Chengdu became aware of the existence of underground water, but their knowledge of geography was not yet complete. They believed that springs and wells connected directly to the sea — why the water in wells and springs wasn't salty seemingly wasn't deeply pondered. Thus, they referred to these sinkholes as “sea eyes” and believed that the stone pillars acted as guardians of the sea eye. If the pillars were removed, seawater would gush out, submerging the entire city of Chengdu.

The legend of the sea eye is actually a psychological remnant left by the worship of water gods. In ancient times, the low—lying and damp areas were constantly plagued by water disasters, so people imagined water monsters causing storms and used real stone pillars, stalagmites, as well as labor-intensive stone towers and wells to suppress these fictional creatures in their minds. The saying “pagoda taming the river monster” actually tames the delusions within their hearts.

In the early years of Chengdu, water disasters were indeed frequent, and the worship of water gods had sunk deep into the collective unconsciousness of the people. The masses were content with the tale of the “sea eye”. However, as an intellectual elite, Du Fu did not believe in it. After researching historical documents, he presented his own views in the poem *An Ode to Stalagmites* .

Du Fu believed that beneath the stalagmite lies the tomb chamber of the ancient Shu aristocrats, while the towering stalagmites above the ground serve as the marker for the burial site, known as the

的瑟瑟，自然就是随葬于墓中的珠宝被大雨冲刷出来了。

一个叫惠嶷的蜀地僧人则说，东晋时桓温带兵攻入成都，剿灭成汉李氏政权时，焚烧了装饰豪华的少城，那些珠宝就是大火之后残留的遗物。

唐朝时，景教（基督教派别之一）在蜀地流传，有外国人在石笋附近建立了大秦寺作为教堂，门楼里有十间房，都用产自大秦（东罗马帝国）的珠宝穿绳为门帘。因此也有人说，大雨中现身的瑟瑟，是大秦寺被毁之后留下的遗物。

这些说法，有一个共同点，那就是：石笋下面并不是海眼，瑟瑟也绝非来自大海之物。

杜甫以石笋为古墓石表之说，以今日历史学、考古学的水准来看，方向也是正确的。21世纪初，在成都市商业街发掘的古蜀国开明王族大型墓葬里，就有残存的木质柱础——很可能就是供安置墓地表面大石柱所用。在文字还不盛行的古蜀国，这种墓地石表，其功能就相当于无字之碑。

在贵族墓室安置石笋这样的大型石柱，是古蜀人一种特别的爱好。成都曾遍布各类大石的遗迹，除了至今存留的支机石和天涯石，还有埋在地下的石镜、已经消失的五块石等

"stone tablets". In this case, Se se, the tiny beads that appeared after the rain, were naturally the precious gems buried with the deceased washed out by the heavy rain.

A Sichuan monk named Huiyi offered a different perspective. According to him, during the Eastern Jin Dynasty(317-420 AD), when Huan Wen led his troops to attack Chengdu and eradicate the Li clan's regime of Cheng Han, the soldiers set fire to the lavishly decorated city. The jewels mentioned were remnants that survived the great fire.

During the Tang Dynasty, Nestorian Christianity spread in the region of Shu (Sichuan). Foreigners built the Daqin Temple near the stalagmite as a church. The temple had a gate tower with ten rooms, and the door curtains were made of strings of jewels from Daqin (the Eastern Roman Empire). Therefore, some people also claim that the tiny beads were remnants left behind after the destruction of the Daqin Temple.

These accounts share a common point— that the area beneath the stalagmite is not a sea eye, and those small, greenish-yellow beads do not originate from the sea.

Du Fu's interpretation of the stalagmites as markers for ancient tombs aligns with the perspective of modern historical and archaeological research. At the beginning of this century, during the excavation of large royal tombs of the Kaiming family of the Shu Kingdom in Chengdu Commercial Street, remnants of wooden pillar bases were found-likely used to support the large stone pillars on the surface of the tombs. In the ancient Shu Kingdom, where writing was not prevalent, these tomb markers served a function similar to inscribed steles.

Placing large stalagmite-like stone pillars in nobleman's burial chambers was favored by the ancient Shu people. In the past, Chengdu was dotted with large stone relics, including the still-existing

（传说这五块叠放的大石头下面也是海眼）。

可是，古代的蜀人，为什么喜欢这么大的石头呢？成都平原并不产石，那么散布于城中的大石头，是从哪儿来的呢？这跟蜀人的发源、迁徙，以及古蜀国的建立密切相关。

Zhiji Stone and Tianya Stone, as well as underground stone mirrors and the disappeared Wukuaishi (five stacked large stones rumored to also contain a sea eye underneath).

But why did the ancient Shu people have a fondness for such large stones? Where did these large stones scattered throughout the city come from? These questions are closely related to the origin, migration, and establishment of the ancient Shu Kingdom.

寻迹“何茫然”

古蜀族兴起于岷江上游的岷山河谷、台地之中，即今四川省茂县叠溪海子一带。因为地质灾害的逼迫，遂在第一代蜀王蚕丛的带领下，开始寻找下山发展的新路径。

蜀族的早期历史，除了近些年来自考古发掘的有限信息之外，在历史文献中鲜有记载。蜀族本身有没有文字，尚无定论，目前发现的被称作巴蜀文字的几百个符号，尚不能为现代人解读。所以，对蜀族最早的记载，仍然要到汉语文献中去寻找。就如匈奴这般纵横于漠北的强悍民族，因为没有自己的文字，其历史也只是存在于《史记》等华夏典籍之中。一旦他们西迁，脱离了与华夏族的接触，那些杂沓又深刻的马蹄痕迹，终湮没于虚无的荒原之上。

古本《竹书纪年》记载，夏桀曾

Tracing the Origin in the Haze of Time

The ancient Shu tribe arose in the Minshan River Valley and terraces in the upper reaches of the Min River, in what is now the region of Diexi Lake in Mao County, Sichuan Province. Due to geological disasters, led by the first Shu king, Cancong, they began seeking new paths for development down the mountains.

The early history of the Shu tribe has limited archaeological evidence and few records in historical documents. It remains uncertain whether the Shu tribe had their own writing system. The hundreds of symbols discovered, known as the Ba-Shu script, cannot be deciphered by modern scholars. Therefore, the earliest records of the Shu tribe must still be sought in Chinese historical literature. Just like the formidable nomadic tribe, the Xiongnu, who roamed across the northern deserts, their history only exists in Chinese classics such as the *Records of the Grand Historian* because they did not have their own writing system. Once they migrated westward and disconnected from contact with the Chinese clans, their miscellaneous and profound hoof traces of history ultimately faded away into the vast wilderness of nothingness.

经征伐岷山，并娶了当地的琬、琰两个女子，这大致是蜀族和华夏族有交集的最早记载，而两大族群的冲突态势则一直延续到了商。殷商甲骨文卜辞中，“蜀”字出现十一次之多。“征蜀”“克蜀”等语，说明商对蜀保持着凌逼、压迫之势。因此，蜀族跟随周武王讨伐商纣，就很自然而然了。

关于蜀人的早期记载，最直接的文献当属扬雄《蜀王本纪》。扬雄的生长年代，距最后一个古蜀王朝开明朝的覆灭不到300年。其时，必然有大量口口相传的神话传说、祭祀史诗可供采摘以成书。他应该也参考过今人不曾见过，甚至未曾听说过的史料。

《蜀王本纪》已亡佚，但古代多种文献曾有辑引。其存世文字虽然甚少，且与神话传说相纠结，却屡屡为后世考古发现所证实。

按照典籍，五代古蜀王为蚕丛、柏灌、鱼凫、杜宇、鳖灵，号称“古蜀五祖”。在古文献乃至后来的论文中，这五个名字的使用往往给阅读者带来巨大的困扰。

它们时而是五个人，时而也是五个部落，是古蜀国的五个王朝，或者某个王朝所有君主的共用称呼——开国君主、末代君主，甚至二者中的任意一位。

In the ancient version *Bamboo Annals*, it is recorded that Xia Jie once launched a campaign against the Minshan region and married two local women named Wan and Yan. This is roughly the earliest record of interaction between the Shu tribe and the Huaxia tribe. The conflict between these two major ethnic groups continued into the Shang Dynasty. The oracle bone inscriptions of the Shang Dynasty, in their divination texts, mentioned the word “Shu” eleven times. Phrases such as “conquering Shu” and “subduing Shu” indicate that the Shang Dynasty exerted dominance and oppression over the Shu people. Therefore, it is natural that the Shu people followed King Wu of Zhou in his campaign against King Zhou of Shang.

Regarding early records of the Shu people, the most direct literary source is Yang Xiong’s *Annals of the Kings of Shu*. Yang Xiong lived less than 300 years after the fall of the Kaiming Dynasty, the last of ancient Shu kingdom, during a time when there would have been a wealth of mythical legends and epic tales passed down through word of mouth, as well as epics about sacrificial rituals, that could be gathered for his writings. He should have also referred to historical records that are beyond the knowledge and awareness of present-day individuals.

The *Annals of the Kings of Shu* is now lost, but it was cited and referenced in various ancient texts. Although it has few surviving written records, which often intertwine with mythology and legends, but repeatedly confirmed by archaeological discoveries.

According to the ancient scriptures, the five ancient Shu kings were Cancong, Boguan, Yufu, Duyu, and Bieling, collectively referred to as the “Five Ancestors of Ancient Shu”. In ancient texts and even later academic papers, the use of these five names often confuses readers.

They can refer to either five individuals or five

搞懂了其概念的适用范围、广义与狭义，接触史料时就不会一头雾水了。在本书中，我们也会遇到这样的情况。

蜀族的第一代首领叫蚕丛。其人功绩，从名字中便可见些端倪。是的，蜀人是世界上最先驯化野蚕的族群，是丝绸的发明者。2020年重启的三星堆考古，发现了大量的丝绸残留物，也为此说法提供了实物证据。

前文曾提及，夏朝的最后一个君主夏桀曾经征伐过蜀地，而蚕丛所在的年代，其实远早于夏。

古蜀由岷山进入四川盆地后，在成都平原建立了宝墩等一批古城，其时间大约距今四千五百年。在考古学文化谱系的时间线上，古蜀族的宝墩文化对应着华夏族的龙山文化早期，即华夏先祖黄帝的活动时期。而宝墩城修建400年之后，华夏族才有夏朝的建立。

tribal groups, representing the five dynasties of the ancient Shu Kingdom, or a collective title for all the monarchs of a particular Dynasty—founding monarchs, last monarchs, or any one of them in between.

Understanding the concept's applicability, both in a broad and narrow sense, will help us navigate through the historical records without confusion. In this book, we will encounter such situations.

The first leader of the Shu tribe was named Cancong. The hints to his achievements are already evident in his name. Indeed, the Shu people were the first in the world to domesticate silkworms ("Can" in Chinese character) and invent silk. The archaeological discoveries at the recently restarted Sanxingdui Site in 2020 revealed a large number of silk remnants, providing tangible evidence for this claim.

As mentioned earlier, the last ruler of the Xia Dynasty, Xia Jie, once campaigned in the land of Shu. However, the era of Cancong predates the Xia Dynasty by a considerable period.

After entering the Sichuan Basin through the Min Mountains, the ancient Shu established a group of ancient cities, including Baodun, on the Chengdu Plain, dating back approximately 4,500 years ago. In the timeline of archaeological cultural pedigrees, the Baodun culture of ancient Shu corresponds to the early stage of the Longshan culture of the Huaxia ethnic group, which is the period when the ancestor of the Huaxia, Huangdi, the Yellow Emperor was active. It was only after the construction of Baodun City for 400 years that the Huaxia ethnic group established the Xia Dynasty.

宝墩古城遗址出土的新石器时代晚期陶敞口圈足尊　余茂智 摄

A Neolithic Late Period pottery round-bottomed vessel with an open mouth unearthed from the Baodun ancient city ruins (Photographer: Yu Maozhi)

《太平御览》引《蜀王本纪》称："从开明已（以）上至蚕丛，凡四千岁。"考虑到华夏族的夏商周三朝一共存续了约一千八百年，从蚕丛至开明共计五个朝代，数千年有一定的合理性。开明王朝的建立，大致是在公元前600年；灭亡是在公元前316年。取二者的中间点公元前458年为下限，再线性前推四千年，则可以得出：第一代古蜀王蚕丛的生活年代距今约六千五百年。

这样的推算方法当然比较粗疏，但结合宝墩古城、营盘山遗址等考古发现，却让人惊异地发现，这个数字是大致合理的。

再来看蜀人的生存状况。

宋代章樵注《蜀都赋》引《蜀王本纪》称："蚕丛始居岷山石室中。"

The *Tai Ping Yu Lan* cites the *Annals of the Kings of Shu*, stating, "From Kaiming to Cancong, it lasts a total of four thousand years." Considering that the Xia, Shang, and Zhou dynasties of the Huaxia ethnic group lasted for approximately 1800 years, with five dynasties from Cancong to Kaiming, a span of thousands of years seems reasonable. The establishment of the Kaiming Dynasty was roughly around 600 BC, and its downfall was around 316 BC. Taking the midpoint of the two, around 458 BC, and applying a simple calculation of 4000 years in reverse, we can estimate that the first generation of the ancient Shu king, Cancong, lived approximately 6500 years ago.

Of course, such a projection is of course rather sloppy, but when combined with archaeological discoveries such as the Baodun ancient city and the Yingpanshan site, Mao County, it is astonishing to find that the estimated timeline is reasonably accurate.

Now let's take a look at the living conditions of the Shu people.

The Song Dynasty's Zhang Qiao's annotations in *Verse on the Shu Capital* quote the *Annals of the Kings of Shu*, stating, "Cancong initially lived in the stone chambers of the Min Mountains."

三星堆雕像的出土，让历代对于"纵目人"的猜想变得具象化　高泓 摄

The discovery of Sanxingdui statues has given concrete form to generations of speculation about the "protruding-eyed people" (Photographer: Gao Hong)

《华阳国志》记载稍详："有蜀侯蚕丛，其目纵，始称王。死，作石棺、石椁。国人从之。故俗以石棺椁为纵目人冢也。"

The *Records of the States South of Mount Hua* provides a slightly more detailed account, stating, "Cancong was the head of Shu. His eyes were oblong. He was the first to claim the title of king. After his death, a sarcophagus and a stone outer coffin were

以上所称“其目纵”“纵目人”为何，数千年来不为人所解，不过三星堆的惊世发现已经给出了线索，本书还会详加讨论。此处先关注蜀人的居住、埋葬方式。可以发现，蜀人对于石头有着一种特别的兴趣，甚至是依恋，他们生前住石头房子，死后又埋葬在石头棺椁里。

石棺椁、石房子是什么样子的？好在虽然已过了数千年，依然可以找到类似的样本。在四川凉山州安宁河畔，散布着两百多座大石墓，它们都是由一块块重达数吨的巨石堆叠而成的；而从阿坝州汶川县向西至理县，沿途可见石块垒砌的羌寨碉楼，里面至今还住着人。

made, and the people of the country followed suit. Later, it became customary to refer to tombs with sarcophagus, and outer coffins as ‘oblong-eyed people’s tombs’.”

For thousands of years, the meaning behind the terms “oblong eyes” and “oblong-eyed people” remained a mystery, but the astounding discoveries at Sanxingdui have provided some clues. They will be discussed in detail in this book. For now, let’s focus on the dwelling and burial practices of the Shu people. It can be observed that the Shu people had a special interest, even an attachment, to stones. They lived in stone houses during their lifetime and were buried in stone coffins after death.

What do these stone houses and stone coffins look like? Fortunately, even though thousands of years have passed, we can still find similar examples. Along the Anning River in Liangshan, Sichuan Province, there are over 200 large stone tombs, constructed by stacking massive stones weighing several tons. And from Wenchuan County to Li County in Aba Prefecture, there are many Qiang ethnic villages and watchtowers built with stone blocks, where people still reside today.

布瓦羌寨的黄泥碉　余茂智 摄
The yellow mud watchtowers of Buwa Qiang Village (Photographer: Yu Maozhi)

石头做的房子——桃坪羌寨　冉玉杰 摄
Stone houses in Taoping Qiang Village (Photographer: Ran Yujie)

石棺椁的习俗，甚至被带到了成都平原。南齐时，齐高帝萧道成之子萧鉴任益州刺史时，发现的古墓里就有石椁。《南史·列传第三十三·齐高帝诸子下》载："（萧鉴）于州园地得古冢，无复棺，但有石椁……金银为蚕蛇形者数斗。又以朱沙为阜，水银为池。"

从墓葬规制来看，应为王族之墓。而蚕虫状的金银制品，显然又是以蚕为图腾。结合石椁等信息来看，此墓极有可能为蚕丛部族在进入成都平原后留下的遗存。

好在萧鉴拒绝了旁人让他取走宝物的劝说，命令重新造坟，将墓重新封闭。也就是说，此墓至今仍有可能埋在成都的地下。

The custom of stone coffins even extended to the Chengdu Plain. During the Southern Qi Dynasty, when Xiao Jian, the son of Emperor Gao of Qi, served as the governor of Yizhou (modern-day Sichuan Province), ancient tombs with stone coffins were discovered. According to the *Biographies of the Sons of Emperor Gao of Qi* in the *Book of Southern Dynasties*, it is recorded that, "(Xiao Jian) found ancient tombs in the gardens, with no coffins but with stone outer coffins instead... and several Dou of gold and silver in the form of silkworms and snakes. Additionally, vermilion sand was used to create hills, and mercury was used to create a pond."

From the burial regulations, it appears to be a royal tomb. The gold and silver artifacts shaped like silkworms clearly indicate that the silkworm was their totem. Combining this information with the presence of stone outer coffins, it is highly likely that this tomb is a remnant left by the Cancong tribe after entering the Chengdu Plain.

Fortunately, Xiao Jian rejected the advice of those around him who urged him to take the treasures and instead ordered the tomb to be reconstructed and sealed again. This means that this tomb may still be buried underground in Chengdu to this day.

不一样的人种？

跋涉于典籍文献，我时常会极其惊讶地发现：从那些看似毫不相关的材料出发，竟然可以神奇地推导出相同的结论。

比如由石室、石棺、石椁，同样能够推断古蜀人的族属、人种，得出与前辈史学大家相同的结论。

A Different Race?

When delving into the classical texts and literature, I often discover with great surprise that seemingly unrelated materials can magically lead to the same conclusions.

For example, by examining the stone chambers, sarcophagus, and outer coffins, we can infer the ethnic and racial origins of the ancient Shu people, arriving at the same conclusions as those of renowned historians.

所谓羌寨碉楼，自然是羌人所建。羌人不是蜀人的主体民族，但是，羌族史诗《羌戈大战》记载，羌人在迁徙过程中，曾经向戈基人学习过修筑石碉房的技术，而戈基人却很可能就跟氐人同种。安宁河畔的大石墓，则是由古邛人修建的，而邛人与羌人不无渊源。

按童恩正先生之说，蜀人即氐人。而大石崇拜的来源，指向的依然是古氐人，是他们构建了古蜀国。

纵目的风尚也一样。在《成汉俑：氐人之眼高悬时间隧道》一章，我们会通过对这种习俗的探索，见到古蜀人、氐人的关联与传承。

氐人已经消失，更别提疑似与其同种的戈基人，关于戈基人的讯息只能到羌人史诗中去找寻。按《羌戈大战》，羌人从青海一带向岷江上游迁徙，因为对生存资源的争夺，与原本居住于此的戈基人发生了强烈冲突，乃至于战争。

关于戈基人的外形，羌人的史诗、传说中主要有两种描述，其中之一说他们个子矮、眼睛竖起。个子矮，是尼格利陀人的特征——这是一种又被称作“矮黑人”的棕种人，他们携带D型Y染色体，是最早走出非洲的智人。所以在《羌戈大战》中，

The Qiang ethnic villages and watchtowers, for instance, were constructed by the Qiang people. Although the Qiang were not the main ethnic group of the Shu people, the Qiang epic *The Great Qiang-Ge Battle* records that the Qiang people, during their migration, learned the technique of building stone watchtowers from the Geji people, who are likely to be the same species as the Di people. The large stone tombs along the Anning River, on the other hand, were built by the ancient Qiong people, who share a historical connection with the Qiang people.

According to Mr. Tong Enzheng, the Shu people were descendants of the Di people. The origin of the worship of large stones points to the ancient Di people, as they were the ones who established the ancient Shu kingdom.

This similarity can also be observed in the cultural trends. In the chapter titled *Cheng Han Figurines: The Eyes of the Di People Suspend in the Time Tunnel*, we will explore the connection and inheritance between the ancient Shu people and the Di people.

The Di people have long vanished, and the same can be said for the elusive Geji tribe, whose information can only be found in the epic poems of the Qiang people, who had once interacted with them. According to the epic *The Great Qiang-Ge Battle*, the Qiang people migrated from the Qinghai region towards the upper reaches of the Min River. Due to competition for survival resources, they encountered intense conflicts and even wars with the original residents of the area, the Geji people.

There are two main descriptions of the Geji people's appearance in the epic and legends of the Qiang people. One of them states that they were short in stature with slanted eyes. The short stature is a characteristic of the Negrito people, also known as "short black people", who carry the D-type Y

羌人是后来者，而戈基人是原住民，这也顺理成章。而眼睛竖起，正与“蜀人纵目”的记载相印证。

蜀人的主体氐作为一个族群，目前已经不见于中国的民族谱系，也就是说，它并不列于五十六个民族之中。不过，发源于今青海、甘肃相接处山岳之间的氐族，曾经在中国历史上大放异彩。

“五胡乱华”这个语句有些贬义，是因为这是从中原史家的视角所见，匈奴、鲜卑、羯、氐、羌，氐族正是五胡之一。在这次历史事件中闪亮登场的氐人苻坚，带着他的族群横扫中国北方，建立了地域广袤的前秦帝国，也给在乱世中艰苦求生之人带来了一线生机。惜乎英明了大半生的苻坚贸然南征东晋，在淝水之战中一败涂地而黯然退场。

苻坚之后，在陇南仇池山，一支杨姓氐人又悄然兴起。他们把王城建在山顶，就像在犬牙交错的南北势力板块中嵌入了一枚楔子，不时让北魏和刘宋两个巨无霸感受到神经疼痛。这个氐人政权在历史上最先被称作前仇池国，被同为氐人的苻坚所灭，不过他们很快复起，又建立起后仇池国。就这样，一次被灭，又一次复国，如是反复者五，在政权如蜉蝣般

chromosome and are among the earliest modern humans to migrate out of Africa. Therefore, in *The Great Qiang-Ge Battle*, the Qiang people are portrayed as the newcomers, while the Ge people are the indigenous inhabitants, which is consistent with this explanation. The depiction of slanted eyes also aligns with the recorded description of the “oblong-eyed Shu people”.

The main body of the Shu people, the Di, as an ethnic group, is no longer present in China’s ethnic classification. In other words, they are not among the 56 recognized ethnic groups in China. However, the Di ethnicity, originating from the mountains between present-day Qinghai and Gansu, once played a prominent role in Chinese history.

The phrase “The turmoil caused by the Five Barbarians” carries a slightly derogatory connotation, as it is a perspective from historians in the Central Plains. The Xiongnu, Xianbei, Jie, Di, and Qiang were the Five Barbarians, with the Di being one of them. In this historical event, the prominent Di leader Pu Jian emerged, sweeping across northern China and establishing the vast Former Qin Empire, which brought a glimmer of hope to those struggling for survival in turbulent times. Unfortunately, after a wise and illustrious reign, Pu Jian impulsively launched a southern campaign against the Eastern Jin Dynasty, only to suffer a devastating defeat at the Battle of Fei River and a humiliating retreat from the stage of history.

After Pu Jian, a branch of the Yang clan among the Di people quietly rose to prominence in the Chouchi Mountains of Longnan. They built their capital on the mountain top, becoming a wedge inserted into the complex landscape of competing northern and southern powers, causing occasional headaches for the formidable Northern Wei and Liu Song dynasties. This Di regime was initially known as Former

朝生暮死的大分裂时期，用三百八十年的时间，向世界诠释了“坚韧”这个词的含义。

蜀人就来自这样的民族。

对纵目的眼崇拜，生居石室，死则石棺葬，正是氐族最显著的文化特征。同华夏人相比，蜀人不仅习俗相异，语言也不同，他们使用的氐语很可能也属于汉藏语系，但因为目前尚未发现文字（或者说不能解读巴蜀文字）而无法让后世窥视更多。他们早年或许跟羌人发生过战争，作为羌族史诗《羌戈大战》中戈基人的形象存留了下来。其人种，甚至跟华夏族也不一样。

现代智人于十万年前走出非洲后，由于基因突变而分为三支：一支是黄种人与白种人的共同祖先；一支是C型棕种人；还有一支是D型棕种人，即前文所述尼格利陀人或矮黑人。

现生活于四川、甘肃交界地带的白马藏族，是氐人分支白马氐的后裔。人类学者曾对三代以内未与外族通婚的白马土著家族采样，发现其父系Y染色体几乎百分之百为Y-D单倍群。就是说，他们是尼格利陀人的直系后裔。

Chouchi State and was conquered by Pu Jian, another Di leader. However, they quickly rose again and established the Later Chouchi State. In this manner, they experienced a cycle of being conquered and rising again, repeating this pattern five times. During the tumultuous era of fragmented regimes, where powers rose and fell like fleeting insects, they, over a span of 380 years, exemplified the meaning of resilience.

The Shu people indeed hail from such an ethnic origin.

The worship of oblong eyes, dwelling in stone chambers, and burial in sarcophagus are indeed the most distinctive cultural characteristics of the Di people. Compared to the Han Chinese, the Shu people not only had different customs but also spoke a different language. The Di language they used likely belongs to the Sino-Tibetan language family. However, due to the lack of discovered writing (or the inability to decipher the Ba-Shu script), we are currently unable to gain further insight. They may have had conflicts with the Qiang people in their early years, and the imagery of the Ge people in the Qiang epic *The Great Qiang-Ge Battle*, could have preserved their appearance. Their ethnic characteristics even differ from those of the Han Chinese.

After modern humans migrated out of Africa around 100,000 years ago, they underwent genetic mutations that led to the formation of three main branches: one branch consists of the common ancestors of East Asians and Caucasians, another branch consists of the C-type Mongoloid population, and the third branch consists of the D-type Mongoloid population, which refers to the previously mentioned Negrito or short black people.

The modern-day Baima Tibetan people, living in the border area between Sichuan and Gansu, are descendants of a branch of the Di people known as the Baima Di. Anthropologists have conducted

白马氐的后裔白马藏族　余茂智 摄
The Baima Tibetan people, descendants of the Baima Di ethnicity (Photographer: Yu Maozhi)

sampling on indigenous Baima families who have not intermarried with outsiders for at least three generations. They have found that their paternal Y-chromosomes are almost 100% Y-D haplogroup, indicating that they are direct descendants of the Negrito people.

科普作家董仁威曾经带队考察氐人后裔生存的四川省平武县、九寨沟县，甘肃省文县等地，他在与韦富章合著的《我们从哪里来——生命女神的魔法》中写道：“（氐人）有着棕色人种D型遗传全结构，是纯血的棕种人。”

其他学者对于这个问题也有不同的看法。黄剑华先生《探寻古蜀国：从三星堆看中华文明》一书认为，从三星堆青铜像的人物造型看，古蜀人具有蒙古利亚人种（俗称“黄种人”）的特征。

古蜀国的民族源流十分复杂。因为缺少历史记载以及分子生物学的印证，研究者目前所掌握的信息碎片，还不足以构成强有力的证据链。但古蜀是以氐人为主体民族建立的国家，这一点得到了部分学者的认同。窃以为，将古氐人描述为古蜀国创立时的

Dong Renwei, a popular science writer, led a team to investigate the survival of the descendants of the Di people in areas such as Pingwu County and Jiuzhaigou County in Sichuan Province, as well as Wen County in Gansu Province. In his co-authored book *Where Do We Come From: The Magic of the Goddess of Life* with Wei Fuzhang, he wrote, “(The Di people) have the complete D-type genetic structure of the brown race and are pure brown people.”

Other scholars have different perspectives on this issue. In the book *Exploring the Ancient Shu State: Understanding Chinese Civilization through Sanxingdui*, author Huang Jianhua believes that based on the appearance of the figures in the bronze statues from Sanxingdui, the ancient Shu people exhibited characteristics of the Mongolian race (commonly known as “East Asian” or “yellow man”).

The ethnic origins of the ancient Shu state are extremely complex. Due to a lack of historical records and molecular biology evidence, the fragments of information currently available to researchers are not sufficient to form a strong chain of evidence. However, it is generally recognized by some scholars that the ancient Shu state was established by the Di people as the main ethnic group. Therefore, at this stage, it may be more accurate to describe the ancient

统治阶层，在目前阶段或更为准确。

古氐人在进入成都平原之后，与当地的土著居民结合交融，形成了一个全新的民族——蜀族。在数千年的时间里，他们都是成都平原的主人，直到在公元前316年被秦灭国。

也是从那个时候开始，蜀族走上了融入华夏之路。

Di people as the ruling class during the establishment of the ancient Shu state.

After the ancient Di people entered the Chengdu Plain, they integrated and merged with the local indigenous population, giving rise to a new ethnic group—the Shu people. For thousands of years, they were the dominant inhabitants of the Chengdu Plain until they were conquered by the Qin Dynasty in 316 BC.

It was during that time that the Shu people began their journey of assimilation into Han Chinese culture.

三星堆合掌青铜人像，其面部特征极具特色　高泓 摄
The distinctive facial features of the bronze clasped-hands statue from Sanxingdui (Photographer: Gao Hong)

自三星堆、金沙的发掘以来，古蜀文明以一种充满陌生感的方式，突然闪现在世人眼前。今天我们知道，习俗、语言乃至人种上的巨大差异，正是古蜀文明神秘莫测的根本原因。

在漫长的中国历史中，“华夷之辨”从未断绝。古蜀自然也是夷狄，如果它能入那些史家之法眼的话。然而，它是一支与华夏并肩生长的文化脉络，一棵共同向天空伸展的文明大树。

所谓“夷夏大防”，是以中原文化为正统的视角，用轻蔑、挑剔的目光来审视其他历史主体。其实，把眼

Since the discoveries at Sanxingdui and Jinsha, the ancient Shu civilization has suddenly appeared before us in a way that is filled with a sense of unfamiliarity. Today, we know that significant differences in customs, language, and even ethnicity are the fundamental reasons behind the mysterious nature of the ancient Shu civilization.

Throughout the long history of China, the distinction between “Huaxia” (Han Chinese) and “Yi” （barbarians）has never ceased. The ancient Shu civilization would naturally be considered as one of the “barbarian” groups if we follow the viewpoint of those historians. However, it is a cultural lineage that grew alongside Huaxia, a civilization that jointly reached towards the sky like a great tree.

The so-called “Yi-xia boundary”, which views Central Plains culture as the orthodox perspective and scrutinizes other historical entities with a condescending gaze, is actually a biased approach. If

光放平就会看到：黄河上空的神灯，并不是唯一的光源。在中国西南方的成都平原，同样有一束光突破厚重云层，照彻远古的蒙昧。

为什么一定要强调华夏尊于其他民族、其他文明呢？唐太宗李世民的观点比很多现代人远为开明，“夷狄亦人，其情与中夏不殊”，如锤击铜钟，轰然作响。然而，这还不够。为什么一定要一样呢？须知，神秘魅力的来源，正是独特性。三星堆之所以能“一醒惊天下”，正是因为它与华夏文明的形态迥然不同。

到了今日，“夷狄”之血液，早已融于华夏之血管。生生不息，源源不绝，吐故纳新。

we broaden our perspective, we will realize that the divine light above the Yellow River is not the only source of enlightenment. In the Chengdu Plain of southwestern China, there is also a beam of light that pierces through the ancient darkness.

Why do we have to emphasize the superiority of the Huaxia (Chinese) over other ethnic groups and civilizations? The viewpoint of Emperor Taizong of the Tang Dynasty, Li Shimin, was far more enlightened than many modern people. His belief that “barbarians are also human, and their emotions are no different from those of the Central Plains” resonates like a hammer striking a bronze bell. However, this is still not enough. Why must everything be the same? It should be understood that the source of mysterious allure lies precisely in uniqueness. The reason why the Sanxingdui culture was able to astonish the world is precisely because it differs greatly from the form of Huaxia civilization.

Today, the blood of “barbarians” has long been integrated into the veins of Huaxia. It continues to flow and renew itself, constantly evolving and embracing new influences.

古蜀人来自巍巍岷山，图为深处的龙溪羌寨　余茂智 摄

The ancient Shu people originates from the mighty Minshan Mountains. Shown is the remote Longxi Qiang Village. (Photographer: Yu Maozhi)

穿越天彭阙

沿国道213从茂县往松潘方向，即将进入海子山隧道时，会看到左侧一汪晶莹澄碧的湖泊，这就是叠溪海子，当年蚕丛部落活动的区域。汉代曾在此置蚕陵县，从名字可以看出它跟蚕丛的关联。

这个长条状的湖泊，海拔超过二千二百米，其实是在高山峡谷中穿行的岷江的一段。这里本来没有湖，直到1933年8月25日的大地震来临——其时天崩地裂，台地垂直下陷数百米，岷江水倾泻而入，将叠溪城及其数千军民沉入水底。

高山上的湖泊，美得如蓝宝石般惊心动魄，原来却是由这样的伤痛结晶而成。

Crossing the Tianpeng Què

When traveling along National Highway 213 from Mao County towards Songpan, just before entering the Haizi Mountain Tunnel, you will see a sparkling and clear lake on the left side. This is the Diexi Lake, the area where the Silkworm Tribe used to reside. During the Han Dynasty, a county called Canling was established here, indicating its connection to the Cancong Tribe.

This elongated lake sits at an altitude of over 2,200 meters and is actually a section of the Min River that meanders through the high mountain valley. Originally, there was no lake here until the massive earthquake of August 25, 1933. In this catastrophic event, the earth trembled and split apart, causing the plateau to sink vertically by several hundred meters. The rushing waters of the Min River poured in, submerging the city of Diexi along with its thousands of soldiers and civilians.

The lake on the mountains, stunning like sapphires, is formed from such a crystallized pain.

拍摄于1910年8月30日的叠溪，所在现为茂县叠溪镇排山营村水沟子组 （英）欧内斯特 · 亨利 · 威尔逊 摄

Diexi, photographed on August 30, 1910, now known as the Shuizigou Group of Paishanying Village in Diexi Town, Mao County. (Photographer: Ernest Henry Wilson, UK)

不时侵扰的地震，必然也给蚕丛部落带来巨大的困扰。他们终于决定离开家园，去山下寻找新的世界。

Frequent and disruptive earthquakes inevitably brought tremendous hardships to the Cancong Tribe. They finally made the decision to leave their homeland and seek a new world down the mountains.

顺着岷江奔往成都平原的方向，离开叠溪海子约六十千米之处，营盘山遗址考古曾经发掘出大量的新时代石器遗迹，包括房屋基址、人祭坑、窑址和灰炕等，距今5500—6000年。这应该就是蚕丛部落南下的第一站。

迁徙之路漫长而艰辛，从叠溪海子到湔江口不过数百千米，用去的时间却要以千年为单位来计。当蜀人来到接近平原之处，"接力棒"交到了柏濩手中。

第二代蜀王柏濩，史籍上的记载极少。《蜀王本纪》里也将其称为柏濩——"濩"的字形与"灌"类似，很可能是传抄中的讹误；另一说，"灌"与"濩"是同一种鸟。

从名字推测，柏灌及其部落活动的区域，很可能处于一个既有柏树也有灌木的地方，即高山与平原的交会处。而存世资料少，说明他开创的王朝存在的时间较短，很可能只是在蚕丛与鱼凫两个朝代之间起到过渡作用。

柏灌留下的遗迹几无，唯温江区寿安镇存有一柏灌王墓，载于清代和民国的地方志。当地百姓不识古意，依"柏灌"之音讹呼为八卦山。

柏灌墓位于成都第二绕城高速内

Continuing along the direction of the Min River towards the Chengdu Plain, approximately 60 kilometers away from Diexi Lake, lies the Yingpan Mountain Site. Archaeological excavations at this site have uncovered a vast number of Neolithic stone artifacts, including house foundations, sacrificial pits, kiln sites, and ash pits, dating back approximately 5,500 to 6,000 years. This is believed to be the first stop of the Cancong Tribe's southward migration.

The journey of migration was long and arduous. From Diexi Lake to the mouth of the Jian River, the distance was only a few hundred kilometers, but it took thousands of years to complete. When the Shu people reached the vicinity of the plain, the baton was passed into the hands of Boguan, continuing the relay of their ancestral heritage.

Very little is recorded about Boguan, the second-generation king of Shu. In the *Annals of the Kings of Shu*, he is also referred to as Bo Huo. The character "Huo" has a similar form to "Guan", indicating a likely transcription error. Another theory suggests that "Guan" and "Huo" are names for the same bird species.

From his name, it can be inferred that Boguan and his tribe were likely situated in an area where both cypress trees and shrubs grew, marking the intersection between mountains and plains. The scarcity of existing historical records indicates that the Dynasty he established had a relatively short existence and probably served as a transitional period between the Cancong and Yufu dynasties.

There are few remaining relics attributed to Boguan, but in Shou'an Town, in the Wenjiang District, there exists a tomb believed to belong to Boguan. It is mentioned in local annals from the Qing Dynasty and the Republic of China. However, the local residents, unfamiliar with its historical significance, mistakenly refer to it as Bagua Mountain

侧，车辆呼啸声清晰可闻。红砂石墓碑上，阴刻着“柏灌王墓”四个宋体大字，两侧为六幅石刻卷轴，显然修葺的年代非常近。碑前石刻香炉上，还有供奉的残香与白酒。碑后方的土堆即墓地，也就是所谓的八卦山，不过以现存的高度来看，实在算不上山。

due to the pronunciation of “Boguan”.

The tomb of Boguan is located on the inner side of the Second Ring Expressway in Chengdu, where the sound of passing vehicles can be heard. The red sandstone tombstone bears the deeply engraved Chinese characters “Tomb of Boguan”, with six scroll-shaped reliefs on either side. The tomb doesn’t have a sense of age and appears to have been renovated quite recently. On the stone incense burner in front of the tombstone, there are remnants of offerings and white liquor. The mound behind the tomb, said to be Bagua Mountain, is where the tomb is located. However, in terms of its present height, it can hardly be considered a mountain.

柏灌王墓　何大江 摄

The Tomb of King Boguan (Photographer: He Dajiang)

一名身着巴宝莉衬衣的当地人告诉笔者，王墓原本很大，占地4亩。20世纪70年代，当地令人在此取土烧砖，因此仅残留一小土堆。

以常理推断墓里所埋者，实在不太可能精确到史料中仅存名字的柏灌。关于此墓的记载，最早可上溯至清代，可见它被视作柏灌王墓的历史并不长。

不过，那位出生于1966年的长者说，在他很小的时候，曾见过堆砌陵墓的大青砖，上面刻有谁也不认识的、弯弯曲曲的文字。其实，这种无人能识的蝌蚪文，则很有可能是尚未破译的巴蜀文字。

A local resident, dressed in a Burberry shirt, told me that the original tomb was quite large, covering an area of 4 Mu（Mu, a unit of area, roughly equals 0.164 Mu）. In the 1970s, local authorities ordered some people to excavate soil and make bricks there, resulting in only a small mound remaining.

Based on common sense, it is highly unlikely that the tomb contained the remains of Boguan, who had minimal historical records and was only known by name. The earliest documentation regarding this tomb can be traced back to the Qing Dynasty, indicating that its association with Boguan’s tomb is relatively recent.

However, the elderly person I spoke to, born in 1966, mentioned that when he was very young, he saw large dark blue bricks used to construct the tomb, were adorned with unfamiliar and intricately curved characters. In fact, the tadpole-like script, which no one can read, is likely to be the undeciphered Ba-Shu script.

墓，的确是古墓，很可能是古蜀国某位贵族甚或王族之墓。不加辨析、夸大说辞，自为人之常情，久之则言之凿凿为柏灌王墓，并载于地方志，当地则据此修葺为柏灌的纪念性坟茔。

蜀人一路走向未知之地，一路回望故乡。而终于走完下山之路，通过天彭阙进入成都平原，这样的伟业则是由第三代开国蜀王鱼凫和他的王朝创下的。

天彭阙之阙，即汉阙之阙，宫门外左右各一的建筑。天彭阙是由湔江进入四川盆地的地标，东北岸的牛心山、西南岸的寿阳山隔江对峙，把守着江口，一幅两岸青山相对出的画面。古蜀人相信，人死之后魂魄会穿过天彭阙，回到远在岷山之上的老家。

天彭阙是具有象征意义的地形，左右相对的山峰构成了一道门，立在盆地西缘。越过天彭阙，就由高峭苦寒之乡进入了蜂蜜与牛奶流淌之地。碧鸡坊的两根石笋，则是一道无形之门，过了此门才能潜入古蜀秘境，与那些往来穿梭的先民之灵对话。

站在天彭阙下，古蜀人抬头回望，是逶迤连绵、积雪覆盖的高岸深谷；低首向下，是一望无垠、富饶

I speculate that this tomb has indeed existed for a long time, and it is likely the tomb of a noble or even a royal of the ancient Shu Kingdom. Without careful analysis, it is common for people to make exaggerated claims, and over time, it is claimed to be the tomb of Boguan, which is then recorded in local annals. Based on this claim, the locals renovated the site as a commemorative burial ground for Boguan.

The ancient Shu people embarked on a journey towards the unknown, continually looking back at their homeland. Finally, they completed the descent from the mountains and entered the Chengdu Plain through the Tianpeng Què, a monumental achievement led by the third-generation founder of the Shu Kingdom, King Yufu, and his Dynasty.

The Tianpeng Què resembles the Han Què, the two watchtowers on either outside the palace gate of the Han Dynasty. It serves as a landmark for entering the Sichuan Basin from the Jianshui River. Niu Xin Mountain on the northeast bank and Shouyang Mountain on the southwest bank stand opposite each other across the river mouth, guarding the entrance and forming a picturesque scene of green mountains on both sides. The ancient Shu people believed that after death, the soul would pass through the Tianpeng Què and return to their ancestral home on the distant Minshan Mountain.

The Tianpeng Què holds symbolic significance as a geographical feature. The opposing peaks of the mountains form a gate standing on the western edge of the basin. Passing through the Tianpeng Què takes one from the harsh and frigid highlands into a land flowing with honey and milk. On the other hand, the two stone spikes of the Biji Neighborhood form an invisible gate. Only after passing through this gate can one venture into the hidden realm of ancient Shu and engage in dialogue with the spirits of the ancestors who passed through.

丰盛的冲积扇平原。在新的家园，鱼凫、杜宇、开明三个王朝接力以继，开创了一种被后世称作古蜀、视为神秘莫测的文明。

蜀人固然热爱成都平原的湿润丰饶，但依然忘不了故乡山风给予的磨砺。他们在山口留下巨石以为路标，希冀不要忘记了归乡的路。

蜀人本来就是一个属于石头的民族。他们早年长在岷山，生，居于石室之中；死，葬于石棺之中，并在地表立石为记。他们以石斧劈木，以石锄犁地，以石箭射猎，以石戈和敌人搏斗。

生和死，蜀人都承受着那些巨大石头给予的庇护。

Standing beneath the Tianpeng Què, the ancient Shu people looked up to behold the winding, snow-covered high cliffs and deep valleys. Looking downwards, they beheld an expansive and fertile alluvial plain. In their new homeland, the Yufu, Duyu, and Kaiming dynasties succeeded each other, establishing a civilization that is now known as ancient Shu, revered as a mysterious and elusive one by later generations.

While the Shu people cherished the lush and fertile Chengdu Plain, they could never forget the ruggedness instilled by the mountain winds of their homeland. They left behind big stones at mountain passes as landmarks, ensuring that the path back home would never be forgotten.

The Shu people were inherently linked to stones. They grew up in the Min Mountains, lived in stone houses, and even in death, were laid to rest in stone coffins, leaving standing stones on the surface as memorials. They wielded stone axes to chop wood, used stone hoes to till the land, shot stone arrows for hunting, and fought enemies with stone spears.

In life and death, the Shu people relied on the protection bestowed by those massive stones.

大石崇拜

前文提到过，成都平原不产大石，那么石笋从何而来？让我们还是把眼光投向古蜀人的来处。从成都中心向西，不到一百千米，便延绵着东北—西南走向的龙门山脉和邛崃山脉，那里也是四川盆地和青藏高原的分界处。山中巨石磊磊，古蜀人为了信仰开山辟路，历经千辛万苦，将它

Worship of the Large Stones

As mentioned earlier, the Chengdu Plain lacks large stones. So where did the stone monuments come from? Let us turn our attention back to the origins of the ancient Shu people. Less than 100 kilometers west of Chengdu lies the Longmen Mountain Range and Qionglai Mountain Range, running northeast to southwest. This area marks the boundary between the Sichuan Basin and the Qinghai-Tibet Plateau. Among the mountains, enormous rocks stood tall. With unwavering faith, the ancient Shu people faced

们搬运回来，树立在成都平原，构筑起奇异的精神世界。

在中国其他地方乃至世界各地，都曾经存在过一个崇拜大石的时期。在四川，在西藏，在东南亚，在地中海，在欧洲，在非洲，在美洲，大石遗迹无处不在。它们呈现的方式也千姿百态，有巨大的独石，也有多块石头组合成的石阵；有尖塔，有列石，有平坊，有园垣，有墓门……

英国的索尔兹伯里巨石阵，是大石遗迹中广为人知者。巨石阵位于伦敦西南一百千米外的旷野，几十个巨大的石柱组成数个同心圆，石阵中心的巨石高达八米，重约三十吨。

巨石阵的用途，主要是天文观测或宗教祭祀。每年夏至时节，太阳初升，跟石阵的主轴连成一线。在巨石下方，人们顶礼膜拜，心怀畏惧。其修筑时间，在公元前4000年至公元前2000年，跟成都的大石遗迹一样，皆为新石器时代、青铜时代交接时的产物。

无论是成都的石笋、石镜、五块石、支机石，还是英国的索尔兹伯里巨石阵，都代表着人类在刚刚进入青铜时代那一刻对石器时代的回望与留恋，映照着人类先祖的精神世界。

巨石无声，默默地诉说着远古的

countless hardships, transporting these stones back to the Chengdu Plain and creating a unique spiritual world.

There existed a period of large stones worship not only in Sichuan but also in other parts of China and around the world. Stone monuments are ubiquitous, scattering across different regions such as Sichuan, Tibet, Southeast Asia, the Mediterranean, Europe, Africa, and the Americas. They exhibit a wide variety of forms, including massive individual stones and stone circles formed by multiple stones. There are towering obelisks, arranged stone columns, flat platforms, enclosed gardens, tomb gates, and more.

One of the most well-known examples of a stone monument is the Stonehenge in Salisbury, England. Located about a hundred kilometers southwest of London, this ancient monument consists of several concentric circles formed by dozens of enormous stone pillars. The central stones of the monument reach heights of up to 8 meters and weigh approximately 30 tons.

The purpose of Stonehenge was mainly astronomical observation or religious rituals. During the summer solstice, as the sun rises, it aligns perfectly with the axis of the stone circle. People gather beneath the gigantic stones to pay their respects and be enchanted by the atmosphere. The construction of Stonehenge took place roughly between 4000 BC and 2000 BC, coinciding with the period of large stone relics in Chengdu, overlapping between the Neolithic and Bronze Ages.

Whether it's the stalagmites, stone mirrors, Wukuaishi,or Zhiji Stone in Chengdu, or the Stonehenge in England, they all symbolize humanity's reflection and nostalgia for the Stone Age at the moment of entering the Bronze Age, reflecting the spiritual world of our ancestors.

These colossal stones speak silently, recounting

故事。

杜甫见过的那两株石笋，南宋时还竖立在成都街头，元代时已不复存在，应毁于南宋末年的战乱之中。宋末元初的战争，是成都建城后数千年来仅有的两次大劫难之一；另一次则发生在明末清初，后文将反复提及。

今日的石笋街，是一条东北—西南走向的僻静小街，其街口则是那两株石笋曾经伫立之处。在石笋街与席草田街交界之处，曾有一家鸿雁皮革厂，某年在此打井，便用残损的石笋作了井口边壁。如今，井已被填封，石笋再无可觅迹，只让凭吊者空自感叹。

ancient stories through time.

The two stone pillars that Du Fu had seen were still standing on the streets of Chengdu during the Southern Song Dynasty. However, they were no longer present during the Yuan Dynasty, presumably destroyed during the wars at the end of the Southern Song Dynasty. These wars marked one of the two major calamities to befall Chengdu in its thousands of years since its founding. The other occurred during the transition from the late Ming Dynasty to the early Qing Dynasty, as will be mentioned later in this book.

Today, Shisun Street is a quiet street running northeast to southwest, and its junction is where the two stone pillars once stood. At the intersection of Shisun Street and Xicaotian Street, there used to be a Hongyan Leather Factory. At some point, when a well was dug at this location, the damaged stone pillars were used as the wellhead lining. Now, the well has been sealed, and the stone pillars are no longer visible, leaving only a sense of emptiness for those who come to pay their respects.

青铜大立人
The Bronze Giant Standing Figure

衣饰华丽，神情霸气，体量巨大，青铜大立人出土于三星堆二号坑，通高2.6米，戴冠人像高1.8米。其身份，公认是古蜀国集神权、王权于一身的大祭司或大巫师。

The Bronze Giant Standing Figure, adorned in magnificent attire and exuding an authoritative aura, was unearthed from Pit No. 2 at Sanxingdui. Standing at an impressive height of 2.6 meters, the figure features a crowned individual measuring 1.8 meters in height. The accepted identity of this figure is that of a high priest or grand sorcerer who possessed both divine and royal authority in the ancient Shu Kingdom.

青铜大立人：鱼凫王幻影
Bronze Giant Standing Figure: Illusion of King Yufu

访鱼凫城故址
清 · 王侃

湔水滔滔送远天，
鱼凫踪迹久茫然。
但闻仙去乘斑虎，
不肯魂归作暮鹃。

Visiting the Ruins of Yufu City
Wang Kan, Qing Dynasty

The Jian River flows ceaselessly, reaching towards the distant sky,

The tracks of Yufu have long been lost, as time passes by.

Only tales remain of the immortal riding on a

万古衣冠沉土壤，
一朝宫殿剩桑田。
欲寻故老谈兴废，
大墓山前霭白烟。

spotted tiger, his departure unknown,
Reluctant to let the soul return, like the evening cuckoo that has not flown.
For thousands of years, his robe and crown sink into the earth,
In just a moment, the palace is reduced to mulberry fields.
Yearning to seek wisdom from the elders, discussing rise and fall,
Before the Grand Tomb Mountain, white mist hovers, unveiling a mysterious call.

清代嘉庆年间温江名士王侃这首诗，怀古于鱼凫城旧址，在鱼凫王墓前追思古蜀国鱼凫王的穷途末路。在王朝更替的争霸战中，第三代蜀王鱼凫败给了第四代蜀王杜宇之后，乘斑斓猛虎化仙而去。

诗中的大墓山，位于温江区寿安镇喻庙社区，距三星堆遗址直线距离不到五十千米。顾名思义，大墓山就是一座山一般的大坟。相传，鱼凫王就埋葬于此。

“乘虎而去”之说出自《成都记》，而《蜀王本纪》则称：“（鱼凫）王猎至湔山，便仙去。今庙祀之于湔。”湔山鱼凫庙已无迹可寻，但大墓山的鱼凫王墓却以实体的方式存在。

五代古蜀王的说法，长期被视作虚无缥缈乃至荒诞不经。然而，随着

During the Jiaqing era of the Qing Dynasty, the renowned scholar Wang Kan expressed his nostalgic sentiments at the ruins of Yufu City and reflected upon the tragic fate of King Yufu, an ancient ruler of the Shu Kingdom. In a battle for supremacy, the third generation king, Yufu, was defeated by the fourth generation king, Duyu. Legend has it that after his defeat, King Yufu transformed into an immortal and departed riding on a magnificent tiger.

The Grand Tomb Mountain mentioned in the poem is located in Yumiao Community, Shou'an Town, Wenjiang District, less than 50 kilometers in a straight line from the Sanxingdui archaeological site. As the name suggests, the grand tomb is a large burial mound resembling a mountain. According to legend, King Yufu was buried there.

The mention of “riding on a tiger” comes from *Records of Chengdu*, while the *Annals of the Kings of Shu* states, “Yufu hunted at Jian Mountain and then transcended into an immortal. His temple is now located on Jian Mountain.”The Yufu Temple on Jian Mountain can no longer be found, but the physical existence of King Yufu's tomb on the grand mound remains.

For a long time, the existence of ancient

三星堆遗址的惊世发掘，界限开始模糊，神话渐成真实。鱼凫王的形象也透过一卷卷竹简、一张张黄纸，以及古城遗址的一道道土埂、一件件文物浮现出来。

Shu kings during the Five Dynasties period was seen as elusive and even absurd. However, with the astonishing discovery of the Sanxingdui archaeological site, the boundaries began to blur, and myths began to transform into reality. The image of King Yufu emerged through bamboo slips, yellowed papers, and the earth mounds of ancient city ruins; and each artifact revealed a part of his story.

以凫之名

三星堆二号坑出土的青铜大立人，威风霸气，睥睨万物。观其面容，如通过一组长焦镜头，将远古人物拉近到眼前。

青铜大立人　高泓 摄

Bronze Giant Standing Figure (Photographer: Gao Hong)

青铜大立人通高260.8厘米，下为底座，上面的人像高一百八十厘米。放在全世界的范围，也是数千年内体量最大的青铜人物雕像，俨然“世界青铜器之王”。

他衣饰华贵，头戴莲花形兽眼高冠，冠顶四片莲花形插片；身着左衽三件套装，其外衣半臂，垂至膝盖，上面绣有黑色的神兽纹、鸟纹、夔龙

In the Name of Cormorants

The bronze figure of the Second Pit at the Sanxingdui archaeological site, known as the Bronze Giant Standing Figure, portrays a majestic and domineering presence, seeming to overlook all things. Observing its facial expression is like looking through a set of telephoto lenses, bringing an ancient figure close to the present.

The Bronze Giant stands an impressive height of 260.8 centimeters, with a figure on top measuring 180 centimeters in height. It is among the largest bronze statues in the world, making it the “king of bronze artifacts” for thousands of years.

The figure is adorned in luxurious attire, wearing a high lotus-shaped crown with animal eyes and four lotus-shaped inserts on the top of the crown. The clothing consists of a three-piece outfit with the left side overlapping the right. The tunic is half-armed and reaches the knees, with elaborate black

纹和卷云纹。

十七厘米的华冠之下，立人身高163厘米，从体形看很可能是一座写实的雕塑。但是，其面部五官却极为夸张——眼、耳、口、鼻、眉撑满了整个面庞，不凡气宇即从此来。鼻居正中，如山岳耸峙；浓眉、鼓目，甚至眼下的法令纹，都一直伸展到正脸轮廓线以外；两耳则上至眉线以上，下达嘴角水平线；口与下巴皆为一字，又平又直；靠近脸庞边沿的双唇紧闭着，透露出无限的威严。

更夸张的是两只手，皆攥成空心拳，单手就比头颅还大。手中所执之物早已不存，或朽于时光，或毁于外力。至于到底所执何物，或说是敬天礼地的玉琮，或说是硕大的象牙。以笔者推断，玉琮外形如立柱，而两手相错，曲直不能相容；而象牙形状有弧度，契合两手中空的位置——毕竟，古蜀国旧都三星堆和金沙，都出土过大量的巨型象牙。

这种猜测，非常类似于世人对希腊雕塑维纳斯两只手臂的推测。1820年，维纳斯女神像出土于爱琴海米洛岛之后，两百年来就不断有人根据肌理走向或文化意象为其制作双臂复原图。在复原图中，有一只手搭在腰间，另一只手托金苹果者；也有两只

embroidery portraying mythological beasts, birds, Kui dragons, and swirling clouds.

Under the 17 centimeters high crown, the figure stands at 163 centimeters tall, appearing to be a realistic sculpture. However, the facial features are highly exaggerated—the eyes, ears, mouth, nose, and eyebrows occupy the entire face, emanating a remarkable presence. The nose stands prominently in the center, resembling a towering mountain. Thick eyebrows, bulging eyes, and even the nasolabial folds extend beyond the contour of the face. The ears extend above the eyebrow line and reach the level of the mouth corners. The mouth and chin are straight and flat. The tightly closed lips near the contour of the face exude immense dignity.

Even more exaggerated are the hands, clenched into hollow fists that are even larger than the head. The objects held in the hands no longer exist, either decayed by time or destroyed by external forces. The exact nature of these objects is a subject of debate, with some suggesting they could be a Jade Cong, symbols used for reverence towards heaven and earth, while others propose the possibility of a large ivory object. Based on my inference, the Jade Cong, which has a columnar shape, would not fit within the interlocked hands, as there is no space to contain it. On the other hand, the curvature of an ivory object would align with the hollow space between the two hands. After all, significant amounts of large ivory have been unearthed from the ancient capitals of the Shu Kingdom, Sanxingdui, and Jinsha.

This speculation is very similar to the case of the Greek sculpture of the Venus de Milo with missing arms. Since its discovery on the island of Milos in the Aegean Sea in 1820, there have been continuous attempts over the past two centuries to recreate the missing arms based on the texture lines or cultural symbolism. In these reconstructions, one hand is placed on the waist, while the other extends

手都前伸，掌中停驻和平鸽者。

好奇心驱使人类探索未知，但是，在有切实的实物证据出来之前，不管是青铜大立人所执何物，还是维纳斯两臂到底长成什么样子，都不可能得出让所有人信服的结论。

青铜大立人究竟是什么身份，引人无限遐想。

一说是群巫之长——统领古蜀神权政治的大祭司或大巫师。

且构想一下那巫师云集的场面：四周是那些或大或小的青铜面具、头像，有的脸上戴着金面罩，有的眼珠像柱子一般突伸出来，有的脸宽阔得接近人展开的双臂，而青铜大立人直端端地挺立在中央。

那是一个众神云集、巫法昌盛的时代。其实，在历史的“大磨”碾压数千年之后，巫的痕迹尚存流风遗韵，飘荡于蜀山蜀水。公元前316年，秦灭蜀建蜀郡，行政归于集权，文明同于华夏，但大一统文化的洪流不可能冲刷至每一个角落。

女曰巫，男曰觋。西汉初年，文翁掌蜀时忧见巫觋之风盛行；到了东汉，张道陵在蜀地创立的天师教，即深受崇拜鬼神的巫术影响。甚至在数十年前，四川农村依然盛产俗称“娘娘婆”的巫和俗称“端公”的觋。

forward, supporting a golden apple, or both hands are extended forward, cradling a dove of peace.

Curiosity drives humans to explore the unknown. However, without tangible evidence, whether it is the object held by the Bronze Giant or the exact appearance of the arms of the Venus de Milo, it is impossible to reach a conclusion that would convince everyone.

The identity of the Bronze Giant raises endless speculation.

One theory suggests that it could be the chief sorcerer or high priest who dominated the ancient Shu Kingdom's religious and political power.

Picture the scene where these sorcerers gather: surrounded by various sizes of bronze masks and sculptures, some wearing golden masks on their faces, others with eyes protruding like pillars, and some with faces so broad they could almost approach a man's spreading arms. Amidst them all stands the Bronze Giant, towering in the center.

The era of the Bronze Giant was a time of gods gathering and flourishing witchcraft. In reality, even after thousands of years of historical changes, traces of witchcraft still lingered between the mountains and rivers of Shu. In 316 BC, the Qin Dynasty conquered Shu and established Shu County, bringing centralized administration and cultural assimilation to the region. However, the sweeping torrents of monolithic culture could not wash over every corner.

Women who practise sorcery are called witches, and men who engage in witchcraft are called wizards. In the early Western Han Dynasty, when Wen Weng governed Shu, he expressed concern over the prevalent practice of witchcraft and divination. During the Eastern Han Dynasty, Zhang Daoling founded the Celestial Masters' teaching in Shu, which was deeply influenced by the worship of ghosts and gods. Even a few decades ago, in rural areas of Sichuan, there were still witches called "Niangniangpo" and wizards

"巫教"一词，仍作为"黑暗""污浊"的同义词广泛存在于四川人的口语之中。1986年，笔者寄居于阆中张飞庙，就见过娘娘婆带着病人请神。病人跪拜在张飞像前，娘娘婆口中念念有词，动作夸张得像一只虚张声势的浣熊。

一说，青铜大立人象征的是某一代蜀王，或者是王与大祭司的合体。若此，具体而微者，按年代等因素推算，他很可能就是第三代蜀王鱼凫，一位集神权和王权于一体的大祭司、王者。

前文提及，古蜀人兴于岷江上游，在第一代蜀王蚕丛、第二代蜀王柏灌的带领之下，顺着河谷往下，朝成都平原迁徙。当中原华夏进入殷商早期时，蜀族则到达了龙门山湔江口，而此时生产方式已发展为渔猎，而文化序列上则为新石器文明与青铜文明的过渡期。

以渔猎为生的蜀族，用他们的生产资料——鱼凫——作了部族之名。鱼凫，学名鸬鹚，在四川也被称为"鱼老鸹"。鱼凫有一长喙，喉部有一囊。用喙捕鱼后，可暂时储于囊内。鱼凫部落驯化了鸬鹚，在其喉部系有一绳，使之捕鱼之后不能咽下，待其回到船上再强令吐出。

called "Duangong". The term "witchcraft" was still widely used in the Sichuan dialect as a synonym for "darkness" and "impurity". In 1986, when I was in high school, I stayed near Zhang Fei Temple in Langzhong and witnessed witches bringing patients to pray before the statue of Zhang Fei, seeking the deity's divine intervention.

One theory suggests that the Bronze Giant symbolizes a specific generation of Shu emperors or a fusion of kingship and high priesthood. If this is the case, taking into account factors such as the timeline, it is highly likely that the Bronze Giant represents Yufu, the third generation Shu King. He embodied the roles of both a high priest and an emperor, combining divine authority and royal power.

As mentioned earlier, the ancient Shu people originated in the upper reaches of the Min River. Under the leadership of the first and second generations of Shu Emperors, Cancong and Boguan, they migrated downstream along the river valley to the Chengdu Plain. Meanwhile, as the Central Plains of China entered the early Yin-Shang period, the Shu people reached the confluence of Longmen Mountain and Jian River. At this time, their production modes had evolved into fishing and hunting, marking a transitional period between the Neolithic and Bronze Age civilizations in terms of cultural development.

The Shu tribe, who lived by fishing and hunting, used their means of production, the Yufu for the name of their tribe. Yufu is a water bird scientifically known as a cormorant, which is also called "Yu Laogua", literally means the old fish crow in Sichuan. The cormorant has a long beak and a pouch in its throat. After catching fish with its beak, it can temporarily store them in the pouch. The Yufu tribe domesticated cormorants, tying a rope around their throats to prevent them from swallowing the fish they caught until they returned to the boat, where the fish would be forcefully spit out.

古蜀人到达湔江口时，以渔猎为生。以鸬鹚捕鱼的方式存留至如今　徐平 摄

When the ancient Shu people arrived at the Jianjiang River mouth, they lived by fishing and hunting. The practice of fishing with cormorants remains to this day. (Photographer: Xu Ping)

蜀人借助鱼凫这种水鸟，在湔江中捕鱼为食，保证了在迁移途中的生存与壮大。鱼凫，对蜀人来说如此重要，以至于不仅成了他们的族名，也成为其图腾和族徽——三星堆出土的鸟形青铜器，多有长喙，而喙的前端是锐利的弯钩，这正是鱼凫（鸬鹚）的典型特征。

The Shu people relied on Yufu, to catch fish in the Jian River, ensuring their survival and growth during their migration. The importance of the cormorant to the Shu people was so great that it not only became their tribal name but also their totem and emblem. Many bird-shaped bronze artifacts unearthed at the Sanxingdui site have long beaks with sharp curved hooks, which is a typical characteristic of cormorants.

三星堆鸟形青铜器，锐钩是鱼凫（鸬鹚）的典型特征　高泓 摄

Sanxingdui bird-shaped bronze artifact, featuring the sharp hook characteristic of cormorants (Photographer: Gao Hong)

鱼凫部族的开创者，就是第一代鱼凫王。

The founder of the Yufu tribe is the first King Yufu (also called Yufu Emperor).

王墓里面埋着谁？

Who is buried inside the royal tomb?

穿过天彭阙的蜀族，如种子一般播撒在成都平原上，迸发出野草一般的蓬勃生命力。他们在平原上建立了

The Shu people, who passed through the Tianpeng Què, spread across the Chengdu Plain like seeds, bursting with vibrant vitality like wild grass. They established numerous cities on the plain,

众多的城市，如星星一般拱卫着王都三星堆。目前发现的古城遗址，有宝墩（新津）、古城（郫都）、鱼凫（温江）、芒城（都江堰）、双河（崇州）、紫竹（崇州）、盐店（大邑）、高山（大邑）等八个。

作为成都平原史前遗址之一的鱼凫村，曾经是古蜀人的聚落。鱼凫村遗址位于温江城以北约五千米六边形的旧址上，报恩寺、冯家墩子、罗家院子、过家院子、戴家院子和雷家院子依逆时针方向环绕一周。

罗家院子位于鱼凫村遗址西侧边缘，占地约三十亩，住户计十九户。清渠从其间穿过，四周花木园圃环绕，青砖砌就的镂空花格墙内，房屋白墙黛瓦，略有几分古朴意趣。

笔者造访的那个下午，阳光和煦，土生土长、五十岁出头的肖四哥正坐在路边修理农机。肖四哥指着面前一片林木间隔的油菜田说，这里曾经有一道一二十米高的土埂子（城墙），由于长年取土烧砖，如今几乎啥都不剩了。几十年前，文物部门的人说不能再烧了，需要保护。肖四哥口中的“保护”，指的是1996年和1999年的两次钻探，两次发掘曾清理出大量文物。

城市是文明的结晶，而城墙是城

arching over the royal capital of Sanxingdui like stars. Among the prehistoric city ruins discovered so far are Baodun (Xinjin), Gucheng (Pidu), Yufu (Wenjiang), Mangcheng (Dujiangyan), Shuanghe (Chongzhou), Zizhu (Chongzhou), Yandian (Dayi), Gaoshan (Dayi), a total of eight ancient cities.

Yufu Village, as one of the prehistoric sites on the Chengdu Plain, was once a settlement of the ancient Shu people. The Yufu Village site is located approximately 5 kilometers north of Wenjiang City, on a hexagonal-shaped site. Surrounding the site in a counterclockwise direction are Bao’en Temple, Fengjia Courtyard, Luojia Courtyard, Guojia Courtyard, Daijia Courtyard, and Leijia Courtyard.

Luojia Courtyard is situated on the western edge of the Yufu Village site, covering an area of about 30 Mu. It consists of 19 households. A clear canal runs through it, surrounded by gardens filled with flowers and trees. Within a lattice wall made of green bricks, the houses have white walls and black roofs, exuding an ancient and rustic charm.

On the afternoon of my visit, the sun was warm and gentle. Xiao sige, a man in his fifties, who was born and raised there, sat by the roadside repairing agricultural machinery. Pointing towards the rapeseed fields interspersed with patches of trees, he mentioned that there used to be a 10 to 20-meter-high earthen embankment (city wall) here, but due to continuous digging and brick-making over the years, almost nothing remains today. Several decades ago, the cultural relics department declared that no further excavation should take place, as protection was necessary. By “protection”, Brother Xiao means the two excavations in 1996 and 1999, a large number of cultural relics were unearthed and cleared out.

Cities are the culmination of civilization, and city walls serve as their protectors.

The construction method of the city walls at

市的保护者。

鱼凫村遗址城墙的建筑方式跟宝墩城一样，皆为堆筑。即先用土堆至一个高度，再由城墙内外两个方向斜向拍夯形成厚度。如是叠加，一层又一层。各层间有鹅卵石，以加固结构。

从剖面看，墙体呈梯形，这意味着墙面并非垂直于地面，而是有一个斜坡。这样的城墙，或许并不能抵御外敌，却可以拒抗水灾。而紧密排列的卵石，也让墙体变得更坚固，能减缓洪水的冲击。这种堆筑的方式，后来也被用于三星堆城垣的修建。

在肖四哥所指的土埂子处，立有全国重点文物单位标志保护碑，上刻“成都平原史前城址”字样。鱼凫村遗址的发现也给当地村民的生活带来了改变。肖四哥说，一二十年前，在文物部门的帮助下，鱼凫村就用上了天然气和自来水，“这在农村是很少见的”。

鱼凫村遗址属于宝墩文化的第三期和第四期，而宝墩文化则是成都平原上迄今能追溯到的最早的考古学文化——产生于新石器时代晚期，距今4500—3700年。

1964年4月，考古学家冯汉骥先生率四川大学历史系考古专业1960级

Yufu Village Site and Baodun City were both made by earthwork. Firstly, soil was piled up to a certain height, and then it was compacted from both the inside and outside of the city walls at an inclined angle to form the desired thickness. This process was repeated layer by layer, with pebbles placed between each layer to reinforce the structure.

From a cross-section perspective, the walls had a trapezoidal shape, indicating that the wall surface was not perpendicular to the ground but sloped. This type of city wall may not have been able to withstand external enemies, but it was effective in resisting floods. The tight arrangement of pebbles on the wall surface also increased its strength and reduced the impact of flooding. This construction method was later used in the construction of the city walls at the Sanxingdui site.

At the location mentioned by Xiao sige, there stands a monument with the inscription “Prehistoric City Site of Chengdu Plain”, indicating its status as a nationally significant cultural heritage site. The discovery of the Yufu Village Site has also brought about changes in the lives of the local villagers. Xiao sige mentioned that with the assistance of the cultural heritage department, Yufu Village was able to access natural gas and tap water one or two decades ago, “which is quite rare in rural areas”.

The Yufu Village Site belongs to the third and fourth phases of the Baodun Culture, which is the earliest archaeological culture known on the Chengdu Plain to date. It originated in the Late Neolithic period, 4,500 to 3,700 years ago.

In April 1964, Mr. Feng Hanji, an archaeologist, led a group of students from the Archaeology Department of Sichuan University to conduct field surveys. They discovered visible remains of city walls on the surface of the Yufu City site, with the tallest section reaching a height of 2.9 meters.

学生进行田野调查，发现当时的鱼凫城遗址地面上保存有明显的城垣，其中最高处残存2.9米。

1996年秋天的发掘表明，二千一百一十米城垣围起的六边形古城面积约三十二万平方米，保存得较为完整的尚有一千八百米左右。遗址内还有灰坑、灰沟和房址，其中房址存基槽或柱洞。

鱼凫村遗址出土的文物以陶器为主，石器较少。第一、二期出土的陶器，其绳纹、篦划纹、瓦楞纹等，与宝墩遗址的文化遗存相一致；而镂孔圈足器则在形制、纹饰上与三星堆一期遗存接近。

成都平原史前遗址，包括温江鱼凫村遗址在内，加上新津宝墩、都江堰芒城、崇州双河等共八座古城址，都是蜀人进入成都平原后创造的新石器晚期文化。因为宝墩古城的面积最大，达到六十万平方米，这一独立的考古学文化因此被命名为宝墩文化。

鱼凫村遗址一、二期，已属于宝墩文化的最后发展阶段；而第三期则介于三星堆遗址的一、二期之间。

在宝墩文化与三星堆文化之间，鱼凫村遗址起着承上启下的作用。实际上，随着考古发掘和研究的深入，宝墩文化—三星堆文化—十二桥文化

According to a survey conducted in the autumn of 1996, the hexagonal ancient city enclosed by a 2,110-meter city wall covered an area of approximately 320,000 square meters. Around 1,800 meters of the city wall remains relatively intact. Within the site, there are also ash pits, ash trenches, and house foundations, some of which still have base grooves or pillar holes.

The cultural relics unearthed at the Yufu Village Site are mainly pottery, with fewer quantities of stone tools. The pottery from the first and second phases of the site exhibits rope patterns, comb patterns, and corrugated patterns, which are consistent with the cultural remains at the Baodun Site. On the other hand, the perforated round-footed vessels show similarities in form and decoration with the first phase remains at the Sanxingdui site.

The prehistoric sites in Chengdu Plain, including the Yufu Village Site in Wenjiang, along with the Baodun Site in Xinjin, the Mangcheng Site in Dujiangyan, the Shuanghe Site in Chongzhou, and four other ancient city sites, were all part of the Late Neolithic culture created by the Shu people after their settlement in the Chengdu Plain. Among them, the Baodun ancient city had the largest area, covering 600,000 square meters. This independent archaeological culture was thus named the Baodun Culture.

The first and second phases of the Yufu Village Site already belong to the last development stage of the Baodun Culture. The third phase falls between the first and second phases of the Sanxingdui Site.

The Yufu Village Site plays a transitional role between the Baodun Culture and the Sanxingdui Culture. In fact, as archaeological excavations and research have progressed, a clear development sequence of ancient Shu culture has emerged: the Baodun Culture—Sanxingdui Culture—Shierqiao

（以金沙遗址为代表）这一古蜀发展脉络也日渐清晰。

在三星堆出土的文物中，有两件能够充分证明它是这一时期古蜀王国的都邑——青铜大立人，以及后文将讲述的金权杖。而鱼凫村遗址，则是修筑得更早的古蜀国大型聚落——从其规模观之，不排除是三星堆城之前的古蜀国都城。

如果说，青铜大立人以鱼凫王为原型，那么这位曾威赫一时的王，在脚下的这片土地上还留下了什么痕迹呢？

就在鱼凫村遗址西北方向十千米，三星堆遗址东南方向五十千米，有文首诗《访鱼凫城故址》中的大墓山，传说鱼凫王就埋葬于此。

喻庙中心道是条不算宽的乡村道路，车停靠在路边，一条十数米长、条石与鹅卵石相间铺就的小径从中心道上分出，通往鱼凫王墓。

在一片绿树红花之中，一个占地三千平方米的封土堆平地而起。这个南北朝向的单冢墓，由四层条石砌成墓基，坟上覆盖着茵茵绿草。墓前石雕香炉上还插着残剩的香烛，一只炉耳已被烟火熏黑。香炉与墓之间，立着一块条形的红砂石碑，上刻“鱼凫王之陵”。从一旁的文物保护单位标

Culture (represented by the Jinsha Site).

Among the artifacts unearthed at the Sanxingdui Site, two items provide strong evidence of its status as the capital of the ancient Shu Kingdom during that period: the Bronze Giant and the Gold Scepter, which will be discussed later. On the other hand, the Yufu Village Site, although similar in scale to Sanxingdui, represents an earlier large settlement of the ancient Shu Kingdom—possibly even the ancient capital before the establishment of Sanxingdui.

If the Bronze Giant was modeled after King Yufu, then what other traces did this once prominent ruler leave on the land he once governed?

Just ten kilometers northwest of the Yufu Village Site, and fifty kilometers southeast of the Sanxingdui Site, lies the Grand Tomb Mountain, mentioned in the opening poem *Visiting the Ruins of Yufu City*. Legend has it that King Yufu was buried there.

The centre road of Yumiao is a narrow rural road. One needs to park the car by the roadside, and walk along a pathway, branching off from the central road and leading to King Yufu's tomb. The pathway, consisting of stone slabs and pebbles, stretches for about a dozen meters.

Amidst the lush greenery and vibrant red flowers, the mound of the tomb rises flatly, occupying an area of 3,000 square meters. This north-south oriented singular burial mound is constructed with four layers of slates as its base, covered with lush green grass. Remnants of incense and candles can be found on the stone-carved incense burner in front of the tomb, with one of its ears blackened from smoke. Between the incense burner and the tomb stands a rectangular red sandstone tablet, inscribed with the words "The Tomb of King Yufu". The nearby monument of the cultural heritage unit reveals that King Yufu's Tomb was officially designated as

志碑上可以看出，鱼凫王墓于2019年1月被确定为“四川省文物保护单位”。

a “Sichuan Provincial Cultural Heritage Unit” in January 2019.

与大墓山相对，距其西北方向1.6千米左右的小墓山，相传曾有鱼凫王妃墓。经不住岁月的侵蚀，载于温江地方志中的古迹小墓山已成平地。当地的村民告诉笔者，小墓山仅仅是留下了一个名字。第二代蜀王柏灌之墓，则在大墓山以东不到三千米。

In contrast to the Grand Tomb Mountain, there is a smaller mountain located approximately 1.6 kilometers northwest, called the Small Tomb Mountain, which is said to be the tomb of King Yufu’s consort. Over the years, due to ages’ erosion,the Small Tomb Mountain, recorded in the local chronicles of Wenjiang, has become a flat ground. Local villagers have informed me that the Small Tomb Mountain now only exists as a name. On the other hand, the tomb of the second-generation Shu Emperor, Boguan, lies less than 3 kilometers east of Grand Tomb Mountain.

俯瞰大墓山。鱼凫王墓处于乡村道路旁，周围散落着农居　师婵 摄

Aerial view of the Grand Tomb Mountain. The tomb of King Yufu lies beside a rural road, surrounded by scattered farmhouses. (Photographer: Shi Chan)

一座王妃墓、一座前朝王墓分布在周围，鱼凫王墓到底有怎样的秘密？

With a princess consort’s tomb and a former emperor’s tomb scattered in the surrounding area, what secrets does King Yufu’s tomb hold?

鱼凫王墓在清乾隆、嘉庆以及民国年间皆记载于温江地方志上，此前数千年的漫长岁月里，更有口口相传。

The tomb of Yufu, passed down orally through countless generations for thousands of years, was recorded in local chronicles during the Qing Dynasty’s Qianlong and Jiaqing reigns, as well as in the Republican era.

这座大墓里面是否真的埋葬着古蜀鱼凫王呢？曾有友人教于笔者：成都平原上的大土堆，若非陵墓则为祭台，要不然即古城墙。

But is it true that the ancient Shu King Yufu was actually buried in this grand tomb? A friend once told me: the large mounds on the Chengdu Plain are either tombs or sacrificial altars, or perhaps ancient city walls.

以常识推之，墓中埋着的，很可

Using common sense, it is more likely that a noble from ancient Shu is buried within the tomb rather than Yufu himself. The situation is quite similar to the Boguan tomb, which is understandable.

能是某位古蜀贵族。若说为鱼凫王本尊，概率要小很多。这与柏灌墓的情况非常相似，也好理解，毕竟夸大其词也是人之常情。

Exaggeration is a common human inclination, after all.

鱼凫王猜想

前文提及，“古蜀五祖”蚕丛、柏灌、鱼凫、杜宇、鳖灵这五个名字的使用混乱给后世带来巨大的困扰，比如我们谈及鱼凫时就会面临这样的困境。鱼凫可能是一个空间上的部族，也可能是一个时间上的王朝；而鱼凫王，则往往被默认为开国君主，但他也可能是末代君主（比如乘斑斓猛虎而去的那位），或者是几百年上千年王朝中的任何一位。

容忍神话的久远吧！原谅巫师吟诵史诗时把众王叫成一个名字的行为吧！毕竟，文学史诗《百年孤独》也在干这样的事，小说里有众多的阿尔卡蒂奥、奥雷里亚诺以及梅蕾黛丝。人名的重复，象征着家族的宿命——无穷无尽的孤独。

鱼凫这个名字，也有同样的隐喻。不是吗？开创、衰败、中兴、灭亡，历史就是一个车轱辘，转了一圈又一圈。

一切都可以解释了。

Speculations on King Yufu

As mentioned earlier, the use of the names Cancong, Boguan, Yufu, Duyu, and Bieling, known as the “Five Ancestors of Ancient Shu”, can cause great confusion for later generations. When discussing Yufu, we are faced with such a dilemma. Yufu could refer to a spatial tribe or a temporal Dynasty. Meanwhile, Yufu is often assumed to be the founding monarch, but he could also be the last ruler (like the one who rode on a bright-colored tiger and vanished), or any ruler within the span of hundreds or even thousands of years.

Let us tolerate the remoteness of the ancient myths and forgive the epics recited by the sorcerers who have assigned a collective name to various emperors. After all, even in the literary epic *One Hundred Years of Solitude*, there are numerous characters named Arcadio, Aureliano, and Remedios. The repetition of names symbolizes the fate of the family—an endless cycle of loneliness.

The name Yufu does indeed carry the same metaphorical meaning, doesn't it? The cycle of creation, decline, revival, and downfall is like the turning of a wheel in history.

Everything can be explained.

The founding monarch of the Yufu Dynasty, who emerged from the mouth of the Jian River, established the capital in Baodun.

Subsequently, one of the rulers, the descendant of the first King Yufu—relocated the capital to Yufu

走出湔江口的那位鱼凫王朝开国君主，把都城建在了宝墩。

其后的某一位君主，也是第一代鱼凫王的后裔，迁都到了鱼凫城。

再以后的鱼凫王，把目光投向了三星堆。毕竟，鸭子河提供了丰盛的食物，水上交通更是带来巨大的便利。三星堆城已然崛起，而鱼凫城老迈了，迁都已成必然。所谓鱼凫城、三星堆城是后人的称谓，我们不知道当时的人如何称呼。

迁都后的鱼凫王朝国力鼎盛，生产力迭代，部族已从石器时代更新到了青铜时代，作为中兴之主的鱼凫王也雄心万丈，把自己站在群巫之中发号施令、直接与神沟通的形象，铸就成青铜，要让后世永远记得他的伟大与威严。三星堆出土的那些造型奇谲、体形巨大、工艺繁复的青铜头像与面具可以为此作注。

City.

In the following era, the Kings Yufu turned their gaze towards Sanxingdui. After all, the Duck River provided abundant food, and water transportation brought great convenience. As Sanxingdui City rose, the old Yufu City aged, and relocation became inevitable. However, the so-called Yufu City and Sanxingdui City are the appellations of later generations. The names by which the ancient Shu people referred to these two cities remain unknown to us today.

The Yufu Dynasty flourished after the capital transfer, with productive forces progressing—the tribe had transitioned from the Stone Age to the Bronze Age. As the ruler of this prosperous period, the ambitious Yufu Kings positioned themselves among the group of sorcerers, issuing orders, and establishing a direct connection with the gods. This image was cast in bronze to ensure that future generations would eternally remember their greatness and dignity. The peculiar, gigantic, and intricately crafted bronze statues and masks unearthed at Sanxingdui bear witness to this ambition.

蜀人沿着湔江进入成都平原，开创了灿烂的古蜀文明，而最后一代鱼凫王又回到了祖先的来处。图为湔江出山口的湔山　冉玉杰 摄

The Shu people entered the Chengdu Plain along the Jianjiang River, creating the splendid ancient Shu civilization. The last King Yufu returned to his ancestral place. Shown here is the Jian River's mountain outlet at Jianshan. (Photographer: Ran Yujie)

最后一代鱼凫王，就没有祖先那么幸运了。他是亡国之君，一个从南

However, the last King Yufu was not as fortunate as his ancestors. He was the ruler of a doomed kingdom, usurped by a man named Duyu, a

边来的叫杜宇的濮人，夺取了他的权力、他的一切。角逐失败的他，带着拥趸逃往祖先的来处——湔山，然后很不甘心地被杀死在那里。但是，篡位者依然忌惮他的余威，为防范那些表面服从的前朝遗民，不得不编出了一个谎言：“你们的王已经成仙了，就在我的治下好好过日子吧。我也怀念他啊，看，我还建了祠庙来祭祀他哩。”而那些不愿服从新朝的子民，为了借助鱼凫的威名，也编出了一个神话：我们的王并没有真正离开，他还骑着猛虎，在山中游荡……

是的，他们都有一个共同的名字，都叫鱼凫王。我们不能准确地知道，其中的哪一位王是青铜大立人的原型，但这并不太重要了——它那睥睨天下、不可一世的威风，正是由一个王朝的霸气所凝聚。

Pu tribe member who came from the south, seizing his power and everything he had. Defeated in the struggle for power, he fled with his loyal subjects to the ancestral land—the Jian Mountains, only to tragically meet his death there, filled with bitter resentment. Nonetheless, the usurper still feared his lingering influence. To prevent any resistance from remnants of the previous Dynasty who outwardly submitted, a lie was concocted: “Your King has ascended to immortality. Under my rule, live peaceful lives. I also miss him. Look, I have even built a temple to worship him.” And for those followers who refused to submit to the new regime, they fabricated a myth: “Our King has not truly departed. He still rides a fierce tiger, roaming the mountains...”

Indeed, they all share a common name, King Yufu. We cannot accurately determine which emperor served as the prototype for the magnificent bronze statue, but it is not of utmost importance. What truly matters is the awe-inspiring and unrivaled grandeur emanating from the hegemony of a Dynasty.

金杖
The Gold Scepter

金杖是由一根金皮包裹的木杖，长一百四十二厘米、宽2.3厘米。于1986年7月27日出土于三星堆一号坑时，木已炭化。金皮铺展开来，宽7.2厘米，上端錾刻有46厘米长的射鱼纹——羽箭穿过鸟身、射进鱼头。

鸟和鱼，都是鱼凫部的图腾。这根同时象征王权与神权的金杖，暗藏着古蜀大地上一段王朝更替的历史。

The Golden Scepter is a wooden staff wrapped in gold foil, measuring 142 centimeters in length and 2.3 centimeters in width. When it was unearthed on July 27, 1986, from Pit No. 1 at Sanxingdui, the wood had already charred; the gold layer, when unfolded, measures 7.2 centimeters in width, with a 46-centimeter-long shooting fish motif carved at the upper end — an arrow piercing through the body of a bird and shooting into the head of a fish.

Both birds and fish are totems of the Yufu tribe. This golden scepter, symbolizing both kingship and divine authority, conceals the history of Dynasty changes that occurred in the ancient land of Shu.

三星堆金杖：射鱼纹的王权密码
The Gold Scepter of Sanxingdui: The Regnal Code of the Shooting Fish Pattern

蜀道难
南北朝 · 阴铿

王尊奉汉朝，灵关不惮遥。

Arduous Journey to Shu
Yin Keng, Southern and Northern Dynasties

Wang Zun, in this divided land, loyal to his

高岷长有雪，阴栈屡经烧。
轮摧九折路，骑阻七星桥。
蜀道难如此，功名讵可要。

cause,

Undeterred by the distant Ling Pass, continues his journey without pause.

The towering Min Mountains bear the weight of snow for miles,

The Yinping plank path have weathered countless fires.

Wheels shatter on the winding roads on ridges,

riders hindered at the Seven Star Bridges,

The arduous road to Sichuan tests every hero's claim.

How can one easily attain glory and fame?

阴铿出身名门，他父亲叫阴子春，是南北朝时期梁朝的名将。阴子春最出名的逸事就是几年才洗一次脚，因为他相信，梁州之败就是因为洗脚造成的。这本是题外话，不过梁州之战他的对手正是北魏征南大将军杨难当，其人跟前后文有些关联，故多提一笔——前文《石笋：由此门潜入古蜀国秘境》里的后仇池国，杨难当任过国主；后文《成汉俑：氐人之眼高悬时间隧道》里的名将杨大眼，则是他的孙子。

阴铿这首诗，讲的是西汉大臣王尊的典故。话说王尊出任益州刺史，走到邛崃山九折阪，看到山高路险，想起了王阳辞官旧事。王阳也曾在赴益州刺史任上经过九折阪，因护送先人遗体而发愁，后托病归乡。王尊到此，道了句“王阳为孝子，王尊为忠

Yin Keng hailed from a prestigious family. His father, Yin Zichun, was a renowned general of the Liang Dynasty during the Northern and Southern Dynasties period. One of the most famous anecdotes about Yin Zichun is that he only washed his feet once every few years because he believed that the defeat of Liangzhou was caused by him washing his feet at the critical moment of the war. Although this may seem unrelated, it is worth mentioning that Yin Zichun's adversary in the Battle of Liangzhou was none other than Yang Nandang, the Northern Wei general who later became the Grand General for the Southern Expeditions. This is connected to the preceding and succeeding context: in the earlier text *Stone Pillars: the Entry into the Secret Realm of Ancient Shu*, it is mentioned that the Yang clan ruled the neighboring state of Later Chouchi State. In the later text, *Cheng Han Figurines: The Eyes of the Di People Suspend in the Time Tunnel*, the renowned general Yang Dayan is mentioned, who happens to be Yang Nandang's grandson.

This poem by Yin Keng tells the story of Wang Zun, a minister of the Western Han Dynasty. It is said that when Wang Zun was appointed as the governor

臣”，仍驱驾前行。

蜀道虽难，但并非没有路。九折阪虽高峻，王尊的车驾毕竟过了。诗中的阴栈，即阴平栈道。当年魏国名将邓艾被姜维阻挡于剑门关，即另辟蹊径，取阴平道裹毡滚坡而下，突袭成都创下不世功业。

古蜀道明月峡 冉玉杰 摄
The ancient Shudao Road at Mingyue Gorge (Photographer: Ran Yujie)

其实，四周高山造成了四川盆地的封闭，是一种持续了数千年的刻板印象。蜀人自进入成都平原，就没有停止过对外界的探索，其心态之开放远远超出后人的臆断——三星堆金杖，就是一件分量十足的证物。

of Yizhou, he came across the treacherous Nine-Bend Slope in the Qionglai Mountains. Standing before the towering mountains and perilous road, he recalled the story of Wang Yang, who was also passing through the Nine-Bend Slope while on his way to assume the post of governor of Yizhou. Wang Yang had worried about escorting his deceased father's remains home and eventually feigned illness and resigned. Inspired by this, Wang Zun uttered the words, "Wang Yang was a filial son, while I, Wang Zun, am a loyal minister", before continuing his journey.

Although the road to Shu is difficult, it is not impassable. Despite the steep and rugged Nine-Bend Slope, Wang Zun's carriage successfully crossed it. The "Yinping plank path" in the poem, which was a secret mountain trail. General Deng Ai of the Wei Dynasty was once blocked by the Shu forces led by Jiang Wei at Jianmen Pass. However, he found an alternative route, taking the Yinping path. He ordered the soldiers to cover themselves with woolen felt and roll down the steep slope, successfully launching a surprise attack on Chengdu, thereby achieving an extraordinary military accomplishment.

In reality, the perception of the Sichuan Basin being isolated by surrounding mountains is a stereotypical impression that has persisted for thousands of years. Since the ancient times, the people of Shu have never ceased their exploration of the outside world. Their open-mindedness far surpasses the presumptions of later generations— a fact well represented by the discovery of the Gold Scepter at Sanxingdui, which carries significant weight as evidence.

金权杖出土

成都平原腹心地带的广汉，史称

The Unearthed Golden Scepter

Located at the heart of the Chengdu Plain,

汉州、雒城或雒县，自古称“蜀省之要衢，通京之孔道”。三国时，蜀国谋士庞统在攻打雒城时中流矢而亡。清康熙二十六年（1687年）始，汉州隶属成都府，民国二年（1913年）改称广汉县。1950年和1953年，分别改属绵阳专区和温江专区。1983年3月，广汉划入成都市，同年8月改由德阳市代管。

广汉县中兴乡（今南兴镇）鸭子河南岸的真武村月亮湾，一直不为外人所知。直到1931年的一天，村民燕道诚和儿子燕保青淘沟底时，那不经意的一锄头挖下去，发出铿锵之声。

月亮湾位于鸭子河与马牧河之间的台地上，鸭子河依然水量丰沛，马牧河却因为泥土淤积，已退化为一条窄窄的水渠。在宽阔的鸭子河以南，马牧河几字形故河道的包围中，有三个被当地老百姓称作“梁子”的土堆，其单个长数十米至百米，宽二三十米，高五至八米。土堆本不稀奇，但以如此巨大的体型突兀在平原上，同样是让人不可忽视的BDO（巨大沉默物体）。而在旧式文人的审美框架中，月色映照下的三个土堆如三颗天上星，于是清代地方志中记为汉州八景之一“三星伴月”。

Guanghan, historically known as Hanzhou, Luocheng, or Luoxian, has always been referred to as the “vital thoroughfare of Shu Province and the key gateway to the capital”. During the Three Kingdoms period, the renowned strategist of Shu, Pang Tong, lost his life by a stray arrow during the siege of Luocheng. Since the 26th year of the Kangxi reign in the Qing Dynasty (1687 AD), Hanzhou was under the jurisdiction of Chengdu Prefecture. In the 2nd year of the Republic of China (1913), it was renamed as Guanghan County. In 1950 and 1953, Guanghan was within the jurisdiction of Mianyang District and Wenjiang District, respectively. In March 1983, Guanghan was incorporated into Chengdu City, and in August of the same year, it was placed under the jurisdiction of Deyang City on behalf of Chengdu.

The Moon Bay of Zhenwu Village, located on the southern bank of Yazi River in Nanxing Town (formerly Zhongxing Township), Guanghan County, remained unknown to the outside world for a long time. It wasn’t until one day in 1931 that a villager named Yan Daocheng and his son, Yan Baoqing, happened to be digging at the bottom of a gully and heard a resounding sound when their hoe struck something.

Moon Bay is situated on a tableland between the Yazi River and Mamu River. While the Yazi River still flows abundantly, the Mamu River has become a narrow channel due to siltation. South of the broad Yazi River, three mounds referred to by the locals as “liangzi” stood, each measuring dozens to hundreds of meters in length, 20 to 30 meters in width, and 5 to 8 meters in height. These mounds may not be particularly extraordinary, but their massive size, abruptly standing out on the plain, is indeed an attention-grabbing BDO (Big Dumb Object). In the aesthetic framework of traditional literati, the three mounds illuminated by moonlight resembled three celestial stars. Therefore, in the local chronicles of

后来的考古证明，这三个土堆其实是夏商时期的城墙废墟。燕道诚父子的那一锄头，惊醒了沉睡数千年的古蜀国，它以三星堆之名重现人间，惊世骇俗。

自1953年始，三星堆遗址上进行过多次考古调查。

the Qing Dynasty, they were recorded as one of "the Eight Scenic Wonders of Hanzhou" known as "Three Stars Accompanying the Moon".

Subsequent archaeological discoveries have confirmed that these three mounds were actually ruins of city walls from the Xia and Shang Dynasties. The swing of Yan Daocheng and his son's hoe awakened the ancient Shu civilization that had remained dormant for thousands of years. It resurfaced in the world under the name of Sanxingdui, stunning and astounding everyone.

Since 1953, multiple archaeological investigations have been conducted at the Sanxingdui Site.

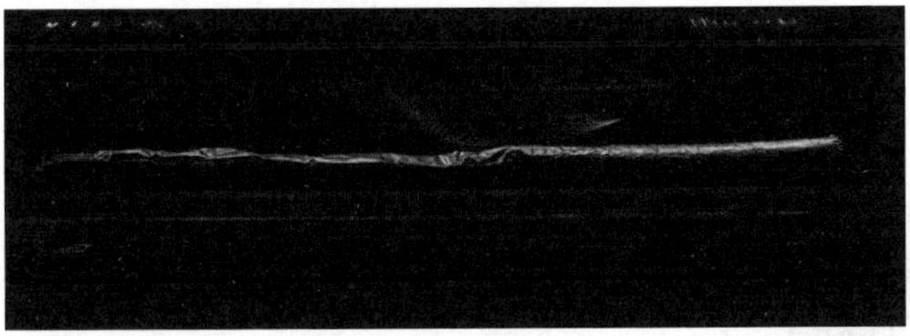

三星堆金权杖　高泓 摄

The Gold Scepter of Sanxingdui (Photographer: Gao Hong)

1986年7月18日，土堆附近砖厂的民工同往常一样采土烧砖时，意外挖得十数件玉器。幸运的是，百米外正在进行一场考古发掘。考古人员闻讯赶来，布起了探方。就这样，长4.5米、宽3.3米的一号祭祀坑被打开了，火烧过的骨灰渣、陶尖底器、玉石器、铜尊、铜盘以及跟真人同等大小的青铜人头像陆续出土。

7月27日凌晨两点半左右，灯光下黑色的灰渣中，一小块耀眼的金黄色跳脱出来。用毛刷细刷之后，能清晰地看到上面的鱼纹，其内侧附有炭

On July 18, 1986, while the laborers at a nearby brick factory were collecting soil for making bricks as usual, they unexpectedly unearthed several jade artifacts. Fortunately, an archaeological excavation was underway just one hundred meters away. When the archaeologists heard the news, they quickly set up probes. As a result, the first sacrificial pit, measuring 4.5 meters in length and 3.3 meters in width, was opened. Burnt bone ash, pointy-bottomed pottery jars, jade artifacts, bronze vessels, bronze plates, and life-sized bronze human head sculptures were gradually unearthed from the pit.

Around 2:30 am on July 27th, amidst the dark grey ashes illuminated by the lights, a small piece of brilliant golden yellow caught the eye. After careful brushing, the fish patterns on its surface became clear, with traces of charred wood on the inner side.

化木痕。而在其近旁二十厘米左右，还发现了一件铜质龙头。经修复后确认，这是一根由金皮包裹木杆的铜龙头杖。

金皮铺展开来，长一百四十二厘米、宽7.2厘米，上端有线刻纹饰图案。因为主体图案为羽箭穿过鸟身、射进鱼头，故被称作“射鱼纹”。说羽箭“穿”过鸟身，是一种简略的叙述，仅从图上看，箭杆其实是压在鸟身上。一种可能是，工匠先錾出了箭杆，再錾鸟时已不可能体现出射进又穿出的遮挡效果。

Approximately 20 centimeters nearby, a bronze dragon head was also discovered. After restoration, it was confirmed to be a gold-plated wooden staff, adorned with a copper dragon head.

The gold-plated surface was unfolded to reveal a length of 142 centimeters and a width of 7.2 centimeters, featuring intricate line-carved patterns on the upper end. This particular pattern, depicting an arrow piercing through a bird's body and into a fish's head, is known as the "Shooting Fish Pattern". The description of the arrow "piercing" through the bird's body is a simplified narrative. The pattern apparently shows that the arrow shaft is actually pressing against the bird's body. One possibility is that the craftsman first carved the arrow shaft, and when carving the bird, it became impossible to depict the effect of it piercing through and coming out of the bird.

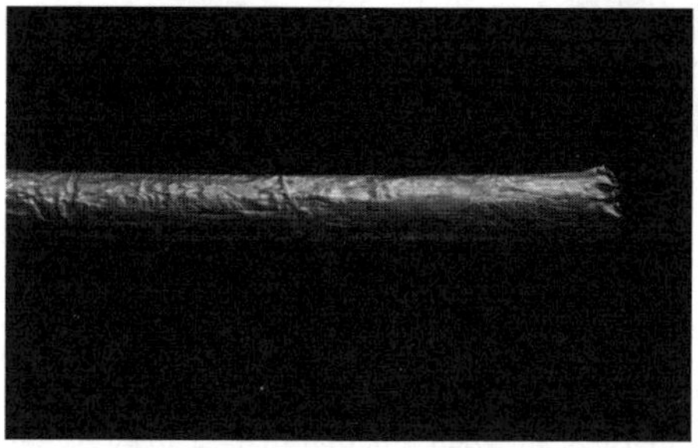

金权杖上射鱼纹清晰可见　高泓 摄

The Shooting Fish Pattern on the gold scepter are clearly visible. (Photographer: Gao Hong)

射鱼纹采用双线勾勒之法，即两条互相平行的线外侧下压、中部凸出，构成一条有宽度的线，使图像显得更为立体、醒目。而这个宽度，也不过1毫米。

长46厘米、宽7.2厘米的射鱼纹，纵向两组完全一样，在包裹成手杖之后体现出了一种对称关系；横向三组，上为鱼，中为鸟，下为人。

The Shooting Fish Pattern is crafted using the method of double-line delineation. This technique involves pressing down on the outer sides of two parallel lines while leaving the center protruding, creating a line with width. This imparts a three-dimensional and eye-catching effect to the image. The width of these lines measures only 1 millimeter.

The Shooting Fish Pattern, measuring 46 centimeters in length and 7.2 centimeters in width, displays a symmetrical relationship after being wrapped around the staff. Vertically, there are two identical sets, while three sets horizontally depict fish at the top, birds in the middle, and human head portraits at the bottom.

射鱼纹解密

射鱼纹所蕴含的信息，藏在人、鸟、鱼和箭里。

人，是对称的两个头像，头戴五齿高冠，左耳垂有一缀饰。戴高冠，说明其身份高贵，不是王就是大巫师，也可能二者的身份合而为一。左耳垂饰，让人联想到青铜大立人左耳上那硕大的孔洞。

观察戴冠者的眼睛，会发现跟三星堆众多青铜人像或面具一样，是典型的丹凤眼，眼角夸张地向上斜吊——蜀人“纵目”的表现方式之一。

鸟，到底是鸬鹚还是杜鹃鸟呢，二者分别是鱼凫、杜宇两代古蜀王的象征。三支象征性的长尾，于鸬鹚和杜鹃都符合，但上喙略弯曲，只是鸬鹚的特点。

鱼，是鱼凫部落在鸬鹚之外的另外一种图腾。

箭，也有两种象征：射鱼、射凫，意味着杜宇部对鱼凫部的征伐；如果仅仅射的是鱼，则是重现鱼凫部落渔猎的生产方式——以镖射鱼。而鱼镖，是一种头带倒钩、尾带长绳的

Decipher the Shooting Fish Pattern

The Shooting Fish Pattern contains hidden information within the depictions of humans, birds, fish, and arrows.

The human heads, depicted symmetrically, wear tall crowns with five teeth and have an earring hanging from their left ears. The presence of the tall crown suggests a noble status, either that of an emperor or a high-ranking sorcerer, or perhaps a combination of both. The earring on the left ear reminds one of the large holes found on the the Bronze Giant’s left ear.

If observing the eyes of the crowned figures closely, one will find that they are typical Phoenix eyes, characterized by their upward-slanted outer corners, much like the numerous bronze figures or masks found in Sanxingdui. This exaggerated upward slant of the eyes represents one of the manifestations of the ancient Shu people’s “oblong eyes”.

As for the bird, it is unclear whether it represents a cormorant or a cuckoo bird. Both birds symbolize different generations of ancient Shu Emperors, with the cormorant representing the Yufu Tribe and the cuckoo representing the Duyu Tribe. The three symbolic long tails correspond to both the cormorant and the cuckoo, but the slightly curved upper beak is a characteristic of the cormorant.

The fish symbolizes another totem of the Yufu Tribe besides the cormorant.

As for the arrow, it also carries two symbolic meanings: shooting fish or shooting cormorants, indicating the conquest of the Yufu Tribe by the Duyu Tribe. If the arrow is depicted as shooting fish, it portrays the fishing and hunting practices of the

箭。图案上羽箭并没有穿进鸟身，到底是射了还是没射？

把这些基本信息摆出来，有助于判断对射鱼纹的两种主流解读方式，这直接关系到金杖的主人是谁。

其一，鱼凫王说。有学者认为，将权杖上的鱼、鸟、人图案顺着读下来，正好是“鱼凫王”。

其二，杜宇王说。这是两个王朝的争霸之战，鱼是鱼凫部的图腾，射鱼即喻意对鱼凫的讨伐。至于被箭杆压着的鸟，到底是鸬鹚还是杜鹃，到底被射了没有，已经不重要了。

笔者曾经是将“鱼、鸟、人”解读作“鱼凫王”之说的拥趸，但经过更深入的思考，倒是越来越偏向于杜宇说——毕竟以射鱼象征讨伐是一种非常直观的表达，而“鱼、鸟、人”的解读则过于隐晦、牵强，涉嫌文字游戏。尤其是金沙遗址出土的金冠带，更是为“杜宇王说”提供了坚实的证据。

Yufu Tribe. This would be represented by a fish spear, which is an arrowhead with a hook-shaped tip and a long rope attached to its tail. In the pattern, the arrow appears to not penetrate the bird's body, leaving ambiguity whether it was shot or not.

Presenting these basic pieces of information aids in determining the two main interpretations of the Shooting Fish Pattern, which directly relates to the identity of the owner of the gold scepter.

The “Yufu King interpretation” suggests that the pattern of fish, birds, and human heads on the scepter can be read in order as “Yu (fish), Fu (cormorant), King (human heads)”. Some scholars believe that this arrangement of patterns represents the title of Yufu.

Secondly, the “Duyu King interpretation” suggests that it represents a battle for supremacy between two dynasties. The fish symbolizes the totem of the Yufu Tribe, and shooting the fish signifies the conquest of the Yufu Tribe. As for the bird being pressed down by the arrow, whether it is a cormorant or a cuckoo and whether it was shot or not becomes less important.

I used to be a supporter of the “Fish, Birds, Human heads” interpretation as “Yufu King”, but after further contemplation, I lean more towards the “Duyu King” interpretation. After all, using shooting fish as a symbol for conquest is a more direct expression, whereas the interpretation of “Fish, Birds, Human heads” seems more obscure and forced, resembling wordplay. Moreover, the discovery of the gold crown band at the Jinsha site provides strong evidence for the “Duyu King interpretation”.

金沙金冠带与三星堆金权杖的射鱼纹高度相似，显示了其文化的延续性　高泓 摄

The shooting-fish motifs on the gold scepter from Sanxingdui closely resemble those on the gold crown band from Jinsha, demonstrating cultural continuity. (Photographer: Gao Hong)

金冠带是一层金箔，厚度仅0.2毫米，比指甲盖还薄。约3厘米宽的金带围成一个直径20厘米的圈，它本是贴附在冠帽之上的。奇的是冠带之上的图饰，同样为鱼、鸟、人、箭。除了人形象不一样外，箭压鸟身穿鱼头，跟三星堆金杖几乎没有差别。将金杖与金冠带放在一起对比，不得不承认三星堆、金沙在文化上的延续性。

细心一点，还是可以发现差别：金冠带上的鱼嘴带一个弯钩。这种具备高度想象力的图形，是凫与鱼的合体，是对被箭矢穿头的鱼的强化，可以确定为鱼凫部落的图腾。

此外，金沙另外出土有一种鱼纹金带，鱼的嘴部也带有锐钩，或者说，它更像是长长的鸟喙。

结合史料的记载，能够明确：这是杜宇部对鱼凫部的征服，他们占有了三星堆，后来又因为战争或水患的原因迁移到了金沙。

三星堆最早的主人是鱼凫部。他们来自岷山，在沿江下山穿越湔江口的路上发现了龙门山中的铜矿，这为后来铸造那些精美的青铜器提供了充足的原料。部族也在下山的路上进化、迭代，把时间线浓缩，就会看到：在山上还拿着石头当武器的人，

The gold crown band is a layer of gold foil, with a thickness of only 0.2 millimeters, thinner than a fingernail. A 3-centimeter-wide gold band forms a circle with a diameter of 20 centimeters, intended to be attached to a cap. Interestingly, the decorative patterns on the crown include fish, birds, human heads, and arrows. Apart from slight differences in the human figures, the arrow pressing against the bird's body and piercing the fish's head is nearly identical to the pattern found on the gold scepter from the Sanxingdui Culture. When comparing the gold scepter and the gold crown band, it becomes difficult to deny the cultural continuity between Sanxingdui and Jinsha.

However, upon closer inspection, one can still identify differences: the fish's mouth on the gold crown band carries a curved hook. This imaginative symbol represents the fusion of a cormorant and a fish, reinforcing the image of a fish with an arrow piercing its head. This confirms it as the totem of the Yufu Tribe.

Furthermore, there have been other discoveries at the Jinsha site, including a gold belt with fish patterns, where the fish's mouth also features sharp hooks. In fact, it resembles a long bird's beak.

Combined with historical records, it becomes clear that this signifies the conquest of the Yufu Tribe by the Duyu Tribe. They occupied Sanxingdui and later migrated to Jinsha, potentially due to war or flooding incidents.

The earliest inhabitants of Sanxingdui were from the Yufu Tribe. They originated from the Min Mountains and, while descending the mountains along the Min River, they discovered copper deposits in the Longmen Mountains. This provided abundant raw materials for the later production of exquisite bronze artifacts. As the tribe evolved and iterated during their descent, a condensed timeline reveals a

在河里会用箭矢射鱼，到了平原上已经变成持着青铜戈的战士；他们放下兵器，围成一圈又一圈，匍匐祈祷，手舞足蹈，惊呼呐喊，中心是体型巨大的青铜面具群，中心的中心伫立着神情威严、正在沟通天地的大巫师。

三星堆换了主人。

新的君主兼大巫师杜宇来自南边的百濮族群，他很可能是借助手里的白银矿资源和家族联姻在古蜀大地上站稳了脚跟，并最终取代了鱼凫。

据文献，杜宇将都城建在了郫邑，后迁都至瞿上；而杜宇之后的开明王朝，则因为君王梦见城郭移动而迁王城至成都——偏偏漏过了对金沙的记载。

上述地名，郫的位置是明确的，瞿上却有争论，或曰彭州海窝子，或曰双流牧马山。试想一下，是否存在这样的可能？

其一，瞿上既不是海窝子，也不是牧马山，而是金沙——杜宇王朝在占领三星堆之后，迁都至金沙。

其二，金沙是开明王朝迁都后的王城。

或许，对金沙的记载并没有遗漏，只是古今名异而已。

实际上，杜宇王朝是非常强盛的，以前松散的部落联盟已开始向权

progression: people wielding stones as weapons on the mountains, fishing with arrows in the river, and ultimately transforming into warriors wielding bronze spears on the plains. They eventually laid down their weapons, forming circle after circle, prostrating themselves in prayer, dancing and leaping, exclaiming and shouting. At the center stood a colossal group of bronze masks. In the very heart of this center stood the grand sorcerer, with a majestic and solemn expression, communicating with the heavens and the earth.

Sanxingdui Changed Hands.

The new sovereign and grand sorcerer, Duyu, hailed from the Bai Pu ethnic group in the south. It is highly likely that he gained a foothold on the ancient land of Shu by leveraging the silver mining resources and forming alliances through marriage, and ultimately replaced the Yufu Tribe.

According to historical records, Duyu initially built his capital in Pi and later relocated it to Qushang. The Kaiming Dynasty that followed Duyu's rule moved the royal city to Chengdu after the king dreamt of the city wall's movement. However, notably missing from the records is any mention of Jinsha.

While the location of Pi is clear, there is debate regarding Qushang. Some argue it could be Haiwozi in Pengzhou, while others suggest it may be Muma Mountain in Shuangliu. Consider for a moment, does such a possibility exist?

Firstly, Qushang is neither Haiwozi nor Muma Mountain, but rather Jinsha. After the Duyu Dynasty occupied Sanxingdui, they relocated the capital to Jinsha.

Secondly, Jinsha became the royal city after the relocation by the Kaiming Dynasty.

Perhaps there is no omission in the records concerning Jinsha; it's just a difference in ancient and modern names.

力集中的国家转型；而开明王朝可以跟北面强大的秦国抗衡，在双方交界的汉中一带反复进行拉锯战。

那么，不管金沙是杜宇的还是开明的，在国力更加强盛、国土幅员更加广阔的情况下，所铸造的祭祀用青铜器从体型、所耗材料以及带给人的震撼感而言，远远不能跟前期的三星堆相比呢？若能排除铜矿资源枯竭的因素，剩下的原因只有一个：神权已开始向王权让步，在城市生活中已经越来越不重要了——从三星堆到金沙，是国土扩张的过程，也是神走下神坛的过程。

In reality, the Duyu Dynasty was incredibly powerful, transforming the previously loose tribal alliances into a centralized state. The Kaiming Dynasty was capable of standing up to the formidable Qin Kingdom in the north, engaging in a repeated tug of war in the border region of Hanzhong.

Regardless of whether Jinsha belonged to Duyu or the Kaiming Dynasty, the bronze ritual artifacts produced during a period of greater national strength and expanded territory cannot compare to those earlier from Sanxingdui in terms of size, materials used, and the awe-inspiring impact they create. If we exclude the factor of copper ore depletion, there is only one remaining reason: divine authority begins to yield to royal authority as it is becoming less significant in urban life. The transition from Sanxingdui to Jinsha represents both territorial expansion and the process of deities stepping down from their altars.

鼎与权杖

与古蜀三星堆、金沙用金杖象征权力不同，早期的中原华夏文明用鼎来代表政权。

《史记·孝武本纪》记载了汉武帝与政府官员关于鼎的对答。武帝问鼎从何而来，官员们都回答道：“黄帝作宝鼎三，象天地人也。禹收九牧之金，铸九鼎……”古人认为，大禹治水成功之后，划分天下为九州，并铸九鼎，以一鼎象征一州。从此，“九州”就成为中国的代名词。

大禹定九州、铸九鼎，虽见于

Ding（鼎）and Scepter

In contrast to the use of gold scepters to symbolize power in the ancient Shu cultures of Sanxingdui and Jinsha, Dings were used by the early Central Plains Huaxia civilization to represent political authority.

The *Annals of Xiao Wu, Records of the Grand Historian* records a dialogue between Emperor Wu of Han and government officials regarding the significance of Ding, which is a vessel in the shape of either a tripod or quadripod. When Emperor Wu asked where the origin of Ding lies, the officials responded, “The Yellow Emperor made three precious Dings, symbolizing heaven, earth, and humankind. Yu collected bronze from Jiuzhou and forged nine Dings...” Ancient people believed that after the successful control of the floods by Yu the Great, he

《左传》《史记》，却一直被视作传说，更别说之前的黄帝铸鼎了。有认为夏尚不具备制鼎技术者，也有否认夏朝存在者。

已有三千二百年历史的后母戊大方鼎，形体巨大，工艺高度复杂，具有震慑人心的力量。国之重器，绝非一天铸成，在后母戊大方鼎之前，制鼎工艺也必然有一个漫长的探索、积累过程。

发掘于河南新郑裴李岗遗址的乳钉纹陶鼎，是中国现存最早的鼎，该遗址距今已有8000余年；现存最早的青铜鼎，则是出土于二里头遗址的方格纹铜鼎。二里头遗址即夏代都城的观点，在学术界已得到越来越多的认同。有实物与典籍的印证，禹铸九鼎之说，甚至黄帝作三宝鼎之说，未可轻易否认。

濮人制作的巫师纹铜鼎　何大江 摄

A bronze Ding with shamanic patterns made by the Pu people. (Photographer: He Dajiang)

divided the world into nine administrative districts, and nine Dings were cast, with each Ding representing a district. From then on, "Jiuzhou" became a synonym for China.

While the story of Yu the Great establishing Jiuzhou and forging nine Dings is found in *Zuo Zhuan* and *Records of the Grand Historian*, it has long been considered a legend, not to mention the casting of Ding by the Yellow Emperor before that. The existence of the Xia Dynasty itself is also a subject of debate, with some suggesting that the Xia Dynasty did not possess the technology to forge ding and others denying the existence of the Xia Dynasty altogether.

The majestic and intricately crafted Houmuwu Great Bronze Ding, which dates back 3,200 years, possesses a formidable presence. Such a significant national artifact was certainly not created overnight. Prior to the creation of the Houmuwu Great Bronze Ding, the art of Ding-making surely underwent a lengthy process of exploration and accumulation.

The discovery of the Nail Pattern Pottery Tripod at the Peiligang Site in Xinzhen, Henan, is the earliest known Ding in China, dating back over 8,000 years. The earliest surviving bronze Ding, on the other hand, was unearthed at the Erlitou Site and features a square grid pattern. The view that the Erlitou Site was the capital of the Xia Dynasty has been increasingly recognized in the academic community. There is physical evidence as well as references in ancient texts that support the claim of Yu forging nine Dings and even the notion of the Yellow Emperor making three precious Dings. Therefore, these accounts cannot be easily dismissed.

鼎，早先只是一种炊器，自大禹铸九鼎，便成为政权的象征。问鼎、鼎革、定鼎，这些词都跟政权相关。

“问鼎”一词，来源于一段史实。楚庄王征伐陆浑戎，到了洛阳，陈兵于周王朝的边境之上。周定王心中惶恐，派出大夫王孙满前去“劳军”。双方通过对鼎的“探讨”，一问一答，展现了高超的外交艺术。

楚庄王问，鼎有多大多重呢？他问的其实不是鼎，而是在说：“周天子的力量到底有多强呢？我想取代他，可不可以呢？”

“在德不在鼎。”使者王孙满的回答，代表了中国人几千年以来一以贯之的对于王权的正统观念——要得天下，仅仅靠强权是不够的，有道义才有合法性；以及一种天人合一的政权观——夏桀昏庸，鼎迁于商，商纣暴虐，鼎迁于周，其间皆有天道所在，只要气数未尽，觊觎者就无可奈何。“周德虽衰，天命未改，鼎之轻重，未可问也。”周王朝虽是军事上的弱者，但使者不卑不亢的回答，展现出智慧，保留了尊严。

楚庄王之后，下一个试探铜鼎、炫耀力量的人是秦武王。秦武王天生神力，秦国经商鞅变法后国力强盛、一路攻城拔寨，所以他也跃跃欲试。

Originally, Ding was just a type of cooking vessel, but it became a symbol of political authority following Yu the Great’s forging of the “Nine Dings”. Expressions such as “seizing the Ding”, “changing the Ding”, and “establishing the ding” are all related to political power.

The phrase “wen ding” (问鼎), meaning “aspire to power”, originates from a historical event. The vassal King Zhuang of Chu led an expedition against the Luhun Rong and arrived at Luoyang, where he stationed his troops on the border of the Zhou Dynasty. Emperor Ding of Zhou felt uneasy and sent the nobleman Wangsun Man on a mission to appease the army. Through a witty repartee centered around the Ding, they displayed remarkable diplomatic artistry.

When King Zhuang asked how big and heavy the Ding was, he was actually implying, “How strong is the power of the Emperor of Zhou? Can I replace him?” It was a veiled way of expressing his intention to challenge the Zhou Dynasty’s authority.

“In virtue, not just the Ding, lies legitimacy.” The response of the envoy Wangsun Man encapsulates the enduring orthodox Chinese belief in the legitimacy of royal authority throughout thousands of years. It signifies that mere power is insufficient to govern a nation; moral integrity is essential to establish legitimacy. It also reflects a concept of harmonizing Heaven and human governance. During the Xia Dynasty, when King Jie ruled incompetently, the Mandate of Heaven shifted to the Shang Dynasty. When King Zhou of Shang became tyrannical, the Mandate shifted to the Zhou Dynasty. In all these transitions, the Heavenly law prevailed. As long as one king’s fate endures, the other covetous individuals will be powerless. “Although the virtue of the Zhou Dynasty may have declined, the Mandate of Heaven remains unchanged, so the Ding’s weight

秦武王不只是嘴巴上问一问，他是真的动手举鼎。不过，力量还不够，鼎摔了下来，砸碎了他的膝盖骨。武王受伤后，很快就死了。

又过了好些年，又有一个天生神力，军事力量也很强大的人，终于成功把鼎举了起来，他就是楚霸王项羽。不过，项羽举的已不是大禹所铸之鼎。大禹之鼎，楚庄王问过，秦武王举过，到了周末和秦始皇的年代，就消失不见了。

自秦始皇始，玉玺成为王权最直接的象征。

然而，古蜀尽管已经熟练掌握了青铜制作工艺，却从来没有发现过青铜鼎。使用手杖来象征权力，是古蜀文明与华夏文明的重大差异。

鼎不是一天铸就的，权杖同理。带有政治属性和文化属性的权杖，不会从天而降，其文化源头何在？

其实，即便在古蜀文明文化序列内部，权杖也并非绝无仅有。2013年7月2日，温江区公平镇一面积约二十万平方米的宝墩时期聚落遗址出土一根象牙权杖。权杖手柄处较粗，下端为尖头，长1.04米，几乎通体笔直。该权柄出土于一竖穴土坑墓，权杖就放在它生前主人的左侧。该墓比聚落遗址内的其他墓葬大近一倍，随

cannot be questioned." Despite the Zhou Dynasty's military weakness, the envoy's response demonstrates wisdom and preserves dignity without displaying subservience.

After King Zhuang of Chu State, the next person attempting to weigh the Ding and showcasing his power was King Wu of Qin State. King Wu was born with extraordinary strength, and under the Qin State's prosperous condition following the reforms by Shang Yang, their national power grew strong, allowing them to conquer cities and establish fortresses along their way. Thus, King Wu of Qin was eager to test his strength. He not only verbally challenged the Ding but actually attempted to lift it. However, his strength was not sufficient, and the Ding fell down, shattering his knee. Shortly after being injured, King Wu died.

Years later, another individual with innate strength and formidable military power finally succeeded in holding the throne. He was Xiang Yu, the Hegemon-King of Chu. However, the Ding he lifted was not the one cast by Emperor Yu, which had been claimed by King Zhuang of Chu and lifted by King Wu of Qin, but by the time of the Zhou Dynasty's end and the reign of Qin Shi Huang, it disappeared without a trace.

Since the reign of Qin Shi Huang, the Imperial Seal became the most direct symbol of royal authority.

However, no bronze tripod or quadripod has ever been found in Ancient Shu, despite their mastery of bronze making craftsmanship. The use of a scepter as a symbol of power represented a significant difference between the ancient Shu civilization and the Chinese civilization.

Dings, like staffs, were not created overnight. Similarly, a staff with political and cultural significance does not come from nowhere. Where does its cultural source lie?

In fact, even within the cultural sequence of

葬品也不相同，墓主生前应为巫师或首领。其入土时期，大致为宝墩文化第三期，距今已四千多年，同三星堆金权杖相比，还要早上一千年左右。

作为一种昭示身份、象征权威的器具，权杖最早出现于两河流域。欧贝德文化晚期的埃利都神庙，21号墓地中即出土有石质权杖头；而一家族墓中有一男性泥雕像，裸体，头部为蜥蜴状，手执一短杖。欧贝德文化分布于美索不达米亚，其活动时期为公元前5000年至公元前3500年。

从美索不达米亚平原到成都平原，直线距离上万里；其间有峡谷、高山，有温度超过七十摄氏度的卢特沙漠，还有极度寒冷的青藏高原；在今天的地图上，则隔着伊朗、阿富汗、巴基斯坦和印度等一众国家——权杖是如何从一个平原传到万里之外的另一个平原的呢？

其实，考察大地上那些曾经出现过权杖的文化遗址，就可以勾画出一道线来。

中国发现的权杖主要集中在西北的新疆、甘肃、陕西等地，年代最早的是甘肃秦安大地湾出土的彩陶权杖头。这是一个泥质红陶扁球，内部中空，上下各有圆孔，可供木杖穿过。

1923年，瑞典地质学家安特生在

the ancient Shu civilization, staffs were not entirely absent. On July 2, 2013, during an excavation at the Baodun period settlement site, an area of 200,000 square meters in Gongping Town, Wenjiang District, an ivory staff was unearthed. The staff had a thick handle and a pointed end, measuring 1.04 meters in length and almost completely straight. The staff was found in a vertical pit grave, placed on the left side of its previous owner. This tomb was nearly twice the size of other graves within the settlement site and contained different burial items, suggesting that the deceased individual held a position of significance, possibly a sorcerer or a leader. The burial can be dated to the third phase of the Baodun culture, over 4,000 years ago, which predates the gold scepter found in Sanxingdui by approximately 1,000 years.

As a tool that signifies status and symbolizes authority, staffs first appeared in the Mesopotamian region. In the late Ubaid period, stone staff heads were discovered in Tomb 21 of the Eridu temple. Additionally, a male clay figurine with a lizard-shaped head holding a short staff was found in a family tomb. The Ubaid culture was distributed in Mesopotamia, and its active period is estimated to be from around 5000 BC to 3500 BC.

The distance from the Mesopotamian plain to the Chengdu plain spans thousands of miles. In between, there are canyons, high mountains, the scorching Lut Desert with temperatures exceeding 70 degrees Celsius, as well as the extremely cold Qinghai-Tibet Plateau. On today's map, it encompasses multiple countries including Iran, Afghanistan, Pakistan, and India. How did the staff travel from one plain to another thousands of miles away?

In fact, by examining the cultural sites where staffs have been discovered throughout the world, we can trace a line.

In China, the discovery of staffs is mainly

洮河流域广河县购得一件白色大理石质地权杖头。该器出自瓦罐嘴遗址，出土时置于墓主手边。瓦罐嘴遗址属于马家窑文化的晚期类型，而马家窑正是古蜀文明的来源之一。从马家窑经岷山到三星堆，正是古蜀人的迁徙路线。

再往西北方向，在甘肃张掖西城驿遗址发掘出土有石质、铜质权杖头。而该处出土的石范，可证明铜杖头在当地铸造。

位于河西走廊玉门镇的火烧沟墓地，十余座墓葬里有石质权杖头，310号墓地里出土有铜权杖头一件。

新疆境内发现权杖头的遗址，则主要分布于天山南北两侧。最东头的若羌县小河墓地，曾出土一件球形白色大理石权杖头，它象征着一名女祭司的权柄。再往西的昌吉州英格堡遗址、乌鲁木齐板房沟镇萨恩萨依墓地，也都发现过权杖头。

由三星堆向西北方向回溯，一条在中国境内由西北向西南延伸的权杖文化传播之路已呼之欲出。

西出中国国境，来到中亚塔吉克斯坦萨拉兹姆遗址、土库曼斯坦松巴尔墓地，它们都是石质权杖头的发现地。在这片广袤的哈萨克大草原，曾有剽悍的哥萨克骑兵纵横呼啸。肖

concentrated in the northwestern regions such as Xinjiang, Gansu, and Shaanxi. The earliest dated staff head was found in the colored pottery from the Dadiwan site in Qin'an, Gansu. This pottery staff head is a hollow, earthenware, flat sphere with circular holes on the top and bottom, allowing it to be attached to a wooden shaft.

In 1923, the Swedish geologist Johan Gunnar Andersson purchased a white marble staff head in Guanghe County, in the Tao River basin. This artifact was discovered at the Waguanzui site, placed beside the owner's hand in a grave. The Waguanzui site belongs to the late phase of the Majiayao Culture, which is considered one of the origins of the ancient Shu civilization. From Majiayao, through the Minshan Mountains, to Sanxingdui, this was the migration route of the ancient Shu people.

Moving further northwest, in the Zhangye Xichengyi Site in Gansu, stone and copper staff heads were unearthed. Interestingly, the stone molds found at this site provide evidence of the local casting of copper staff heads.

The Huoshao Gou burial site, located in Yumen Town in the Hexi Corridor, contains several stone staff heads in more than ten tombs. Additionally, a copper staff head was unearthed in Tomb 310.

In Xinjiang, the sites where staff heads have been discovered are mainly distributed on both sides of the Tianshan Mountains. At the easternmost edge, the Xiaohe Cemetery in Ruoqiang County yielded a spherical white marble staff head, symbolizing the authority of a priestess. Further west, staff heads have also been found at the Yinggebao Site in Changji Prefecture and the Sa'ensai Cemetery in Banfanggou Town, Urumqi.

Tracing back from Sanxingdui in a northwestern direction, we can vividly see a cultural diffusion route of staffs that extends from northwest to southwest

洛霍夫的《静静的顿河》里面，就多次提到过这种镶着铜头的权杖——在哥萨克地区，不仅村长之间的权力更替要移交权杖，克拉斯诺夫少将当选为顿河司令官，也以接过权杖为标志。

一路向西，终于回到了（今人所知的）第一根权杖制作出来的地方——美索不达米亚平原。将近八千年前，第一个人类文明——苏美尔文明就在此产生。

人类凭借大脑里的想象，虚构出了意识形态，并产生合作，团队的力量由此远胜于个体，体能和搏击力并不出众的人类，得以站上生物链的顶端。

这就是协作的力量。而指挥这些协作的，就是部落酋长手里的权杖。那不仅仅是一根顶着一坨石头或青铜的木棍，而是昭示权威、象征神圣，蕴含着开山劈水之力的奇异魔法杖。

权杖产生于两河流域。对权杖的尊崇，向北传入欧洲，向西经死海地区传入埃及，向东则经中亚细亚传入中国境内，并沿着青藏高原东沿，一直抵达三星堆，这才有了那根暗藏着权力密码、亮得炫目的金权杖。

within Chinese territory.

In the west, it reached beyond the borders of China into Central Asia, where significant discoveries of stone scepter heads were made at the Sarazm Site in Tajikistan and the Songbal Cemetery in Turkmenistan. These regions were once vast Kazakh grasslands, home to fierce Cossack cavalry. In Sholokhov's *Quiet Don*, the scepter adorned with a copper head is mentioned multiple times. In the Cossack region, the transfer of power between village chiefs was symbolized by handing over the scepter. When General Krasnov was elected as the commander of the Don River, it was also marked by receiving the scepter.

Continuing on this westward path, we finally arrive at the Mesopotamian Plain, which is believed to be the birthplace of the first known scepter. It was here, nearly 8,000 years ago, that the first human civilization, the Sumerian civilization, emerged.

Driven by their imaginations, humans constructed ideologies and formed cooperative teams, surpassing the capabilities of individual beings. Despite lacking exceptional physical strength or combat prowess, humans were able to ascend to the top of the biological chain.

Indeed, this is the power of collaboration. The scepter, held in the hands of tribal chiefs, signifies the ability to command this collaboration. It is not merely a wooden stick with a stone or bronze head; it represents authority, symbolizes the sacred, and contains the mystical power to part mountains and rivers.

The scepter originated in the Mesopotamian Valley. The reverence for the scepter spread northward into Europe, westward through the Dead Sea region into Egypt, and eastward through Central Asia into China. Along the eastern edge of the Qinghai-Tibet Plateau, it finally arrived at Sanxingdui, where it transformed into a stunning gold scepter, concealing the secrets of power within its dazzling appearance.

巴比伦神庙与羊子山土台的应和

美索不达米亚平原，或称两河流域，是人类历史上最早出现文明的区域之一，这里诞生了世界上首部成文法典《汉谟拉比法典》、首部英雄史诗《吉尔伽美什》。

城市，是文明最具象的结晶。而巴比伦城，曾经是这片土地上最繁华、最有名的城市。它的位置，在今日伊拉克首都巴格达以南一百千米。

巴比伦城被北面的亚述帝国摧毁之后，在新巴比伦时代得以重建，尼布甲尼撒二世时期，它成为当时世界上最大的城市。尼布甲尼撒二世是新巴比伦最有名的国王，他曾于公元前589年攻陷耶路撒冷，掳掠上万名犹太人为奴。二千五百多年后，在《巴比伦河》这首歌里，还可以听到犹太人的倾诉："当我们想起锡安，忍不住悲伤抽泣。"

巴比伦城被幼发拉底河分成两个区域。东岸是国王的宫殿与神的庙宇；西岸则被称作新市，它应当是城市扩张之后新兴的商业区与居住区。祭祀主神马杜克的神殿，就在河东岸，其中最重要的建筑是一座金字形

The convergence between the Babylonian temple and the earthen platform of Yangzishan

The Mesopotamian Plain, also known as the fertile crescent, is the region where civilization first emerged in human history. It gave birth to the world's first written legal code, the *Code of Hammurabi*, and the first epic heroic poem, the *Epic of Gilgamesh*.

Cities are the tangible crystallization of civilization, and the city of Babylon was once the most prosperous and famous city in this region. Its location was approximately 100 kilometers south of present-day Baghdad, Iraq.

After being destroyed by the Assyrian Empire, the city of Babylon was rebuilt during the Neo-Babylonian period, and during the reign of King Nebuchadnezzar Ⅱ, it became the largest city in the world. Nebuchadnezzar Ⅱ is the most renowned king of Neo-Babylon, known for capturing Jerusalem in 589 BC and enslaving thousands of Jewish people. Over 2,500 years later, in the song *the Rivers of Babylon*, one can still hear the outpouring of the Jewish people: "We wept, when we remembered Zion."

Babylon was divided into two regions by the Euphrates River. The eastern bank housed the king's palace and the temples of the gods. The western bank, known as the New City, emerged as a commercial and residential district after the city expanded. The temple dedicated to the chief god Marduk was located on the eastern bank, with its most significant structure being a ziggurat in the shape of a tiered pyramid.

After the destruction of the ancient Babylonian kingdom's ziggurat, It was rebuilt during the reign of

神塔。

古巴比伦王国的金字塔被摧毁之后，又在尼布甲尼撒时期得以重建。建成的金字塔高至少五十米，基座边长九十一米，共七层，之字形的斜坡可通往塔顶的圣所。

耸立在美索不达米亚平原的这座高塔，未必就是《圣经·创世纪》中的巴别塔，但它很可能是巴别塔的原型之一。

无独有偶，在远古的成都平原上，也曾经有一座巨大的祭祀台。它在时光长河的冲刷下伫立数千年，直到1950年代还遗迹尚存。

这座祭祀台便是羊子山土台。它位于老川陕公路西侧，驷马桥以北约一千米处——这座桥也是成都一处著名古迹。当年司马相如赴长安求取功名，曾于桥上立誓："他日若不乘高车驷马，不过此桥。"

羊子山是一座基底边长约为140米的正方形土台，高约10米，共有三级方台。每级方台外围，都是土坯砖砌成的围墙，砖体巨大，长0.65米、宽0.36米、高0.1米。这种土砖是放在木制模具里面捶打而成的，未经烧结，但有过日光下的暴晒，土里还掺有茅草以增加承载力。砖层之间，用灰白色细泥黏合。

Nebuchadnezzar. This reconstructed ziggurat stood at least 50 meters high with the base measuring 91 meters in length, and seven tiers and a zigzagging ramp to the sacred sanctuary.

This magnificent tower may not be the exact Tower of Babel as in *Genesis*, the *Bible*, but it likely served as one of the prototypes of the Tower of Babel.

It is no coincidence that there was once a colossal sacrificial platform on the ancient Chengdu plain. For thousands of years, it withstood the test of time, until the 1950s when remnants were still prime.

This revered sanctuary was known as the Yangzishan Earthen Altar. It is located on the west side of the Old Sichuan Shaanxi Highway, about one kilometer north of Sima Bridge—a bridge that stands as a famous ancient heritage. It was here that Sima Xiangru, seeking fame and glory in Chang'an, made a solemn oath on the bridge, "If I do not ride in a grand carriage drawn by four steeds in the future, I shall not cross this bridge again."

Yangzishan is a square earthen platform with a base measuring approximately 140 meters on each side. It stands about 10 meters high, comprised of three tiers, with each surrounded by walls of adobe bricks. These adobe bricks were enormous in size, measuring 0.65 meters in length, 0.36 meters in width, and 0.1 meters in height. They were formed by pounding clay in wooden molds, unsintered but with exposure to sunlight, and the earth was mixed with straw to increase the load-bearing capacity. Between the layers of bricks, a fine greyish-white clay is used to bind them together.

At the heart lies a central brick wall, encompassing a soil platform measuring 31.6 meters on each side. Resembling a well, yet not filled with water, but with compacted soil. The soil, diligently rammed and pressed, bears the imprints of 9-centimeter diameters. These brick walls, three in

最中心的砖墙，围成一个31.6米见方的土台。这很像是一口井，不过这口砖井里装的不是水，而是土。土都经过夯筑，留有直径9厘米的夯窝。像这样的砖墙一共有三道，三级土台也因此而成。

四川省文物管理委员会发布的《羊子山土台遗址清理报告》里估算，土台总共夯土加墙体七万余方，共使用土砖约一百三十八万余块。进行这样大的工程，背后没有强大的国力支撑是做不到的。而实施这项大工程的，应当就是三星堆或金沙时期的古蜀国。土台的功用，是举行大型祭祀。那么，土台最中心站立的大祭司，是不是三星堆青铜大立人的原型呢？祭司手中握着的，是不是那根刻有射鱼纹的金权杖呢？

巧合的是，羊子山土台使用的时代，跟巴比伦城金字形神塔大致相当。

土台废弃于战国晚期，原因很好理解。公元前316年秦灭巴蜀，在古蜀盛行的原始宗教就此消亡，大型祭祀台也再无用武之地。羊子山土台在尘土的掩盖下，逐渐跟一座天然的土丘没有差别了。而土丘的一大用处，便是成为墓葬的承载地。自1953年始，两年半的清理中，发现了上自战

total, form a tri-level platform, and the three levels of earthen platforms were formed as a result.

According to *the Clearance Report of the Yangzishan Earthen Platform Site* released by the Cultural Relics Management Committee of Sichuan Province, it is estimated that the total amount of soil used for the platform's rammed earth walls is approximately 70,000 cubic meters, with a total of about 1.38 million clay bricks used. The execution of such a large-scale project would not have been possible without strong national support. It is believed that the ancient Shu Kingdom, either during the Sanxingdui or Jinsha period, was responsible for carrying out this monumental construction. The purpose of the earth platform was to hold large-scale ceremonies and rituals. One may wonder whether the central figure standing on the platform, the grand sorcerer, could be the prototype of the Bronze Giant statues found in Sanxingdui? Could the gold scepter held by the sorcerer possibly feature the Shooting Fish Pattern that were commonly depicted?

It is a coincidence that the era in which the Yangzishan Earthen Platform was used roughly corresponds to the time of the Babylonian ziggurat.

The platform was abandoned during the late Warring States period, which is quite understandable. In 316 BC, the state of Qin conquered the Ba and Shu regions, leading to the demise of the primitive religion that thrived in ancient Shu. Consequently, the need for large-scale ceremonial platforms vanished. Over time, the Yangzishan Earthen Platform gradually became indistinguishable from a natural mound, hidden under layers of dust. Such mounds, however, served a crucial purpose as burial grounds. During the two and a half years of excavation starting from 1953, a total of 211 tombs were discovered. These tombs ranged from the late Warring States period to the Han, Jin, Tang, Song, and even the Ming dynasties.

国末期，涵盖汉晋唐宋，下至明代共计二百一十一座墓葬。

到了近现代，羊子山土台在未清理之前，是一座直径一百四十米、高十米的土丘。1953年底，附近一砖瓦厂投产，在此取土。同时西南博物院也派人到此勘察，当时仅以为羊子山是一座大墓的封土。到了1956年，羊子山仅剩中心部分四十米左右见方的土堆，其高度也被削去了两米多，几千年来的土坯砖和夯土，都被烧制为砖瓦。

2018年，笔者写作以杜宇取代鱼凫一战为题材的科幻小说《猛犸金沙》时，曾经实地探访。土台遗址处于羊子山路、横桥街的交会处，在水岸雅居和华宇阳光两个楼盘的包围中，徒留一片三角形的空地。稍远处，有地铁站，也有正待拆迁的城中村。

在科幻小说中，外星人创造了BDO这样的巨大沉默物以昭示人类。而巴比伦城金字塔形神庙和羊子山土台都是人类创造的BDO，是幼年时的人类对于几何这种抽象之美的理解。而羊子山土台更有特别的内涵：中轴线以北偏西55度的方向，指向蜀人的来处——岷山；四面三角形锥体，则是对岷山众山顶的模仿。

In modern times, before the excavation, the Yangzishan Earthen Platform existed as a 140-meter diameter and 10-meter high earthen mound. By the end of 1953, a nearby brick factory commenced operations and utilized the soil from the site. Simultaneously, experts from the Southwest Museum also conducted surveys, initially assuming that Yangzishan was simply the covering soil of a large tomb. By 1956, only the central part of Yangzishan remained, a roughly 40-meter square soil heap. Its height had been reduced by more than two meters, as thousands of years worth of rammed earth and clay bricks were transformed into burnt bricks and tiles.

In 2018, during the writing of my science fiction *Mammoth Jinsha* based on the theme of the conflict between Duyu and Yufu, I had the opportunity to visit the site. The Yangzishan Earthen Platform is located at the intersection of Yangzishan Road and Hengqiao Street, surrounded by the Waterfront Residence and Huayu Sunshine apartment complexes, leaving behind only a triangular vacant space. Just a short distance away, there is a subway station, as well as a nearby urban villages awaiting demolition.

In the science fiction novel, extraterrestrial beings create colossal silent objects like the BDO to communicate with humanity. The ziggurat of Babylon and the Yangzishan Earthen Platform are both man-made BDOs, an early human understanding of the abstract beauty of geometry. However, the Yangzishan Earthen Platform carries a special significance: the central axis, with a deviation of 55 degrees northwestern from true north, points to the origins of the Shu people — the Min Mountains. The triangular pyramid shape on all sides is a reflection of the multiple peaks of the Min Mountains.

The ancient Shu civilization and the Mesopotamian civilization were separated by thousands of miles, with the formidable barriers of the Hengduan

古蜀文明和美索不达米亚文明相距万里，中间隔着横断山脉、喜马拉雅山脉及青藏高原、恒河平原以及印度大沙漠、伊朗高原，然而，这些对古人来说无异于天堑的艰难地形，却未曾将它们真正隔绝。

Mountains, the Himalayas, the Qinghai-Tibet Plateau, the Gangetic Plain, the Indian Thar Desert, and the Iranian Plateau in between. However, these challenging terrains, which seemed like insurmountable obstacles to ancient people, did not truly isolate them.

形状各异的三星堆青铜人像　高泓 摄
Bronze human figures in various forms in Sanxingdui. (Photographer: Gao Hong)

中原文明没有作青铜雕像的传统。三星堆一号坑和二号坑出土的青铜立人像、人头像、人面具、兽面具共计82具，与殷墟文物的风格迥然相异。而在遥远的美索不达米亚，最迟在约公元前3000年就开始制作青铜雕像，在乌尔发现的青铜人头像是其一例。在尼尼微，有阿卡德·萨尔贡一世的青铜人头像；在印度河，有戴手镯、臂钏的青铜舞女像；在更遥远的埃及，则有第六王朝法老佩比一世和其子的全身青铜像。

古蜀和美索不达米亚之间的沟通与文化传播显而易见。不过，古蜀文明是独立萌发于四川盆地的原生文明，则毋庸置疑。

Indeed, the Central Plains civilization did not have a tradition of creating bronze sculptures. The bronze human figures, heads, masks, and animal masks unearthed from the No.1 and No.2 pits of Sanxingdui, totaling 82 in number, bear a strikingly different style compared to the artifacts found in the Yin ruins. In the distant Mesopotamia, the production of bronze sculptures began as early as around 3000 BC. An example of this is the bronze head discovered in Ur. In Nineveh, there is a bronze head of Akkadian ruler Sargon I. Along the Indus River, there are bronze sculptures depicting dancing girls adorned with bracelets and armlets. In the far-off land of Egypt, there are full-body bronze statues of Pharaoh Pepi I and his son from the Sixth Dynasty.

The communication and cultural dissemination between the ancient Shu civilization and Mesopotamia are indeed evident. However, there is no doubt that the ancient Shu civilization emerged independently in the Sichuan Basin as an indigenous culture.

望丛祠
The Wang Cong Shrine

两个巨大的封土堆，里面真的埋葬有古蜀国望帝杜宇、丛帝鳖灵吗？两帝陵上古柏森森，鳖灵湖内莲荷摇曳。望丛祠位于成都市郫都区，这里也被认为是杜宇旧都。

祭祀望帝的祠庙，原建于灌县玉垒山，南北朝由灌迁郫，与祭祀丛帝的祠庙合二为一，称望丛祠。相爱相杀的望帝与丛帝，由此相伴相随千年。

Do the two colossal mounds truly hold the remains of the ancient rulers Duyu and Bieling of Shu Kingdom? Ancient cypress trees adorn the tombs, while lotus flowers sway in the Bieling Lake. The Wang Cong Shrine, nested in the Pidu District of Chengdu, is said to be the former capital of Duyu.

Originally erected on Mount Yulei in Guan County, the temple devoted to Duyu, the Emperor Wang was relocated to Pidu during the Southern and Northern Dynasties period. It merged with the temple dedicated to Bieling, the Emperor Cong and became what is now known as the Wan Cong Shrine. Throughout the ages, the intertwined fate of the appreciating and conflicting Emperors Du and Bie has endured for millennia.

望丛祠迷雾：杜宇、鳖灵的相爱相杀
The Wang Cong Shrine Myth: Duyu and his frenemy, Bieling

谒望丛祠

清·何绍基

蜀王坟上草青青，
翠柏苍松护鳖灵。
一代勋名高禹绩，
千秋揖让近虞廷。
荆尸浮处人争异，
蜀魄啼时梦乍醒。
无限荒丘环寝殿，
丹枫老树作人形。

Pilgrimage to the Wang Cong Shrine

He Shaoji, Qing Dynasty

On the tomb of Duyu and Bieling, the grass grows green,
Emerald cypresses and towering pines guard Bieling.
Achievement in flood control, surpassing even Yu the Great,
Entrustment of state, like Yao's abdication, surpassing any debate.
Disputes arise over the floating corpse from Jingchu, a fragmented clue,
Shu's restless spirit weeps, awakening from its slumber askew.
Endless deserted mounds encircle the palace halls, a solemn scene,
Aged maple trees take on human forms, with an aura so serene.

望丛祠　冉玉杰 摄

Wang Cong Shrine (Photographer: Ran Yujie)

何绍基以书法闻名于世，至今杜甫草堂工部祠还悬挂着他撰书的对联“锦水春风公占却，草堂人日我归来”。清咸丰二年，何绍基授四川学政，三年后辞官，游历蜀、秦、鲁，授学往来于湘楚吴越。他这首《谒望丛祠》，凭吊古蜀两位君主，缅怀望

He Shaoji was renowned in the world of calligraphy, and even today, his written couplet “Amidst the embroidered waters, the spring breeze is claimed by the Poet; as a visitor to the Thatched Cottage, I return on this auspicious day” still hangs in the Gongbu Temple at Du Fu's Thatched Cottage. In the second year of the Xianfeng era of the Qing Dynasty, He Shaoji was appointed as the educational official of Sichuan. Three years later, he resigned

帝杜宇、从帝鳖灵劝农、治水的功绩，并对两者之间通过禅让实现政权的和平交接而赞叹不已。

杜宇与鳖灵的故事，中国人耳熟能详，是因为李商隐《锦瑟》的名句“望帝春心托杜鹃”，这两位古蜀国君主由此有了全国性的影响。

在这个故事里，古蜀国的君主杜宇教会了老百姓种庄稼，深受拥戴。又因为遭遇严重的水患，而拜荆楚人鳖灵为相，让他带领民众治水。后来，杜宇因跟鳖灵之妻有私情而羞愧，便将王位让给治水成功的鳖灵。隐居西山之后，杜宇却又心有不甘，便化为杜鹃，每年春耕时节以“布谷布谷”的啼叫，提醒蜀民莫忘农时。

类似的传说很多，大同小异，真实的情况又如何呢？关于古蜀史，历来所依据者多为扬雄《蜀王本纪》及常璩《华阳国志》。扬雄和常璩都是大家，但由于年代的久远以及认知上的时代局限，即便是这样重要的著作，在今天看来也颇有些匪夷所思之处。

from his official position and embarked on a journey through the regions of Shu, Qin, and Lu, engaging in scholarly exchanges in Xiang, Chu, Wu, and Yue. In his poem *Pilgrimage to the Wang Cong Shrine*, he pays homage to the two ancient Shu monarchs, Duyu and Bieling, recalling Duyu's agricultural merits and Bieling's water management achievements. He admires the peaceful transfer of power through abdication between the two rulers.

The story of Duyu and Bieling is well-known among the Chinese people, largely due to the famous line from Li Shangyin's poem: "The longing of the emperor's heart is placed upon the cuckoo." This line has bestowed a nationwide influence upon these two ancient rulers of the Shu Kingdom.

In this story, the ancient ruler of the Shu Kingdom, Duyu, taught the common people how to cultivate crops, earning their admiration and support. However, when the kingdom faced severe flooding, Duyu sought the assistance of Bieling, a skilled water management expert from the Jingchu region. Bieling successfully led the people in combating the floods. Later, Duyu, feeling ashamed due to his illicit relationship with Bieling's wife, decided to abdicate the throne in favor of Bieling, who had proven himself in water management. Retreating to the Western Mountains, Duyu couldn't shake off his lingering discontent and transformed into a cuckoo bird. Every spring, during the sowing season, he would remind the people of Shu with his repetitive call of "bu gu, bu gu", urging them not to forget the timing of sowing.

Similar legends abound, each with its own variations, but what is the true account? The primary sources for ancient Shu history have long been Yang Xiong's *Annals of the Kings of Shu* and Chang Qu's *Records of the States South of Mount Hua*. Although both Yang Xiong and Chang Qu were esteemed scholars, their works were composed centuries ago, and are subject to the limitations of their era and understanding. Even these significant works, when viewed today, may present some perplexing aspects.

天上，井里，江中
神秘的来处

最让人疑惑的，是这两位君主以及杜宇妻子的来处。

《蜀王本纪》记载，“后有一男子名曰杜宇，从天堕，止朱提。一女子名利，从江源井中出，为杜宇妻……荆有一人名鳖灵，其尸亡去，荆人求之不得。鳖灵尸随江水上至郫，遂活，与望帝相见。”

杜宇之名，在《蜀王本纪》中又作“蒲泽”，记为“蜀之先，称王者有蚕丛、柏濩、鱼凫、蒲泽、开明”。到了常璩写《华阳国志》，综合各种版本，将其统一为杜宇。

看到了吗？望帝杜宇是从天上掉下来，落到一个叫朱提的地方的。他的妻子利，则是从江源这个地方的井里面冒出来的。

丛帝鳖灵，又称开明，他的身世更为传奇。

生活在荆楚的鳖灵本来已经死了，尸体却不顺流东下进入大海，而是通过复杂的水系逆流而上，向西来

Their origins remain a mystery
From the heavens, the well, and the river

What perplexes most is the origin of these two monarchs and Duyu's wife.

Annals of the Kings of Shu states, “There was a man named Duyu who descended from the heavens and settled in Shushi. There was a woman named Li who emerged from a well at the source of the river, and she became Duyu's wife... In Jing, there was a man named Bieling. After his death, the people of Jing searched for his body in vain. Bieling's body floated up the river to Pi County and miraculously came back to life, meeting with Emperor Duyu.”

In *Annals of the Kings of Shu*, Duyu is also known as Pu Ze. It records, “Among the early Emperors of Shu, there were Cancong, Boguan, Yufu, Pu Ze, and Kaiming.” However, when Chang Qu wrote the *Records of the States South of the Mount Hua*, he synthesized various versions and unified it as Duyu.

Did you see it? The Emperor Duyu descended from the heavens and landed in a place called Shushi. His wife, Li, emerged from a well in the source of the river.

As for Emperor Bieling, also known as Kaiming, his origins are even more legendary.

Bieling was dead in Jingchu. However, his body did not flow downstream to the sea but defied the natural course of the water, moving against the currents. It traveled upstream, westward, and arrived in the Shu region, specifically in Pi County. Even

到了蜀地郫邑。更神奇的是，他到了郫之后，不仅复活，后来还做出了治理水患这样的大功业，更进一步成为蜀王，开创了一个传承十二世的开明王朝。

读史，尽信书不如不读书。这三位的来处，肯定不是现实意义上的真实。但若仅视之为不值一提的荒诞无稽，则为视瑰宝如敝屣，入宝山而空手归。

传说与神话，通过先民心灵与意识的棱镜，折射出历史的真实。

more astonishing, upon reaching Pi County, he was not only resurrected but also accomplished great feats in water management, eventually becoming the Emperor of Shu. He founded the illustrious Kaiming Dynasty, which endured for twelve generations.

When it comes to studying history, it's better to read books critically rather than blindly believing everything written. The origins of these three figures are certainly not to be taken in a literal sense. However, if we dismiss them as mere absurdities, we would be overlooking the value and significance they hold. Just like returning empty-handed from a treasure-filled mountain.

Most of the time, legends and myths reflect the true essence of history through the prism of our ancestors' minds and consciousness.

从天堕，止朱提
杜宇从哪儿来?

《蜀王本纪》称，杜宇“从天堕，止朱提”。从天上掉下个古蜀王，就跟“天上掉下个林妹妹”一样，不具备简单的真实性。破解杜宇的来处，密码藏在后半句，“止朱提”。

朱提的地理位置很明确，即云南昭通。昭通海拔最高四千零四十米，最低二百六十七米，处于云南与贵州、四川交界处，古代就以产银闻名。

乌蒙山腹地的万山丘壑中，有一块不大也不小的平地——面积五百二十五平方千米的昭鲁坝子。地

Where did Duyu come from? Descending from the heavens and settling in Shushi

According to the *Annals of the Kings of Shu*, Duyu' descended from the heavens and settled in Shushi. Similar to the saying "sister Lin falling from the sky", this does not hold a simple literal truth. To unlock the origin of Duyu, the clue lies in the latter half of the sentence: "settled in Shushi."

The geographical location of Shushi is explicitly mentioned as Zhaotong in Yunnan Province. Zhaotong ranges from an altitude of 267 meters to the highest point of 4040 meters. It is located at the border of Yunnan, Guizhou, and Sichuan. In ancient times, Zhaotong was renowned for its silver production.

In the heart of the Wumeng Mountains, amidst the myriad hills and valleys, lies a relatively large plain—the Zhaolu Basin, with an area of 525 square kilometers. The terrain is flat, and with abundant

势平坦，再加之水资源丰富，为赤水河源头，很适于发展农业。这就是朱提之所在。

杜宇所在的百濮部族，原本生活在朱提以西的高山地区。杜宇也是一种鸟的名字，即杜鹃，又叫子规或子巂——很可能就是杜宇部族当时的图腾，这从后来三星堆出土的大量鸟形器物也可以得到印证。前文已述，三星堆出土的青铜鸟，带有锐钩的，是鱼老鸹（鸬鹚）的象征，是鱼凫部落的图腾；而鸟喙不带锐钩的，则多是杜鹃鸟，非杜宇部莫属。

朱提西北方向直线距离约一百五十千米处，有一座巂山（今凉山彝族自治州越西县西南），古地名越巂或以此山而得名。

子巂（guī）、巂（xī）山，虽然字同音不同，但二者之间的联系是显而易见的——相对于字形来说，读音很容易发生变化。生活在巂山一带的杜宇部族向东迁徙，越过高山，下到朱提。在昭鲁坝子的原住民看来，就如同天神下凡一般，或便是“从天堕，止朱提”的由来。

杜宇是濮人。濮是中国南方一个古老的民族，“牧誓八国”之一。武王伐纣时，与庸、羌、蜀、茅、微、卢、彭、濮八个方国成为同盟。决战

water resources as it is the source of the Chishui River, it is well-suited for agricultural development. This is the location of Shushi.

The Baipu tribe to which Duyu belonged, originally lived in the high mountainous areas west of Shushi. Duyu is also the name of a bird, the cuckoo, also known as zigu or zixi. It is highly likely that the cuckoo was the totem of the Duyu tribe at that time, as evidenced by the large number of bird-shaped artifacts unearthed from the Sanxingdui site. As mentioned earlier, the bronze birds unearthed from Sanxingdui, with sharp hooks, symbolized the fish-cormorant, the totem of the Yufu tribe. On the other hand, birds with beaks without sharp hooks were mostly cuckoos, undoubtedly representing the Duyu tribe.

Approximately 150 kilometers northwest of Shushi, there is a mountain called Xishan (now located in the southwest of Yuexi County, Liangshan Yi Autonomous Prefecture). It was known as Yuexi in ancient times, named after this mountain.

Although the characters “Gui”（巂）and “Xi”（巂）have similar form but different pronunciations, their connection is apparent. In terms of written characters, it is common for the pronunciation to undergo changes over time. The Duyu tribe, living in the vicinity of Guishan, migrated eastward, crossing over the high mountains and settling in Shushi. To the indigenous people of Zhaolu Basin, it seemed as though divine beings had descended from the heavens or, perhaps it was the origin of the saying “falling from the sky, settling in Shushi”.

The Duyu tribe is part of the Pu people, an ancient ethnic group in southern China and one of the “Eight Allied Tribes”. During the campaign against King Zhou of Shang, King Wu of Zhou formed an alliance with the tribes of Yong, Qiang, Shu, Mao, Wei, Lu, Peng, and Pu. Before the decisive battle at

前在牧野誓师时，周武王还问候道："远来辛苦了啊，你们这些从西边来的人。"濮人遍布于荆楚巴蜀，其族群众多，故又称百濮。到了汉代，濮人又被称为僰人，以制作悬棺而名传于后世。

杜宇从高山下到朱提之后，并未一直停留下来，而是继续向北，经过今日的宜宾、乐山一带，到达蜀中。

朱提地处南丝绸之路要冲，号称"锁钥南滇，咽喉西蜀"。秦时建"五尺道"，南抵滇池，北通蜀南，朱提正处中间。在修筑"五尺道"之前，就有不少断断续续甚或隐秘的道路存在。因此，杜宇从朱提至蜀，并不是难事。

一个外来者，怎样成了古蜀国的帝王，已不可考证了，但极可能跟他对先进农业技术的掌握——濮是长于农业的民族——或者跟对朱提白银资源的把控有关。甚至不排除，也有政治联姻的支持。五个古蜀王朝，曾有过那么多首领，而只有杜宇的妻子"利"在史籍上留下了名字，也很可能是因为她的家族不同凡响。

前文曾提及，杜宇的妻子利的身世也很神秘，"从江源井中出"。首先要确定"江源"为何处？史学大家

Muye, King Wu greeted them, saying, "You have traveled a long way, you people from the west." The Pu people were scattered throughout the regions of Jing, Chu, and Bashu, and their population was abundant, hence they were also known as the Bai (hundreds) Pu. During the Han Dynasty, the Pu people were also referred to as the Bo people, renowned for their production of hanging coffins on cliffs that left a lasting legacy.

After descending from the high mountains to Shushi, the Duyu tribe did not remain there permanently but continued their journey northward. They passed through the present-day areas of Yibin and Leshan, eventually reaching the Shu region.

Shushi is located at a crucial junction of the Southern Silk Road, often referred to as the "lock and key of South Dian and the throat of Western Shu". During the Qin Dynasty, the "Five-Foot Road" was constructed, extending south to Dianchi and north to southern Shu, with Shushi situated in the middle. Even before the construction of the "Five-Foot Road", there were already intermittent or even hidden pathways in existence. Therefore, it was not difficult for the Duyu tribe to travel from Shushi to Shu.

It is difficult to establish with certainty how an outsider became the emperor of the ancient Shu kingdom. However, it is highly likely that it was due to their mastery of advanced agricultural techniques, as the Pu people were known for their agricultural expertise. It could also be attributed to their control over the abundant silver resources in Shushi. Additionally, it is not unlikely that political alliances played a role as well. Among the five ancient Shu dynasties, there were numerous leaders, but only the wife of Duyu, named Li, is mentioned in historical records, which may suggest the significance of her family background.

As previously mentioned, the background of

任乃强先生认为，江源是松潘草原，“亦蜀族所由来处”。

如果说“从天降”是杜宇下自高山的隐喻，那么，松潘草原平均3400米的海拔也不低，为什么利就成了从“井中出”呢？其实，这样的视角，是由松潘草地的地理特征所决定的。

松潘草原地势平缓，处于西倾山、岷山和巴颜喀拉山等山脉之间，周围尽是4000米左右的雪山。由草原环顾四周，就如同站在一口巨井的底部，仰望井壁。原来，井也是先民的一个隐喻。

而且，这一带沼泽密布、汊河横生，随便挖一个坑就能成井。水坑，就是天然之井。（一位北方朋友告诉笔者：她老家地下水位高，挖井非常容易，用手拎桶就能把井水打上来，根本不需要井绳。）这也是对利神秘来处的解释之一吧。

杜宇时的古蜀国，已经掌握了在当时非常先进的耕作技术，以节令行农事，说明种植业进入精耕细作阶段，农耕文明已趋于成熟。这也造就了古蜀的国力强大、疆域广阔，它北抵褒斜道，将汉中囊括在内；西达宝兴，往南则达到云南。

按照《蜀王本纪》和《华阳国志》的说法，杜宇治下的古蜀国，将

Duyu’s wife, Li, is also mysterious, as she was said to have emerged from a well in the source of the river. The first step is to determine the location of this “river source”. Prominent historian Mr. Ren Naiqiang believes that the “river source” refers to the Songpan Grassland, which is also believed to be the origin of the Shu people.

If “descending from the sky” is a metaphor for Duyu’s descent from the mountains, then why is Li described as emerging from a “well”? In fact, this perspective is influenced by the geographical features of the Songpan Grassland. Located at an average elevation of 3,400 meters, the uniqueness contributes to this imagery.

The terrain of the Songpan grassland is gentle, located amidst the Xiqin Mountains, Min Mountains, Bayan Har Mountains, and other mountain ranges, all being snow-capped mountains of around 4,000 meters. Looking around from the grassland, it feels like standing at the bottom of a giant well, gazing up at the well walls. In fact, the well was a metaphor used by the ancestors.

Moreover, this area is dotted with marshes and intersected by rivers, making it easy to dig a well anywhere. Water holes are natural wells. (A friend from the north once told me that the groundwater level is high in her hometown, and digging wells is remarkably easy. They can draw water up with a bucket using their hands, without the need for a rope.) This may also be one of the explanations for Li’s mythical origin.

During the time of Duyu, the ancient Shu Kingdom had already mastered highly advanced agricultural techniques for that era, practicing seasonal farming. This demonstrates that the cultivation industry had entered a stage of meticulous and refined farming, and the agricultural civilization had matured. This also led to the great strength and vast territory

玉垒山、峨眉山视作城墙，岷江、嘉陵江、绵远河、石亭江视作池塘，以岷山下的草地为牧场，南中（四川西南、宜宾以南及云贵一带）为花园。其气魄之大，令人瞠目。

杜宇将都城建在了郫（今成都市郫都区），又因水患而迁都至瞿上。瞿上究竟在何处，学术界对此尚有争论，一说在双流牧马山，任乃强则称在彭州海窝子。

位于双流牧马山一说，源自南宋罗泌撰、罗苹注的《路史》。而罗泌、罗苹父子是江西人，撰注《路史》皆辑采于典籍，可能并未到蜀地进行过实地探访。

海窝子则位于湔江河谷，两侧山脉连绵，海拔近千米。向下，如鹰隼俯瞰成都平原——瞿是一个会意字兼形声字，隹（鸟禽类）上双目，注视状；向上，则通往岷山脚下草原，那也是利的来处。利背后强大的家族，可给予杜宇经济、政治甚至军事上的支撑，从地缘利益的角度考虑，古蜀帝迁都至此不是没有道理的。

在本书《三星堆金杖：射鱼纹的王权密码》一文中，笔者推断瞿上不排除是金沙的可能——若是，则文献与遗址发掘则得到了完美的印证。

of ancient Shu, as it extended northwards to the Baoxie Trail, incorporating Hanzhong; westwards to Baoxing; and southwards reaching Yunnan.

According to the *Annals of the Kings of Shu* and *Records of the States South of Mount Hua*, under the rule of Duyu, the ancient Shu Kingdom considered the Yulei Mountains and Mount Emei as their city walls, and they viewed the Min River, Jialing River, Mianyuan River, and Shiting River as their ponds. They used the grasslands at the foot of the Min Mountains as their pastures, and the Nanzhong region (southwest Sichuan, Yibin, and part of the Yun-Gui region) as their gardens. The grandeur of their spectacles was truly astonishing.

Duyu built the capital city in Pi (present-day Pidu District, Chengdu), but due to frequent flooding, he relocated the capital to Qushang. The exact location of Qushang is still debated in academic circles. Some believe it was located at Shuangliu Muma Mountain, while Mr. Ren Naiqiang claims it was at Haiwozi in Pengzhou.

The claim that Qushang was located at Shuangliu Muma Mountain is based on the *Lu Shi* written by Luo Mi and annotated by Luo Pin during the Southern Song Dynasty. However, Luo Mi and Luo Pin were both from Jiangxi and their work on *Lu Shi* was based on existing records, so it's possible that they did not personally visit the Shu region.

On the other hand, Haiwozi is situated in the Jian River Valley, with continuous mountain ranges on both sides, reaching an elevation of nearly a thousand meters. Looking down, it overlooks the Chengdu plain like a falcon in flight. Qu is known as a joint ideogram and pictophonetic character. The upper part of the character represents a bird (specifically a bird of prey) with its two eyes focused and alert. Looking up, it leads to the grasslands at the foot of the Min Mountains, which is also the origin of Li—a place of

沱江受龙泉山脉阻挡，形成“沱江小三峡” 冉玉杰 摄

The Tuo River, blocked by the Longquan Mountains, forms the “Three Gorges of Tuo River” . (Photographer: Ran Yujie)

advantage. Behind the scenes, the powerful Li family could provide economic, political, and even military support to the Du family. Considering the strategic interests, it is not without reason that the ancient Shu Emperor relocated the capital here.

In the article of *The Gold Scepter of Sanxingdui: the Regnal Code of the Shooting Fish Motif* in the book, I speculates that Qushang may possibly refer to Jinsa. If this is the case, it would provide a perfect confirmation between historical records and archaeological discoveries.

“尸随江水上至郫”
鳖灵何处治水

从帝鳖灵，又称鳖令。灵、令声相近、义相通，皆为首领，灵更含有巫觋之意。

鳖灵一族聚居之地，在长江南岸的乌江与沅江之间，当时属于楚国或其附属国，即今日贵州东部与湖南西部一带。说鳖灵是荆楚之人，是就区域或国别而言，就其族属来说，他可能是僚人。

僚，又称獠，是中国南方的一个古老民族。《北史》对其生活习性有详尽的记载，说他们在树上搭干阑，住在这种类似吊脚楼的房子里；水性极好，能躺在水底以刀刺鱼；饮食方式很独特，“其口嚼食并鼻饮”。用

the Corpse follows the river up to Pi Bieling’s Efforts at Baopingkou and Jintang Gorge

Emperor Bieling (Ling means “spirit”) is also known as Bieling (here Ling means “chieftain”). The two words are homophones, both referring to leaders, with the first one also implying shamans or sorcerers.

Bieling’s clan resided in the area between the Wu River and Yuan River on the southern bank of the Yangtze River, which at that time belonged to the state of Chu or its vassal states, corresponding to the eastern part of present-day Guizhou and western part of Hunan. To say that Bieling was a native of Jing Chu is to speak in terms of the region or country he belonged to; as for his ethnicity, he may have been a the Liao people.

The Liao people, also called and written as Liao 獠, were an ancient ethnic group in southern China. *The Book of Northern History* provides detailed records of their customs and way of life. It describes how they built raised platforms on trees as their homes, resembling suspended houses. They had excellent swimming abilities and could lie at the

鼻孔饮水，是古代南方一些少数民族的习性，到了清代才彻底消失。世界之奇，在我们这些视以口饮水为本能的人看来，鼻饮很难想象，而且毫无必要。无论如何，善鼻饮的民族是很难呛水的，这跟他们擅水性也相辅相成。

生活在这样的地方，跟水打交道是理所当然。由此可以推断，作为鳖邑首领的鳖灵具备几个特长：一是水性极好；二是会治水；三是有管理能力。

当鳖邑部族与强大的楚国发生冲突之际，作为首领的鳖灵选择了向蜀国逃亡。其路线则是沿着长江倒溯而上，由今日的宜宾沿岷江直至岷山（汶山）之下。最初的场景也可以想象：由于追兵紧急，鳖灵跳入江中，凭借独特的水中生存能力，浮在水面上诈死，然后逆流潜泳，脱离追杀之后再上到岸边。

上文提及，杜宇又名蒲泽，后面这个名字透露出的信息是：望帝治下的古蜀，曾经大水泛滥，一片泽国。当此时带着治水技术东来的鳖灵，立即找到了发挥才能之地。他被望帝起用为蜀相，投入对洪水的治理之中。

鳖灵作为楚国边缘地带的一个

bottom of the water to spearfish with knives. Their eating habits were unique, as they would "chew food with their mouths while drinking through their nostrils". Nasal drinking, a habit of some ancient ethnic groups in the southern regions, gradually disappeared during the Qing Dynasty. It is quite unimaginable and seemingly unnecessary to us, who instinctively drink water through our mouths. Nonetheless, a people who excel at nasal drinking are less likely to choke on water, which complements their swimming skills.

Living in such a environment, it is natural for them to have a close relationship with water. From this, we can deduce that Bieling, as the leader of the Liao clan, possessed several remarkable abilities: exceptional swimming skills, water management expertise, and strong leadership capabilities.

When the Liao clan clashed with the mighty Chu Kingdom, Bieling made the choice to flee to the Shu Kingdom. His route was to follow the Yangtze River upstream, starting from present-day Yibin along the Min River until reaching the foot of the Min Mountains (also known as the Wen Mountains). We can imagine the initial scenes: with pursuers close behind, the Bieling leapt into the river, leveraging his unique aquatic survival ability to float motionless on the water's surface, feigning death. He then swam underwater against the current. After escaping the pursuit, he eventually made his way up to the riverbank.

As mentioned earlier, the name "Pu Ze" (the Chinese character "Ze" means lakes, streams, swamps, and marshes) is another name for Duyu. The information conveyed by this name implies that in the ancient Shu under the reign of Emperor Duyu, there were massive floods that turned the land into a vast marshland. At this time, Bieling, who brought with him water management techniques from his homeland, immediately found a place to showcase his talents. He was appointed by Emperor Duyu as the

小部族首领，只身跳水逃亡，初到蜀地时一无所有，而此时创下的功业同在鳖邑相比时，已经有过之而无不及了。“鳖灵尸亡，诉（溯）江而上”，不仅是对他逃亡时的现实描述，也是对他在蜀国卷土重来、登上高位的隐喻。

鳖灵究竟在哪里治水？有一种说法是，鳖灵凿巫峡，使潴塞在成都平原的积水有了个去处，陆地才开始显现出来。鳖灵凿巫峡的说法，见于记述古蜀国历史与传说的《本蜀论》（已亡佚，《水经注》有引文）。然而，巫峡的位置在巴东，是古蜀国敌对国古巴国的辖地，蜀相是不可能到那儿去治水的。更何况巫山巫峡跟成都平原相距千里以上，通巫峡而蜀得陆地，很明显是南辕北辙的说法。或有巫峡为金堂峡之说，但尚无明确证据。

其实，《蜀王本纪》上说得很明白：“使鳖灵决玉山，民得安处。”

玉山即玉垒山，又叫九峰山（九顶山、九鼎山），属青藏高原东部边缘龙门山脉中段，其最高峰为太子城，海拔四千八百一十八米。因湔江发源于太子城—九峰山区，故又称湔山。玉垒山呈东北—西南走向，走到末端，一个神龙摆尾甩向东南，伸进

Prime Minister of Shu and dedicated himself to the task of flood control.

As the leader of a small tribal group on the outskirts of the Chu Kingdom, Bieling fled alone by diving into the water. When he first arrived in the land of Shu, he had nothing. However, the achievements he made during this time surpassed those in his previous clan. “Bieling’s corpse, tracing the river upstream” not only describes the reality of his escape but also metaphorically represents his rise to power and prominence in the Shu Kingdom.

The exact location where Bieling carried out water management project remains uncertain. One theory suggests that the Bieling carved the Wuxia Gorge, providing an outlet for the accumulated water on the Chengdu plain and causing the emergence of land. This notion of Bieling carving the Wu Gorge is mentioned in *Ben Shu Lun* (alreay lost, referenced in *Commentary on the Water Classic*), which contains accounts of ancient Shu Kingdom history and legends. However, the location of the Wuxia Gorge is in Badong, which was under the jurisdiction of the hostile ancient Ba Kingdom, making it highly unlikely for the Prime Minister of Shu to travel there for water management. Furthermore, the Wuxia Gorge and the Chengdu plain are separated by over a thousand kilometers, making the idea of unchoking the Wuxia Gorge to obtain the land of Shu contradictory. There is also a theory that the Wuxia Gorge refers to the Jintang Gorge, but there is no clear evidence to support this claim.

In fact, the *Annals of the Kings of Shu* provides a clear explanation, stating: “Bieling was tasked with breaking the Jade Mountain, allowing the people to find a land to live.”

Jade Mountain, also known as Yulei Mountain or Jiufeng Mountain, is part of the middle section of the Longmen Mountain Range on the eastern edge of the Qinghai-Tibet Plateau. Its highest peak is Taizi

都江堰市城区，即今日玉垒山公园所在。开明所凿之宝瓶口，即在玉垒山公园西南侧。

玉垒山西南方向为岷江，水量丰沛；东侧为湔江等河流，相对水量较少。虽有地质运动造成的天然缺口宝瓶口，却比较狭窄，过水量不够。鳖灵带领蜀民，将其拓宽、挖深，引岷江之水过近四十米峡口，向东形成柏条河。柏条河流至郫都区石堤堰，又分流为府河和毗河。其中，前者流入成都城区，成为锦江；毗河则成为千里沱江的三大支流之一。这就是《尚书·禹贡》上讲的“岷山导江，东别为沱”。郦道元《水经注》则称：“江水又东别为沱，开明之所凿也。”

岷江之水进入柏条河，既减轻了玉垒山西南侧的水患，又为其东侧的成都平原提供了灌溉资源。

毗河流经今日的新都、青白江地界，在金堂注入沱江。然而，此处还有一个瓶颈，那就是金堂峡。金堂峡全长十二千米，由鳖灵峡、明月峡和九龙峡组成，号称“沱江小三峡”。从名字就看得出来，首当其冲的鳖灵峡又跟鳖灵治水有关。

龙泉山脉呈东北—西南走向，逶迤于成都平原东部，全长三百余千

Cheng, reaching an elevation of 4,818 meters. The Jian River originates from the Taizi Cheng-Jiufeng Mountain area, hence the name Jianshan Mountain. It runs in a northeast to southwest direction, with its tail resembling a dragon swinging toward the southeast, extending into the urban area of Dujiangyan City, where the Yulei Mountain Park is located today. The Baopingkou, a strategically carved water passage by Kaiming, is situated on the southwest side of Yulei Mountain Park.

To the southwest of Yulei Mountain flows the abundant Min River, while on the eastern side are rivers like the Jian River with relatively smaller water volumes. Although there is a natural gap called the Baopingkou caused by geological movement, it is quite narrow and does not allow sufficient water flow. Bieling led the people of Shu to widen and deepen this gap, allowing the waters of the Min River to pass through the nearly 40-meter-wide gorge and form the Baitiao River, which flows eastward. The Baitiao River then reaches the Shidiyan area of the Pidu District, where it divides into the Fu River and the Pi River. The former flows into the urban area of Chengdu, becoming the Jin River, while the Pi River becomes one of the three major tributaries of the Thousand Mile Tuo River. This is what is described in the *Shang Shu* as “guiding the river from the Min Mountains to form the Tuo River in the east”. In Li Daoyuan’s *Commentary on the Water Classic*, it is also mentioned, “The river water also diverges east to become the Tuo River, which was created by the work of Kaiming.”

The waters of the Min River flow into the Baitiao River, relieving the water disaster on the southwest side of Mount Yulei and providing irrigation resources for the Chengdu Plain to the east.

The Pi River flows through the present-day boundaries of Xindu and Qingbaijiang, merging into the Tuo River in Jintang. However, there is a bottleneck here, known as Jintang Gorge. Stretching

米。川西坝子上的河要东流归海，都会遭遇它的阻挡。金堂峡便是沱江突破龙泉山脉中段低缓山丘，过云顶山麓而形成的通道，原本非常狭窄；龙门山以东又是鹿头山暴雨区，沱江支流绵远河、石亭江、湔江均发源于此——一旦大雨滂沱、山洪暴发，金堂峡峡口若再因山体崩塌等原因而堵塞，成都平原就会变成泽国。

鳖灵在金堂峡所为，跟在宝瓶口大同小异。传说他率民以水激火烧之法，拓宽峡口，清理河道堵塞物。如此，成都平原的潴水得以找到出口，民得陆处，千里沃野才能得以利用。

治水成功的鳖灵，在蜀国取得了极大的威望，这让他取代杜宇有了合法性。

相爱相杀的望帝与丛帝　冉玉杰 摄
Emperor Wang, and his frenemy Emperor Cong. (Photographer: Ran Yujie)

for twelve kilometers, Jintang Gorge consists of Bieling Gorge, Mingyue Gorge, and Jiulong Gorge, collectively known as the “Three Gorges of the Tuo River”. From the name itself, it is evident that Bieling Gorge is closely associated with Bieling’s water management.

The Longquan Mountain Range stretches over 300 kilometers in a northeast-southwest direction, winding through the eastern part of the Chengdu Plain. The rivers from the western basin flow eastward towards the sea, but encounter obstacles along the way. The Jin Tang Gorge serves as a passage for the Tuo River to break through the gentle hills of the middle section of Longquan Mountain Range and flows past the foothills of the Yunding Mountain. Originally, the gorge was very narrow. To the east of the Longmen Mountain lies the rain-prone area of Lutou Mountain. The tributaries of the Tuo River, such as the Mianyuan River, Shiting River, and Jian River, originate from this area. In the event of heavy rainfall and flash floods, if the mouth of the Jin Tang Gorge were to be blocked due to landslides or other reasons, the Chengdu Plain would be at risk of turning into a waterlogged land.

The efforts of Bieling in Jin Tang Gorge are quite similar to what he did at the Baopingkou. Legend has it that Bieling led the people to widen the gorge by setting fire to the rock, then they quickly poured cold water over it to make the rock to contract and produce cracks. After cracking, people used tools such as chisels, hammers, and shovels to strike and pry open the rock cracks, so the blockages in the river were cleared. This allowed the waterlogging on the Chengdu Plain to find an outlet, giving the people a place to settle and enabling the fertile land to be utilized.

Bieling’s success in controlling the water brought him great prestige in the state of Shu, establishing his legitimacy and overshadowing the authority of Duyu.

“开明肇其端，李冰集大成”望帝祠为何变成二王庙?

宝瓶口以北不到一千米处的玉垒山上，有一座二王庙，里面立着李冰和其子二郎的塑像。其实，这座庙宇的前身跟李冰全无关系，它本是为纪念杜宇而建立的望帝庙。

为什么要在玉垒山为望帝建祠，自然是因为“决玉山”治水。但治水的不是丛帝鳖灵吗，为什么是望帝祠而不是丛帝祠？其实，历史不可以简单类推。鳖灵是在杜宇的起用之下治水的，在这种意义下，望帝与丛帝即为一体。在鳖灵还没有完全取代杜宇之前，若建丛帝祠，那是再明显不过的僭越。类似可比之于著名的君臣合祠武侯祠，它其实是埋葬刘备的惠陵——汉昭烈庙，将祭祀诸葛亮的武侯祠与汉昭烈庙合二为一，已是在刘备、诸葛亮君臣去世一千多年后的明洪武年间了。

那么，为什么望帝祠会变成祭祀李冰的二王庙呢？最主要的原因还在于，两千年封建王朝，都是以中原华夏为正统进行叙事的。所谓“华夷之防”，来自岷山的蜀族是西戎，它的两位首领——濮人杜宇、

Kaiming lays the foundation; Li Bing excels in his achievements. Why the Temple of Emperor Duyu becomes the Temple of the Two Kings?

Located less than a kilometer north of Baopingkou, on the Yu Lei Mountain, stands the Temple of the Two Emperors, adorned with statues of Li Bing and his son Erlang. However, the origin of this temple have nothing to do with Li Bing. It was originally built as a memorial to Duyu, known as the Temple of Emperor Duyu.

The reason for establishing the Temple of Emperor Duyu on Yu Lei Mountain is indeed related to one water management achievement known as “carving a water passage through the Jade Mountain”. However, despite Bieling’s involvement in managing the water, the temple was not dedicated to him as the primary figure. Instead, it was dedicated to Duyu. Actually, it is necessary not to make simple assumptions or comparisons of the past events. Since Bieling was appointed by Duyu to assist in controlling floods, in that sense, the two Emperors are regarded as one. Before Bieling completely replaced Duyu in his role, inappropriately building a temple dedicated solely to him would have been seen as arrogation. This can be compared to the famous combined temple of the Emperor Liu Bei and the marquis Zhuge Liang, which is actually the Han Zhaolie temple housing Liu Bei’s mausoleum. The merging of the worship of Zhuge Liang in the Wuhou Temple with Han Zhaolie temple took place over a thousand years after the deaths of Liu Bei and Zhuge Liang, during the Ming Hongwu period.

The main reason for the transformation of the Temple of Emperor Duyu into the Temple of the Two Kings

獠人鳖灵——都是南蛮，皆为广义之夷。

南齐建武年间（494—498年），望帝祠被改建为崇德庙，以纪念兴建都江堰水利工程李冰父子。到了宋代，李冰父子被敕封为王，崇德庙即更名为二王庙。秦蜀郡守李冰兴修水利的名声于是更盛，鳖灵治水的功绩，倒渐渐湮没于历史的烟波之中。吊诡的是，立像于庙中、享香火上千年的李冰儿子二郎，其实在现实世界中并不存在，乃是由神话中的二郎神杨戬穿凿附会生成。

望帝祠留给李冰父子之后，迁到了郫邑，与原来就在此处的丛帝祠合为一体，成为望丛祠。由此算来，它距今已有一千五百多年的历史了。

不过，望帝、丛帝回到当年立都之处，也算是得其所哉。

李冰的事迹千古流传，而鳖灵则多被世人遗忘。古人亦有为鳖灵鸣不平者，清人孙澎就在《岷阳二帝前志序》中感叹道："天下有同一功德，一传一不传。"

孙澎曾以望丛旧事询问过郫邑的老百姓，大家都回答："地老天荒的事，从何说起呢？"他不甘心，又去问官吏士绅，这些人则回答他："古

dedicated to Li Bing lies in the narrative framework of the feudal dynasties, which upheld the Central Plains as the orthodoxy of the Han Chinese civilization. The concept of "Sino-Barbarian dichotomy" arose from the fact that the Shu people from the Min Mountains were considered as Western Barbarians, with their two leaders, Duyu, from the Pu clan, and Bieling, of the Liao clan, being broadly categorized as barbarians.

During Jianwu era of the Southern Qi Dynasty (494-498 AD), the Temple of Emperor Du was rebuilt as the Chongde Temple to commemorate Li Bing and his son's construction of the Dujiangyan irrigation system. In the Song Dynasty, Li Bing and his son were posthumously elevated to the status of kings, leading to the renaming of the temple as the Temple of the Two Kings. The fame of Li Bing, the Qin Shu Prefect who built the water conservancy project at Dujiangyan, overshadowed the merits of Bieling in water management, leading to the latter's reputation to be gradually lost into the mist of history. It is indeed ironic that Li Bing's son, Erlang, whose statue has stood in the temple and received worship for thousands of years, does not actually exist in the real world. It was a creation born out of the association with the mythical figure of Erlang God, also known as Yang Jian. This juxtaposition of historical figures and mythical beings is a testament to the blending of history and folklore in Chinese culture.

After the Temple of Emperor Duyu was dedicated to Li Bing and his son, it was later moved to Pi County and merged with the original Temple of Emperor Bieling. By this reckoning, this combined temple, known as the Wan Cong Shrine, is over 1,500 years old.

Indeed, the return of Emperor Duyu and Emperor Bie to this location can be seen as a fitting tribute, symbolizing the continuity of their legacy and the connection to the historical capital of ancient Shu Kingdom.

籍上记载蚕丛距今已有四万八千年（李白《蜀道难》：尔来四万八千岁，不与秦塞通人烟），都是些很荒唐的事，无从稽考。”当地人的反应，让孙澎不仅失望，甚至有几分悲愤。

当然，并不是所有的后世子孙都对伟大的祖先一无所知、遗忘殆尽。

北宋时，鳖灵之坟划在净林寺的地界内，僧人们削平坟顶，在上面修筑台观。邑人张俞担心丛帝之墓连同其功迹皆被湮没，便向郡守请求为其立碑，并在墓上建祠。

到了宋仁宗皇祐年间，净林寺的和尚死了，寺庙和鳖灵坟都被人占为民田。张俞听说此事，再一次向县令建言。县令被深为触动，便亲自前往察看。就在县令去后第二天，以进士杜常为首的五十八名邑人联名提交诉状，要求不得侵占丛帝之墓为田地。在得到郡守的嘉许后，县令把望帝和丛帝的墓茔都划给净林寺，又访到有声望的僧人垂白来主持寺庙，以使先人之功德不致被遗忘。

两次主持这件事的郫邑人是隐士张俞，他因一首《蚕妇》而名传于后世：“昨日入城市，归来泪满巾。遍身罗绮者，不是养蚕人。”

张俞曾被录用为秘书省校书郎，却把职位让给了父亲，后来又七次拒

The achievements of Li Bing have been celebrated throughout the ages, while Bieling has often been forgotten by the world. Ancient scholars also expressed their dissatisfaction with the neglect of Bieling. Sun Peng, a Qing Dynasty scholar, lamented in his *Preface to the Records of the Two Emperors of Minyang*: “In the world, there are those with equal merits, yet some are remembered, and some are not.”

Sun Peng once inquired about the old events of Emperor Duyu and Emperor Bieling, asking the local people in Pi County. However, they all responded, “Those are ancient matters that date back to the beginning of time. How can we even begin to talk about them?” Disheartened, Sun Peng sought answers from officials and scholars, but they answered, “The ancient books record that Cancong existed 48,000 years ago (Li Bai in his poem *the Arduous Journey to Shu* mentions that it has been 48,000 years since the establishment of the Shu Kingdom, but the Shu region is still isolated from the Qin region and the road to Shu is uninhabited and desolate). It is an absurd and unverifiable claim.” The reactions of the local people not only disappointed Sun Peng but also filled him with a sense of sadness and frustration.

Of course, not all descendants in later generations are completely ignorant or have forgotten about their great ancestors.

During the Northern Song Dynasty, the tomb of Bieling was located within the territory of the Jinglin Temple. The monks flattened the top of the tomb and built a platform on it. However, the local resident Zhang Yu was concerned that the tomb of Bieling, along with his achievements, would be lost and forgotten. He requested the county magistrate to erect a stele and build a temple at the tomb.

During the reign of Emperor Renzong in the Song Dynasty, the abbot of Jinglin Temple passed away, and both the temple and the tomb of Bieling were occupied by the local people as farmland. Zhang

绝诏用。至今，在望丛祠内立着一块碑，刻有宋代陈皋的《杜宇鳖灵二坟记》，上面记载了张俞两次出面力主修复古蜀帝墓的事迹，从中也可以看出其尊重历史、推崇教化的衷心。而张俞自己撰写的《蜀望丛帝新庙碑记》，也被勒铭于石，立在望丛祠内。

把首开宝瓶口归于鳖灵，并不是要否认李冰。李冰的功绩，主要在于修飞沙堰，开辟经过成都的郫江、检江，以及在沫水（青衣江）上开凿离堆。鳖灵开凿宝瓶口之后，李冰再次开凿、将其扩宽淘深也是可能的。总言之，鳖灵为李冰的治水打下了基础。今日的望丛祠，在那面巨大的屏壁背面的右侧，刻着十个字，作为对鳖灵、李冰治水功绩的评价，可谓非常精到："开明肇其端，李冰集大成。"

司马迁与扬雄，同为彪炳千秋的文史大家。《史记》中只记载了李冰治水，并没提及鳖灵。而扬雄生长的年代，距司马迁并不太远，他作为郫邑人，对乡梓更为熟悉，也更有深情。扬雄于乡中父老之间采集世代流传的说法，将"鳖灵决玉山，民得安处"载之于册，今人不可不察。

Yu, upon hearing this news, once again advised the county magistrate. Deeply moved, the magistrate personally went to investigate. Just one day after the magistrate's visit, a group of fifty-eight local residents, led by Du Chang, an accomplished scholar, jointly submitted a petition, demanding that the tomb of Emperor Wang and Emperor Cong not be encroached upon for agricultural purposes. With the permission of the prefect, the county magistrate assigned the tombs of Emperor Wang and Emperor Cong to Jinglin Temple. He also sought out the respected monk, Chui Bai to preside over the temple, ensuring that the merits and virtues of the ancestors would not be forgotten.

The person who twice stood up to handle this matter in the county of Pi was the recluse Zhang Yu. He gained fame in later generations for a poem titled *the Silkworm Breeder*, which goes as follows: "Yesterday, I entered the bustling city, and upon my return, my tears soaked my handkerchief. Those wearing silk and satin garments, are not the ones who rear the silkworms."

Zhang Yu was once appointed as a position in the Secretariat in the imperial court, but he gave up the post to his father. He later declined seven royal appointments. To this day, a stone stele stands in the Wan Cong Shrine, bearing an inscription of the *Epitaph for the Twin Tombs of Duyu and Bieling* by Chen Gao of the Song Dynasty. It records Zhang Yu's efforts in advocating for the restoration of the ancient tombs of the Shu emperors on two occasions, reflecting his deep respect for history and reverence for cultural enlightenment. Zhang Yu also authored the *Epitaph for the New Temple of the Shu Emperors of Wan Cong*, which was engraved on another stone and placed in the Wan Cong Shrine.

Attributing the carving of the Baopingkou to Bieling does not mean to deny the contributions of Li Bing. Li Bing's major achievements lie in the construction of the Feishayan weir, the excavation of

望帝陵，其碑为辛亥革命元老但懋辛手书　冉玉杰 摄

Tomb of Emperor Wang with its handwritten tablet by Dan Maoxin, a veteran of the 1911 Revolution. (Photographer: Ran Yujie)

the Pi River and Jian River that pass through Chengdu, and the digging of irrigation channels on the Mo River (Qingyi River). After Bieling opened the Baopingkou, it is possible that Li Bing widened and deepened it further. In summary, Bieling laid the foundation for Li Bing's water control efforts. At the Wan Cong Shrine in present times, on the backside of a huge screen wall, there are ten characters engraved on the right side. They aptly summarize the achievements of Bieling and Li Bing in water management: "Kaiming lays the foundation; Li Bing excels in his achievements."

Simultaneously renowned in the annals of literature and history, Sima Qian and Yang Xiong were both prominent scholars. *Records of the Grand Historian* only documented Li Bing's water management achievements without mentioning Bieling. As for Yang Xiong, he lived not too long after Sima Qian and being a native of Pi County, he had a deeper familiarity and emotional connection to his hometown. Yang Xiong collected the oral traditions passed down among the older generation in his village and recorded the phrase "Bieling was tasked with breaking the Jade Mountain, allowing the people to find new land" in his works. This is something that present-day individuals should not overlook.

"乃委国授之而去，如尧之禅舜"
既是以德服人，何有杜鹃泣血？

十来年前，笔者曾经探访过望丛祠。它处于城区边缘，红墙之中，二陵并峙，古木荫天，萍浮于池。夏天，鳖灵湖东西湖七百平方米湖面上

"Thus, he entrusted the governance of the state and departed, just like Yao's abdication." If indeed it was through Duyu's virtuous abdication that he gained the loyalty of Bieling, why would the cuckoo' mouth weep blood?

About a decade ago, I had the opportunity to visit the Wang Cong Shrine. Situated on the outskirts of the city, within its red walls, stand the twin tombs,

荷花盛开，随风摇曳。春天，听鹃楼旁杜鹃怒放，姹紫嫣红。传说望帝杜宇死后，精魂化为杜鹃鸟，口中泣血滴于春天开的第一种花之上，杜鹃花由此而得名。杜鹃鸟与杜鹃花，是望丛祠内最应景的动物与植物，必不可少。

望帝陵位于望丛祠西侧偏南，丘堆高十五米，呈椭圆形，周长约二百五十米。丛帝陵位于祠内东侧偏北，丘堆高十米，呈圆形，周长约一百米。二陵之上，皆有古柏森森。这些柏树都种植于清道光年间，距今有近两百年的历史。

沿着石阶向上，就可以分别来到二陵的“古望帝之陵”和“古丛帝之陵”石碑前。两碑皆由当时兼摄四川军民两政的熊克武立于民国八年，由辛亥革命元老但懋辛手书，距今已过百年。

杜宇将政权交给鳖灵后，隐居于西山。西山何所在？一说是青城山，但笔者以为，任乃强先生所言西山为“岷江西岸诸山之统称”者，更具可信性。后者包含前者，但范围大得多，甚至可以延展到成都平原以西岷山脚下的松潘草原。结合《华阳国志》中“以褒斜为前门，熊耳、灵关为后户……汶山为畜牧，南中为园

overshadowed by ancient trees, and adorned with floating water plants. In the summer, lotus flowers bloom gracefully on the 700-square-meter surface of the Bieling Lake, swaying gently in the breeze. And in the spring, near the Tingjuan Tower, rhododendrons burst forth with vibrant purples and reds. According to legend, after the passing of Emperor Wang, Duyu, his spirit transformed into a cuckoo bird, and its blood fell upon the first blossoming flower of spring, thus giving the flower the name “du juan” or cuckoo flower. The cuckoo bird and the cuckoo flower are the most fitting and indispensable creatures and plants within the Wang Cong Shrine.

The tomb of Emperor Wang is situated to the southwest of the Wang Cong Shrine. Its mound is 15 meters high, oval-shaped, with a circumference of approximately 250 meters. The tomb of Emperor Cong is located to the northeast within the shrine. Its mound is 10 meters high, circular, with a circumference of around 100 meters. Both mounds are adorned with ancient cypress trees that were planted during the reign of Emperor Daoguang in the Qing Dynasty, making them nearly two hundred years old.

Ascending the stone steps, one can reach the respective stone tablets of Tomb of the Ancient Emperor Wang and Tomb of the Ancient Emperor Cong. Both tablets, more than a century old, were erected by Xiong Kewu, who concurrently held leading military and civilian positions in Sichuan, in the eighth year of the Republic of China. They were handwritten by Dan Maoxin, a veteran of the 1911 Revolution.

The hand-written stone tablets of the Emperor Wang and Emperor Cong by Dan Maoxin.

After Emperor Duyu handed over political power to Bieling, he retired to the Western Mountain. The exact location of the Western Mountain is a subject of debate. Some believe it refers to Qingcheng

苑”之说，今人或应反思，是否把古蜀人的活动范围想得太局限了？

前文还曾提及望帝与丛帝的政权交接，作为德行直追尧舜的禅让，被人称颂了几千年。望丛祠两个侧门的匾额，分别刻着“功在田畴”和“德垂揖让”。功在田畴是真，无论是杜宇还是鳖灵都当得起这四个字。但真的是德垂揖让吗？稍一思索，就会发现问题：既然是以德服人的禅让，杜宇何以心有不甘，甚而至于化为泣血的杜鹃？“泣血”二字，暗藏有多少的悲恸、愤懑与不平？！

就“禅让”本身来说，它绝非温文尔雅的以德服人。回顾中国历史上那些耳熟能详的禅让故事，曹丕代汉、司马炎代魏、刘裕代晋、萧道成代宋、萧衍代齐，其间多有胁迫、杀戮，以及欲迎还拒、半推半就的故作姿态。

上古尧舜禹之间的禅让，为儒家文化所赞美、推崇，然而，在儒家学说一统天下之后几百年，西晋太康年间出土的春秋时晋、战国时魏的史书《竹书纪年》，却有几条让人读之心惊的记载：

“尧之末年，德衰，为舜所囚。”

“舜囚尧，复偃塞丹朱（尧之子），使不与父相见也。”

Mountain, but I personally find the interpretation by Mr. Ren Naiqiang, who refers to the Western Mountain as a collective term for “all the mountains on the west bank of the Min River”, to be more credible. This broader interpretation encompasses Qingcheng Mountain and extends far beyond, even to the Songpan Grassland at the foothills of the Min Mountains west of the Chengdu Plain. Considering the description in *Records of the States South of Mount Hua*, which mentions “Baoxie Pass as the front gate, Xiong’er and Lingguan as the back door... Wenshan Mountain as pastures, and Nanzhong as gardens”, it leads one to reflect on whether we have too narrowly confined the scope of ancient Shu people’s activities.

As mentioned earlier, the transfer of power from Emperor Duyu to Emperor Bie, regarded as a benevolent act comparable to the abdication of Yao and Shun, has been praised for thousands of years. The inscriptions on the side doors of the Wang Cong Shrine, 功在田畴 (Merits in the farmland) and 德垂揖让 (Virtues of humble abdication), hold significant meaning. It is true that both Duyu and Bieling lived up to the phrase 功在田畴. However, can we truly say that there was virtuous abdication? Upon further reflection, we discover a question: If it was truly an abdication based on virtuous conduct, why did Duyu harbor discontent, to the extent of transforming into the cuckoo bird with tearful bloodshed? The phrase “weeping blood” implies profound sorrow, resentment, and dissatisfaction.

Regarding the concept of abdication itself, it is far from a gentle and virtuous act of winning people over with moral conduct. Reflecting on well-known abdication stories in Chinese history, such as Cao Pi taking over Han, Sima Yan taking over Wei, Liu Yu’s replacement of Jin, Xiao Daocheng’s theft of the Song Dynasty, and Xiao Yan’s usurpation of Qi,

“舜囚尧于平阳，取之帝位。”

“舜篡尧位，立丹朱城，俄又夺之。”

古本《竹书纪年》为信史，由是可见，即便是历代赞颂的尧舜禹之间的禅让，也并非所谓的礼让恭谦、温情脉脉。舜并非儒家史观中那个宽厚的道德完人，而是一个精通宫廷政变的阴谋家。对尧，囚而篡位，冷酷无情；对丹朱，立而又夺，也无非历史中常见的掩人耳目却又急不可耐。

再把视线移回杜宇和鳖灵身上。鳖灵在外治水，杜宇和他的妻子私通，感到悲愤的不应当是他吗？为什么反倒是杜宇泣血悲号，表现得像受害者呢？

杜宇跟臣妻有私，可能会有内疚，但要说会因此而让出王位，这实在是过分高看了道德和超我的力量，低估了权力的魅力。历史上因为这个原因杀掉臣子而霸占其妻的君主，倒是数不胜数。

鳖灵用了什么手段，让杜宇“被迫心甘情愿”地退位，实在让人好奇。

people should find many of them involve coercion, killing, posturing and feigning.

The abdication between Yao, Shun and Yu in ancient times was praised and revered by Confucian culture. However, a few hundred years after Confucianism reigned supremely, *Bamboo Annals*, the Bamboo Slips Chronicle, a history book of Jin in the Spring and Autumn Period and Wei in the Warring States Period, which was unearthed during the Taikang period of the Western Jin Dynasty, contains a few entries which are shocking to the mind when reading it:

“In the final years of Yao’s reign, his virtue declined, and he was imprisoned by Shun.”

“Shun imprisoned Yao and held his son Danzhu in confinement, preventing them from seeing each other.”

“Shun imprisoned Yao in Pingyang and seized the imperial throne.”

“Shun usurped Yao’s throne, set up a city especially for Danzhu, but later captured the city.”

The ancient book *Bamboo Annals* is considered to be a reliable historical record. From this, we can see that even the revered acts of peaceful transition of power between Yao, Shun, and Yu were not exactly the selfless and humble gestures they have been portrayed to be. Shun, contrary to the Confucian view, was not the paragon of virtue but rather a master of palace intrigue. He imprisoned Yao and usurped his position, showing a cold and ruthless side. His treatment of Danzhu, feinting to establish him as the heir and then impatiently taking it away, was merely a common tactic to disguise his true intentions.

Now, let’s shift our focus back to Duyu and Bieling. Bieling was tasked with flood control, while Duyu had an illicit affair with Bieling’s wife. Shouldn’t Bieling be the one feeling anger and sorrow in this situation? Why is it that Duyu is depicted as the victim, shedding tears and lamenting as if he's the one being wronged?

It is possible that Duyu felt guilt over his affair with a minister's wife, but to assume that he would willingly relinquish his position of power because of it is overly idealistic, underestimating the allure of power and overestimating the power of morality. Throughout history, there have been countless rulers who have killed their ministers and claimed their wives for this very reason.

As for the means by which Bieling compelled Duyu to willingly abdicate, it remains a mystery that piques curiosity.

"始立宗庙，以酒曰醴，以乐曰荆"
蜀王改制，爱荆楚，慕华夏

按前文，五代蜀王蚕丛、柏灌、鱼凫、杜宇、开明，有时指一个传承了数百年历史的王朝，有时也指这个朝代中的某一位君主。

那么，本文所述的杜宇，"从天堕，止朱提"的杜宇，跟起用鳖灵、退隐西山、泣血化鹃的杜宇，也并不是同一个人。他们分别应当是杜宇王朝开国蜀王和末代蜀王——只是在传说与历史的纠缠中，被合二为一了。

查阅对望帝、丛帝记载最为详细的《华阳国志》，还会发现一个特点：时间由远及近，资料也由简及详。前

"(Aligning with those in the Central plains), they established the ancestral temple, called the libation as 'Li', and adopted the rites and music from Jing" the Shu king implemented reforms, showing fondness for the regions of Jing and Chu, while also admiring the culture of the Central Plain.

As mentioned earlier, the Five generations of Shu emperors, including Cancong, Boguan, Yufu, Duyu, and Kaiming (Bieling), at times refer to a dynasty that spanned several hundred years, and at times to a specific monarch within that Dynasty.

Therefore, the Duyu described in this passage, who descended from heavens to stop at Shushi, and the one who appointed Bieling, secluded himself in the Western Mountains, and wept blood after transforming into a cuckoo, are not the same person. They respectively represent the founding emperor and the last emperor of the Duyu Dynasty—they have simply

三代蜀王蚕丛、柏灌、鱼凫，多一笔带过，各代君主之名混为一谈。而到了杜宇，不仅有来处、去处，有历史功绩，有爱恨情仇。对鳖灵的着墨则更多，除了治水，还有他开创的王朝数百年的兴衰史——有神话传说一般的山精、五丁、金牛，也有接近信史的蜀国与秦国在政治、军事上的战略博弈。君王之名杂糅的现象也得到很大改善。

从帝鳖灵接过望帝杜宇的政权，开创的开明王朝共传承十二代。十二代君主中，开国者开明一世即鳖灵，号丛帝；二世号卢帝；三世号保子帝。卢帝和保子帝时古蜀国力极度强盛，卢帝北击秦国至凤翔，保子帝南攻僰人和僚人，让疆域进一步扩张。这三位有作为的君主，都在历史上留下了自己的名字。

公元前400年，中原进入战国时期已经七十六年，古蜀国也迎来了变革时期，即位的开明九世改制，开始大幅度向华夏文明靠拢。且来看一看《华阳国志》中的这段文字透露的讯息："始立宗庙，以酒曰醴，以乐曰荆，人尚赤，帝称王……未有谥列，但以五色为主，故其庙称青、赤、黑、黄、白帝也。"

立宗庙，以五色为主。宗庙，帝

been intertwined in a mix of legend and history.

When we consult the detailed records found in the *Records of the States South of Mount Hua*, which provide extensive information on the monarchs of Shu, particularly Emperor Wang and Emperor Cong, a notable pattern emerges: the information progresses from distant to recent times, with increasing levels of detail. The first three emperors of Shu, Cancong, Boguan, and Yufu, are briefly mentioned, and the names of each successive monarch become somewhat blurred. However, when it comes to Duyu, there is a wealth of information available, including his origins, achievements, and emotions of love and resentment. Bieling receives even more prominence, with a focus not only on his flood control efforts but also on the rise and fall of his Dynasty, spanning several hundred years. This includes mythical legends such as the goblin, Wuding (literally means five strong men), and the stone oxen (oxen claimed to be able to poop gold), as well as strategic political and military maneuvering between the states of Shu and Qin, which is closer to reliable historical accounts. The phenomenon of mixed names and confusion among monarchs is significantly improved in these records.

Emperor Cong Bieling took over the political power from Emperor Wang Duyu and established the Kaiming Dynasty, which lasted for twelve generations. Among the twelve generations of monarchs, the founder was Kaiming the First, also known as Bieling, titled Emperor Cong. The second emperor was known as Emperor Lu, and the third emperor was titled Emperor Bao Zi. During the reigns of Emperor Lu and Emperor Bao Zi, the ancient state of Shu reached its pinnacle of strength. Emperor Lu led expeditions northward, assaulting the Qin region up to Fengxiang, while Emperor Bao Zi launched successful campaigns against the Bo and Liao tribes in the south, expanding the territorial boundaries even

王、诸侯祭祀祖宗之处，也是华夏文化中祖先崇拜的具象体现。若帝王宗庙被毁，就意味着政权的倾颓，其重要性可见。古蜀国虽然还没学到中原的谥法和左昭右穆的排序，但也制作了五种颜色的祖先神主牌位以供膜拜。

人尚赤。喜欢红色，推崇红色，倒不是为了时尚，而是因为出自商周时期的一种哲学观念——五行。西周早期的文字《尚书·洪范》里有一段商朝贵族箕子与周武王的对话："五行一曰水，二曰火，三曰木，四曰金，五曰土。水曰润下，火曰炎上……"五行可以囊括万事万物，材质、方位、颜色、味觉……到了战国，阴阳家邹衍集大成创立"五德终始说"，把五行跟王朝的更替联系在一起，深远地影响了中国的文化和政治。

荆楚在华夏之南，南方属火，主赤色——蜀人尚赤，已能充分说明对楚文化的偏好、对先进文明的倾慕。

以酒曰醴。醴是未经过滤、滓汁不分的甜酒、浊酒，类似数十年前川渝地区流行的用竹管从陶罐中吸取的高粱咂酒，或者至今仍在普遍食用的醪糟。醴是一个古老的汉字，古蜀

further. These three accomplished monarchs left their marks in history with their achievements.

In the year 400 BC, which marked the 76th year of the Warring States Period in the Central Plains, the ancient state of Shu entered a period of transformation. The ninth generation emperor, Kaiming, implemented reforms, bringing the state closer to the civilization of Huaxia. Let's take a look at the information revealed in the *Records of the States South of Mount Hua*: "(Aligning with those in the Central plains), they established the ancestral temple, called the libation as 'li', and adopted the rites and music from the region of Jing. People dressed in red, and the emperor was titled as the king... There were no posthumous titles, but the five colors served as the main criteria, hence the temple was named after the Green, Red, Black, Yellow, and White Emperors."

The establishment of ancestral temples with the emphasis on the five colors holds significant meaning. An ancestral temple is a place where emperors and feudal lords worship their ancestors, serving as a tangible embodiment of ancestor worship in Chinese culture. If an emperor's ancestral temple were to be destroyed, it would symbolize the decline of their political power, highlighting its importance. Although the ancient state of Shu had not yet adopted the posthumous title system and the specific ordering of the patriarchal system, they still created ancestral tablets in the five colors to pay reverence to their ancestors.

People dressing in red is not merely a fashion trend but has its roots in the philosophical concept of Wu Xing, which originated in the Shang and Zhou dynasties. In an early Western Zhou text called *Shang Shu, the Book of Documents*, there is a dialogue between the noble Ji Zi of the Shang Dynasty and King Wu of Zhou, which states, "The five elements are water, fire, wood, metal, and earth. Water moistens and descends, fire blazes and ascends..."

人把酒叫作醴，显示当时古蜀国已经在使用汉语和汉字了，文化上趋同于中原。

曾侯编钟是战国早期曾国国君的大型礼乐重器，曾国又称随国，后被楚国所灭　何齐铁 摄

The Zenghou bronze chime bells, a large ceremonial musical instrument from the early Warring States period, belonged to the ruler of the Zeng State (also called the Sui State), which was later conquered by the Chu State. (Photographer: He Qitie)

以乐曰荆，帝称王。荆即楚，以乐曰荆，是指古蜀国采用楚国的礼乐制度。帝称王，则是政治制度上向楚国靠齐。

华夏政治制度，在周朝时唯天子称王，诸侯国君主则按爵位分别称公、侯，如齐桓公、晋文公和魏文侯等。楚国不管是文化还是政治地位，都处于华夏文明的边缘地带，楚国国君被周王室分封为子爵，是公、侯、伯、子、男五级爵位中的第四等。被视为蛮夷的楚国，先后于周夷王、周桓王时期两次称王，后一次称王保持

The five elements can encompass all things, including materials, directions, colors, and even tastes. During the Warring States period, Zou Yan, a practitioner of Yin-Yang philosophy, further developed the theory of the Five Virtues and the cycle of them, linking the concept of the five elements with the succession of dynasties. This had a profound influence on Chinese culture and politics."

Jingchu, situated in the southern region of China, has the fire as its predominant element and the color red as its symbol. The fondness of the people of Shu for the color red demonstrates their affinity for the culture of Chu and their admiration for advanced civilizations.

They referred to wine as "Li". Li is an unfiltered, sweet and turbid wine, similar to the alcoholic sorghum wine popular in the Sichuan-Chongqing region decades ago, which was consumed by sipping through bamboo tubes from clay jars; or it resembles the fermented grains still widely consumed today, known as "Lao zao". The term "Li" is an ancient Chinese character, indicating that the ancient Shu people were already using Chinese language and characters, demonstrating cultural convergence with the central plains.

They referred to music as "Jing". "Jing" is synonymous with Chu. The first phrase refers to that the ancient Shu state adopted the rites and music system of Chu; the emperor being titled as king also indicates a political alignment with the Chu state.

In the political system of ancient China, only the emperor of the Zhou Dynasty was titled as king, while the monarchs of the vassal states were titled as duke or marquis according to their noble ranks. Examples include Duke Huan of Qi, Duke Wen of Jin, and Marquis Wen of Wei. Both culturally and politically, the Chu state was on the periphery of Huaxia civilization. The Chu ruler was bestowed the title of "Zijue", which was the fourth level among the five ranks of nobility: duke, marquis, earl, viscount, and

到灭国之时。

古蜀国君主此前称帝，如望帝、丛帝、卢帝等，此帝并不等同于中原自秦始皇开始的皇帝称谓，或可视为转型为国家之后古蜀国对首领的一种特定称谓。学楚国称王，是一种信号非常明显的政治语言：跟楚国一样不愿意臣服于周王室，而是有一种敢于与之平起平坐的气魄。

楚国尽管不为中原诸侯待见，但毕竟同文同种，好歹是华夏一支。而蜀国不管是从文化、制度、语言乃至人种来说，都算是典型的异类了。倾慕强势、先进的中原文化是内心的渴望，但毕竟隔得太远，哪怕向北越过秦岭，能接触到的秦国也只是华夏的边缘。从地缘、文化甚至民族属性来说，蜀国跟楚国倒是更为接近，毕竟百濮众生是两国的共同子民，甚而至于，开明王朝的先祖也来自楚国。除了文化上的倾同性，甚至不排除二者结为政治或军事同盟，共同对抗北面强秦的可能。

baron. The Chu state, regarded as barbarians, declared themselves kings twice during the reigns of King Yi of Zhou and King Huan of Zhou, with the latter continued to hold the royal title until its eventual downfall.

The ancient rulers of the Shu state were previously addressed as emperors, such as Emperor Wang, Emperor Cong, Emperor Lu, and so on. However, this title of emperor is not equivalent to the title of emperor that began with Qin Shihuang in the Central Plains. It can be seen as a specific designation for leaders of the ancient Shu state after its transition into a nation. The decision to proclaim themselves as kings, similar to the Chu state, was a highly significant political statement. It signified their unwillingness to submit to the Zhou royal family and instead displayed a determination to stand on equal footing with them.

Although the Chu state was not well-regarded by the Central Plains feudal lords, they were ultimately of the same cultural and ethnic background, at least belonging to a branch of Huaxia civilization. On the other hand, the Shu state, in terms of culture, system, language, and even ethnicity, can be considered a distinctive outlier. Admiring the dominant and advanced culture of the Central Plains was an inner longing for the Shu people, but the distance between the two regions was significant. Even if they crossed the Qinling Mountains to the north, they would still encounter the peripheral regions of Huaxia, represented by the Qin state. In terms of geographical proximity, cultural affinity, and even ethnic attributes, the Shu state was closer to the Chu state. After all, the Bai Pu tribes were shared subjects of the two states. Furthermore, the ancestors of the Shu kingdom came from the Chu state, which adds another layer of connection. Apart from cultural similarities, it is not unthinkable that the two states could form a political or military alliance in order to jointly resist the powerful state of Qin to the north.

铜建鼓座出土于擂鼓墩1号墓，此墓也曾出土曾侯乙编钟。铜建鼓座上数十条大龙与小龙纠结穿插，风格奇谲莫测 白曦 摄

The bronze drum stand unearthed from Tomb No. 1 at Leigudun, which also yielded the Zenghou Yi chime bells. The stand features dozens of intertwining large and small dragons, exhibiting a mysterious and intricate style. (Photographer: Bai Xi)

成都市青白江区大弯街道双元村，迄今已发现春秋、战国时期的古蜀国墓葬二百七十余座，其中154号墓葬出土的青铜器、漆器等，除了巴蜀本土文化因素外，还显示出楚国礼制的强势影响。

154号墓葬的墓主是开明朝的王族或高级贵族，这位30岁左右的女性躺在一艘长六米、由整段楠木刳凿而成的船棺之中。来自荆楚的开明氏，一生都在与水打交道，船是他们最重要的生产工具和生活工具。这位王族女性，用乘船而葬的方式，完成了对故乡的回归。

船棺中部下方有一个长一米、宽0.59—0.65米的腰坑，这是一种来自中原的丧葬习俗。腰坑中有鼎、甗（yǎn，饪食器）、尊缶（盛酒器）、匜（yí）、盆等五件青铜器，它们或曾有过实用价值，但同时也是陈列于宴

In Shuangyuan Village, Dawan Street, Qingbaijiang District, Chengdu, more than 270 ancient tombs from the Spring and Autumn and Warring States periods of the Shu state have been discovered to date. Among them, the unearthed bronze and lacquerware from Tomb No. 154 not only reflect the local culture of Ba and Shu, but also demonstrate a strong influence of the Chu state's ritual system.

The tomb owner of Tomb No. 154 was a member of the Kaiming Dynasty, belonging to the royal family or high-ranking nobility. This woman, approximately 30 years old, was laid to rest in a boat-shaped coffin hewn from a 6-meter-long piece of nanmu wood. The Kaiming clan, originally from the Jingchu region, had a close relationship with water throughout their lives, as boats were their most important production and daily-use tools. By being buried in a boat, this noblewoman completed her final journey, returning to her homeland in a symbolic way.

In the lower middle section of the boat-shaped coffin, there is a pit measuring approximately 1 meter in length and 0.59-0.65 meters in width. This is a burial custom originating from the Central Plains. Inside this pit, there are five bronze vessels, including a Ding (cooking vessel), a Yan (food container), a Zunfu (wine container), a Yi (food vessel), and a

飨、祭祀和典礼的礼器。

匜，是一种外形如瓢的盥器。侍女执匜，水自流口出，清濯过贵族之手后，落入下方的盘中。船棺中的这件青铜，錾刻有十分精美的纹路。流口是三条尾、鳍都特别夸张的小鱼，中间那条头朝向匜内，左右两条朝外。匜壁上刻有小树、大树、仙鹤、人物，人有递物者、斟酒者、弯弓搭箭欲射者。这或许是一个观赏圈养仙鹤的飨礼场面，一旁还有人表演射猎。匜底盘踞两物，身子粗大，互相勾搭，如蛇似蟒，具有抽象几何图案的意趣——刻纹铜器和水蛇纹，最早都出现于吴越，通过楚文化区传播到了巴蜀。

楚地风格的青铜敦 何大江 摄

A bronze dun (ritual vessel) with Chu-style motifs. (Photographer: He Dajiang)

就这样，上游的巴蜀文化、中游的荆楚文化、下游的吴越文化，在这座古蜀开明氏王族墓葬中，串起了一条长江文化的传播线。

教民务农、功在田畴，贯穿了杜

Pen (basin). These bronze vessels may have served practical purposes at one point, but they were also used as ceremonial utensils displayed during feasts, rituals, and ceremonies.

The Yi is a ladle-shaped vessel used for pouring water. The attendants would hold the Yi, and water would flow out from the spout, cascading down on the noble hands and into the basin below. The bronze Yi found in the boat-shaped coffin is exquisitely engraved with intricate patterns. The spout features three small fish with exaggerated tails and fins, with the middle fish facing inward towards the Yi and the other two facing outward. The walls of the Yi are adorned with depictions of trees, cranes, and figures engaged in various activities such as offering objects, pouring wine, and preparing to shoot a bow and arrow. This scene likely depicts the etiquette of serving guests at banquet where cranes were being displayed and admired, while a performance of archery was taking place nearby. At the bottom of the Yi, there are two serpentine-like creatures with intertwined bodies, resembling snakes or pythons, featuring abstract geometric patterns. The art of engraving patterns on bronze and the use of snake motifs originated in the Wu and Yue regions and later spread to the Ba and Shu regions through the influence of Chu culture.

In this ancient tomb belonging to the Kaiming clan of the Shu state, the upstream Ba and Shu culture, the midstream Jingchu Culture, and the downstream Wuyue culture interweave, forming a transmission line of Yangtze River Culture.

The emphasis on educating the people in

宇王朝的始终，鳖灵开创的开明王朝更将之发扬光大。杜宇将精耕细作带到了成都平原，鳖灵整治水利，古蜀农业水平得以提档升级，古蜀国也开始步入最强盛时期。

望丛祠屏壁刻着一句话，总结了杜宇与鳖灵的功绩：“蜀国破天荒，德高追尧舜。”望帝来自朱提，丛帝来自荆楚，两个古老的“蓉漂”，在成都平原开创了千秋功业。

agriculture, highlighting the importance of farming, persisted throughout the Duyu Dynasty, and was further developed by the Kaiming Dynasty founded by Bieling. Duyu brought the practices of meticulous farming to the Chengdu Plain, while Bieling focused on water management, elevating the agricultural standards of ancient Shu and propelling the kingdom towards its peak of prosperity.

On the screens of the Wang Cong Shrine, there is an inscription that summarizes the achievements of Duyu and Bieling: “The two emperors make ground-breaking history for the ancient Shu; their virtues are comparable to those of the ancient sages Yao and Shun.” Emperor Wang hailed from Shushi, while Emperor Cong came from Jingchu, representing two ancient “Chengdu drifters” who made significant contributions to the Chengdu Plain.

武担山
WuDan Mountain

占地数亩、高七丈的山，是从千里之外搬到成都来的，只为了让妃子能够在故乡的泥土中长眠。

这是一名对女人用情至深的蜀王，同时，也是一名昏庸无道的蜀王。重心放错了位置，浪漫就变成了残酷。普通人家的万滴血，抵不过君王思念妃子的那一滴泪。

山精化妃、石牛便金、五丁拽蛇……拨动一个个奇异神话的灰烬，其实能够找寻到古蜀国亡国的线索。

Wudan Mountain, occupying several Mu and standing seven Zhang (Zhang, a unit of length, equals $3^1/_3$ metres) tall, was transported from a thousand Li (Li, a unit of length, roughly equals 0.31 miles) away to Chengdu, all to ensure that the concubine could rest eternally in her homeland's soil.

This was a Shu king who loved a woman with utmost passion, yet at the same time, he was a king who ruled with incompetence. Once his focus was misplaced, the romance turned into cruelty. The countless drops of blood shed by ordinary people could not compare to the single tear shed by the king yearning for his concubine.

The goblin turns into the concubine, the stone oxen excrete gold, the Wuding pulls a snake... Stirring up the ashes of each peculiar myth, one can actually find clues to the demise of the ancient Shu kingdom.

武担山往事：古蜀国"泰姬陵"骊歌
Wudan Mountain: The Tale of a Farewell Song of the Ancient Shu Kingdom's Taj Mahal

武担山

北宋·宋京

君不见蜀王妃子墓突兀，
成都城中若山积。
墓头寒镜涩无光，
妒月欺烟化为石。
鸿荒无根凭野史，
直谓山妖化妃子。
临终未免怀首丘，
运土山中葬于此。
山名武担锦江边，
用是得名千万年。
如今佛阁倚空翠，
老木盘郁摩苍天。
晴云入穴西山出，
卷帘坐见岚光滴。
安得文如汲冢书，
免使后人疑往昔。

Wudan Mountain

Song Jing, Northern Song Dynasty

In the city of Chengdu, so grand,
The tomb of the Shu King's beloved wife,
Stands abrupt, a mountain-like pride.
The cold mirror atop, devoid of light,
Envied by the moon, satirized by the mist, turns to stone in plight.
Legend tells of a mountain goblin, a wild tale,
Claiming the concubine transformed, much to bewail.
In her final moments, thoughts of her homeland befall,
Her remains were buried here, in the earth carried from her ancestral mound, standing tall.
Named Wudan, by the banks of Jinjiang,
Its fame has endured for thousands of years, lingering.
Now a Buddhist pagoda nestled amidst the green,
Old trees embracing the sky, a serene scene.
Clear clouds enter caves, exit from the western peak,
Through parted curtains, the misty radiance we seek.
If only we had historical records like Bamboo Annals from the ancient tomb,
To free future generations from doubting tales of doom.

北宋徽宗崇宁年间进士宋京是双流人，自然对蜀中非常熟悉，他留下的二十来篇诗歌，大多跟四川有关。这首《武担山》，几乎就是一首叙事诗，它讲述了一个跟泰姬陵十分相似的故事。

Song Jing, a Jin Shi during the reign of Emperor Huizong of the Northern Song Dynasty and a native of Shuangliu, had a deep understanding of the Shu region. He left behind around twenty poems, most of which were related to Sichuan. This poem, *Wudan Mountain*, is almost a narrative poem, telling a story that is strikingly similar to that of the Taj Mahal.

印度的泰姬陵始建于1631年，是莫卧儿王朝皇帝沙·贾汗为已故妃子修建的一座白色大理石陵园。而武担山的修垒，时间大致在公元前337—公元前316年（自秦惠王即位至秦灭巴蜀），比泰姬陵差不多早了两千年。

The Taj Mahal in India was built in 1631 by Emperor Shah Jahan of the Mughal Dynasty as a white marble mausoleum for his deceased wife. The construction of Wudan Mountain, on the other hand, took place roughly between 337 BC to 316 BC (from the reign of King Hui of Qin to the annexation of the Ba-Shu region by the Qin Dynasty), making it nearly two thousand years older than the Taj Mahal.

一座山 从武都搬到了成都

故事一开始就非常奇幻，带有《笑傲江湖》中东方不败的色彩。说是在武都这个地方，有一个男子变成了女人，因为极其美艳，被好色的蜀王纳为妃子。对于以男化女，《华阳国志》给的解释是：山精。

因为水土不服，王妃想回家乡，蜀王却舍不得放她走。没多久，王妃病故，蜀王十分哀痛。想到王妃生前思念故土，便派遣五丁（字面意义为“五个大力士”）到其故乡武都担土为冢。

工程量巨大，因为墓地占地数亩，高达七丈（换算成现在的尺度约十七米）。如此，蜀王妃便可在家乡的泥土中长眠了。

整个墓地由两个土堆构成，中间连接地带凹了下去，从侧面看，像一对驼峰。在西侧的土堆上，还立着一

A mountain moved from Wudu to Chengdu

The story itself begins with a great mystery, seemingly carrying shades of Dongfang Bubai, an undefeatable man from the east who castrates himself only for mastering matchless Gongfu, a character from the novel *the Smiling, Proud Wanderer*. It is said that in Wudu, there was a man who transformed into a woman and possessed extraordinary beauty. The amorous King of Shu took her as his consort. Regarding the transformation from male to female, *Records of the States South of Mount Hua* provides an explanation: it is a goblin.

Because she couldn't adapt to the new environment, the concubine desired to return to her hometown. However, the King of Shu was unwilling to let her go. Before long, the concubine passed away, leaving the King of Shu in deep sorrow. Recognizing her longing for her homeland, the king dispatched Wuding (literally meaning five men of unusual strength) to Wudu, her ancestral land, to bring back soil for her tomb.

The scale of the project was enormous, as the tomb occupied several Mu of land and reached a height of seven Zhang (roughly 17 meters in today's measurements). With such a size, the Shu king's concubine could rest in eternal peace in her hometown soil.

面石镜。镜面澈莹，似乎真的可以当镜子用。

石镜的大小，《蜀王本纪》称“径一丈，高五尺”，《太平寰宇记》则称“厚五寸，径五尺”。其实，“高五尺”和“径五尺”并不矛盾。石镜呈椭圆形，五尺是短径，一丈是长径。

“径一丈，高五尺”的表述非常精妙，六个字就清清楚楚地说明，石镜是一个横长竖短的椭圆。如果说“宽一丈，高五尺”，可能会被当成一个矩形；即便用专门描述椭圆的数学语言说成“长径一丈，短径五尺”，也有可能被视作一个竖长形的椭圆。

按现代度量衡换算，这个椭圆的石镜短径约1.15米，长径约2.3米，厚度约11厘米。

1905年3月，日本学者山川早水进入四川考察，留下了有二十多万字和约150幅图片的游记。让人遗憾的是，没有武担山的照片，但也有值得兴奋之处——山川早水亲眼见到过石镜。

“石镜今尚在。”山川早水见到的石镜，已被弃置于山腰，一半埋于土中。而露出来的部分，他判断，其大小与文献或传说是相吻合的。

The entire tomb was composed of two mounds of earth, with a concave area connecting them in the middle, resembling a pair of camel humps when viewed from the side. On the western mound, there was even a stone mirror standing. The mirror's surface was clear and bright, as if it could truly be used as a mirror.

The size of the stone mirror is described differently in different sources. *Annals of the Kings of Shu* states that it had a diameter of one Zhang and a height of five Chi, while *Taiping Huanyu Ji* states that it had a thickness of five Cun and a diameter of five Chi. In fact, these descriptions of “height of five Chi” and “diameter of five Chi” are not contradictory. The stone mirror has an oval shape, with five Chi referring to the shorter diameter and one Zhang referring to the longer diameter.

The description of “diameter of one Zhang and height of five Chi” is very exquisite. With just six characters, it clearly indicates that the stone mirror is an oval with a longer horizontal length and a shorter vertical length. If it were described as “width of one Zhang and height of five Chi”, it might be mistaken for a rectangle. Even if using the mathematical language specifically for describing ovals, saying “long diameter of one Zhang and short diameter of five Chi”, it could still be perceived as a vertically elongated oval.

In modern measurements, this oval stone mirror would have a shorter diameter of approximately 1.15 meters, a longer diameter of about 2.3 meters, and a thickness of 11 centimeters.

In March 1905, Japanese scholar Yamakawa Sousui visited Sichuan for research purposes and wrote a travelogue consisting of over 200,000 words and approximately 150 illustrations. Unfortunately, there were no photographs of Wudan Mountain, but there was still something exciting to behold—Yamakawa Sousui personally laid eyes on the stone mirror.

至于山中到底有没有妃子墓，山川早水则未亲见。明代学者、官员曹学佺在《蜀中名胜记》中的记载，就有点让人惊悚了。这段文字的原文是："武陵王萧纪掘之，得玉石，棺中美女，容貌如生，体如冰。"

萧纪是梁武帝萧衍的第八子。537年，他以武陵郡王的身份被父亲派到成都作益州刺史。548年，侯景作乱，天下崩溃。552年，萧纪在成都称帝，随即带兵东进去跟哥哥萧绎争天下，不久兵败身死。以此推算，掘开蜀王妃墓的时间，大致就在537—552年。不过，以成都潮润的气候，尸体不腐烂，且在下葬八九百年后还"容貌如生，体如冰"，实在有些离奇。仅从目前掌握的史料来看，这则记述尚不足以采信。

山川早水听到的传说是，除了山上有王妃墓，山下还有开明王墓——这位多情的君王，死后也要跟妃子葬在同一座山。在开明王墓的旁边，据说还有一个稍小的墓，人称"太子墓"。山川早水是四川高等学堂的日文教师，关于这几座古墓，他的判断就更具现代考古学意识——他认为，这几座墓的主人可能是古代贵族。

蜀王妃墓到底是否存在，尚不能

"The stone mirror still exists." The stone mirror that Yamakawa Sousui saw had been abandoned and left halfway up the mountain, partially buried in the soil. However, the exposed portion led him to conclude that its size was consistent with the descriptions in historical records or legends.

As for whether there is a tomb of the concubine in the mountain, Yamakawa Sousui did not personally witness it. The account by Ming Dynasty scholar and official Cao Xuequan in his book *Records of Famous Places in Shu* is rather chilling. The original text reads: "Wuling Prince Xiao Ji excavated it, and inside the coffin, he discovered jade stones and a beautiful woman, whose appearance was lifelike, with a body as cold as ice."

Xiao Ji was the eighth son of Emperor Wu of the Liang Dynasty, Xiao Yan. In the year 537, he was conferred Wuling Prince and sent by his father to Chengdu as the prefectural governor of Yizhou. In 548, the rebellion of Hou Jing led to the disintegration of the empire. In 552, Xiao Ji declared himself emperor in Chengdu and marched east to contend for supremacy with his brother, Xiao Yi. However, he was soon defeated in battle and died. Based on this timeline, the excavation of the tomb of the Queen of Shu would have taken place roughly between the years 537 and 552. However, it seems rather peculiar that the body of the concubine, buried for several hundred years in the humid climate of Chengdu, would remain uncorrupted and maintain a lifelike appearance. Based on the current available historical records, this account cannot be fully substantiated.

Yamakawa Sousui heard a legend that not only was there a tomb of the concubine on the mountain, but also a tomb of the Kaiming emperor beneath the mountain—an amorous ruler who wanted to be buried alongside his concubine. Next to the tomb of the emperor, there was said to be a slightly smaller

完全确定。因为年代的久远，在跟武担山相关的系列史料中，留有太多谜团、太多的不确定性。比如，武都到底在何方，五丁到底是什么……

可以很明确定位的，是武担山所在。成都老城墙还没有拆的时候，武担山位于成都城内的西北角，在西城墙之内。今天的位置，则在武都路、江汉路之间，新华宾馆以北。武担山西侧，清代为练兵用的北较场。清末和民国，都在此地建有军校。目前，在北较场西路与五丁桥相接处，还保留有北较场古城墙遗迹。

tomb known as the Prince's Tomb. As a Japanese teacher at the Sichuan Higher School, Yamakawa Sousui approached these ancient tombs with a more modern archaeological perspective, speculating that the owners of these tombs may have been ancient nobles.

The existence of the tomb of the concubine of Shu cannot be completely confirmed. Due to the distant timeframe, there are many mysteries and uncertainties in the series of historical records related to Wudan Mountain. For example, the exact location of Wudu, or the true identity of the "Wuding" mentioned, remain elusive.

It can be easily identified that Wudan Mountain is located there. Before the old city walls of Chengdu were demolished, Wudan Mountain was situated in the northwest corner of Chengdu city, within the west city walls. Today, it is located between Wudu Road and Jianghan Road, north of Xinhua Hotel. On the west side of Wudan Mountain, there was a northern training ground used for military purposes during the Qing Dynasty. Military academies were established in this area during the late Qing Dynasty and the Republic of China. Currently, remnants of the ancient city walls of the northern training ground can still be found at the junction of Bei Jiaochang West Road and Wuding Bridge.

一条路
潜藏在古蜀国的"特洛伊木马"

在《华阳国志》里，关于这位葬妃于武担山的蜀王着墨不多，却生动、完整地勾勒出了其形象。跟他有关的几个故事，大致都发生在公元前337年。这一年，雄才大略的秦惠王

A Hidden "Trojan Horse" in Ancient Shu

In *Records of the States South of Mount Hua*, there is not much mention of the emperor who buried his concubine on Wudan Mountain, but it vividly and comprehensively outlines his image. Several stories related to him mostly took place around the year 337 BC. It was also during this year that the talented and ambitious King Hui of Qin had just risen to the stage of history.

也刚刚登上历史舞台。

正处于上升期的秦，位于蜀的东北方向。此时，经过商鞅变法后的秦国雄心四溢，小小的关中已经盛不下了。这一年，蜀王来到褒谷（今汉中西北）打猎，与刚刚即位的秦惠王不期而遇。

汉中古称南郑，是秦、蜀交界之处，其归属长时期在两国之间拉锯，也是检验两国实力和关系的风向标。

秦王出现在有争议的、此时归属蜀王的土地上，此事十分可疑。但蜀王似乎倒也并不认为是多大个事，并不想加以深究。为了回报秦惠王的那一竹箱子金子，他还送了些珍宝玩件。

然而，诡异的事情发生了。秦惠王回去之后，发现蜀王送的珍玩全部化作泥土。《华阳国志》虽为信史，但这一段记载大可不必当真。其间究竟发生了什么——是蜀王大方许诺之后又后悔了，还在某一环节被人调了包？抑或记录者常璩并不具备唯物的世界观，而采信了某种传说？无可考证。有意思的是接下来发生的事。

秦惠王感觉自己被蜀王戏耍了，非常愤怒，群臣却表示祝贺，说这是将拥有蜀国土地的吉兆。类似的故事，在“春秋五霸”之一晋文公重耳

At that time, the rising power of Qin was located northeast of Shu. After the reforms carried out by Shang Yang, Qin had expanded its ambitions, and the small region of Guanzhong was no longer able to contain him. In the same year, the King of Shu arrived in Baogu (now northwest of Hanzhong) for a hunting expedition and unexpectedly encountered the newly enthroned King Hui of Qin.

Hanzhong, formerly known as Nanzheng, was the border between Qin and Shu. Its ownership had long been contested between the two states and served as an indicator of their strength and relationship.

The appearance of the king of Qin on the disputed land, which at that time belonged to the King of Shu, was highly suspicious. However, the King of Shu seemed unfazed by it and did not wish to delve deeper into the matter. In return for the bamboo box filled with gold from King Hui of Qin, he even presented some precious treasures and playthings.

However, something peculiar happened. After King Hui of Qin returned, he discovered that all the precious items from the King of Shu had turned into mud. Although *Records of the States South of Mount Hua* is considered a reliable historical record, this particular account should not be taken literally. What exactly transpired— did the King of Shu have a change of heart after making such a generous promise, or was there tampering involved at some stage? Alternatively, could it be that the recorder Chang Qu didn't possess a materialistic worldview and thus believed in a certain legend? There is no concrete evidence. However, what happened next is quite intriguing.

King Hui of Qin felt that he had been played by the King of Shu and was filled with anger. However, his ministers congratulated him, saying that it was an auspicious sign that he would possess the land of Shu. A similar story occurred with one of the "Five

身上也曾发生过一次。

那时，重耳还处于逃难途中。在卫国边境，重耳公子见到农夫在田间吃饭时产生了条件反射，肚子鸣叫起来，越发饿得难以忍受，便让跟随者去讨点吃的。谁知农夫却十分无礼，捡起一块土扔过来，说："吃吧，吃这个。"重耳大怒，想要动粗，一路跟随的赵衰却拉住了他，并说："公子，这意味着将来有土有地啊！倒应该恭恭敬敬地拜谢才是。"

这两个故事相似性如此之高，不是用巧合就能解释的，它们其实有更深层次的含义。

在秦惠王的故事里，我们可以看到他对开疆拓土的渴望；而流浪途中的公子重耳最盼望的，则是回到故土，坐上国君的位置。农耕时代，土地就意味收成、人丁、赋税，土地就是一切。一块泥土，成了拓展政权或执掌政权的象征。

秦惠王和晋文公后来都成为一代雄主，他们对于制造舆论、操控人心都是非常有心得的。天降泥土，就是"授命于天"，意味着其政权的合法性有了保障。这类神迹或者吉兆，对于那个时代的黔首百姓是非常具有说服力的。

话说秦惠王听了群臣的话，跟重

Hegemons of the Spring and Autumn Period", Duke Wen of Jin, also known as Chong'er.

At that time, Chong'er was still on the run. On the border of the state of Wei, the young Chong'er saw a farmer eating in the field and his stomach growled instinctively, making him even hungrier. He sent his followers to ask for some food. However, the farmer was extremely rude and threw a clod of dirt at them, saying, "Eat this!" This angered Chong'er, and he wanted to retaliate, but his follower Zhao Cui held him back and said, "Master, this means that in the future, you will have land and territory! Instead, we should respectfully thank him."

The striking similarities between these two stories cannot be explained by mere coincidence. They actually hold a deeper, symbolic meaning.

In the story of King Hui of Qin, we can perceive his fervent desire to expand his territory. On the other hand, the wandering prince Chong'er longed to return to his homeland and assume the position of ruler. In an agricultural society, land represented harvest, population, and tax revenue — it meant everything. A clod of dirt, therefore, became a symbol of expanding or seizing political power.

King Hui of Qin and Duke Wen of Jin both went on to become powerful rulers of their respective states. They were highly adept at manipulating public opinion and controlling the hearts of the people. The offering of the clod of dirt, seen as a "divine mandate", meant that the legitimacy of their rule was now assured. Such miracles or auspicious signs held great persuasive power over the common people in that era.

In the case of King Hui of Qin, he heeded the advice of his ministers and turned his anger into joy, following the belief that the clod of dirt was a sign of good fortune. Moreover, he took a series of actions in response to this event.

耳一般转怒为喜。此外，更是采取了一系列行动。

秦惠王派人刻制了五头石牛，并建立了一支数量多达百人的养牛队。这支规模庞大的养牛队是不是要给石牛洗澡、喂草不好说，但他们有个明确的任务，就是早上起来，把金子放到石牛身后，说是它们拉的。

King Hui of Qin had five stone oxen carved and established a large team of cattle farmers consisting of hundreds of people. While it is unclear whether this massive cattle team attended to bathing and feeding the stone oxen, they had a clear task-every morning, they would place gold behind the stone oxen, claiming that the oxen had pooped out gold.

成都金牛坝，是传说中蜀王安置金牛处。金牛坝上建有“金牛台”，以作纪念　何大江 摄

Jinniuba in Chengdu, the legendary site where the Shu King placed the golden ox. A “Golden Ox Terrace” was built here as a memorial. (Photographer: He Dajiang)

消息传到蜀王耳中（高度疑似秦王有意散布），便向秦王讨要这五头牛。秦王倒是同意了，但自古蜀道难啊，蜀王倒有办法，他派了五丁一路逢山开道、遇水架桥，硬是修通了一条路，将五头石牛（又称金牛）迎了回来。

When news of this reached the ears of the King of Shu (likely deliberately spread by King Hui), he requested the five oxen from King Hui. Surprisingly, King Hui agreed, but as the saying goes, “The road to Shu is difficult.” Nevertheless, the King of Shu found a way. He sent the team of Wuding, building roads through mountains and constructing bridges over rivers, eventually bringing the five stone oxen (also known as the Gold Oxen) back to Shu.

“五丁开山”雕塑。五丁，指五名大力士，但实际上是古蜀国工程兵部队的隐喻　何大江 摄

The sculpture of “Five Strongmen Opening the Mountains”. The five strongmen symbolize the engineering corps of ancient Shu. (Photographer: He Dajiang)

蜀王满心喜欢地得到这五头牛，却发现它们并不屙金，便又愤怒地将牛送了回去，并给秦人取了一个“东方放牛娃儿”的绰号来挖苦他们。秦国人倒也不含糊，回答道：“我虽然放牛，但是要放到你地坝头。（吾虽牧犊，当得蜀也。）”秦国毫不掩饰自己的虎狼之心，蜀国人却并没有因此警惕。

秦王行使的，是一条堪比古希腊“特洛伊木马”的计策，不仅没有打草惊蛇，而且是靠敌手达到了目的，还远远比“特洛伊木马”来得隐忍，直到二十一年后，作用才显现。

秦惠王即位那一年，就一而再再而三地送美女给蜀王（以秦的虎狼之心，肯定藏有其他想法），蜀王因此还专门去秦国见了秦王，表示感谢。这一次，秦又嫁了五个美女给蜀王，而没心没肺的蜀王依然笑纳，并派遣五丁前去迎接。

沿着上次接金牛时开辟的金牛道，迎亲的队伍回程走到梓潼，又遇到一桩怪事，见到一条巨大的蛇钻入山洞中。这个时候，五丁中有一丁偏又童心爆棚，要去拖大蛇的尾巴，把它从洞中拖出来。偏偏蛇力气太大，于是，其他几人又去帮忙，五人一起拖，竟然拖得山崩地裂。大山塌了，五丁被压在山下，他们迎来的五个美女也一道

The King of Shu was thrilled to receive these five oxen, but soon discovered they did not excrete gold, so he angrily sent them back and mockingly nicknamed the Qin people “the Eastern Oxherd”. The people of Qin, not to be outdone, replied, “Though we may herd oxen, we will graze them on your doorstep.” Qin did not hide their ambitions, yet the people of Shu remained unaware.

The strategy employed by the King of Qin was as cunning as the Trojan Horse of ancient Greece. It did not raise suspicions and was successful in deceiving their enemy. Moreover, it was far more patient than the Trojan Horse, as its effects took 21 years to emerge.

In the year King Hui of Qin ascended the throne, he repeatedly sent beautiful women to the King of Shu (with undoubtedly hidden motives, given Qin’s cunning nature). In gratitude, the King of Shu personally visited the King of Qin. On this occasion, Qin once again sent five beautiful women to the King of Shu, who, heedless and carefree as ever, graciously accepted them and appointed the Wuding to receive them.

Following the path of the Gold Oxen Road, which was opened during the previous reception of the stone oxen, the wedding procession reached Zitong and encountered a strange incident. They witnessed a massive snake entering a cave. At that moment, one of the Wuding, fueled by his childlike curiosity, decided to grab the snake’s tail and pull it out of the cave. Unfortunately, the snake was too powerful, so the other four came to his aid. Together, they pulled with such force that the mountain crumbled. The Wuding were buried beneath the collapsing mountain, along with the five beauties they were welcoming. Deeply saddened by this tragedy, the King of Shu built a “Memorial for my Wives” on the mountaintop to mourn his five

做了冤魂。对于此事，蜀王又十分哀伤，居然又在山顶建了个思妻台，来悼念他那还没过门的五个媳妇。

soon-to-be wives.

险峻的金牛蜀道　余茂智 摄

The perilous Jinniu Shu Road. (Photographer: Yu Maozhi)

五丁拖蛇而致山崩的故事，绝非真实。但是，它完全可能是某些历史现象在蜀人先民意识中的映射。

比如，仅靠五人就能修通艰难蜀道的大力士五丁，自然也是不存在的。任乃强先生在《华阳国志校补图注》中称：“（五丁）可能是此蜀王有忠勇奴隶，编为五军。”也就是说，五丁其实是工程兵部队或者禁卫军。将其当作五个大力士，也是一种心理投射。

五丁入秦接美女，当年周显王三十二年，即公元前337年。而《华阳国志》在讲述开明九世时，就曾提到“时蜀有五丁力士，能移山，举万钧”——开明九世时间约在公元前400年，与五丁入秦隔着将近七十年的时光。一个人不可能在七十年后还是壮汉，这也从另一个侧面证

The story of the Wuding causing a mountain collapse by pulling a snake is not true. However, it could very well be a reflection of certain historical phenomena in the consciousness of the ancient Shu people.

For example, the existence of the mighty Wuding, who were able to complete the arduous road to Shu with just five people, is highly unlikely. Mr. Ren Naiqiang in his book *Annotation and Supplement to the Illustrations in Records of the States South of Mount Hua* suggests that the Wuding were possibly loyal and courageous slaves organized into five military units. In other words, the Wuding were actually corps of engineers or imperial guards. Portraying them as five men of unusual strength is a psychological projection.

The event of the Wuding going to Qin to escort the beauties took place in the 32nd year of King Xian of Zhou, around 337 BC. However, in the *Records of the States South of Mount Hua* when describing the reign of Kaiming the Ninth, it mentions, “During that time, there were five mighty men in Shu, capable of moving mountains and lifting ten thousand Jun (a unit of weight).” The reign of Kaiming the Ninth is estimated to be around 400 BC, which is nearly

明了五丁非五人，而是一支常设的部队。

又比如巨蛇，任乃强先生说，“(事故发生地)梓潼水蜿蜒似蛇行，《汉志》称为蛇水”，那么巨蛇致山崩，有没有可能是山洪暴发导致山体滑坡的隐喻？

至此，蜀王的性格特点已经非常明显了。他贪色，却又有情有义，时不时会为妃子伤心一场；他贪财好货，却智商不在线；他也时常为了自己的私欲而挥霍民力，实在算不得一个好君王。

“黯然销魂者，唯别而已矣”，何况死别。蜀王开明离别妃子，其哀痛也真。对妃子的情真意切是真实的，但换一个角度来说，对人民的残暴也是真实的。世人多赞美泰姬陵，但泰姬陵何尝不是如此？普通人家的千滴泪、万滴血，也抵不过君王思念妃子的那一滴。

而蜀王的潜在对手秦惠王，一上台就杀掉了商鞅，实在是个杀伐决断的狠角色。如此呆萌的蜀王，在秦惠王眼中无疑是一只待宰的好肉鸡。

21年之后，秦惠王的机会终于来了。

汉中，对秦、蜀来说，既是前线也是缓冲地带，镇守此重地的，是蜀

seventy years before the incident of the Wuding going to Qin. It is implausible for an individual to remain as a strong man after seventy years. This further supports the notion that the Wuding were not actually five individuals, but rather a permanent unit or corps.

Regarding the giant snake, Mr. Ren Naiqiang states, “The location of the incident, Zitong, has a winding river resembling a snake, which is referred to as Snake River in the *Han Annals*.” With this in mind, the possibility arises that the giant snake causing the mountain collapse could be a metaphor for a flash flood leading to a landslide.

By now, the character traits of the King of Shu have become quite apparent. He is lustful, yet also has affection and faith in love, occasionally experiencing heartbreak for his consorts. He is greedy for wealth and possessions, but lacks intelligence. He often squanders the labor of the people for his own desires, making him far from a good ruler.

“To part is the ultimate sadness, even more so in death.” The separation of the King of Shu from his consorts truly brought him immense grief. His genuine and intense love for his consorts is undeniable, but from a different perspective, his cruelty towards his people is also evident. While the world often praises the Taj Mahal, the mausoleum of the Queen Mumtaz, but that Ji was no exception. The thousands of tears and bloodshed from ordinary families pale in comparison to the single teardrop shed by a king longing for his consort.

On the other hand, the King of Shu’s potential rival, King Hui of Qin, wasted no time in eliminating Shang Yang after taking power. He was undoubtedly a ruthless and decisive character. In the eyes of King Hui, the seemingly foolish King of Shu was nothing but a ready-made target for slaughter.

And after 21 years, King Hui’s opportunity finally arrived.

王的弟弟苴侯。但这个苴侯也是个不懂事的，蜀与东边的巴国是世仇，他却偏偏要跟巴国交好。蜀王心中气不顺，就带兵讨伐自己的兄弟。蜀王封苴侯在秦灭蜀71年前。准确地说，此时的蜀王与苴侯应为堂兄弟。

苴侯打不过，就逃到了巴国，并向秦国求救。

还有一个问题需要讨论：跟苴侯开战的末代蜀王、开明十二世，跟那位深情地为妃子建武担山墓葬的蜀王是不是同一人？

开明王朝自九世始立宗庙，却并未有谥列，再加上古人行文过于简略，造成的直接后果就是——只称“蜀王”，指代不明。不过，二十一年的时间对一个人的职业生涯来说并不算太长。当年刚即位的秦惠王十九岁，如今正值盛年，他的蜀国对手若还是同一人，也很正常。更何况，史料中两个蜀王的颟顸、昏庸，倒是非常一致。他们是同一人的可能性非常大。

接到苴侯求救信的秦国有些犹豫：到底打不打蜀国？

朝堂上两种意见，一种认为蜀国比较偏僻，好处不多，不如去打楚国。唯有名将司马错、中尉田真黄认为：蜀国物产丰富，足以提供军资；

Han Zhong, for both Qin and Shu, served as both a front line and a buffer zone. It was guarded by the younger brother of the King of Shu, the Marquis Ju. However, the Marquis Ju was also disobedient. While Shu and the neighboring Ba kingdom were archenemies, he insisted on forming an alliance with Ba. This displeased the King of Shu, who led his troops to attack his own brother. The King of Shu granted the title of Marquis of Ju to his brother 71 years before the fall of Shu to Qin. To be precise, at this time, the King of Shu and the Marquis of Ju should have been cousins.

Unable to win the war, the Marquis of Ju fled to the Ba kingdom and sought help from the Qin state.

Another question that needs to be discussed is whether the last King of Shu, who waged war against the Marquis of Ju, and the King of Shu who tenderly built the Wudan Mountain tomb for his consort are the same person.

The Kaiming Dynasty established its ancestral temple starting from the Kaiming Ninth, but they were not given any posthumous titles. In addition, the ancient texts are often overly concise, resulting in the lack of clarity when referring to the King of Shu. However, 21 years is not a significant amount of time in one's career. When King Hui of Qin ascended the throne, he was only nineteen years old. It is reasonable to assume that his antagonist from Shu may still be the same person. Moreover, the consistent description of the two kings of Shu in historical records as being foolish and dim—witted adds to the likelihood of them being the same person.

When Qin received the call for help from the Marquis Ju, there was some hesitancy: whether to attack the State of Shu or not?

Two opinions emerged in the court. One argued that Shu was relatively remote with few advantages, thus suggesting an attack on Chu instead. Only the

巴国多健儿，足以补充兵源；取巴蜀之后，顺江东下，则可轻易灭楚，乃至得天下。

秦惠王最终采纳了司马错等的建议，并让张仪、司马错、都尉墨带兵，从蜀国自己修好的石牛道进军侵蜀。二十一年前的“特洛伊木马”，终于发挥作用了。

石牛道又称金牛道。它起自今陕西眉县，经斜谷、褒谷栈道入汉中，在勉县向西出阳平关，由山道抵白水关（今四川青川县沙州镇），然后沿白龙江河谷至葭萌（广元昭化），经剑门关而直至成都。这也是秦汉至南北朝由关中入蜀的主道。

蜀王带兵到葭萌抵抗，打了败仗，逃到武阳（今彭山东北）被秦军杀了。他的大臣和太子则战死于白鹿山（今彭州白鹿镇）。

renowned general Sima Cuo and the lieutenant Tian Zhenhuang believed that Shu possessed abundant resources, sufficient to supply the military; Ba State had many strong men to replenish the troops. After gaining control of Ba and Shu, advancing downstream along the river, they could easily conquer Chu and even conquer the world.

King Hui of Qin ultimately adopted the advice of Sima Cuo and others, appointing Zhang Yi, Sima Cuo, and Mo as commanders. They led the troops to invade Shu using the Shiniu Road, which was constructed by Shu itself. The “Trojan Horse” from twenty-one years ago finally proved its effectiveness.

The Shiniu Road (the Stone Oxen Road), also known as Jinniu Road (the Gold Oxen Road), starts from Meixian County in present-day Shaanxi Province. It passes through Xiegu and Baogu plank road into Hanzhong, then heads west from Mianxian county through Yangping Pass. It follows mountain trails to Baishuiguan (now Shazhou Town, Qingchuan County, Sichuan Province), then continues along the Bai Long River valley to Jiameng (Zhaohua in Guangyuan), and finally passes through Jianmen Pass to Chengdu. This was the main route from Guanzhong to Shu during the Qin, Han, and Northern and Southern Dynasties.

The King of Shu led his troops to resist in Jiameng but suffered a defeat. He escaped to Wuyang (now northeast of Pengshan) and was killed by the Qin Army. His ministers and crown prince perished in the Battle of Bailu Mountain (now Bailu Town, Pengzhou).

昭化古城古称葭萌关，《三国演义》中，张飞在此挑灯夜战马超　冉玉杰 摄

The ancient city of Zhaohua, historically known as Jiameng Pass. In *The Romance of the Three Kingdoms*, Zhang Fei fought Ma Chao here under torchlight. (Photographer: Ran Yujie)

在此事件中，蜀王、苴侯兄弟俩犯了三个大错：

一是苴侯不懂地缘政治，行事令亲痛仇快；

二是蜀王不懂唇亡齿寒的道理，兄弟阋于墙；

三是苴侯所托非人，开门揖盗。

不管怎么说，古蜀亡了，自蚕丛开创的五个王朝，开明王朝传下来的十二代君王，到此皆成往事。

In this event, the brothers of Shu King and Marquis Ju made three major mistakes:

Firstly, the Marquis Ju lacked understanding of geopolitics and acted in a way that quickly turned friends into enemies.

Secondly, the King of Shu failed to grasp the principle of mutual dependence, leading to conflicts with his own brother at home.

Thirdly, Marquis Ju misplaced his trust in the wrong people, opening the door to the invaders.

Regardless of the reasons, the ancient kingdom of Shu fell, bringing an end to the five dynasties that originated from Cancong and the twelve generations of Kaiming monarchs that followed.

一座城
纵横家的创建之功

张仪、司马错灭掉蜀国，一鼓作气又顺道灭了巴国，在两地分设蜀郡与巴郡。巴与蜀两个邦外之地就此走上全面融入华夏文明之路。

然而，最初的蜀郡人心未稳，彻底的中央集权很难推行，因此秦立末代蜀王开明十二世的后人公子通为蜀侯，以陈壮为相——这意味着，秦还暂时保留了蜀的宗庙，开明氏尚未绝祀。既有蜀侯、又有蜀郡守，这种双重管理制度该如何理解？

可参照本书后文《蜀王城：十三代皇族的楼起楼塌》，秦封的蜀侯可比明代蜀王，绝大部分时间并不参与

A City
The achievements of the Political Strategist School

Zhang Yi and Sima Cuo destroyed the state of Shu and, with great momentum, also conquered the state of Ba, establishing the Shu Commandery and the Ba Commandery in the respective territories. These once foreign regions Shu and Ba began their journey to full integration into the Chinese civilization.

However, in the early days, the people of Shu Commandery were not stable, and the complete centralization of power was difficult to implement. Therefore, the descendant of the Kaiming 12th generation of the last king of Shu, Prince Tong, was appointed as the Marquis of Shu, with Chen Zhuang as his prime minister— which meant that Qin temporarily retained the ancestral temple of Shu, and the clan of the King of Shu, the Kaiming family, had not yet been extinguished. With both the Marquis of Shu and the commander of Shu Commandery, how should we understand this dual management system?

地方管理；郡守则如主理一省民政之布政使。以相为辅佐的方式，又颇类西汉初年的封国制。任乃强先生则以为，蜀侯其实是一种监察官，巡察的区域包括蜀、巴和汉中三郡，相当于汉代实行的刺史制。

将在外，主有疑。疑的不仅仅是作为封疆大吏的蜀郡守，蜀侯同样受到猜忌，所以郡守、蜀侯是一种相互监督、相互牵制的关系。

有疑必乱。蜀国灭亡后第七年，蜀侯公子通欲叛秦，为蜀相陈壮所杀。借公子通人头降秦的陈壮，又思割据蜀地，再次被秦国攻灭。

这一次，秦王派了自己人来，秦武王异母弟公子恽成为新的蜀侯。公子恽远在蜀国，在哥哥因为举鼎砸脚弃世之后无法接班，因而与新继位的另一兄弟秦昭襄王之间存在着一种微妙的关系。当了七年蜀侯之后，公子恽被昭襄王生母诬陷，说他在进贡的食物中下毒，赐死，夫妻双双自尽。

新封的蜀侯是恽的儿子绾。父母死于非命之痛，必然让他与秦昭襄王存在嫌隙。

恽死三年之后得以昭雪，发生了一系列的异事。

恽夫妇在冤死后平反，灵柩被

Referring to the later chapters of this book, *The City of the King of Shu: The Rise and Fall of Thirteen Generations of Imperial Family*, the Marquis of Shu appointed by Qin can be compared to the Ming Dynasty Kings; for the majority of the time, they did not actively participate in local governance. The Commandery Governor, on the other hand, acted as the chief administrator, similar to the provincial governor in charge of civil affairs. This dual system, with the prime minister serving as an advisor, bears similarities to the early Western Han Dynasty's system of enfeoffment. Mr. Ren Naiqiang believes that the Marquis of Shu actually served as a supervisor, responsible for inspections in the three commanderies of Shu, Ba, and Hanzhong. This can be seen as equivalent to the provincial governor system implemented during the Han Dynasty.

When the general is out, the emperor is in doubt. The Commandery Governor and the Marquis of Shu were both subject to suspicion and distrust, resulting in a relationship of mutual surveillance and restraint.

Suspicion breeds chaos. In the seventh year after the fall of the Shu state, the Marquis of Shu, Prince Tong, plotted to rebel against Qin but was killed by the Shu Prime Minister, Chen Zhuang. Chen Zhuang, who surrendered Prince Tong's head to Qin, harbored thoughts of establishing his own regime in Shu and was subsequently attacked and destroyed by the Qin forces.

This time, the King Wu of Qin appointed his own man, Prince Yun, his half-brother as the new Marquis of Shu. When Prince Yun was in distant Shu, he found himself unable to succeed his brother after the latter's death due to an accident involving a falling tripod. This led to a delicate relationship between him and the newly ascended King Zhaoxiang of Qin. After serving as the Marquis of Shu for seven years,

迎入城内重葬。这一年先是大旱，后又淫雨连绵。迁葬时，灵车在积水中艰难通行，好不容易到了成都城的北门，突然地陷车坠。蜀人于是又干了两件事：把成都北门改名为咸阳门；为恽修建祠庙，缺雨水时就去拜祭他，据说灵验得很。

“蜀人因名北门曰咸阳门”，这句话初看无头无脑，车陷北门、命名咸阳门之间哪有因果关系呢？多问一句咸阳在何处，或许便可识破端倪。那是秦昭襄王生活的地方，把北门叫作咸阳门，就是在说：看哪，就是住在咸阳的那个家伙制造了冤案，导致天作异象，记住他！而把冤死者奉为有灵异的雨神，与其说是蜀人怀念恽，倒不如说是在继续打昭襄王的脸。

最初的旱和后来的雨，是真的，但车陷北门有没有人在幕后操作，整幕大戏有没有人导演，就很值得怀疑了。那为什么要在平反之后才会发生这些怪事呢？非如此，不足以诠释“腹诽心谤”这个词。毕竟，绾在翅膀没长硬之前，再有怨气也只能腹诽，而且也只有在理由充分的情况下才能把这种腹诽表现出来一点点。

然而，腹诽必有罪。绾在当了十五年蜀侯之后，又被秦王诛杀。“疑蜀侯绾反”，一个“疑”字，道

Prince Yun was falsely accused by the birth mother of King Zhaoxiang of poisoning the tribute food and was sentenced to death. He and his wife chose to commit suicide together.

The newly appointed Marquis of Shu was Wan, the son of Prince Yun. The tragic deaths of his parents undoubtedly created resentment between him and King Zhaoxiang of Qin.

Three years after Yun's death, he was finally vindicated, and a series of strange events took place.

Following the posthumous exoneration of Yun and his wife, their coffins were welcomed back into the city for a reburial. That year, there was a severe drought followed by continuous downpours. During the procession to the new burial site, the funeral carriage struggled to pass through the accumulated water. Finally, when it reached the northern gate of Chengdu, the ground suddenly collapsed, causing the carriage to fall. In response to these events, the people of Shu did two things: they renamed the northern gate of Chengdu as Xianyang Gate, and they built a temple to honor Yun. They would pray to him in times of drought, and it was said that their prayers were answered.

The statement “The people of Shu renamed the northern gate as Xianyang Gate” may initially appear confusing, giving no clear cause-and-effect relationship between the carriage incident and the gate renaming. However, by asking where Xianyang is located, the clue might become evident. Xianyang was the place where King Zhaoxiang of Qin resided. By renaming the northern gate as Xianyang Gate, the people were essentially saying, “Look, it was that guy who lives in Xianyang who caused this wrongful case and the unusual phenomena. Remember him!” Regarding the deification of the wrongfully deceased as a rain god, it is less about the people of Shu reminiscing about Yun and more about continuing to

尽了这对王室叔侄之间的不信任和罪名的莫须有。权力面前无至亲，果然近乎真理。

绾被诛之后，秦国不再封蜀侯，大概是觉得与之斗心眼太劳心了，从此，蜀地进入郡守独治的时代。后来，蜀郡守中出了个名垂青史之人，那就是至今还在被人怀念的李冰。

在李冰之前，第一代蜀郡守叫张若。其实，秦国最初占领蜀国时，在蜀郡守、蜀侯这两支政治力量之上，权力最大的是领兵入蜀的张仪——著名外交策略“连横说”的创造者。而蜀侯公子通作为前朝王子，大概仅仅是安抚蜀人情绪的一个摆设。

对成都来说，张仪与张若最大的功绩是筑城。成都城始筑于公元前311年，这在长时间内被认为是成都城市史之始。那么，此前成都平原上没有城吗？非也。

在张仪筑城两千多年前的宝墩，就已经有城墙了。三星堆也有城墙，但跟宝墩的一样，都是堆筑的土埂子；而且二者的土墙都是斜坡，只能防洪，不能抵御外敌。宝墩、三星堆之城，跟张仪所筑之成都城，在功用上还是存在差别的。此外，成都城、成都平原之城在概念的外延上也是种属关系。

abash King Zhaoxiang of Qin.

The initial drought and later rainfall were indeed true, but whether someone manipulated the incident of the carriage getting stuck at the North Gate and whether someone directed the entire spectacle is questionable. Why did these strange events occur only after the injustice was corrected? Without this, it is insufficient to explain the term “malicious calumniation and vindictiveness”. After all, before the wings grow strong, any resentment can only be kept within, and it can only be expressed in bits and pieces when there are sufficient reasons.

However, harboring such thoughts is not without guilt. After serving as the Marquis of Shu for fifteen years, Wan was eventually executed by the King of Qin on the grounds of suspected rebellion. With just a single word of suspicion, it revealed the lack of trust between the royal uncle and nephew, and the unfounded charges. In the face of power, even close relatives are treated with suspicion, almost resembling the truth.

After Wan was executed, the state of Qin ceased to appoint a Marquis of Shu, probably realizing that it was too tiresome to contend with such a cunning mind. Thus, Shu entered an era of governance by regional officials. Later on, a figure who would go down in history emerged among the commandery governors of Shu, and that person is none other than Li Bing, who is still fondly remembered today.

Before Li Bing, the first regional official of Shu was Zhang Ruo. In fact, when Qin initially occupied the state of Shu, the most powerful figure above the commandery governor and the Marquis of Shu was Zhang Yi, the commander who led the troops into Shu and the renowned creator of the diplomatic strategy known as “Lianheng Shuo” (Vertical and Horizontal Strategies). As for the Marquis of Shu, Prince Tong, being a prince of the former Dynasty, he was likely

当然，说成都城初建于公元前311年没错，但成都这个概念已经扩大了很多倍之后，再来讨论成都城市史，就不应该只限定于自张仪至清末民初的那座城了。

张仪新筑的成都城用的是砖墙，更经过精心规划设计，以秦国都城咸阳为蓝本。咸阳城始建于公元前350年，参照鲁国、卫国等重要诸侯的都城营建。在秦始皇吞并六国、迁入富户以充实人口之前，咸阳的人口在二十万人以上，已是一个区域性大城市。

新筑起的成都城，起点不俗。“周回十二里，高七丈”，砖砌的城墙又高又直，上面还建有瞭哨望敌之观楼、阻蔽敌箭之射阑，具备系统性的军事防御功能。

张仪以外交上的纵横捭阖闻名于世，但并不是一个只会耍嘴皮子的政客，对建设成都的通盘考虑，显示了他的大才。

新建的成都城分为太城和少城两部分，太即大，少即小。大城在东，内有权力中心郡府，以及盐官、铁官和市官等衙署，分别类似于现代的盐务局、冶金局和工商局。少城在西，紧靠大城，主要供普通百姓居住，还建有市场和货栈，生活便利与商业繁

just a figurehead to appease the emotions of the Shu people.

For Chengdu, the greatest achievement of Zhang Yi and Zhang Ruo was the construction of the city. The construction of Chengdu City began in 311 BC, which was long regarded as the starting point of Chengdu's urban history. However, does this mean that there were no cities on the Chengdu Plain before that? Not really.

Over two thousand years before Zhang Yi built the city, there was already a city wall at Baodun. Sanxingdui also had city walls, but like Baodun, they were earthen ramparts built with soil. Moreover, the walls of both Baodun and Sanxingdui had a slope, only capable of preventing floods but not defending against external enemies. The cities at Baodun and Sanxingdui had functional differences compared to the Chengdu City built by Zhang Yi. Furthermore, Chengdu City and the cities on the Chengdu Plain can be seen as belonging to a categorical relationship in terms of conceptual extension.

Of course, it is true that Chengdu City was initially built in 311 BC. However, when discussing the urban history of Chengdu, it should not be limited to just the city that existed from the time of Zhang Yi until the late Qing Dynasty and early Republican period. The concept of Chengdu has expanded many times since then, and any discussion of Chengdu's urban history should encompass this broader perspective.

The newly constructed Chengdu City by Zhang Yi used brick walls and was meticulously planned and designed, taking the Qin capital of Xianyang as a blueprint. Xianyang City was first built in 350 BC, modeled after the important capitals of states like Lu and Wei. Before Emperor Qin Shi Huang merged the six states and relocated wealthy households to increase the population, Xianyang already had a

华互为倚重。沿着城墙，则建有一间间仓库，作为赋税上交的谷物都储存在这里。此时的成都，已经是一座农、工、商皆备的大城。

成都平原上，同时立起来了三座“现代化”城市。除成都城之外，其西南方向有临邛城，西北方向有郫城。三座城池互为犄角，军事上相呼应，经济上相依存。尤其是临邛，城如其名，正对着邛、笮、僰、僚等少数民族地区，既有交通贸易之便利，又扼军事攻防之要冲。

民国初年的郫县县城 （美）西德尼 · 甘博 摄
The county seat of Pixian in the early Republican era. (Photographer: Sidney David Gamble, USA)

population of over 200,000, making it a regional metropolis.

The newly built Chengdu City had an impressive starting point. “With a circumference of twelve Li (about 6 kilometers) and a height of seven Zhang (about 24 meters)”, the brick walls were tall and straight. Observation towers were built on top to watch for enemies, and shooting galleries were designed to shield against enemy arrows, having a comprehensive military defense function.

Zhang Yi was renowned for his diplomatic skills, but he was not simply a politician skilled in rhetoric. His comprehensive considerations for the construction of Chengdu demonstrate his great talents.

The newly built Chengdu City was divided into two parts: Taicheng (the Grand City) and Shaocheng (the Lesser City). Taicheng was in the east and served as the power center, housing the regional government office, as well as the salt, iron, and market officials, similar to modern-day Salt Administration Bureau, Metallurgical Bureau, and Commerce Bureau respectively. Shaocheng was located to the west, adjacent to Taicheng, and primarily served as a residential area for ordinary people. It also had markets and storehouses, creating a place both for convenience of daily life and bustling commercial activities. Along the city walls, individual warehouses were built to store the grain collected as taxes. At this time, Chengdu had already become a major city with a well-developed agricultural, industrial, and commercial sector.

On the Chengdu Plain, three “modernized” cities were simultaneously established. In addition to Chengdu City, there were Linqiong to the southwest and Picheng to the northwest. These three cities formed a triangular formation, complementing each other in military coordination and economic interdependence. Especially Linqiong, its name

即便如此，以铁血起家的强秦仍不放心。它像狼一样，咬住了猎物，眼神也绝不放弃警戒。移民，是秦在军事手段之后的后续策略。方向却有两种，如迁秦民万户数万人至蜀，此谓掺沙子；反之，灭并六国之后，徙关东十二万户入咸阳，这是放在身边监视——如何选择，全看当时形势。

成都城更新换代，这片大地也换了主人，换了血液。

古蜀时代结束了。持续数千年的氐人王朝，转身走进历史深处。迎面而来的，是一个被称作秦汉的全新世代。

perfectly reflects its location facing minority areas such as Qiong, Ze, Bo, Liao, providing both convenience for trade and transportation and serving as a crucial military stronghold.

However, even with this arrangement, the powerful Qin Dynasty, born from iron and blood, remained cautious. Like a wolf, it held onto its prey and never let down its vigilant gaze. Migration was the subsequent strategy after military means. There were two directions to choose from: relocating tens of thousands of Qin people to Shu, which is like mixing sand; on the other hand, after eradicating and annexing the six states, relocating 120,000 households from the eastern frontier to Xianyang, which served as a means of surveillance. The choice depended entirely on the prevailing circumstances at the time.

Chengdu City underwent a process of regeneration, and this land changed its owners, its blood.

The era of ancient Shu came to an end. The Dynastic rule of the Di people, which lasted for thousands of years, stepped into the depths of history. In its place emerged a brand new era, known as the Qin and Han dynasties.

一艘船
从荆楚到红河平原

然而，古蜀虽亡，余绪未了。

将近一百年之后，距成都数千里之外的交趾（今越南北部）突然出现了一支数万人的军队，领军者称蜀王子。

当时的交趾生活着一个叫雒的部族。雒人滨海垦田，因潮水涨落而不

A Boat
Sailing from Jingchu to Red River Delta

Yet, though ancient Shu had fallen, its remnants remained.

Nearly 100 years later, thousands of miles away from Chengdu, in Jiaozhi (present-day northern Vietnam), a sudden appearance of a tens of thousands strong army led by a leader claiming to be a prince of Shu, took the stage.

At that time, there was a tribe called Luo living in Jiaozhi. The Luo people lived by the coast and

时被淹，生产方式还处于比较粗放的阶段。蜀军不是秦军的对手，但是要打统治雒民的雒王、雒将，还是比较有心得。征服雒地之后。蜀王子便在此建国，自称安阳王。

虽然开明十二世死于彭山，太子死于白鹿山，公子通当了几年秦的傀儡后被杀，却还有残部逃出了生天。经过多年流亡、辗转，来到交趾。蜀人政权真如野火一般，在成都平原熄灭了，却又在几千里外的南海北部湾海滨重新燃烧了起来。这跟耶律大石在大辽灭亡之后远走西域又建起西辽王朝的旧事如出一辙。

安阳王之事迹，在中国和越南的史书上都有记载，二者可互相印证。在越南史籍上，他还有个名字叫泮，被称作蜀王子泮。不过，此王子并非末代蜀王开明十二世之子，因为开明十二世亡于公元前316年，而安阳王亡于南越王赵佗之手，而赵佗称王已是在公元前206年——因此安阳王之亡距开明十二世之亡至少隔着一百一十年，二者绝非父子关系。

不过，在一则带有传奇色彩的史料里，安阳王倒跟他的祖辈——为妃子从千里之外搬了一座山到成都的那位蜀王——非常相似，都是行事有些颟顸的。

cultivated fields, which were occasionally flooded due to the tides. Their mode of production was still in a relatively primitive stage. The Shu army was not a match for the Qin army, but they had some experience in dealing with the Luo king and Luo generals who ruled the Luo people. After conquering the Luo territory, the prince of Shu established a kingdom there and proclaimed himself the King of Anyang.

Although the Kaiming twelfth ruler died in Pengshan, the crown prince died in Bailu Mountain, and Prince Tong served as a puppet under the Qin rule for several years before being killed, a remnant of the Shu people managed to escape and find refuge in Jiaozhi after years of exile and wandering. The political power of the Shu people was extinguished in the Chengdu plain, but it rekindled like a wildfire on the coast of the northern part of the South China Sea, thousands of miles away. This is parallel to the story of Yelü Dashi, who fled to the Western Regions after the fall of the Khitan Empire and established the West Liao Kingdom.

The deeds of King Anyang are recorded in both Chinese and Vietnamese historical texts, and these accounts can mutually corroborate each other. In Vietnamese historical records, he is also referred to as Prince Pan, known as the Prince of Shu, Pan. However, this prince is not the son of the last ruler of Shu, King Kaiming Twelfth who died in 316 BC, while King Anyang met his demise at the hands of the Southern Yue king Zhao Tuo, who declared himself king in 206 BC. Therefore, there is at least a 110-year gap between the deaths of King Anyang and King Kaiming Twelfth, ruling out any possibility of a father-son relationship between them.

However, in a legendary historical account, King Anyang bears a striking resemblance to his ancestor—the Shu king who moved a mountain from a thousand miles away to Chengdu for his consort. Both of them are depicted as somewhat eccentric in their actions.

南越武王赵佗本是秦朝人，公元前219年，作为副将带兵五十万平定岭南而留在当地，此时他才二十一岁。又过了十年，陈胜吴广起兵反秦，天下大乱。产生了割据之心的赵佗便断绝了跟中原的交通，关起门来建国称王。赵佗带兵西击安阳王，是在称王之后。

传说赵佗的军队打不过安阳王，是因为后者手下有一个神人叫皋通，他制作了一张神弩，一箭射出去，能够杀死三百人。安阳王因为不识皋通本事，言语中有些无理，便惹恼了他。皋通离去之前，给安阳王留下两句预言："拥有此弩则可称王，失去此弩必将败亡。"

赵佗因为向安阳王称臣，便把儿子赵始送到安阳王处当人质。没想到安阳王有个女儿叫瑞珠，见赵始外貌俊俏，便私下交好。赵始让瑞珠取来神弩，悄悄锯断后逃走。赵佗再次发兵，这一次，安阳王没有了神弩的助力，大败，只得乘船出海逃亡。《水经注》引《交州外域记》称：道平县（今越南永福省福安市）还有当年安阳王的王宫遗迹。

这个类似于参孙被大利拉剪掉头发而失去神力的故事，当然是传说，但南越武王赵佗带兵击溃安阳王，却

Zhao Tuo, the King Wu of Nanyue, was originally from the Qin Dynasty. In 219 BC, at the age of 21, he was left in Lingnan as a deputy general with an army of 500,000 to pacify the region. Ten years later, the uprising led by Chen Sheng and Wu Guang against the Qin Dynasty plunged the land into chaos. Influenced by separatist tendencies, Zhao Tuo cut off communication with the central plains and declared himself king, establishing his own kingdom. It was after proclaiming himself king that Zhao Tuo led his army to the west to attack King Anyang.

According to legend, Zhao Tuo's forces were unable to defeat King Anyang due to a divine figure named Gao Tong, who served under King Anyang. Gao Tong crafted a divine crossbow that could kill three hundred men in a single shot. King Anyang, unaware of Gao Tong's abilities, spoke in a manner that offended him. Before leaving, Gao Tong left King Anyang with two prophecies: "With possession of this crossbow, one can be king; without it, one will be doomed to fail."

In order to demonstrate his submission to King Anyang, Zhao Tuo sent his son Zhao Shi as a hostage to King Anyang's court. Unexpectedly, King Anyang had a daughter named Rui Zhu who was attracted to Zhao Shi's handsome appearance. They secretly formed a bond, and Zhao Shi persuaded Rui Zhu to retrieve the divine crossbow for him. After sawing through the crossbow, Zhao Shi quietly escaped. Then, Zhao Tuo launched another military campaign, and without the assistance of the divine crossbow, King Anyang suffered a major defeat and was forced to flee by ship. The *Commentary on the Water Classic* quotes the *Jiao Zhou Wai Yu Ji* in stating that there are still remnants of King Anyang's palace in Daoping County (now Fuan City, Yongfu Province, Vietnam).

This story bears similarities to the tale of Samson losing his strength after his hair was cut by Delilah, but it is, of course, a legend. However, the

是真实的历史。

historical fact remains that the King Wu of Nanyue, Zhao Tuo led his army to defeat King Anyang.

开明王族墓地的船棺，船棺葬是古代巴蜀人和一些傍水而居的民族特有的丧葬习俗　何大江 摄

The boat-shaped coffins in the royal cemetery of the Kaiming Dynasty. Boat burials were unique funeral customs of ancient Ba-Shu peoples and other water-dwelling ethnic groups. (Photographer: He Dajiang)

当年开明十二世不能抵抗秦国的虎狼之师，向南逃亡，行至不远的彭山便被杀。而蜀人却并没有被斩草除根，另有王族率残部继续向南。他们经过雅安芦山，一部分留在了大凉山；到了南中，又有一部分留在了楚雄州大姚一带。最终，安阳王率领的残部出现在交趾。

古蜀人就像种子一样，把人种和习俗留在他们行经的轨迹上。在越南朱芹、朱清等地，曾发现过秦至东汉末的船棺葬，这跟成都的商业街、双元村船棺葬存在着传承关系。死后乘船归故乡，是楚人的风俗，鳖灵将这一习俗带到成都平原，而安阳王又将它带到了红河平原。

During the reign of King Kaiming Twelfth, he was unable to resist the mighty army of the Qin Dynasty and was forced to flee south. However, he was killed in Pengshan, not far from Chengdu. The Shu people, however, were not completely eradicated. Another group of royal descendants led the remaining survivors southward. They passed through Lushan in Ya'an, with some settling in Daliangshan, and others in the Da Yao area of Chuxiong Prefecture. Ultimately, a remnant led by King Anyang emerged in Jiaozhi.

The ancient Shu people, like seeds, left behind their ethnicity and customs along the paths they traveled. In places such as Zhuqin and Zhuqing in Vietnam, boat coffins from the Qin Dynasty to the end of the Eastern Han Dynasty have been discovered, showing a connection to the boat coffins found in Chengdu's commercial streets and Shuangyuan Village. The tradition of returning to one's homeland by boat after death was a custom of the Chu people, which was brought to the Chengdu plain by the Bieling clan and further spread to Red River Delta by King Anyang.

一抔土
让人喟叹的武担山往事

A Handful of Soil
A sigh-inducing tale of Wudan Mountain

武担山，是蜀王的泰姬陵，也是

Wudan Mountain is Taj Mahal of the Shu King,

古蜀国的墓志铭。

武担山附近，今日有几个地名都跟蜀王葬妃的故事相关。

北面，沿着府河呈东西方向延伸的，是武都路——其名字来源是蜀王妃的故乡武都。

西北方向，横跨府河的是五丁桥，这座桥南连北较场西路，北通五丁路。五丁桥和五丁路，都是以本文反复出现过的五丁命名。在古蜀国开明王朝的后期，五丁多次出场，他们承担了接石牛、修路、担土、迎亲等重大任务，直到山崩时被埋于梓潼附近。

问题是，蜀王妃的故乡武都到底在哪里？

刘琳《华阳国志校注》中称，武都“在今绵竹，非甘肃之武都”，是指绵竹县北三十里之武都山（紫岩山），这也是《蜀中名胜记》和《方舆纪要》里的说法。

任乃强则认为，武都山是甘肃的仇池山。然而，任乃强也并不以为武担山的土来自仇池，他说这其实是高骈筑罗城、为郫江改道时挖壕沟堆的土。

任先生之学问笔者如仰望高山，此处却不能苟同。一是未见给出证据；二是《华阳国志》记载此事是

as well as a memorial to the ancient Shu Kingdom.

In the vicinity of Wudan Mountain, there are several place names today that are related to the story of the Shu King burying his consort.

To the north, along the Fu River, stretching from east to west, there is Wudu Road—named after the hometown of the Shu King's consort, Wudu.

To the northwest, spanning across the Fu River, is Wuding Bridge, which connects Bei Jiaochang West Road in the south and Wu Ding Road in the north. Both the Wuding Bridge and Wuding Road are named after the character "Wuding" that has been mentioned repeatedly in this text. During the late period of the Kaiming Kingdom of Ancient Shu, the Wuding played significant roles in tasks such as transporting stone oxen, constructing roads, carrying soil, and welcoming the royal bride. However, they were buried near Zitong when the mountains collapsed.

The question remains, where was the hometown of the Shu King's consort, Wudu?

Liu Lin's *Annotation to the Records of the States South of Mount Hua* mentions that Wudu is present-day Mianzhu, not the Wudu in Gansu. This refers to Wudu Mountain (Ziyan Mountain) located thirty miles north of Mianzhu County. This is also mentioned in the *Records of Famous Places in Shu* and the *Summary of Regional Geography*.

Mr. Ren Naiqiang claims that Wudu Mountain is referring to the Chouchi mountain, Gansu. However, he does not believe that the soil of Wudan Mountain actually came from Chouchi. He argues that it was soil excavated by Gao Pian to build Luocheng and redirect the Pi River.

I hold great respect for Mr. Ren's knowledge, like admiring a towering mountain. However, I cannot agree with him on this matter for several reasons. Firstly, there is no evidence provided to support his claim. Secondly, according to the records

在晋代，远早于高骈挖壕；三是若土堆成于唐代，那么对于早就存在的石镜、南梁时发现的古墓也不能做出很适当的解释。

那么，蜀王妃的故乡到底是在甘肃还是在绵竹呢？

仇池山，位于甘肃陇南市西和县，其西南侧紧靠陇南市武都区。今日要从成都开车过去，里程大致是四百六十千米。想来，二千三百多年前，要把“占地数亩，高七丈”的土从近千里外的地方运回来，难度也实在是太大了些。从这种意义上讲，倒是绵竹要更可靠一些。

当然，如果使用现代科技对武担山的土质进行化验，同甘肃仇池山、绵竹紫岩山以及成都本地的土质进行比较，得出的结论会更加可靠。

至于那面石镜，清末时山川早水见过，却并没有说镜面澈莹。其实，山上既然有墓，它显然也是墓表石，跟前文讲过的石笋、天涯石等同属大石遗迹。

《华阳国志》里有一个小故事，说成都城里还有一根石笋，长约三丈许（折合七米出头），周长约六尺（约1.5米）；在城北外的毗河边，也有差不多同样大小的另一根石笋——它们都是五丁去武都担土时，使用的

in the *Records of the States South of Mount Hua*, this event took place during the Jin Dynasty, well before Gao Pian's excavations. Thirdly, if the soil mound was created during the Tang Dynasty, it would not adequately explain the existence of ancient mirrors already present at the time or the ancient tombs discovered during the Southern Liang Dynasty.

So, was the homeland of the Shu King's concubine in Gansu or in Mianzhu?

Chouchi Mountain is located in Xihe County, Longnan City, Gansu Province. It is adjacent to the southwest side of Wudu District, Longnan City. If one were to drive from Chengdu today, the distance would be approximately 460 kilometers. It is difficult to imagine that over 2,300 years ago, transporting soil that covered several Mu and was seven Zhang high from a location hundreds of kilometers away would have been feasible. In this sense, Mianzhu seems to be more reliable.

Of course, if modern technology were used to analyze the soil composition of Wudan Mountain and compare it with Chouchi Mountain in Gansu, the Ziyan Mountain in Mianzhu, and the local soil in Chengdu, the conclusions would be more reliable.

As for the stone mirror, it was seen by Yamakawa Sousui in the late Qing Dynasty, but there is no mention of its clear and transparent reflection. In fact, since there are tombs on the mountain, it is clearly a tombstone, similar to the described stone stalagmites and Tianya stone, which are all large stone relics.

There is a story in the *Records of the States South of Mount Hua* that mentions another stone stalagmite in Chengdu City, which is about three Zhang long (approximately 7 meters) and has a circumference of about six Chi (approximately 1.5 meters). There is another stone stalagmite of similar size near the Pi River outside the northern part of

扁担。

现实世界里，当然不会存在这样的扁担，它们同样是古蜀人留下的大石遗迹。这两根巨人尺度的“扁担”，毁于西汉末年公孙述称帝时。山川早水见过的石镜，也不知所终；也有人说，它还埋在武担山上。

数千年的古蜀史，已经拉下了帷幕，唯有武担山的一抔泥土，供人伤怀往事。

the city. The story goes that they were both used as carrying poles when transporting soil from Wudu to Chengdu.

In the real world, such carrying poles do not exist. They are, like the mentioned stone stalagmites, remnants left behind by the ancient Shu people. These two giant-sized “carrying poles” were destroyed during the late Western Han Dynasty when Gongsun Shu declared himself emperor. The stone mirror seen by Yamakawa Sousui has also disappeared without a trace. Some people speculate that it may still be buried on Wudan Mountain.

The ancient history of Shu, spanning thousands of years, has come to a close. Only a handful of soil from Wudan Mountain remains, evoking a sense of nostalgia for the past.

第二卷

Volume 2

文翁石室
Wen Weng Stone Chamber

由汉白玉和花岗岩建成的石室精舍，外形古朴，庄严巍然。它曾经是中国历史上第一所由地方政府主办的官学，凭教化之功改变了一方风气。

它作过祭祀先贤的周公礼殿，也曾改建为孔庙。还曾有超过一千块石碑屹立于此，上面镌刻着儒家十三经，成为一座石质图书馆。

直至清代，它都是四川地区官办最高学府。

它，就是文翁石室。

Crafted from white marble and granite, this stone chamber stands as a sanctuary of wisdom, a spiritual haven. Its exterior exudes an ancient simplicity, dignified and majestic. Once the foremost official academy sponsored by local governance in Chinese history, it wielded transformative influence, reshaping the educational and cultural landscape of its surroundings.

It served as the ceremonial hall for venerating the virtuous Zhou Gong and underwent transformations to become a Confucian temple. Over a thousand stone tablets once stood here, each bearing inscriptions of the thirteen classics of Confucianism, turning it into a bibliotheca of stone.

Until the Qing Dynasty, it remained the preeminent official institution of learning in the Sichuan region.

Such was the grandeur and significance of the Wen Weng Stone Chamber.

文翁石室：汉白玉砌就精神殿堂

Wen Weng Stone Chamber: A Spiritual Hall Built with White Marble

文翁讲堂

唐 · 卢照邻

锦里淹中馆，岷山稷下亭。
空梁无燕雀，古壁有丹青。
槐落犹疑市，苔深不辨铭。
良哉二千石，江汉表遗灵。

The Lecture Hall of Wen Weng Stone Chamber

Lu Zhaolin, Tang Dynasty

In City of Brocade at the foot of Mount Min,
Stands the deserted Stone Chamber tall,
Which still echoes the scholars' din,
Of the legendary Jixia Pavilion and Yanzhong Hall.
The rafters now echo a vacant tune,
No swallows grace the beams, under the aged moon.
Ancient walls adorned with crimson strokes,
Yet moss-covered, the inscriptions evoke.
Locust trees' whispers hint at the market's past,
The engraved tales beneath the deep moss forever last.
Oh, praise the virtuous ruler, his wisdom draws nigh,
In the Jianghan region his legacy gleams high.

"初唐四杰"之一的卢照邻，在他生活年代见到的文翁石室，已经非常凋敝了。屋梁空空，青苔横生，石梁上连燕子也不来筑巢。只是古老的石壁上，依旧有近千年前壁画的痕迹，青苔之下，依稀还能看得到当年刻下的铭文。

尽管如此，卢照邻对这座残存的石室评价却非常高，将之比作孔子故里淹中，比作战国时期的学术中心稷下宫。站在石室之前，槐花飘落一身，仿佛回到当年的长安太学槐市。

As one of the "Four Greats of Early Tang", Lu Zhaolin beheld the Wen Weng Stone Chamber during his lifetime, now greatly dilapidated. With the above beams bare, green moss rampant, and not even a swallow comes to build its nest in the stone hollow. Yet, on the ancient stone walls, traces of a nearly thousand-year-old mural still persist. Beneath the green moss, one can faintly discern the inscriptions carved back in ancient days.

Despite this, Lu Zhaolin highly praises this remaining stone chamber, likening it to Confucius' hometown of Yanzhong and comparing it to the academic center of Jixia Palace in the Warring States period. Standing in front of the stone chamber, with locust flowers drifting down and covering him, it felt as if he were transported back to Huaishi (the locust market), the former Imperial Academy in Chang'an.

建一座人心中的殿堂

石室的创建者，人称文翁。

文翁姓文名党，字仲翁，是汉景帝和武帝时期蜀郡的最高长官——郡守。《汉书·循吏传》称其文翁是尊称，即“文老先生”。文翁之所以受到如此尊重，跟他创立石室精舍并以此为基地教化一方，是分不开的。

文翁创建的石室，位置在今日文庙前街以北、文翁路西侧，即石室中学校址。在汉代，则处于外江和内江之间那块狭长地带“市”之内。两条江夹着一块商业区，在当时有个名字，叫“二江珥市”。

中国古代建筑多以木为主，而文翁所建的郡学，却以汉白玉、花岗岩为材。无论是材质还是做工，石都比木造价高很多，汉白玉尤为名贵。成都平原并不产石，为何要舍近求远、花费巨大，来建一座石室呢？

隔着两千多年的时光，来猜想其意图：石材坚实，不仅能够抵御腐朽，对于木建筑最大的隐患——火灾，也毫不惧怕。东汉永初、中平年间，石室都遭遇过大火。尤其是后一场大火，将学观的厢房、廊庑吞噬殆尽，而石室独存。

Erecting a sanctuary in the hearts of all

The founder of this chamber is known as Scholar Wen. With the surname Wen and given name Dang, and courtesy name Zhongweng, Wen was the highest official of Shu County during the reigns of Emperors Jing and Emperor Wu. The *History of the Han Dynasty: Biographies of Exemplary Officials* reveres him as Wen Weng, a term of respect, meaning “Mr. Wen the Elder”. The reason why Wen Weng is so respected is inseparable from his establishment of the Shishi Jingshe (Stone Chamber Academy) and using it as a base to educate the people.

The stone chamber established by Wen Weng stood north of the present-day Wenmiao Front Street, on the west side of Wenweng Road—the current location of Shishi High School. In the Han era, it occupied a narrow strip of land between the outer and inner rivers within the confines of the marketplace, known then as “the Earring—like Twin Rivers of the Market”.

In ancient Chinese architecture, wood was the primary material, but Scholar Wen’s prefectural school defied convention, utilizing white marble and granite. Both in terms of materials and craftsmanship, stone was a more precious and expensive choice than wood. Since the Chengdu Plain lacked a local stone source, why did Wen opt for the distant and costly endeavor of constructing a stone chamber?

Across the span of more than two millennia, we can infer his intent: Stone is sturdy and not only resistant to decay but also impervious to the greatest threat to wooden structures—fire. During the the Yongchu and Zhongping periods of Eastern Han Dynasty, the stone chamber faced severe fires, particularly in the later conflagration that consumed

the study rooms and corridors of the academy, leaving the stone chamber alone unscathed.

汉代凤阙画像砖，两阙之间栖息着一只凤凰，寓意“有凤来仪”，象征吉祥　何大江 摄

A Han Dynasty brick depicting the Fengque (Phoenix Towers), with a phoenix perched between the towers, symbolizing auspiciousness and harmony. (Photographer: He Dajiang)

到了宋代，李清照的丈夫赵明诚在《金石录》中记载，当时的成都府学（地方官学）还存有汉代文翁石室和周公礼殿留下的屋柱。这些柱子都是正正方方，上小下大。屋楹上，刻于东汉末年的《周公礼殿记》依然完好，而此时距赵明诚所处时代已近千年。

石头保存的时间固然很长，但是文章教化泽被后世，持续更为久远，这大概也是文翁的初衷。事实上，文翁石室的创立开启了蜀学的先声，也影响了中国数千年的文官选拔制度。

文翁是庐江舒地人（今安徽省庐江县、舒城县一带），其地自西周始，皋陶（尧舜时司法长官）后人在这一带建立了众多小方国，如舒、龙舒、舒庸等，合称群舒。群舒多为楚所灭，汉置舒县。此地还出了一个名气

By the Song Dynasty, Zhao Mingcheng, husband of the renowned poet Li Qingzhao, recorded in *Jin Shi Lu* that Chengdu Prefectural School still retained the Han-era stone chamber built by Scholar Wen and the columns from the Hall of Zhou Gong Rituals. These columns were perfectly square, tapering from larger bases to smaller tops. On the lintel, the inscription from the end of the Eastern Han Dynasty (184-220 AD) still remained intact. By Zhao Mingcheng's time, nearly a millennium had passed since these columns were erected.

Though stone endures the test of time, Scholar Wen's teachings resonate through the ages, a legacy that surpasses the longevity of mere rock. This enduring impact was likely Wen Weng's original intent. In reality, the establishment of Wen Weng's Stone Chamber marked the inception of Shu Studies, namely, the literary and educational endeavors to spread Confucianism in Sichuan, influencing China's civil servant selection system for millennia.

Hailing from Lujiang (in the present-day areas of Lujiang County and Shucheng County in Anhui Province), Wen Weng's roots trace back to the early Western Zhou Dynasty. In this region, descendants

比文翁更大的人，那就是雄姿英发、羽扇纶巾的周瑜周公瑾。

文翁为官之前的记载极少。刘宋一朝的志怪小说《异录传》说他少时即有神异。成年后，曾想开垦一块水田，需要斫除草木，当晚就有百十头野猪来帮忙，用鼻子载着土往柴草上堆。到了天亮的时候，水田就建成了。《太平广记》收录此说时，还多了一个“文翁掷斧”的故事。说文翁断树，想砍之处离地面一丈八尺，他祝告道：“如果我能砍中，就会当俸禄两千石的大官。”一斧头飞去正中其处，后来果然当了蜀郡守。

这类神话的价值本不大，从中却可以得知，文翁少年时家贫，却心怀大志。正史则说他少年时酷爱读书，通晓《春秋》。

文翁当过郡县小吏，在这一过程中培养了行政管理能力，熟悉了民间疾苦。因在任上干得不错而得到提拔，到汉景帝末期，出任蜀郡守。

郡守即一郡之太守，在实施郡县制的秦汉，算是封疆大吏了。西汉在郡之上虽然设有州，但州为监察区而非行政区，刺史巡视考察州内的郡、封国而无管理职能，其俸禄亦不足郡守的三分之一。刺史变为有实权的官员，位居郡守之上，已是东汉末年天

of Gao Tao, the judicial chief during the time of Yao and Shun, established numerous small fiefdoms such as Shu, Longshu, and Shuyong, collectively known as Qunshu. Many of these were later conquered by the Chu state, and the Han Dynasty established Shu County in their place. This land also produced a figure of greater renown than Wen Weng himself – the resplendent Zhou Yu, or Zhou Gongjin, with his striking presence, feathered fan, and silk headscarf.

Little is recorded about Wen Weng's pre-official years. According to the Liu Song Dynasty's fantastical novel *Yi Lu Zhuan*, it suggests that even in his youth, he displayed signs of the supernatural. Upon reaching adulthood, he endeavored to reclaim a patch of waterlogged fields. That night, a multitude of wild boars numbering in the hundreds arrived, using their snouts to transport soil onto piles of straw. By daybreak, the waterlogged fields were transformed. Another tale in *Tai Ping Guang Ji* adds an episode where Wen Weng, tossing an axe into the air, hoping to strike a tree branch high off the ground. He prayed, “If I hit the target, I shall become a high official with an annual stipend of two thousand Dan.” True to his words, he later assumed the position of Shu Commandery Governor.

While such myths may hold limited historical value, they hint at Wen Weng's humble beginnings and lofty aspirations in his youth. Official accounts describe his passion for reading and his proficiency in the *Spring and Autumn Annals*.

Wen Weng began his career as a minor official in the counties, cultivating administrative skills and becoming familiar with the hardships of the common people. Due to his commendable performance in office, he was gradually promoted. By the end of Emperor Jing's reign, he assumed the role of Shu Commandery Governor.

In the Qin and Han periods, during the

下即将大乱的时节了。

班固《汉书·循吏传》将文翁列为循吏之首。循者，因循也，遵循也，但所谓循吏，并非仅仅指奉公守法的官员。若仅论守法，则循吏、酷吏并无差别。颜师古注《汉书》，对“循吏”的解释是，“循，顺也，上顺公法，下顺人情。”一句“下顺人情”，辨明循吏绝非老好人、书呆子，反而要多一分对人性的洞察、对人心的关怀——这也是循吏与酷吏的最大区别。

《循吏传》之后即是《酷吏传》，二者紧挨而放，是有心对比。在《酷吏传》之首，班固先后引用了《论语》《道德经》《史记》来阐明理念：严刑峻法，或许可以吓住老百姓；而道德教化，才会让人从内心知善恶并不断自省。

当然并非空口谈道德，只高谈道德难免虚假伪饰。文翁是如何做的呢：以办学为抓手，以教育易风俗、正人心。

文翁就任蜀郡守之后，干了两件大事。

第一件是“穿湔江口”，即在湔江上开凿分渠，灌溉繁县一千七百顷田地（今都江堰市东部以及彭州、新都一带），从而成为继鳖灵、李冰之后第三个因兴修水利惠民而在四川历

implementation of the prefecture and county system, the position of Commandery Governor (Jun Shou) was considered a significant title. Though the Han Dynasty had provinces above commanderies, provinces were primarily supervisory regions rather than administrative ones. The Inspector (Ci Shi), responsible for overseeing and examining commanderies and fiefdoms within the province, did not hold administrative powers and received less than one-third of the stipend of a Commandery Governor. The shift to a more authoritative role for the Inspector marked the approaching chaos at the end of the Eastern Han Dynasty.

In Ban Gu's *History of the Han Dynasty: Biographies of Exemplary Officials*, Wen Weng is acknowledged as the foremost among the "Xunli" (Exemplary Officials). "Xun" signifies adherence, compliance, and conformity, but when applied to officials, it extends beyond merely upholding laws and regulations. If it were solely about legal adherence, there would be no distinction between "Xunli" (Exemplary Officials) and "Kuli" (Harsh Officials). Yan Shigu, annotating the *History of the Han Dynasty*, interprets "Xunli" as "following, obeying; above, conforming to public laws; below, conforming to human sentiments." The phrase "conforming to human sentiments" clarifies that Exemplary Officials are not mere sticklers for rules; rather, they possess insight into human nature and exhibit genuine concern for people—a crucial distinction from Harsh Officials.

Following the *Biographies of Exemplary Officials* is the *Biographies of Harsh Officials*, intentionally juxtaposed for comparison. At the beginning of the latter, Ban Gu references the *Analects of Confucius*, the *Tao Te Ching*, and the *Records of the Grand Historian* to elucidate the philosophies at play: severe punishments and rigorous laws might intimidate the

史上留名之人。

《水经·江水注》编了个神话故事，说江神曾经发洪水淹死了人，而文翁来到蜀地之后，特地在祭祀时向其敬酒。然而江神不吃敬酒吃罚酒，文翁于是拔剑砍击，从此不再有江神之害。

当然，这种祭祀带有鲜明的表演性质。文翁明白以那时老百姓的文化水平，是听不进去大道理的，郡守这样的大官亲自登台演戏，必然广受欢迎，更能安定人心。其实，斗江神这种把戏，李冰就表演过。看来，在诸葛亮治蜀之前，便有"攻心""审时"这样的治民之术。

第二件事是修筑石室精舍。文翁就任郡守时的情况是，"蜀地辟陋有蛮夷风"。事实上，古蜀文化与中原华夏文化的差别很大，除了民风民俗、社会组织结构不同，甚至连语言也不一样——前文已述，蜀人的主体民族为氐族，并不讲汉语。虽然古蜀被秦国吞并后，大量移民进入蜀地，语言互相渗透并逐渐统一，但百姓受教育水平低、人才匮乏、民间巫觋之风盛行却是文翁面临的现状。

以站在局外的现代人眼光来看，蜀地迥异于中原的奇风异俗是极有魅力的，其民俗学上的价值当然不可否认，但是，倘若真生活在那样的环境

common people, but true moral education encourages individuals to recognize right from wrong and engage in continuous self-reflection.

However, this emphasis on morality is not a mere rhetorical flourish. Wen Weng's actions speak louder: he addressed the root through the establishment of an educational institution, leveraging education to shape customs and rectify the human heart, thus fostering societal transformation in the end.

Upon assuming the role of Shu Commandery Governor, Wen Weng undertook two significant initiatives.

The first was the "Channeling of Jian River Mouth", involving the excavation of diversion channels on the Jian River to irrigate approximately 1,700 hectares of land in Fanxian County. This encompassed the eastern regions of Dujiangyan City, as well as areas in Pengzhou and Xindu. Wen Weng thus became the third historical figure in Sichuan, following Bieling and Li Bing, to leave a lasting legacy through the improvement of water resources for the benefit of the people.

The *Water Classic* compiled a mythological story, claiming that the River God had caused flooding and death. Wen Weng, after arriving in Shu, made a special offering of wine during a ritual. Nevertheless, the River God refused the libation, prompting Wen Weng to draw his sword and strike. Supposedly, after this encounter, the River God ceased to bring harm.

It's important to note that such rituals had a performative nature. Wen Weng understood that the common people at that time did not possess such a cultural level to easily comprehend profound principles. As a high-ranking official, personally engaging in such theatrics would likely be well-received and contribute to stabilizing the populace. Interestingly, the performance of challenging river deities was not unique to Wen Weng; Li Bing had

中，必然是离蒙昧近、距文明远。

文翁最先采取的策略是，派人到京城留学。他从郡县小吏中挑选了十八个聪慧有才干的，送到长安成为博士门下弟子，学习儒家七经（《诗》《书》《礼》《乐》《易》《春秋》《论语》）。其中的一些专门学习律令，以备将来充实行政管理系统。

东汉讲经画像砖，反映了当时崇师重教的风气　何大江 摄
An Eastern Han portrait brick depicting a lecture scene, reflecting the prevailing respect for teachers and education. (Photographer: He Dajiang)

数年后，这些青年才俊学成归乡，文翁把他们都安排到重要位置上，并且根据考察情况加以提拔。后来，有人做到郡守、刺史这样的高官。其中一个姓张名宽字叔文者曾为汉武帝近臣侍中，著有《春秋章句》，共计十五万字。张宽在《华阳国志》中有传与赞，列于司马相如之前，其赞曰："叔文播教，

done something similar. This suggests that strategies such as "winning hearts" and "timing assessments" were already present in governance before Zhuge Liang's administration of Shu.

The second major undertaking was the construction of the Stone Chamber Academy. When Wen Weng assumed office, the situation in Shu was described as "rudimentary with the influence of barbarian customs." Indeed, the ancient Shu culture differed significantly from the Central Plains Han culture. Besides varying customs, social structures, and even languages—remember that the main ethnic group in ancient Shu was the Di people, who did not speak Chinese. Although a significant influx of immigrants occurred after the Qin Dynasty annexed Shu, resulting in language assimilation, the populace's low education level, a scarcity of talent, and prevalent shamanistic practices were challenges Wen Weng faced.

From the perspective of a modern observer standing outside of that historical context, the unique customs and traditions of Shu, distinct from those of the Central Plains, hold a certain charm with anthropological value. However, living in such an environment would likely bring one closer to ignorance and farther from civilization.

Recognizing this, Wen Weng implemented a strategic move–sending individuals for education in the capital. From the pool of local minor officials in the commanderies and counties, he carefully selected eighteen intelligent and capable individuals. These chosen few were dispatched to Chang'an, the capital, to become disciples under the scholars, learning the seven Confucian classics (The Book of Poetry, The Book of Documents, The Rites, The Music, The Changes, The Spring and Autumn Annals, The Analects). Some of them specialized in the study of laws and regulations, preparing to enrich the

变风为雅。道洽化迁，实我西鲁。”

《搜神记》中也有一段关于张宽的神话。话说张宽曾跟随汉武帝到甘泉、泰畤祭天，路过渭河时，见一女子在河中洗浴。武帝感觉很奇怪，便问她是谁，女子回答：“你后面第七辆车上的侍中知道，问他吧。”数过去，第七辆车上坐的正是张宽。张宽答道：“天上有星辰主祠祀，如果有祭祀者斋戒不洁的话，就会化作女子出来相见。”武帝闻言后有所感悟，于是检点自己行为中的不当。张宽则因为敢于直谏，被汉武帝派为扬州刺史，同时给后世留下了一个“七车张”的名号。

成都羊子山遗址出土的东汉讲经画像砖。经师坐于榻上，头顶有遮灰的承尘，六名弟子手执简牍，跪坐两侧　何大江 摄

An Eastern Han portrait brick unearthed from the Yangzishan site in Chengdu. It shows a teacher seated on a platform, shaded by a ceiling canopy, with six disciples kneeling on either side, holding bamboo slips. (Photographer: He Dajiang)

administrative management system in the future.

After several years of education in the capital, the young talents Wen Weng had sent to study returned to their hometown. Wen Weng strategically placed them in important positions, promoting them based on their performance and evaluations. Some of these individuals eventually rose to high-ranking positions such as Commandery Governors and Inspectors. One notable individual, named Zhang Kuan, courtesy name Shuwen, had served as a close aide to Emperor Wu of Han. He authored a work titled *Chapters and Verses of the Spring and Autumn Annals*, comprising 150,000 words. In the *Records of the States South of Mount Hua*, there is a biography and commendation for Zhang Kuan, placing him ahead of Sima Xiangru. The commendation states, "Shuwen spread education, transforming customs into elegance. The Way flourished, and culture shifted, truly our Western Confucius."

The *Soushen Ji,* In Search of the Supernatural also recounts a myth related to Zhang Kuan. It tells of an incident when Zhang Kuan accompanied Emperor Wu of Han to offer sacrifices at Ganquan and Taishi. While passing the Wei River, he noticed a woman bathing in the river. Intrigued, Emperor Wu inquired about her identity, and the woman replied, "The assistant sitting in the seventh carriage behind you knows. Ask him." Counting carriages, Zhang Kuan was indeed seated in the seventh carriage. When questioned, he explained, "In the heavens, there's the celestial being overseeing sacrifices. If the one offering sacrifices is not properly cleansed, the celestial being may transform into a woman to appear before him." Emperor Wu, upon hearing this, was enlightened and examined the improprieties in his own behavior. Zhang Kuan, for his courage in offering straightforward advice, was appointed as the Inspector of Yangzhou by Emperor Wu. This incident

话题回到文翁。对于远在长安的学子，文翁十分关切。为了结好教学的博士，让他们更尽心尽力，文翁特意减少郡府用度，派人购买蜀刀与蜀布等特产馈赠。

文翁又在全国率先建立郡学，面向全郡选拔各县子弟入学，这便是石室精舍之由来。文翁办学，是为国家培养人才，而入学的家庭也得到了实惠。入学者可免除徭役，减少了后顾之忧。学得好的，便选来填补郡县官吏的空缺，保持行政体系的正常运转；差一等的，也授予“孝悌”“力田”之称。

文翁办学，有强烈的经世致用的特点。他会从石室中选出些年轻人跟随在身边，让他们出入官府，观摩自己如何处理政务。到各县巡视时，则又会挑选一些品学俱佳的学生随行，让他们去宣传政府的法令。

与文翁石室相关的，还有个比张宽出名得多的人物——司马相如。《三国志·秦宓传》录有秦宓写给蜀郡太守王商的信：“蜀本无学士，文翁遣相如东受七经，还教吏民，于是蜀学比于齐鲁。”也就是说，司马相如不仅是文翁派到长安的学子，而且学成归来，还在石室担任教职。不过，蒙文通等学者考证

also gave rise to the epithet “Zhang of the Seventh Carriage” for Zhang Kuan in later generations.

Returning to the topic of Wen Weng, he showed great concern for students in Chang’an. In order to win the favor of teaching scholars and encourage them to put in more effort, Wen Weng deliberately reduced the expenses of the commandery, sending people to purchase local specialties such as Shu knives and Shu fabric as gifts for them.

Furthermore, Wen Weng pioneered the establishment of a commandery school nationwide, selecting talented youths from all counties to attend. This was the origin of the Stone Chamber Academy. Wen Weng’s approach to education aimed at cultivating talents for the country, and the families of the students benefited as well. Those who enrolled could be exempted from corvée, alleviating their worries. Those who excelled were chosen to fill vacancies in commandery and county offices, maintaining the normal operation of the administrative system. Even those with slightly lower achievements were granted titles such as “Filial Piety” and “Diligent Farming” to encourage them.

Wen Weng’s educational style was characterized by a strong emphasis on practicality. He personally selected young individuals from the Stone Chamber to accompany him to the offices, allowing them to observe how he handled governmental affairs. During inspections of various counties, he would also choose students with outstanding character and academic achievements to accompany him, letting them disseminate government laws and regulations.

Associated with Wen Weng’s Stone Chamber, there is another figure much more famous than Zhang Kuan—Sima Xiangru. In the *Record of Qin Mi* from the *Records of the Three Kingdoms*, there is a letter from Qin Mi to Wang Shang, the Prefect of Shu Commandery, which states: “Originally, Shu

过，在文翁办郡学之前，司马相如已经到了长安，所以很可能是秦宓搞错了。

说司马相如执教于石室，也有曹学佺《蜀中广记》引《太平寰宇记》称："石室，司马相如教授于此，从者数千人。"查北宋乐史《太平寰宇记》下"孔子庙"条，原文为："昔司马相如教授于此。"但汉代成都并无孔庙，乐史所指当为石室，故曹学佺有此论。而最为权威的《汉书》原文为："繇文翁倡其教，相如为之师。"其实，班固所论为蜀学，而非石室，言及文翁倡教、相如授经的贡献，二者是并列关系，并不能得出授经是在石室的结论。或因二人为同时代蜀地名人，后世学人未详加辨析，便得出了司马相如授经于石室的结论，如此而已。

在石室读书的弟子，不仅有了学问，有了出路，也有了社会地位，以至于整个蜀郡的人都想把子弟送至石室读书。那些富裕的家庭，宁愿花上大价钱也要创造机会进石室。至此，便能明白文翁在成都缺乏石材的情况下，非要建一座石室精舍的深意：要的不只是校舍能够防火，能够保存久远；更要它威严庄重、富丽堂皇、为人敬仰，要在蜀民心中树立起一座不

had no scholars. Wen Weng sent Sima Xiangru to the east to study the Seven Classics, and upon his return, he taught officials and the people. Thus, Shu's education became comparable to that of Qi and Lu." This indicates that Sima Xiangru was not only one of the students Wen Weng sent to Chang'an but also returned to take a teaching position at the Stone Chamber. However, scholars like Meng Wentong have pointed out that Sima Xiangru had already arrived in Chang'an before Wen Weng established the commandery school, suggesting a possible error in Qin Mi's account.

There are different historical accounts regarding Sima Xiangru's role at the Stone Chamber. Cao Xuequan's *Shu Zhong Guang Ji,* the Geography in Central Sichuan quotes *the Tai Ping Universal Records* stating, "Sima Xiangru taught and instructed here, with several thousand followers." The authoritative *History of the Han Dynasty* original text states, "Wen Weng initiated its teachings, and Xiangru was its teacher." In fact, Ban Gu's discussion pertains to Shu Studies, rather than specifically the Stone Chamber. The contributions of Wen Weng and Sima Xiangru in promoting education are mentioned in parallel, and it cannot be conclusively inferred that Sima Xiangru taught the Classics at the Stone Chamber. The confusion might stem from the fact that both figures were prominent personalities in Shu during the same era, and subsequent scholars may not have thoroughly analyzed the details, leading to the assumption that Sima Xiangru taught at the Stone Chamber.

The disciples who studied at the Stone Chamber Academy not only gained knowledge and prospects but also attained social status, to the extent that people throughout Shu Commandery aspired to send their children to study here. Wealthy families were willing to spend a considerable amount of money

倒的精神殿堂。

秦代禁办私学，因此文翁刚到蜀地，满目所见皆是教育凋敝的景象，而经过这一番教化，崇文重教之风深入人心。蜀人不仅要送孩子上学，有条件的还要送到教育条件最好的京城长安去。文翁时期，在长安求学的蜀郡子弟已跟来自圣人之乡齐鲁的一样多。

汉武帝元光年间，丞相公孙弘巡视西南夷（今四川西南部及云贵）途经成都，得知文翁之事后深为赞赏，回到长安后开始向全国推广，下令所有的郡国（在西汉，郡直属中央，封国由分封诸王治理）都要设置“学校官”。因此，说文翁开创了中国兴办地方官学之举，这一点是毫无疑义的。

to create opportunities for admission. At this point, one can understand the deeper meaning behind Wen Weng's decision to build the Stone Chamber Academy despite the lack of local stone resources in Chengdu. It was not just about having a school building that could resist fire and endure the test of time; more importantly, Wen Weng aimed for a dignified and magnificent structure that commanded respect, establishing an enduring spiritual sanctuary in the hearts of the people of Shu.

During the Qin Dynasty, private schools were prohibited, so when Wen Weng arrived in Shu, he encountered a scene of educational decline. Through his efforts, a culture of valuing education and literature took root deeply in the hearts of the people. Shu residents not only sent their children to school locally but, if possible, also to the capital city Chang'an, where educational conditions were deemed the best. During Wen Weng's era, the number of students from Shu Commandery seeking education in Chang'an was comparable to those coming from the renowned educational regions of Qi and Lu in Shandong.

During the reign of Emperor Wu of Han in the Yuanguang era, Prime Minister Gongsun Hong conducted an inspection tour of the southwestern regions inhabited by various ethnic groups (modern-day southwestern Sichuan and parts of Yunnan and Guizhou). While passing through Chengdu, he learned about the achievements of Wen Weng and was deeply impressed. Upon returning to Chang'an, he initiated a nationwide promotion of Wen Weng's educational model, ordering all commanderies and princedoms (in Western Han, commanderies were directly governed by the central government, while princedoms were ruled by appointed princes) to establish "educational officials." Therefore, it is indisputable to say that Wen Weng pioneered the establishment of local official schools in China.

蜀学三宝

文翁殁于蜀地。他去世之后，蜀人在石室为他立像，“岁时祭祀不绝”。文翁虽然离世了，蜀学却在他创立石室、教化人民的基础上肇端，历经两千年而不绝，成为华夏文明的重要组成部分。古蜀则在文翁时代完成转型，彻底融入华夏文明。

关于蜀学，北宋学者吕陶有非常精彩的评价：“蜀学之盛，冠天下而垂无穷者，其具有三：一曰文翁之石室，二曰周公之礼殿，三曰石壁之九经。”

这段话一共提到蜀学的三个标志，除了文翁石室这个原点之外，周公礼殿和孟蜀石经其实也都建在文翁石室的旧址上。

周公礼殿是一座先贤纪念堂，文翁在创建石室时，又在其旁建立了礼殿，绘有孔子及其弟子像。汉献帝兴平元年（194年），郡守高眹（同“朕”，也有典籍作“昳”，音shùn。“眹”“昳”形似，易有传抄之误）在修复被火焚烧的石室同时，于其东侧建立了周公礼殿，祭祀周公、孔子等历代圣贤及儒林人物。

高眹所建周公礼殿，壁上画有三皇五帝、孔子及七十弟子，并有大学

The Three Treasures of Shu Studies

Wen Weng passed away in Shu. After his death, the people of Shu erected a statue for him in the Stone Chamber, and they continued to offer annual sacrifices. Although Wen Weng was no longer alive, Shu Studies, founded on the basis of his creation of the Stone Chamber and the education of the people, continued for two thousand years and became an integral part of Chinese civilization. Ancient Shu completed its transformation during the era of Wen Weng, thoroughly integrating into Chinese civilization.

Regarding Shu Studies, the Northern Song scholar Lü Tao offered a vivid assessment: “The flourishing of Shu’xue, surpassing all others and extending endlessly, is characterized by three elements: firstly, the Stone Chamber of Wen Weng; secondly, the Ritual Hall of Zhou Gong; thirdly, the Nine Classics on Stone Tablets.”

In this passage, there are three key symbols of Shu Studies mentioned. In addition to Wen Weng’s Stone Chamber, the Ritual Hall of Zhou Gong and the Mengshu Stone Classics were also built on the site of Wen Weng’s Stone Chamber.

The Ritual Hall of Zhou Gong is a memorial hall for eminent sages. When Wen Weng created the Stone Chamber, he also built a Ritual Hall beside it, adorned with images of Confucius and his disciples. In the first year of the Xianping era of Emperor Xian of Han (194 AD), the commandery administrator Gao Zhen restored the Stone Chamber damaged by fire and concurrently erected the Ritual Hall of Zhou Gong on its east side. This hall served as a place of worship for Zhou Gong, Confucius, and various sages and scholars throughout history.

The Ritual Hall of Zhou Gong, built by Gao Zhen, featured paintings on the walls of the Three

者蔡邕书写的《周公礼殿记》。

南齐永明年间，画家刘王真重新作画。此后历代亦有补画，如五代丘文播画山水、黄筌画湖滩。

Sovereigns, Five Emperors, Confucius, and the Seventy Disciples. The renowned scholar Cai Yong wrote the *Record of the Ritual Hall of Zhou Gong* displayed in this hall.

During the Southern Qi Dynasty's Yongming era, the painter Liu Wangzhen created new paintings. Subsequently, there were additions by artists from different dynasties, such as Qiu Wenbo's landscape paintings during the Five Dynasties and Huang Quan's depiction of lakeshores.

熹平石经《毛诗》残片。熹平石经是中国最早的官定儒家经典刻石，始刻于东汉灵帝熹平四年，立于洛阳太学　何大江 摄

A fragment of the *Classic of Poetry* from the Xiping Stone Classics. The Xiping Stone Classics, carved during the reign of Emperor Ling of the Eastern Han, were the earliest official Confucian texts engraved on stone tablets in China and were erected at the Luoyang Imperial Academy. (Photographer: He Dajiang)

五代时建石经堂，刻“孟蜀石经”于此。刻石经是太学的配置，可知此时建在此处的学校已升格为后蜀的国家最高学府。

所谓石经，是刻在石碑上的儒家经典。在印刷术发明之前，无论是用刀刻在竹简上，还是用笔写在丝帛或纸张上，文字在传抄的过程中都有可能产生错讹。而将其刻于石碑，立于殿堂，就相当于建立了一种国家标准。对于自己手上的儒家经典存有疑义的士子学人，都可以到石经前比较、订正。

In the Five Dynasties, the Stone Classics Hall was established, and the *Mengshu Stone Classics* were engraved here. Engraving the stone classics was only fitted for the Imperial Academy, indicating that the school established here had been upgraded to the highest educational institution in the later Shu kingdom.

The so-called "Stone Classics" refers to Confucian classics engraved on stone tablets. Before the invention of printing, whether carved on bamboo slips with a knife or written with a brush on silk or paper, errors could occur during transcription. By engraving them on stone tablets and placing them in halls, a national standard was established. Scholars who had doubts about the Confucian classics they possessed could compare and correct them in front of the stone tablets.

抗战时期出土于成都南城墙的孟蜀石经《毛诗》残片，双排小字为注释　何大江 摄
A fragment of the Mengshu Stone Classics' *Classic of Poetry* unearthed from the southern city wall of Chengdu during the War of Resistance Against Japan, the annotations are in twin-row, small characters. (Photographer: He Dajiang)

孟蜀石经《尚书》残片　何大江 摄
A fragment of the Mengshu Stone Classics' *Book of Documents*. (Photographer: He Dajiang)

孟蜀石经始刻于后蜀广政七年（944年），由宰相毋昭裔主持。其时雕版印刷术已经发明，但并非所有人都有条件置办整套的儒家经典书籍，所以石经仍然承担着一种“石质图书馆”的功能，可供莘莘学子抄录。

孟蜀石经最初所刻经典为《周易》《尚书》《毛诗》《周礼》《仪礼》《礼记》《春秋左氏传》（未完成）《论

The Mengshu Stone Classics was first engraved in the seventh year of the Guangzheng era of the Later Shu (944 AD), under the supervision of Prime Minister Wu Zhaoyi. Although woodblock printing had already been invented at that time, not everyone had the means to acquire a complete set of Confucian classics. Thus, the Stone Classics continued to serve as a "stone library," available for diligent students to transcribe.

Initially, the Mengshu Stone Classics included ten works: *Zhou Yi* (the Book of Changes), *Shang Shu* (the Book of Documents), *Mao Shi* (Mao Poetry),

语》《孝经》和《尔雅》十部。后蜀灭亡，宋朝又补刻了《春秋左氏传》的后半部分以及《春秋公羊传》《春秋穀梁传》。

1123年《孟子》的镌刻完成，是一个标志性的时间点——儒家“十三经”的概念因此诞生。从此，儒家文献由“五经”“六经”“九经”等范式定型为“十三经”。

中国历史共出现过七种石经，唯一带注释的则是孟蜀石经。注文为双行，列于经文之下。有经有注，显然是一种信息含量更丰富的读本。

孟蜀石经规模宏大，其中《左传》三十卷共计三十四万五千八百四十四字，《礼记》二十卷共计十九万六千七百五十一字（皆含序、注）。逾千块石碑，立于石经堂之中，这是一种怎样让人震撼的场景，是一种怎样厚重的文化沉潜。

高朕所建周公礼殿，在唐初改为孔庙。

事实上，春秋末年开始的祭祀孔子的建制典礼，仅仅限于曲阜，且为私家性质，而由官方建立的孔庙，差不多还要在周公礼殿三百年后才出现。周公礼殿，不仅是中国古代“庙学合一”的最早标本，也与文翁石室一道，成为蜀学的精神家园。

Zhou Li (the Rites of Zhou), *Yi Li* (the Etiquette), *Li Ji* (the Book of Rites), *Chun Qiu Zuo Shi Zhuan* (Zuo's Spring and Autumn Annals, incomplete), *Lun Yu* (the Analects of Confucius), *Xiao Jing* (the Classic of Filial Piety), and *Er Ya* (Exegesis). After the downfall of the Later Shu, the latter half of the *Chun Qiu Zuo Shi Zhuan* was supplemented in the Song Dynasty, together with the *Chun Qiu Gong Yang Zhuan* and the *Chun Qiu Gu Liang Zhuan* (Spring and Autumn Annals of Guliang) added.

In 1123, the engraving of *Mencius* was completed, marking a significant moment to gave rise to the concept of the Confucian “Thirteen Classics”. From this point onward, Confucian literature transitioned from paradigms like “Five Classics”, “Six Classics”, “Nine Classics” to the established “Thirteen Classics”.

In Chinese history, seven editions of Stone Classics emerged, with the Mengshu Stone Classics being the only one annotated. The annotations were written in two lines beneath the text, providing readers with a richer source of information.

The monumental Mengshu Stone Classics consisted of 30 volumes of *Zuo Zhuan* with a total of 345,844 characters and 20 volumes of *Li Ji* with a total of 196,751 characters, including prefaces and annotations. With over a thousand stone tablets standing in the Stone Classics Hall, the scene is awe-inspiring, representing a profound cultural legacy.

The temple initially established by Gao Zhen as the Zhou Gong Lidian (The Ritual Hall of Zhou Gong) was later converted into the Confucius Temple during the early Tang Dynasty.

In fact, formal ceremonies honoring Confucius began in the late Spring and Autumn Period, mainly centered in Qufu and of a private nature. It took almost three hundred years after the establishment of the Zhou Gong Lidian for officially sanctioned Confucius Temples to appear. The Zhou Gong Lidian,

到了唐代，房玄龄建议取消周公之祀，改为专祭孔子，这也是成都孔庙（文庙）的起源。而一直到民国，每年的全省祭孔典礼亦都在此处。

礼殿虽然改为文庙，但建筑整体风貌依然保持，外形古朴，柱子方正，此即南宋赵明诚在千年后之所见。

不管是礼殿还是孔庙，都传承了文翁崇文重教的宗旨，不仅具有祭拜功能，同时还一直是教育机构之所在。

西汉末年，公孙述据蜀称帝，文翁所创郡学自然提档为国家级的教育机构——太学。

公孙述被灭，改回郡学。

东汉末年，刘焉为益州牧，改郡学为州学。

刘备称帝，改太学。

后蜀时立石经于此，亦为太学。

南宋赵明诚所见，为府学。

元代，建石室书院于此。

明代，设府学；用于乡试的贡院、士子考前必拜的文昌宫，也建于此。

清顺治二年（1645年），孔庙失火被焚，顺治十八年（1661年）重建孔庙，康熙四十三年（1704年）于孔庙西侧建锦江书院。

serving as an early example of the integration of temple and school in ancient China, along with the Wen Weng's Stone Chamber, became the spiritual home of Shu Studies.

During the Tang Dynasty, Fang Xuanling proposed discontinuing the worship of Zhou Gong and instead dedicating the temple solely to Confucius, marking the origin of Chengdu Confucius Temple. This practice continued until the early 20th century, where annual Confucius worship ceremonies for the entire province were held at this location.

Although the Lidian was transformed into a Wenmiao (Confucian Temple), the overall architectural style remained simple and ancient, with square pillars, as witnessed by Zhao Mingcheng during the Southern Song Dynasty, almost a millennium later.

Regardless of being a Lidian or a Confucian Temple, both continued the educational mission of Wen Weng, focusing not only on worship but also serving as educational institutions.

In the late Western Han period, Gongsun Shu declared himself emperor in Shu, and the county school created by Wen Weng naturally evolved into a national-level educational institution–the Taixue (Imperial Academy).

After the defeat of Gongsun Shu, it reverted to being a county school.

In the late Eastern Han period, when Liu Yan became the Governor of Yizhou, he changed the county school to a provincial school. When Liu Bei declared himself emperor, it was upgraded to Taixue.

During the Later Shu regime, stone classics were established in the Taixue.

In the Southern Song Dynasty, as witnessed by Zhao Mingcheng, the institution was referred to as Fuxue (Prefectural School).

During the Yuan Dynasty, the Shishi Shuyuan

郡学、太学、州学、府学，名称的改变，意味着行政区划的调整，或者政权的更迭，但基本上一直到清代，文翁石室之所在，一直是成都乃至四川地区官办最高学府。

1902年，对于两千年皆为文教重地的这一方地来说，具有划时代意义。这一年，文翁石室旧址上建起了成都府师范学堂，这是成都历史上首所近现代意义的中等学校；1905年，清政府宣布废除科举，该校更名为成都府中学堂。1913年，更名为成都联合县立中学校，从一张老照片上“石室同学联合会”的称谓以及上方的横匾可以看出，当时的学子亦以文翁石室的传人自居。

今日的文翁路之上，最显眼的标识便是石室中学的仿古建筑。那由方形柱构成的大门，是符合《金石录》对周公礼殿门柱的描述的。

学校之传承，校史之延续，是一个综合因素，校址、师生、经费来源、行政规划、所有权归属，都应该考虑。仅就文翁所建郡学，实际上最迟在西汉灭亡、公孙述称帝之际即已断绝。能够传承的，无非是精神而已。而文翁之精神是否得到传承，也非自我标榜即可认定。

从清末的成都府师范学堂以

(Stone Chamber Academy) was established here.

In the Ming Dynasty, it was designated as Fuxue (Prefectural School), and structures such as the Gongyuan (Imperial Examination Hall) used for the provincial examinations and the Wenchang Palace, where scholars would pray before exams, were also built on this site.

In the second year of the Shunzhi era in the Qing Dynasty (1645), a fire destroyed the Confucius Temple, but it was rebuilt in the eighteenth year of Shunzhi's reign (1661). In the forty-third year of Kangxi's reign(1704), the Jinjiang Shuyuan (Jinjiang Academy) was established on the west side of the Confucius Temple.

Despite changes in the names from Junxue (County School), Taixue (Imperial Academy), Zhouxue (Provincial School), Fuxue (Prefectural School), reflecting adjustments in administrative divisions or shifts in political power, up until the Qing Dynasty, the site of Wenweng Shishi (Wen Weng Stone Chamber) remained the location of the highest official educational institution in Chengdu and the broader Sichuan region.

In the year 1902, a momentous transformation took place in this region, which had been a center of culture and education for two millennia. On the old site of Wen Weng Shishi, the Chengdu Prefectural Normal School was established, marking the inception of the first modern secondary school in Chengdu's history. In 1905, following the Qing government's decision to abolish the imperial examination system, the school was renamed Chengdu Prefectural Middle School. By 1913, it underwent another name change to Chengdu United County Public Middle School. From an old photograph displaying the title “Shishi Students Union” and the horizontal plaque above, it is evident that the students of that time identified themselves as descendants of Wen Weng Shishi.

降，在石室旧址上建校，能否视为对文翁石室（其实质是西汉官办学校——成都郡学）的传承，其实大可商榷。若不问青红皂白，强纳古人入校史，恐有拉大旗作虎皮之嫌；更以司马相如、卓文君、扬雄为校友，则未免贻笑于天下。倒是若真能传承文翁之志，便不负其卓然深远之教化。

The present-day Wen Weng Road prominently features the replica of ancient architecture belonging to Shishi Middle School. The gate, composed of square pillars, conforms to the description of the door pillars of Zhou Gong Lidian in the *Jin Shi Lu*.

The heritage of the school and the continuation of its history involves a comprehensive set of factors such as the school's location, faculty and students, funding sources, administrative planning, and ownership. Concerning the county school established by Wen Weng, it had effectively ceased no later than the downfall of the Western Han Dynasty and the self-proclamation of Emperor by Gongsun Shu. What can be passed down is essentially the spirit. Whether Wen Weng's spirit has been inherited cannot be solely determined by self-proclamation.

Since the late Qing Dynasty, starting with Chengdu Prefectural Normal School on the site of Shishi, the establishment of schools of different names has taken place. Whether this can be regarded as the inheritance of Wenweng Shishi (essentially the official school of the Western Han Dynasty – Chengdu County School) is a matter open to debate. Without delving into the details, forcibly incorporating ancient figures into the school's history might be seen as an attempt to exaggerate its prestige. Moreover, claiming figures like Sima Xiangru, Zhuo Wenjun, and Yang Xiong as alumni might invite ridicule. However, if the school truly embodies the spirit of Wen Weng, it would not disappoint his profound influence on education.

支机石
Zhiji Stone

一块褐色的大石头，高约两米，半腰处浅窝旁曾有篆文“支机石”三字。

巨石既然在成都街头立了数千年，便一定会附着些神话。有故事说，它是天上织女的垫机石，去成都找严君平就可以知道答案。

严君平倒是真有其人，他就在支机石旁边卖卜，给人算命。他是个小人物，不过成都有三条街道以他命名。

A brown boulder stands roughly two meters high, with a faint hollow at its waist where once bore the seal characters “Zhiji Stone”. Since this colossal stone has stood in the streets of Chengdu for thousands of years, it undoubtedly carries with it some myths. There’s a story that claims it to be used by the celestial Weaver Girl for supporting her loom, and to unveil the answers, one must seek out a man named Yan Junping in Chengdu.

Indeed, Yan Junping was a real person, sitting right next to the Zhiji Stone, practicing divination and fortune-telling. Though a humble figure, he left an indelible mark on Chengdu, with three streets named in his honor.

支机石：*BDO* 见证算命先生的傲娇

Zhiji Stone: BDO Witnessing the Capriciousness of the Fortune-Telling Sage

严君平卜肆

唐 · 岑参

君平曾卖卜，卜肆芜已久。
至今杖头钱，时时地上有。
不知支机石，还在人间否。

Yan Junping's Divination Stall

Cen Shen, Tang Dynasty

Junping once sold fortune's game,
The divination stall, overgrown with grass, bears its name.
Coins at the end of his walking cane,
Scattered on the ground, still there remain.
But where has the divining stone flown?
Does it linger in this earthly zone?

767年，唐代大诗人岑参从成都赴任嘉州刺史，为官不过一年即被罢官。因时局纷乱、东归受阻而滞留成都，769年秋冬之季病逝于客舍。

诗中的卜肆，是汉代严君平算命卖卜之处。数千年来，此地还竖着一块富有传奇色彩的巨石，因严君平居于此，后世也就编出一段他与此石相关的神话。严君平大隐于世，却因学问道德而名传千古。

对于这样的前贤，岑参自然是高山仰止，但发出“不知支机石，还在人间否”的疑问，显然并未至严君平故居一拜。究其原因，应当是因为一病沉疴，处于生命最后阶段了。

In the year 767 AD, the renowned Tang Dynasty poet Cen Shen set out on a journey from Chengdu for an official post in Jiazhou. After just a year of service, he was dismissed from office. Then, he was stranded in Chengdu and was unable to return to the east, due to the turmoil of the times. In 769 AD, he died of illness at a guesthouse in Chengdu.

The poem speaks of Yan Junping's divination stall, where he foretold the future for a living. Next to his stall was a legendary stone, thus myths were created about his association with this stone. Yan Junping, a recluse known for his wisdom and morals, left a lasting legacy.

For such a sage, Cen Shen naturally admired deeply, yet he expressed uncertainty about the Stone's whereabout with the question, "Does it linger in this earthly zone?" The reason likely lies in Cen Shen's advanced illness, indicating that he was approaching the end of his life, and apparently he didn't pay a visit to Yan Junping's former residence.

一块被神话的石头

这是一块褐色的大石头，高约2米，宽0.8米，半腰处有一圆锥形的

A Mythologized Stone

A large brown stone, about two meters high and 0.8 meters wide, bearing a shallow, conical hollow at its waist. On the side of the hollow, there once existed

浅窝。浅窝旁，曾有唐人铭勒的篆文“支机石”三字，如今早已蚀灭。背面的棱上，还有一道长方形的凿痕。

支机石是一块被神话的石头，石的被神话来源于人的被神话。最早将严君平神话的，是西晋张华《博物志》。然而《博物志》中，并没有提及此石。

seal characters engraved by a Tang poet, stating “Zhiji Stonc”, which have now eroded away. On the back, there is a rectangular chiseled mark along its edge.

The Zhiji Stone is a mythical stone, and the myth surrounding the stone originates from the myth surrounding a person. The earliest mention of the mythologized Yan Junping is found in the *Bowu Zhi,* the Record of Strange Things, by Zhang Hua of the Western Jin Dynasty. However, Zhang Hua’s work does not mention this stone.

民国时期上海抛球场系列明信片上的支机石（资料图片）
Zhiji Stone featured in a series of postcards depicting the Shanghai Ball-Tossing Grounds during the Republic of China period. (Archival Image)

明代曹学佺《蜀中广记》将支机石和名人张骞加入其中，故事变得更为丰满。说是汉武帝时，博望侯张骞出使大夏（今阿富汗北），在一条河的尽头看见一个女子在织锦，她丈夫则牵着一头牛在吃草。张骞问这是什么地方，那女子指着旁边一块大石头

In the Ming Dynasty, Cao Xuequan included the Zhiji Stone and the famous figure Zhang Qian in his *Shuzhong Guangji*, making the story more elaborate. It is said that during the reign of Emperor Wu of the Han Dynasty, Zhang Qian, the Marquis Bowang, was sent as an envoy to Daxia (north of present-day Afghanistan). At the end of a river, he saw a woman weaving brocade, while her husband was grazing a cow. Zhang Qian asked about the place, and the

说，把它运到成都去问严君平吧。

张骞找到严君平，后者掐指一算，说："怪不得去年我看星相，见有客星侵入牛郎星和织女星之间，原来是你坐船跑到天上的银河去了。"那块石头，是织女拿来垫织机用的；那个浅窝，则是用来置放织机机脚的。

世人编撰这个故事，将读万卷书的严君平、行万里路的张骞强行拉来背书，总算给伫立街头的BDO找了个来历，强行纳入既有的认知框架。

其实，《博物志》里来往于银河、大海之间的浮槎，是诞生于一千七百年前的宇宙飞船，是古人的想象力之舟，而支机石上的圆锥形浅窝对应于织机机脚置放处，则有一种奇异的时空转换感——如此具有未来感的想象，最终却又进入"掐指一算"的套路，想象力的宇宙飞船，本可以探索星辰大海，但还未启航就熄火，殊为可惜。

即便是古人，只要具有思考能力，也不会相信这类穿凿附会。张骞和严君平虽然都是西汉人，但前者去世多年后者才出生，自然不可能对话。严君平为张骞解惑，属于"关公战秦琼"，但严君平被人景仰是真的。自六朝至唐宋，其卜肆故居一直为人

woman pointed to a large stone nearby, suggesting that he should take it to Chengdu and ask Yan Junping about it.

When Zhang Qian found Yan Junping, the latter calculated with fingers and said, "No wonder last year when I observed the stars, I saw a guest star entering between Altair and Vega. It turns out it was you, sailing on a boat to the Milky Way in the sky." That stone was used by the celestial Weaver Girl to support her loom, and the shallow hollow was used to place the loom's legs.

People have fabricated this story, forcefully pulling in Yan Junping, who read thousands of books, and Zhang Qian, who traveled thousands of miles, to serve as endorsements. So, they managed to give this BDO standing on the street, a somewhat plausible origin, forcibly fitting it into an existing cognitive framework.

In reality, the floating raft traveling between the Milky Way and the sea in *Bowu Zhi* was the cosmic spaceship born 1,700 years ago—an imaginative vessel of ancient people. The cone-shaped shallow hollow on the Zhiji Stone corresponding to the placement of the loom's legs creates a peculiar sense of space-time transformation. Such futuristic imagination, ultimately reduced to the routine of "calculating with fingers", could have been applied in exploring the vast cosmos but stalled before even setting sail, which is a pity.

Even ancient people with thinking capabilities would not easily believe such far-fetched associations. While Zhang Qian and Yan Junping were both from the Western Han era, the former had passed away many years before the latter was born, making their conversation impossible. Yan Junping explaining things to Zhang Qian is akin to the drama of "Guan Gong fighting Qin Qiong", in which the characters of different times

供奉祭祀。

严君平长于老庄之学，被尊为“严真人”。不过，严真人去世了一百多年，道教的起源天师道才产生。这是因为严之学问路数近于道家，被教徒追封而致。到了五代，道教领袖杜光庭在前蜀当大官，改君平故居为严真观继续崇奉。

为弘教故，杜光庭还编了一本《道教灵验记》，专门讲些灵异事件，其中对于支机石上的那条凿痕，也有个故事。说是太尉敦煌公喜欢新奇的事物，让人从支石机上凿一块下来，以制作器物。敲凿之时，周遭风起雾涌。停止凿打则风雾消失，再次凿打风雾又起。这位敦煌公好奇心极度强烈，又叫人把它挖起来，结果这一次是天色昏暗、雷鸣电闪。

故事里的太尉敦煌公，笔者考据应是北魏并州刺史李宝或其子李茂，至于他们是否到过成都、见到过支机石，当然不重要，因为这本来就是拉大旗作虎皮，仅供愚民。

然而，街头之BDO，总是会引人揣想其来历，附加些故事。晚清傅崇榘编《成都通览》，将支机石与天涯石一道视为从天而降之陨星。傅氏之说，已具有一定现代科学意识。但实际上，它们也并不是陨石，而是跟前

are messed up; but Yan Junping's revered status is genuine. From the Six Dynasties to the Tang and Song Dynasties, people continuously offered sacrifices to his former divination dwelling.

Yan Junping was honored as "Yan Zhenren" (Yan, the immortal) for his proficiency in the teachings of Laozi and Zhuangzi. However, Yan Zhenren had been gone for more than a hundred years when Taoism's origin, the Celestial Masters Dao, emerged. This was because Yan's studies were close to Taoism, leading believers to posthumously confer honors. During the Five Dynasties, Taoist leader Du Guangting held a high position in the Former Shu, turning Yan's former residence into the Yan Zhen Temple for continued reverence.

To propagate the teachings, Du Guangting compiled a book titled *Records of Taoist Miracles*, specifically recounting supernatural events. Among them is a story about the chiseled mark on the Zhiji Stone. It tells of General Dunhuang liking novel things, instructing people to chisel a piece from the Zhiji Stone to make a utensil. During the chiseling, the surroundings became misty and windy. When the chiseling stopped, the wind and mist disappeared; upon resuming, they returned. Intrigued, General Dunhuang ordered the stone to be excavated, resulting in darkening skies, thunder, and lightning.

As I see it, the General Dunhuang mentioned in the story is likely to be Li Bao, the Inspector of Bingzhou during the Northern Wei Dynasty, or his son Li Mao. Whether they visited Chengdu or saw the Zhiji Stone is not crucial, as it is clearly an exaggeration, crafted solely for the purpose of duping the public.

However, the BDO on the street always prompts people to speculate about its origin and add some stories. In the late Qing Dynasty, Fu Chongju compiled *A Comprehensive Overview of Chengdu* and

文杜甫所见的巨大石笋一般，都是大石崇拜的遗迹。而支机石上的浅窝，或为宋末元初的某一次战争中，被用于支垫发炮石机所致；棱上的长痕，则可能是将大石放倒后在地上拖曳而造成的。

categorized both the Tianya Stone and the Zhiji Stone as a meteorite fallen from the sky. Fu's interpretation already reflected a certain level of modern scientific awareness. However, in reality, these stones are not meteorites but remnants of the ancient worship of large stones, similar to the enormous stone stalactite mentioned by Du Fu in the previous text. The shallow hollows on the Zhiji Stone may have resulted from being used as a support for a cannon during a war in the late Song or early Yuan Dynasty, while the long groove on the edge could have been caused by dragging the stone on the ground after it was toppled.

严真观与关帝庙

世外高人的故居，加一块神秘的巨石，是严真观的主要构成。

到了明代，支机石上建有一小亭，以避日晒雨淋。

清初因八旗驻防成都，在大城西侧建满城，供八旗兵及家眷居住，严真观即在满城之中。

君平故居及支机石所在，建成街道最初名叫仁里二条胡同。“胡同”是北方对里弄街巷的称呼，一说源于蒙古语中的“水井”。因为严君平的名气太大，这条街也被称为君平胡同。

Yanzheng Temple and Guandi Temple

The abode of this reclusive sage, combined with a mysterious giant stone, forms the main structure of Yanzheng Temple.

In the Ming Dynasty, a small pavilion was built on the Zhiji Stone to provide shade from the sun and protection from rain.

In the early Qing Dynasty, due to the presence of the Eight Banners stationed in Chengdu, a residential area called "Mancheng, the Manchu City" was built on the west side of the city, accommodating the Eight Banners soldiers and their families. Yanzheng Temple was located within this Manchu city.

The street where the former residence of Junping and the Zhiji Stone are situated was originally named Renli Second Hutong. "Hutong" is a term used in the north of China to refer to narrow lanes or alleys, possibly originating from the Mongolian word for "water well". Due to the great fame of Yan Junping, this street was also called Junping Hutong.

1910年的满城关帝庙 （英）恩内斯特·亨利·威尔逊摄
The Guandi Temple in Mancheng, photographed in 1910. (Photographer: Ernest Henry Wilson, UK)

修筑满城时，在原严真观旧址上，建立了祭祀“武圣”关羽的关帝庙。

关帝庙毁于清末。民国年间，君平胡同更名为支机石街。到了1924年，卢作孚先生在此处建支机石公园。袁庭栋先生《成都街巷志》称，因为战乱纷频，公园并未建成。不过，一张支机石公园的老照片，让此说并不成立。

由出版家舒新城1924年拍摄的公园大门，竖匾上“支機石公園”几个字清晰可见，“機”字旁还挂着一盏玻璃灯。另有数份资料显示，支机石公园还有数百株或上千株大楠木树，也因此被称为“森林公园”。

支机石公园东至同仁路，西临老西门城墙，占地十余亩，呈长条状。原支机石庙包含在公园之内，进入公园大门就能见到耸立的支机石。园中那些生长了上百年的大楠木，在抗日战争期间尽被砍伐。战火中的成都

During the construction of Mancheng, a Guandi Temple was erected on the original site of Yanzheng Temple, dedicated to the worship of the “Martial Saint” Guan Yu.

Guandi Temple was destroyed in the late Qing Dynasty. During the Republican era, Junping Hutong was renamed Zhijishi Street. In 1924, Mr. Lu Zuofu built the Zhijishi Park at this location. According to Mr. Yuan Tingdong’s *Chengdu Streets and Alleys Chronicle*, due to frequent wars, the park was not completed. However, an old photo of Zhijishi Park disproves this claim.

A photo of the park’s entrance taken by the publisher Shu Xincheng in 1924 shows the words “支 機 石 公 園” (Zhijishi Park) on the vertical signboard, and next to the character “機”, there is a glass lamp hanging. Several sources also indicate that Zhijishi Park had several hundred or even thousands of large Nanmu trees, earning it the title of a forest park.

Zhijishi Park extends from Tongren Road in the east to the Old Ximen City Wall in the west, covering an area of over ten Mu in an elongated shape. The original Zhijishi Temple is included within the park, and upon entering the park gate, one can see the towering Zhijishi stone. During the Chinese People’s War of Resistance Against Japanese Aggression, the large Nanmu trees in the park, which had grown for over a hundred years, were all cut down. The people

人，整日忙于跑警报、躲空袭，公园自然就荒废了。

对于支机石的去处，《成都街巷志》称："1985年，支机石终于得以移入文化公园。"然而，数位亲历者证实了1958年的说法。《成都街巷志》之说，实为笔误。

of Chengdu, caught in the flames of war, were busy with air raid alerts and seeking shelter, leaving the park neglected.

Regarding the relocation of Zhiji stone, *Chengdu Streets and Alleys Chronicle* states that "in 1985, Zhiji stone was finally moved to the Cultural Park." However, several eyewitnesses have confirmed the 1958 account. The mention in *Chengdu Streets and Alleys Chronicle* is indeed a typographical error.

迁于文化公园内支矶山上的支机石　何大江 摄

Zhiji Stone relocated to Zhiji Mountain within the Cultural Park. (Photographer: He Dajiang)

据原四川师范大学影视学院新闻中心主任王华回忆：1959年春节前后，他就读于宁夏街小学时，低年级八个班的同学曾在少先队大队辅导员的带领下，自带锅碗柴火，到文化公园搞野餐。同学们看到支机石，都非常好奇，更有调皮的学生用弹弓瞄准射击。

According to Wang Hua, former director of the News Center at the School of Film and Television of Sichuan Normal University, in the spring of 1959, when he was attending Ningxia Street Elementary School, lower-grade students from eight classes, led by the Young Pioneers instructor, brought pots, bowls, and firewood for a picnic in the Cultural Park. The students were curious when they saw the Zhiji stone, and some mischievous ones aimed at it with slingshots and shot the stone.

作家杨彤小学期间（1976—1981年）去文化公园玩耍时，总要把脑袋放进支机石的浅窝里，一比大小。此事多年来还一直被家人取笑。

土生土长的成都人、知青文化研究者谢光治，也曾于1970年代初在文化公园见到过支机石。谢光治说，1958年成都扩建公园时，迁移了很多居民大院里的古树名木以及散落在街头的文化遗存到各公园内。他回忆道，支机石曾伫立在文化公园湖边，他还于1980年代初在报纸上发表过文章，建议修亭保护。

如今的支机石已被迁至文化公园一小山顶，整块石头被封进玻璃之内，上再置亭，以免受风雨侵蚀。

Yang Tong, the author, used to play in the Cultural Park during his elementary school days from 1976 to 1981. He would often put his head into the shallow pit of the Zhiji stone to compare sizes, a childhood memory that his family still teases him about.

Chengdu native and researcher of Intellectual Youth culture, Xie Guangzhi, also saw Zhiji stone in the early 1970s at Cultural Park. He recalled that in 1958, when Chengdu expanded its parks, many ancient trees and cultural relics from residents' courtyards and scattered in the streets were moved to various parks. Xie Guangzhi reminisced that Zhiji stone used to stand by the lake in Cultural Park, and in the early 1980s, he published an article suggesting the construction of a pavilion for its protection.

Nowadays, Zhiji stone has been relocated to the top of a small hill in Cultural Park, encased in glass, with a pavilion on top to prevent erosion from wind and rain.

“支机石”还是“支矶石”？

整篇文章都在说“支机石”，那为什么这条街却叫“支矶石街”呢?

不时有市民向报社反映，说他们所在的街道本来是支机石街，路牌上却写成了“支矶石街”。到底是“机”还是“矶”，几乎成了一段公案。且以一种非常有价值的原始资料——历年出版的地图为脉络，去探究一番。

光绪五年（1879年）地图上，支矶石街被称作“仁里二条胡同”，这

“支机石” or “支矶石”?

Why is this street called “支矶石街” when the whole article is about “支机石”?

Regarding the name of the street, there has been confusion among citizens who claim that their street was originally “支机石街” (Zhijishi Street), but the road sign reads “支矶石街”(Zhijishi Street). Whether it is “机” or “矶” has almost become a public case. Let's take a very valuable source material - maps published over the years - as a powerful common strand to explore.

The article examines historical maps to trace the origin of the name. In the map from the fifth year of the Guangxu era (1879), the street is called “Renli

也是它最初的名字。而于光绪二十年（1894年）绘制出版的《四川省城街道图》，也沿用了此名称。

宣统三年（1911年），清王朝覆灭前夕出版的《成都街道二十七区图》，注明为“君平胡同”。严君平的人格力量，穿越两千年的时光，再次显现。

到了民国年间出版的《成都明细图》，标明为“支机石街”，这也合情合理。有学者根据地图上“中山纪念碑”的建成时间——1928年，以及“四川大学校”“国立成都大学”“四川农业学校”等几所学校存在的时间——皆于1931年合并到国立四川大学，考据、分析得出结论：此版地图制作于1928—1931年。

而到了民国二十二年（1933年）年底制作的《成都街市图》上，却变成了“支矶石街”。

“机”和“矶”一字之差，意义却并不相同。“矶”的本义为水边突出的岩石或石滩，比如长江边有采石矶——南宋时，名将虞允文在此大败金兵；传说诗仙李白因为酒后在矶边捉月，溺亡于此。而“机”的意思，在此处即为织机，显然跟这条街的由来更为相符。

“支机石”这一文化意象中，有

Second Hutong," which was its original name. The street retained this name in the street map of Sichuan Province drawn and published in the twentieth year of the Guangxu era (1894).

In 1911, the third year of the Xuantong era, during the last days of the Qing Dynasty, the *Map of Chengdu Streets in Twenty-Seven District* was published, designating the street as "Junping Hutong" (君平胡同). The force of Yan Junping's personality, spanning two thousand years, began to manifest itself again.

In the *Chengdu Detailed Map* published during the Republican era, the street is labeled as "Zhiji Stone Street" (支机石街), which seems reasonable. Scholars, based on the completion time of the "Zhongshan Memorial" in 1928 and the existence of several schools such as "Sichuan University", "National Chengdu University", and "Sichuan Agricultural School"— all merging into National Sichuan University in 1931— concluded that this version of the map was created between 1928 and 1931.

However, by the end of the year 1933, on the *Chengdu Street Map* created during the 22nd year of the Republic of China (1933), the name changed to "Zhiji Stone Street" (支矶石街).

The difference between "机" (ji) and "矶" (ji) may be a single character, but their meanings are distinct. The original meaning of "矶" refers to a protruding rock or stone beach by the water, such as the Chai Shi Ji on the Yangtze River where General Yu Yunwen achieved a great victory over the Jin army during the Southern Song Dynasty. Legend has it that the poet Li Bai drowned here after attempting to catch the moon while intoxicated. On the other hand, the meaning of "机" in this context refers to a weaving machine, which is more in line with the street's origin.

"机"又有"石"，很容易被写作兼具"石"之意、"机"之音的"矶"字。因为用字不规范，加之不知源流的望文生义，"支机石街"就变成了"支矶石街"。

据曾经生活在这条街多年的老居民回忆，在他们小的时候街名叫"支机石街"，改为"支矶石街"的时间大致是在1986年，并一直延续至今日。

这条街的名字，曾在"支机石街"与"支矶石街"之间来回变动，而最终被确定为后者。不过，地名的确立是具有唯一性的。在现阶段，"支矶石街"才是规范的表述，那块石头却不能叫作"支矶石"——如果像把支矶石街的支机石复制品下直接标注为"支矶石"，就有忘却街名本原或不识字义之嫌。

The cultural imagery of "支机石" incorporates both "石" (stone) and the sound of "机" (ji), making it easy for the character "矶" to be mistakenly used due to unclear sources and misinterpretation. "支机石街" thus became "支矶石街".

According to the recollections of long-time residents who lived on this street, the name was initially "支机石街", changed to "支矶石街" around 1986, and has continued in this form to the present day.

Despite the fluctuation between these variations, "支矶石街" is now the standardized expression for the street's unique name, while the stone itself should not be referred to as "支矶石". If a replica of the Zhiji Stone on Zhiji Stone Street is directly labeled as "支矶石", it might lead to the oversight of the original street name or a misunderstanding of its meaning.

空谷幽兰

一条街道，如果以一个人的名字命名，该是何等的荣耀。严君平之名跟三条成都街道有关，分别是支矶石街（君平胡同）、君平街和君平巷，而他不过一个视名利若无物的隐士。

严君平是西汉时期蜀郡成都人，辞赋大家扬雄的老师。他本来姓庄，

A hermit, As an orchid in a hollow valley

It's an extraordinary honor to have a street named after an individual. The name of Yan Junping is associated with three streets in Chengdu, namely Zhiji Stone Street (formerly Junping Hutong), Junping Street, and Junping Lane. However, Yan Junping was merely a hermit who disregarded fame and fortune.

Yan Junping was a native of Chengdu in Shu County during the Western Han Dynasty. He was the teacher of Yang Xiong, the famous master of Ci

叫庄遵，字君平。到了东汉，班固写《汉书》，其中的《王贡两龚鲍传》收录了一系列隐逸、清节之士，因为要避汉明帝刘庄的讳，就把庄改成了严，严君平其名由此得以传世。

庄遵是易经学者、哲学家，他以《周易》阐释《老子》，代表作为《老子指归》，凡十万余言。“无身者生，有身者死；趋利者逢患，求福者得祸；不召自来，不迎而遇……听造化者，煞之不忧，生之不喜……”这段见于《老子指归》中的文字，很能体现出他的哲学观和处世之道：祸福相依，有即是无。有了这样的心态，自然就明白自己要在世上追求什么了。

搞哲学研究并不是严君平的职业，他的本职是占卜——借用蓍草、龟甲等工具，形成一定的卦象，再以周易之理解读。

即便在汉代，卜筮也是一种底层职业。然而，严君平却乐此不疲。他认为这种职业可以为人言明吉凶，而这种祸福却并非全由天定，可以靠人力转换，其中有是非正邪之大道。因此，作为卜筮者应当因势利导，借以改良社会风气。

有些人抱着整人害人之心来问命，严君平则给他指出危害，避免其走上歪路。对于当儿子的，就在解卦

and Fu. Originally surnamed Zhuang, his name was Zhuang Zun, and his courtesy name was Junping. During the Eastern Han Dynasty, when Ban Gu wrote *Biographies of Wang, Gong, Gongsheng, Gongshe and Bao* in *Book of the Han*, he recorded a series of reclusive and morally upright individuals. To avoid the taboo of mentioning the Emperor's name, Liu Zhuang, the character "庄" (Zhuang) in Zhuang Zun's name was changed to "严" (Yan), and thus Yan Junping's name was preserved for posterity.

Zhuang Zun was a Yijing scholar and a philosopher who interpreted the *Tao Te Ching* through the *Book of Changes*. His representative work, *Laozi Zhigui*, consisted of over a hundred thousand words. "Those without a body live, those with a body die; Those who seek benefits encounter troubles, while those who seek blessings get misfortunes; weal and woe come uninvited... Those who submit to the will of nature do not either worry or rejoice", the excerpt from *Laozi Zhigui* reflects his philosophical views and principles of living: misfortune and fortune are interconnected, and having something implies having nothing. With such a mindset, one naturally understands what to pursue in life.

Despite being a philosopher, Yan Junping's primary profession was divination, using tools such as yarrow stalks and tortoise shells to form hexagrams and interpreting them based on the principles of the *Book of Changes (Yijing)*.

Even in the Han Dynasty, divination was considered a low-status occupation. However, Yan Junping enjoyed this work and believed that divination could provide guidance on good and bad fortunes. He saw divination not as predetermined by heaven but as a way to change weal and woe through human effort, emphasizing the importance of morality and righteousness in this process, so as to improve societal values.

时讲明应当孝敬老人；有兄弟的，就助其团结友爱；帮国家或个人办事的，就让他要学会忠诚。君平先生略加统计，发现超过一半的顾客听从了自己的劝告，于是也从中得到了莫大的满足感。

卜筮业从业者虽然地位不高，却很能挣钱。不过，君平先生却志不在此，每日只给数人解卦指路，赚够了一天的伙食费就收摊回家。岑参诗中“至今杖头钱，时时地上有”句，说的就是此事。所谓“杖头钱”，指的是挂在杖头用于买酒的百文铜钱。时时有，是说先生需要花点小钱时，才去摆摊。

当然，君平先生回家也不是虚度光阴，而是收了数名弟子，讲解《道德经》；或者，在竹简上写他的《老子指归》和《易学骨髓》。

君平先生的子弟，后来出了个大人物，就是与司马相如齐名的辞赋大家扬雄。扬雄扬名于京师之后，多次在朝廷诸贤面前称颂君平的道德文章。扬雄说，不要看诸位都是当大官的，我老师还不一定想见你们哩。扬雄有个官朋友叫李强，偏不信邪。后来机缘偶合，李强出任益州牧，就想检验一下扬雄那句话。扬雄告诫他：“你见我老师不要摆官威。礼贤下士

Some people approached Yan Junping with malicious intentions, seeking to harm others through divination. However, Yan Junping would caution them about the harm they intended and advise them to avoid the wrong path. For those seeking advice on family matters, he emphasized filial piety; for those with brothers, he encouraged unity and friendship; and for those involved in national affairs or someone else's business, he stressed the importance of loyalty. Yan Junping, after a brief statistical analysis, found that over half of his clients heeded his advice, bringing him great satisfaction.

While diviners in this trade could earn a decent income, Yan Junping was not focused on accumulating wealth. He provided divination services to only a few people each day, earning enough for his daily meals before closing his stall and returning home. The line in Cen Shen's poem, “至今杖头钱，时时地上有” (“Coins at the end of his walking cane, Scattered on the ground, still there remain.”), refers to this practice. The term “杖头钱” (Zhangtou Qian) refers to copper coins hanging on the cane for purchasing wine. It indicates that Yan Junping would only set up his stall when he needed a little money for expenses.

Certainly, Mr. Junping did not loaf away his time after he returned home. He took on several disciples, expounding on the *Tao Te Ching*, or he wrote his own works such as *Laozi Zhigui* and *Yixue Gusui*, the Quintessence of Yi on bamboo slips.

Mr. Junping's disciples included a prominent figure, Yang Xiong, a master of Ci and Fu who gained fame in the capital. Yang Xiong often praised Mr. Junping's moral writings in front of the wise men at the court. He once said that not everyone had the privilege to meet his teacher, implying that Mr. Junping might not be willing to see everyone. A friend of Yang Xiong, named Li Qiang, was skeptical.

的话，可能还见得到他。不过，要是想让他出山辅佐你的话，我劝你还是早日打消这个念头。”

李强不信，到了成都之后，果然去见了君平先生。他对严君平居所的阴冷潮湿颇感不适，提议出去走走，晒晒太阳。

“你到蜀地来，众人都想捧场，要给你接驾。我们这一出门，扰民。”君平先生拒绝了，而且不以大官前来拜访为荣，反视之为耻，“再者，人家看见我跟你在一起，还会误以为我跟你有啥交情，这也不好。”会面结果是，李强被君平先生淡定而强大的气场所震慑，根本不好意思把请他出山辅佐的话说出口。

当时蜀地还有个富豪叫罗冲，他对君平先生说：“你为什么不出去当官呢？你要去当官，我可以给你提供车马和服装。”

君平先生却回答道：“别，你这么穷，还来救济我，我哪里敢收哩？”罗冲对有人说自己穷感到不解且愤怒。

“你不穷，为啥每天要熬更守夜，四处奔忙，这么辛辛苦苦地挣钱呢？”君平先生道，“你看我，想花钱的时候才出门，给人解解卦，钱就到手了。现在还有几吊铜钱，摆在桌

Later, when Li Qiang was appointed as the governor of Yizhou (Sichuan), he wanted to test Yang Xiong's claim. Yang Xiong warned him, “If you meet my teacher, don't display your official authority. Using words of respect and humility, you might be able to see him. However, if you wish to persuade him to come out of seclusion and assist you, I advise you to abandon that idea.”

Li Qiang didn't believe him and, upon arriving in Chengdu, decided to visit Mr. Junping. Feeling uncomfortable with the cold and damp conditions of Mr. Junping's residence, Li Qiang suggested going out for a walk in the sun.

“When you come to Shu, everyone wants to welcome you, and they want to escort you. If we go out together, it will disturb the people,” Mr. Junping refused. He didn't see the visit of a high-ranking official as an honor but rather considered it shameful. Moreover, he thought that if people saw him with Li Qiang, they might mistakenly assume he had some relationship with the official, which he found undesirable. The meeting concluded with Li Qiang being awed by Mr. Junping's calm and powerful aura, and he didn't dare express his desire for Mr. Junping to come out of seclusion and assist him.

At that time, there was also a wealthy man named Luo Chong in Shu. He said to Mr. Junping, “Why don't you go into government service? If you want to take an official position, I can provide you with vehicles and clothing.”

Mr. Junping replied, “No, you're so poor, and yet you want to support me. I dare not accept.” Luo Chong, feeling puzzled and angered by being called poor.

“If you are not poor, why do you toil day and night, running around, working so hard to earn money?” Mr. Junping replied, “You see, when I want to spend money, I go out, interpret a few divinations,

子上灰尘都好厚了，还不晓得咋用。这不是钱多得用不完了吗？”听了君平先生的话，罗冲瞬间窒息，说不出话来。

对于名利场，君平先生总结了一句：“益我货者损我神，生我名者杀我身。”总之，这个淡泊名利者活了九十六岁，一直到死都只是个卜筮者，这也证明他隐居于世并不是要走终南捷径，所谓身后之名，完全是无心插柳。

曾经有人问他的学生扬雄：“一个君子，最怕在世上活了一辈子而声名不显。为什么不借那些有名望者之手，成就自己的名声呢？”

扬雄回答道：“君子立德为先，德立则名自立。梁齐楚赵等诸侯，都既富且贵，但他们的名声是如何得来的呢？……蜀郡的严君平先生，深沉无欲，不结交有权势者和富贵者，也不苟且求利。他长时间幽居而不改操守，这样的人才是国家的珍宝啊。即便是随侯之珠、和氏之璧，又岂能与之相比？”

前文提到，成都的支矶石街、君平街和君平巷的得名，都跟严君平有关。支矶石街曾叫君平胡同，而君平街原本是修建满城时，在其南垣所筑的蓝旗官街永济胡同。同样是在民国

and the money is coming. Now, I still have a few copper coins on the table, covered in dust, and I don't know how to use them. Isn't it because I have so much money that I can't spend it all?" Hearing Mr. Junping's words, Luo Chong was momentarily choked and unable to speak.

Regarding the pursuit of fame and wealth, Mr. Junping summarized it with a saying: "What adds to my wealth harms my spirit, and what adds to my reputation detracts from my health." In essence, this person who lived a simple life without seeking fame and wealth lived to be ninety-six years old. Until his death, he remained a diviner, proving that his seclusion from the world was not a shortcut to fame. The posthumous fame was completely unintentional.

Once, someone asked Yang Xiong, Mr. Junping's student, "A nobleman fears nothing more than living a lifetime without gaining recognition in the world. Why not use the hands of those who are renowned to establish one's own reputation?"

Yang Xiong replied, "A nobleman prioritizes virtue, and with virtue established, fame naturally follows. The rulers of states like Liang, Qi, Chu, and Zhao were wealthy and powerful, but how did they get their fame?... Mr. Junping from Shu County has profound virtues, remaining deep and without desire. He avoids associating with those in power and the wealthy, and he isn't resigned to circumstances to seek profit hastily. He has secluded himself for a long time without changing his principles. Such a person is truly a treasure for the country. Even the rare and valuable pearls and jades cannot compare to him."

The previous text mentioned that the names of Chengdu's Zhiji Stone Street, Junping Street, and Junping Lane are all related to Yan Junping. Zhiji Stone Street was once called Junping Hutong, and Junping Street was originally a Blue Banner Official Street called Yongji Hutong, built when the Manchu

年间那次满城大改名中，永济胡同改成了君平街。今日之君平街，东起横陕西街北口接陕西街，西至小南街南口，全长四百二十米。

君平街东段南侧，有一条宽不足四米，长不足二百米的小巷子。这条小巷，原称火巷子，因为重名，在1981年的地名普查中被更名为君平巷。

当年的君平胡同（支矶石街），和今天的君平街离得很近，不到两千米。君平巷则更是与君平街紧紧相连。这三条街的得名，都是为了纪念这位不想当大官也不想挣大钱却有大学问的世外高人。

city was established. Similarly, during the renaming of the city in the Republican era, Yongji Hutong was changed to Junping Street. Today's Junping Street stretches from the north entrance of Hengshanxi Street to the south entrance of Xiaonan Street, with a total length of 420 meters.

On the south side of the eastern section of Junping Street, there is a narrow alley that is less than 4 meters wide and less than 200 meters long. This alley was originally called Huo Lane, but due to the duplicate name, it was renamed Junping Lane in the 1981 geographical name census.

The former Junping Hutong (Zhiji Stone Street) was very close to today's Junping Street, less than two kilometers away. Junping Lane is even more closely connected to Junping Street. The names of these three streets are all in commemoration of Yan Junping, a recluse who didn't aspire to be a high official or earn a fortune but possessed profound knowledge.

第三卷

Volume 3

成汉俑
Cheng Han Figurines

成汉俑最突出的特点，是脸上那双无法忽视的眼睛，它们大得拉满了整个脸颊，而上下眼睑也突出于面部，形成两个大框——让人无法不联想到三星堆青铜面具上那些奇谲之眼。

这，就是纵目吗？

The most striking feature of Cheng Han figurines is their eyes, which dominate the face to an extent that is impossible to ignore. These eyes are so large they span the entire cheeks, with the upper and lower eyelids protruding from the face, forming two prominent frames. This distinctive characteristic irresistibly calls to mind the enigmatic eyes of the bronze masks from Sanxingdui.

Is this what is meant by "Vertical eyes"?

成汉俑：氐人之眼高悬时间隧道
Cheng Han Figurines: The Di People's Eyes Suspend in the Time Tunnel

成都杂诗

清·李调元

纷纷割据竟何存，
天府休言控剑门。
试向筹边楼上望，
暮云低处李雄坟。

Miscellaneous Poem of Chengdu

Li Tiaoyuan, Qing Dynasty

In endless strife, what remains of fractured state?

No boast of Jianmen Pass, the displaced Di fleeing through the natural defensive gate.

From border tower, cast your gaze far and wide,

Where evening clouds over Emperor Li Xiong's tomb abide.

清代文学家李调元这首诗，讲的是西晋因“八王之乱”而分崩离析的年代，氐人流民过剑门关入蜀，在成都建立大成政权的旧事。大成后改国号为汉，史称成汉，李雄则是其开国皇帝。

This poem by Li Tiaoyuan, a literary figure from the Qing Dynasty, tells about the era of the Western Jin Dynasty, which fell apart due to the "Upheaval of the Eight Princes". During this time, the Di people fled through the Jianmen Pass into Shu, establishing the Dacheng regime in Chengdu. This regime later changed its name to Han, known in history as Cheng Han, with Li Xiong as its founding emperor.

李雄是氐人流民首领李特之子，李特起事时充任前将军。李雄还有个哥哥叫李荡，在李荡出生之前，他俩的母亲梦见两道彩虹自门前升空，其中一道却断裂了。其母曾对人讲：“我这两个儿子，要是有一个先死了，另一个必然显贵。”后来李荡不幸死于军中，李雄果然当了皇帝，治蜀三十一年。

Li Xiong was the son of Li Te, the head of the Di people refugees. During Li Te's uprising, Li Xiong served as the Front General. Li Xiong had an elder brother named Li Dang. Before Li Dang was born, their mother dreamt of two rainbows rising from their doorstep, but one of them broke. She once said, "If one of my two sons dies first, the other is destined for greatness." Later, Li Dang unfortunately died in the army, and Li Xiong indeed became emperor, ruling Shu for thirty-one years.

诗中提到的李雄坟，即安都陵，方志称在成都县北七里，推算起来，大致是在凤凰山、升仙湖一带。也有文章称，李雄安都陵在黉门后街放生池。

The Li Xiong tomb mentioned in the poem refers to Andu Mausoleum, which is noted in local records to be seven Li north of Chengdu County. This places it roughly in the area of Phoenix Mountain and Shengxian Lake. Some sources suggest that Li Xiong's Andu Mausoleum is located at the Release Pond behind Hongmen Street.

黉门后街以前确实有个放生池，至今还存有“放生池四十一号大院”之名。其实，此处倒也真有个成汉墓，此墓在很长时间内还曾被当作张飞衣冠墓。

There was indeed a Release Pond behind Hongmen Street, and the name "Release Pond No. 41 Courtyard" still exists today. In fact, there is indeed a Cheng Han tomb in this location, which for a long time was mistakenly thought to be the cenotaph for Zhang Fei.

传说中的张飞衣冠墓

与黉门后街相垂直的，有一条叫作桓侯巷的小街，两条街分别构成了华西医院的北界和西界。

“桓侯”二字，得名于巷内曾有的桓侯庙。在庙里享受香火的，是汉桓侯张飞。庙后一圆丘形土冢，高十米，旁立石碑，上书“汉张夫子衣冠墓”。该庙建于清代，为成都屠宰业祭祀张飞所用——传说张飞在桃园结义之前的职业是屠夫，故被奉为杀猪匠祖师爷。

作家杨彤于1981—1984年就读的成都市二十五中初中部，就在桓侯巷，同学则大多住在附近。班上几个调皮的学生经常去附近的“张飞墓”玩耍，他们称之为“皇坟”。其中有个女同学叫陈文松，性子很野。有一次，杨彤听到班主任在课堂上大骂：“陈文松，西班牙（该女生是龅牙）。站在皇坟上头，向下面的男娃子撒烟。下头的几副颜色，憨口水都流出来了，像啥子话？！”

时至今日，庙已不存，土冢则位于华西医院第三住院部和第四住院部之间的小池塘边。当年不少华西子弟也曾像陈文松和她的烟友一般，在土

The Legendary Zhang Fei's Cenotaph

Vertical to Hongmen Street, there is a small street called Huanhou Alley, forming the northern and western borders of Huaxi Hospital.

The name “Huanhou” comes from the Huanhou Temple that once stood there. This temple was dedicated to Han Dynasty's Marquis Zhang Fei. Behind the temple stood a round mound, ten meters high, with a stone stele inscribed “Tomb of Zhang Fei's Clothing and Hat”. The temple was built during the Qing Dynasty by the butchery guild of Chengdu, as Zhang Fei, according to legend, was a butcher before his oath of brotherhood in the Peach Garden, thus being revered as the patron saint of butchers.

From 1981 to 1984, writer Yang Tong attended the junior high department of Chengdu No. 25 Middle School, which was located on Huanhou Alley. Most of his classmates lived nearby. Some mischievous students often played at the “Zhang Fei Tomb”, which they called the “Grand Mound”. One of his classmates, a girl named Chen Wensong, was wild and untamed. On one occasion, Yang Tong heard their homeroom teacher angrily scold in class: “Chen Wensong, you, the buck teeth, stood on the tomb, spreading cigarettes down at the boys below. And the looks on their faces, drooling like fools. What kind of behavior is that?!”

Today, the temple no longer exists, and the mound is now located beside a small pond between the third and fourth inpatient departments of Huaxi Hospital. Many children of Huaxi staff also used to play wildly on the mound, just like Chen Wensong and her smoking friends.

Today, the earthen mound, now several meters high, is enclosed and protected by a wire fence,

堆上疯玩。

如今封土约高数米，已被铁丝网封闭保护起来，铁网上蔷薇盛开。土丘下方的石碑因风蚀剥落，字迹已荡然无存。墓前建一汉阙风格仿古亭，时常有病人或家属在此休憩。

1985年，这个传说中的“张飞衣冠冢”开始考古发掘。打开封土，内为一高2.5米、长近十三米的墓室。在已发现的成汉墓葬中，此墓规模最大。

adorned with blooming roses. The stone stele at the base of the mound has been weathered away, leaving the inscription illegible. In front of the tomb, there is a pavilion built in the style of a Han Dynasty Que, where patients and their families often rest.

In 1985, archaeological excavations began on the legendary "Tomb of Zhang Fei's Clothing and Hat". Upon opening the earthen mound, a tomb chamber measuring 2.5 meters high and nearly 13 meters long was discovered. Among the Cheng Han tombs found, this one is the largest.

成汉墓镇墓俑，最突出处是两只眼睛　何大江 摄
Tomb guardian figurines from the Cheng Han tomb, noted for their prominent, striking eyes. (Photographer: He Dajiang)

墓葬虽多次被盗，依然出土了丰富的随葬品——近百件陶俑及陶制动物模型，陶俑种类有文吏、击鼓、吹箫、侍俑等。墓中最让人惊奇的是镇墓俑：高鼻子、大扁嘴、凸眉弓，尤其是一对大眼睛拉满了整个脸颊，而上下眼睑也突出于面部，形成两个大框。

纪年砖上的年号太康、玉衡、玉恒、汉兴，泄露了墓葬的秘密。除太康为晋武帝年号之外，余者皆为成汉

Despite being looted multiple times, the tomb still yielded a wealth of burial goods, including nearly a hundred clay figurines and clay models of animals. The figurines varied, depicting civil officials, drummers, flute players, and attendants. The most astonishing find in the tomb was the guardian figurine: it had a high nose, large flat mouth, prominent brow ridges, and, most notably, a pair of large eyes that spanned the entire cheeks, with protruding upper and lower eyelids forming two large frames.

The secret of the tomb was revealed by the era names on the chronicle bricks: Taikang, Yuheng (玉衡), Yuheng (玉恒), and Hanxing. Except for Taikang, which was the reign title of Emperor Wu of Jin, the

年号。其中，“玉衡”为开国皇帝李雄年号，“玉恒”为第三代皇帝、李雄之子李期年号，“汉兴”为第四代皇帝、李雄堂弟李寿年号。从年号、随葬品、陵墓规模等可以判断，墓主为成汉贵族。

李雄离世时，尚无玉恒、汉兴年号，此墓当然不可能是安都陵。

而张飞衣冠冢的说法，则完全不值一驳。很显然，清代成都的杀猪匠联盟需要一位精神领袖，需要一件图腾来凝聚人心，于是行业就指定了这座祖师爷之墓。

屠宰业选择这座大墓有两个原因：一是它没有主人，年代太久远了，无人知其来历；二是它够大够显赫，封土堆够高，里面躺的肯定是位大人物。选择它，只是因为它满足作为精神象征的条件。

操弄人心、指鹿为马的行径，从来不绝于史。也因为这个原因，对于前文所述之柏灌王墓、鱼凫王墓、武担山开明王妃墓，笔者总是怀着几分警惕之心，在未见切实证据之前，不肯轻易相信。

rest were Cheng Han reign titles. Yuheng (玉衡) was the reign title of Li Xiong, the founding emperor; Yuheng (玉恒) was the reign title of Li Qi, the third emperor and Li Xiong's son; and Hanxing was the reign title of Li Shou, the fourth emperor and Li Xiong's cousin. From these reign titles, the burial goods, and the scale of the tomb, it can be deduced that the tomb's owner was a Cheng Han noble.

When Li Xiong passed away, the Yuheng (玉恒) and Hanxing era names did not yet exist, so this tomb certainly cannot be the Andu Mausoleum.

The idea of it being Zhang Fei's tomb of clothing and hat is entirely baseless. It is evident that the butchers' guild of Qing Dynasty Chengdu needed a spiritual leader and a totem to rally around, so they designated this tomb as the resting place of their patron saint.

The butchers' guild chose this large tomb for two reasons: firstly, it had no known owner—its antiquity meant that no one knew its origins; secondly, its grandeur and the height of the earthen mound suggested that it belonged to an important figure. The selection of this tomb was solely because it met the criteria for a symbolic figurehead.

The manipulation of public perception and the substitution of the false for the true have always been present throughout history. For this reason, I'm always a little wary about the previously mentioned tombs of Boguan King, Yufu King, and the consort of King Kaiming in Wudan Mountain. Without concrete evidence, I'm reluctant to believe these claims readily.

成汉立国

成汉建立者李雄，其祖上为巴

The Founding of Cheng Han

The founder of Cheng Han, Li Xiong,

人的一支——賨人。东汉末年天下大乱，賨人自巴西郡宕渠县迁于汉中杨车坂，被称作“杨车巴”。曹操大军过境征服汉中时，李雄的曾祖父李虎是杨车巴首领，他带着五百户部民众投诚曹操，得封将军，再受命迁往氐人居住的略阳（今甘肃省秦安县）。

到了西晋元康六年（296年），关中频岁大饥，天水、略阳、武都、阴平等六郡十万余氐人，不得不进入蜀地就食——蜀地有粮，饥民通过受雇用解决生存问题——李雄的父亲李特即成为六郡流民的主要领袖。

descended from the Cong people, a branch of the Ba people. During the turmoil at the end of the Eastern Han Dynasty, the Cong people moved from Dangqu County in Baxi Prefecture to Yangcheban in Hanzhong, becoming known as the “Yangche Ba”. When Cao Cao’s army passed through and conquered Hanzhong, Li Xiong’s great-grandfather, Li Hu, who was the head of the Yangche Ba, surrendered with 500 households to Cao Cao. He was granted the title of general and was later ordered to relocate to Lueyang, the dwelling place of the Di people (modern-day Qin’an County, Gansu Province).

By the sixth year of Yuan Kang (296 AD) during the Western Jin Dynasty, a severe famine struck Guanzhong. Over 100,000 Di people from the six counties of Tianshui, Lueyang, Wudu, and Yinping, among others, were forced to migrate to Shu for sustenance. Shu had food, and the starving people could survive by working as hired laborers. Li Xiong’s father, Li Te, became the primary leader of the refugees from these six counties.

剑门雄关地势险要，引来李特无限遐想　冉玉杰 摄
The perilous terrain of Jianmen Pass sparked endless musings in Li Te. (Photographer: Ran Yujie)

李特身长八尺，“雄武善骑射，沉毅有大度”。带领十数万流民到了剑门关，素怀大志的他见山势雄险，遂箕踞于地叹息道：“刘禅有如此之地而面缚于人，岂非庸才耶？！”所谓箕踞，是指伸开两腿坐在地上，在古代算是极不拘礼节的行为。

笔者故乡四川省营山县，在晋

Li Te, with a towering figure at eight chi in height, was “valiant and skilled in horse riding and archery, steadfast and magnanimous.” Leading over 100,000 refugees to Jianmen Pass, he, harboring great ambitions, saw the imposing mountains and sighed as he sat down with legs outstretched, saying, “Liu Shan had such a formidable land yet surrendered—what a mediocrity!” This act of sitting with legs stretched out was considered highly informal and disrespectful in ancient times.

My hometown, Yingshan County in Sichuan

代属巴西郡宕渠县，而笔者在少年时即知县里太蓬乡有李特遗迹——天子读书堂。海拔七百余米的太蓬山山巅有一石室，石室下面的狭长岩穴即读书堂所在。李特生前未称帝，但建立过实际上的割据军政府，也有过自己的年号，再加上死后被儿子追封为皇帝，勉勉强强可称天子。不过，宕渠只是李特祖籍，他并没有生长于此，多半也没来过；而高山之巅，也绝非日常读书去处——“天子读书堂”无非是借祖籍地之名，附会于李特而已。

永宁元年（301年），借“八王之乱”再起、关陇局势混乱的机会，李特在绵竹聚众起义，两年后死于战事。304年，李特之子李雄攻下成都，即皇帝位，国号大成，后改为“汉”，史称“成汉”。同月，匈奴人刘渊在左国城（今山西离石）建国，即历史上的前赵。此时，西晋王朝的“八王之乱”还没有结束，而中国历史上大分裂时期的“十六国”已经有两国建立起来了。

成汉政权控制区域最大时，大致包括今日之四川全境加上云南北部、陕南和甘南，以及湖北和贵州的一部分，而其统治中心一直在成都。

成汉的行政区划，前后有过司隶

Province, was part of Dangqu County in Baxi Prefecture during the Jin Dynasty. As a youth, I knew of the “Emperor’s Study Hall” in Taipeng Township within the county, associated with Li Te. At the summit of Mount Taipeng, which rises over 700 meters, there is a stone chamber, and beneath it, a narrow rock cave known as the Study Hall. Although Li Te never proclaimed himself emperor, he did establish a de facto separatist military government and had his own era name. After his death, his son posthumously honored him as emperor, allowing for the loose title of “Emperor”. However, Dangqu was merely Li Te’s ancestral home; he neither grew up there nor likely ever visited. Moreover, a mountaintop would hardly be a suitable everyday study location. The “Emperor’s Study Hall” is simply a name borrowing from his ancestral ties, attaching significance to Li Te.

In the first year of Yongning (301 AD), amid the resurgence of the “Upheaval of the Eight Princes” and the chaotic state of affairs in the Guanlong region, Li Te mobilized a mass uprising in Mianzhu. Two years later, he perished in battle. In 304 AD, Li Te’s son, Li Xiong, captured Chengdu and declared himself emperor, naming his state Dacheng, later renamed to “Han”, known historically as “Cheng Han”. In the same month, the Xiongnu leader Liu Yuan founded a state in Zuo Guo City (present-day Lishi, Shanxi), which is historically known as Former Zhao. At this juncture, the “Upheaval of the Eight Princes” within the Western Jin Dynasty continued unabated, while the period of significant fragmentation in Chinese history known as the “Sixteen Kingdoms” had already witnessed the establishment of two states.

The Cheng Han regime, at its prime, controlled an area roughly encompassing the entirety of present-day Sichuan, alongside northern Yunnan, southern Shanxi, southern Gansu, and parts of Hubei and

部（益州）、梁州、宁州、荆州、交州、安州和汉州等。有意思的是，与成汉同时期的东晋，有数州的名称与成汉相同。

比如我们常说的荆州。《三国演义》中的荆州，其实是一个文化概念；在地理上，则分属成汉与东晋。当时，荆州是成汉与东晋的前线，二者各占据了一部分。两个政权，在行政建制上都有各自的荆州。

成汉的建立，似乎应了“天下未乱蜀先乱”一语，其实也未尽然。考察成汉和后文前蜀的建立过程，就会发现，它们都是在天下初乱、中央政府失去对全国局势的控制时，利用地理形势上的特点而割据的；而当天下最乱、战火最旺、杀声最响之时，此处反倒是一片宁静。

成汉统治者李氏家族虽然为巴人后裔，但实际上已经氐化了。李氏移于略阳后即称“巴氐”。李特率流民入蜀之前，李氏在氐人的传统居住区略阳居住了八十三年，已融于氐人之中。

Guizhou. The administrative center of Cheng Han was consistently based in Chengdu.

Throughout its existence, Cheng Han's administrative divisions included several prefectures: Silibu (Yizhou), Liangzhou, Ningzhou, Jingzhou, Jiaozhou, Anzhou, and Hanzhou. Interestingly, the Eastern Jin Dynasty of the same period also had several prefectures with names identical with Cheng Han's.

For instance, the frequently mentioned Jingzhou, as depicted in *Romance of the Three Kingdoms*, is actually a cultural concept. Geographically, Jingzhou belonged to Cheng Han and the Eastern Jin respectively. Jingzhou served as the frontier between Cheng Han and Eastern Jin, with each regime controlling a segment of it, and both maintaining their own administrative establishments of Jingzhou.

The establishment of Cheng Han seems to corroborate the saying, "When chaos has yet to arise in the empire, Shu falls into turmoil first". However, this is not entirely accurate. By examining the formation of Cheng Han and, later on, Former Shu, one finds that both entities founded separatist regime respectively by leveraging their geographical advantages precisely when the central government was losing its grip on the national situation in the early stages of sprawling disorder. Paradoxically, during periods of greatest turmoil, when wars were fiercest and the clamor of battles loudest, these regions remained tranquil.

The ruling Li family of Cheng Han, though descended from the Ba people, had actually assimilated into the Di ethnic group. After relocating to Lueyang, the Li clan began to identify itself as "Ba-Di". By the time Li Te led his exiled people into Shu, the family had inhabited the traditional Di dwelling area of Lueyang for 83 years, fully blending into the Di community.

无法忽视的眼睛

能够认定的成汉地下遗存很少，除了桓侯巷，还分布于成都万年场、双流广福村以及西昌等数个地区。这或许是因为成汉国祚不长，也有另一种可能，即氐人入蜀之后迅速汉化，其墓葬因为民族特色的丧失而不能被辨认。

总之，存世的成汉文物特色鲜明，尤其是成汉俑那一双双具有极高辨识度的眼睛。

每件文物身上都携带着时代的信息。比如气冲牛斗的兵马俑之于秦代，诙谐滑稽的说唱俑之于东汉，面如满月、樱桃小口的三彩女俑之于唐代，手按兵器、怒目而视的武士俑之于宋代。而成汉俑最突出的特点，就是脸上那双无法忽视的眼睛。

成汉，是李氏集团带领氐人流民入蜀建立的政权。成汉俑，反映的是氐人的民族习俗。

氐人这个名字听起来似乎挺熟悉，是的，古蜀国的主体民族就是氐族，是他们创造了三星堆和金沙的璀璨。

Eyes that can’t be ignored

There are very few ascertainable Cheng Han archaeological remains. Aside from Huanhou Alley, remains are scattered in several regions including Wannianchang in Chengdu, Guangfu Village in Shuangliu, and Xichang. This scarcity could be attributed to the relatively short duration of Cheng Han’s rule. Another possibility is the rapid Chinesization of the Di people after entering Shu, causing their burial customs to lose distinctive ethnic characteristics, thereby making the tombs hard to recognize.

Nevertheless, the extant artifacts from Cheng Han are unmistakably distinctive, particularly the highly identifiable eyes of Cheng Han figurines.

Each artifact carries the imprint of its era. For example, the majestic terracotta warriors of the Qin Dynasty, the humorous and whimsical crosstalk figurines from the Eastern Han, the Tang Dynasty’s tri-color glazed female figurines with full moon faces and cherrylike mouths, and the warrior figurines from the Song Dynasty, typically depicted with hands on their weapons and glaring fiercely, exemplify the spirit of each era. In contrast, the most striking feature of Cheng Han figurines is their unignorable eyes.

The Cheng Han regime was established by the Li family leading the Di exiles into Shu; Cheng Han figurines mirror distinct Di people’s customs.

The name “Di people” may sound familiar, and indeed, the ancient Shu state’s main ethnic group was the Di, the very creators of the brilliant Sanxingdui and Jinsha civilizations.

三星雕像最独特、最具辨识度的是那一对眼睛　高泓摄

The most distinctive and recognizable feature of statues in Sanxingdui is their protruding eyes. (Photographer: Gao Hong)

1986年，四川省广汉市三星堆遗址一号坑和二号坑共出土了青铜人像六十九件，其造型都非常奇异，其中最独特、最具辨识度的是那一对眼睛，大且外凸。其中，最大的青铜面具高六十五厘米，宽一百三十八厘米，最为奇特的是，它的两只眼球竟然是圆柱形的，凸出眼眶达16.5厘米，完全就是两根柱子。三星堆青铜像的这些眼睛，又引起了人们探讨“纵目”的兴趣。

对于成汉俑和三星堆青铜像，众多的传说、史料和考古发现都有两个指向：一是其来源都跟古氐人相关，二是都有着“纵目崇拜”。

当然，同三星堆的青铜像相比，无论是气势之恢宏还是制作之精美，成汉俑都不在同一个层次上。这固然是由于前者乃倾国之力，后者只是私人墓葬，也从侧面反映出成汉身处乱世，没有多余的财力和心思投放于艺术。

In 1986, from Pits No. 1 and No. 2 at the Sanxingdui site in Guanghan, Sichuan Province, a total of 69 bronze human figures were unearthed. Their designs are extraordinarily unique, with the most distinctive and recognizable feature being their large, protruding eyes. The largest bronze mask measures 65 centimeters in height and 138 centimeters in width, with its most peculiar feature being cylindrical eyeballs that protrude 16.5 centimeters out from the eye sockets, essentially resembling two columns. These eyes have sparked renewed interest in the concept of “vertical-eye” worship.

Regarding Cheng Han figurines and the bronze statues from Sanxingdui, numerous legends, historical records, and archaeological discoveries converge on two points: their origins are linked to the ancient Di people, and both feature elements of “vertical-eye worship”.

Of course, compared with the Sanxingdui bronzes, the Cheng Han figurines do not match up in terms of grandeur or craftsmanship. This disparity is naturally due to the former were created with a national effort, whereas the latter are mere private tomb artifacts. It also indirectly testifies the fact that Cheng Han existed in a time of turmoil, without the surplus funds or leisure to invest in the arts.

三星雕像的眼睛，很容易让人联想到成汉俑　高泓 摄
The eyes of statues in Sanxingdui readily evoke connections to the Cheng Han figurines. (Photographer: Gao Hong)

笔者曾经采访过考古专家索德浩，他说，第一次看到收藏于成都博物馆的成汉俑时，脑海里马上浮现出三星堆青铜塑像的面容。此后，他两次参与成汉俑的考古发掘，包括2011年双流华阳镇广福村的成汉崖墓，以及2012年的田家寺崖墓群。两次出土的镇墓俑，跟万年场、桓侯巷和西昌地区出土的成汉俑都有着共同特点：粗眉弓高高凸起，双眼呈橄榄形并外鼓。

无论如何，三星堆青铜雕像与成汉俑这两种氐人的艺术品，对眼睛的重视都无以复加。两种雕像的制作者，两个蜀人族群，隔着近两千年的时光，草蛇灰线犹可溯其本源。

I once interviewed the archaeological expert Suo Dehao. He mentioned that the first time he saw the Cheng Han figurines in the Chengdu Museum, the images of the Sanxingdui bronze statues immediately sprang to his mind. After that he participated in two archaeological excavations of Cheng Han figurines, including the Cheng Han cliff tomb in Guangfu Village, Huayang Town, Shuangliu in 2011, and the Tianjiasi Cliff Tombs in 2012. The tomb guardian figurines unearthed from these sites share commonalities with those from Wannianchang, Huanhou Alley, and Xichang regions: thick, high brow ridges with almond-shaped, protruding eyes.

Regardless, both the Sanxingdui bronze statues and the Cheng Han figurines—artifacts of the Di people—exhibit an unparalleled emphasis on the eyes. Despite nearly two millennia separating these two artistic representations, one can trace a continuous cultural thread linking the creators of these sculptures and the two Shu ethnic groups.

纵目之辨

“有蜀侯蚕丛，其目纵，始称王。死，作石棺石椁，国人从之，故俗以石棺椁为纵目人冢也。”《华阳国志》先说蜀王蚕丛的眼睛是竖着长的，再把整个蜀人称作“纵目人”，可见纵目是蜀族的普遍现象，非蚕丛独有。从人种学的角度来说，还可以扩展为氐人纵目。

纵目之说，见于《山海经》《华阳国志》等典籍，但何为纵目，则众说纷纭。

《山海经·海内北经》称：“袜，其为物，人身、黑首、从目。”袜即魅，鬼怪，《康熙字典》上称之为老山精；从即纵，从目即纵目。清代蒋应镐版的绘图，袜的眼睛旋转了九十度，竖着长在额头之下。

Vertical Eyes: A Cultural and Ethnological Inquiry

“King Cancong of Shu had vertical eyes and proclaimed himself king at the start of his reign. Upon his death, he was buried in a stone coffin with stone outer chambers, hence a practice followed by the people of Shu, and customarily associated with the vertical-eyed people.” This excerpt from *Records of the States South of Mount Hua* first describes the eyes of King Cancong as vertically oriented and subsequently refers to the Shu people as “vertical-eyed people”, indicating that vertical eyes were a widespread characteristic among the Shu tribe, not unique to Cancong. From an ethnological perspective, this can be extended to suggest that the Di people also had vertical eyes.

The concept of vertical eyes is mentioned in classical texts such as the *Classic of Mountains and Seas* and *Records of the States South of Mount Hua*, but interpretations of what vertical eyes entail vary widely.

The *Classic of Mountains and Seas: Classic of Regions within the Seas–North* states: “Mei, who possesses a human body, a black head, and vertical eyes.” Mei refers to a demon, which is also identified in the *Kangxi Dictionary* as an old mountain spirit; 从 translates to “vertical”. In the Qing Dynasty illustrations by Jiang Yinghao, the eyes of a Mei are depicted as rotated ninety degrees, vertically positioned under the forehead.

袜的纵目，为两只眼睛呈九十度旋转（摘自蒋应镐绘图版《山海经》）

Mei’s protruding eyes are depicted as rotated 90 degrees. (Source: *Classic of Mountains and Seas* of Jiang Yinghao’s illustration version)

后世也有学者猜测，纵目是指氐人因缺碘而眼球突出。

历史学家马长寿先生则认为，氐人的眼角多朝两额角斜吊，即俗语所谓丹凤眼，此为纵目。《红楼梦》里描绘王熙凤，说她“一双丹凤三角眼，两弯柳叶吊梢眉”。吊梢眉指眉尾斜插入鬓，与之相匹配的，则是眼角斜吊——此形象为马长寿纵目说作了一个具象而艺术化的注解。

科普作家董仁威也持有跟马长寿相同的观点。他曾两次深入氐人后裔白马藏人生存的四川省平武县白马乡考察。他发现，白马藏人中存在着大量的“纵目人”（丹凤眼）。在他调查过的三个家庭中，每家至少有一个“纵目人”。其中的田小美一家，田小美及其丈夫、女儿皆为纵目。董仁威因此推断：“这似乎预示着其中有一些遗传规律可循。”

且列举一下纵目可能的种类：

其一，类似缺碘者的眼球突出；

其二，三星堆雕像的圆柱形眼球，亦可视作上一种的艺术夸张；

其三，眼角斜吊的丹凤眼；

其四，《山海经》中两只眼睛旋转九十度；

其五，如成汉俑一般极度醒目，几乎占了脸庞一半。

In more recent times, some scholars have speculated that the Di people had protruding eyes, due to iodine deficiency.

Historian Ma Changshou offers a different perspective. He believes that the Di people typically had eyes that slanted upward towards the temples, a characteristic often referred to as phoenix eyes in common parlance. As described in *Dream of the Red Chamber*, Wang Xifeng has “a pair of slanted phoenix eyes and two arched eyebrows like willow leaves.” The term “arched eyebrows like willow leaves” suggests the tips of her eyebrows slope upward towards the temples, complementing the upward-slanting eyes. This artistic depiction serves as a concrete, artistic interpretation of Ma Changshou’s theory regarding vertical eyes.

Popular science writer Dong Renwei shares a similar viewpoint with Ma Changshou. Dong has conducted two extensive field studies in Baima Township, Pingwu County, Sichuan Province, where the descendants of the Di people, known as the Baima Tibetans, live. He observed that a significant number of these Baima Tibetans exhibit the “vertical eyes” (or phoenix eyes) trait. In the three families he surveyed, at least one family member in each household had these distinctive eyes. One notable example is the family of Tian Xiaomei, where Tian Xiaomei, her husband, and their daughter all have vertical eyes. Based on these findings, Dong Renwei surmises that “there seems to be some hereditary patterns at play here.”

Here I list the possible types of vertical eyes:

1. Eyes that protrude prominently, similar to those seen in individuals with iodine deficiency.

2. Round, columnar eyeballs as depicted in Sanxingdui bronze sculptures, possibly an artistic exaggeration of the aforementioned protruding eyes.

3. Eyes with corners that tilt upwards towards

除了以上五种，还有“纵目”吗？

有，我们每个人都在影视中见过。那就是眉心处竖立着的眼睛——二郎神的天眼。

the temples, commonly known as phoenix eyes.

4. Eyes Rotated 90 Degrees (from *Classic of Mountains and Seas*).

5. Eyes that are extremely striking and occupy almost half of the face, characteristic of the Cheng Han figurines.

In addition to the above five, is there any other types of “vertical eyes”?

Yes, almost all of us have seen Erlang Shen’s “celestial eye”. As often portrayed in mythology and popular media, he had an eye positioned vertically at the center of his forehead.

崇拜眼睛的民族

在古氐人发祥地仇池国故地——甘肃陇南的仇池山，至今还流传着“立眼人”的故事。

传说中的立眼人除了跟常人一般并列横排的双眼之外，在前额中间还有一只纵立的眼睛。下雨时，其纵眼因无眉骨、睫毛遮护，会被雨水侵入。立眼人因此而得病，并绝种。

与传说对应的真实情况是，氐族先民有着一种“剠额为天”的习俗。剠，即黥，原指在面上刺字且涂墨的刑罚；天，即头顶。所谓“剠额为天”，就是用刀刻额头，形成永久性痕迹。有“眼睛崇拜”习俗的氐人，在额头上刻的是一只竖着的眼睛——没错，这就是二郎神杨戬的“天眼”。

二郎神的来源，有多种说法，其

The Eye-Worshipping People

In Chouchi Mountain, located in Longnan, Gansu Province—the ancestral land of the ancient Di people and the former Chouchi state—a legend about the “vertical-eyed people” still circulates today.

According to the legend, in addition to the normal pair of horizontally aligned eyes, these vertical-eyed people possessed an additional eye on their foreheads. This vertical eye lacked the natural protection of brow ridges and eyelashes and was thus susceptible to rainwater. As a result, these individuals supposedly fell ill from rainwater entering their unprotected eye, leading eventually to their extinction.

Historically, this legend aligns with the Di people’s custom known as “engraving the forehead” (剠额为天). “剠” refers to “黥”, an archaic form of punishment in which characters were tattooed and inked on the face. “天” means the top of the head. Therefore, it involved carving a permanent mark on the forehead with a knife. For the Di people, who practiced eye worship, the mark of a vertical eye on the forehead symbolizes their reverence for eyes. Indeed, this aligns with the mythical depiction of the

文字记载最早见于唐代。一说为灌江口的李二郎，因为帮助父亲李冰修筑都江堰而被奉为神灵，其实李冰并没有这样一个儿子；一说为隋朝时隐居青城山学道、后官拜嘉州太守的赵昱赵二郎，他曾与蛟龙搏斗而被奉为神明，唐人为其立庙于灌江口。

这两个二郎神，虽说都是穿凿，但也都跟氐人有些关系。灌江口所在之地，在汉代为湔氐道属地，从名字就看得出来，这是氐人活动区域。

流传最广的说法，二郎神为玉皇大帝的外甥杨戬，曾劈华山救母，然而玉皇大帝本身也是个神话。但二郎神必有原型，此人姓杨，而杨姓为氐族大姓，二郎神原型正是氐王杨难当，一个实实在在的历史人物。

"马王爷三只眼"，这句民间俗语众人耳熟能详，却不知其意。其实，那个第三只眼，就是额头上竖着的"天眼"。马王爷最初也是氐族神祇，后来成为道教神明，而道教中还有王灵官等也是纵目三眼。

celestial eye (天眼) of Erlang Shen.

The origins of the deity Erlang Shen have various accounts, with the earliest literary mention dating back to the Tang Dynasty. One account identifies Erlang Shen as Li Erlang from Guanjiangkou (Guanjiang River Estuary), who was deified for helping his father, Li Bing, construct the Dujiangyan irrigation system—although in reality, Li Bing did not have such a son. Another account attributes Erlang Shen to Zhao Yu, also known as Zhao Erlang, who in the Sui Dynasty secluded himself in Qingcheng Mountain to practice Taoism. Zhao later became the prefect of Jiazhou and was deified for his legendary battle with a Jiaolong (a mythical flood dragon). The Tang people built a temple in his honor at Guanjiangkou.

While both narratives seem rather contrived, they do have some connections to the Di people. The area around Guanjiangkou, known in the Han Dynasty as Jiandi Dao, was an activity zone for the Di people, as indicated by its name.

The most widely accepted story describes Erlang Shen as Yang Jian, the nephew of the Jade Emperor (the Supreme Deity of Taoism), who split Mount Hua to save his mother. The Jade Emperor himself is a mythological figure, but Erlang Shen surely has a historical prototype. This individual bore the surname Yang, a prominent surname among the Di people. The true historical prototype of Erlang Shen is believed to be Yang Nandang, a Di king who was a significant historical figure.

The saying "Lord Ma with three eyes", well-known in folklore, is a metaphor for someone not to be messed with, yet its meaning is often misunderstood. The third eye refers to the vertically oriented "celestial eye" (天眼) on the forehead. Lord Ma was originally a deity of the Di people, later becoming a Taoist deity. In Taoism, other deities, such as Wang Lingguan, also possess the characteristic of having three eyes with one being vertically oriented.

喇嘛庙的三眼神祇 （美）西德尼 · 甘博 摄

A three-eyed deity in a lama temple. (Photographer: Sidney David Gamble, USA)

袁枚《子不语 · 卷十八》讲了一个妖魅附身新妇与道士斗法的故事。起初僵持不下，最终，“三目神擒一白猴，大五尺许”。

既然说纵目为氐人习俗，为何道教中又有如此多的三目神灵呢？其实，追溯一下道教的起源就不难理解了。道教的前身为五斗米教，东汉张道陵在蜀郡鹤鸣山创立五斗米教时受到蜀地原始宗教——巫觋信仰——的强烈影响，而氐人曾经是古蜀的主体民族。从氐人纵目到道教三目神，纵然流变复杂，但其中明显的相关性是非常明晰的。

氐人之纵目习俗，甚至到了近代还有留存。王国维先生关门弟子、考古大家卫聚贤1943年在《说文月刊》上发表《二郎考》一文，其中关于三目人现身成都街头的记载，极具

Yuan Mei's *Zi Buyu, Volume 18* recounts a story about a demon possessing a bride and battling a Taoist priest. Initially, there was a stalemate, but ultimately, “the three-eyed deity captured a white monkey, about five feet tall”.

Given that vertical eyes (纵目) are described as a custom among the Di people, why then are there so many three-eyed deities in Taoism? To understand this, one needs to trace the origins of Taoism. Taoism evolved from Wudoumijiao (五斗米教), the Five Pecks of Rice movement, which was founded by Zhang Daoling in the Eastern Han Dynasty on Heming Mountain in Shu Commandery. This movement was significantly influenced by the primitive shamanistic beliefs of the Shu region. Considering that the Di people were once a major ethnic group in ancient Shu, it's clear that there is a strong connection.

The custom of vertical eyes among the Di people even persisted into modern times. In 1943, Wei Juxian, the last disciple of the renowned scholar Wang Guowei and a prominent archaeologist, published an article titled *The Investigation on Erlang* in the *Shuowen Monthly*. This article contains a highly

价值："直到清光绪三十年左右，有二十余人自西藏赴北京朝贡。其人皆三只眼，路过成都时被围观。详察其额，正中一眼非真眼，乃幼时刻其额外一小直孔，含以黑珠，及长，珠位肉内，酷似纵目。"

氐人作为一个族别虽已流散消失于时间之河，但在这一过程中，已与邻近民族发生了深度融合。卫聚贤所言三目人，也正是氐人习俗的流传。

valuable account of three-eyed individuals appearing on the streets of Chengdu: "Until around the 30th year of the Guangxu reign in the Qing Dynasty, over twenty individuals traveled from Tibet to Beijing to pay tribute. These people all had three eyes and were surrounded by onlookers as they passed through Chengdu. Upon close inspection, the third eye in middle was not a real eye but rather a small vertical hole carved in their foreheads during childhood, containing a black bead. As they grew, the bead embedded itself into the flesh, resembling a vertical eye."

Although the Di people as an ethnic group have faded away over time, they have deeply integrated with neighboring ethnicities throughout this diaspora. The three-eyed individuals as described by Wei Juxian, exemplify the enduring legacy of Di customs.

白马藏族傩戏曹盖舞，面具上有一只竖眼　余茂智 摄
The Baima Tibetan exorcism ritual dance, known as the Caogai Dance, features masks with a vertical third eye. (Photographer: Yu Maozhi)

作为古氐人后裔的白马藏族，其民俗曹盖舞，则至今存留着纵目的痕迹。白马藏族生活在四川省平武县涪江上游的山间谷地，每年正月初五，各村寨辞旧迎新的大型祭祀中，跳曹盖舞是其最主要的活动。

曹盖舞是一种傩舞，舞蹈者戴着面具跳跃，模仿野兽动作，粗犷而刚猛。面具是神灵的形象，双目圆瞪，张嘴似怒吼，极为类似汉族地区的吞口，而最大的区别是：曹盖面具额头

Among the Baima Tibetans, descendants of the ancient Di people, their traditional dance, the Caogai Dance, still retains traces of the vertical eye. The Baima Tibetans reside in the mountainous valleys of the upper Fujiang River in Pingwu County, Sichuan Province. Each year, on the fifth day of the first lunar month, during the large-scale ceremonies of bidding farewell to the old and welcoming the new year, dancing the Caogai Dance is the main event in various villages.

The Caogai Dance is a type of exorcism dance (Nuo dance). Dancers wear masks and perform jumps while imitating the movements of wild animals, portraying a rough and vigorous style. The masks represent divine figures, with eyes glaring and mouths

间多了一只竖立的第三只眼。

纵目，其实是氐人“眼睛崇拜”习俗的曲折反映。考察与氐相关的文化、习俗、名人，都可以发现与眼睛崇拜的关联。

open as if roaring, closely resembling the "swallowing mouth" designs found in Han Chinese regions. The most distinct difference, however, is that Caogai masks feature an additional vertical third eye on the forehead.

The concept of vertical eyes is, in essence, a manifestation of the Di people's tradition of eye worship. Delving into the culture, customs, and notable figures associated with the Di people reveals a consistent emphasis on eyes.

北魏名将杨大眼

二郎神杨戬的原型、后仇池国国王杨难当，就是氐人。

仇池的国土面积并不算太小，它以今日甘肃南部的仇池山为中心，占据了川陕甘交界处大约几十万平方千米的土地。这个时而独立、时而半独立、时而灭亡、时而复兴的国家，处于北魏与南朝的夹缝之中，在两个大国之间摇来摆去、左右逢源。

杨难当有两个孙子，一个叫杨大眼，一个叫杨小眼。等到杨大眼出生时，国家已经倾覆。出身于王室的他，只是北魏一个沦落民间、生活困顿的子民。连吃饭都颇成问题的杨大眼，决定进京寻找出路。

当时，北魏高祖孝文帝拓跋宏准备南征，正派尚书李典选取军官。杨大眼前去应征，却没被看上，因为个

Northern Wei General Yang Dayan

Erlang Shen (Yang Jian) is thought to be based on the historical figure of Yang Nandang, a king of the later Chouchi state, who was a Di person.

Yang Nandang's Chouchi is notably centered around present-day Chouchi Mountain in southern Gansu. This region covered an area spanning hundreds of thousands of square kilometers, encompassing parts of modern Sichuan, Shaanxi, and Gansu provinces. Chouchi was a state that experienced periods of independence, semi-independence, annihilation, and revival. Situated between the Northern Wei and the Southern Dynasties, Chouchi adeptly navigated the political landscape, maintaining a delicate balance of affiliation and disobedience between these two powers.

Yang Nandang had two grandsons: Yang Dayan (Big Eyes) and Yang Xiaoyan (Small Eyes). By the time Yang Dayan was born, their kingdom had already fallen. Although born into a royal lineage, Yang Dayan found himself reduced to the status of a commoner living in hardship within Northern Wei. Struggling even to secure daily sustenance, Yang Dayan decided to venture to the capital in search of opportunities.

子不高，体魄不壮，没有战场上吃香的将军肚。

眼看要被淘汰了，杨大眼忙道："大人莫急，看我使个绝招。"于是，找来根三丈长的绳子系在发髻上，朝前猛冲，跑起来的速度之快，连马也追不上。越来越快，绳子离地了，在脑袋后面拉伸成了一根线，像射出去的箭一样直。

李宰相见了大惊，"这到底是什么功夫？！"于是，杨大眼自然入选，领了军主的职位，相当于一入伍就当上了连长。

杨大眼的速度到底有多快？千百年后，他家乡所在的陇南师专蔡副全教授曾做了个实验。蔡教授找了一根长8.40米（按北魏的计量单位约三丈）、直径一毫米的棉线，绑在疾驰的摩托车后。他发现，只有当摩托车的速度达到五十千米/小时，才能出现那种像箭一样直的情形。

当今世界上冲刺速度最快的人，非牙买加运动员博尔特莫属，然而，以博尔特创下的9.58秒的百米世界纪录换算，时速也不到三十八千米。难道说，杨大眼的冲刺速度能超过博尔特的百分之三十？

显然不可能。一个没有高科技跑鞋，没有教练，没有营养师、按摩

At that time, Emperor Xiaowen of Northern Wei, Tuoba Hong, was gearing up for a southern expedition. He had dispatched the Prime Minister, Li Dian, to select military officers. Yang Dayan went to enlist but was initially turned away because he did not have the imposing stature and a potbelly typically desired for generals on the battlefield.

Facing imminent rejection, Yang Dayan quickly interjected, "Please, my lord, allow me to demonstrate a special skill." He then fetched a rope, three Zhang (approximately ten meters) in length, and tied it to his topknot. With a sudden burst of speed, he sprinted forward so swiftly that even a horse could not catch up with him. As Yang Dayan ran faster and faster, the rope lifted off the ground, stretching taut behind his head like an arrow shot from a bow.

Prime Minister Li was astounded by the display, exclaiming, "What on earth is this kung fu?!" Naturally, Yang Dayan was selected and appointed as a military leader, equivalent to a company commander right upon enlistment.

How fast was Yang Dayan actually? To explore this, centuries later, Professor Cai Fuquan from Longnan Normal College, located in Yang Dayan's hometown, conducted an experiment. Professor Cai used a cotton thread 8.40 meters long (approximately three Zhang according to the Northern Wei measurement) with a diameter of 1 millimeter. He tied it to the back of a speeding motorcycle. He discovered that only when the motorcycle reached a speed of 50 kilometers per hour did the thread stretch straight and taut, resembling the arrow-like effect mentioned in the story.

It's certainly intriguing to compare Yang Dayan's legendary sprinting speed with contemporary records. Jamaican sprinter Usain Bolt holds the world record for the 100-meter dash at 9.58 seconds, translating to a speed of just under 38 kilometers

师，没有数据分析团队，更没有受过现代科学训练的古人，是不可能跑过博尔特的。那么，《魏书》上描述的"绳直如矢"的惊奇场景，是不是胡说呢？

非也。杨大眼跟博尔特并非同台竞技，蔡教授做实验时，也并没有考虑风向、风速和坡度等因素。试想，如果是在一个斜坡上朝下冲，又逆着风的话，应该不用达到博尔特的速度，就可以"绳直如矢"了。《魏书》上李典对杨大眼"自千载以来，未有逸材若此者也"的评价是可信的。

杨大眼性格张扬，从他投军成功以后的表现也可见一斑。话说杨大眼当上军主之后，就对兄弟伙说了一句话："从今天开始，我就是蛟龙入水，鹰飞冲天。以后，就不会跟各位在同一张桌子上吃饭了。"

当年陈胜辍耕于垄亩之上，道"苟富贵，无相忘"，以田野耕夫而言鸿鹄之志，也够张扬的，但毕竟不忘相互提携，这跟杨大眼直接把同侪踩在脚下简直不可以道里计。要说张扬，还没有大眼的十分之一。

战场上的杨大眼，果然勇冠三军，攻城拔寨，一路升迁。任荆州刺史之时，听闻辖地有虎害，大眼亲自下场与之搏斗，斩虎头悬于市中。当

per hour. Could Yang Dayan's sprinting speed really exceed Bolt's by 30%?

Clearly, it would be improbable for an ancient individual—lacking modern high-tech running shoes, coaches, nutritionists, massage therapists, data analysis team and even advanced training methods—to outpace Usain Bolt. Thus, whether the astonishing scene described in the *Book of Wei* (魏书), where Yang Dayan's rope stretches taut like an arrow, is a mere exaggeration that deserves no closer look?

Not quite. Yang Dayan and Usain Bolt were not competing under the same conditions, and Professor Cai's experiment did not account for variables such as wind direction, wind speed, and slope inclination. Imagine if Yang Dayan was running downhill against the wind—it wouldn't be necessary to reach Bolt's speed to achieve the "arrow-straight rope"effect. Therefore, the depiction in the *Book of Wei*, along with Li Dian's praise of Yang Dayan as "an exceptional talent unseen for a thousand years" is credible.

Yang Dayan's bold personality was evident through his actions after successfully joining the military. Upon becoming a military leader, he confidently declared to his comrades, "From today onwards, I am like a dragon diving into the water or an eagle soaring into the sky. In the future, I will no longer dine with you at the same table."

Indeed, when Chen Sheng, a farmer who led a peasant uprising against the Qin Dynasty, famously declared, "If one day I become wealthy and powerful, I will not forget you," he spoke of grand aspirations as a plowman while still emphasizing mutual support among peers. This stands in stark contrast to Yang Dayan, who directly asserted his superiority over his companions. In terms of flamboyance and bravado, Yang Dayan certainly surpasses Chen Sheng.

On the battlefield, Yang Dayan's courage was unmatched, leading to numerous victories and

地为盗寇的荆蛮闻之惊骇，变得规规矩矩。那一带的老百姓恐吓哭闹的小孩，说“再哭杨大眼来了”，以此止哭，果然百试百验。

南齐王秉为名门之后，“旧时王谢堂前燕”中的王家，说的就是其先祖。王秉后来逃至北魏，见到了杨大眼，对其相貌颇有些失望，道：“在南朝就听到过将军的大名，都说关羽、张飞的勇猛也不过如此，还真以为你眼睛大如车轮哩。等到今天见面，才发现与常人无异。”

这种疑问杨大眼可能也遇得多了，倒也不惊不诧，回答道：“当跟敌军遭遇，相互都看得见之时，我眼睛里燃烧的怒火，让敌人不敢与我直视，这就足够了，何必要瞪得跟铜铃一样大呢？”

可见，他眼睛并不特别大，他弟弟杨小眼也并未见得眼睛就特别小。那么，两个王子王孙为什么会取两个如此奇怪的名字呢？

杨大眼、杨小眼兄弟是氐人后裔，而“纵目崇拜”或称“眼睛崇拜”“眼球崇拜”，正是氐人的独特风俗。对于氐人来说，眼睛不只是人体的一个器官，而是一件很重要、很神圣的物什。

现在就很清楚了，哥哥取名为

continuous promotions. When he served as the Governor of Jingzhou, he heard reports of a tiger causing havoc in his jurisdiction. True to his bold nature, Yang Dayan personally engaged the tiger in combat, slaying it and hanging its head in the marketplace. This act instilled such fear in the local bandits and outlaws that they quickly reformed their behavior. The local populace even used his name to discipline children. When children cried, parents would say, “If you keep crying, Yang Dayan will come!” This tactic proved highly effective time and again.

Wang Bing, a descendant of a prestigious lineage from the Southern Qi and his family referred to in the phrase “the swallows under the eaves of Wang and Xie’s halls”, eventually escaped to Northern Wei. Upon meeting Yang Dayan, he was somewhat disappointed by his appearance. He remarked, “In the Southern Courts, your name was famed, and it was said that your bravery rivaled that of Guan Yu and Zhang Fei. I even imagined your eyes to be as large as cart wheels. But now, seeing you in person, you appear no different from any other man.”

Such doubts were likely something Yang Dayan had encountered frequently. Unfazed, he responded, “When facing the enemy, in those moments when we can see each other clearly, the fire burning in my eyes is enough to cow my foes. They dare not meet my gaze directly. There is no need for my eyes to be as large as copper bells.”

It’s evident that Yang Dayan’s eyes were not particularly large, nor were his brother Yang Xiaoyan’s eyes notably small. So why did these two princely brothers receive such unusual names?

The brothers, being descendants of the Di people, came from a culture that practiced “vertical eye worship” or “eye worship”. For the Di people, eyes were not just organs but were considered highly significant and sacred.

大眼，并不是因为眼睛大；弟弟叫小眼，也不是因为眼睛小——而是因为他俩所属的民族崇拜眼睛，故以“眼”为名，兄弟俩序长者称大眼，序幼者为小眼。

与杨氏兄弟差不多同时期，北魏还有个将军叫傅竖眼。其籍贯地清河，大致在今日河北邢台、山东临清交界一带，但史载清河傅氏有自北地迁徙者——北地郡治义渠，春秋时即为氐羌故地。竖眼其名，带有明显的纵目习俗痕迹，以此推断，傅竖眼很有可能是义渠氐人的后裔。

傅竖眼以平定武兴（今陕西略阳）氐人叛乱而得以升迁，算得上是打回老家去。以氐平氐而不自知，类萧峰抗辽而实为“辽狗”，历史的吊诡尽在其中。

Given this cultural background, it becomes clear that Yang Dayan and Yang Xiaoyan were named not based on the actual size of their eyes. Instead, their names are a testament to the ethnic group's reverence for eyes, and the elder brother, named "Big Eyes", signifies his seniority; the younger brother, named "Small Eyes", indicates his position as the junior sibling.

Around the same time as the Yang brothers, there was another Northern Wei general named Fu Shuyan. Fu hailed from Qinghe, roughly located at today's border area between Xingtai in Hebei and Linqing in Shandong. Historical records indicate that originally the Fu family had migrated from Beidi Commandery, whose administrative center was Yiqu—a region historically inhabited by the Di and Qiang peoples in the Spring and Autumn period. The name "Shuyan" literally means "vertical eye", which suggests a clear trace of the vertical eye worship custom. This naming convention leads to the strong possibility that Fu Shuyan was a descendant of the Di people from Yiqu.

Fu Shuyan rose through the ranks by quelling the Di rebellion in Wuxing (present-day Lueyang, Shaanxi). In a sense, he was "returning to his roots" by fighting in a region that once belonged to his ancestral homeland. The irony of history is quite striking here—just as the character Qiao Feng in the *Dragon Oath* fought against the Khitans while being a Khitan.

道教治国

农耕时代的时光流逝是缓慢的。

东汉汉安二年（143年），早年曾任巴郡江州（今重庆）县令的张道陵在鹤鸣山创立五斗米教时，距古蜀

Taoism in national governance

In agrarian times, the passage of time moved at a leisurely pace.

By the second year of Han'an reign during the Eastern Han Dynasty (143 AD), Zhang Daoling, who had previously served as the magistrate of Jiangzhou

国灭亡已四百五十四年，其时原始宗教在那一片大地仍有流风遗韵。张道陵就地取材，以蜀地巫觋杂以老庄学说创教，凡供奉五米斗者即可拜在门下，一时门徒云集。中国历史上规模和影响最大的本土宗教——道教，就此诞生。

张道陵共划分了二十四个教区，即二十四治，其中有一半在成都地区，如阳平治、鹤鸣山治、葛贵山治以及位于南门外锦江畔的玉局治。

张陵死后，子张衡、孙张鲁相继承其业。初平二年（191年），张鲁攻下汉中，并烧毁栈道，断绝交通，在此建立了政教合一的政权。

李雄家族自祖上迁往汉中杨车坂之后，开始接触道教。其实，李氏所属賨人是巴人一支，在其原居住宕渠与蜀人相邻而生，对巫觋原本就十分敬奉。到了张鲁在汉中传播五斗米教，自然是趋之若鹜。待到李特率领数量庞大的氐人流民进入蜀地，以至李雄建立成汉，同氐人原始信仰关系密切的道教之于氐人政权，便如水之于鱼。

in Ba Commandery (modern-day Chongqing), founded the Five Pecks of Rice movement on Heming Mountain. This occurred 454 years after the fall of the ancient Shu state, a period in which elements of primitive religion still lingered in the region. Drawing from local traditions, Zhang Daoling combined Shu shamanistic practices with the philosophies of Laozi and Zhuangzi to establish his new faith. The core principle was simple: anyone who offered five pecks of rice could become his follower. This straightforward and accessible requirement attracted a multitude of disciples. Thus, Taoism, the largest and most influential indigenous religion in Chinese history, was born.

Zhang Daoling divided his movement into twenty-four parishes, with half of them located in the Chengdu area. Notable parishes included Yangping Parish, Heming Mountain Parish, Gegui Mountain Parish, and Yuju Parish along the Jin River outside the southern gate of Chengdu.

Upon Zhang Daoling's death, his son Zhang Heng and later his grandson Zhang Lu took over the leadership of the movement. In the second year of Chuping (191 AD), Zhang Lu seized control of Hanzhong. He then strategically isolated the region by destroying plank roads and cutting off transportation routes. In doing so, he established a theocratic regime that combined religious authority with political governance.

After the Li family's ancestors relocated to Yangcheban in Hanzhong, they began to encounter Taoism. The Li family belonged to the Cong people, a branch of the Ba people, who originally lived in Dangqu and were neighbors to the Shu people. The Ba people had a strong reverence for shamanistic practices and witchcraft long before their exposure to Taoism. Thus, when Zhang Lu started propagating the Five Pecks of Rice movement in Hanzhong, the

青城山天师洞古银杏需六七人才能合抱，树身钟乳密集悬垂，相传此树为道教创始人张天师手植　冉玉杰 摄

The ancient ginkgo tree at Tianshi Cave on Mount Qingcheng requires six to seven people to encircle it. The tree, with densely hanging stalactite-like roots, is said to have been planted by Zhang Tianshi, the founder of Taoism. (Photographer: Ran Yujie)

在李氏家族建立成汉政权的过程中，道教领袖范长生起了重要作用。范长生生于汉献帝建安二十三年（218年），历经东汉、蜀汉、西晋、成汉四朝。如是算来，他与李氏开始接触时，已经八十五岁了。这个年龄略有些夸张，但不算离谱。范长生擅天文术数，也懂得长生之道，他在青城山率上千户人结寨而居，拥有大批部曲和积粮。太安二年（303年），李特死于兵事，又加之军中缺粮，一时人心浮动，形势极为艰难。此刻，范长生伸出援手，为流民队伍提供了军粮。

Li family naturally gravitated towards it. When Li Te led a large number of displaced Di people into the Shu region, and later when Li Xiong established the Cheng Han state, Taoism became deeply intertwined with the Di people's original beliefs. For the Di-led Cheng Han regime, Taoism was as vital and natural as water is to fish.

A Taoist leader named Fan Changsheng played a crucial role in the establishment of the Cheng Han regime by the Li family. Born in the 23rd year of the Jian'an reign (218 AD) during Emperor Xian of Han's era, he lived through the Eastern Han, Shu Han, Western Jin, and Cheng Han dynasties. By the time he began interacting with the Li family, he was already 85 years old—a seemingly exaggerated age but not implausible given historical records. Fan Changsheng was well-versed in astronomy, divination, and the teachings of longevity. He led over a thousand households to form a settlement in Qingcheng Mountain, amassing a considerable following and stockpiling substantial grain reserves. In the second year of the Tai'an reign (303 AD), the situation became dire after Li Te died in battle, and the army faced a severe shortage of provisions, causing unrest among the people. At this critical juncture, Fan Changsheng supplied the displaced population with much-needed military provisions.

In the leap month of the lunar calendar, Li Xiong captured Chengdu. Fan Changsheng arrived in a plain carriage, and Li Xiong personally greeted him at the city gate, offering him the seat of honor and proposing to make Fan the king. However, Fan Changsheng declined and urged Li Xiong to proclaim himself ruler instead. In gratitude and recognition of Fan's support, Li Xiong appointed Fan Changsheng as Chancellor and honored him with the title "Grand Master of Heaven and Earth". Additionally, Fan's followers were exempted from paying taxes,

当年闰十二月，李雄攻占成都。范长生乘坐素车来到成都，李雄立于城门前迎接，执版让座，欲迎范长生为君王，而范长生反劝李雄自立。李雄也投桃报李，封范长生为丞相，加号“天地太师”。特别优惠的是，范的部曲得以免缴赋税。五斗米教由此成为国教，教首范长生成为国师，道教的传播和成汉政权的巩固，可谓相辅相成。

李雄欲让大位于范长生，大概率是真心诚意而非故作姿态，原因有三：一是李雄对道教虔诚，对范尊重且有感激之情；二是氐族流民入蜀之初，与土著民多有冲突，李特就死于当地大姓组织的反叛之中，故李雄欲借助范长生的影响力来弥合外来者与当地人的矛盾；三是李雄对权力并没有执念。不渴望权力者，在历史上是异数，但并非没有，李雄对接班人的安排可以印证这一点。

春秋时，吴国国王寿梦欲传位给贤明的幼子季札，却被推辞，于是想了个主意，要让王位在四个儿子之间依序传递。等到三个哥哥都死了，终于传到四弟季札时，他却一躲了之。于是，老大的儿子阖闾觉得既然四叔不当国王，王位就应当回到自己的手里，于是刺杀了三叔的儿子、坐在国

which was a significant privilege. This event marked Taoism's elevation to the status of the state religion. Fan Changsheng, as its patriarch, became the State Preceptor. The support and integration of Taoism played an instrumental role in consolidating the Cheng Han regime and the spreading of Taoism.

Li Xiong's offer to cede the throne to Fan Changsheng was likely genuine rather than a mere gesture, and there are three main reasons to support this: first, Li Xiong was a devout follower of Taoism and held Fan Changsheng in high regard. He was deeply grateful for Fan's crucial support, especially during the challenging times; second, the displaced Di people faced numerous conflicts with the indigenous population upon entering Shu. Li Te himself was killed during a rebellion led by local elites. Li Xiong likely sought to leverage Fan Changsheng's influence to foster social harmony and bridge the gap between the newcomers and the natives; lastly, Li Xiong did not exhibit an obsession with absolute power, a rarity in history but not unprecedented. His approach to succession planning provides further evidence of this disposition.

Li Xiong's approach to succession indeed finds an interesting parallel in historical anecdotes. During the Spring and Autumn period, King Shoumeng of the State of Wu wanted to pass the throne to his wise youngest son Ji Zha. However, Ji Zha refused the throne, prompting Shoumeng to plan for the throne to be passed sequentially among his four sons. After the elder three brothers died, Ji Zha evaded his responsibility, leading to a conflict where the eldest brother's son, Helü, claimed the throne by assassinating the third brother's son, King Liao.

A similar scenario replayed in the Cheng Han state under Li Xiong's rule.

Despite having ten sons, Li Xiong insisted on appointing his nephew, Li Ban, the son of his

君位上的吴王僚。

类似的剧情，又在李雄生后重演。

李雄自己有十来个儿子，却不顾大臣反对，坚持要立哥哥李荡的儿子李班为太子，理由有二：一是基业是由父亲李特创下的，哥哥李荡本应是继承人，却在即将胜利之时死于战争之中（其母罗氏梦到门前两道彩虹升空，一道断裂，即指此事）；二是李班为人仁厚孝敬，又好学重儒，将来会是一个好皇帝。

李班作为李特亲孙子、李雄钦定王储，继位是有合法性的。可是，架不住有人更有合法性，李雄的儿子李越就不服气，遂暗中与弟弟李期图谋，杀李班于殡宫之中。为斩草除根，还杀了李班弟弟李都，逼得李班另一个兄弟李玝投降了西晋。

李班在位一年，被杀后由李雄第四子李期即位。李期治国无方，政事决于数人，且好杀戮，大臣皆惶恐不安，道路以目的场面现于国中。李期在位三年，被堂叔李寿囚禁，心中郁闷，自缢而亡，时年二十五岁。李寿则一鼓作气，将李雄的儿子全部杀掉。

经过这一系列的自相残杀，成汉的国运一日不如一日，李雄死后十多

deceased elder brother Li Dang, as his heir. This decision was made despite significant opposition from his ministers and can be attributed to two main reasons: first, Li Xiong believed that the foundation of their state had been established by his father, Li Te, and the inheritance of their state rightfully belonged to his brother Li Dang, who tragically died in battle just as victory seemed within reach. This was symbolically represented by a dream Li Dang's mother, Lady Luo, had, wherein two rainbows rose in front of their gate, but one broke—an omen foretelling Li Dang's untimely death; second, Li Ban was known for his benevolence, filial piety, and dedication to learning in Confucianism. Li Xiong saw these qualities as indicative of a promising future emperor who would rule with wisdom and compassion.

Li Ban, as the direct grandson of Li Te and the heir designated by Li Xiong, had a legitimate claim to the throne. However, legitimacy alone was insufficient to deter those with competing claims and ambitions. Li Xiong's son Li Yue was dissatisfied with the naming of Li Ban as the successor. Along with his younger brother Li Qi, they conspired to seize power. They orchestrated a plot and ultimately killed Li Ban in the funeral palace. To ensure their hold on power and eliminate any potential threats, they also murdered Li Ban's brother Li Du, forcing another brother, Li Wu, to seek refuge by defecting to the Western Jin.

After Li Ban's assassination, Li Xiong's fourth son, Li Qi, ascended to the throne. However, Li Qi's reign proved disastrous. He made an ineffective ruler, relying on a small coterie of advisors to make decisions, and he had a penchant for violence, instilling fear and insecurity among his ministers. The pervasive fear and instability led to a situation where "people on the road dared not to say anything but to exchange their hatred with eyes." Li Qi's reign

年，就被东晋桓温带兵灭国了。

李雄在世之日，性情宽仁，行法简约，颇能听进谏之言，与丞相范长生的配合也是相得益彰。集道教领袖和成汉丞相两种职位于一身的范长生，以道家思想无为而治，与民休养生息。对待老百姓，减役宽政，男丁每年只交三斛谷子——比西晋丁男的田赋少一斛，女丁则减去一半，生病者亦减半；按户征调的赋税每年也只有数丈缎、数两绵，不及西晋的三分之一。

此外，成汉还兴办学校，设置史官，出现了一派民风质朴、社会安定的局面。当时的西晋王朝，“八王之乱”尚未结束，给社会带来的创痛依然惨烈，“五胡乱华”方兴未艾，可谓内忧外患、板荡难已，而此时的蜀地，却人民乐悦、远离刀兵，成为乱世之中的桃源。只可惜，这一切在李雄生后就戛然而止了。

按理说，李雄传贤不传子，于国于民是有利的，但他没想到的是，美好的愿望敌不过人心的残酷。过于先进的理念，出现在不恰当的时间，可能会带来巨大灾难。就像他那位半个同族人、雄才伟略的大秦天王苻坚一样，存宏愿而不逢时——后者心怀民族大同的理想，却最终被现实导入

lasted only three years before he was imprisoned by his paternal uncle, Li Shou. Overcome with depression, Li Qi committed suicide by hanging at the age of twenty-five. Li Shou, seizing the opportunity to consolidate power, eliminated all of Li Xiong's remaining sons.

The internecine strife and brutal purges significantly weakened the Cheng Han state. With its fortunes waned steadily over the years, just over a decade after Li Xiong's death, the Cheng Han regime was conquered by Eastern Jin's Huan Wen.

During Li Xiong's reign, his benevolence and straightforward administration gained him respect and loyalty. He was open to advice and had a good rapport with Fan Changsheng. Fan, who combined his roles as the Taoist patriarch and Chancellor of Cheng Han, implemented lenient and considerate policies inspired by Taoism's principles of non-exertion. His government reduced corvée labor requirements and implemented lighter governance measures. Male adults were required to pay only three bushels of grain per year, which was one bushel less than the tax imposed by the Western Jin. Female adults, as well as those who were sick had their tax obligations cut by half. Taxes levied per household yearly comprised only a few bolts of silk and a few liangs of cotton, amounting to less than one-third of what the Western Jin required.

Besides, Cheng Han established schools to promote literacy and learning among the populace. Official historians were appointed to document the events and governance of the state. The society was characterized by simplicity and stability, contrasting starkly with the concurrent chaos of the Western Jin Dynasty, where the "Rebellion of the Eight princes" continued to wreak havoc, and the "Upheaval of Five Barbarians" further exacerbated the widespread devastation. Cheng Han became a refuge of peace and

"非我族类，其心必异"的旧轨。

惜哉。

李氏集团带领十数万流民入蜀成就霸业，是古蜀国的辉煌之后氐人又一次高光时刻。随着苻坚战败于淝水、前秦帝国土崩瓦解，仇池国屡灭屡复而最终倾灭于北周杨坚，"氐"这个字在史籍中出现的次数越来越少，在历史的隧道中渐行渐远，步向永恒的未知深处。

唯有从三星堆青铜像到成汉俑，那一只只奇诡的眼睛，依然悬挂在时间的上空，透露出无尽的好奇。

joy. Unfortunately, it all came to an abrupt end after Li Xiong's death.

Li Xiong's decision to pass the throne to a capable and wise successor rather than his own son was, in principle, beneficial for both the state and its citizens. However, he underestimated the harsh realities of human nature and its ruthless desire for power. Li Xiong's progressive notion of merit-based succession came in inopportune times, shattered and produced tragic outcomes, much like his partially kin-related counterpart Pu Jian of the Former Qin Dynasty, who harbored grand visions of national unity among diverse ethnic groups. In the end, Fu was channeled into the old track of "non-kin must have different hearts", likewise met with failure.

What a pity.

The Li clan's leading of tens of thousands of displaced people into Shu and the establishment of a dominant regime was a significant high point for the Di people, following the ancient glory of the Shu Kingdom. However, as Pu Jian's catastrophic defeat at the Battle of Feishui, the Former Qin empire disintegrated. The state of Chouchi experienced numerous cycles of destruction and revival but ultimately succumbed to Northern Zhou under Emperor Yang Jian. The name "Di" slowly began to vanish from historical records, receding into the obscurity of history's long passage.

Though the Di People prominence's waned, from the enigmatic bronze statues of Sanxingdui to the distinctive Cheng Han figurines, the unique and mysterious eyes continue to captivate.

万里桥
Wanli Bridge

它是成都最古老的桥，年龄二千二百岁。它出身名门，由蜀郡守李冰修建；诸葛亮、费祎点石成金。

治蜀名臣在桥上怀念诸葛亮的功绩，大诗人如杜甫、刘禹锡、岑参、张籍、薛涛、苏轼、陆游留下了咏吟它的诗篇。

它当得上“成都第一桥”之名吗?

It is the oldest bridge in Chengdu, aged 2200 years. It has a noble origin and was built by Li Bing, the Governor of Shu; Zhuge Liang and Fei Yi turned this stone bridge into a golden signboard.

Famous officials governing Shu memorialized Zhuge Liang's achievements on the bridge, and great poets such as Du Fu, Liu Yuxi, Cen Shen, Zhang Ji, Xue Tao, Su Shi, and Lu You left behind verses chanting it.

Does it deserve the title of"The First Bridge of Chengdu"?

万里桥：成都第一桥
Wanli Bridge, the first bridge in Chengdu

万里桥

清・骆成骧

长江万里涉波涛，
慷慨登舟使节劳。

Wanli Bridge

Luo Chengxiang, Qing Dynasty

Through Yangtze's surging billows, a thousand miles we trace,
Embarking boldly, envoys toil with grace.

山隔巫庐云盖迴，
江连吴楚浪花高。
三分鼎立东西帝，
百战关临上下牢。
朱雀桥边回首处，
连天春草似青袍。

Mountains separate Mount Wu and Mount lu, clouds in distant veil,
River merges the ancient states Wu and Chu, high waves prevail.
Three kingdoms stand, East and West divided,
Hundred battles fought here, fortress exchanged.
By Vermilion Bird Bridge, I turn and see,
Spring grass blending with the heavens, a green sea.

万里桥是一座承载着历史的桥梁　何大江 摄
Wanli Bridge, a structure steeped in history. (Photographer: He Dajiang)

临三国遗迹而咏史，诗与文不可胜数，而清末状元骆成骧的《万里桥》是艺术价值被低估了的一首诗。作者站在成都万里桥边怀古，目光越过猿啼云绕的三峡和曾有折戟沉沙的赤壁，抵达东吴首都建业。串连起三千里长江，跨越两千年废兴，这首诗当得起状元之才。诗中“慷慨登舟使节劳”之句，就涉及万里桥的得名。

联吴抗曹，是诸葛亮在隆中时就制订的战略，但吴蜀两国为了争夺荆州，进行了一系列的战争，后果是关羽被杀、刘备败死白帝城。刘备去世

Poems and essays commemorating the relics of the Three Kingdoms are innumerable, yet “Wanli Bridge” by Luo Chengxiang, the top scholar of the late Qing Dynasty, is a poem whose artistic value has been underestimated. Standing by the Wanli Bridge in Chengdu, the author reflects on history, his gaze traversing the Three Gorges, where apes cry and clouds coil, and the sands of Red Cliffs where broken spears once lay submerged in, and reaching Jianye,the capital of Eastern Wu. This poem links the three thousand miles of the Yangtze River and spans two thousand years of rise and fall, befitting the talent of a top scholar. The line “Embarking boldly, envoys toil with grace”alludes to the origin of the name Wanli Bridge.

The alliance with Wu against Cao Cao was a strategy devised by Zhuge Liang during his retreat in Longzhong. However, the states of Wu and Shu waged a series of wars over Jingzhou, with the

后，诸葛亮调整策略，着手修复战争造成的创痕。建兴三年（225年），诸葛亮平定南中之乱后回到成都，以费祎出使东吴，重修盟好。此时，距夷陵之战不过三年。

因为此行关系重大，诸葛亮亲自到成都城南锦江上的水码头饯行。船之将发，深孚厚望的费祎对着一旁的大桥叹曰："万里之路，始于此桥。"桥，因此更名为万里桥，之前它本叫长星桥。

从此之后，众多治蜀地方官员、无数文人学子便在桥边缅怀诸葛亮。一声感慨，一千八百年后犹有回响。

1988年，对万里桥进行维修时，人们在桥下曾发现汉砖，这为谱画该桥的历史年轮增添了实物佐证。

consequences of Guan Yu's killing and Liu Bei's defeat and death at Baidi City. After Liu Bei's decease, Zhuge Liang adjusted his strategy and began to work on repairing the wounds caused by the war. In the third year of Jianxing (225 AD), Zhuge Liang returned to Chengdu after pacifying the Nanzhong Rebellion, and dispatched Fei Yi as an envoy to the Eastern Wu to renew the alliance. At this time, it was only three years after the Battle of Yiling.

Because of the journey was very important, Zhuge Liang personally went to the dock by the Jin River, which was seated on the south of the Chengdu City, to bid farewell. Before the ship was about to depart, Fei Yi, bearing great expectations, gazed at the bridge and exclaimed: "thousand miles of the road starts from this bridge."The name of this bridge, therefore, was changed into the Wanli Bridge (Thousand Miles Bridge); previously it was called the Changxing Bridge.

Since then, many Shu local officials, countless literati and students would stand at the bridge to commemorate Zhuge Liang. Their exclamations still reverberate after 1800 years.

In 1988, during the restoration of Wanli Bridge, Han Dynasty bricks were discovered beneath it, providing tangible evidence to trace the bridge's historical timeline.

李冰建造
北斗七星映七桥

万里桥的建成，年代则更为久远，可以追溯到李冰修都江堰、引二江入成都之际。锦江是想象力的产物，等同于将岷江搬到了成都。其实，锦江之上万里桥的建造也非常富

Seven Stars shining up Seven Bridges build by Li Bing

The construction of the Wanli Bridge was even older, dating back to the time when Li Bing constructed the Dujiangyan and drew the two rivers into Chengdu.The Jin River is a product of imagination and is equivalent to moving the Min River to Chengdu. In fact, the construction of the Wanli Bridge over the Jin River was also very

于想象力。秦汉时的两江，分别从北和西两个方向流到成都城西南角。北面的那条叫郫江，又叫内江，即今日之府河；南面的那条叫流江、检江，也叫外江，即今日之南河。在唐之前，两条江在成都城南并肩而行，又离得非常近。其间的狭长地带，在汉代即是繁华的商业区，被称作“市”。两条河一内一外，像是挂在“市”两边的耳环，这就是当时成都“二江珥市”的格局。

李冰是个极度有想象力的官员，他在这两条江上造了七座桥，而这七座桥正对应天上的“北斗七星”。内江之上，从东至西分别为江桥、市桥、冲治桥、长升桥和永平桥；外江之上，为长星桥（万里桥）和笮桥。内江上的江桥、市桥和外江上的两桥座，组成七星阵的斗勺，而万里桥则正对应着北斗星上天璇星的位置。

imaginative.The two rivers in Qin and Han Dynasty, flew respectively from the north and west to the southwest corner of Chengdu City. The one on the north side was called the Pi River, aka the Inner River, that is today's Fu River; the one on the south side was called the Liu Jiang River or Jian Jiang River, aka the Outer River, today's Nanhe River. Before the Tang Dynasty, the two rivers ran shoulder to shoulder in the south of the Chengdu City and they were very close. The narrow strip of land in between was a bustling commercial area known as the "Market" as early as in the Han Dynasty. The two rivers, one inside and one outside, looked like earrings hanging on both sides of the "Market", which was the pattern of Chengdu's "two earring-like rivers encircle the market"at that time.

Li Bing was an incredibly imaginative official. He constructed seven bridges over these two rivers, corresponding to the Big Dipper constellation in the sky. On the Inner River, from east to west, there are Jiang Bridge, Shi Bridge, Chongzhi Bridge, Changsheng Bridge, and Yongping Bridge; on the Outer River, there are Changxing Bridge (Wanli Bridge) and Zuo Bridge. The Jiang Bridge, Shi Bridge on the Inner River, and the two bridges on the Outer River form the dipper's bowl in the Big Dipper formation, with Wanli Bridge corresponding to the star Megrez.

20世纪20年代的万里桥。河里的竹篓里面，是餐馆养的活鱼。桥头的枕江楼始创于1907年，是以河鲜、海产品著称的餐馆，民国时期的成都文人常在此雅集（资料图片）

Wanli Bridge in the 1920s. The bamboo baskets in the river were used by restaurants to keep live fish. At the bridgehead stood Zhenjiang Tower, established in 1907, a restaurant famous for river and seafood dishes. During the Republican era, it was a popular gathering spot for Chengdu's literati. (Archival Image)

到了唐僖宗乾符元年（874年），南诏入侵成都，能臣高骈紧急调任剑南西川节度使进行抵御。击退南诏之后，高骈决定一劳永逸地解决城区太小无余地回旋、城防缺少屏障等问题，遂兴筑罗城。同时，还让内江改道，从縻枣堰（今九里堤）改向东流——成为今日府河雏形，并仍在原来的两江汇合处（今合江亭）与外江相交。这样，新的郫江保护着城的北面与东面，检江则继续保护着南面，成都的城市格局也从“二江珥市”变成了“两江环抱”。

这一次大改造，基本没有涉及检江。因失去功用，原内江上的桥逐渐被湮没，而万里桥则一直伫立在南河之上。

In the first year of the Qianfu reign of Emperor Xizong of the Tang Dynasty (874 AD), the army of Nanzhao Kingdom invaded Chengdu, and Gao Pian, an able minister, was urgently transferred to the position of Military Governor of the Western Sichuan Province in Jiannan to defend against the invasion. After defeating the Nanzhao troops, Gao decided to solve once and for all the problems of the city being too small to maneuver and lacking a barrier in its defense, so he built Luo Cheng. At the same time, he ordered the diversion of the river from Mizaoyan (now Jiuli Dike) to the east—becoming the prototype of the current Fu River, and the convergence to the Outer River was still at the original joint (now the Hejiang pavilion). That being done, the new Pi River protects the north and east of the city, and the Jian River continues to protect the south; whereupon Chengdu's urban pattern from the "two earring-like rivers encircling the market" into the "two rivers embracing the city".

This major renovation basically did not involve the Jian River. Due to the loss of its functionality, the original bridge over the Inner River was gradually obliterated, while the Wanli Bridge has always been standing over the Nanhe River.

四方辐辏
诗人自古多吟咏

“扬一益二”是唐代俗语，益即益州，实指其首府成都。实际上，在唐人卢求看来，所谓扬州繁华天下第一，只是因为名声在彼耳尔。他在《成都记》序言中如此比较两大名镇：“江山之秀，罗锦之丽，管弦歌舞之

Attention from all directions; poets have been singing and chanting since ancient times

The Tang Dynasty saying "Yang ranks first, Yi second" refers to Yizhou, specifically its capital Chengdu. In fact, according to the Tang poet Lu Qiu, the reputed splendor of Yangzhou was only because of its fame. In his preface to *Record of Chengdu*, he compares the two great towns: "The beauty of its rivers and mountains, the elegance of its brocade,

多，伎巧百工之富；其人勇且让，其地腴以善熟。较其妙要，扬不足侔其半。”

侔者，相等也。卢求是幽州范阳（今北京）人，这个北方人来到成都，对这里的山川物产、风俗人情都热爱得无以复加。在他看来，扬州连成都的一半都比不上。而在当时的成都，万里桥一带的“市”又是繁华之最，真可谓“最是红尘中一二等风流富贵之地”。

这等繁盛的由来，跟万里桥附近的大型水码头有关。李白的“云帆龙舸下扬州”、杜甫的“门泊东吴万里船”，都能证明成都与江南的水路往来。岑参《万里桥》里的“沧江东流疾，帆去如鸟翅”则描绘了江面细节，更加具有画面感。除了水路交通，万里桥还占据着陆路交通的要津。直到明清，出城向南通往新津，乃至更远的雅安、乐山和康定，万里桥都是主通道上的必经之处。

在高骈筑罗城改内江之前将近一百年，韦皋镇蜀时，就在万里桥以南创办了新南市。他令人平整坟墓、开通街道。实际上，这是因为当时成都商业发达、人口膨胀，夹在两江之中的“市”已不敷使用，需要向外扩展，另辟新区。成都尹、剑南西川

the abundance of music and dance, the plenty of its skilled artisans; its people are both brave and courteous, and its land is fertile and well-cultivated. In terms of its excellence, Yangzhou does not even compare to half of it.”

Lu Qiu, a native of Fanyang in Youzhou (present-day Beijing), fell deeply in love with Chengdu’s natural beauty, products, customs, and people. To him, Yangzhou could not even match half of Chengdu’s splendor. In those times, the market area around Wanli Bridge was the most prosperous, truly a place of “supreme elegance and wealth amidst the worldly dust.”

This prosperity can be attributed to the large river dock near Wanli Bridge. Li Bai’s “Cloud sails and dragon boats descend to Yangzhou” and Du Fu’s “outside the door, moor the boats going to the Easter Wu, a thousand miles journey” testify to the waterborne traffic between Chengdu and Jiangnan. Cen Shen’s poem *Wanli Bridge* describes the river scene vividly, “The blue river flows swiftly east, sails depart like bird wings”, adding a picturesque touch. Besides water transportation, Wanli Bridge also occupied a crucial point in land transportation. Until the Ming and Qing dynasties, it was the main route south out of the city, leading to Xinjin, and further to Ya’an, Leshan, and Kangding.

Nearly a hundred years before Gao Pian built Luocheng and diverted the water passage of the Inner River, Wei Gao founded Xinnan City to the south of Wanli Bridge when he was in charge of the administration of Shu. He had the graves leveled and new streets opened. In fact, Chengdu was so commercially developed and populated that the “market” sandwiched between the two rivers was no longer adequate and needed to be expanded outward to create a new area. Wei Gao, the Military Governor of Yin and Jiannan/Western Sichuan exerted a huge

节度使韦皋的力度很大，在万里桥南岸建好的新区商铺楼阁相连，规模宏大，民户过万。

不过，夜间的新南市跟白天完全是两个世界。夜色里鬼声呜咽，砾石乱飞，将人吓得不轻。韦皋于是请来道士，置办了黄箓道场，连做三天法事才算消停。此后，神仙托梦给韦皋：因为建新南市平坟，造就了一大批孤魂野鬼，他们因失去家园而痛哭，不过后来法事做得好，上帝受感动，决定超拔野魂三万，剩下的则去各处投生了。

故事要分两部分来看。上半部分讲述事实，下半部分生发意义。这段记载首见于《云笈七签》，这是一本道教类书，编者是宋真宗时的官员张君房。真宗崇道，上有好下必甚，此书的目的便可以想见。不过，倒不必因为书中夹有私货，而将宝贵的史料弃若敝屣。研究历史，亦如沙里淘金。

由于水陆通达、商贾云集，唐代的万里桥一带，旅舍酒肆业极为发达。

“锦江近西烟水绿，新雨山头荔枝熟。万里桥边多酒家，游人爱向谁家宿。”在唐代诗人张籍的《成都曲》里，因为酒店、宾馆多得让人眼花缭

power. Under his stewardship, new commercial stores and pavilions connected one another on the south bank of the Wanli Bridge, the scales being more than 10,000 households.

However, the Xinnan City at night was a completely different world as opposed to its daytime scenery. In the night, ghost-like whimper can be heard, gravels were seen flying about and people were scared out of wits. Wei Gao then invited Taoist priests to conduct the religious ceremony for three days before the weird incidents stopped. After that, a Taoist immortal sent a dream to Wei Gao: because of the construction of the Xinnan City, graveyards were levelled; as a result, a large number of lonely ghosts were displaced. They cried because of the loss of their homes, but after the ceremony was done, God of Underworld was moved and decided to save the wild souls of 30,000, and the rest of them reincarnated elsewhere.

The story should be viewed in two parts. The first part recounts the facts, while the second part elaborates on their significance. This account first appeared in the *Seven Sticks of Yunji,* a Taoist text compiled by Zhang Junfang, an official during the reign of Emperor Zhenzong of the Song Dynasty. Zhenzong revered Taoism, and what the emperor favored was often pursued with great enthusiasm by his subjects. The intent of this book is therefore understandable. However, we should not discard valuable historical materials just because some personal biases may be interwoven. Studying history is akin to panning for gold in the sand.

Due to its accessible waterways and land routes, and converging merchants, the area around Wanli Bridge in the Tang Dynasty thrived with inns and taverns.

In the Tang poet Zhang Ji’s Song of Chengdu, he describes the abundance of hospitality establishments

乱，游人竟然有了选择恐惧症。

这幅成都版的“清明上河图”上，作为陪衬的景物也非常迷人：新雨初霁，锦江上薄雾升腾，刚被雨水洗过的荔枝在枝头颤颤巍巍，引人垂涎欲滴。顺带说一句，唐时成都气候比现在更温暖，能够种植荔枝。

在有关成都的古诗词里，万里桥是被吟诵得最多的名胜。

“万里桥西一草堂，百花潭水即沧浪。”杜甫在这里安息身心，观百花潭水而感到身心自足。尽管跟官朋友断绝了往来，儿子也总是挨饿，但不妨碍他“自笑狂夫老更狂”。

“凭寄狂夫书一纸，家住成都万里桥。”杜甫之外，还有个刘禹锡写万里桥时也用到了“狂夫”一词，不过他这是在模仿思念丈夫的怨女的口吻：你在外谈生意进货，倒是风流快活，可不要忘了我们在万里桥边的家啊。

“楚客过此桥，东看尽垂泪。”荆州江陵人岑参在万里桥头的酒楼里怀念家乡，道不尽游子孤寂。

“拿舟直入修篁里，坐听风湍澈骨清。”在桥边竹林丛里划船吹风，是吕大防为官之外的乐趣。

“我欲归寻万里桥，水花风叶暮萧萧。”经历过“乌台诗案”的苏轼，

around Wanli Bridge, making travelers so overwhelmed by choices that they experience a sort of decidophobia:

Jin River close by, misty and green, New rain, lychees ripening, sheen.

Wanli Bridge flanked by taverns galore,

Which one to stay in? Tourists implore.

In this Chengdu version of “Along the River During the Qingming Festival”,the supporting scenery is equally enchanting: a fresh rain has just ceased, thin mist rises from the Jin River, and the recently washed lychees dangle tantalizingly from their branches. Incidentally, the climate in Tang-era Chengdu was warmer than it is now, allowing for the cultivation of lychees.

In the ancient poems about Chengdu, Wanli Bridge is the most recited famous place.

“West of Wanli Bridge, a thatched hut, the Hundred Flowers Pool, I wash my hat-strings in the clear water.”

Here, Du Fu found solace, facing the waters of Hundred Flowers Pool and feeling self-sufficient. Though he severed ties with his official friends and his son often went hungry, it didn’t stop him from jesting about his own eccentricities:“Laughing at myself, a madman growing madder with age.”

“Awaiting a letter from the madman, his home by Wanli Bridge.” Besides Du Fu, Liu Yuxi also referenced Wanli Bridge, using the term “madman” in a playful mimicry of a longing wife’s voice: “While you are out conducting business, enjoying yourself, don’t forget our home by Wanli Bridge.”

“Chu traveler crossing this bridge, looks east and weeps.” Cen Shen, from Jiangling in Jingzhou, reminisced about his hometown at the tavern near Wanli Bridge, expressing the solitude of a wanderer.

“Paddle straight into the bamboo grove,

Sit and listen to the clear winds rinsing my

更加迷恋生活中可以把握的美好，明明是送别朋友，他却思念蜀地了。

“扫眉才子知多少，管领春风总不如。”王建用诗歌来赞美小他三岁的小姐姐——“万里桥边女校书”薛涛；而薛涛自己则叹道：“万里桥头独越吟，知凭文字写愁心。”

说到跟万里桥有关的历史名人，不可不提《松窗杂录》里记载的一件轶事。

开元十二年，唐玄宗临幸东都洛阳，游天宫寺阁，高僧一行（天文学家张遂）随行。此时秋色将尽，万木凋零，玄宗触目伤怀，接连叹气四次。此时才三十九岁的他，问一行：“吾甲子得终无患乎？（不知在我有生之年，会不会遇上忧患？）”一行答道：“陛下行幸万里，圣祚无疆。”

又过了三十一年，安史之乱爆发，玄宗狼狈逃到成都。一日，至一桥边，问道：“是桥何名？”剑南节度使崔园打马上前，答道：“万里桥。”

唐玄宗突然想起多年前一行所言“行幸万里”，顿时心安。一行所说的“万里”，指的是行万里路，但若视作双关，便是谶语，便藏玄机。

后来，崔园因为在万里桥上接驾玄宗有功升了官，当上中书令，并进

bone marrow.” Boating and enjoying the breeze in the bamboo thickets near the bridge was one of Lü Dafang’s pleasures outside his official duties.

“I wish to return to Wanli Bridge, where water flowers and wind leaves whisper in the dusk.”

Having experienced the “Wutai Poetry Case”, Su Shi grew even more enamored with the beauties of life he could grasp. Though bidding farewell to a friend, his heart yearned for Sichuan.

“Talented women are not many, who knows the subtlety of literature better than her.” Wang Jian used the poem to praise Xue Tao, a young lady three years younger than him, who was the “Blue stocking by the Wanli Bridge”; while Xue Tao herself lamented, “I have been singing alone at the Wanli Bridge, only to drown my sorrows in my writings.”

Speaking of historical figures related to Wanli Bridge, we cannot fail to mention an anecdote recorded in the *Miscellany of Pine Windows*.

In the twelfth year of Kaiyuan, Emperor Xuanzong of the Tang Dynasty visited Luoyang, the eastern capital, and traveled to the Heavenly Palace, accompanied by the prestigious monk Yixing (Zhang Sui, an astronomer). At that time, the autumn colors were fading out and all the trees were withering. Touched by this bleakness, Xuanzong, 39, sighed four times in a row and he asked Yixing: “Will my reign see no calamities?” Yixing replied, “Your Majesty’s journey will span ten thousand miles, and your reign will be eternal.”

Thirty-one years later, the An Shi Rebellion broke out, and Emperor Xuanzong fled to Chengdu in distress. One day, he went to a bridge and asked, “What is the name of this bridge?” Cui Yuan, the Military Governor of Jiannan came forward on his horse and replied, “Wanli Bridge (Thousands of Miles Bridge).”

Emperor Xuanzong suddenly recalled the

封赵国公——不知是否跟唐玄宗领悟“万里”的那一刻，心中大石头落了地有关系。

words Yixing said many years ago, "journey spanning ten thousand miles" and immediately felt at ease. What Yixing said "thousands of miles" referred to thousand miles distance, but if regarded as a pun, it is a prophecy, a hidden mystery.

Later, Cui Yuan got promoted because of his merit in escorting Emperor Xuanzong on the Wanli Bridge. First he was promoted as Secretariat Director and was further granted Mr. Zhao — it remained unknown whether his promotion had anything to do with relief of Emperor Xuanzong when he suddenly apprehended the meaning of "Thousands miles".

一桩谜案 杜甫在万里桥还有草堂？

万里桥由李冰所建，出身不凡，经诸葛亮、费祎点石成金，又有历代诗人妙笔生花，关注度一直非常高。然而，当笔者偶然接触到陆游《老学庵笔记》上的一则史料时，仍然禁不住又惊又喜。惊的是，名人留胜迹，如此重要之事，怎会从来未听说过？喜的是，似乎解开了笔者对一句杜诗的疑惑。

《老学庵笔记》上的那段文字是这样的：“杜少陵在成都有两草堂，一在万里桥之西，一在浣花，皆见于诗中。万里桥故迹湮没不可见，或云房季可园是也。”

看，陆游也提到诗。哪句诗？上

A mystery case: did Du Fu has another thatched house by the Wanli Bridge?

The Wanli bridge was built by Li Bing. It has unusual origin and its reputation, buttressed by Zhu Geliang and Fei Yi as well as poets from different generations, is nothing short of brilliance so the attention it attracts has been very high. However, when the author accidentally came upon a historical material recorded in *Notes on Laoxuean Thatched House* written by Lu You. I cannot help being surprised and happy. What surprised me was why I didn't know such a celebrity had ever visited this important site. What made me joyful was that it seems to solve a mystery in Du Fu's poem which baffles me.

The passage from *Old Schoolyard Notes* reads: "Du Shaoling had two cottages in Chengdu, one west of Wanli Bridge and one in Huanhua, both mentioned in his poems. The original site of Wanli Bridge has vanished and is no longer visible, though some say it was the Garden of Fang Ji."

The poem Lu You referred to is also mentioned above, in which two verses read "A thatched house

文的“万里桥西一草堂，百花潭水即沧浪”。还有一句杜诗，往往被今人记作“万里桥西宅，百花潭北庄”。

唐代的百花潭，并非今日百花潭公园，而是在杜甫草堂西南的龙爪堰。清水河在此一分为三，中为清水河主流，向北分出浣花溪，向南分出肖家河，三股水形似龙爪，而明代在此筑堰溉田，故称“龙爪堰”。

草堂倒正是在古百花潭东北面，靠得很近，正是所谓“百花潭北庄”。但是，顺着清水河向东，与磨底河汇成南河，再到万里桥，还有八九里路哩。这么远的距离，能纳入一处来写吗？

如果按陆游所说，杜甫有两处草堂，一处在万里桥西，另一处在浣花溪，不是完美解决了疑问吗？

说杜甫草堂为“万里桥西宅”，是“诗意”的误会
冉玉杰 摄
Referring to Du Fu’s Thatched Cottage as “the residence west of Wanli Bridge” is a poetic misunderstanding. (Photographer: Ran Yujie)

locates to the west of the Wanli Bridge, the water of the Hundred Flowers Pond is like the water in The Canglang River”. There’s another verses from Du’s poem, often remembered today as “A house on the west of the Wanli Bridge, and a cottage on the north of the Hundred Flowers Pond”.

The Hundred Flowers Pond in Tang Dynasty was not today’s Hundred Flowers Pond Park, but the Longzhuayan in the southwest of Dufu Thatched House Park. The Qingshui River is divided at here into three tributaries, with the mainstream in the middle, to the north it branching out the Huanhuaxi Creek and to the south it diverging the Xiaojia River. The three streams shaped like a dragon’s claw, and in Ming Dynasty a weir was built here to irrigate the fields, so it is called the Longzhuayan (Dragon’s Claw Weir).

The Thatched House is precisely located to the northeast of the Hundred Flowers Pond and they are very close, that is “a cottage on the north side of the Hundred Flowers Pond”. However, there are eight or nine miles between the Thatched House and the Wanli Bridge. One has to walk along the Qingshui River to the east, and passes the Modi River before coming to Nanhe River, and finally arrives at the Wanli Bridge. Can such a long distance be treated as one place?

If, according to Lu You, Du Fu had two thatched houses, one on the west of the Wanli Bridge and one at the Huanhua Creek, wouldn’t that be a perfect solution to my question?

且慢，稍加研究，却又发现了新的问题，前文提及“万里桥西宅，百花潭北庄”，一查杜甫原诗，居然不是“西宅”，而是“南宅”——所以笔者才说“往往被今人记作”。

那似乎也说得通，杜甫两处草堂，一处在浣花，另一处在万里桥西南方附近——既是“西宅”，也算“南宅”。

但是，笔者再三思考，否定了这样的判断。

理由一，杜甫之贫困人所共知，很难有能力建两处草堂。

理由二，若真有两处草堂，为什么不卖掉一处，来修补为秋风所破的另一处呢？至少得让儿子吃饱吧？

理由三，以杜甫的名声，真有两处草堂，应当会有多处记载，而不会只见于《老学庵笔记》一处。对于史料，笔者的态度是：凡有可疑者，若只此一说即为孤证，不足采信。

理由四，杜诗写自己的心理感受，见景生情，即便写两处景，也当为转眼之见所见。若只是展开联想，写两处相距甚远、几无关联的场景却不注明，断无此理。

再读一下他那两首《怀锦水居止》中的一首吧，明明是由自己所住之地扩展到整个锦城，怎么也看不出

Wait a minute. A new problem occurred after a little research. The verses “A house on the west of the Wanli Bridge, and a cottage on the north of the Hundred Flowers Pond” mentioned earlier should be “A house on the south side of the Wanli Bridge” when I checked Du Fu’s original poem; it is actually not “west”, but “south”! — That’s why I said “often remembered today”.

That also seems to make sense because Du Fu had two houses, one in Huanhua Creek, the other in the southwest of the Wanli Bridge near — “west”, or rather “south”.

However, upon further reflection, the author rejects such a judgment.

Reason one: Du Fu’s poverty was well known, and he could hardly afford to build two thatched houses.

Reason two: if there were really two thatched houses, why wouldn’t he sell one of them to repair the other one that was broken by the autumn wind? At least let his son have enough to eat, right?

Reason three: given Du Fu’s renowned status, if he truly had two cottages, there would be multiple records of them rather than just a mention in the *Old Schoolyard Notes*. The author’s stance on historical materials is: anything suspicious, if it is a solitary mention, is not credible.

Reason four: Du Fu’s poem was his own psychological reflections and his feelings were aroused when he saw some scenes. Even if he wrote two scenes, those scenes were what he saw at present. If he let his imagination expand, it is unreasonable to have two scenes juxtapose that are far away from each other and have no connection.

Let us read the whole poem, *Missing My Residence in Jinjiang*. When he wrote about his residence,he practically looked beyond his residence to the entire city and people can barely see that he is

写的是两处宅子——

万里桥南宅，百花潭北庄。

层轩皆面水，老树饱经霜。

雪岭界天白，锦城曛日黄。

惜哉形胜地，回首一茫茫。

那么问题出在何处？

这是因为从浣花溪至万里桥皆在唐代成都南城门之外，沿途并无别的标志性建筑，因此杜甫将桥作了参照物，以表明草堂方位。

万里桥实在是名气太大，所以往往成为描述方位的标杆。如雍正年间《四川通志》，说关帝墓（衣冠庙）和张桓侯墓俱“在华阳南万里桥侧”，但实际上，衣冠庙距万里桥三里左右；张桓侯墓其实是成汉贵族墓，在今华西医院内，距万里桥约一里。说墓在桥侧，其实相距甚远，杜甫只说“桥西”“南宅”，便可以理解了。

那么，到底是南宅，还是西宅呢？杜甫原诗确为“南宅”，为何改为“西宅”，参见清人梁章钜《楹联丛话》所言：“草堂集句联云：‘万里桥西宅，百花潭北庄。’”

将“西宅”作为对联刻在杜甫草堂正门的匾额上，自然广布天下。久而久之，倒没人记得杜甫原诗了。

就实际方位而言，草堂确实在万里桥以西，“西宅”是准确的描述。

writing about two residences—

Residence south of Wanli Bridge, village north of Hundred Flowers Pool.

Layered pavilions face the water, old trees weathered by frost.

Snow-capped peaks touch the sky white, Jin City's dusk sun glows yellow.

Alas, this splendid place, looking back, vast and vain.

Then what is the problem?

This is because the area from Huanhua Creek to Wanli Bridge was outside the south gate of Chengdu in the Tang Dynasty, and there were no other landmarks along the way, so Du Fu used the bridge as a reference to show the location of his thatched house.

The fame of the Wanli Bridge is so popular that it is often used as a benchmark to describe the location. In the *History of Sichuan* published in Yongzheng reign, it is said that Guan Di Temple (cenotaph) and Zhang Huanhou Tomb were "in the south of Huayang by the side of the Wanli Bridge" — but in fact, the Guan Di Temple is about three miles from the Wanli Bridge while Zhang Huanhou Tomb, a tomb among the aristocrats' tombs of the Cheng Han Dynasty (in today's Huaxi Hospital), is about one mile from the bridge. The tombs "by the side of the Wanli Bridge" are actually far from each other. Therefore, it is understandable when Du Fu said "west" and "south".

Then why the "south" house in Du Fu's original poem was changed into "west" house? In *Couplets* written by Liang Zhangjui in Qing Dynasty, it is recorded that "A house on the west of the Wanli Bridge, a cottage on the north of the Hundred Flowers Pond"

The verses containing "west" was engraved as a couplet on the plaque at the main entrance of Du Fu's Thatched House, which was naturally widely

那么是在西南方吗？若此，“南宅”倒也说得通。

不，在西北方。那么，“南宅”从何而来？

还是跟着杜甫的脚步，从草堂往万里桥走一走吧。草堂所在浣花溪，从清水河分出，只流了短短几里路便汇入磨底河，很快又跟清水河汇合成南河——古今水系有变，但他一直走在南河的南岸。

从汇合点开始，南河呈西北—东南流向，但这个幅度很小，沿着河走的人是感觉不出来的。再走上几里路，就来到万里桥了。此时，杜甫的位置正在桥之南桥头，吟出“万里桥南宅”便是自然而然的事了。

至于宋代为什么会有杜甫有两处草堂的说法，应该还是因为那两首诗的误导，加之对方位的理解不同所致。

publicized. Over time, no one remembers Du Fu's original poem.

In terms of physical orientation, the Thatched House is indeed at the west of the Wanli Bridge, so "west house" is an accurate description. Is it in the southwest? If so, "south house" would make sense as well.

No, it's in the northwest. So, where does "south house" come from?

Let's follow Du Fu's footsteps and walk from the Thatched Hose to Wanli Bridge. He walked along the Qingshui River to the east, and passed the Modi River before coming to Nanhe River, and finally arrived at the Wanli Bridge—the water system has changed since ancient times, but he always walked on the south bank of the Nanhe River.

From the confluence, the Nanhe River flows in a northwest-southeast direction, but this magnitude is so small that it is not perceptible to those walking along the river. A few more miles up the road, one will come to the Wanli Bridge. Du Fu's position was at the south end of the bridge, and it was natural for him to recite "A house on the south of the Wanli Bridge".

In Song Dynasty, the question regarding why Du Fu had two thatched houses should be ascribed to the misleading meaning of the two poems, coupled with a different understanding of the orientations.

四个赵公
究竟是谁修了万里桥？

万里桥到底什么模样，宋之前已不可考。

南宋一位崇拜诸葛亮的赵姓地方官在成都知府任上，命人整修了古

All four gentlemen are surnamed Zhao, who indeed repaired Wanli Bridge?

What exactly the Wanli Bridge looks like is not available before Song Dynasty.

During his tenure as Prefect of Chengdu, a Southern Song Dynasty official surnamed Zhao, who worshipped Zhuge Liang, ordered the renovation of

柏祠和万里桥两个跟诸葛相关的三国遗迹。他最初见到的万里桥已经很破败了，于是增加石鱼（水标），将水分为五道——由是可知当时是一座五孔桥——并在石桥墩上用木材搭建房屋，让之成为一座廊桥。

此事被宋人刘光祖写于《万里桥记》。这名修桥的地方官，在文中被称作侍御赵公。幕僚刘光祖受赵公委托写此记，颇有范仲淹受滕子京嘱写《岳阳楼记》之意味。两文相同之处还有，写景非意在写景，总是会落脚到天下为公的儒家理想。

文中说，千年间人事兴废，而桥独以孔明之故传世。走在赵公新建好的桥上，人们匆匆忙忙无暇欣赏风景，即便欣赏风景者也很少有人能明白赵公之深意。那么，这位以诸葛亮为榜样的赵公是谁呢？

有文章称其为绍兴年间两度为相的赵鼎，笔者之前也曾采用过这样的说法。

嘉庆《华阳县志》称其为成都路转运判官赵开，其人曾在四川进行财政改革。

《都江堰文献集成》“万里桥记”条下注释称其为成都知府赵抃，其人在历史上与西汉文翁、蜀汉诸葛亮、北宋张咏并称“四大治蜀名臣”。赵

the Gubai Shrine and the Wanli Bridge, two relics of the Three Kingdoms associated with Zhuge. The Wanli Bridge he initially saw was already in a state of disrepair, so he added stone fishes (water markers), divided the water into five channels—from which it can be seen that it was a five-hole bridge at that time—and used timber to build houses on the stone piers to make it into a corridor bridge.

This deed was written by Liu Guangzu in Song Dynasty, in the *Book of Wanli Bridge*. The prefect who repaired the bridge was called Mr. Zhao, Imperial Consul, in the text. Commissioned by the Mr. Zhao, Liu Guangzu wrote this record, which is quite similar to *The Record of Yueyang Tower* written by Fan Zhongyan who was commissioned by Teng Zijing. The two texts are also alike in that the writing of scenery is not meant to be scenic, but always comes down to the Confucian ideal of the whole world is one community.

People rise and fall in thousands of years, so are worldly affairs, according to the text, and the bridge exists only because of Zhuge Liang. Walking on the newly built bridge by Mr. Zhao, people are in a hurry and have no time to appreciate the scenery, and even if they appreciate the scenery, few can understand the deep meaning of Mr. Zhao. So, who is this Mr. Zhao that models himself after Zhuge Liang?

Some articles claim that he was Zhao Ding, who was a Grand Councilor twice during the Shaoxing era, and the author had also adopted such a statement before.

The Record of Huayang County published in the Jia Qing era calls him Zhao Kai, a magistrate of Chengdu, who initiated fiscal reforms in Sichuan.

An entry *Records of Wanli Bridge* in the *Literatures Collection of Dujiangyan* identifies that he is the Prefect of Chengdu, Zhao Bian, who is historically known as one of the "Four Famous

抃著过一本讲述成都沿革、地理的《成都古今记》，且又担任过殿中侍御史，与侍御赵公的称呼也相符，应该是他了吧？

然而以上三人中，年龄最大的赵抃比写《万里桥记》的刘光祖大一百三十四岁；年龄最小的赵鼎去世时，刘光祖不过五岁，显然不能为其幕僚。

检索《宋史》，发现与刘光祖交往甚密者，有四川制置史赵汝愚。

赵汝愚，宋太宗赵光义八世孙，虽为天潢贵胄，但自幼家贫。汝愚至孝，少有大志，常说："丈夫得汗青一幅纸，始不负此生。"后来果然考中状元，成为一代名相。

查《南宋制抚年表》，赵汝愚于南宋淳熙十二年（1185年）入蜀为官，在四川制置使任上共三年。而《万里桥记》称，在赵公之前，"前帅沈公常修广之"。赵汝愚入蜀之前二十二年，确有沈介担任同职。如是，确定修缮万里桥者为赵汝愚。

经赵公汝愚修葺的万里桥存在了约四百六十年，明末毁于战火。在张献忠攻陷成都城的战斗中，成都同知方尧相被执不降，遇害于万里桥。临终留下绝命诗："江水茫茫须借力，此身飘荡赴团风。"他希望自己的魂

Ministers of Shu" along with Wen Weng of the Western Han Dynasty, Zhu Geliang of the Shu Han Dynasty, and Zhang Yong of the Northern Song Dynasty. Zhao Bian authored a book about the history and geography of Chengdu, *Records on Ancient and Contemporary Chengdu*, and also served as a royal official in the palace, and his title also matches Mr. Zhao, Imperial Consul. So, should the Mr. Zhao be him?

However, of the above three, the oldest, Zhao Bian, was 134 years older than Liu Guangzu, who wrote *Book of Wanli Bridge*, while the youngest, Zhao Ding, died when Liu Guangzu was only five years old, so obviously Liu Guangzu could not be Zhao Ding's advisor.

Searching the *History of the Song Dynasty*, it is found that the person who had a very close relationship with Liu Guangzu was Zhao Ruyu, a city planner in Sichuan.

Zhao Ruyu, an eighth grandson of Zhao Guangyi, Emperor Taizong of Song. Although born with a silver spoon in mouth, Zhao Ruyu came from a humble start. Pious and aspirational, he often said: a man of character must leave reputations in history so as not to waste his life. Later on, he really won the *Zhuang Yuan* (top scholar), and became a famous Grand Councilor.

Checking the *Governor's Chronology of Southern Song Dynasty*, we find that in twelfth year of Chunxi (1185) of Southern Song Dynasty, Zhao Ruyu came to the Shu to perform his duty. He three years as a city planner. According to *Book of Wanli Bridge*, before Zhao Ruyu, "the former Duke of Shen often repaired the Wanli Bridge". Twenty-two years before Zhao Ruyu, came to Sichuan, Shen Jie indeed served in the same position. As such, the one who repaired the Wanli Bridge is Zhao Ruyu for certain.

The Wanli Bridge, which was repaired by the

魄能够顺着锦江水，从万里桥回到家乡黄冈团风。

到了清康熙五年（1666年），以巡抚张德地为首的四川官员捐出俸禄，重建廊桥。

乾隆五十年（1785年）再次修缮：两侧加装石栏杆，江水中增加石墩，万里桥就这样变成了一座七孔石砌拱桥。

Duke Zhao Ruyu, existed for about 460 years before it was destroyed in a war at the end of the Ming Dynasty. During the battle when Zhang Xianzhong captured Chengdu, Fang Yaoxiang, a government official, was killed on the Wanli Bridge after he refused to surrender. On his last moment, he left behind a parting poem:"Boundless river, may I borrow your strength, my soul adrift, to consign this body to Tuanfeng." He hoped that his soul could follow the water of the Jin River under the Wanli Bridge and return to his hometown, Tuanfeng, Huangang.

By the fifth year of the Kangxi reign of the Qing Dynasty (1666), Sichuan officials, led by Grand Coordinator Zhang Dedi, donated their salaries to rebuild the corridor bridge.

In the fiftieth years of Qianlong (1785) the Wanli Bridge was repaired again: stone railings were added on both sides of the bridge and stone pillars were installed in the water, turning the Wanli Bridge into a seven-hole stone arch bridge.

"忒修斯之船"
万里桥还是万里桥吗?

万里桥因为处于成都南门外，成都人通常呼之为南门大桥。1939年，下游锦江上又新建了一座南门大桥，此桥便被称为“老南门大桥”。

1953年、1987年和1989年三个时间点，万里桥数次进行维修、加固，两侧增设钢桁架人行道，铺筑沥青混凝土桥面。

因为府南河整治工程的需要，老万里桥于1995年2月23日下午3时15

"Ship of Theseus":
Is Wanli Bridge still the same bridge?

The Wanli Bridge is often referred to as the Nanmen Bridge because it is located just outside the south gate of Chengdu, and in 1939 a new Nanmen Bridge was built over the Jin River downstream, which became known as the "Old Nanmen Bridge".

In 1953, 1987 and 1989, the Wanli Bridge was repaired and strengthened, augmented with steel truss sidewalks and asphalt concrete decking on both sides.

The old Wanli Bridge was demolished by blasting at 3:15 p.m. on February 23, 1995, because of the needs of the Funan River Improvement Project. With a span of 53 meters, a width of 40 meters, and a

分爆破拆除。跨度五十三米、桥宽四十米，混凝土结构，一座新的万里桥在原址上建了起来。

那么，这座桥还是不是万里桥呢？这似乎又是一个类似“忒修斯之船”的哲学命题。

古希腊的英雄忒修斯带领勇士，驾着一艘船，杀死了怪物，因此深受敬仰。罗马帝国时代的希腊哲学家普鲁塔克于是借此神话进行了一个思想实验，他设想：那艘船因为风雨的侵蚀而破败，人们为了维修，开始一块块更换船上木板和其他部件，终于有一天，船上所有的木板都被换光了——那么，这艘“新”船跟忒修斯驾回来的那艘船相比，已经没有一块板、一个部件相同了——它们还是同一条船吗？

想起来，万里桥甚至还远远比不上忒修斯的那条船。它并不是一块石板一块石板、一个石墩一个石墩地拆换，而是被整体炸毁了。还是不是同一座桥，也更加没有悬念。

不过，人们依旧把这座混凝土桥视作万里桥，或许是因为心中有着敬仰和念想吧。用人类的感情解开了普鲁塔克给出的难题。

“忒修斯之船”还有进一步的推想：拆下来的木板被运到了另一座码头，重新拼装成了一条船——那么，

new concrete structure Wanli Bridge was built on the same site.

So, is this bridge still the Wanli Bridge? This seems to be another philosophical proposition similar to the “Ship of Theseus”.

The ancient Greek hero Theseus was greatly admired for leading warriors, sailing a ship, and slaying monsters. Plutarch, a Greek philosopher during the Roman Empire, then used this myth to conduct a thought experiment, in which he envisioned that the ship had been worn out by the elements, and that in order to repair it, people began to replace the planks and other parts of the ship piece by piece, and that one day, all the planks on the ship had been replaced—so the “new” ship was no longer the same as the one that Theseus had sailed back, not a single plank and a single part—was it still the same ship?

The Wanli Bridge was not even remotely close to the ship of Theseus. It wasn’t removed and replaced slab by slab, pillar by pillar, but was blown up as a whole. Whether it’s still the same bridge or not is even less suspenseful.

However, people continue to regard this concrete bridge as the Wanli Bridge, perhaps because of the admiration and thoughts in their hearts. The puzzle given by Plutarch was solved with human feelings.

The “Ship of Theseus” is further hypothesized: if the planks that were dismantled, were transported to another dock, and reassembled into another boat—was it the real Ship of Theseus?

The fate of Wanli Bridge seems to coincide with the second step of Plutarch’s thought experiment: at the end of 1997, between Qingyang Hengjie Street and Wangxianchangjie Street on the north and south bank of the Nanhe River, another five-hole bridge across the Jin River was erected—modelled after

它才是真正的忒修斯之船吗？

万里桥的际遇，似乎跟普鲁塔克思想实验的第二步又正相吻合。1997年底，在南河北岸的青羊横街和南岸的望仙场街之间，又一座跨越锦江的五孔桥立了起来——它正是依照七孔古万里桥的形制建造的。虽然它的名字叫“望仙桥”的，也没有一块石头来自古万里桥，但毕竟在典籍资料和老照片之外，给成都人增添了一个更加生动的凭吊之处。

其实，当人们去追寻文物古迹之时，经常会遭遇“忒修斯之船”的哲学命题。

文物修复，若不能修旧如旧，便多会遭人诟病，这不仅是因为破坏了文物，也有着更深层次的哲学原因。

此外，异地搬迁也是文物保护的常态。比如位于文殊坊的肇第，原本是民国军阀石肇武的公馆，2006年由鼓楼南街迁来；又比如本书《蜀王陵：十三代皇族的楼起楼塌》一文中的蜀昭王陵，则是从白鹤村搬到了现址，利用全部的原材料，按原来的样式重建。

在对待文物古迹的拆迁与修复，如果人们能多一分哲学意义上的思考，便会给后世多留一分幸运。

且放下关于“忒修斯之船”的思考，再回到这座桥本身。

and built in the shape of the ancient seven-hole Wanli Bridge. Although its name is “Wangxian Bridge”, and there is no stone from the ancient Wanli Bridge, but after all, in addition to the canonical data and old photos, a more vivid place was added for the people of Chengdu to pay homage to for the old-time sake.

In fact, the philosophical proposition of the “Ship of Theseus” is often encountered when people are in search of cultural relics and monuments.

When it comes to restoration of cultural relics, if you cannot restore as they were, you will be criticized, not only because of the destruction of cultural relics, but also a deeper philosophical reason.

In addition, relocation is also the norm in heritage conservation. For example, the *Zhaodi*, which is located in Wenshufang, was the original residence of a warlord, Shi Zhaowu, in Republic of China, and was moved in 2006 from South Gulou Street; the Royal Residence of King of Shu, which is introduced in this book, was relocated from Baihe Village to the current site. Following the original pattern and style and using original raw materials, people rebuilt a new one.

In dealing with the demolition and restoration of cultural relics and monuments, if people can think a little more philosophically, they will leave a bit of fortune for future generations.

Let’s put aside our thoughts about the “Ship of Theseus” and return to the bridge itself.

The Wanli Bridge has been called by its name for more than 1,800 years; and in the more than 2,200 years since it was built by Li Bing, its location has never changed, regardless of repair or rebuilding, making it the oldest known bridge in Chengdu.

万里桥的名字叫了一千八百多年；而从李冰建桥至今二千二百多年的时间里，不管修葺还是重建，它的位置也从来没有变更过，是已知成都最为古老的桥。

建于1997年的望仙桥，保存了古万里桥的神韵　何大江 摄

Wangxian Bridge, built in 1997, preserves the charm of the ancient Wanli Bridge. (Photographer: He Dajiang)

今日成都，运用新技术、新材料，充满科技感的桥层出不穷。这些桥甫一竣工，往往就成为网红打卡地，引人搔首弄姿。

今日的万里桥，从外形上看，它没有新桥的酷炫，也没有古桥的典韵；同前贤后辈相比，它显得那么普通。

不过，在成都还找不出另外一座桥，比它存在的年月更久长；更找不出一座桥，附着有那么多的人文内涵，有那么多著名的诗歌来吟诵。如果诗中的万里桥、我们心中的万里桥不是“成都第一桥”，那么哪座桥又敢说自己是呢？

In Chengdu today, there are numerous bridges full of new technologies and materials. Upon completion, these bridges often become internet hotspots, attracting people to take photos and selfies.

Today's Wanli Bridge does not have the coolness of these new bridges, nor the elegance of those ancient bridges from its appearance; compared with the former and later generations, it seems so ordinary.

However, in Chengdu you cannot find another bridge whose age was older than it; nor can you find a bridge that is attached with so many humanistic connotations and is recited by so many famous poems. If the Wanli Bridge in the poems and in our hearts is not the "No. 1 Bridge in Chengdu", who else dares to proclaim it is?

第四卷

Volume 4

大慈寺
Daci Temple

号称“震旦第一丛林”的大慈寺，极盛时期计有96院、8542房、佛像万尊、壁画千面。

一生传奇的玄奘大师，既与大慈寺有着殊胜因缘，也留下不少谜案：比如，玄奘圆寂之后九十三年才规建大慈寺，为什么众多高僧大德认为他受戒于此？又比如，玄奘逝于长安，他的顶灵骨为何又曾保存于大慈寺？

Daci Temple, known as the “foremost monastery in Cathy”, in its heyday, had 96 Buddhist colleges, 8,542 halls, tens of thousands of Buddha statues, and countless murals.

The legendary monk Xuanzang had a special connection with Daci Temple, leaving behind several intriguing mysteries. For instance, why did numerous esteemed monks and masters believe that Xuanzang received his ordination at Daci Temple, even though it was established 93 years after his parinirvana? Furthermore, Xuanzang passed away in Chang’an, so why were his parietal bone once preserved in Daci Temple?

大慈寺：唐玄奘谜案
Daci Temple: The Mystery of Tang Xuanzang

天申节前三日大圣慈寺华严阁燃灯甚盛游人过于元夕

宋·陆游

万瓦如鳞百尺梯，
遥看突兀与云齐。
宝帘风定灯相射，
绮陌尘香马不嘶。
星陨半空天宇静，
莲生陆地客心迷。
归途细踏槐阴月，
家在花行更向西。

Three days before the Tian Shen Festival, the Great Holy Compassionate Temple's (Daci Temple) Huayan Pavilion is brightly lit, with more visitors than at the Lantern Festival

Lu You, Song Dynasty

Ten thousand eaves like scales of the dragon, a hundred feet of stairs,
From afar they rise, in unison with clouds they share.
Silken curtains still in breeze, lamps pierce through night's gleam,
Flowery paths, dust and fragrance, horses without a single whinnying stream.
Stars cascade, half the sky, cosmos in tranquil hue,
Lotus blooms on earth's expanse, traveler's heart askew.
On the homeward journey, treading the acacia shade,
Moonlight guides my path, the florist's further laid.

红尘中宁静的去处——大慈寺　余茂智 摄
Daci Temple, a tranquil retreat amidst the bustling world. (Photographer: Yu Maozhi)

在传统民俗中，岁时节令多有燃灯环节，意在祈求福佑。到了唐宋，燃灯会更具规模。南宋初期，以宋高

In traditional folk customs, there are often lantern lighting ceremonies during various festive seasons, symbolizing prayers for blessings and

宗赵构的生辰（农历五月二十一）为天申节，陆游在成都大慈寺参与的这一次燃灯会，则算是其预热。

那天的大慈寺灯会摩肩接踵，游人锦衣绣袿、珠翠香粉，骑马坐轿而至。寺内灯轮高立，上面摆放着盛满了清油的灯盏。等到夜色降临，一一点亮，顿时火树华灯，开启璀璨之夜。

悬在高处的灯火，如半空坠星。地上的莲花灯，则代表寺庙燃灯会的独特性，“我为沙门，处于浊世，当如莲华，不为泥污”。

观灯之后戴月而归，陆游一路上还在回味当时的心醉神迷。

protection. During the Tang and Song dynasties, lantern festivals grew in scale. In the early Southern Song Dynasty, the birthday of Emperor Gaozong (Zhao Gou) on the 21st day of the fifth lunar month was designated as the Tian Shen Festival. The lantern festival that Lu You participated in at Daci Temple in Chengdu could be considered a prelude to this grand event.

On that day, the lantern festival at Daci Temple was crowded with visitors. People came dressed in luxurious attire, adorned with silk garments, embroidered robes, and precious jewelry. They arrived on horseback or in sedans. Inside the temple, towering lantern wheels were adorned with oil lamps, shining brightly. As night fell, the lamps were lit one by one, illuminating the surroundings with a brilliant display of lights, creating a dazzling night of splendor.

The lanterns hanging high resembled stars shining in the sky, while the lotus-shaped lanterns on the ground represented the distinctive nature of the Buddhist temple. They symbolized the purity and enlightenment of monks, who, like lotus flowers, remain unaffected by the impurities of the world.

After enjoying the lantern festival, as Lu You made his way back home under the moonlight, he couldn't help but reminisce and cherish the intoxicating and enchanting experience he had just witnessed.

老成都人叫它太子寺是讹读还是跟太子有关？

在老一辈成都人的口中，大慈寺其实另有称呼。

生于1952年的林子女士（化名），小时候曾跟着爷爷奶奶、爸爸妈妈

The old Chengdu locals call it Taizi Temple, Is it a mispronunciation or related to the prince?

In the mouths of the old generation of Chengdu locals, Daci Temple has another name.

Mrs. Lin, born in 1952 (pseudonym), used to visit with her grandparents and parents when

前去游玩，一家人都把它叫作“太子寺”。而她上中学时，大慈寺成为“成都警备区司令部”的办公场所，于是又有了新称呼——警司。

20世纪80年代末，林子以知青身份回城在市税务局工作好些年头了，一天坐公交车路过，突然听见普通话报站名“大慈寺站到了”，不由得大吃一惊：什么时候改的名字？

其实，叫大慈寺还是叫太子寺，二者并不矛盾。

“大”跟“太”在古代相通，而“慈”跟“子”发音近似——不过，大慈寺被叫作太子寺，并不是简单的读音讹误，而是真的跟一名“太子”相关，即新罗国（唐代朝鲜半岛上的国家）国君圣德王金兴光的三王子。

在中国佛教史尤其是禅宗史上，这位三王子是绕不开的人物，他是禅宗七祖无相禅师，也是著名的八祖马祖道一的师父。据称，为了回避可能发生的王室内部纷争，唐开元十六年（728年）三王子渡海来到大唐，受到玄宗召见。

“安史之乱”爆发之际，无相禅师正在蜀中访道。其时，为了赈济逃难入蜀的百姓，僧人英干设粥厂，在大街上向饥饿之民供粥，并祈祷国家渡过难关。而这个时候，唐玄宗也

she was a child. They all called it “Taizi Temple” (Taizi, the crown prince). However, when she was in middle school, Daci Temple became the office of the Chengdu Garrison Command. Hence, it acquired a new name—Jingsi.

In the late 1980s, as an “Educated Youth”, Ms. Lin returned to the city and had worked in the Municipal Tax Bureau for many years. One day, while she was taking a bus, she suddenly heard the station name announced in Mandarin, “you’ve arrived at the Daci Temple.” She couldn’t help but be surprised, wondering when the name was changed.

In reality, whether it is called Daci Temple or Taizi Temple, the two names are not contradictory.

The word “大” is synonymous with “太” in ancient times, and “慈” sounds similar to “子”. However, calling Daci Temple “Taizi Temple” is not simply a mispronunciation; it is actually related to a prince, pronounced as Taizi in Chinese. This prince was the third son of King Jin Xingguang, the ruler of the Silla Kingdom (a country on the Korean Peninsula during the Tang Dynasty).

In the history of Chinese Buddhism, particularly in Zen Buddhism, this prince is an important figure. He is the seventh patriarch, Master Wu Xiang, and also the teacher of the famous eighth patriarch, Master Ma Zu Dao Yi. It is said that in order to avoid potential internal conflicts within the royal family, the third prince crossed the sea to the Tang Dynasty in the 16th year of the Kaiyuan era (728 AD) and was summoned by Emperor Xuanzong.

During the turmoil of the Anshi Rebellion, the monk Wu Xiang was traveling through Shu region in search of spiritual enlightenment. At that time, in order to aid the refugees who had sought shelter in Shu, the monk Ying Gan established a porridge factory on the main streets, providing food to the starving populace and offering prayers for the

因为避难驻跸成都，听闻高力士奏报此事，心生感动，遂赐田一千亩用于大慈寺扩建，并手书“大圣慈寺”匾额。一个“圣”字，意味着大慈寺和皇家有了关联。唐武宗时期的“会昌毁佛”事件中，大量寺庙被拆毁、僧尼被强制还俗、佛像被销熔，而因为跟唐玄宗的渊源，大慈寺得以幸免于难。

除了题匾赐地，唐玄宗还敕令无相禅师规制大慈寺，并于757年动工。大慈寺的兴盛，以无相禅师始；无相禅师的一生，则以大慈寺终。762年，无相禅师坐化于他作为总规划师参与建设的大慈寺。

无相禅师规制建成的大慈寺，共计“九十六院，八千五百区”，规模极为宏大，号称“震旦第一丛林”。极盛之时，北至今日武城大街，南抵镗钯街一线（镗钯街为当年武僧放置习武兵器镗钯之所），西至红星路二、三段，东临府河。

至于大慈寺诞生的年代，寺内的介绍称“始建至今有一千六百多年”。然而，于此尚有争论。

country to overcome this difficult time. Learning of this act, Emperor Xuanzong of Tang, who had taken refuge in Chengdu, was deeply moved by the report from his trusted advisor Gao Lishi. In response, he bestowed a thousand Mu of land for the expansion of the Daci Temple and personally inscribed the plaque “Great Holy Compassionate Temple (“大圣慈寺” in Chinese character)”. The inclusion of the character Holy in the plaque signaled the connection between the Daci Temple and the imperial family. During the iconoclastic events of the Huichang Persecution under Emperor Wuzong of Tang, many temples were destroyed, monks and nuns were forcibly secularized, and Buddha statues were melted down. However, due to its association with Emperor Xuanzong, the Daci Temple was spared from such destruction.

In addition to bestowing land and inscribing the plaque, Emperor Xuanzong also issued a decree for Wu Xiang to oversee the construction and regulations of the Daci Temple, which began in the year 757. The prosperity of the Daci Temple can be attributed to Wu Xiang’s guidance, and it marked the culmination of his life’s work. In the year 762, Wu Xiang passed away within the Daci Temple that he had helped plan and construct.

Under Wu Xiang’s regulations, the Daci Temple was completed, consisting of “ninety-six colleges and eight thousand five hundred sections”. It was an immense complex, proudly known as the “foremost monastery in Cathy”. During its height, the temple stretched from Wucheng Street in the north to the line of Tangba Street in the south (where the martial monks used to practice with weapons such as spears and halberds), from sections two and three of Hongxing Road in the west to the Fuhe River in the east.

As for the exact birthdate of the Daci Temple, there is some debate. The temple’s internal records claim that it has been in existence for over 1,600 years. However, there are differing opinions on this matter.

玄奘西行归来译《心经》在流沙河念诵的《心经》从何而来?

大慈寺玄奘像　余茂智 摄

贞观三年，玄奘决意西行求法。

西出玉门关，五座烽燧遥遥相接。第一座烽火台的守将王祥赠送了装水的皮囊，更叮嘱玄奘：不宜从第五烽经过，因为当地守将粗鲁，恐于突破禁令走出国门的僧人不利；绕过第五烽，可于野马泉取水。

于是玄奘遵照指点，开始了西行路上最艰难的一段旅途——走进莫贺延碛。

“八百里流沙界，三千弱水深。鹅毛飘不起，芦花定沉底。”《西游记》里，唐僧就在这里收服了沙和尚，此地则被描绘为宽八百里、长万里，波浪汹涌、凶险万分的流沙河。然而，真实的流沙河并不是河，它是戈壁滩上的流沙，是上无飞鸟下无走

After returning from his journey to the West, Xuanzang began the work of translating the Heart Sutra Where did the Heart Sutra that Xuanzang chanted at the flowing Sands River originate?

Statue of Xuanzang at Daci Temple. (Photographer: Yu Maozhi)

In the third year of the Zhenguan era, Xuanzang made the determination to embark on a journey to the West in search of Buddhist scriptures.

Passing through the Yumen Pass, five beacon towers stood in a row, their fires flickering in the distance. The commander of the first beacon tower, Wang Xiang, presented Xuanzang with a water-filled leather bag and advised him not to pass through the fifth beacon tower. He warned that the local commander there was rough and might cause trouble for the monk who had violated the ban by leaving the country. Instead, Xuanzang should bypass the fifth beacon tower and obtain water at the Wild Horse Spring.

Following the guidance, Xuanzang embarked on the most difficult part of his journey to the West - crossing the treacherous Mohe Yan Gobi Desert.

“It’s all quicksand for 800 miles, and three thousand deep no-buoyance rivers. Even goose feathers cannot float, and reeds sink to the bottom.” In the novel *Journey to the West*, Tang Monk tamed the Monk Sha at this location, which is depicted as a

兽的生命禁区。

莫贺延碛，即今日的噶顺戈壁。这里极端干旱，几乎寸草不生，且大风呼啸，雅丹遍布，唯有骡马、骆驼的白骨一路相连。

偏偏在这里，玄奘饮水时失手将皮囊打翻，大漠中最宝贵的生存资源——水，瞬息间全部丧失。这之后四五天的时间，玄奘没有沾过一滴水，虽然还带有干粮，但也因为太渴而无法下咽。唯一能做的，便是以头顶的星月和脚下的骨骸为路标，朝着西北方向继续前行。

干渴、饥饿、温差、大风、孤独、恐惧，让玄奘产生了幻觉，他见到各种各样奇形怪状的恶鬼，缠绕于身前身后。虽然口中称颂着观音菩萨的名号，但恶鬼并不退去。后来，玄奘念诵《心经》，方才战胜幻觉，驱退魑魅魍魉。

“宁可就西而死，岂归东而生？”第五日夜半，有凉风拂身，人与马体力稍有恢复，终于在识途老马的带领下找到水源。经过这一场磨难，玄奘完成了心理上的嬗变，继续西行之路。

问题来了：现在最流行的《心经》汉译版本是归在玄奘名下的，而他在到达天竺之前还未学会梵文，还

wide and long river, spanning eight hundred miles in width and ten thousand miles in length, with turbulent waves and extreme danger. However, in reality, the Flowing Sands River is not actually a river; it refers to the shifting sands on the Gobi desert, a forbidden zone devoid of any living creatures, where neither birds nor animals can be found.

The Mohe Yan Gobi, now called Gashun Gobi, is extremely arid, with almost no vegetation. Strong winds howl through the area, and it is covered in wind-eroded dunes, with only bones of mules, horses, and camels scattered along the way.

Yet, in this harsh environment, Xuanzang accidentally spilled the water from his leather pouch while trying to drink, losing the most precious resource for survival in the desert— water— in an instant. For the next four to five days, Xuanzang went without a drop of water. Although he still had some dry rations, he was too thirsty to swallow them. The only option left was to use the stars above and the scattered bones beneath his feet as landmarks, continuing to march northwestward.

Dehydration, hunger, extreme temperature fluctuations, strong winds, loneliness, and fear caused Xuanzang to experience hallucinations. He saw all sorts of grotesque and monstrous demons swirling around him, tormenting him from all sides. Even though he chanted the name of Avalokiteshvara Bodhisattva, the demons did not retreat. It wasn't until he recited the *Heart Sutra* that he was able to overcome the illusions and drive away the malevolent spirits.

"Would I rather die to the west than be born to the east?" On the fifth night, at midnight, a cool breeze brushed against Xuanzang's body, and both he and his horse regained a bit of strength. Finally, guided by the experienced horse, they discovered a water source. After enduring this trial, Xuanzang

不可能翻译《心经》，那么，在莫贺延碛拯救了玄奘、给了他精神力量的《心经》又是怎么来的呢？

《大慈恩寺三藏法师传》给出了答案。

618年，才十六岁的玄奘入蜀问道，在成都曾遇一病人。此人一身恶臭，长满脓疮，衣服也破破烂烂，十分肮脏。玄奘心生慈悲，便将他带回寺庙照顾，给予饮食衣物。病人十分感激，便传授一部佛经给玄奘作为报答，这即是玄奘在莫贺延碛所念诵的《心经》的来源。

病人传授给玄奘的《心经》又从何而来？

《心经》的汉译版本非常复杂。传世的七个版本译文中，除玄奘本外，另有东晋时期姚秦高僧鸠摩罗什的译本。比较两位大师的翻译，可以发现高度一致。那么便存在这样一种可能：玄奘从病人处习得鸠摩罗什翻译的《心经》，又过了若干年，在天竺那烂陀寺学会了梵文并取经东归，然后在鸠摩罗什译本的基础上，按照自己的理解重新进行了翻译。

也有人认为，鸠摩罗什出生虽然早于玄奘两百多年，但鸠摩罗什译本却是在唐朝才出现，很可能鸠摩罗什并没有翻译《心经》，所谓译本

underwent a profound transformation in his mindset, and he continued on his journey to the west.

The question is: The most popular translated version of the *Heart Sutra* is attributed to Xuanzang, however, he had not yet learned Sanskrit before he arrived in India, so it would have been impossible for him to have it translated. So, how did he come across the *Heart Sutra* that had saved and given him spiritual strength in the Mohe Yan Gobi?

The answer can be found in the *Biography of Tripitaka Master of Great Mercy Temple*.

In the year 618, when Xuanzang was only 16 years old, he came to Sichuan in search of the Dharma. In Chengdu, he encountered a sick man. This man emitted a strong odor, covered in festering wounds, wearing tattered and filthy clothes. Xuanzang felt compassion and brought him back to the temple to take care of him, providing him with food and clothing. The grateful sick man then imparted a Buddhist scripture to Xuanzang as a token of gratitude. This was the origin of the *Heart Sutra* that Xuanzang recited in the Mohe Yan Gobi Desert.

Where did the *Heart Sutra* that the sick man imparted to Xuanzang come from?

The Chinese translations of the *Heart Sutra* are quite complex. Among the seven extant versions, apart from Xuanzang's translation, there is another translation by the eminent monk Kumarajiva during the Eastern Jin Dynasty. Comparing the translations by these two masters, a high degree of consistency can be observed. Therefore, there is a possibility that Xuanzang learned Kumarajiva's translation of the *Heart Sutra* from the sick man, and after several years, he learned Sanskrit and obtained the scriptures in Nalanda, India. Then, based on Kumarajiva's translation and his own understanding, Xuanzang retranslated the sutra.

Some people also believe that although

乃是后人在玄奘译本基础上的托伪之作。

Kumarajiva was born more than two hundred years before Xuanzang, his translation of the *Heart Sutra* only appeared during the Tang Dynasty. Therefore, it is highly possible that Kumarajiva did not actually translate the *Heart Sutra*, and the so-called translation attributed to him is a later fabrication based on Xuanzang's version.

去世后百年才建大慈寺 玄奘能在大慈寺受戒吗？

玄奘将病人带到寺庙照顾，这寺庙便是本文的主角大慈寺吗？

玄奘生于隋朝，十岁时出家。隋末因为关中战乱，佛教的兴盛之地已由长安转移至成都。618年，即隋政权的最后一年，玄奘入蜀求法。而他于622年受具足戒的场所，史料上没有明确记载。（具足戒：又称大戒，意为戒品具足，为佛教徒全面接受戒律的仪式。佛教徒受具足戒后，才能取得正式资格，成为真正意义上的僧人。）

高僧圣钦和尚自1931年起担任大慈寺方丈多年，他在自传中说："当时各丛林以成都大慈寺为唐玄奘大师受戒处。"

按照四川省文史研究馆馆员冯修齐《玄奘在成都大慈寺受戒考论》一文的推论，玄奘大师在成都受具足戒处有两种可能：大慈寺，或大慈寺

It was not until a hundred years after Xuanzang's death that the Daci Temple was built. How could Xuanzang receive ordination at the Daci Temple?

When Xuanzang brought the sick man to the temple for care, was this temple the protagonist of this story, the Daci Temple?

Xuanzang was born during the Sui Dynasty and became a monk at the age of ten. Towards the end of the Sui Dynasty, due to the turmoil in the Guanzhong region, the center of Buddhist flourishing shifted from Chang'an to Chengdu. In the year 618 AD, which was the last year of the Sui Dynasty, Xuanzang went to Sichuan in search of the Dharma. However, there is no clear historical record regarding the specific location where he received the full ordination in 622 AD. (Full ordination, also known as the "Great Ordination",means fully receiving the precepts and is a ceremony in which Buddhist practitioners fully accept the Buddhist code of conduct. Buddhist practitioners can only become true monks in the full sense after receiving full ordination.)

The venerable monk Sheng Qin had served as the abbot of Daci Temple for many years since 1931. In his autobiography, he mentioned: "At that time, Daci Temple in Chengdu was regarded as the place where Master Xuanzang received his ordination."

的前身——多宝寺律院。以上只要有一处成立，即可认为玄奘受戒于大慈寺。

多宝寺遗址，在成都东郊外沙河边，距大慈寺直线距离约3.5千米。唐时的多宝寺，环境清幽，时有高僧大德在此讲法，座下听众多达数百人，是个学修佛法的好去处。然而，它却离城较远，对受戒的僧人来说并不方便。冯修齐考证称，多宝寺的律院应当设在大慈寺内。的确，唐代的大慈寺内，真还有一座多宝塔——相同的名字，似乎暗示着两座寺庙之间的渊源。

据冯修齐推断，后来多宝寺僧众、地盘都归并于大慈寺，直到明代中期复建。近年出土的文物也为这种说法提供了新的证据。在恢复开放大慈寺的建设施工中，2004年元月，大雄殿与藏经楼之间地下两米处，发现了一座多宝寺的石经幢。两年之后，大慈寺再次出土清初石幢《重修多宝寺碑记》。

对于玄奘受戒于大慈寺的说法，反对者也很多，文史作家郑光路即其中之一，他在《宋代成都之七：宋代大慈寺记》一文中明确说道："有人又说玄奘法师是在大慈寺受戒。664年，玄奘逝世。过了九十三年后的

According to the inference made by Feng Xiuqi, a researcher at the Sichuan Provincial Institute of Cultural and Historical Research, in his article *A Study on Xuanzang's Ordination in Chengdu's Daci Temple*, there are two possible locations where Master Xuanzang received his full ordination in Chengdu: Daci Temple or its predecessor, Duobao Temple Monastic Court. If either of these locations can be established, it can be concluded that Xuanzang received his ordination at Daci Temple.

The site of Duobao Temple was located on the outskirts of Chengdu, near the Sha River, at a straight-line distance of approximately 3.5 kilometers from Daci Temple. During the Tang Dynasty, Duobao Temple was a serene environment where esteemed monks would preach, with hundreds of listeners sitting beneath them. It was a good place for studying and practicing Buddhism. However, it was relatively far from the city and not very convenient for monks seeking ordination. Feng Xiuqi's research suggests that the monastic court of Duobao Temple was actually located within the premises of Daci Temple. Interestingly, there was indeed a Duobao Pagoda within the Tang-era Daci Temple, bearing the same name and indicating a possible connection between the two temples.

According to Feng Xiuqi's inference, the monks and territory of Duobao Temple were eventually merged with Daci Temple and were reconstructed in the mid-Ming Dynasty. In recent years, the discovery of cultural relics has provided new evidence for this claim. During the construction of the restoration of Daci Temple in January 2004, at a depth of two meters between the Main Hall and the Scripture Hall, a stone stele from Duobao Temple was found. Two years later, another stone stele titled *Inscription on the Restoration of Duobao Temple* from the early Qing Dynasty was unearthed at Daci Temple.

757年，大慈寺才开始建寺。玄奘法师已经死了将近一百年了，怎会在大慈寺受戒呢？”

大慈寺创始年代，若确定为无相禅师757年规制之时，至2020年止，为1263年。那么，大慈寺内部介绍所称该寺有1600年历史，又是从何而来？

两种说法的矛盾可归结于一点：无相禅师规建大慈寺，是新建还是重建？

若是新建，自然郑的说法是正确的；若是重建或扩建，那么在此之前，大慈寺所在位置上，必然有寺。

禅宗典籍《五灯会元》中有这样的说法：印度人宝掌和尚“魏晋间东游此土，入蜀礼普贤，留大慈”。可见当时蜀地有名为大慈的佛寺无疑。曹魏建于220年，东晋灭于420年，看来大慈寺一千六百年历史的说法即来源于此，并保守地取其下限。

当然，这种说法也有值得质疑之处。

一是宝掌所留大慈，并不一定就是本文所述大慈寺，也可能只是名字相同。

二是《五灯会元》所述，带有明显的神话色彩。宝掌自述出生于周威烈王十二年（公元前414年），有一日

There are indeed many opponents to the claim that Xuanzang received his ordination at Daci Temple, and one of them is the writer Zheng Guanglu. In his article *Chronicles of Chengdu in the Song Dynasty: Chronicles of Daci Temple in the Song Dynasty*, he explicitly states, “Some people claim that Master Xuanzang received his ordination at Daci Temple. Xuanzang passed away in 664 AD. It was not until 93 years later, in 757 AD, that Daci Temple began its construction. Xuanzang had already been dead for nearly 100 years, so how could he have received his ordination at Daci Temple?”

If we determine the founding year of Daci Temple to be 757 AD, as stated by the regulations of Wu Xiang, and calculate until 2020 AD, it would be 1263 years. So, where does the claim of Daci Temple having a history of 1600 years, as mentioned in their internal introductions, come from?

The contradiction between the two arguments can be narrowed down to one point: was the construction of Daci Temple by Master Wu Xiang a new construction or a reconstruction?

If it was a new construction, then Zheng’s argument would naturally be correct. However, if it was a reconstruction or expansion, it indicates that there must have been a temple on the site of Daci Temple before its construction.

The Zen Buddhist scripture *Wudeng Huiyuan* contains the following statement: “During the Wei and Jin dynasties, the Indian monk Baozhang traveled to this land and paid respects to Samantabhadra Bodhisattva, and stayed in Daci.” This clearly suggests that there was a Buddhist temple named Daci in the Shu area at that time. The Cao Wei Dynasty was established in 220 AD, and the Eastern Jin Dynasty ended in 420 AD. It seems that the claim of Daci Temple having a history of 1600 years comes from this period, and has been conservatively estimated.

对众人说："吾有愿住世千岁，今年六百二十有六。"以此计算，宝掌说此话的时间为公元213年，跟曹魏建国还有七年时间，"魏晋间东游此土"一说也是大致时间。

以上，只能说明来自《五灯会元》的证据还不够充分，当然亦无法反证其伪。宝掌自述六百岁非真，但并不等于入蜀留大慈为假。

笔者倒以为，2004年大慈寺工地出土的南北朝石佛残躯，是一个比较坚实的证据，说明在无相禅师规建之前，此处曾有寺庙——无论它叫不叫大慈寺。

郑光路文谈及过寺内接引殿的一尊高二丈余的铜佛像："铜佛的背面刻有'永镇蜀眼李冰制'七个比拳头还大的字，字为秦篆体……一千多年来，这尊佛像逃过了历次战火，但毁于1958年的'全民炼钢'。有'老成都'之称的冯水木先生曾告诉我：铜佛基座有一米高，仅铜皮就有约两寸厚。他目睹工人抡大锤乱砸；头部无法砸烂，为实心红铜。"

关于这尊佛像，《志林大观》1999年第2期刊登的王治平《大慈寺及其兴衰史》之文可与之印证。该文指出：李冰是战国时秦郡守，小篆为秦相李斯所创，其时距李冰去世已有

Of course, this argument also has its questionable aspects.

Firstly, the Daci where Baozhang stayed may not necessarily refer to the Daci Temple mentioned in this context; it could simply be a temple with the same name.

Secondly, the description in the *Wudeng Huiyuan* carries obvious mythical elements. Baozhang claimed to have been born in the twelfth year of King Weilei of the Zhou Dynasty (414 BC), stating that he had been alive for six hundred and twenty-six years, though expecting to live in this world for one thousand years. According to this calculation, Baozhang's statement would date back to 213 AD, which is seven years before the establishment of the Cao Wei Dynasty. The mention of "during the Wei and Jin dynasties" also roughly corresponds to that timeframe.

Indeed, the evidence from *Wudeng Huiyuan* may not be sufficient, but it also cannot be completely dismissed. While Baozhang's claim of living for six hundred years is not true, it does not necessarily invalidate the possibility of his visit to the Shu region and the existence of a temple known as Daci.

Furthermore, the discovery of the remains of stone Buddha statues from the Southern and Northern Dynasties at the construction site of Daci Temple in 2004 provides solid evidence that there was a temple at the location before Master Wu Xiang's reconstruction, regardless of whether it was called Daci Temple or not.

In Zheng Guanglu's writings, he mentioned a bronze Buddha statue in the Daci Temple's Jieyin Hall that stood over two zhang (approximately 7 meters) tall. "The back of the bronze Buddha was inscribed with seven characters in Qin seal script, which read 'Eternal Protector of Shu, Made by Li Bing'. This inscription, according to Zheng, was as large as a clenched fist. Over the course of more than

九十年；另，佛教在东汉明帝时传入中土，距李冰则隔着四百年的时光——李冰是根本不可能去塑造刻有小篆的佛像的，只能是后人托伪。

“据考证，这尊佛像是南北朝时候的造像。我记得在这尊佛像前，还悬了一个‘法侔宝志’的横匾，‘宝志’是梁武帝的国师志公的法号，那么这尊佛像也就是梁武帝时铸造过的。”《大慈寺及其兴衰史》提供的这个细节，还是具有一定的说服力。

侔者，齐也。“法侔宝志”一语，如此赞叹志公禅师，而志公作为梁武帝的国师，在南梁时的影响力肯定是最大的。以此判断，此佛像建于当时的可能性为最大。

如此看来，在唐代无相禅师规建之前，大慈寺的存在是大概率事件，是有着多重证据的。

即便解决了大慈寺在唐代之前是否存在的问题，也未可说玄奘即受戒于此。

《成都城坊古迹考》称，据《大唐大慈恩寺三藏法师传》及唐《续高僧传·玄奘传》载，玄奘受戒于位于现西胜街的石犀寺（又称空慧寺、圣寿寺）。袁庭栋先生的《成都街巷志》也支持此说法。

查《大唐大慈恩寺三藏法师传》

a thousand years, the Buddha statue had survived numerous wars, but it was unfortunately destroyed during the 'Great Leap Forward' movement in 1958 when people were engaged in impractical steel production. Feng Shuimu, a well-known Chengdu local, once told Zheng that the bronze Buddha's base stood one meter high, and the outer bronze skin alone was about two inches thick. Feng had witnessed workers wielding heavy hammers, but despite their efforts, they couldn't fully destroy the Buddha statue's head, as it was made of solid red copper."

The information provided in Wang Zhiping's article *The History of Rise and Fall of Daci Temple* published in the 1999 issue of Zhilin Daguan magazine supports this view. According to the article, Li Bing was a Qin Dynasty official, serving as the governor of Qin commandery during the Warring States period. Qin seal script was created by Li Si, a chancellor of the Qin Dynasty, at a time that was already 90 years after Li Bing's passing. Additionally, Buddhism was introduced to China during the reign of Emperor Ming of the Eastern Han Dynasty, which is approximately 400 years after Li Bing's time. Therefore, it is highly unlikely that Li Bing would have been involved in creating a Buddha statue inscribed with Qin seal script. This suggests that the inscription was most likely a later addition or fabrication.

"According to research, this Buddha statue was made during the Southern and Northern Dynasties. I remember that in front of this Buddha statue, there was also a horizontal plaque that read 'Fa Mou Bao Zhi', where 'Bao Zhi' is the Dharma name of Master Zhi Gong, the national teacher of Emperor Wu of Liang." Therefore, this Buddha statue was likely cast during the reign of Emperor Wu of Liang. This detail provided in *The History of Rise and Fall of Daci Temple* is quite convincing.

“侔” means matching. The phrase “法侔宝志”

原文为:“法师兄因住成都空慧寺……于成都受具坐夏学律。”《续高僧传》则称:“(玄奘)晚与兄俱住益南空慧寺。”

从古籍中,只能看出玄奘在成都受戒、曾住宿于空慧寺等史实,未可轻易得出受戒于成都空慧寺的结论。

前文冯修齐先生称玄奘受戒于多宝寺,其证据之一为玄奘跟驻锡于多宝寺的道因法师、宝暹法师关系密切,从天竺取经归来还特邀法师赴长安译经。细较之,证据也并非十分过硬。

总言之,玄奘到底受具足戒于何寺,仍是一桩谜案,空慧寺、多宝寺和大慈寺俱不能排除。

不过,不管玄奘是否受戒于此,他与大慈寺确实是有着殊胜因缘的。圆寂1298年之后,他的灵骨回到了大慈寺。

praises Zen Master Zhi Gong, and as the national teacher of Emperor Wu of Liang, his influence during the Southern Liang Dynasty was undoubtedly significant. Therefore, it can be inferred that this Buddha statue was most likely built during that period.

In this case, the existence of Daci Temple before the establishment by Zen Master Wu Xiang in the Tang Dynasty is highly probable and supported by multiple pieces of evidence.

However, even if we determine whether Daci Temple existed before the Tang Dynasty, it cannot be concluded that Xuanzang received ordination there.

According to *A Study of Chengdu's Ancient City Districts and Historical Sites*, it is mentioned in *The Biography of Tripitaka Master Xuanzang of Daci En Temple in the Great Tang Dynasty* and *The Continued Biographies of Eminent Monks: Biography of Xuanzang* in the Tang Dynasty that Xuanzang received ordination at Shixi Temple, which is located on Xisheng Street (also known as Konghui Temple or Shengshou Temple). This claim is also supported by Mr. Yuan Tingdong in *Chengdu's Street and Lane Chronicles*.

According to the original text of *The Biography of Tripitaka Master Xuanzang of Daci En Temple in the Great Tang Dynasty*, it states, “The Master's brother resided in Chengdu's Konghui Temple... and received the full ordination with ‘Sitting in Summer’, a three months' meditation in summer in Chengdu.” In *The Continued Biographies of Eminent Monks*, it is mentioned, “(Xuanzang) later resided with his brother at Konghui Temple south of Chengdu city.”

From these ancient texts, we can only ascertain the historical facts that Xuanzang received ordination in Chengdu and stayed at Konghui Temple, among other details. It is not easy to conclude definitively that he received ordination at Chengdu's Konghui Temple.

In the previous text, Mr. Feng Xiuqi mentioned that Xuanzang received ordination at Duobao Temple.

One of the pieces of evidence he presented is the close relationship between Xuanzang and two masters, Dao Yin and Bao Xian, who resided at Duobao Temple. After Xuanzang's return from India with the Buddhist scriptures, he specifically invited these masters to Chang'an to assist with translation. Upon closer examination, however, the evidence is not entirely conclusive.

In conclusion, the question of which temple Xuanzang received the full ordination at remains a mystery, and the possibilities of Konghui Temple, Duobao Temple, and Daci Temple cannot be ruled out.

Regardless of whether Xuanzang received ordination at any of these temples, he indeed had a special connection with Daci Temple. After his passing in 1298, his relics were brought back to Daci Temple.

圆寂于长安
玄奘灵骨怎么到了大慈寺?

玄奘圆寂于长安，顶灵骨为何曾经保存于大慈寺呢?

玄奘的灵骨是在南京报恩寺发现的。报恩寺位于金陵机器制造局附近，内有纪念玄奘的三藏殿和三藏塔墓。1937年，南京沦陷于日军之手，金陵机器被开辟为军工修械厂。

1942年，日军军工厂在平整三藏殿后的土地时，发现一石函，上铭文字："大唐三藏大遍觉法师玄奘顶骨，早因黄巢废塔，今长干演化大师可政于长安传得，于此葬之。"

这段刻于宋仁宗天圣年间的文字，讲述了玄奘灵骨迁播的过程。唐

Xuanzang passed away in Chang'an, and it is indeed a mystery as to how the relics of his bone ended up in Daci Temple.

Xuanzang passed away in Chang'an, so why were his parietal bone once preserved in Daci Temple?

Xuanzang's relics were actually discovered in Bao'en Temple in Nanjing. Bao'en Temple is located near the Jinling Machinery Manufacturing Bureau and houses the Sanzang Hall and Sanzang Pagoda in commemoration of Xuanzang. In 1937, Nanjing fell into the hands of the Japanese army, and the Jinling Machinery was converted into a military machineray repair factory.

In 1942, during the leveling of the land behind the Sanzang Hall by the Japanese military factory, a stone casket was found with the inscription: "The skull relic of the Great Tang Tripitaka Master Xuanzang, the embodiment of great awakening, was originally buried here due to the destruction of the

高宗麟德元年，玄奘大师圆寂，安葬于白鹿原，五年后高宗下令迁葬于兴教寺墓塔内。到了唐末，黄巢大军占据长安，塔墓被毁，玄奘灵骨暴于荒野，被僧人可政发现后带到金陵，安葬于天禧寺（明宣德六年改名为报恩寺）。

元代与明代，玄奘灵骨又曾两次在寺内迁葬。到了清代咸丰年间，太平天国运动爆发，在社会动荡中再一次失去下落——直到在金陵机器制造局重见天日。

在发掘现场，玄奘灵骨置放在石函下面一铜质小龛中。小龛内，装有舍利子及玄奘顶灵骨，灵骨宽约两寸、长约四寸。

日军自然是想将玄奘灵骨据为己有，但在中国人的压力下，不得不于1943年举行了移交仪式。

中国奉迎回玄奘灵骨后，将其分为数份，送往各地，以建灵骨塔。主持分配灵骨的白隆平是四川西充人，决意留下一份在玄奘曾经居住、受戒的四川成都。而玄奘灵骨保存于大慈寺的经历，更有几分传奇色彩。

蒙文通先生是著名历史学家，也对玄奘唯识论有着精深的研究。1949年，时任华西大学（原华西协合大学）教授的蒙文通在家中接待了一位神秘的客人。来客递给蒙文通一个小

pagoda by the rebel Huang Chao. It is now entrusted by the eminent Master Kezheng of Chang Gan Ashram in Chang'an for safekeeping and burial here."

This inscription, dating back to the Tian Sheng reign of Emperor Renzong of the Song Dynasty, narrates the process of the relocation of Xuanzang's relics. In the first year of Emperor Gaozong's Linde reign in the Tang Dynasty, Master Xuanzang passed into Parinirvana and was buried in Bailu Plain. Five years later, Emperor Gaozong ordered the relocation of his remains to the funerary pagoda of Xingjiao Monastery. However, during the late Tang Dynasty, the rebel army led by Huang Chao occupied Chang'an, and the pagoda and tomb were destroyed, leaving Xuanzang's relics exposed in the wilderness. They were later discovered by the monk Kezheng and brought to Nanjing, where they were reinterred at Tianxi Temple (renamed Bao'en Temple during the 6th year of the Ming Dynasty's Xuande reign).

During the Yuan and Ming dynasties, the relics of Xuanzang were relocated twice within the temple. During the Xianfeng reign of the Qing Dynasty, when the Taiping Rebellion broke out, amidst the social turmoil, the relics were once again lost. They remained missing until they were rediscovered at the Jinling Machinery Manufacturing Bureau.

On the excavation site, Xuanzang's relics were placed in a small bronze niche beneath a stone casket. Inside the niche, there were sarira and Xuanzang's skull relic, which measured about two inches wide and four inches long.

The Japanese army naturally wanted to claim possession of the relics, but under pressure from the Chinese, they were obliged to hold a handover ceremony in 1943.

After the relics were returned to China, they were divided into several portions and sent to various

圆木盒，托他交给近慈寺住持能海法师。同时移交的文字《唐三藏法师玄奘灵骨显隐转移之迹》，赫然道出了盒中所藏之物的来历——在金陵机器局挖出的玄奘遗骨。

玄奘灵骨经白隆平、蒙文通、能海之手，安置于成都南郊石羊场附近的近慈寺，后存放于川西博物馆。1962年，大慈寺奉迎了玄奘灵骨。

20世纪60年代中期，大慈寺被用作他途，玄奘灵骨被转移至文殊院保存。

玄奘大师十六岁来到成都，一共待了五年的时间，在成都受戒，并借助在成都得授的《心经》渡过了西行取经途中最大的难关。因为这一段殊胜因缘，他的灵骨存放于成都，可谓是题中应有之义。

苏轼曾与弟苏辙夜游大慈寺，盛赞其间的唐代壁画“精妙冠世” 余茂智 摄

Su Shi and his brother Su Zhe once visited Daci Temple at night, marveling at its Tang Dynasty murals, which they praised as “unrivaled in their brilliance”. (Photographer: Yu Maozhi)

locations to build reliquary stupas. Bai Longping, who was in charge of distributing the relics, was from Xichong, Sichuan province, and decided to keep a portion in Chengdu, where Xuanzang once resided and received ordination. The journey of Xuanzang's relics to Daci Temple adds a touch of legend to their story.

Mr. Meng Wentong, a renowned historian and a scholar with profound research on Xuanzang's Yogacara philosophy. In 1949, while he was a professor at Huaxi University (formerly Huaxi Allied University), Mr. Meng received a mysterious visitor at his home. The visitor handed him a small wooden box and asked him to deliver it to Master Nenghai, the abbot of Jin Ci Temple. The accompanying document, titled *The Journey of Transfer and Manifestation of the Relics of Tripitaka Master Xuanzang from the Tang Dynasty*, revealed the origin of the contents inside the box: Xuanzang's remains unearthed at the Jinling Machinery Bureau.

Through the hands of Bai Longping, Meng Wentong, and Master Nenghai, the relics were eventually enshrined at Jin Ci Temple near Shiyang Field in the southern outskirts of Chengdu. Later, they were placed in the West Sichuan Museum. Finally, in 1962, Daci Temple welcomed the arrival of Xuanzang's relics once again.

In the mid-1960s, Daci Temple was repurposed, and the remains of Xuanzang were moved to Wenshu Monastery for safekeeping.

At the age of 16, Master Xuanzang arrived in Chengdu and stayed for a total of five years. During his time in Chengdu, he received the ordination and overcame the greatest obstacle on his journey to the west by relying on the *Heart Sutra* he obtained in Chengdu. Due to this remarkable affinity, his remains are kept in Chengdu, living up to their poetic significance.

大慈寺极盛时期为唐宋，此后数毁数建，历经千年沧桑。

明宣德十年（1435年）的一场大火将寺院烧为荒墟，大慈寺僧众迁往与之渊源极深的多宝寺。十一年后再将大慈寺重修一新。

明末张献忠攻陷成都城，大慈寺也迎来了一场大劫难：先是被当作战俘营，关押明朝官员；后又因藏匿一逃亡明朝宗室，全寺近千僧人几遭屠戮殆尽。

明清以降，大慈寺规模已大幅缩减。

圣钦和尚在自述中说，他于1932年任方丈时，全寺被军阀马德斋部占据，另有街房二十余间为一陈姓恶霸所占，俱多方设法才得以收回。

1939年3月，七千八百二十七箱故宫文物运抵大慈寺。这些文物是为了躲避日寇、传承文脉，而自故宫迁出的。1933年，近两万箱文物从故宫出发，其中将近三分之一辗转南京、洛阳、西安、宝鸡、汉中，历时六年终抵成都。

1950年，大慈寺有常住僧四十八人，土地二百三十亩，出租街房350余间。

1967年，成为成都警备区司令部驻地，即前文林子口中的“警司”。

Daci Temple reached its peak during the Tang and Song dynasties, but it has since experienced numerous destructions and reconstructions over the centuries.

In the 10th year of the Ming Dynasty’s Xuande era (1435 AD), a great fire reduced the temple to ruins. The monks of Daci Temple relocated to Duobao Temple, which shares a deep connection with Daci Temple. Eleven years later, the temple was rebuilt.

During the late Ming Dynasty, Zhang Xianzhong captured Chengdu, and Daci Temple suffered a great calamity. It was first used as a prisoner of war camp, where Ming officials were imprisoned. Later, because it sheltered a fleeing member of the Ming royal family, the temple’s nearly thousand monks were mercilessly massacred.

Since the Ming and Qing dynasties, the size of Daci Temple has significantly reduced.

In his autobiography, Monk Sheng Qin stated that when he served as the abbot in 1932, the entire temple was occupied by the warlord Ma Dezhai’s troops. Additionally, more than twenty street houses were occupied by a bully surnamed Chen, and it took great effort to regain control of them.

In March 1939, 7,827 boxes of cultural relics were transported to Daci Temple. These cultural relics were moved from the Forbidden City to evade the Japanese invaders and preserve the cultural heritage. In 1933, nearly 20,000 boxes of cultural relics started their journey from the Forbidden City. Among them, almost one-third were transported to Nanjing, Luoyang, Xi’an, Baoji, and Hanzhong before finally arriving in Chengdu after six years.

In 1950, Daci Temple had 48 resident monks and a land area of 230 Mu. Over 350 street houses were rented out.

In 1967, it became the headquarters of the Chengdu Garrison Command, referred to as “Jing Si”

1983年，设成都市博物馆于寺内。

2004年，大慈寺重修并对外开放。

因为附近分布有四川省作协、文联的办公地点和宿舍，以及《四川日报》《成都日报》等数十家新闻单位，众多文人墨客和媒体人时常茶聚于大慈寺的庭院之中。笔者记得，盖碗茶的单价约是两元。

大慈寺当年的坝坝茶园　余茂智 摄

The open-air tea garden of Daci Temple. (Photographer: Yu Maozhi)

收藏家彭雄在茶聚中问学于学者流沙河，回家后将所得写成系列文章《茶馆问学记》，发表于博客，一时读者甚众。

大慈寺修复施工始于2004年1月7日。仅仅两天之后，就发现了镇寺之宝——清光绪六年腊月初八，由经学家、二品官员黄云鹄（著名学者黄侃之父）题写的“古大圣慈寺”匾额。

匾额初发现时，尚被水泥封住。2004年1月10日的《成都日报》，以《敲开水泥 石匾露了一横》为题，描述了那块石匾重见天日的细节：“石

by the locals.

In 1983, the Chengdu Museum was established within the temple premises.

In 2004, Daci Temple underwent restoration and was opened to the public.

Due to the presence of the Sichuan Provincial Writers' Association, Federation of Literary and Art Circles, as well as dozens of media organizations such as Sichuan Daily and Chengdu Daily in the vicinity, many writers, intellectuals, and media professionals often gathered for tea in the courtyards of Daci Temple. I remember that a covered bowl tea cost approximately two yuan.

During the tea gatherings, collector Peng Xiong sought knowledge from the scholar Liu Shahe. Inspired by their discussions, Peng Xiong went home and wrote a series of articles titled *Records of Learning in the Tea House*, which he published on his blog. These articles gained a large number of readers.

The restoration and construction of Daci Temple began on January 7, 2004. Just two days later, a treasured item was discovered—the plaque of 'Ancient Great Holy Compassionate Temple' inscribed by Huang Yunhu, an expert in classics and a second-ranking official, was discovered. Huang Yunhu was also the father of the famous scholar Huang Kan.

When the plaque was first discovered, it was still covered in cement. An article titled *Knocking Open the Cement, Revealing a Horizontal Line* was published on January 10, 2004 in the Chengdu Daily, describing the details of the unveiling of the stone

块一点点地脱落，石匾也渐渐露出一角。只见一块淡红色的石板上，清晰地刻着一横的右端。”文中提到的那“一横”，就是“圣”字最下面的那一笔。如今，这块高约七十厘米、宽约三米，已有一百四十年历史的石匾正镶嵌于大慈寺山门顶端。

plaque: “Piece by piece, the stone chips fell away, gradually revealing a corner of the plaque. On a pale red stone slab, a clear right end of a horizontal line could be seen.” The “horizontal line” referred to in the article is the stroke at the bottom of the character “圣” (shèng). This stone plaque, measuring about 70 cm in height and 3 meters in width, with a history dating back 140 years, used to be embedded at the top of the main gate of Daci Temple.

清代经学家黄云鹄题写的匾额 余茂智 摄

A plaque inscribed by Qing Dynasty Confucian scholar Huang Yunhu. (Photographer: Yu Maozhi)

2014年，毗邻大慈寺、汇聚国际一线品牌的成都远洋太古里开业。在红尘喧嚣、潮流时尚的三面环抱中，存一块虚静空灵之地。幸甚。

In 2014, the Chengdu IFS (International Finance Square) opened its doors, adjacent to Daci Temple and gathering renowned international brands. Amidst the bustling and trendy atmosphere, there exists a serene and tranquil place. How fortunate it is indeed.

永陵
Yongling

川西坝子一望无垠，平地上突兀的大土堆，多半是古代帝王或贵族的陵墓，但以前的成都人并不明白这个道理。老成都城西门外，一高十五米、直径八十米的土丘，多年来被讹传为汉代司马相如、卓文君的抚琴台。其实，它是一座罕见的地上皇陵——永陵。

永陵的主人叫王建，五代十国时期前蜀的开国皇帝。当皇帝之前很多年，他曾干过盗墓、偷牛等勾当。他用一生的行为艺术，为汉语贡献了“王八”和“豹变”两个词。

As far as the eye can see in the flat plains of western Sichuan, there are prominent mounds of earth which mostly conceal the tombs of ancient emperors or nobles. However, the people of old Chengdu did not understand this. Outside the west gate of old Chengdu, there is a 15-meter-high and 80-meter-diameter mound, which has long been mistakenly believed to be the zither-stroking platform of Sima Xiangru and Zhuo Wenjun, two figures from the Han Dynasty. In reality, it is a rare above-ground imperial tomb called Yongling.

The owner of Yongling is Wang Jian, the founding emperor of Former Shu during the Five Dynasties and Ten Kingdoms period. Many years before he became emperor, Wang Jian was involved in tomb raiding and cattle theft. Through his life's actions, he contributed two Chinese words “wangba” (swearword, meaning turtle) and “baobian” (meaning astonishing transformation).

永陵传奇：从盗墓贼到皇帝的豹变人生
The Legend of Yongling: An Astonishing Transformation From Tomb Raider to Emperor

陈情献蜀皇帝

前蜀·贯休

河北江东处处灾，
唯闻全蜀少尘埃。
一瓶一钵垂垂老，
千水千山得得来。
秦苑幽栖多胜景，
巴歈陈贡愧非才。
自惭林薮龙钟者，
亦得亲登郭隗台。

Tribute to the Emperor of Shu

Guanxiu, Former Shu

In Hebei and Jiangdong, woes abound,
Yet word of distant Shu bears little dust around.
A flask and a bowl, now aged, in hand,
A thousand waters, a thousand mountains, over the land.
The royal gardens such a thrilling sight.
The imperial Gala an event so delight.
Humbled, I, a hermit, worn with age,
Too, ascend the Guowei Tower as a sage.

在五代画僧贯休的这首诗里，唐末的战乱纷扰尚未平息，唯有王建治下的前蜀，算得上是乱世中的桃源。贯休以一瓶一钵一驴入蜀，求见前蜀开国皇帝王建，并将之比作筑台招贤的燕昭王。

向皇帝献这样的诗，很容易被认为是阿谀之词。但历史上，贯休留下的恰恰是一种完全相反的形象。《唐才子传》对贯休的评价是："一条直气，海内无双。"

贯休云游海内时已在花甲之年。他于唐乾宁年间来到吴越，其时乱世已至，镇东军节度使钱镠控制了两浙十三州。贯休到时，钱镠正因功加检校太师，画像已上凌烟阁。贯休持诗祝贺，留下了"满堂花醉三千客，一

In this poem by Guanxiu, a painter-monk of the Five Dynasties period, the turmoil and chaos of the late Tang Dynasty had not yet subsided. Amongst this unrest, the regime of Wang Jian in the Former Shu could be likened to a utopia. Guanxiu, armed only with a bottle, a bowl, and a donkey, ventured into the Shu territory. He sought an audience with the founding emperor of the Former Shu, Wang Jian, and likened him to the wise and benevolent King Yan Zhao, known for building a platform to recruit talented individuals.

Presenting such a poem to the emperor might easily be seen as flattery. However, in history, Guan Xiu left behind a completely different image. *Tang Caizi Zhuan*, the Talented Scholars of the Tang Dynasty, appraised Guanxiu as having "a straightforward disposition, unparalleled in the realm."

Guanxiu, a wandering poet, had already reached his sixtieth year when he traveled through the vast expanse of the realm. During the reign of Tang's Qianning, he arrived in the domain of Wuyue. At that time, the chaotic era was in full swing, and the military commissioner of Zhen Dong, Qian Liu,

剑霜寒十四州”“他年名上凌烟阁，岂羡当时万户侯”等名句。岂料钱镠此时已有帝王之意，非要将“十四州”改为“四十州”才能满足自己的野心。利与威之下，贯休并不相从，反而愤怒地拂袖而去。

贯休以“僧中之一豪”的人品，对文首诗描述的前蜀安稳的社会状态，做了有力背书。

held control over the thirteen prefectures of Eastern and Western Zhejiang. Upon Guanxiu's arrival, Qian Liu was newly honored with the title of Jian Jiao Tai Shi (a false rank to a seignior) due to his military achievements, and his portrait was already enshrined in the Lingyan Pavilion. Guanxiu, offering his congratulations in verse, left behind the lines: "Amidst the intoxicating flowers, three thousand guests in revelry, With one sword, chilling frost engulfs fourteen prefectures." He also wrote, "In later years, if my name grace the Lingyan Pavilion; shall I envy the countless marquises of that time?" Little did Guanxiu know, at this very moment, Qian Liu harbored imperial ambitions. He insisted on changing "fourteen prefectures" to "forty prefectures" to satiate his own desires for power and prestige. Faced with coercion and cajoling, Guanxiu did not yield. Instead, he departed indignantly, sweeping his sleeves in defiance.

With the persona of a "distinguished hero among the monks", Guanxiu served as a strong endorsement of the peaceful social state of the former Shu Kingdom, as described in the opening poem.

琴台原是帝王陵

民国时期，成都西城墙外是一大片农田。在农田中间，立着一个巨大的土堆，直径八十米，高出地面十五米。在平畴千里的川西坝子，特别显眼。当时的成都人一致认为，此处是西汉司马相如和卓文君的故居，而那个大土堆则是琴瑟和谐的司马相如夫妻二人抚琴之处，故称之为“抚琴台”。因为这个缘故，这一带形成的

Qin Tai, originally an imperial tomb

During the Republican era, outside the western city walls of Chengdu, there was a vast expanse of farmland. In the midst of the farmland stood a massive earthen mound, 80 meters in diameter and rising 15 meters above the ground. It was particularly conspicuous in the vast Chengdu Plain. The people of Chengdu unanimously believed that here was the former residence of Sima Xiangru and Zhuo Wenjun from the Western Han Dynasty. The large earthen mound was believed to be the place where the harmonious couple played the zither together, thus it was called the "Fuqin Tai" (literally meaning

居民区被命名为”抚琴小区”。此外，还有二十多条以“抚琴”为名的街道，包括所谓“抚琴台”南侧的抚琴东路。

1999年，抚琴东路改名为永陵路。为什么会有这次改名呢，还得从“抚琴台”说起。

20世纪30年代末，抗日战争已进入战略相持阶段，日机多次轰炸作为中国大后方的成渝两地。为了让老百姓“跑警报”，1940年，当局决定由天成铁路局在这个大土堆上挖掘防空洞。

工程从“抚琴台”北面开始，挖了四米就发现一堵砖墙。墙砖巨大，竟然厚达两米，此为墓壁外层；而内层，则由厚度为一米的巨型石条构成。因为有抚琴台的传说，砖墙自然而然被认作琴台基脚。然而，时任四川大学历史系教授的冯汉骥先生在现场勘察之后，得出了迥然不同的结论——这是一座陵墓，跟抚琴台根本没有关系。

究竟是谁的陵墓？

因为处于抗战时期，发掘工作差不多两年后才开始。从1942年9月15日开挖，到当年11月底结束第一阶段勘察，结果出来了。墓中出土的玉册表明：陵墓叫永陵，其主人是前蜀开

"zither-stroking platform"). Due to this connection, the residential area that developed in this area was named the Fuqin Neighborhood. Additionally, there were more than twenty streets named after "Fuqin", including the Fuqin East Road located south of the so-called "Fuqin Tai".

In 1999, the name of Fuqin East Road was changed to Yongling Road. To understand this renaming, we need to go back to the story of the Fuqin Tai.

In the late 1930s, the War of Resistance against Japan had entered a phase of strategic stalemate, and Japanese aircraft repeatedly bombed the Chengdu-Chongqing region, which served as the rear area of China. In order to alert the local residents to take cover during bombings, in 1940, the authorities decided to let Tiancheng Railway Bureau to excavate air-raid shelters in this large earthen mound.

The project began from the north side of the "Fuqin Tai" and after digging four meters, a brick wall was discovered. The bricks were massive, with a thickness of two meters, forming the outer layer of the tomb, while the inner layer was made up of giant stone slabs, each one meter thick. Due to the legend of the Fuqin Tai, the brick wall was naturally assumed to be the foundation of the zither-stroking platform. However, Mr. Feng Hanji, a professor in the History Department of Sichuan University, came to a completely different conclusion after conducting a survey at the site—this was a tomb, unrelated to the Fuqin Tai.

Whom does the tomb belongs to?

Due to the ongoing war, the excavation work at the tomb didn't commence until nearly two years later. It began on September 15, 1942, and the first phase of exploration concluded by the end of November of the same year, yielding conclusive results. The unearthed jade register left no doubt as

国皇帝王建。

to the identity of the tomb's owner—it is known as the Yongling, the final resting place of Wang Jian, the founding emperor of the Former Shu Kingdom.

兔子上金床

前蜀皇帝王建之墓永陵出土的文物，有两件被评定为国宝，谥宝即其一。

谥宝，是帝王在阴间的玉玺。王建出生、登基都在兔年，故谥宝外形为兔，而身上又有鳞甲，寓意其真龙天子身份　何大江 摄

何为谥宝？谥者，谥号也；宝者，玉玺也——帝王之印，自秦始皇之后专称“玺”，而武则天改之为“宝”。所谓谥宝，即刻有谥号的玉玺，它是皇帝死后的印信，是皇权在阴间的象征。

谥宝被发现时，置于王建石造像前的精美双层宝盝中。

谥宝的印面接近一正方形，长11.7厘米，宽10.7厘米，上刻14个篆字——高祖神武圣文孝德明惠皇帝。前面的“高祖”即其庙号，后面充满溢美意味的“神武圣文孝德明惠皇

On the Golden Bed Lies the Rabbit

From the tomb of Wang Jian, the emperor of Former Shu, the cultural relics unearthed at Yongling include two rated National Treasures, with “Shi Bao” being one.

The *Shi Bao* is the imperial jade seal of the underworld. As Wang Jian was born and ascended the throne in the Year of the Rabbit, the seal is shaped like a rabbit, with scales symbolizing his status as a true dragon emperor. (Photographer: He Dajiang)

Shi Bao refers to the jade seal inscribed with the emperor's posthumous title. It symbolizes the imperial authority in the afterlife. Since the time of Emperor Qin Shi Huang, the emperor's seal has been known as “Xi” (玺), but Empress Wu Zetian changed its name to “Bao” (宝).

When Shi Bao was discovered, it was found to be placed inside an exquisite double-layered treasure chest in front of the stone statue of Wang Jian.

The imprint on Shi Bao is nearly square, measuring 11.7 centimeters in length and 10.7 centimeters in width. It is inscribed with fourteen seal characters, “Gaozu Shenwu Shengwen Xiaode Minghui Huangdi”, which can be translated as “Emperor Gaozu, the Divine, Martial, Wise, Filial, Virtuous, Bright, and Benevolent”. The term “Gaozu” refers to Wang Jian's temple name, while the

帝”则是其谥号。

谥号、庙号有何区别？谥号，是皇帝或重臣去世后所得的称号，亦含有褒贬之意；庙号则是太庙中供奉大行皇帝时所称名号。谥号原本简短，后来被那些马屁精搞得越来越长，恨不得把所有的褒义词都加上去，称呼起来便十分不便。于是从唐代起，史家便以庙号称呼帝王。因此，汉高祖、汉武帝是谥号，称呼王建用的蜀高祖却是庙号，看似相类却有着实质差别。

印台的顶面并不平整，中间微微隆起，厚度为3.4—3.7厘米；印台四个立面刻有花纹，主持永陵发掘的冯汉骥先生所撰《前蜀王建墓发掘报告》描述为：“谥宝的前方刻凤，两边刻龙，后方刻兽形纹及云纹。”

其实，四方立面所刻，更有可能是古代所谓“天之四灵”——青龙、白虎、朱雀、玄武。发掘报告所称印台后方所刻“兽形纹”，其实是一个昂头乌龟的正面像，而龟背上则曲伏着一条张口之蛇，而龟与蛇的组合，正是传统文化中玄武的形象；凤与朱雀，原型均为禽类，极易混淆；唐宋时期，青龙、白虎形状相似，这大概是发掘报告中“两边刻龙”一语之由来。所谓“前朱雀，后玄武，左青龙，右白虎”，谥宝上四面所刻，方

elaborately crafted complimentary title represents his posthumous title.

What is the difference between a posthumous title (shi hao) and a temple name (miao hao)? A posthumous title is a name or honorary title bestowed upon an emperor or esteemed minister after their passing, often reflecting praise or degrading. A temple name, on the other hand, is the name used to venerate an emperor in the ancestral temple during worship. Originally, posthumous titles were brief, but over time, flattery led them to become increasingly long, including as many positive terms as possible, making them cumbersome to use. From the Tang Dynasty onwards, historians began using temple names to address emperors. Thus, Emperor Gaozu and Emperor Wu of Han were posthumous titles, while the temple name used for emperor Wang Jian of Former Shu Kingdom appears similar, but holds a substantial difference.

The top surface of the seal is not smooth, slightly raised in the middle, with a thickness of 3.4-3.7 centimeters; the four sides are carved with patterns, described in the *Excavation Report of the Yongling Tomb* by Mr. Feng Hanji as follows: “In front of the posthumous seal is carved a phoenix, dragons are carved on both sides, and the back is decorated with animal motifs and cloud patterns.”

In fact, the carvings on the four sides are more likely to represent the ancient Four Spiritual Creatures of Heaven—the Azure Dragon, White Tiger, Vermilion Bird, and Black Tortoise. The so-called “animal motifs” carved on the back of the seal platform, as described in the excavation report, actually depict the front view of a raised tortoise, with a coiled snake on its back—symbolizing the traditional image of the Black Tortoise. The phoenix and the Vermilion Bird both have similar bird-like attributes, which can easily be confused. During the

位正与此相应——可知实为青龙、白虎、朱雀、玄武“四大神兽”。

印台之上的印纽，已呈现两处断裂。实际上，整个纽身已经从印台上脱落了。热胀冷缩，上千年的岁月之力，即使在暗黑、密闭的墓穴之中也显示着力量。温润美玉雕成的谥宝，表面也风化了，展现着时光的粗粝。

印纽之外形，为一只傍地之兔，兔头、兔足齐全，还有头顶兔耳，以及偏向右侧的尾。

然而，这又并非一只纯粹的兔子。制作时，前后兔足之间被掏空了，使整个身体呈条状——没错，这是龙的形状，而身与腹上的鳞甲，也证明此点。

兔与龙的奇特组合，构成了谥宝之钮。

在传统文化中，以龙象征帝王，故帝王专用的玉玺、谥宝之印纽多雕刻为龙形。而王建谥宝之印钮却造型为兔首龙身，兼具龙、兔两种元素。龙的元素好理解，而钮之兽首为兔头，则跟王建的生世有关。

公元847年是一个丁卯年，也是生肖计年的兔年，这一年，王建生于许州舞阳。六十年后，王建于成都称皇帝，这又是一个丁卯年。生于兔年，又在兔年成为真龙天子，算不算

Tang and Song Dynasties, the shapes of the Azure Dragon and White Tiger were quite similar, which might explain the mention of “dragons are carved on both sides”. The saying goes, “the Vermilion Bird is in the front, the Black Tortoise in the back, left is the Azure Dragon, right is the White Tiger.” The carvings on all four sides of the seal correspond exactly to this arrangement, indicating that they represent the “Four Great Divine Beasts”.

The seal knob has shown two fractures. In fact, the entire knob has detached from the platform. The power of time, spanning thousands of years, with its thermal expansion and contraction, is evident even within the dark and sealed tomb. The exquisite jade carving of the posthumous seal has also weathered on the surface, revealing the roughness brought by time.

The shape of the knob resembles a crouching rabbit, with a complete head and feet, as well as ears on top, and a tail angled towards the right side.

However, this is not merely a pure rabbit. During its production, the space between the front and rear feet of the rabbit was hollowed out, giving the whole body a cylindrical shape. Yes, it resembles a dragon, and the scales on its back and abdomen further confirm this.

The unique combination of a rabbit and a dragon forms the knob of the posthumous seal.

In traditional culture, the dragon symbolizes the emperor. Therefore, the knobs of jade seals and posthumous seals used exclusively by emperors are often carved in the shape of a dragon. However, the knob of Wang Jian’s posthumous seal is formed by a rabbit head and a dragon body, incorporating both dragon and rabbit elements. The dragon element is easy to understand, but the rabbit head on the knob is related to Wang Jian’s birth and life.

In the year 847 AD, which was a Ding Mao

是一种特别的缘分？

即便只是一种巧合，但对于以操弄人心为基本功的帝王术来说，绝对是一个进行舆论宣传的大好机会。“兔子上金床”的谶语，在唐代就有，这对王建来说，简直是不用白不用。于是登基之时，便真的以金装饰御床以应谶言。

year in the Chinese zodiac, Wang Jian was born in Wuyang, Xuzhou. Sixty years later, he became the emperor of Chengdu, also in a Ding Mao year. Being born in the Year of the Rabbit and then becoming the emperor in the Year of the Rabbit, could this be considered a special fate?

哀册是书写帝王生前功德的文体。王建哀册为玉石册，被发现时与谥宝等同置于棺床之上　何大江 摄

The *Ai Ce* is a eulogy inscribed to commemorate an emperor's virtues and achievements during his lifetime. Wang Jian's *Ai Ce* is made of jade and was found placed alongside the *Shi Bao* on the coffin bed. (Photographer: He Dajiang)

此谶并不只流行于蜀中；生于兔年，并在兔年登基的，也并不只有王建一人。先行者便是建立大越罗平国的董昌。

董昌与王建同年出生，属相皆为兔。董本为地方豪强，在唐末的动荡中成为浙东一带的实际控制者。或许是受到“兔子上金床”这句谶语的刺激，董昌的欲望愈发膨胀，决心称帝，并为此将三个劝谏他的大臣灭族。895年，又是一个兔年，48岁的董昌在越州（今浙江绍兴）称帝，建立大越罗平国。但不到一年，便被原

Even if it is just a coincidence, for a ruler skilled in manipulating public opinion, it is undoubtedly a great opportunity for propaganda. The prophetic saying “A rabbit hops on a golden bed” existed during the Tang Dynasty, and for Wang Jian, it was a perfect fit. So when he ascended the throne, he truly decorated his royal bed with gold to fulfill the prophecy.

This prophecy was not only popular in the region of Shu. There were also others who were born in the Year of the Rabbit and ascended to the throne in the Year of the Rabbit, besides Wang Jian. One such predecessor was Dong Chang, the founder of the Luoping State of Da Yue.

Dong Chang was born in the same year as Wang Jian and both belonged to the Rabbit zodiac sign. Originally a local powerful figure, Dong Chang

手下头号大将、后来的吴越国开国国君钱镠灭国。董昌被俘，在押解过程中投水自尽。

罗平国因为立国时间太短，并未得到史家承认，明代郭之奇有诗讥讽道：“四月山禽称鸑鷟，痴心兔子上金床。”鸑鷟，凤之一种。飞上枝头的山鸡，并未能变成凤凰，反而成为后世笑谈。

谥宝之外，永陵出土的另一件国宝文物为玉大带。

玉大带出土于棺床之上，当为王建遗体身佩之物。七块方形銙和末端的长条形獭尾上均雕刻有龙　何大江 摄

The jade belt unearthed from the coffin bed is believed to have been worn by Wang Jian. Its seven square plaques and elongated otter-tail tip are engraved with dragon motifs. (Photographer: He Dajiang)

玉大带即玉带，是古时代表品级地位的饰品，由玉銙片缀于皮革之上制成。五代十国时期前蜀开国皇帝王建生前佩戴过的这根玉带，由七块玉銙片和末端的长条形獭尾构成。所用

became the de facto ruler of the eastern part of Zhejiang during the turmoil of the late Tang Dynasty. Perhaps inspired by the prophecy of “A rabbit hops on a golden bed”, Dong Chang’s desires grew and he became determined to establish himself as an emperor. In pursuit of this, he even exterminated three ministers who had advised him against it. In the year 895 AD, also a Year of the Rabbit, at the age of 48, Dong Chang declared himself emperor in Yuezhou (present-day Shaoxing, Zhejiang), establishing the Luoping State of Dayue. However, within a year, he was overthrown by his former top general and later the founding ruler of the Wuyue State, Qian Liu. Dong Chang was captured and, while being escorted, he chose to jump into the water and ended his own life.

The Luoping State did not receive recognition from historians due to its short existence. In the Ming Dynasty, Guo Zhiqi mocked it in a poem, saying, “In April, mountain birds claim to be golden pheasants, a foolish rabbit hopping on a golden bed.” The golden pheasant, a type of phoenix, refers to the mountain chicken, which despite landing on the branch, failed to transform into a phoenix and became a subject of ridicule in later generations.

Apart from the posthumous seal, another national treasure excavated from the Yongling Tomb is a jade belt.

The jade belt, also known as a Jade Big Belt, was an ornament in ancient times that represented one’s status and rank. It was made by attaching jade plaques to a leather base. This particular jade belt, which was worn by Wang Jian, the founding emperor of the Former Shu kingdom during the Five Dynasties and Ten Kingdoms period, consists of seven jade plaques mounted in gold and a long strip of otter tail at the end. The jade used for this belt is of extremely high quality and comes from the Hetian region.

材料，为一块品质极高的和田美玉。

玉大带以鞓（tīng）和缀附于其上的玉带板为主要构件，而玉带板又由銙片和獭尾两部分构成。鞓，指作为玉带基底的皮带。獭尾，又作鉈尾，是玉带的收尾构件，它穿过带扣之后，垂头朝下，在穿佩者后腰像水獭尾巴一样垂吊着。王建玉大带被发现时，其鞓多已腐朽，而玉銙片、獭尾及银扣则保存完好。

以皮革为带，本是胡服制式，即游牧民族使用的蹀躞带，具有很强的收纳功能。腰带之上缀有蹀躞，蹀躞上小带，以悬挂弓、剑、小刀、磨刀石、佩巾、贮物袋等随身用品。

蹀躞带传入中原之后，丧失了功能性，演化为一种纯粹表示等级的礼仪性饰品。蹀躞上面垂下的、用于悬物的小带消失了，蹀躞则变成附缀于皮带上的銙片。作为一种表示品级的服饰，玉大带出现的时间其实很晚，考古发现的最早的玉大带，也是唐朝产物。

关于永陵的这条玉大带，还有一个神异的故事，后文述之。

The main components of the jade belt are the belt base called "Ting" and the jade plaque attachments. The otter tail serves as the finishing component of the belt. It hangs down from the belt clasp, resembling the tail of a water otter, behind the wearer's waist. When the jade belt worn by Wang Jian was discovered, the leather belt base had mostly decayed, but the jade plaques, otter tail, and silver clasp were well-preserved.

Using leather as the belt, Die Xie was originally a Hu-style attire, specifically used by nomadic peoples, with strong carrying capacity. Above the waist belt are adorned with Die Xie with small straps attached and used to hang bows, swords, knives, whetstones, handkerchiefs, and storage bags for personal belongings.

After the introduction of the belt to the Central Plains, it lost its functionality and evolved into a purely ceremonial accessory representing hierarchy. The small straps hanging from the Die Xie and used for hanging items disappeared, and the Die Xie itself transformed into an ornament attached to the leather belt. As a garment symbolizing one's rank, the appearance of the jade belt was actually quite late, with the earliest discovered jade belt dating back to the Tang Dynasty.

There is also a mystical story about the jade belt at the Yongling Mausoleum, which will be described later in the text.

此曲只在地下有

王建墓，地面封土高15米、直径80余米；内由14道石券拱构成地前、

This Tune Should Only be Heard Underground

The Yongling Mausoleum is buried underground, with a mound of soil measuring over 15 meters

中、后三室，长度共计30.8米。

前室只是一个通道，类似于住宅的玄关。

面积最大的中室，置一红砂石须弥座棺床（须弥座又名“金刚座”，是安置佛像、菩萨像的台座，从侧面看，上下凸出、中间凹入）。棺床长7.45米、宽3.35米、高0.89米，如此大的一个空间，足以安放两组具有极高价值的石刻。

其一曰“十二神”。

“十二神”为立体雕像，分置于棺床东、西两侧。神像是半身像，高50—63厘米，股以下尽没于土中。这十二个神像中六人着冠，六人戴盔，皆身披铠甲。冠、盔、甲都雕刻得十分精细，刚出土时，甲皆上色贴金。

按照冯汉骥先生的考古发掘报告，十二神分别是天一、腾蛇、朱雀、六合、句陈、青龙、天后、太阴、玄武、太常、白虎、天空。神像之手托起棺床下沿，皆怒目圆睁，威风凛凛，似乎要用尽全力把这石头棺床抬将起来。

in height and 80 meters in diameter. Inside, there are three chambers divided by 14 stone arches, comprising the front, middle, and rear chambers, with a total length of 30.8 meters.

The front chamber serves as a passage, similar to the entrance hall of a residence.

The middle chamber, which has the largest area, contains a red sandstone Buddhist altar (also known as a vajrasana, which is a pedestal for placing Buddha or Bodhisattva statues. This altar protrudes at the top and bottom while being concave in the middle). The dimensions of the altar are 7.45 meters in length, 3.35 meters in width, and 0.89 meters in height. With such a large space, it is capable of housing two sets of highly valuable stone carvings.

The first is the Twelve Deities.

The Twelve Deities are three-dimensional sculptures placed on the east and west sides of the altar. These deity statues are half-length figures, measuring approximately 50 to 63 centimeters in height, with their lower bodies buried in the ground. Among the twelve statues, six are wearing crowns while the other six are wearing helmets, all adorned with armor. The crowns, helmets, and armor are intricately carved, and when they were first unearthed, they were painted and gilded.

According to Mr. Feng Hanji's archaeological excavation report, the Twelve Deities are Tianyi (Heavenly One), Tengshe (Soaring Snake), Zhuque (Vermilion Bird), Liuhe (Six Harmonies), Gouchen (Kylin), Qinglong (Azure Dragon), Tianhou (Goddess of Heaven), Taiyin (Lunar Deity), Xuanwu (Black Tortoise), Taichang (Great Constant), Baihu (White Tiger), and Tiankong (Heavenly Sky). The hands of the deity statues hold up the lower edge of the altar, with eyes glaring fiercely, exuding a powerful and majestic aura as if they are exerting all their strength to lift up the stone coffin.

怒目圆睁的抬棺力士　余茂智 摄

Coffin bearers with fierce, glaring expressions. (Photographer: Yu Maozhi)

其二曰“二十四伎乐”。

伎乐刻于棺床南、东、西三面，为高度二十五厘米左右的浮雕。这是一支刻在石头上的宫廷乐队，其中有舞者二人，乐器演奏者二十二人。

二十四伎皆圆领上衣，华袂广袖。刚发掘时，还可以见到衣皆为红色，裙皆为杏黄色，袂和领的颜色却各不相同，或红，或绿，或黄。至于发髻，则发之梳法相同，髻之挽法各异，共计二十二种。这种细节上的差别，既说明雕刻者匠心独具，又展示了其精湛技艺。

当然，更为丰富多彩、千差万别的是这支石刻宫廷乐队的乐器。乐器不同，则演奏方式不同，体现在石刻上则是姿态各异，却又生动形象。

The second is the Twenty-Four Performers.

The twenty-four Performers are engraved on the southern, eastern, and western sides of the altar, in the form of low reliefs measuring about 25 centimeters in height. It depicts a court musical ensemble carved on the stone, consisting of two dancers and twenty-two musicians.

The performers are all depicted wearing round-collared robes with wide sleeves. When first excavated, the robes were found to be red in color, while the skirts were apricot yellow. However, the colors of the sleeves and collars varied, some being red, some green, and some yellow. As for their hairstyles, they were all combed in a similar manner, but the bun styles differed, totaling twenty-two different styles. These subtle differences in details not only showcase the artistic creativity of the sculptors but also demonstrate their exquisite craftsmanship.

Of course, even more colorful and diverse are the musical instruments of this stone-carved court ensemble. Different instruments require different playing techniques, which are reflected in the varied and vivid postures depicted in the carvings.

二十二个演奏者，共有二十种乐器，诸如琵琶、羯鼓、竖箜篌、横笛、筚篥、排箫……既有汉族传统乐器，又有从域外传入的乐器，显示出自唐至前蜀的文化包容性。

后室则设一宽大的石床，依照皇帝上朝时的御座制作而成。御座上的石刻王建，其相貌很符合《新五代史》上“隆眉广颡，状貌伟然”的描绘，他袖手端坐，神情稳重，似乎正安详地看视着这片土地。

Among the twenty-two musicians, there are a total of twenty different instruments, including instruments such as the pipa (a kind of chinese lute), jiegu (a type of drum), vertical konghou (harp), transverse flute, bili (a kind of wind instrument), pan flutes, and more. This collection includes traditional Han instruments as well as instruments imported from other regions, demonstrating the cultural inclusiveness from the Tang Dynasty to the Former Shu Kingdom.

In the rear chamber, there is a large stone bed designed in the style of the emperor's throne during court sessions. The stone carving of Wang Jian on the throne, depicted a striking resemblance to the description in the *New History of the Five Dynasties* as “broad forehead, prominent eyebrows, with a magnificent appearance”. He sits with folded hands, displaying a dignified and serene expression, seemingly calmly observing the land.

伎乐共使用了二十种乐器，包括从域外传入的琵琶、羯鼓等　余茂智 摄

Musical ensembles included 20 types of instruments, such as the Pipa and the *Jiegu* drum, introduced from abroad. (Photographer: Yu Maozhi)

纷扰尘世有净土

“五代之乱极矣。”这是欧阳修的感叹，“传所谓‘天地闭，贤人隐’之时欤？当此之时，臣弑其君，子弑其父……”其时军阀混战，百姓惨遭屠戮，政权朝生而暮死。

然而，乱世之中也有不多的净土，王建治下的前蜀就是其中之一。

王建称帝第二年，发布《武成

Amidst the turmoil and chaos of the world, there exists a pure land

“The chaos of the Five Dynasties has reached its extreme.” This was the lament of Ouyang Xiu. “Is this the time when heaven and earth close, and the virtuous hide? At such a time, ministers kill their kings, and sons kill their fathers...” During this era, warlords fought against each other, and the people suffered from massacres. Political power rose and fell rapidly.

However, amidst the chaos, there were few sanctuaries, and the Former Shu under the rule of

诏》，称：“有利于民者，不得不用；有害于民者，不得不除。”前蜀武成三年六月，王建再次下诏课劝农桑，令地方官员不得侵扰百姓。

通过减轻赋税、赦免犯人等一系列休养生息的政策，蜀中呈现出了百业兴盛的局面。

王建治蜀的另一个亮点是：选贤能，纳人才。王建自己是个文盲，却能善待读书人。

为避乱世，很多唐朝名臣的后代进入蜀中。比如花间派词人韦庄，是韦应物四世孙（《新五代史》称其为唐宰相韦见素之孙），后来在前蜀当了宰相。张格，是唐末宰相张浚的儿子，他在父亲被杀后入蜀投奔王建，做了翰林学士。这一批人熟悉唐代的典章规制，前蜀开国时的顶层设计，就出于他们之手。

杜光庭是留下了很多神异传说的道士，他学识渊博，精通儒道两家典籍，在前蜀朝廷里官至户部侍郎。王建对杜光庭极为赏识，称他一个人就比得上汉初的“商山四皓”。

前文提到的贯休，入蜀后也得到了厚遇。王建游龙华禅院，命贯休诵诗。贯休以“锦衣鲜华手擎鹘”“艰难稼穑总不知”讽刺公子哥的轻薄无知，令在座权贵十分怨怼，而王建却

Wang Jian was one of them.

In the second year of Wang Jian's reign, he issued the *Wu Cheng Edict*, proclaiming, "What benefits the people must be duly utilized; what harms the people must be eradicated." In the third year of the Wu Cheng era in Former Shu, in June, Wang Jian issued another edict to encourage agricultural development, forbidding local officials from harassing the common people.

Through policies such as reducing taxes and granting pardons to prisoners, the region of Shu witnessed a flourishing of various industries, allowing for a period of rejuvenation and prosperity.

Another highlight of Wang Jian's rule in Shu was his focus on selecting talented and capable individuals. Despite being illiterate himself, Wang Jian respected and valued scholars.

To seek refuge from the chaotic times, many descendants of renowned Tang Dynasty officials came to the region of Shu. For example, Wei Zhuang, a poet of the Huajian School, was the great-grandson of Wei Yingwu (claimed as the grandson of Wei Jiansu, a prime minister of the Tang Dynasty in the *New History of the Five Dynasties*). He later became a chancellor in the Former Shu. Zhang Ge, the son of Zhang Jun, a prime minister in the late Tang Dynasty, sought refuge in Shu after his father was killed. He became a member of the Hanlin Academy under Wang Jian's rule. This group of individuals, well-versed in the regulations and customs of the Tang Dynasty, were instrumental in the top-level design of the Former Shu during its founding.

Du Guangting was a Taoist who left behind many miraculous legends. He was knowledgeable and well-versed in the works of both Confucianism and Taoism. He rose to the rank of Assistant Minister of the Ministry of Revenue in the former Shu Dynasty. Wang Jian held Du Guangting in high regard,

加以称颂，认为有警醒之用。

considering him to be on par with the "Shangshan Four Scholars" of the early Han Dynasty.

As mentioned before, Guan Xiu also received great favor after entering Chengdu. Wang Jian visited the Longhua Zen Monastery and commanded Guan Xiu to improvise a poem. Guan Xiu used verses such as "In bright and ornate embroidered garments, holding a falcon in hand" and "In extravagance, I know nothing of sowing and reaping" to satirize the ignorant frivolity of young gentlemen. This caused resentment among the privileged individuals present, but Wang Jian praised and regarded it as a means of sobering.

王八蛋的豹变人生

有句骂人的俗语叫“王八蛋”或“王八”。关于这个词的来历，有人说是“忘八端”的错讹，指忘记了儒家的“八端”——孝、悌、忠、信、礼、义、廉、耻。另一种说法是，它源自本文的主人公王建。相较之下，笔者更偏向于后一说。“忘八端”之说，明显有文人穿凿的痕迹，老百姓骂人不会这么引经据典的。

王建，早年有一个外号叫“贼王八”。这个称呼其实很贴切，他姓王，排行第八，最初成名是因为在乡里做贼。因为王建，“王八”变成了骂人之语。

王建字光图，生于许州舞阳（一说陈州项城），家中世世代代做饼师，也算是清白人家。待及成年，他并不

The transmutation of Thief Wang the Eighth's Life

In colloquial language, there is a derogatory term "王八蛋 Wang Ba Dan" or "王八 Wang Ba" used to insult someone. There are different theories about the origin of this term. Some suggest that it is a corruption of "忘八端" (Wang Ba Duang means forgetting the Eight Virtues), referring to neglecting the Confucian principles of filial piety, brotherly respect, loyalty, trustworthiness, propriety, righteousness, honesty, and a sense of shame. Another theory is that it is derived from the protagonist of this story, Wang Jian. Comparatively, I lean towards the latter theory. The explanation of "忘八端" seems to be an attempt by literary scholars and doesn't align with the vernacular usage of an insult.

Wang Jian, in his early years, had a nickname "Thief Wang the Eighth". This nickname was actually quite fitting as his surname was Wang and he was the eighth child in his family, and initially gained fame for his thieving activities in the village. Due to Wang Jian, the term "Wang the Eighth" became a derogatory term used to insult others.

愿意继承普普通通的祖业，烤一辈子烧饼。彼时乱世将至，他的人生也迎来了变数。

Wang Jian, with the courtesy name Guangtu, was born in Wuyang, Xuzhou (some say Xiangcheng, Chenzhou). His family had been bakers for generations, and they were considered to be an honorable household. However, as he grew older, Wang Jian was not content with inheriting the ordinary family business of baking. He did not want to spend his whole life making pancakes. As the chaotic times were approaching, his life was about to undergo significant changes.

狡诈、凶狠与忠诚、宽厚，是王建性格中的两面。永陵地宫中发掘出的王建坐像容貌端庄、神态安详　余茂智 摄

Wang Jian's personality combined cunning and cruelty with loyalty and magnanimity. His serene and dignified seated statue, uncovered in Yongling's underground palace, reflects this duality. (Photographer: Yu Maozhi)

王建年轻时，从事过的"职业"有杀牛、偷驴、贩私盐、盗墓、结伙抢劫等，用现在的话来说，都是些写在刑法上的"挣钱"行当。从这些经历看得出来，他是个枭勇之徒。其绰号"贼王八"，就得名于此。

王建其实长得不错，体魄健、个子高、脑门阔、眉毛浓。有一年，王建犯了重罪被关在许州监狱里，被狱卒私下放出来后，因藏躲于武当山而偶遇僧人处洪。处洪惊奇于王建骨相，认为贵不可言，便建议他改行从军，报效国家，以"自求豹变"。

When Wang Jian was young, he engaged in various "professions", including poaching cows, stealing donkeys, smuggling salt, tomb raiding, and participating in gang robberies, and so on, all of which, in today's parlance, are "money-making" professions written in the penal code. Based on these experiences, it is evident that he was a daring and ruthless individual. His nickname "Thief Wang the Eighth" derived from his notorious reputation.

In terms of appearance, Wang Jian was actually quite handsome, with a strong physique, tall stature, broad forehead, and thick eyebrows. One year, Wang Jian committed a felony and was imprisoned in Xuzhou. After being secretly released by a prison guard, he happened to encounter a monk named Chuhong while hiding in Wudang Mountain. Chuhong was astonished by Wang Jian's phrenological features

所谓“豹变”，是说花豹幼小时皮毛花纹似金钱，而到成年则变成类似虎纹的“扁担纹”，威风非常。处洪的提点，开启了一代平民皇帝的传奇人生。

王建离开武当山，到忠武军投军，因征讨王仙芝、救护唐僖宗等累计军功而升迁，成为神策军（唐廷直接控制的武装力量）将领。他的发迹，与当时的权宦田令孜也很有些关系。田令孜是王建的义父，二人纠葛不休的一生充满了悲喜剧。

唐昭宗即位后，田令孜与其兄陈敬瑄（西川节度使）在成都叛乱，二人对在阆州（今阆中）拥兵自重的王建颇为忌惮。田令孜说：“王八是我儿子，我一封信就可以把他叫来。”

田令孜和陈敬瑄招王建到成都，是为了控制他。但他们没想到的是，王建手头有兵，岂能任人摆布？经过手下提醒，田令孜兄弟终于明白：本是想囚虎于笼，搞不好就成了引狼入室。于是，赶紧加强城防，同时派人阻止王建前行。

王建绝非召之即来、挥之即去之辈，闻讯之后大怒，挥鞭夺关，兵临成都。也许，对方的反悔正中王建下怀，不然他真还没有借口撕破脸皮，毕竟田令孜对他有恩。

and believed that he possessed a rich and powerful future. He then suggested that Wang Jian change his path and join the military to serve the country and seek a transformation (豹变) for himself.

The term “豹变” refers to the leopard’s coat pattern resembling coins when it is young, but as it grows into adulthood, the pattern transforms into a tiger-like pattern, exuding great majestic presence. Chuhong’s guidance opened the doors to a legendary life for Wang Jian, who started as a commoner and would eventually become an emperor.

After leaving Wudang Mountain, Wang Jian joined the Zhongwu (Loyal and Mighty) Army and accumulated military achievements through campaigns against Wang Xianzhi and the rescue of Emperor Xizong of Tang. He was promoted and became a general of the Shence Army, which was directly controlled by the Tang court. His rise to power was also closely related to the influential official Tian Lingzi at that time. Tian Lingzi was Wang Jian’s adoptive father, and the lives of these two individuals were filled with both tragedy and comedy, with constant entanglement between them.

After Emperor Zhaozong ascended the throne, Tian Lingzi and his brother, Chen Jingxuan (the military governor of Xichuan), rebelled in Chengdu. They were wary of Wang Jian, who had a strong military presence in Langzhou (now Langzhong). Tian Lingzi said, “Wang Jian is my son, I can summon him with just one letter.”

Tian Lingzi and Chen Jingxuan summoned Wang Jian to Chengdu with the intention of controlling him. However, they didn’t anticipate that Wang Jian had his own troops and wouldn’t be easily manipulated. After being reminded by their subordinates, Tian Lingzi and Chen Jingxuan finally realized that their intention to confine a tiger in a cage might turn into inviting a wolf into their home. As a

王建围了成都三年，都没有打下来。唐昭宗有意休兵，派宰相韦昭度为成都尹，另在邛州（今邛崃）置永平军，以王建为节度使。但成都这块到口的肥肉，王建并不愿吐出来，便想了个匪夷所思的招数来驱赶韦昭度。他派手下把韦昭度的亲吏骆保抓来，切片食之。进士出身的韦昭度，一介书生，哪里见过这么野蛮的行径，顿时魂魄俱散，当天就交出官印，逃回了长安。

随即，王建威逼利诱，让田令孜、陈敬瑄交出了成都。再通过软禁、诬告、暗杀等方式，终于在同一天除掉了这对权倾一时的哥俩。陈敬瑄手下曾评价王建为奸雄，说他“狼顾久矣，必不为人下”，终于得到了应验。但人的性格都是复杂的，枭勇机诈也只是王建的一面。

时间轴拉到三年前。

河中节度使王重荣联合河东军叛乱，兵犯长安，田令孜挟唐僖宗逃往宝鸡。王建则背着玉玺，跟随在皇帝身边。到了大散岭，栈道被焚烧，王建扶着僖宗穿过火焰浓烟。

夜间宿于郊外，僖宗枕着王建的膝盖睡了一晚。为了不惊动皇帝，王建始终保持着坐姿。僖宗醒来之后，涕泣感佩不已，于是脱下身上御衣给

result, they quickly strengthened their city defenses and sent people to stop Wang Jian from advancing.

Wang Jian was not the kind of person who could be summoned and dismissed at will. Upon hearing the news, he was furious and wielded his whip to seize the pass, leading his troops to Chengdu. Perhaps the other party’s betrayal was exactly what Wang Jian had hoped for, as it gave him the perfect excuse to confront them openly, considering that Tian Lingzi had shown him kindness.

Wang Jian besieged Chengdu for three years but was unable to capture it. Emperor Zhaozong of Tang intended to cease hostilities; he appointed Wei Zhaodu, the Prime Minister, as the governor of Chengdu, and established a garrison in Qiongzhou (now Qionglai) with Wang Jian serving as the military governor. However, Wang Jian was reluctant to let go of the lucrative opportunity of ruling over Chengdu. Therefore, he resorted to a bizarre and unthinkable tactic to drive out Wei Zhaodu. He had his subordinates capture Wei Zhaodu’s trusted attendant, Luo Bao, sliced and consumed his flesh. Wei Zhaodu, a scholar-official, had never witnessed such barbaric behavior and was utterly terrified. On that same day, he handed over his official seal and fled back to Chang’an.

Immediately after that, Wang Jian used various methods of coercion and cajoling to make Tian Lingzi and Chen Jingxuan surrender Chengdu. Through tactics such as confinement, false accusations, and assassination, he finally eliminated the once powerful pair on the same day. Chen Jingxuan’s subordinates had once praised Wang Jian as a cunning hero, stating that “he has been like a wolf for a long time and will never be subservient to others.” This statement eventually proved to be accurate. However, the nature of human character is complex, and Wang Jian’s cunning and ruthlessness were only one aspect of his personality.

Let’s go back three years on the timeline.

王建，并解释之所以解衣相赠，是因为上面有自己的泪痕。

这很容易让人想到西晋“八王之乱”时的另外一个故事。当叛军要伤害晋惠帝司马衷时，侍中嵇绍上前护卫而被杀，鲜血溅了惠帝一身。惠帝是“何不食肉糜”的发明者、历史上著名的傻子皇帝，却表现出了不少聪明人不具备的重情重义，他不让宫人涤洗那件沾血的御衣，说上有嵇绍之血，要留作念想。这个典故，也是文天祥《正气歌》中“为嵇侍中血”的来历。

两个落难天子，两个忠心臣子，两件“皇帝的旧衣”，历史又开始押韵合辙。

王建进入蜀地，四处攻城略地，想的是成为割据一方的藩镇。随着实力和地盘的膨胀、对他有知遇之恩的唐僖宗离世，以及唐末政治格局的变化，终于产生了自立为帝的想法。

907年，朱温逼唐哀帝让位，以梁代唐。此前已焚栈道、锁关隘，独立经营蜀地数年的王建闻讯，朝着北方痛哭，遂效法刘备于成都称帝，建立蜀王朝，史称前蜀。

跟同样在蜀称帝的刘备相比，对于他们宣称要效忠的前朝来说，王建其实远远比刘备做得多。刘备打仗，

The military governor of Hezhou, Wang Chongrong, joined forces with the Hedong Army in a rebellion that reached Chang'an. Tian Lingzi, taking Emperor Xi Zong with him, fled to Baoji. Wang Jian, carrying the imperial seal, accompanied the emperor. When they reached Dalian Ridge, the plank road was set on fire, but Wang Jian supported Emperor Xi Zong and guided him through the flames and thick smoke.

They spent the night on the outskirts, and Emperor Xi Zong slept with his head resting on Wang Jian's knee. To avoid disturbing the emperor, Wang Jian maintained a sitting position throughout the night. When Emperor Xi Zong woke up, he was moved to tears and deeply admired Wang Jian. He took off his imperial robe and gave it to Wang Jian, explaining that the reason why he unclothed it and gave it to him was because there were traces of his own tears on it.

This easily reminds people of another story during the "War of the Eight Princes" in the Western Jin Dynasty. When the rebels were about to harm Emperor Hui of Jin, the Assistant Minister Ji Shao stepped forward to protect him and was killed, splattering the emperor's body with blood. Emperor Hui was the inventor of the saying "Why not let the people eat minced meat? (When the world was in a state of desolation and the people were starving to death) and is famous in history for being a foolish emperor. However, he showed a sense of righteousness and affection that many intelligent people do not possess. He refused to let the palace attendants clean the blood-stained imperial robe, saying that it had the blood of Ji Shao on it and wanted to keep it as a reminder. This anecdote is also the origin of the line "For the blood of the loyalist Ji Shao" in Wen Tianxiang's poem *The Song of Righteousness*.

Two emperors in distress, two loyal ministers, and two "old robes of the emperor"—history begins to rhyme and echo once again.

基本上都是为自己而打，而王建的前半生多是在为唐王朝出生入死。

至此，以“贼王八”身份出道的王建，终于在六十岁的时候成为中国历史上为数不多的平民皇帝，完成了人生豹变。

Wang Jian entered the land of Shu and launched numerous attacks, seeking to establish himself as a local power in the region. As his strength and territory grew, and with the passing of Tang Xizong who had favored him, as well as the changing political landscape towards the end of the Tang Dynasty, Wang Jian finally entertained thoughts of becoming an emperor.

In the year 907 AD, Zhu Wen forced the abdication of Emperor Ai of Tang and established the Liang Dynasty as a successor to the Tang Dynasty. Upon hearing this news, Wang Jian, who had burnt the plank road and locked the passes, independently governing the land of Shu for several years, burst into tears to the north. Following the example of Liu Bei, who had declared himself emperor in Chengdu, Wang Jian also declared himself emperor and established the Shu Dynasty. This period in history is known as the Former Shu.

Compared with Liu Bei, who also declared himself emperor in Shu, Wang Jian actually did much more in terms of pledging his loyalty to the former Dynasty. Liu Bei primarily fought for his own interests, while Wang Jian spent the majority of his early life risking his life for the Tang Dynasty.

Thus, Wang Jian, who started his career as a “Thief Wang the Eighth”, finally became one of the few commoner emperors in Chinese history at the age of 60, undergoing a remarkable transformation in his life.

用怎样的历史观评价王建?

如何评价王建，首先应当看他作为一个皇帝对社会所起的作用，是稳定、建设，还是破坏；其早年人品若何，次之；至于当皇帝是否名正言顺，则不足道矣。

What historical perspective is used to evaluate Wang Jian?

To evaluate Wang Jian, we should first consider the impact he had on society as an emperor—whether it was stabilizing and constructive or disruptive. His personal character in his early years would come next. As for whether he had a legitimate claim to the

《旧五代史》将王建置于《僭伪列传》,《五国故事》称“伪蜀先主建”,《蜀梼杌》也视其为“自古奸雄窃据成都者”，都是受到传统史观的影响。

这种历史观讲究正朔和所谓的传承，以中原政权视角观天下。司马光著《资治通鉴》，在唐朝之后仅作《后梁纪》《后唐纪》《后晋纪》《后汉纪》《后周纪》，其余政权如前蜀、后蜀、南唐、吴越，几视若无物。

这种历史观，从“五代十国”的命名也可见端倪。五代，其实质就是五国，梁、唐、晋、汉、周——跟王建的前蜀、李煜的南唐并无区别。史家却将这五个国家专门拎了出来，呼之为五代，何也?

代者，替也。梁、唐、晋、汉、周才是大唐的继承者（哪怕是篡权也算传承），是正统政权的五次更迭，此外皆为僭越——这是命名法里面潜藏的价值观。

五代十国时期，所谓“五代”的中原王朝已经不再是经济中心和文化中心。而如果称“五代”为政治中心，则“十国”一定会坚决反对。

其时，中国经济重心已经完成了向南转移，长江流域开始取得对黄河流域的压倒性优势。当时经济最繁

throne, that is of lesser importance.

The *Old History of the Five Dynasties* categorizes Wang Jian under the section of *Usurpers and Pretenders*, while the *Stories of the Five Kingdoms* refers to him as “the Bogus Founding Emperor of Shu”. In *Shu Tao Wu*, he is also depicted as a “treacherous hero who seized control of Chengdu”. These accounts are influenced by traditional historical perspectives.

This historical perspective emphasizes legitimacy and the concept of inheritance, viewing the world from the perspective of the Central Plains regime. The *Zizhi Tongjian* by Sima Guang, for example, only includes the records of the Later Liang, Later Tang, Later Jin, Later Han, and Later Zhou Dynasties after the Tang Dynasty, largely ignoring other regimes such as Former Shu, Later Shu, Southern Tang, and Wuyue.

This perspective is evident in the naming of the period as the *Five Dynasties and Ten Kingdoms*. In reality, the Five Dynasties essentially refers to the five major kingdoms of Liang, Tang, Jin, Han, and Zhou—no different from the Former Shu under Wang Jian or the Southern Tang under Li Yu. However, historians have singled out these five kingdoms and labeled them as the Five Dynasties,Why?

“Dynasty” refers to a replacement or substitution. The Liang, Tang, Jin, Han, and Zhou Dynasties were the true successors of the Great Tang (even if they came to power through usurpation), representing the five legitimate transitions of power. The other regimes were considered to be usurpers—this underlying value judgment is reflected in the naming convention.

During the period of the Five Dynasties and Ten Kingdoms, the so-called “Five Dynasties” in the Central Plains were no longer the economic and cultural centers. If we refer to the “Five Dynasties” as the political center, the “Ten Kingdoms” would surely

华者为南唐、吴越两国，南唐的都城金陵是江南也是全华夏最为重要的商业中心，钱氏治下的吴越则如苏轼在《表中观碑记》所称，“铸山煮海，象犀珠玉之富甲于天下……是以其民至于老死不识兵革，四时嬉游，歌舞之声相闻”。乱世之中，居然还有细民百姓终身未被战火烤燎，只知游玩歌舞，这足以让人热泪盈眶。

“蜀险而富。”其时的蜀中，经济发达仅次于江南，而文化上则可以与之并驾齐驱。当时中国两大文化中心，一为南唐之金陵，一为前、后蜀之成都。江南有歙砚，蜀中则有雕版印刷；南唐有李煜的“问君能有几多愁，恰似一江春水向东流”，前蜀则有韦庄的“垆边人似月，皓腕凝霜雪。未老莫还乡，还乡须断肠”。

五代十国时期，“五代”能够拿出来一说的，仅有军事优势而已。但不要忘了，正是所谓的这种优势，导致了当时中国北方的经济凋敝、人口流失，让百姓痛不欲生。

史家立论，往往重国祚而轻民生。也可以从其极为看重的国祚进行一个比较：“五代”之中，有三个的存续时间不超过十年，其中后汉仅仅三年，最长的后梁也不过十六年；“十国”里面的前蜀、后蜀尽管都

strongly object to this classification.

During that time, the economic center of China had indeed shifted towards the south, with the Yangtze River region gaining overwhelming advantages over the Yellow River region. The most prosperous economies were found in the Southern Tang and Wuyue kingdoms. Jinling, the capital of the Southern Tang, was not only the commercial center of Jiangnan but also the most important one in the entire region of China. Under the rule of the Qian family, Wuyue, as described by Su Shi in his *Record of Viewing Steles in Biaozhong Guan,* was known for its immense wealth, comparable to “Mining copper ore from the mountains to mint coins, boiling seawater to produce salt, thus possessing treasures like rhinoceros horns and jade. This led to its citizens living their whole lives without experiencing the ravages of war, knowing only the pleasures of leisure, with the sounds of singing and dancing echoing throughout the four seasons.” In such chaotic times, it is heartwarming to think that there were common folk who lived their whole lives untouched by the flames of war, and instead, only knew merriment and revelry. This is enough to move a person to tears.

“The Shu region was rugged yet prosperous.” During that era, the Shu region, while geographically challenging, was economically thriving, trailing only behind the wealth of the Jiangnan region, while its cultural achievements were on par with it. At the time, there were two major cultural centers in China: Jinling of the Southern Tang, and Chengdu of the Former and Later Shu. In Jiangnan, there were exquisite Shexian inkstones; in Shu, there was woodblock printing. The Southern Tang boasted Li Yu’s “How much sorrow can one bear? Like a river flowing east, without despair.” The Former Shu presented Wei Zhuang’s “By the fireside, the beauty glows, fair arms, frosty like snow. Do not return home till old, heartache

毁于"废二代"，但王建之前蜀存世十八年，孟知祥之后蜀二十八年，最长的吴越则长达七十一年——比"五代"前后相加的五十三年还要长得多——难怪其治下百姓可以唱歌跳舞、游山玩水一辈子。

可以设想一下，你如果生于五代十国时期。是愿意生活在天天打仗的正统王朝，搞不好就房子被烧，或者挨一刀；还是愿意生活在前后蜀、南唐、吴越这种"伪僭"之国，可以嬉游歌舞，还可以吟诗作赋？

传统史家最为看重的正朔与伪僭，究其实质无非是政治阐释，读史若不能辨，则入其彀矣。

awaits when homeland unfolds."

During the Five Dynasties and Ten Kingdoms period, the only thing that can be boasted about the Five Dynasties is their military advantage. But let's not forget that it was precisely this advantage that led to economic decline and population loss in northern China, causing immense suffering for the people.

Historians often prioritize the fate of empires over the well-being of the people. We can compare this by looking at the significant emphasis placed on the fate of these empires. Among the Five Dynasties, three of them lasted for less than ten years. The Later Han Dynasty, for instance, existed for a mere three years, and the longest, Later Liang, lasted only 16 years. In the case of the Ten Kingdoms, both the Former Shu and Later Shu were destroyed by succeeding generations. However, the Former Shu, under the rule of Wang Jian, existed for 18 years, while the Later Shu, under Meng Zhixiang, lasted 28 years. The longest of them all was the Wuyue Kingdom, enduring for a remarkable 71 years – much longer than the combined total of the Five Dynasties' span of 53 years. It is no wonder that under their governance, the people could sing, dance, and enjoy their lives, indulging in activities like mountain excursions and river boating.

Imagine if you were born during the period of the Five Dynasties and Ten Kingdoms. Would you prefer to live in a legitimate Dynasty where battles are fought every day, risking your house being burned down or facing harm? Or would you choose to live in a "pseudo" regime like Former Shu, Later Shu, Southern Tang, or Wuyue, where you can enjoy leisurely pursuits like singing, dancing, and composing poetry?

The emphasis traditional historians place on legitimacy and pseudo regimes ultimately boils down to political interpretations. If we cannot discern and analyze history critically, we may fall into their traps.

帝王心病以神玉为药

晚年的王建有两大心病。

第一个是早年的恶名。王建年轻时曾因作奸犯科受过杖刑，当了皇帝之后，仍对此耿耿于怀。有一天，当着众人的面问御史大夫冯涓："我听见有人在背后议论，说我曾被打过棍子。你说说，有这事吗？"

王建期待的回答是什么，谁都知道，但冯涓偏偏脆生生地答道："有。"

于是，王建也顾不得皇帝的尊严了，当即脱下衣服，把背露给冯涓："你再仔细看一下哩，我背上有伤痕吗？有挨了打背上还这么光滑的吗？"

"真是稀奇啊。"冯涓也是个没眼水的，竟然伸手摸着王建的背说，"那么，这么好的膏药，是从哪儿弄来的呢？"

冯涓当年以敢于直言著称，也曾反对过王建称帝，王建选择冯涓来接这个话，是经过筹划的，正是要借冯之美名来洗刷己之恶名，倒没想到对方这么不配合。

冯涓也果然毒舌，敢摸皇帝后背并出言挖苦，千年之后依然让人震惊。好在皇帝倒并不以为忤，而是仍

The Emperor's anxiety was treated with a divine jade

In his later years, Wang Jian had two major concerns.

The first one was his infamous past. When Wang Jian was young, he had received corporal punishment for committing wrongful acts. Even after becoming an emperor, his past actions still rankled with him. One day, in front of the crowd, he asked the Chief Censor Feng Juan, "I have heard people talking behind my back, saying that I was beaten with a stick. Tell me, is this true?"

Everyone knew what answer Wang Jian was expecting, but Feng Juan unexpectedly replied, "Yes."

Instantly, Wang Jian disregarded his imperial dignity, taking off his clothes and exposing his back to Feng Juan, saying, "Take a closer look, are there any scars on my back? Can someone who has been beaten still have such smooth skin?"

"It's truly remarkable," Feng Juan, with unwavering composure, even reached out to touch Wang Jian's back and said, "In that case, where did you get such an excellent ointment?"

Feng Juan, known for his fearless outspokenness, had previously opposed Wang Jian's ascension to the throne. Wang Jian intentionally chose Feng Juan to address this matter, planning to use Feng's reputation to cleanse his own tainted past. However, he did not anticipate Feng's uncooperative response.

Indeed, Feng Juan's tongue was sharp, daring to touch the emperor's back and sarcastically comment. Even after a millennium, it still astounds people. Fortunately, the emperor did not take offense but continued to be at ease and even exchanged banter. From this incident, we can see that Wang Jian

旧谈笑自若。从这件事看，王建还是有肚量的。

第二个心病倒不奇怪，接班人问题。这是帝王家的常见病，也是疑难杂症。那些雄才伟略的君主，如秦始皇嬴政、汉高祖刘邦、隋文帝杨坚、明太祖朱元璋，都曾遇到过这样的问题。处理得不好，庞大的帝国就二世而亡。

接班人问题大致有以下几类：没有儿子，儿子太多，儿子太笨，儿子太聪明……是的，儿子太聪明也是问题。隋炀帝杨广就是个具有超级智商和能力的人，但是他一手埋葬了国家。

那么，王建的心病何在？

王建当年征战时，为了笼络人心，收了不少能征善战的部下当义子。说起来吓人，干儿子的数量竟然上百，其中史籍有载者四十五人。干儿子就够多了，王建自己还生了十一个儿子，难怪前蜀宫廷里会为了谁接班乱成一锅粥。

王建的干儿子中，最能打的叫王宗佶，是王建在忠武军中当兵时抢来的——居然儿子也能靠抢，足见唐末军队的风纪。

王宗佶为前蜀建国立有大功，存非分之想也是自然。等王建的亲生

possessed a broad-mindedness and tolerance.

The second concern, the issue of succession, is not unusual. It is a common ailment for imperial families and a challenging problem to tackle. Great rulers with remarkable talents, such as Qin Shi Huang, Emperor Gaozu of Han, Emperor Wen of Sui, and Emperor Taizu of Ming, all faced similar dilemmas. If not handled properly, their vast empires would perish in the hands of their successors.

The issue of succession can be categorized in several ways: having no sons, having too many sons, having sons who are not capable, and even having sons who are excessively talented. Yes, having overly intelligent sons can also be a problem. Emperor Yang Guang of the Sui Dynasty was a person with extraordinary intelligence and abilities, but his actions eventually brought downfall to the nation.

So, what were Wang Jian's concerns?

During his military campaigns, Wang Jian recruited numerous combative and capable subordinates as adopted sons to gain their loyalty and support. It's quite staggering to think about it; he had hundreds of adopted sons, with historical records mentioning 45 of them. With such a large number of adopted sons, coupled with his own 11 biological sons, it's no wonder that the issue of succession in the court of Former Shu became chaotic.

Among Wang Jian's adopted sons, the most skilled in warfare was Wang Zongji, whom Wang Jian had seized as a soldier during his time in the Zhongwu Army. The fact that even sons were acquired through seizing highlights the discipline of the military during the late Tang Dynasty.

Wang Zongji made great contributions to the founding of the former Shu state, so it is natural for him to harbor aspirations beyond his position. As Wang Jian's biological son grew up, Zongji began to feel uneasy and sought to obtain the position of Grand

儿子逐渐长大，宗佶开始感到不安，于是谋求到大司马一职。统领六军，刀把子捏在手里，但仍然未能拯救自己。

宗佶跟枢密使唐袭关系不好，后者只一句话就让王建起了杀心："宗佶功臣，其威望可以服人心。"于是在朝堂之上，命武士将其扑杀。时为武成元年，前蜀王朝在头年才刚刚建立。

杀了干儿子，王建立次子王元膺为太子。王元膺相貌丑陋，猪嘴，蛀牙，但箭法奇佳，能射中钱孔，马背上抛球而射，百发百中。王建让学识渊博的户部尚书、道教领袖杜光庭当太子的老师，应该说存有这样的考虑：万一发生动荡，或可借助杜在宗教界的影响力稳定局势。

王建教育太子说，"你一切行事参照我的行为，就可以保护国家"，可以说是寄予了厚望，但这也是个不省心的。

同义子之死一样，太子之死也跟唐袭有直接关系。唐袭原本是王建的舞僮，深得宠爱，后来竟然当了枢密使这样的大官，以皇帝心腹的身份出掌军政。《新五代史》说，"唐袭，建之嬖也"。嬖，本指身份低微而受宠爱者。王建大概率有男风之好，跟唐

Marshal. Although he commanded six armies and held the power, he was still unable to save himself.

Zongji had a bad relationship with Tang Xi, the Prime Minister, and with the latter's one word, saying, "Zongji, as a meritorious general, his prestige can win the hearts of the people," Wang Jian developed the intention to kill him. Thus, he was assassinated by warriors in the court. This happened in the first year of Wucheng, just one year after the establishment of the former Shu Dynasty.

After killing his adopted son, Wang Jian appointed his second son, Wang Yuanying, as the Crown Prince. Wang Yuanying had an ugly appearance, with a pig-like mouth and rotten teeth. However, he had exceptional archery skills and could shoot coins through a hole and throw and hit balls while on horseback, never missing a single shot. Wang Jian appointed Du Guangting, the knowledgeable Minister of the Ministry of Revenue and leader of the Taoist community, as the tutor for the Crown Prince. This decision was likely made with the consideration that in case of any unrest, Du's influence in the religious community could help stabilize the situation.

Wang Jian taught the Crown Prince, saying, "Follow my actions in all your conduct, and you will be able to protect the country." This was undoubtedly a heavy expectation, but also a source of worry for Wang Jian.

Just like the death of the adopted son, the death of the Crown Prince is also directly related to Tang Xi. Tang Xi was originally a dancer and favorite of Wang Jian, but later he unexpectedly rose to the position of Prime Minister, holding military and political power as a trusted confidant of the emperor. *The New Five Dynasties History* describes Tang Xi as "Jian's favorite". "Favorite" originally referred to someone of low status who is favored. It is highly probable that Wang Jian had an intimate sexual

袭有着不可描述的关系。

当年宗佶跟唐袭发生冲突，是因为瞧不起他，即便他当了枢密使还是直呼其名——古人社交礼仪是称人表字，直呼其名则极其不礼貌，所谓“指名道姓”。皇太子元膺犯了同样的错误，经常在朝堂上挖苦唐袭。

然而，舞僮出身的唐袭，其学识才具、心胸格局都不足以治国。俗语说，“宁得罪君子不得罪小人”，王宗佶、王元膺两位皇子用生命诠释了这句话，唐袭则用生命为“小人”这个词做了终极诠释。

终于有一天，唐袭找到机会挑唆王建：“太子要造反，赶快调兵进宫护卫。”太子原本没有防备，听到唐袭调兵，既愤怒又恐惧，遂召集人马攻打皇宫，激战于神武门。

这是一个两败俱伤的结局。唐袭在乱战中被流箭射中，坠马而死，太子则兵败逃亡，后为卫兵所杀。

王元膺跟唐袭的冲突，像极了汉武帝时的“巫蛊之祸”。

汉武帝太子刘据跟宠臣江充有隙，江充怕太子将来即位自己不得好死，便诬陷刘据用巫术诅咒皇帝。太子因被阻挡，无法进宫申辩，只能起兵造反，杀江充，兵败，亡。

这件事发生之后，对汉武帝的打

relationship with Tang Xi, which cannot be explicitly described.

The conflict between Zongji and Tang Xi back then was due to Zongji looking down on him, even after he became the Prime Minister, Zongji still called him by his name directly. In ancient social etiquette, it is impolite to directly call someone by their name, it is considered as “pointing fingers and name-calling”. Crown Prince Yuanying made the same mistake, often mocking Tang Xi in court.

However, Tang Xi, who came from a dancer background, lacked the knowledge, talent, and broad-mindedness needed to govern a country. As the saying goes, “It is better to offend a nobleman than to offend a villain.” Wang Zongji and Wang Yuanying, the two imperial princes, demonstrated the truth of this saying with their lives, while Tang Xi ultimately embodied the term “a vile character” with his actions.

Finally, one day, Tang Xi found an opportunity to incite Wang Jian: “The Crown Prince is planning a rebellion. Quickly deploy troops to guard the palace.” The Crown Prince was caught off guard and became both angry and fearful upon hearing that Tang Xi was mobilizing troops. He then gathered his forces and attacked the imperial palace, engaging in a fierce battle at the Shenwu Gate (the Gate of Divine Prowess).

This is a mutually destructive outcome. Tang Xi was struck by stray arrows during the chaotic battle and died after falling from his horse. The Crown Prince, on the other hand, was defeated and fled, only to be killed by his entourage.

The conflict between Wang Yuanying and Tang Xi mirrors the infamous “Witchcraft Incident” during the reign of Emperor Wu of Han.

The Crown Prince, Liu Ju, had disagreements with the emperor’s favored advisor, Jiang Chong. Fearing that the Crown Prince would seek revenge

击其实是非常大的。父子反目，儿子自杀，帝国也失去了接班人。汉武帝醒悟过来之后，在太子刘据身亡之处修建“归来望思之台”，来寄托对儿子的思念，表达自己的悔恨。此外，为了泄愤，还把江充的一家人都杀了，灭了三族。

历史，会重复发生吗?

法国作家米兰·昆德拉在小说《生命中不能承受之轻》里，提到一个“永劫回归”的哲学概念：“想想我们经历过的事情吧，想想它们重演如昨，甚至重演本身无休无止地重演下去！”

不妨把王元膺、唐袭的冲突，跟汉代的“巫蛊之祸”比较一下，看一下有哪些相似。

其一，皇帝都有一个宠臣，汉武帝有江充，王建有唐袭；

其二，宠臣跟太子的关系，都非常差；

其三，宠臣都诬陷太子；

其四，太子都起兵反抗；

其五，太子、宠臣都死于非命。

这种重复发生的历史，其哲学意义，正如昆德拉所说：“它将变成一个永远隆起的硬块，再也无法归复自己原有的虚空。”

明白了汉武帝的悔恨，就能理解

once he ascended to the throne, Jiang Chong falsely accused Liu Ju of using witchcraft to curse the emperor. The Crown Prince was unable to enter the palace to defend himself and had no choice but to rebel, leading to Jiang Chong’s death. However, the rebellion failed, and the Crown Prince perished.

After this incident, it had a profound impact on Emperor Wu of Han. The rift between father and son, the son’s suicide, and the loss of a successor greatly affected the empire. Emperor Wu of Han, upon realizing the gravity of the situation, constructed the “Platform of Yearning and Remembrance” at the location where his deceased son, Liu Ju, passed away. This served as a place for him to express his remorse and longing for his son. Additionally, in a fit of anger, he had Jiang Chong’s entire family executed, resulting in the extermination of three generations.

Can history repeat itself?

French writer Milan Kundera, in his novel *The Unbearable Lightness of Being*, mentioned the philosophical concept of “eternal return”: “Imagine we experience the same events over and over again, infinitely recurring as if they happened just yesterday, without end!”

It is interesting to compare the conflict between Wang Yuanying and Tang Xi with the “Witchcraft Incident” during the Han Dynasty and identify the similarities:

Firstly, both emperors had a favored advisor: Emperor Wu of Han had Jiang Chong, while Wang Jian had Tang Xi.

Secondly, the relationship between the favored advisor and the Crown Prince in both cases was extremely poor.

Thirdly, both favored advisors falsely accused the Crown Princes.

Fourthly, the Crown Princes rebelled against their respective emperors.

王建的内心伤痛。父子反目发生在帝王家，对国家政治格局的冲击，也是难以估量的。

不过，生活还是要继续，政权也还是要继续，王建遂立宠妃徐氏生的幼子王衍为嗣。而就是这个幼子，最终把前蜀送上了不归路。

其实，王衍的荒唐，王建在生前就曾察觉，并萌生了换信王王宗杰为太子的想法。王宗杰倒是贤明，但在王建动了换储念头几个月之后，却突然暴病而亡。

在信王莫名其妙死去的前几年，皇宫中还发生了一场莫名其妙的大火，烧毁了满储奇珍异宝的百尺楼。面对这场蹊跷的大火，王建也做出了一个非常蹊跷的反应：严闭宫门，将前来救火的将士挡在门外，任由一夜大火将那些珍宝烧得干干净净。

他防的是另外一把火。

这把火，在西晋时就曾被一个五岁的孩子提及。

那一回皇宫中失火，晋武帝司马炎登楼查看，五岁的孙子司马遹（yù）拉着他的衣裾，让他躲入暗处，以备非常。生在深宫之中，对于人世间的阴谋耳濡目染，五岁孩子都懂得火光中潜藏的危险。当然，司马遹的聪颖是毋庸置疑的。也正因为

Lastly, both the Crown Princes and the favored advisors met tragic ends.

The recurrence of such historical events, as Kundera stated, carries a philosophical significance: "It becomes an ever-increasing solid mass from which it is impossible to escape back into the lightness of emptiness."

Understanding Emperor Wu of Han's remorse helps us comprehend Wang Jian's inner pain as well. When the estrangement between father and son occurs within a royal family, the impact on the political landscape of the country is immeasurable.

However, life must go on, and the reign of power must continue. Therefore, Wang Jian designated his youngest son, Wang Yan, born to his favored concubine Xu, as his heir. Yet, it was this very son who eventually led the former Shu state down an irreversible path.

In fact, Wang Jian had already sensed the recklessness and foolishness of Wang Yan even before his passing and had considered replacing him with one of his trusted sons, the Prince Xin, Wang Zongji, as the Crown Prince. Wang Zongji was indeed wise. However, just a few months after Wang Jian entertained the idea of changing his successor, Prince Xin suddenly fell seriously ill and passed away.

In the years leading up to the inexplicable death of Prince Xin, there was also a mysterious fire in the palace, which engulfed the Hundred-Foot Tower that housed numerous rare and valuable treasures. Faced with this suspicious fire, Wang Jian responded in an equally perplexing manner: he ordered the palace gates to be tightly shut, preventing the soldiers who came to extinguish the fire from entering. He allowed the blaze to consume all the treasures throughout the night, leaving them completely destroyed.

He was guarding against another fire. This fire had been mentioned by a five-year-old child during

此，晋武帝终于下定决心把傻儿子司马衷定为继承人，以便皇位有一天能传给这位聪明的孙子。

同时期还有一把火，如果真烧起来了的话，也许就不会有西晋实质上的二世而亡，不会有分裂三百年的南北朝了。

司马衷即位，就是著名的晋惠帝，此时大权归于晋武帝第二任皇后杨芷的父亲杨骏之手。杨芷是司马衷母亲杨艳的堂妹，也算是司马衷的继母。太傅杨骏擅权，就跟渴望权力的新任皇后贾南风产生了剧烈冲突。皇家的婆媳矛盾一旦爆发，来得远比普通人家的惨烈。儿媳妇贾南风先下手为强，拿到皇帝诏书，立即派人去抓婆婆的老爹。

得到风声的杨骏急召部下商讨对策，太傅主簿朱振建议："立即火烧禁宫前的云龙门，造成震慑，趁乱进宫擒杀贾氏一党，然后以太傅的身份立太子为帝。"主意是好主意，但是太费门了，杨骏嗫嚅道："云龙门是魏明帝时建造，花费巨大，烧了可惜。"

反而是来抓杨骏的，到了杨府就先放一把火试探虚实。结局是，勤俭节约、不愿放火的杨骏被杀死在马棚里，强悍又愚蠢的贾南风上位。不久

the Western Jin Dynasty.

At that time, there was a fire in the imperial palace. Emperor Wu of Jin, Sima Yan, went up to a tower to inspect the situation. His five-year-old grandson, Sima Yu, pulled on his clothes and urged him to hide in a dark corner in case of emergency. Being born in the deep palace and exposed to the world of conspiracies, even a five-year-old child understood the dangers hidden in the flames. Of course, Sima Yu's intelligence was unquestionable. It was precisely because of this incident that Emperor Wu of Jin finally made up his mind to designate his seemingly foolish son, Sima Zhong, as his successor, so that the throne could one day be passed on to this intelligent grandson.

At the same time, there was another fire. If it had really started, perhaps the Western Jin Dynasty wouldn't have met its downfall, and the division of the unified China into the Northern and Southern Dynasties for three hundred years might have been avoided.

When Sima Zhong ascended to the throne as Emperor Hui of Jin, the real power was in the hands of Yang Jun, the father of Empress Yang Zhi, who was the second empress of Emperor Wu of Jin. Yang Zhi was the cousin of Sima Zhong's mother, Yang Yan, so she was also his stepmother. Grand Tutor Yang Jun, grasping power, clashed fiercely with the newly appointed empress, Jia Nanfeng, who eagerly desired authority. The conflicts between the mother-in-law and daughter-in-law in the royal family were far more intense than those in ordinary households. Jia Nanfeng made the first move by obtaining an imperial decree and immediately sent people to arrest her mother-in-law's father.

Upon receiving the news, Yang Jun urgently summoned his subordinates to discuss countermeasures. Zhu Zhen, the Chief Secretary of the Grand Tutor,

后即引发“八王之乱”，开启了一个血与火交织的大黑暗时代。

放火，不是宫廷政变的标准配置，但对于发生在夜间的政变来说，火，是混乱制造机，是信号发射枪，也是方向指示灯。雄猜多疑的枭雄王建，自然是懂得这把火的妙用的。危局时刻，老谋深算的老江湖靠定力稳住了局面。

火把所有的珍宝都烧得一干二净了吗？也没有，还单单剩下一块宝玉。这块来自和田的玉石，温润洁白异常，有着良匠也从未见过的高品质。经过烈火锻炼的神石，王建让人做成了玉大带，亲自佩戴于腰。

玉大带由七块方形銙和末端的长条形獭尾构成，銙方二寸，獭尾六寸五分，皆雕有龙。銙为方形，龙身盘曲为C字形或D字形，然而也是曲中有伸，颇具张力。獭尾上的龙，尾在上，身在下，龙头却高高昂起，前爪一上一下，威武非常，而满身细鳞清晰可见。

更难得的是，獭尾背面有一篇铭文，记载了此玉的来历。

永平五年乙亥孟冬下旬之七日，荧惑次尾宿，尾主后宫，是夜火作，翌日于烈焰中得所宝玉一团，工人皆曰：“此经大火，不堪矣。”上曰：

suggested, “Immediately set fire to the Yunlong Gate in front of the Forbidden Palace to create shock and chaos. Take advantage of the situation to enter the palace and capture and kill the supporters of Jia Nanfeng’s faction. Then, in the position of the Grand Tutor, establish a new emperor.” It was a good idea, but it was quite extreme. Yang Jun hesitated and said, “The Yunlong Gate was built during the reign of Emperor Ming of Wei at great cost. It would be a pity to burn it.”

Ironically, it was those who came to arrest Yang Jun that set fire to his residence as a means of testing the situation. The outcome was that Yang Jun, who valued frugality and was reluctant to resort to arson, was killed in the stable, while the ruthless and foolish Jia Nanfeng seized power. Shortly afterward, the “Upheaval of the Eight Princes” broke out, ushering in a dark era of bloodshed and turmoil.

Setting fire may not be the standard approach in a palace coup, but for a coup that occurred at night, fire serves as a device to create chaos, a signal flare, and a guiding light. Wang Jian, the cunning and suspicious warlord, naturally understood the ingenious use of fire. In a critical moment, the experienced old-timer relied on his composure to stabilize the situation.

Did the fire burn all the treasures to ashes? Not quite. There was still one precious item left: a piece of jade. This jade stone, from Hetian, was exceptionally smooth and pure, possessing a quality that even skilled craftsmen had never seen before. After being forged in the intense flames, Wang Jian had it made into a jade belt and personally wore it around his waist.

The jade belt consisted of seven square jade plaques and a long strip of otter tail at the end. Each plaque was two inches long, and the otter tail measured six inches and five fen, with dragons engraved on them. The plaques were square-shaped, and the dragon’s body coiled in a “C” or “D” shape,

"天生神物，又安能损乎？！"遂命解之。其温润洁白异常，虽良工目所未睹。制成大带，其胯方阔二寸，獭尾六寸有五分。夫火炎昆岗，玉石俱焚，向非圣德所感，则何以臻此焉？谨记。

这是一个神异的故事。

915年阴历十二月十七，荧惑停驻于尾宿（二十八星宿之一）。荧惑即火星，古人视之为灾星。传统文化中，荧惑次尾宿，意味着后宫将有灾变。

獭尾背面的铭文记载了那场奇异的大火　何大江摄

Inscriptions on the otter-tail tip document that mysterious great fire. (Photographer: He Dajiang)

but with a sense of expansion within the curve, creating a powerful and dynamic effect. The dragon on the otter tail had its tail positioned upward, its body below, and its head held high. With one forelimb raised and the other lowered, it exuded a mighty presence, while its scales were intricately and clearly visible.

What is even more rare is that there is an inscription on the back of the otter tail, which records the origin of this jade.

In the seventh day of the end of the tenth month in the fifth year of Yongping (59 AD), Mars passed through the Tail mansion, which governs the imperial harem. On that night, a fire broke out. The following day, amidst the intense flames, this precious piece of jade was discovered. The craftsmen all said, "It has been through a great fire and is no longer usable." However, His Majesty said, "Heavenly treasures are naturally indestructible!" Thus, it was ordered to be preserved. Its exceptionally smooth and pure quality was beyond the scope of any skilled artisans. It was made into a large belt, with a width of two inches at the waist and the otter tail measuring six inches and five fen. The fire would ravage even mountain, reducing both jade and stone to ashes. Without the influence of the virtuous deeds of His Majesty, how could it be obtained? Duly record this.

This is a miraculous story.

On the seventeenth day of the twelfth lunar month in the year 915, Mars came to a halt in the Tail mansion, which is one of the twenty-eight constellations. Mars was seen as an ominous star in ancient times. In traditional culture, Mars lingering near the Tail mansion indicated an impending disaster in the imperial harem.

That evening, a mysterious fire broke out in the palace, engulfing the hundred-foot tower that housed countless rare and precious treasures. Strangely enough, all the other treasures were completely

当天晚上，皇宫里就发生了一场莫名其妙的大火，烧毁了满储奇珍异宝的百尺楼。奇的是，其他的珍宝都被烧得干干净净，独留下一块质地极佳的美玉。皇帝王建让良工雕琢美玉，将其制成大带，佩戴于腰——这便是国宝级文物玉大带的由来。

此事蹊跷有三。

其一，大火来得毫无缘由。

其二，美玉经火不坏，让“玉石俱焚”这一成语落空。

其三，獭尾之文没有记载的是：王建不许人救火，他下令严闭宫门，将前来救火的将士挡在门外，任由一夜大火将那些珍宝烧得干干净净。这之后的举动，其实揭示了真相。根据《资治通鉴》的记载，大火到第二天早上仍未熄灭。王建则出义兴门见群臣，令百官巡视全城。

可见，他对于那把火因何而起，心中存在着极大的疑虑，甚至有了自己的答案。

宝玉为何经火不坏，王建本人的说法是：“天生神物，又安能损乎？”神物一说自然是骗人的把戏，“玉石俱焚”的常识也未可轻易被突破。

统治者对于利用舆论来操控人心，往往有非常多的心得。铭文末尾的那句话“向非圣德所感，则何以

consumed by the fire, leaving behind only a piece of excellent-quality jade. Emperor Wang Jian had skilled craftsmen carve and fashion the jade into a large belt, which he wore around his waist. This became the origin of the national treasure, the Jade Belt.

There are three peculiarities to this incident.

Firstly, the fire broke out inexplicably, without any apparent cause.

Secondly, the fact that the beautiful jade remained unharmed by the fire contradicted the saying “all jade and stone burned to ashes”.

Thirdly, the inscription on the otter tail doesn’t mention that Wang Jian forbade people from extinguishing the fire. He ordered the palace gates to be tightly shut, preventing the soldiers who came to put out the fire from entering, allowing the fire to consume all the treasures completely. His actions afterwards, however, revealed the truth. According to the records in the *Zizhi Tongjian*, the fire was still burning on the morning of the next day. Wang Jian then went out of the Yixing Gate to meet his officials and ordered them to inspect the entire city.

It is evident that he had great doubts about the origins of the fire, and even had his own answer.

As for why the Precious Jade remained unharmed in the fire, Wang Jian himself stated, “A divine object by nature, how could it be damaged?” The notion of a divine object is nothing more than a clever deception, and the common knowledge that “jade and stone burn together” cannot be easily overcome.

Rulers often have a profound understanding of using public opinion to manipulate the masses. The sentence at the end of the inscription, “Without the influence of the virtuous deeds of His Majesty, how could it be obtained?” attributes the miraculous event to the emperor’s virtue. However, it could also be a trick similar to concealing the silk with writing on it in a fish’s belly, as in the case of “The Great Chu

臻此焉”，把异象归结于皇帝的圣德，还是鱼腹藏书“大楚兴、陈胜王”的把戏，说到底，王建是要借这块美玉、这根玉大带，来稳定前蜀最后的基本盘。王朝接班人未妥的危机，被王建向后延缓了，但心病终究未能治愈。

神玉现身后三年，潜在接班人信王暴毙，又过了几个月，出身“贼王八”的开国皇帝油尽灯枯。而神玉制成的玉大带，则在地下陪伴了他上千年。

虽然埋葬王建的永陵早就发掘了，虽然抚琴台已被证明只是一个误解，但它太深入人心，地宫外面的道路便被命名为抚琴东路。直到1999年，终于正本清源改为永陵路。

依托永陵所建园林，在成都人的口中称作王建墓。多年以前笔者就常去喝茶，极爱其清幽。2009年10月1日，在王建墓基础上改建的永陵公园正式开放。

公园广场上，有二十四伎乐，只是她们不再是棺床上的浮雕，而都变成了立体雕像。

十二神也在，只是他们抬的也不是棺床，而是王建谥宝。这件雕塑的绝对体量并不算太大，但由于将真实的谥宝放大了很多倍，在广场上也有一种BDO的效果。路过时的惊鸿一瞥，能感受到内心的震颤。

Rises and Chen Sheng becomes the King”. Ultimately, Wang Jian intended to use this beautiful jade and jade belt to stabilize the fundamental support of the former Shu state. The imminent crisis of succession for the Dynasty was delayed by Wang Jian, but the underlying issues were never truly resolved.

Three years after the appearance of the divine jade, the potential successor to the throne, Prince Xin, met a violent death, and a few months later, the founding emperor with a questionable background passed away. Meanwhile, the jade belt made from the divine jade remained buried underground, accompanying Wang Jian more than 1000 years.

Although the Yongling Mausoleum, where Wang Jian was buried, was excavated long ago, and the Fuqin Tai has been proven to be a misconception, it had already deeply ingrained itself in people’s hearts. The road outside the underground palace was named Fuqin East Road. It was not until 1999 that it was finally renamed Yongling Road to correct the misconception.

The garden built around the Yongling Mausoleum, known as Wang Jian’s Tomb among the people of Chengdu, has been my cherished place for tea drinking for many years due to its serenity. On October 1, 2009, the Yongling Park, built on the foundation of Wang Jian’s tomb, was officially opened.

In the park square, the twenty-four performers are no longer mere reliefs on a sarcophagus. They have been transformed into three-dimensional sculptures.

The twelve deities are also present, but they are not lifting a sarcophagus; instead, they are carrying Wang Jian’s posthumous seal. Although the sculpture itself is not of significant size, it creates a powerful effect of the BDO on the square due to the magnification of the true posthumous seal. A fleeting glance while passing by can evoke a profound sense of awe and resonance within one’s heart.

第五卷

Volume 5

合江亭
Hejiang Pavilion

古代成都的城市格局，曾经有过两次大变动。但无论是“二江珥市”还是“两江环抱”，合江亭始终处于这两条河的交汇处。

自唐宋以来，合江亭一直是成都的游宴胜地，也是文人墨客吟诗作赋之处。范成大和路岩两名蜀地主政者，都在合江亭辞别成都，前者记录沿途胜景，以《吴船录》流传千年；后者则在流放途中被诛，昔日煊赫尽化作云烟。

In the ancient urban layout of Chengdu, there have been two major changes. However, whether it was “Two Earring-like Rivers Encircle the Market” or “Two Rivers Embrace the City”, Hejiang Pavilion has always been located at the confluence of these two rivers.

Since the Tang and Song Dynasties, Hejiang Pavilion has been a popular destination for leisure and entertainment in Chengdu, as well as a place for literati and intellectuals to chant poems and write essays. Two notable political figures in the Shu region, Fan Chengda and Lu Yan, bid farewell to Chengdu at Hejiang Pavilion. Fan Chengda recorded the beautiful scenery along his journey in his famous work *Record of Wu Boats*, which has been passed down for a thousand years. Lu Yan, on the other hand, was executed during his exile, and the glory of his past faded away like dispersing smoke.

合江亭：诗人的吟唱与大吏的殊途

Hejiang Pavilion:
The Chanting of Poets and the Separate Paths of High Officials

合江亭

宋 · 周焘

却暑追随水上亭，
东郊乘晓戴残星。
余歌咽管来幽浦，
薄雾疏烟入画舲。
兴废江湖驰象魏，
情钟原隰咏飞鸰。
故溪何时垂纶去，
天末遥岑寸寸青。

Hejiang Pavilion

Zhou Tao, Song Dynasty

Avoiding the heat, we reach the waterside pavilion,
In the eastern suburbs, under a fading morning star's dominion.
The song fades, the flute weeps in a secluded creek,
Thin mist, sparse smoke, into a painted boat they streak.
Rise and fall, echo of the vanity fair's might,
Flatland and marsh, singing of a soaring wagtail.
When will I cast my fishing-rod in the boyhood creek's flow,
At the world's end, a distant peak, inch by inch it grows green and slow.

合江亭处于府河与南河的交汇点上，两条河在这里汇成锦江　冉玉杰摄

Hejiang Pavilion stands at the confluence of the Fu River and Nan River, where they merge to form the Jin River. (Photographer: Ran Yujie)

周焘是名门之后，理学家、《爱莲说》作者周敦颐的次子，这首诗写于他在成都知府的任上。

那是夏日合江亭旁的一场欢歌夜宴，此时华章已过，仅留下些余绪。星星尽管还挂在天上，但东方欲晓，

Zhou Tao, the author of this poem, was the second son of Zhou Dunyi, a prominent scholar and author of *Ailian Shuo* (On Love for the Lotus). Zhou Tao wrote this poem during his tenure as the magistrate in Chengdu.

It was a summer night feast by the side of Hejiang Pavilion, where the festivities had reached their height, now only leaving behind remnants.

晨雾升腾飘入画舫。而诗人在这一场尽兴的狂欢之后，正被无边的虚无笼罩着。对于公务繁剧、官场倾轧，以及夜夜笙歌的应酬已心生厌倦，他更向往与怀念的，是原野上的飞鸟，是垂钓于家乡的小河边，望着远处青草覆盖的山崖发呆。

合江亭在那时就是一个重要的游宴之地，名人在此处留下的诗文之多或仅次于万里桥。

沿着水津街往南走，右侧是由北向南流的府河；街的左侧，便是2010年10月开业的兰桂坊街区，著名的酒吧聚集处。很快便来到了府河汇入南河之处。两河相交之地，盘踞着一个外形独特的双亭建筑，那便是合江亭。

合江亭的亭顶为双檐，下有十根亭柱支撑着。双亭相连，构成一个整体，翘角飞檐张开，像一只大鸟伸展双翼欲飞。

站在合江亭上，朝下俯瞰，府河自北而来，南河向东而去。

亭既称合江，必与两江相合有关。战国末期，秦蜀郡守李冰建都江堰，引郫江、流江入成都，在城南门外形成二江并流之势。到了唐贞元年间（785—805年），为解决成都城

Though the stars still hung in the sky, the eastern horizon hinted at dawn, with morning mist rising and drifting into the painted boat. After this merry celebration, the poet finds himself enveloped in boundless emptiness. He is tired of the busy official duties, political struggles, and the superficiality of the night revelries. Instead, he yearns and reminisces about the birds flying over the meadows and the angling moments by the riverside of his hometown, gazing at the distant green-covered cliffs.

During that time, Hejiang Pavilion was an important venue for leisure and entertainment, and the literary works left by famous individuals there were second only to the poems written on the Wanli Bridge.

Walking south along Shuijin Street, on the right flows the Fuhe River from north to south; on the left of the street is the Lan Kwai Fong community, opened in October 2010, which is famous for its concentration of bars. Soon, we arrive at the confluence of the Fuhe River and the Nan River. At this junction, there stands a uniquely shaped twin pavilion, known as Hejiang Pavilion.

The roof of Hejiang Pavilion is double-eaved, supported by ten pavilion columns below. The twin pavilions are connected, forming a unified structure, with protruding corners and flying eaves, resembling a bird spreading its wings, ready to take flight.

Standing on the Hejiang Pavilion and looking down, we see the Fu River flows from the north, while the Nan River flows to the east.

The name "Hejiang Pavilion" implies its connection to the confluence of the two rivers. In the late Warring States period, Li Bing, the governor of Qin in Shu, constructed the Dujiangyan Irrigation

中的用水问题，剑南西川节度使韦皋开凿解玉溪，由西北方向引水穿城而过，在合江亭北面附近汇入锦江。同时，在两江汇合之处修建了合江亭。

到了高骈任节度使时，为了重构城市军事防御系统而筑罗城，改郫江从城北面、东面流过。郫江虽然改道，但两江汇合之处依然未变，并一直延续至今日。

占据形胜之地，这样的地标性建筑自然而然成为名胜。实际上，双亭相连的建筑构造，也是对两江合流的寓喻。

System, diverting the waters of the Pi River and the Liu River into Chengdu. This created a confluence of the two rivers outside the southern gate of the city. During the Zhenyuan era in the Tang Dynasty (785-805 AD), Wei Gao, the military governor of Jiannan West Sichuan, dug the Jieyu Canal to solve the water supply issues in Chengdu. The canal was constructed to divert water from the northwest, passing through the city and merging with the Jin River near the northern part of Hejiang Pavilion. At the confluence of these two rivers, Hejiang Pavilion was built.

In order to restructure the city's defense system, Gao Pian, the military governor built a city wall and redirected the Pi River to flow from the north and east of the city. Although the Pi River was diverted, the confluence of the two rivers remained unchanged and has continued to this day.

Occupying such a strategic location, this iconic building naturally became a famous attraction.The connected pavilions also symbolize the convergence of the two rivers.

范成大：送君千里的传奇

与合江亭有关的古时名人，唐多名将，如韦皋、高骈；宋多文人，如周焘、吕大防、范成大和陆游等。其实，唐之武、宋之文，也各自正是中国历史上的武功与文治的巅峰。

北宋神宗年间，吕大防知成都府时，合江亭已久未打理，杂草丛生，便将其开辟为船舶管理官员的办公处。整治后的合江亭视野开阔，往东

Fan Chengda: A Legendary Farewell Across a Thousand Miles

Many famous figures in ancient times have been associated with Hejiang Pavilion, including renowned Tang Dynasty generals such as Wei Gao and Gao Pian, and renowned Song Dynasty literati such as Zhou Tao, Lü Dafang, Fan Chengda, and Lu You. In fact, the Tang Dynasty was known for its military achievements, while the Song Dynasty reached the pinnacle of literary and cultural accomplishments in Chinese history.

望过去，缓坡之上茂林修竹，烟雾如织，鸥鹭翻飞，鸣声悠扬。而江面之上，商旅之船和打鱼小舟悠缓而行。这样的场景，正适合拿来下酒。

南宋名臣范成大任四川制置使时，便把摆酒亭上变成了一项工作。既然是工作，其意义绝不仅是公款吃喝，中有教化社会、传播文化、与民同乐的深意。

合江亭旁有芳华楼，四周多植梅树。巡检司会密切关注花事，一旦花开三分，便向上申报，摆下宴席。

巡检司是掌管地方治安的机构，看花、摆酒显然非其本职，不过是因为办公场所在亭旁，而就近为上司打杂而已。其实，不只是巡检司干过这样的事，范成大有诗《雨后，东郭排岸司申梅开方及三分，戏书小绝，令一面开燕》，从长长的诗名看得出来，同样在附近办公的船纲管理机构排岸司，也承担过园林局和招待所的职责。

亭上摆酒，邀请文人饮酒作诗、广为传播；庶民百姓也呼朋引伴、乘兴而来，望月赏梅、兴尽而归。作为蜀地的主政官员，范成大自然不会缺席这种亲民的仪式。“司花好事相邀勒，不著笙歌不肯春。”在他的诗里，百花女神是个事儿妈，竟然逼人摆酒

During the reign of Emperor Shenzong of the Northern Song Dynasty, when Lü Dafang served as the magistrate of Chengdu Prefecture, Hejiang Pavilion had been neglected for a long time, overrun with weeds. Lü Dafang then decided to convert it into an office for managing ships and boats. With the renovation completed, Hejiang Pavilion offered a broad view: looking eastward, one could see lush woods and bamboo groves on gentle slopes, with wisps of smoke and egrets soaring in the air, their melodious songs echoing. On the river surface, merchant ships and fishing boats glided leisurely. Such a scene was perfect for enjoying a drink.

When Fan Chengda, a famous statesman during the Southern Song Dynasty, served as the Governor of Sichuan, he turned holding banquets on the pavilion into a form of official duty. Since it was considered an official engagement, its significance went beyond mere extravagance at public expenses. It held deep meaning in terms of educating society, spreading culture, and enjoying festivities with the people.

Near Hejiang Pavilion stands the Fragrant Tower, surrounded by plum trees. The Inspectorate closely monitored the blooming of flowers, and once the blossoms reached three-tenths of their full bloom, a report would be submitted, and a banquet would be arranged.

The Inspectorate was an institution responsible for maintaining local security, so it may seem out of their jurisdiction to be involved in flower-watching and banquets. However, it happened because their office happened to be located near the pavilion, and they were assigned to assist their superiors. It was not only the Inspectorate that engaged in such activities. Fan Chengda's poem *After the Rain, Inspectorate Reported Plum Blossom Opening to Three-Tenths, I Parodied of a Quatrain, Ordering him to Hold a Banquet* reveals that the Pai'an Inspectorate, the

请客，否则就不放春天来到人间。有司摆酒，大员亲临，文人赋诗，万民同乐——难怪，那么多读书人有梦回宋朝的情结。

在蜀为官两年后，范成大因病离任，在合江亭下登舟归吴。此次离蜀，多名好友搭船相送至乐山，其中更有二位则一直送到川、渝、贵交界的合江县。

范有诗记之：

合江亭前送我来，
合江县里别我去。
江流好合人好乖，
明日东西南北路。
千里追随不忍归，
一杯重把知何处。
临歧心曲两茫然，
但祝频书无别语。

送君千里终有一别，都以为是修辞夸张，但于范这次旅途却是真实。从成都合江亭登船，在彭山进入岷江，经眉山、乐山、犍为、屏山、宜宾并入长江主流，再经江安、泸州抵达合江县，里程刚刚超过一千里。合江县是长江与赤水河的交汇处。刚好送君千里，有主动作为之意，但起点、终点皆为“合江”，倒真是无巧不成书，刚好送范成大一首诗。

Ships and Boats Management Institution, which also had its office nearby, assumed the responsibilities of the garden bureau and the guesthouse.

Setting up feasts on the pavilion and inviting literati to drink and compose poetry helped spread the cultural influence. Common people, too, would gather and enjoy the moon and appreciate the plum blossoms, and leave when the excitement wanes. As the chief official in the Shu region, Fan Chengda naturally wouldn't miss out on such a popular event. "For such a delightful flower-viewing event, a lack of music and singing would delay the arrival of spring." In his poems, the goddess of flowers is depicted as a taskmaster, demanding banquets and gatherings, or else she won't bring spring to the mortal realm. With the Inspectorate arranging banquets, high-ranking officials attending, literati composing poetry, and the common people joining in the celebration—it's no wonder that so many intellectuals today yearn for a dreamlike return to the Song Dynasty.

After serving as an official in Shu for two years, Fan Chengda left his post due to illness and boarded a boat under Hejiang Pavilion to return to Wu. On this departure from Shu, many good friends accompanied him on the boat until they reached the city of Leshan. Two of them even continued to escort him to Hejiang County, which lies at the junction of Sichuan, Chongqing, and Guizhou.

Fan Chengda recorded this journey in his poem:

Before Hejiang Pavilion, you sent me on my way,
In Hejiang County, we bid goodbye today.
The river flows, joining seamlessly, people part in grace,
Tomorrow, roads diverge in every direction we face.
A thousand miles you'd follow, reluctant to retreat,
With one more cup, where shall we meet?
At this parting, hearts twist, lost in their own

千里送友的是哪两位呢？谭德称，崇庆府学教授；杨商卿，富顺知监。

合江亭内的藻井　何大江 摄
The ornate ceiling inside Hejiang Pavilion. (Photographer: He Dajiang)

一个市教育局局长，一个县长，如果仅仅是以官职论，级别是远远够不上范成大这种从皇帝身边出来的大官的，但他们还有一个共同身份——诗人。或许，他们就是在合江亭的宴饮上相识、相知的。

送君千里，真的是终有一别。舟离合江县数里，仍依依不舍："船尾竹林遮县市，故人犹自立沙头。"

相别之时，自然有再会的约定，

plight,

But I wish you well in every letter I write.

Farewells after a thousand miles may seem exaggerated in rhetoric, but in Fan Chengda's case, it was a reality. Starting from Chengdu's Hejiang Pavilion, he and the friends who saw him off boarded a boat and traveled through Pengshan, entering the Min River. Passing through Meishan, Leshan, Qianwei, Pingshan, and Yibin, they joined the mainstream of the Yangtze River. Continuing through Jiang'an and Luzhou, they arrived at Hejiang County, with the total distance just surpassing a thousand miles. Hejiang County is precisely the confluence of the Yangtze River and the Chishui River. The fact that the journey covered exactly a thousand miles and both the starting and ending points were "Hejiang", is a remarkable coincidence, almost as if it was destined to inspire Fan Chengda's poem.

The two individuals who accompanied Fan Chengda on his journey were Tang Decheng, a tutor at Chongqing Prefectural School, and Yang Shangqing, the magistrate of Fushun County.

In terms of official positions, a municipal education bureau director and a county magistrate would not be on the same level as Fan Chengda, who held a high-ranking position as an official close to the emperor. However, they shared a common identity—poets. Perhaps, they became acquainted and developed a friendship through the banquets and gatherings at Hejiang Pavilion.

Facing the inevitable parting, their hearts entwined in sorrow. Even when the boat departed from Hejiang County, they were still reluctant to part ways, as the poem says: "At the stern, bamboo groves obscure the county' silhouette, old friends still stand on the sandy shore, reluctant to part."

When parting ways, there is often an agreement to meet again, each leaving behind an address to be found.

留下可以找寻的地址。但以当时的交通、通信条件，谁都知道，若非因缘际会，几乎不可能再见——因此，古人才有那么多伤别离的诗赋。

范成大离开成都五个月之后，回到临安（杭州）就任礼部尚书，主管外交、教育及意识形态。此后，又在明州（宁波）、建康（南京）等地辗转为官。六年之后，因为眩晕病而五次提出致仕。

合江一别九年之后，卧病于床的范成大某天惊奇地发现，推门进屋的竟然是故人杨商卿。任何人处于此境，第一反应怕都是：这不是在梦中吧？

这个场景，让人不由得想起网络上流传的混搭诗句："垂死病中惊坐起，笑问客从何处来。"网友将元稹与贺知章的诗各取一句相凑，倒真能描绘此时此境，除了那个"笑"字很是违和。当然，作为南宋"中兴四诗人"之一的范成大于此也不可能无诗，"我今抱病塘蒲衰，君归报政还复来"。

那一年，范成大已经六十岁，自叹风烛残年，如池塘中的香蒲草一样衰败。而杨商卿也刚刚退休交卸公事，终于有了自己的生活。于是，从

However, given the transportation and communication conditions of that time, it was almost impossible to meet again, unless by chance - hence, ancient people had so many poems lamenting the pain of separation.

After five months of leaving Chengdu, Fan Chengda returned to Lin'an (Hangzhou) and took office as the Minister of Rites, in charge of diplomacy, education, and ideology. He held various official positions afterwards in places such as Mingzhou (Ningbo) and Jiankang (Nanjing). Six years later, due to frequent dizziness, he proposed retirement five times.

In the ninth years of separation in Hejiang County, the bedridden Fan Chengda was surprised to find one day that the person entering the room was his old friend Yang Shangqing. In such a situation, anyone's first reaction would likely be: Is this a dream?

This scene inevitably brings to one's mind the blended poetry lines circulating online: "In the throes of near-death, startled to sit up, I laugh and ask, from where does the guest arrive?" Netizens have combined lines from Yuan Zhen and He Zhizhang's poems, which indeed captures the current situation, except for the jarring word "laugh". Of course, as a poet of the Southern Song Dynasty and one of the "Four Great Masters of the Zhongxing Period", it's unlikely that Fan Chengda would be without a poem for this occasion: "I now embrace illness by the withering pond reeds, weakened and weary; your return, the report on governance, and the rapport come back once more."

In that year, Fan Chengda was already sixty years old, lamenting his dwindling years like the withering reeds in a pond. As for Yang Shangqing, he had just retired and handed over his official duties, finally having his own life. So, he traveled from Sichuan to Suzhou, thousands of miles away by water, solely to fulfill the promise of reuniting with his old friend.

四川赶赴万里水路之外的苏州，只为履行与老友重逢的诺言。

窃以为，跟“合江亭前送我来，合江县里别我去”这样有着事实支撑的诗句相比，“桃花潭水深千尺”倒是显得空洞了些。而杨商卿万里赴约，同九年前的千里送友相比，情意又更厚重一层。真君子之诺也。

I must say, compared to verses like “Before Hejiang Pavilion, you sent me on my way; in Hejiang County, we bid goodbye today”, which have a reality basis, “The water in Peach Blossom Pool is a thousand feet deep” does feel somewhat hollow. On the other hand, in Yang Shangqing’s journey of thousands of miles to keep the appointment, when compared to the thousand-mile farewell of nine years ago, the depth of his sentiment adds an even deeper layer. It truly exemplifies the pledge of a true gentleman.

陆游：亭边爱梅人

合江亭千里送友两人中的另一位谭德称，同杨商卿相比，在诗人圈中更为活跃。南宋“中兴四大诗人”中的三位——范成大、陆游、杨万里，均跟谭德称有诗歌唱和、文字应答。其中，陆游跟其交往最为密切。

谭德称是以科举中进士而入宦途的，曾授崇庆府府学教授，是主管当地教育的官员。四年之后，迁成都府吏部，因为任命搁置不批，又回到崇庆。陆游曾任崇庆府通判，在这里写下上百首诗，范成大主任四川之后，又调至成都为官。他与谭德称的交往，就发生在这两个时期。

他俩曾在烛火通照的江边酒楼上痛饮，也曾骑着马一前一后共逛花市。二人情意相投，都并不汲汲于功

Lu You: a lover of plum blossoms by the Pavilion

In the duo of “Thousand-Mile Farewell at the Hejiang Pavilion”, the other person involved, Tan Decheng, was more active in the circle of poets compared to Yang Shangqing. Among the “Four Great Poets of the Zhongxing Period in the Southern Song Dynasty”, Fan Chengda, Lu You, and Yang Wanli, all had poetic exchanges and literary responses with Tan Decheng. Among them, Lu You had the closest association with him.

Tan Decheng achieved the rank of Jin Shi (successful candidate in the imperial examinations) and entered the realm of officialdom. He was once appointed as the tutor of Chongqing Prefectural School, holding the position of an official in charge of local education. After four years, he was transferred to Chengdu as an official in the Ministry of Personnel. However, due to delayed approval of his appointment, he returned to Chongqing. Lu You had served as the assistant magistrate of Chongqing, where he wrote hundreds of poems. After Fan Chengda became the chief official of Sichuan, Lu You was transferred to Chengdu for an official position. His interaction with

名，互称锦里先生、玉霄散吏。

陆游的诗作中，有大量写给谭德称的。其中有一首悼亡诗，说在某年正月十一的梦中，在合江亭附近的小东门见到谭德称迎面而来，于是二人勒马交谈。陆游要等梦醒时分才明白，谭已经去世了。

“岂料今宵清梦里，东门交辔说春寒”，可拟于杜甫夜梦李白之“落月满屋梁，犹疑照颜色”。

“何方可化身千亿，一树梅花一放翁。”陆游爱梅，古今咸知。合江亭以梅著称，自然也会出现在他的诗中。“几年不到合江园，说著当时已断魂。”回到老家山阴，合江园的梅依然让他魂萦梦牵。

“山鸡飞起乱花落，下上青林穿翠壑。”合江园是以合江亭为原点、因亭而衍生的园林，虽是人工，却宛如天作，有几分原始森林的野趣。园中芳华楼，楼前楼后都是梅花，陆游为此写下了《芳华楼赏梅》等诗。咏梅不只是咏梅，更是述志。从驿外断桥边，到芳华楼；从“零落成泥碾作尘，只有香如故”，到“天工丹粉不敢施，雪洗风吹见真色”，一以贯之。

虽然陆游爱梅如痴，但对梅花盛开的合江园，却并非总是溢美之

Tan Decheng took place during these two periods.

They had enjoyed hearty drinking sessions at riverside taverns illuminated by candlelight, and strolled together on horseback in the flower market, one leading the way while the other followed. The two shared a deep bond, not being overly concerned with fame and fortune, referring to each other as “Mr. Jinli” and “Official Yuxiao” in a spirit of camaraderie.

There are numerous poems by Lu You dedicated to Tan Decheng. Among them, there is a mourning poem in which Lu You describes a dream he had one January 11th. In the dream, he encountered Tan Decheng near the Hejiang Pavilion, by the small Eastern Gate. They halted their horses and engaged in conversation. Lu You only realized, upon awakening from his dream, that Tan had already passed away.

“Little did I expect, in this lucid dream tonight, by the Eastern Gate, bridles brushed past, we discussed the spring chill.” This verse can be likened to Du Fu’s dream of Li Bai: “Moonlight fills the beams, casting uncertain hues.”

“Whence can one transform into billions, in every tree of plum blossoms, there resides a lonely wanderer?” Lu You’s love for plum blossoms is renowned throughout history. Hejiang Pavilion, famed for its plums, naturally finds its place in his poetry. “Years have passed without visiting Hejiang Garden; speaking of it now, my soul is already shattered.” Returning to his hometown in Shanyin, the plum trees in Hejiang Garden still hold his soul captive, entwined in his dreams.

“Mountain birds take flight, petals scatter, up and down through a verdant forest and emerald gorges.” Hejiang Garden, deriving from Hejiang Pavilion, has evolved into a garden that, though man-made, resembles the work of nature, exuding a wild charm akin to a primitive forest. In the midst of the garden, there is the Fragrance and Splendor Pavilion, surrounded by plum blossoms in every direction. Lu

辞。“冷淡生涯元不恶，却嫌歌吹合江园”，表面上是在厌弃游宴的喧嚣，更深层次则是在针砭自唐代以来的文恬武嬉。作为饯饮胜地的合江亭，见过酒酣欢歌，见过离愁别恨，也见过太多的酒中荒唐。

You composed poems such as *Appreciating Plum Blossoms at the Fragrance and Splendor Pavilion* in response to this scenery. His verses on plum blossoms go beyond mere appreciation; they articulate aspirations. From the broken bridge outside the relay station to the Fragrance and Splendor Pavilion, from "scattered and ground into dust, only the fragrance remains as before" to "not daring to apply artificial colors, the snow washes away to reveal true hues", there is a consistent theme.

Although Lu You was passionately fond of plum blossoms, he did not always sing praises for the blooming Hejiang Garden. "Indifferent to a desolate existence, yet disdained the singing and music at Hejiang Garden." On the surface, he expressed a defiance of the noisy revelries of festivities, but on a deeper level, it was a critique of the superficiality and extravagance that had prevailed since the Tang Dynasty. As a gathering place for banquets and celebrations, the Hejiang Pavilion had witnessed scenes of drunken revelry, the heartache of parting, and too many instances of debauchery within the realm of alcohol.

路岩：从这里走向地狱

唐代的剑南西川节度使路岩是个“官二代”，他自己三十六岁时也当上了类似于宰相这样的大官，又有一副盛世美颜，还打扮得帅绝人寰。到了成都之后，整日带着一群乐妓到处吃酒，一时间男羡女爱，有过于潘安。当时的成都人，在街巷之中见到著华服、精容妆者，便会出言挖苦：“你以为你是谁？还真把自己当成路大人

Lu Yan: On the Road to Hell

Lu Yan, the military commissioner of the Jiannan West Sichuan during the Tang Dynasty, was born into an influential family. At the age of thirty-six, he achieved a high-ranking position similar to that of a prime minister. With his stunning beauty and extraordinary appearance, he was the epitome of elegance. Upon arriving in Chengdu, he would frequently accompany a group of musicians and entertainers, indulging in feasts and pleasures. His charm and popularity among women were comparable to the legendary figure Pan An. The people of Chengdu would mock anyone they saw on the streets

了？”足见时人独美路岩。

路岩也是个时尚引领者，他裹头巾裹得绰有风姿，蜀人纷纷效仿。但奢侈品必因其稀缺方显优越，路岩也深谙其理，于是他又剪掉纱巾脚，以凸显其差异化。

这些官妓中，最跟他打得火热者叫行云。到了迁任荆南节度使时，路岩跟行云依依难舍，饯别于合江亭时，还填了一首《感恩多》相赠，内中有“离魂何处断，烟雨江南岸”之语。此词一出即成顶级流量，在各家妓院广为传唱。

单就辞章而言，这两句同柳永的“今宵酒醒何处，杨柳岸晓风残月”意境颇似，却还早上几百年，柳词或化自其中也未可知。不过，对一位封疆大吏来说，为妓女写的词火了，并不是件值得炫耀的事。

好酒贪色，若仅限于私人领域，原也无可指责，但路岩作为主政一方、掌百姓生死的高官，行径如此不羁，就值得商榷了。柳永花酒生涯，却无人指责其私德；而路岩即便拥权势、财富、帅气于一身，受尽艳羡，却并不得人尊重——这就是原因。

曾经有人经过猪市，见到猪贩子指着一头猪说：“这猪长得漂亮，连

dressed in fine attire and delicate makeup, saying, “Who do you think you are? Do you consider yourself a high-ranking official like Lu Yan?” This demonstrates the unmatched allure of Lu Yan during that time.

Lu Yan was also a trendsetter. He wrapped his headscarf in a unique and graceful manner, and the people of Shu eagerly followed suit. However, scarcity heightens the value of luxury goods. Understanding this concept, Lu Yan cut off the fringes of his scarf to accentuate his distinctiveness.

Among all the official courtesans, the one who had the most passionate relationship with Lu Yan was called Xingyun. When Lu Yan was reassigned as the military commissioner of Jingnan, he found it hard to part with Xingyun. As they bid farewell at the Hejiang Pavilion, Lu Yan even composed a poem titled Gratefulness to present to her, which included the lines “Where does the departing soul sever, on the misty and rainy southern bank of the river.” This poem instantly became a hit, widely circulated in various brothels.

In terms of poetic expression, these two lines bear a resemblance to the poetic imagery of Liu Yong’s verse: “Where am I when I wake from this night’s revelry, on the bank of willows, beneath a waning moon in the dawn breeze.” However, they preceded Liu Yong’s work by several hundred years, and whether or not his poem drew inspiration from them remains unknown. Nevertheless, for a high-ranking official, gaining fame for writing verses for a courtesan was not something to boast about.

Indulging in fine wine and pursuing physical pleasures might be beyond reproach if confined to one’s private domain. However, as a high-ranking official with the power to govern and control the lives of the people, Lu Yan’s unrestrained behavior is indeed questionable. Unlike Liu Yong, who lived a life of indulgence in drunkenness and debauchery, but faced no criticism of his personal morality, Lu Yan,

路大人也比不上。”路岩或许是一个超我不够强大之人，头顶的星空和内心的道德律没能唤起他的敬畏与惊奇。人们都想拥有他拥有的，对他却也缺少敬畏。

路岩其实是被赶到成都来的。他曾在朝堂上权倾一时，却与另一宰相韦保衡不能相容。主人不收敛，爪牙会更张狂。二人之党羽，被时人称作“牛头阿旁”。牛头好懂，即地狱使者牛头马面；阿旁，梵语之鬼卒也——用一句四川俗话，叫“衣襟角角都要抽人”。

晚唐时国力衰退，四境不宁，蜀地作为边疆西接吐蕃，南临南诏，时有战事。路岩党争失败被逐出朝廷，为官蜀地之后，开始整治边事。他在邛州设置军队，修补旧关隘，扼守大渡河，并组织边州民兵进行军事训练，补充为屯垦将士。这一系统举措足见成效，于是边境安靖，西山八国等羌部纷纷前来朝拜，他也因此升迁，被封魏国公。

路岩治理边疆一事，充分说明人与事的多面性、复杂性。其为人，不仅有权、多金、帅气，而且有才华、有能力，惜乎不能内敛自省。路岩在蜀为官，对亲信不加约束，任其飞扬

despite possessing power, wealth, and charm that stirred envy, did not earn the respect of others. This is the crux of the matter.

There was once an incident where someone passing by a pig market heard a pig vendor pointing at a pig and saying, “This pig is so beautiful, even Lord Lu can’t compare.” Lu Yan may have lacked a strong sense of self-restraint. The vastness of the starry sky above his head and the moral compass within failed to evoke a sense of awe and wonder in him. People may covet what he possessed, but they also lacked reverence for him.

In fact, Lu Yan was sent to Chengdu. He once held great power in the imperial court but had a conflict with another prime minister, Wei Baoheng. When the master fails to restrain himself, his subordinates become even more unruly. The factions of Lu Yan and Wei Baoheng were derogatorily referred to as Niu Tou A Pang by the people of that time. Niu Tou refers to the ox-headed and horse-faced messengers of hell, while A Pang is a Sanskrit term for grim reapers—expressed in a Sichuan idiom, it means “to pester someone relentlessly.”

During the declining period of the Later Tang Dynasty, the country’s strength weakened and the borders were restless. As Sichuan bordered Tubo to the west and Nanzhao to the south, there were frequent military conflicts. After Lu Yan’s faction lost in the power struggle, he was expelled from the imperial court and appointed as an official in Sichuan. He began to address border issues by establishing military forces in Qiongzhou, repairing old passes, controlling the Dadu River, and organizing local militias for military training and recruitment. These comprehensive measures proved effective, bringing stability to the border regions. All the Qiang tribes of the Western Mountains came to pay homage to him. As a result, he was promoted and bestowed the title of Duke of Wei.

跋扈、为非作歹。后来，两名属吏被疑谋反，他也受牵连，因此迁官荆南节度使——这是合江亭别姬赠词一幕的前因。

不过，朝廷行的是调虎离山、釜底抽薪之计，路岩的厄运才刚刚开始。还在赴任路上，新的任命来了，再迁新州刺史。唐代州刺史仅为郡守，已属贬官；新州在岭南，更具有流放性质。

等他到了江陵，又来了一道指令，免官，抄家，流放儋州——此地因苏轼流放而闻名，从这个意义上讲，路岩倒算得上是苏东坡的先“驱”。路岩以美髯出名，而在江陵待了不过两天，四十七岁的他就因焦虑而胡须全部变白。此时的他，应该十分清楚朝廷的整人步骤了。

流放并不是最坏的结局，甚至死也不是。等路岩到了新州，收命符来了，赐死，然后剔下喉管，送去验明正身。如此残酷的刑罚，其实是路岩得势之时自己提议的，专用于三品以上的被诛高官，没想到作茧自缚，这跟商鞅逃亡时无人敢收留颇为相类。

两位自合江亭离蜀的大员，范成大乘舟南下，作《吴船录》而流播天下；路岩却一步一步走向地狱，其

The governance of the borderlands by Lu Yan fully illustrates the complexity and multifaceted nature of both individuals and their actions. He possessed not only power, wealth, and charisma but also talent and capability, yet he lacked introspection and self-restraint. During his time as an official in Sichuan, he failed to impose any restraints on his trusted aides, allowing them to act recklessly and commit wrongdoing. Later, two of his subordinates were suspected of plotting against the government, implicating Lu Yan himself. As a result, he was reassigned as the military commissioner of Jingnan, which set the stage for the scene of farewell at the Hejiang Pavilion.

However, the imperial court employed the strategy of “luring the tiger down the mountain” and “taking away firewood from under the pot”. Lu Yan’s misfortune had only just begun. While he was on his way to assume his new post, a new appointment arrived, relocating him once again as the governor of Xinzhou. During the Tang Dynasty, the position of a Zhou governor was considered a demotion from the role of a prefect, and being assigned to Xinzhou, located in the Lingnan region, had even more of an exile-like nature.

Upon his arrival in Jiangling, another decree was issued, stripping him of his official position, confiscating his property, and exiling him to Danzhou. This place was renowned for being the location of Su Shi’s exile. In this sense, Lu Yan could be seen as a precursor to Su Dongpo. Lu Yan was famous for his magnificent beard, but in Jiangling, where he only stayed for two days, the anxieties he faced turned all of his facial hair white. At this point, he should have been well aware of the imperial court’s scheme to torment him.

Exile was not the worst outcome, nor was death. When Lu Yan arrived in Xinzhou, the execution order arrived—he was to be put to death, his larynx

权势、财富与容貌，皆湮没于浩瀚史籍，几无人所知。

文章千古事，信乎？

removed and sent for verification. This brutal punishment was actually suggested by Lu Yan himself during his time of power, specifically targeting high-ranking officials of the third rank and above. Little did he know that he had woven his own cocoon, similar in a way to when Shang Yang, while on the run, found no one willing to offer him shelter.

Indeed, the two high-ranking officials who left Chengdu from the Hejiang Pavilion went on quite different paths. Fan Cheng embarked on a journey southward, composing the famous *Records of Wu Boats* that spread throughout the world. Meanwhile, Lu Yan gradually descended into a personal hell, his power, wealth, and beauty all fading into the vast annals of history, known to few.

Truly, the impact and endurance of one's writings are eternal, don't you think?

双亭毗连：人亦为景观

合江亭不仅是唐宋时成都的游宴胜地，也是其园林的原点——有了合江亭这个地标性建筑，便以此为根基伸发，在周围种植嘉木修竹，修筑亭台楼阁——芳华楼、合江园，以及江对岸的赵园皆是如此。

赵园跟合江园一样，也以红梅和海棠著称，陆游曾经为它写过多首诗，其中有“诗句带花香，东风不敢吹”这样的妙语，更为出名的则是《自合江亭涉江至赵园》：“政为梅花忆两京，海棠又满锦官城。鸦藏高柳阴初密，马涉清江水未生。”至今，

Twinned pavilions stand adjacent: People constitute the scenery

Hejiang Pavilion, not only stood as a venue for banquets and pleasure in Chengdu during the Tang and Song Dynasty, but also as the origin of its gardens. With Hejiang Pavilion as the landmark, it expanded and blossomed, with precious woods and bamboo planted around, and pavilions and tower buildings constructed—such as Fanghua Tower, Hejiang Garden, and the Zhao Garden on the other side of the river.

Similar to Hejiang Garden, the Zhao Garden is renowned for its red plum blossoms and begonias. Lu You once wrote several poems for it, including the exquisite line "Poetic verses carry the fragrance of flowers, where the east wind dares not blow." Even more famous is his poem "Crossing the River from Hejiang Pavilion to Zhao Garden", which goes:

这首诗以对联的形式悬挂于合江亭廊柱。从诗里看得出，在丰水期到来之前，宋代时锦江某些地段的水并不深，甚至可以打马过河，从合江亭到对岸的赵园去赏梅。

郫江上原有两个著名的景点，一为今汪家拐与文庙西街之间的张仪楼，二为今烟袋巷附近的散花楼。李白曾有诗咏吟："北地虽夸上林苑，南京犹有散花楼。"诗中的南京，则是方位上相对于长安处于南边的成都。自韦皋治蜀建亭之后，锦江之上，张仪楼、散花楼、合江亭连成一线，为一时风物之盛。

到了876年，高骈筑罗城，改郫江道，因为失去了河流的依托，张仪楼与散花楼渐渐衰败，很少再为人提及。所幸的是，郫江与流江的交汇处并没有变，合江亭依然屹立于原处，占据着两江的形胜之地。

郫江改道之后，锦江上的主要港口，从老南门万里桥转移到了合江亭。锦江通航的时间很早，原本舟楫往来、白帆点点，有了码头，合江亭就更添繁忙装卸、更添迎来送往，以及送别时的诗词唱和。

自宋至元，合江亭一直是锦江水路的起点。直到明清，外运港口转移到九眼桥以下，才盛况不再。

"Thinking of plum blossoms evokes memories of the two capitals, while begonias once again fill the city of Jin. Ravens conceal themselves in the dense shade of lofty willows, and horses ford the clear river not yet swollen." To this day, this poem hangs as a couplet on the columns of Hejiang Pavilion. From the poem, we can infer that prior to the period of abundant water, certain sections of the Jin River in Chengdu during the Song Dynasty were not deep, and one could even cross on horseback, from the Hejiang Pavilion to the Zhao Garden on the opposite bank, to admire the plum blossoms.

On the original Pi River, there were two famous attractions: Zhangyi Tower between today's Wangjiaguai and West Wenchang Street, and Sanhua Tower near Yandai Alley. Li Bai once composed a poem, saying, "Although the north boasts of the Shanglin Garden, Nanjing still has the Sanhua Tower." In this poem, Nanjing refers to Chengdu, positioned to the south relative to Chang'an. Since Wei Gao governed Shu and built pavilions along the river, Zhangyi Tower, Sanhua Tower, and Hejiang Pavilion were strung together to form a beautiful urban waterscape, showcasing the flourishing scenery of the time.

However, in the year 876 AD, Gao Pian built the Luocheng City and changed the course of the Pi River. Due to the loss of the river's backdrop, Zhangyi Tower and Sanhua Tower gradually declined and are rarely mentioned today. Fortunately, the confluence of the Pi and Liu River remained unchanged, and Hejiang Pavilion still stands in its original position, occupying the picturesque land where the two rivers converge.

After the diversion of the Pi River, the main port on the Jin River shifted from the Wanli Bridge near the Old South Gate to the Hejiang Pavilion. Navigation on the Jin River began quite early on,

经历上千年的沧桑，当年陆游赏梅的赵园自然早已湮没。今日的合江亭对面，是建于1997年的府南河音乐广场。从音乐广场顺着锦江向东，一直到九眼桥桥头，是一条被叫作“丝管路”的小街。

丝管路的白天似乎平淡无奇，一排低调的仿古建筑滨江而立，路上也静悄悄的，似乎连行人也没有几个。但一到夜幕降临，这条路瞬间便生动了起来。

霓虹灯照亮了飞檐，店招又把自己的流光溢彩投射到江里，产生出万花筒一般的光影效果——这条长五六百米的临水小街，鳞次栉比排列着四十余家酒吧、咖啡馆。

跟别处相比较，此处的特色在于，有的酒吧开设在四合院中。其中有一家，前院是河边露天坝子摆着酒桌，中院还有一口井，最里面才是光线幽暗、音乐低回的室内酒吧。

还记得十年前，有一家的店名给人留下了深刻印象，店招上四个字——两河流域。以合江亭旁的府河与南河，对应最早产生人类文明的幼发拉底河、底格里斯河，不可谓不巧妙。

府河与南河环绕着的合江亭，毁于宋末元初的战乱之中。明代在此辟有锦官驿，清代置有船税所。这块土

with boats and sails dotting the river. With the establishment of a dock, Hejiang Pavilion became even busier with loading and unloading activities, as well as the recitation of poems during farewells.

From the Song to the Yuan Dynasty, Hejiang Pavilion served as the starting point for water transportation on the Jin River. It was not until the Ming and Qing Dynasties that the main port moved downstream to below Jiuyan Bridge, leading to a decline in the prominence of Hejiang Pavilion.

After experiencing thousands of years of changes, the once-famous Zhao Garden where Lu You admired the plum blossoms has long been lost. On the opposite side of today's Hejiang Pavilion is the Funan River Music Square, built in 1997. From the music square, following the Jin River eastward all the way to Jiuyan Bridge, there is a small street called Siguan Road.

In the daytime, Siguan Road may seem unremarkable, with a row of low-key buildings of ancient Chinese style standing by the river, and the street itself quiet with few pedestrians in sight. But as night falls, the road instantly comes to life.

Neon lights illuminate the flying eaves, while store signs cast their colorful glow onto the river, creating a kaleidoscope-like visual effect. This stretch of waterfront street, about five to six hundred meters long, is lined with over forty bars and cafés.

What sets this place apart from others is that some of the bars are located within traditional courtyard houses. Among them, there is one where the front courtyard has outdoor tables by the riverside, while the middle courtyard features a well. It is only in the innermost part that one finds a dimly lit indoor bar with soft music playing.

I still remember the impression left by a particular shop name ten years ago. Its signboard displayed four characters—Mesopotamia. It cleverly

地又寂寞了很多年，直到1989年新的合江亭重建于原址。1991年合江亭入选新的“蓉城八景”，其景之名曰“解玉双流”。这个名字其实说的是盛唐时，合江亭下郫江、流江和解玉溪三江汇流的盛景。

合者，合两江为一。合二为一的寓意，双亭毗连的象征，诞生了一种都市新景象——每逢良辰，便有新人来合江亭拍摄婚纱照。最多的时候，拍照新人一天多达两百多对。

合江亭下，人观景致，人亦为景观。

corresponded to the Fu River and the Nan River beside Hejiang Pavilion, which symbolize the Euphrates and Tigris Rivers, where human civilization first emerged.

Hejiang Pavilion at the junction of the Fu River and the Nan River was destroyed during the warfare in the late Song Dynasty and early Yuan Dynasty. In the Ming Dynasty, the Jin Guan Yi Courier Station was established here, and in the Qing Dynasty, a boat tax office was set up. This land remained desolate for many years until the new Hejiang Pavilion was rebuilt on the original site in 1989. In 1991, Hejiang Pavilion was included in the new “Eight Scenic Spots of Rong City”, with the name “Jieyu Shuangliu”. This name actually refers to the magnificent scene during the prosperous Tang Dynasty when the Pi River, Liu River, and Jieyu Creek converged under Hejiang Pavilion.

“He” represents the convergence of two rivers into one. The symbolism of merging two into one, the connection between twin pavilions, has given birth to a new urban phenomenon—couples coming to Hejiang Pavilion to take wedding photos on auspicious occasions. At its peak, there would be over two hundred pairs of newlyweds taking photos in a single day.

Under Hejiang Pavilion, people observe the scenery, and people themselves become part of the landscape.

安顺廊桥
Anshun Corridor Bridge

它是《马可·波罗游记》中的桥，“两边各有一排大理石桥柱，支撑着桥顶”。不过，马可·波罗曾广受质疑，被视作骗子与吹牛大王。如果马可·波罗都未曾真正来过中国，那么他游记中的安顺廊桥也就来历不明了。

其实，历史有记忆，故纸里有证据。

It is the bridge mentioned in *The Travels of Marco Polo*, described as “a bridge with rows of marble pillars on both sides, supporting the roof.” However, Marco Polo himself has faced much skepticism and been regarded as a fraud and a great braggart. If Marco Polo had never truly visited China, then the origins of the Anshun Corridor Bridge mentioned in his travelogue would be uncertain.

However, history holds its memories, and evidence can be found in ancient texts.

安顺廊桥：让马可·波罗印证
Anshun Corridor Bridge: Marco Polo’s Confirmation

成都竹枝辞
清·吴好山

安顺桥头看画船，
武侯祠里问灵签。

Chengdu Zhu Zhi Ci
Wu Haoshan, Qing Dynasty

On Anshun Bridge, watching the painted boats,
In the Wuhan Shrine, we inquire with divination sticks.

呼郎伴妾三桥去，
桥底中间望四川。

With my beloved by my side, crossing the three bridges,
Underneath the bridge, we gaze upon the rivers conflux.

这首《竹枝辞》，描绘的是清末成都人的游冶之乐。所谓“三桥”，乃是虚数，言其多，也可理解为以诗人视角观，脚下站立的安顺廊桥，以及上游的万里桥、下游的九眼桥——尤其是后者，仅在数百米之外，清晰可望。而所谓“四川”，当然不是指省级行政区，同样虚指。若一定实指，则视为其上游刚刚交汇于合江亭的南河、府河，以及老成都城西面的两条重要河流磨底河、清水河。

安顺廊桥因为外形华丽——尤其是夜晚，华灯璀璨，晶莹剔透——而知名度奇高。它横跨锦江之上，其南岸为酒吧林立、摩肩接踵的丝管街，北岸是占地超过四万平方米的另一酒吧聚集区兰桂坊。

This Zhu Zhi Ci (ancient Chinese poems written for music) depicts the leisurely pleasure of the people of Chengdu during the late Qing Dynasty. The “three bridges” mentioned in the poem are just notional and represent the abundance of bridges. It can also be understood as the bridges, from the poet’s perspective, the Anshun Corridor Bridge he stands on his feet, the Wanli Bridge upstream and the Jiuyan Bridge downstream - especially the latter, which is just a few hundred meters away and clearly visible. As for “Sichuan”, which literally means Four Rivers, it is not referring to the provincial administrative region, but is also figurative. If it must refer to something concrete, it can be seen as the Nan River and the Fu River, which converge just upstream of Hejiang Pavilion, as well as the important rivers of Modi River and Qing Shui River in the western part of old Chengdu city.

The Anshun Corridor Bridge is well-known for its magnificent appearance, especially at night when it is adorned with dazzling lights, sparkling and translucent. It spans across the Jin River, with a south bank lined with bustling bars on the vibrant Siguan Street, and a north bank occupied by the Lan Kwai Fong, another bar-focused area covering over 40,000 square meters.

夜晚的安顺廊桥，流光溢彩，玲珑剔透　冉玉杰 摄
Glowing with vibrant colors and delicately translucent, Anshun Corridor Bridge illuminates the night. (Photographer: Ran Yujie)

安顺廊桥的名满天下，得自一本奇书，旅行家马可·波罗的《东方见闻录》(又称《马可·波罗游记》)。不过，目前众人所知的安顺廊桥，是不是《竹枝辞》里的安顺桥，是不是马可·波罗所说的廊桥呢?

The fame of the Anshun Corridor Bridge spread far and wide, thanks to a remarkable book called *The Book of the Marvels of the World* (also known as *The Travels of Marco Polo*). However, it remains uncertain whether the Anshun Corridor Bridge mentioned in the book is the same as the Anshun bridge in the *Zhu Zhi Ci* or if it is indeed the Corridor Bridge Marco Polo referred to.

马可·波罗口中的廊桥

想象一幅画面：1298年，热那亚的一个监狱里，两个衣衫褴褛的囚徒斜靠着墙，对坐在地板上。一个手拿鹅毛笔，面前的地板上摊着一张羊皮纸；而对面的那个则用手梳理着已经打结的大胡子，时而长时间沉默，好似在捕捉思绪，时而又开始讲述，或磕磕巴巴，或酣畅淋漓。鹅毛笔跳动着，马可·波罗口中的法意混合语变成文字，出现在羊皮纸上。

拿着笔的叫鲁思梯谦，来自比萨；而梳着胡子的，则是后来闻名于世的马可·波罗，他来自水城威尼斯。此刻，他们都是热那亚的战俘。

二十八年前，马可·波罗曾经跟随父亲和叔叔进行了一次跨越亚洲大陆的旅行，并且见到了有“众王之王”之称的忽必烈大汗。向鲁思梯谦讲述旅途中的奇闻逸事，是打发狱中艰难时光的好办法。马可·波罗是个

The corridor bridge that Marco Polo talks about

Imagine a scene: It is the year 1298, inside a prison in Genoa. Two ragged prisoners lean against the wall, sitting on the floor. One holds a goose feather pen, with a piece of parchment spread out before him, while the other untangles his matted beard. Occasionally, he falls into deep contemplation, as if capturing his thoughts, only to begin speaking again, sometimes haltingly, sometimes with fervor. The goose feather pen dances, and Marco Polo’s words, a blend of French and Italian, take form on the parchment.

The one holding the pen is Rustichello from Pisa, while the bearded man is none other than Marco Polo, who would later become renowned throughout the world. He hails from the aquatic city of Venice. In this moment, they are both captives in Genoa.

Twenty-eight years ago, Marco Polo embarked on a journey across the Asian continent alongside his father and uncle. During this journey, they had the incredible opportunity to meet Kublai Khan, the renowned “King of Kings”. To pass the difficult time in prison, Marco Polo delighted in recounting the extraordinary tales and adventures he experienced along the way to his cellmate. Marco

文盲，而鲁思梯谦曾经写过小说，职业习惯驱使他拿起了笔，要把这一切记录下来。

羊皮纸上的记录后来流传出去，就成了《东方见闻录》最初的稿本，而关于成都桥梁的文字，收录于该书第二卷《忽必烈大汗和他的宫廷 西南行程中各省区的见闻录》中。

“有许多大川深河发源于远处的高山上，河流从不同方向围绕并穿过这座城市，供给该城所需的水。这些河流有些宽达半英里，有些宽两百步，而且都很深。”

用成都的情形来对应《东方见闻录》中的文字，庶几可以严丝合缝。老成都城正是一座被水环抱的城市，河流不仅保卫着城市安全，更提供生养之利。成都人在河上通航运输，在河中游泳洗衣、捕鱼捞虾，并挑起一担担河水，沉澄后冲泡成河水香茶。

以锦江为主导的成都河流都来自都江堰，再往上则可追溯至岷山融雪。那条温润的母亲河，原本是清冷彻骨的雪水。而元代高山融雪更为丰沛，河面远比现在宽阔，或与书中的“宽达半英里”相去不远。

“城内有一座大桥横跨其中的一条大河，从桥的一端到另一端，两边各有一排大理石桥柱，支撑着桥顶，

Polo, being illiterate, relied on Rustichello, who had previously written novels, to pick up the pen and record everything Marco Polo encountered on his travels.

The recorded accounts on the parchment later made their way into the initial draft of *The Travels of Marco Polo*. The descriptions of the bridges in Chengdu were included in the second volume of the book, titled *The Journeys and Observations through the Provinces during the Southwest Itinerary of Kublai Khan and His Court.*

“There are many great rivers and deep streams originating from distant mountains. These rivers surround and traverse this city from various directions, providing the necessary water supply for the city. Some of these rivers are as wide as half a mile, some are two hundred paces wide, and all of them are quite deep.”

Drawing parallels between the descriptions in *The Travels of Marco Polo* and the situation in Chengdu, there is a almost seamless fit. The old city of Chengdu is indeed a city surrounded by water, where rivers not only defend the city but also provide benefits for its inhabitants. The people of Chengdu navigate the rivers for transportation, swim and wash clothes in them, and fish for shrimp and fish. They even fetch water from the rivers, which, after settling and clarifying, is used to brew fragrant tea.

The rivers in Chengdu, mainly the Jin River and its tributaries, are sourced from the Dujiangyan irrigation system and can be traced back to the melted snow from the Min Mountains. The gentle mother river, icy cold with snow melt, “was more abundant with meltwater during the Yuan Dynasty. The river’s width was much broader in the past, not far from the description of “as wide as half a mile” in the book.

“Inside the city, there is a large bridge spanning

桥顶是木质的，装饰着红色的图案，上面还铺着瓦片。”

可以推断，这是一座廊桥。

何为廊桥？顾名思义，就是像走廊一样的桥。跟一般的拱桥和平板桥相比，它的上面多了一个顶。廊桥，就是有屋檐的桥。因为可以挡风避雨，又叫风雨廊桥。

“整个桥面上有许多别致的小屋和铺子，买卖众多的商品，其中有一个较大的建筑物是收税官的居所。所有经过这座桥的人都要缴纳一种通行税，据说大汗每天仅从这座桥上的收入就有一百金币。”

桥梁，作为连接江河两岸的必经之路，自然流量繁忙，是做生意的好地方；而有了廊顶的庇护，无论下雨落雪、风吹日晒，生意都不会耽搁，因此廊桥又往往发展成为固定的集市。

“你可见过这样的一个城？”在意大利作家卡尔维诺《看不见的城市》中，忽必烈大汗对公务劳形心生倦怠，似乎马可·波罗描绘的一个又一个神奇的城市更能引起他的兴趣。

“再讲一个城罢。”“还欠一个。”大汗总像一个贪婪地向父母索要故事的孩子。或许他也隐约地觉得，帝国那所向披靡的军队所到达的土地，甚至还不如一个商人多。

across a mighty river. From one end of the bridge to the other, there are rows of marble pillars on each side, supporting the wooden roof. The roof is adorned with red patterns and covered with tiles.”

From this description, we can infer that this is a covered bridge, often referred to as a “Langqiao” in Chinese.

As the name suggests, a Langqiao is a bridge that resembles a corridor. Unlike typical arched or flat bridges, it has an overhead roof. The Langqiao is also known as a “wind and rain sheltered bridge” because it provides shelter from wind and rain.

“The entire bridge is adorned with many quaint small houses and shops, selling a variety of goods. Among them, there is a larger building that serves as the residence of tax collectors. Everyone passing through this bridge is required to pay a toll, and it is said that the Great Khan earns a hundred gold coins a day from the revenue collected on this bridge.”

Bridges, as essential pathways connecting the two banks of rivers and streams, naturally witness bustling traffic and become favorable places for conducting business. With the shelter provided by the covered roof, regardless of rain, snow, wind, or scorching sun, business can continue without interruption. Consequently, covered bridges often transform into permanent marketplaces.

“Have you ever seen such a city?” In Italo Calvino’s *Invisible Cities*, Kublai Khan expresses weariness from administrative duties, seemingly more intrigued by Marco Polo’s vivid descriptions of one magical city after another.

“Tell me about another city.” “You still owe me one more story.” The Great Khan always craves stories like a child beseeching his parents for more. Perhaps he too vaguely senses that the land conquered by his all-powerful armies may not offer as much as

《看不见的城市》里，马可·波罗没有向忽必烈提及成都的安顺廊桥，因为小说的城市都是卡尔维诺虚构的，是作家用来展现人类想象力的意趣和极限的。而在热那亚监狱里，鲁思梯谦记下的，却是万里之外的实体。那座“河流从不同方向围绕并穿过”的城市，就是成都；而“两边各有一排大理石桥柱，支撑着桥顶”的桥，就是安顺廊桥。

an enterprising merchant.

In *Invisible Cities*, Marco Polo does not mention the Anshun Corridor Bridge to Kublai Khan because the cities depicted in the novel are fictional creations by Calvino. These cities serve as a means for the author to explore the depths and limits of human imagination. However, in the prison in Genoa, Rustichello recorded real experiences from thousands of miles away. The city described as being “surrounded and traversed by rivers from different directions” is Chengdu, while the bridge with “rows of marble pillars on each side, supporting the wooden roof” refers to the Anshun Corridor Bridge.

他是个大忽悠吗？

然而，《东方见闻录》甫一问世，即受到了强烈的质疑。马可·波罗应该是一个性格热烈、张扬的人，他的讲述中充满了“百万”这样的大词，百万的马匹、百万的人口、百万的房舍。

在回到威尼斯招待亲朋的时候，三位“波罗”——马可和他的父亲、叔叔，更是用刀划破身上的袍子，让藏在里面的红宝石、蓝宝石、金刚石、翡翠等珠贝倾泻一地。

这些带有强烈优越感的炫耀，让当时的欧洲人非常不适应。他们用刻薄的反讽，把这本见闻录直呼为《百万》，马可·波罗的住宅被称为“百万宅”，他本人则是“百万君”或

Was Marco Polo a great pretender?

However, as soon as *The Travels of Marco Polo* was published, it faced strong skepticism. Marco Polo was likely a passionate and flamboyant individual, and his narratives were filled with words like “millions”—millions of horses, millions of population, millions of dwellings.

When the three Polos returned to Venice to entertain their relatives and friends, they even cut their robes with knives, causing the pouring out of precious gems such as rubies, sapphires, diamonds, and jade hidden inside.

These displays of superiority made the Europeans of that time very uncomfortable. They sarcastically referred to Marco Polo’s travelogue as “Millions” and his residence as the “Million Mansion”. Marco Polo himself was called “Million Lord” or “Marco the Million”— these designations directly labeled him as a big fraud and a great trickster. Such judgments naturally had an impact on future generations.

“马可百万”——这简直就是直接将其认定为大骗子、大忽悠了。这样的判断自然影响到后世。

“马可·波罗根本就没有来过中国，前面更加险恶的漫漫长路吓住了他，他们就在西亚转悠了几年，后来这人把从那里道听途说来的传闻讲给了那位作家狱友，后者写成了那本伟大的游记。”

这是刘慈欣科幻小说《镜子》里的一段话。这部神奇的小说诠释的是决定论这个哲学概念，否定的是自由意志的存在。在小说中，主人公凭借一部超弦计算机，能够在原子级别上模拟整个宇宙。

何谓决定论？宇宙的一切，在大爆炸的时候就已经决定了。一切都是因果，一条无休无止的因果链贯穿了宇宙从生到死的整个过程。这条因果链，也是佛教里面“空”的概念。（然而，现在我们知道，人的思想、意愿是可以改变因果的，而人的思维来自真正随机的量子层面，那个世界却是不受决定论、因果关系束缚的。）

按照《镜子》的设定，既然一切在宇宙之初就决定了，而超弦计算机可以模拟宇宙，那么这个宇宙所产生的所有画面，都可以在计算机上看到镜像。书中人检索马可·波罗，看到

"Marco Polo never actually came to China. The treacherous and endlessly long journey ahead scared him off, so he wandered around Western Asia for a few years. Later, he told the rumors he had heard there to his writer cellmate, who turned them into that magnificent travelogue."

This is a passage from Liu Cixin's science fiction novel *The Mirror*. This amazing novel explores the concept of determinism and denies the existence of free will. In the story, the protagonist possesses a superstring computer that can simulate the entire universe at the atomic level.

What is determinism? It suggests that everything in the universe was determined at the moment of the Big Bang. Everything is intertwined in a never-ending chain of cause and effect, encompassing the entire process of life and death in the universe. This chain of causality is also a concept of "emptiness" in Buddhism. (However, we now know that human thoughts and intentions can alter causality, and human thinking originates from the truly random quantum level, which is not bound by determinism or causal relationships).

According to the premise of *The Mirror*, since everything was predetermined at the beginning of the universe, and the superstring computer can simulate the universe, then all the scenes generated by this universe can be mirrored on the computer. The book characters search for Marco Polo and see that he "stole someone's water five times and someone's bread twice", in short, he never actually came to China.

The opinions expressed in the novel are, of course, not sufficient to argue the matter. However, they do reflect the perceptions of some people towards Marco Polo, which are based on reality. The cultural talk show program *Xiaosong's Qitan* also holds the same view, directly referring to Marco Polo

他“五次偷别人的水喝，两次偷别人的饼”，总之，他根本就没来过中国。

小说家言，当然不足以辩。然而，它所反映的部分人对马可·波罗的认识，却是真实的。文化脱口秀节目《晓松奇谈》也持有相同观点，直接把马可·波罗称作妄人，列入《妄人列传》。

那么，马可·波罗真的是一个骗子、一个大忽悠吗？

质疑他到过中国的学者，主要理由如下：一是中国所有的典籍资料里，没有马可·波罗的名字；二是游记中并未提及许多中国的独有事物，比如长城、方块字、妇女缠足、茶叶和印刷术等。

关于第一点，诸位研究历史的学者，大概是过于低估了个人在历史长河中的渺小了；对于时光淘选历史人物的无情，也有着不恰当的认识。马可·波罗游历中国的多种意义，诸如为由哥伦布引发的大航海时代播下种子、成为东西方文化交流的使者等，在公元13世纪还不曾显露，故而采用天朝大国视角的典籍中没有留下一个外国商人的名字，实在是再平常不过。

第二个所谓的理由，更是存在着方法论上的明显谬误。要论证马可·波罗是否来过中国，其重点当在于关注他看到并记叙了什么，而不是

as an imposter and including him in *the Imposter Biography*.

So, is Marco Polo really a fraud, a great trickster?

The scholars who question Marco Polo's visit to China generally provide the following reasons: First, there is no mention of Marco Polo's name in any Chinese historical documents. Second, his travelogue does not mention many unique aspects of China, such as the Great Wall, square characters, foot binding, tea, and printing.

Regarding the first point, it is possible that historians may underestimate the insignificance of an individual in the long river of history. They may also have an inappropriate understanding of how time selects historical figures. The various meanings of Marco Polo's travels in China, such as sowing the seeds for the Age of Discovery sparked by Columbus or serving as a cultural ambassador for East-West exchange, were not fully evident in the 13th century. Therefore, it is quite ordinary that the annals from the perspective of a celestial empire like China do not record the name of a foreign merchant.

The second reason provided is indeed a clear methodological fallacy. When it comes to determining whether Marco Polo visited China, the focus should be on what he saw and described, rather than what he may have omitted.

In the second chapter alone, which is related to China in his travelogue, Marco Polo recounts the armed rebellion of King Nai Yan, member of the Golden Family, the life in the court of Kublai Khan, the military and postal systems of the Yuan Dynasty, the legal codes, astrology, and even the custom of ghost marriage.

Among the cities he passed through, Marco Polo describes the city of Beijing and the Lugou Bridge on the Yongding River, even mentioning

他漏掉了什么。

仅仅是在游记跟中国相关的第二章，他讲述了黄金家族成员、宗王乃颜的武装叛乱；讲述了忽必烈的宫廷生活，元朝的军事制度、驿站制度、法律条规、占星术甚至阴婚习俗。

在走过的城市中，他讲述了北京城、永定河上的卢沟桥，甚至桥上的石狮子；讲述了大同府和它的皇家狩猎园林；讲述了黄河（喀拉摩拉河）和它两岸的城市，以及城里面的商人；讲述了西藏，以及把装饰品戴在脖子上的女子；讲述了宏伟壮丽的昆明城（押赤）、出产金沙的河道、用作货币的贝壳，以及捕捉巨蟒的方法；讲述的城市还有宜宾（叙州）、涿州、沧州（河间府）、济南、扬州、南京、襄阳、九江、镇江、常州、苏州和杭州……他说苏州是“地上的城市”，杭州又称“天城”——这大概是“上有天堂，下有苏杭”那句话的讹误。

the stone lions on the bridge. He describes Datong Prefecture and its royal hunting grounds, the Yellow River (referred to as the Caramoran) and the cities on its banks, as well as the merchants within the cities. He also discusses Tibet, including the women wearing ornaments around their necks. He recounts the magnificent city of Kunming (known as Iaci), the river that produces gold sands, the use of seashells as currency, and the method of capturing pythons. Other cities he mentions include Yibin (Xuzhou), Zhuozhou, Cangzhou (Hejian Prefecture), Jinan, Yangzhou, Nanjing, Xiangyang, Jiujiang, Zhenjiang, Changzhou, Suzhou, and Hangzhou. He refers to Suzhou as the “city on earth” and Hangzhou as the “heavenly city” — though this may be an error for the famous saying “Heaven above, Suzhou and Hangzhou below.”

As for why Marco Polo did not mention the Great Wall, those scholars may have forgotten that most of the existing sections of the Great Wall in China were built during the Ming Dynasty, nearly a hundred years after Marco Polo left China. As for foot-binding, it was a practice mainly confined to secluded women and not easily seen by outsiders.

美国社会经济学家西德尼·甘博在1908—1932年曾五次来到中国，在中国西部地区拍摄了大量珍贵照片。这张安顺桥旧影就拍摄于这一时期 （美）西德尼·甘博 摄

The American socio-economist Sidney Gamble visited China five times between 1908 and 1932, capturing numerous precious photographs of western China. This vintage image of Anshun Corridor Bridge was taken during that period. (Photographer: Sidney Gamble, USA)

至于马可·波罗为何没有提及长城，那些学者大概是搞忘了，中国现存的长城多为明长城，要在他离开中国将近一百年后才开始修筑。而缠足的妇女多在深闺，不是能轻易见着的。

方块字没能引起马可·波罗的兴趣，也实在不难理解：一个有翻译陪同的，连母语文字也不认识的文盲商人，会有多大可能把注意力放在像天书一样难懂的方块字上？

It is also understandable why Marco Polo did not show interest in Chinese characters. As an illiterate merchant who relied on translators, it is unlikely that he would pay much attention to complex characters, resembling arcane scripts that were unfamiliar to him.

故纸里的证据

历史学家杨志玖终身研究马可·波罗，1941年尚在云南昆明北京大学文科研究所（西南联合大学）读元史研究生时，他就从典籍中发现了马可·波罗来过中国的铁证。那是《永乐大典·站赤》上元世祖至元二十七年（1290年）的一段公文：

平章沙不丁上言：“今年三月，奉旨遣兀鲁䚟、阿必失呵、火者取道马八儿，往阿鲁浑大王位下。同行一百六十人，内九十人已支分例，余七十人，闻是诸官所赠遗及买得者，乞不给分例口粮。”

公文中所提兀鲁䚟、阿必失呵、火者三位使者，经马八儿（今印度东南海岸），前往波斯，回报其国王阿

Evidence in Ancient Documents

Historian Yang Zhijiu dedicated his life to the study of Marco Polo. In 1941, when he was a graduate student studying Yuan Dynasty history at the Humanities Research Institute of Peking University (Southwest Associated University) in Kunming, Yunnan, he discovered conclusive evidence of Marco Polo's visit to China in ancient texts. It was a passage in the *Yongle Encyclopedia* from the 27th year of Emperor Shizu of the Yuan Dynasty (1290 AD):

Shahab al-Din, Grand Councilor, submitted a report, saying, "In March of this year, by imperial order, we dispatched three envoys named Wuludai, Abishihe, and Huo Zhe to go through Ma Baer and reach the court of the King Aluhun. Accompanying them were a hundred and sixty people, of whom ninety had already received their allotted provisions, while the remaining seventy people acquired theirs as gifts from various officials or through purchases. Request that provisions not be given based on regulations."

鲁浑大王一段史实，正与波罗家族三人回国一事可互相印证。

《东方见闻录》讲道，马可的父亲尼可罗·波罗，有一次恳请大汗同意他们回国，被拒绝了。正在此时，波斯君王阿鲁浑派遣了三名男爵为专使来到中国，请求挑选一名女子为偶，以填补他亡妻的位置。因为他的妻子来自元朝境内，临死前留下遗言：只有自己家族的女子才能继承后位。这三位男爵的名字分别为Oulatai、Apousca、Coja，翻译过来就是上述公文中的兀鲁䚟（dǎi）、阿必失呵、火者。

游记还记载了这件事情的后续。在大汗的关照下，一位十七岁的美丽姑娘阔阔真被挑选出来，准备送到波斯。游记说："大汗为表示对阿鲁浑未来王后的敬重，特地挑选了大批的扈从随行侍卫"，这也可跟公文中的"同行一百六十人，内九十人已支分例"相印证。

没想到的是，使团在归程中遭遇鞑靼诸王之间的战争，不能继续向前，只好返回。这给熟悉海上航行的波罗家族提供了机会。他们再次觐见大汗，极言海上航行的便捷与安全，终于得到陪伴使团从海路前往波斯的机会。就这样，马可·波罗终于踏上

The three envoys mentioned in the document, Wuludai, Abishihe, and Huo Zhe, traveled through Ma Baer (now the southeastern coast of India) and arrived in Persia. They then reported to King Aluhun, the ruler of Persia, providing historical facts that can be corroborated by the accounts of the Polo family.

In the book *The Travels of Marco Polo*, it is mentioned that Marco Polo's father, Niccolo Polo, once pleaded with the Great Khan to allow them to return home but was refused. At this time, the king of Persia, Aluhun, sent three barons as envoys to China, requesting the selection of a woman to be his bride and fill the position left vacant by his deceased wife. According to her dying wish, only a woman from the her family could inherit the position. The names of these three barons were Oulatai, Apousca, and Coja, which correspond to the names mentioned in the aforementioned ancient document as Wuludai, Abishihe, and Huo Zhe.

The travelogue also recorded the follow-up of this event. Under the great Khan's care, a beautiful seventeen-year-old girl named Kuo Kuo Zhen was selected and prepared to be sent to Persia. The travelogue states, "In order to show respect to Queen Aluhun, the Great Khan specially selected a large group of attendants and guards to accompany her," which aligns with the official document's mention of "160 people traveling together, with 90 people already allocated their provisions."

Unexpectedly, the envoy encountered wars among the various Tartar kings on their return journey and could not proceed further. This provided an opportunity for the Polos, who were familiar with sea navigation. They once again visited the Great Khan and emphasized the convenience and safety of sea travel, finally obtaining the chance to accompany the envoy by sea to Persia. And so, Marco Polo finally set

了归途。

然而海上旅程也并非所说的那样便捷与安全，三名男爵中只有火者到达了目的地，其他两位与众多船员、乘客一同都客死海上，好在总算完成了护送新王后的任务。马可·波罗与父亲、叔叔经君士坦丁堡回到家乡威尼斯，已是五年以后。而在头一年，曾经庇护过他们一家的忽必烈大汗已经离世，听到消息的马可知道，他再也不会回到中国了。

又是三年之后，威尼斯与热那亚爆发战争，作为威尼斯富商的马可·波罗贡献出了家族的一艘战船，并担任船上的荣誉司令，却不幸战败被俘而投入监狱，这才有了那部伟大的《东方见闻录》。

然而，对于杨志玖先生提出的如此确凿的证据，也并非所有的人都能被说服。执怀疑论的集大成者是曾在北京学习过的汉学家吴芳思（时任英国不列颠图书馆中国部主任的弗兰西丝·伍德博士），其理由是：波罗家族陪伴三名使臣返回波斯一事，可能是采自其他资料。

想来竟然有些好笑：吴芳思实在是高看了马可·波罗这名文盲，以为他有识读汉字、查阅元朝公文的机会、能力和动机，完成了众多饱学之

foot on the homeward journey.

However, the sea journey was not as convenient and safe as claimed. Out of the three barons, only Coja reached their destination, while the others, along with numerous sailors and passengers, perished at sea. Fortunately, the mission of escorting the new queen was accomplished. Marco Polo, along with his father and uncle, returned to their hometown of Venice through Constantinople, but it took them five years. In the previous year, news reached Marco that the great Khan Kublai, who had once sheltered their family, had passed away. This meant that Marco would never return to China.

Three years later, a war erupted between Venice and Genoa. Marco Polo, a wealthy Venetian merchant, contributed one of his family's warships and served as an honored commander onboard. However, unfortunate defeat led to his capture and imprisonment, which ultimately led to the creation of his monumental work, *The Travels of Marco Polo*.

However, not everyone can be convinced by Mr. Yang Zhijiu's compelling evidence. The epitome of skeptical thinking was the sinologist Wu Fangsi, who had studied in Beijing (Dr. Frances Wood, then director of the China section at the British Library). His argument was that the Polo family accompanying the three envoys back to Persia might have been sourced from other materials.

It is quite amusing to think about it. Wu Fangsi greatly overestimated Marco Polo, the illiterate, believing that he had the opportunity, ability, and motivation to read Chinese characters and access official documents of the Yuan Dynasty, accomplishing feats that even many learned scholars were incapable of achieving.

Actually, if skeptical scholars can put aside their biases and read *The Travels of Marco Polo*

士都无能为力的壮举。

其实，质疑派的学者们只要能放下偏见，像普通人一样读一读《东方见闻录》，就会被其中可与现实印证的巨大信息量及细节所震撼，而不得不承认：那是不可能依据道听途说编出来的。

like ordinary people, they will be shocked by the immense amount of information and details that can be corroborated with reality. They will have no choice but to admit that it could not have been fabricated based on hearsay.

三星堆的海贝从哪儿来？

在游记中，马可·波罗多次提及云南一带将贝壳当作货币使用，尤为值得探讨。

在昆明城，用海里才有的白贝壳为币，"八十个贝壳可兑换一个银币"。

在下一个城市，他继续记述了以贝为币的情形："离开押赤城，向西走十日，便到达哈剌章省的一个主要城市，这里也隶属于大汗，由他的儿子忽哥赤在此行使皇家的职权。"马可·波罗明确地说道：在这个城市，用作货币的贝壳是从印度输入的——这是一条非常有价值的线索，它也是破解三星堆深海贝壳之谜的关键。

原文中的押赤城，即元代蒙古人对昆明的称呼。而哈剌章省，则有广义与狭义之分，狭义即大理地区，广义则指整个云南。而游记称忽哥赤在

Where do the sea shells in Sanxingdui come from?

In his travelogue, Marco Polo repeatedly mentions the use of shells as currency in the Yunnan region, which is particularly worth exploring.

In the city of Kunming, white shells, which can only be found in the sea, are used as currency, "eighty shells can be exchanged for one silver coin."

In the next city, he continued to describe the use of shells as currency. "Leaving Iaci City and traveling west for ten days, we arrived at a major city in the province of Caragian, which is also under the rule of the Great Khan. His son, Hugochi, exercises the imperial authority here." Marco Polo explicitly states: in this city, the shells used as currency are imported from India. This is a valuable clue and a key to unraveling the mystery of the deep-sea shells in Sanxingdui.

In the original text, Iaci City refers to the Mongolian name for Kunming during the Yuan Dynasty. As for the province of Caragian, there is a distinction between a broad and narrow sense. In the narrow sense, it refers to the Dali region, while in the broad sense, it refers to the entire Yunnan province. The travelogue's mention of Hugochi exercising imperial authority here is also consistent with

此行使皇家职权则，也是符合史事的。忽哥赤是忽必烈大汗的第五子，1267年被封为云南王。

那么，游记中的这个重要城市是哪儿呢？打开地图就能看到，昆明往西略偏北，直线距离约270千米即大理——崎岖的山路远不止于此，十日的行程是合理的。而忽哥赤驻扎之地正是大理——云南首府从大理迁往昆明已是1274年之事。

另一句话，“该处的每条河道都出产金沙”，也为这座城市的定位提供了佐证。大理北面数十千米则是金沙江，那里出产黄金早就记载于书。“金生丽水，玉出崑岗”，丽水即金沙江之古称，古人诚不我欺也。

“从哈剌章省西行五日，便到达了匝儿丹丹省……这个地区的货币是黄金，有时也用贝壳。”游记里的省，并非当时元代的行省，视作一个区域即可，马可·波罗对中国的行政区划大概就没有弄清楚过。匝儿丹丹是傣族生活之地，大致为沿怒江、澜沧江一带的今日云南西部与缅甸东部。按游记，从大理西行五日即可到达此地，而当地居民则有以薄金片为牙套作装饰、男子纹身的习俗。

秃剌蛮也使用来自印度的贝壳为货币。然而，让人震惊的却是接下来

historical events. Hugochi was the fifth son of Kublai Khan and was appointed as the King of Yunnan in 1267.

So, which city is this important city mentioned in the travelogue? By looking at a map, it can be seen that if you go slightly north-west from Kunming, the distance is approximately 270 kilometers in a straight line, and you will reach Dali. The rugged mountain roads extend beyond this distance, so a ten-day journey is reasonable. And the place where Hugochi stationed himself was indeed Dali. The capital of Yunnan was moved from Dali to Kunming in 1274.

Another sentence, “Every river channel in that place produces gold sand,” provides further evidence for locating this city. Several dozen kilometers to the north of Dali is the Jinsha River (Golden Sand River), where the production of gold has long been recorded in books. “Gold comes from Li Shui, jade comes from Kun Gang”, Li Shui is the ancient name for the Jinsha River, and the ancients were indeed not deceiving us.

“After five days of travel west from Caragian Province, we arrived at Çardandan Province... The currency in this region is gold, and sometimes shells are also used.” The provinces mentioned in the travelogue do not correspond to the administrative provinces of the Yuan Dynasty at that time. They can be considered as regional references. Marco Polo probably did not have a clear understanding of China’s administrative divisions. Çardandan was the land of the Dai ethnic group, roughly corresponding to the western parts of present-day Yunnan and eastern parts of Myanmar along the Nu River and Lancang River. According to the travelogue, it takes five days of travel west from Dali to reach this place, where the local residents have customs such as using thin gold sheets as dental decor and tattooing for men.

The Tulaman also uses as currency shells imported from India. However, what is shocking is

的记载："此地的市镇和城堡有许多位于高山之上。这里的人死后，实行火葬，不能化为灰的骨头，就被放入木箱中，带到山上，藏在岩石洞中，以免受到野兽的侵扰。"

当我读到这一段文字时，心脏禁不住扑棱起来：天哪，这不就是僰人悬棺吗？

秃刺蛮在何处，借《元史·列传第八·速不台》可以确定。"遂出乌蒙，趋泸江，刬秃剌蛮三城，却宋将张都统兵三万，夺其船二百艘于马湖江，斩获不可胜计。遂通道于嘉定、重庆，抵合州，济蜀江……"

文中记载的行军路线，按今之地理名称为：在从云南昭通赴金沙江——诸葛亮《出师表》中的"故五月渡泸，深入不毛"亦指此处，击破秃刺蛮；在至宜宾一带的长江江面上击败宋军，夺船两百艘，于是溯岷江上至乐山、顺长江下到重庆的通路都被打开了。

没错，昭通至宜宾这一片土地，曾经的主人就是制作悬棺的僰人。

我们的叙述再回到贝壳，用作货币的贝壳，来自印度的贝壳。前文说过，它是破解三星堆深海贝壳之谜的关键。

1986年，三星堆一号坑、二号坑

the following account: "The towns and fortresses in this area are located on high mountains. After people die here, they are cremated, and if their bones cannot turn to ashes, they are placed in wooden boxes and brought to the mountains to be hidden in rock caves to avoid disturbance from wild beasts."

When I read this passage, my heart couldn't help but race: Oh my goodness, isn't this the hanging coffins of the Bo people?

As for the location of the Tulaman, we can determine it through *Yuan History, Biography, Volume 8, Su Butai*. "Then they left Wumeng, headed towards the Lujiang River, obliterated three cities of the Tulaman, and defeated Song Dynasty General Zhang's army of 30,000 and seized 200 boats from the Mahu River, with an immeasurable number of beheadings and captures. They then traveled through Jiading, Chongqing, reached Hezhou, and crossed the Shu River..."

The marching route recorded in the text, in modern geographical names, would be: From Zhaotong in Yunnan to the Jinsha River — "crossing the Lujiang River, deep into the barren land in May" mentioned in Zhuge Liang's *Norther Expedition Memorandum* also refers to this place, where the Tulaman was defeated. Then, in the area around Yibin, they defeated the Song army on the Yangtze River, seized 200 boats, and opened up the passage along the Min River to reach Leshan and open the passage down the Yangtze River to Chongqing.

Indeed, the land from Zhaotong to Yibin was once inhabited by the Bo people, who were known for crafting hanging coffins.

Let's return to the discussion of shells, specifically the shells used as currency, imported from India. As mentioned earlier, they are the key to unraveling the mystery of the deep-sea shells in Sanxingdui.

出土了数千枚海贝。从海贝上的穿孔看，是被穿成串用于流通。海贝贮存于罍、彝、尊或人头像之内，三星堆的古蜀人显然将这些青铜器当作了存钱罐或者保险柜。

成都平原是不产海贝的，它们必然是来自沿海地区。2014年，笔者曾在三星堆博物馆采访过副馆长邱登城，他告诉笔者，出土的海贝中有一种货齿贝，“只产于印度洋的深海区域”。

且把目光投向遥远的古印度，那些生活在海边的人们，正是将海贝穿磨成孔，以绳为串，用于贸易流通。跟三星堆相较，关山阻隔、相距数千千米的两地，为何使用货币的方式如此一致呢?

从三星堆到古印度，在高岸低谷与原始森林之间，其实暗藏着一条古老的国际贸易通道——蜀身毒道。“身毒”为印度古称，读作juāndū，《史记》上便是这样的叫法。又称天竺或贤豆，其实是一个词的不同译法，到了玄奘大师，才译为读音更为准确的“印度”。蜀身毒道，又由灵关道、五尺道、黔中古道和永昌道四段构成。其中的五尺道，在《望丛祠迷雾：杜宇、鳖灵的相爱相杀》一文中曾提及，那也是杜宇从朱提至成都

In 1986, thousands of sea shells were unearthed from Pit 1 and Pit 2 in Sanxingdui. The perforations on these shells indicate that they were strung together for circulation. The sea shells were stored inside jars, Yi vessels, Zun vessels, and even within human figurines. The ancient Shu people of Sanxingdui clearly considered these bronze objects as money boxes or safes for storing their wealth.

The Chengdu Plain does not naturally produce sea shells, so they must have come from coastal areas. In 2014, I interviewed Vice Curator Qiu Dengcheng at the Sanxingdui Museum, and he informed me that among the unearthed sea shells was a type called dentalium shell, which “is only found in the deep-sea areas of the Indian Ocean.”

If we cast our gaze towards ancient India, those living along the coast were known to perforate sea shells, string them together, and use them for trade and circulation. Compared to Sanxingdui, these two distant locations separated by mountains and thousands of kilometers share such a similar currency system. Why is that?

From Sanxingdui to ancient India, hidden between steep cliffs and primitive forests, lies an ancient international trade route known as the Shu Juandu Dao. “Juandu” was the ancient Chinese term for India, pronounced as “juāndū”, as mentioned in the *Records of the Grand Historian*. It was also referred to as Tianzhu or Xian Dou, which are different translations of the same term. It was not until the time of the great master Xuanzang that the more accurate pronunciation and translation of “Yindu” (India) were adopted. The Shu Juandu Dao consisted of four sections: Lingguan Road, Wu Chi Road, Qianzhong Ancient Road, and Yongchang Road. The Wu Chi Road, mentioned in the article *The Wang Cong Shrine Myth: Duyu and his frenemy, Bieling* was the path taken by Duyu when he established his

创建功业所经由的道路。

在马可·波罗的游记中，提到以海贝为币的地区共有五个：秃剌蛮（川南、滇北）、押赤（昆明）、哈剌章（大理）、出产苏木和大象的罗斛国（泰国）、“省城”为永昌的匝儿丹丹（云南西部、缅甸东部）。简单把这五个区域用线串起来，就可以看出，这条线大致与蜀身毒道重合。三星堆的海贝从哪儿来，已经不言自明。

是的，蜀身毒道。

这条数千千米长的古道，或盘旋于峻岭，或蜿蜒于密林，或开凿于峭壁。4000年间，因人事兴废而隐隐绰绰，时断时续。通过这条路，靠人背，靠马驮，汉代蜀地的布料和邛竹杖到了大夏（阿富汗）——此为汉使张骞所见，而印度洋的深海贝也到了三星堆。

马可·波罗自然没见过三星堆的海贝，但历史就是这么奇妙。他笔下的叙述，却也能够从一个断面揭示三星堆海贝的来源之谜，也从另一个侧面证实了《东方见闻录》的真实性。

achievements from Zhuti to Chengdu.

In Marco Polo's travelogue, it is mentioned that there were five regions using sea shells as currency: Tulaman (south of Sichuan, north of Yunnan), Iaci (Kunming), Caragian (Dali), Luohuguo (Thailand) that produces sappanwood and elephants, and the "provincial capital" Yongchang of Çardandan (western Yunnan, eastern Myanmar). By connecting these five regions with a simple line, we can roughly see that this line coincides with the ancient Sichuan-Tibet Tea and Horse Ancient Road. Where the sea shells in Sanxingdui come from is already self-evident.

Yes, the Shu Juandu Dao, the ancient road connecting Sichuan and India.

This ancient road, which stretches for thousands of kilometers, either winds around steep mountains, meanders through dense forests, or is carved into cliffs. Over the course of 4000 years, it has existed in a sporadic manner due to the rise and fall of human activities. Through this road, relying on human backs and horse carriages, the fabrics and bamboo staffs from the Han Dynasty's Sichuan reached Daxia (Afghanistan)—as witnessed by the Han envoy Zhang Qian and the deep-sea shells from the Indian Ocean also reached Sanxingdui.

Marco Polo naturally had not seen the sea shells in Sanxingdui, but history is just so magical. His descriptions can still uncover the mystery of the source of sea shells in Sanxingdui from a certain perspective, and also indirectly confirm the authenticity of *The Travels of Marco Polo*.

时间河流上的桥

关于安顺廊桥最早修建的时间，据李贵平先生《安顺廊桥：构架成都

The Bridge on the River of Time

Regarding the earliest construction time of the Anshun Corridor Bridge, according to Mr. Li Guiping's article *Anshun Corridor Bridge: An*

历史的古桥》一文，有资料称为1277年。若此，则马可·波罗见到此桥是在十年后。对于一座桥来说，十年正值其最好年华。

嘉庆《华阳县志》里的安顺廊桥
The Anshun Corridor Bridge as recorded in the Jiaqing Edition of the *Huayang County Chronicles*.

安顺廊桥再一次在史料中出现，是在嘉庆版《华阳县志》中。其“安顺桥”条目称：旧名长虹桥，治东城外大佛寺前。

长虹桥更名为安顺桥，是乾隆十一年（1746年）的事了。这一年，华阳县令安洪德在原址上再建风雨廊桥，桥长二十丈，宽一丈，桥面上还供有神像，设有摊市。安洪德为新的风雨廊桥题额“安顺”。

从嘉庆《华阳县志》的《大佛寺图》上可以清晰地看到，廊桥横跨锦江，南桥头正对着大佛寺，北桥头上

Ancient Bridge that Frames Chengdu's History, there are records indicating that it was built in 1277. If this is the case, then Marco Polo would have seen this bridge ten years later. For a bridge, ten years is when it reaches its prime.

The Anshun Corridor Bridge appears once again in historical records, specifically in the Jiaqing edition of the *Huayang County Chronicles*. Its entry for the “Anshun Bridge” states that it was previously known as the Changhong Bridge and was located in front of the Dafosi (Great Buddha) Temple outside the eastern city.

The Changhong Bridge was renamed the Anshun Bridge in the 11th year of Qianlong's reign (1746). In that year, the county magistrate of Huayang, An Hongde, rebuilt the Fengyu Corridor Bridge on the original site. The bridge was 20 Zhang long and 1 Zhang wide, with statues placed on the bridge deck and a market set up. An Hongde inscribed the new Fengyu Corridor Bridge with the words “Anshun”.

In the *Map of the Great Buddha Temple* of the Jiaqing edition of the *Huayang County Chronicles*, it is clearly visible that the corridor bridge spans across the Jin River, with the southern end of the bridge directly facing the Great Buddha Temple. At the northern end of the bridge, there is a plaque inscribed with the words “Anshun”. Twelve stone piers stand in the river. The piers are constructed with stacked stones, covered with wooden boards, and topped with roofs, representing a typical wooden-structured corridor bridge style. During the time when the Jin River was navigable, the spaces between the piers were passable for boats as illustrated in the drawing—three wooden boats, two flowing downstream, and one vigorously paddling upstream. The houses by the river stilted on pillars inserted into the water, while on both sides, willows and ginkgo trees flourished.

端有匾，上书“安顺”二字。十二个石桥墩立于江中。桥墩由条石堆砌而成，上面铺以木板，并覆有屋顶，是典型的木结构廊桥样式。当年的锦江通航，图上的桥墩之间是可以过船的——三条木舟，两条顺流而下，一条奋力朝上。江边的房子，以吊脚楼的方式将立柱插入水中，而两岸柳叶婀娜、银杏茂密。

在明代的天启年间《成都府志》，笔者查到了一条相关信息，“普安桥”条：华阳东，水津街。只有六个字，却透露出不一般的信息。笔者推测，它很有可能是安顺廊桥曾经的称呼：

其一，水津街的位置非常确定，它正是安洪德所建的安顺廊桥北端所对之处；其二，安县令将重建的风雨廊桥命名为安顺桥，安顺之安，或许就来自普安之安。

从忽必烈时代到华阳县令安洪德重修安顺廊桥，近四百六十年，其间发生了些什么，又经历了几毁几建，那些或多姿多彩或沉痛悲泣的故事，都已随滔滔锦江，东入大海，不复为后来的探寻者所知。

自得名“安顺”之后，廊桥果然“安安顺顺”地在锦江之上立了两百年之久。从安洪德建桥至今，安顺桥再经毁建，桥名从未更改，大概也

In the Tianqi period of the Ming Dynasty, in the *Chengdu Prefecture Chronicles*, I found a related piece of information. Under the entry for “Pu’an Bridge”: “east of Huayang, in Shuijin Street.” Although it consists of only six characters, it reveals extraordinary information. I speculate that it was highly likely the former name of the Anshun Corridor Bridge.

Firstly, the location of Shuijin Street is very specific, and it is precisely where the northern end of the Anshun Corridor Bridge built by An Hongde was located. Secondly, the county magistrate named the rebuilt Fengyu Corridor Bridge as the Anshun Bridge, and the sense of “safety” or “smoothness” in Anshun may have originated from the name Pu’an (universally safe).

From the time of Kublai Khan to the reconstruction of the Anshun Corridor Bridge by Huayang county magistrate An Hongde, nearly 460 years have passed. What happened in between, how many times it was destroyed and rebuilt, and the colorful or mournful stories associated with it have all been carried away by the surging Jin River, flowing into the sea, no longer known to later explorers.

Since it was named Anshun, the corridor bridge indeed stood peacefully and smoothly over the Jin River for two hundred years. From the time of An Hongde’s bridge construction until today, despite being destroyed and rebuilt, the name of Anshun Bridge has never changed. This perhaps reflects people’s longing for “safety” and “smoothness” from a certain perspective.

To this day, some elderly people still remember seeing the two-story Anshun Corridor Bridge during their childhood, remarking that “business was very good on the bridge.” Around 2006, I interviewed Mr. Chen, who had lived in this area for about seventy years, near the new Anshun Corridor Bridge.

从一个侧面反映了人们对于“安”和“顺”的向往吧。

时至今日，锦江边还有些老人记得，幼年时见到的安顺廊桥有两层，“上面生意好得很”。2006年左右，笔者在新的安顺廊桥边采访了于此居住了七十年左右的陈大爷。

陈大爷生于1930年代，七十来年后，他仍清楚地记得，小时候经常去廊桥上买邻居罗婆婆的花生吃。花生装在竹篾条编的笼子里面，一百元就可以买一笼。陈大爷所说的一百元，是旧币制的最小单位，相当于新币制的一分钱。至于罗婆婆，推算起来，应该是1870年代生人。

陈大爷见到的廊桥，就是乾隆十一年安洪德建的安顺桥，他在桥上买竹笼花生的时间，大致是在1940年代。这座桥在1947年7月被一场特大洪水冲毁，仅仅剩下些桥墩。1950年代，人们借用乾隆年间残余的两个桥墩，在其上架设木板，形成简易便桥。1994年出版的《成都市交通志》称：“今仍存。”

因为位置靠得很近，人们时常将安顺廊桥与另一座桥——十二北街桥——混为一谈，很多文章甚至工具书也犯了这样的错误。李贵平《安顺廊桥：构架成都历史的古桥》一文对

Mr. Chen was born in the 1930s, and even after seventy years, he still vividly remembers going to the corridor bridge to buy peanuts from his neighbor, Aunt Luo. The peanuts were stored in a cage woven with bamboo strips, and one could buy a cage for one hundred yuan. The one hundred yuan mentioned by Mr. Chen was the smallest unit of the old currency system, equivalent to one cent of the current currency system. As for Aunt Luo, based on estimations, she was likely born in the 1870s.

The corridor bridge that Mr. Chen saw was the Anshun Bridge built by An Hongde in the 11th year of the Qianlong reign. He bought peanuts on the bridge in the 1940s. This bridge was partially destroyed by a major flood in July 1947, with only a few piers remaining. In the 1950s, people used the remaining two piers from the Qianlong era to construct a makeshift wooden bridge. The *Chengdu City Transportation Chronicles* published in 1994 stated that it “still exists” at that time.

Due to their close proximity, people often confuse the Anshun Corridor Bridge with another bridge, the Shierbeijie Bridge. Many articles and even reference books make this mistake. Li Guiping’s article *Anshun Corridor Bridge: An Ancient Bridge that Frames Chengdu’s History* provides a detailed analysis on this.

The Shierbeijie Bridge was first built in 1974 and opened to traffic four years later. It spans from the northern end of Shierbeijie to Qinglian Xiajie, crossing the Nanhe River. On July 14, 1981, it was destroyed by a massive flood.

In July 1981, Chengdu was suddenly hit by a heavy rainstorm. Due to the flooding of the houses near the river, the residents had to find temporary shelter elsewhere. It was not until mid-July that the floodwaters began to recede. It was reported that on the afternoon of the 14th, someone accidentally

此有很详细的辨析。

十二北街桥，始建于1974年，四年后通车。其南起于十二北街北端，跨南河接于青莲下街。1981年7月14日，被一场特大洪水冲毁。

1981年7月，成都骤降暴雨，因江边平房被淹，居民们不得不另寻他处暂住。到了7月中旬，洪水才开始消退。据称，14日下午，有人从桥上路过时，不慎把自行车掉入河中。下河打捞时，吸引了不少人到桥上看热闹。悲剧瞬间发生，桥突然垮塌，数十多人落水。张先德在《成都：近五十年的私人记忆》一书中，记下了自己的亲眼所见：

"但见断桥斜插入河中，士兵们还在两河口宽阔湍急的河面上寻找幸存者或打捞死者。两岸人山人海，围着附近居民，听他们绘声绘色地讲述如何听得一声巨响，挤在桥上把栏观望水情的群众倒饺子般被倾入河中急流，水性好反应灵敏者怎样拼死捡得一条命，其他人怎样被迅速卷进百米外的湍急漩涡不得生还，救人好汉又怎样托起别人而牺牲了自己……"

现场描述非常生动，但也将十二北街桥当成了安顺桥，笔者在多年前的文稿中也犯过类似错误。

真正的古安顺桥，还要在十二北

dropped the bike into the river while passing by the bridge. The act of retrieving the bike from the river attracted a crowd of curious onlookers on the bridge. In a tragic turn of events, the bridge suddenly collapsed, and dozens of people fell into the water. Zhang Xiande, in his book *Chengdu: Personal Memories of Nearly Fifty Years*, recorded what he witnessed with his own eyes:

"I saw the broken bridge slanting into the river, soldiers were searching for survivors or retrieving the dead. The crowd on both sides of the river, like a sea of people, listened intently to nearby residents, as they vividly described how they heard a loud noise, the crowd on the bridge, squeezed against the railings, like dumplings, were thrown into the rushing water. Some nimble and quick to react, saved themselves, while others were swiftly swept into the turbulent whirlpools a hundred meters away, and heroes sacrificed themselves to save others..."

The on-site description was vivid. But it mistakenly identified the Shierbeijie Bridge as Anshun Bridge. I also made a similar mistake in my previous writings long ago.

The true ancient Anshun Bridge is located more than 200 meters downstream from the Shierbeijie Bridge, in close proximity to Hejiang Pavilion. Its northern end is almost directly facing Tianxianqiao South Road and Shuijin Street on the northeast bank of Jin River.

I have verified this information through multiple maps. Among them, the *Guangxu Five-Year Map* (published in 1879) provides a rough representation of the location and is not reliable for reference. However, the *Newly Revised Map of Chengdu's Twenty-Seven Districts* (published in June 1911, during the Xuantong era) is more detailed. The *Detailed Map of Chengdu City* published between 1928 and 1931, as well as the *Chengdu Street and Market Map* published

街桥下游两百余米处，邻近合江亭极近，其北端几乎正对着锦江东北岸的天仙桥南路和水津街。

笔者查证过多幅地图，其中《光绪五年图》(1879年出版）位置关系十分粗疏，不足为参考，而宣统三年（1911年）六月出版的《新订成都街道二十七区图》就比较精细了，而1928年至1931年出版的《成都市明细图》和民国二十二年（1933年）出版的《成都街市图》就非常准确了。在后三份地图上，古安顺桥都邻近合江亭，斜对着汇入锦江的府河口以及两侧的大安街（天仙桥南路）、水津街。

十二北街桥在垮塌的第二年重建，是一座可通行汽车的钢筋混凝土桥。而古安顺桥在洪水之后仍旧铺上木板继续作为便桥。

随着城市进程的发展，古旧的安顺廊桥彻底失去了使用功能，终于完成了使命。从1277年到2002年，它在时光之河中站立了七百二十五年。在拆除旧安顺廊桥的同时，一座明清风格的三孔仿古石桥在原安顺桥下游约三百米左右处动工。2003年8月4日，新安顺廊桥开桥。新桥只过行人，不通车辆，其红柱黛瓦、雕栏飞檐，颇具古韵。

廊桥北侧，有魏明伦撰写的《廊

in the 22nd year of the Republic of China (1933), are more accurate. In the latter three maps, the ancient Anshun Bridge is depicted near Hejiang Pavilion, diagonally facing the confluence of Fu River, which flows into Jin River, and the surrounding Da'an Street (Tianxianqiao South Road) and Shuijin Street.

The Shierbeijie Bridge was rebuilt in the second year after its collapse, as a reinforced concrete bridge that could accommodate vehicles. On the other hand, the ancient Anshun Bridge, after the flood, continued to be covered with wooden boards and served as a makeshift bridge.

With the development of the city, the old Anshun Bridge completely lost its functional use and finally fulfilled its mission. From 1277 to 2002, it stood for 725 years along the river of time. Alongside the dismantling of the old Anshun Bridge, construction began on a new three-arched stone bridge in the style of the Ming and Qing dynasties, located approximately 300 meters downstream from the original bridge. On August 4, 2003, the new Anshun Bridge opened. The new bridge is only accessible to pedestrians and not vehicles, adorned with red columns, black-tiled roofs, and intricately carved railings, capturing the charm of antiquity.

On the north side of the bridge, there is an *Ode to Corridor Bridge* written by Wei Minglun: "With a new appearance on the old site, vermilion pavilions and azure waters. A corridor extends from north to south, with twin pavilions gazing east and west." On the south side, there is an engraved statue of Marco Polo, along with a map depicting his route across the Asian continent over seven centuries ago, as a tribute to this great traveler who made the name of the Chengdu Corridor Bridge known throughout the world.

Although the bridge has a new location, its name remains the same. The rhythmic essence of

桥赋》："旧址新颜，朱楼碧水。一廊穿南北，双亭望东西。"南侧，镌刻有马可·波罗像及其七百多年前横穿亚洲大陆的线路图，以表达对这位让成都廊桥名传天下的伟大旅行家的敬意。

桥虽新址，其名依旧。马可·波罗曾向全世界传播过的中国韵律，又重新在钢筋水泥之间跃动。

《东方见闻录》成书之后，当时的欧洲人对于东方之富庶颇难置信，很长一段时间，"马可·波罗"这个名字是被戏谑的对象，是虚假的代名词。

1324年，这位曾经用破旧衣服裹藏大量宝石带回，曾被嘲弄为"百万君"的伟大旅行家离世。在他临死之际，有人让他撤回谎言，好让灵魂能上天国。面对这样的质疑，马可·波罗说道："我未曾说出我亲眼看见的事物的一半。"

好在还有成都的廊桥，它与马可·波罗之言互相印证，让人明白历史并非一团空洞和虚无。

China that Marco Polo once spread to the world now dances again between the steel and concrete.

After the compilation of *The Travels of Marco Polo*, Europeans at that time found it hard to believe in the wealth and prosperity of the East. For a long time, the name Marco Polo became a subject of mockery and a synonym for falsehood.

In 1324, the great traveler, who had once returned with a vast quantity of gemstones hidden in tattered clothing and was sarcastically referred to as the "Million Lord", passed away. When his death was imminent, someone urged him to retract his lies so that his soul could ascend to heaven. In response to such a challenge, Marco Polo said, "I have not even told half of what I saw with my own eyes."

Indeed, the existence of the Chengdu Corridor Bridge serves as confirmation and affirmation of Marco Polo's words, allowing us to understand that history is not just a hollow and empty concept.

第六卷

Volume 6

蜀王城
Royal Residence of King of Shu

它是明代的蜀王府，崔巍壮丽；它是明代皇权在蜀地的象征，让人心生敬畏。

它的中轴线，就是城市中轴线。从它开建的那一天，就奠定了成都几百年来的城市格局。640年了，那条中轴线从来都没有更改或废弃。

它最后毁于一把大火，成为不折不扣的人间炼狱。

It was the Royal Residence of King of Shu in Ming Dynasty, resplendent and magnificent; it stood as a symbol of the imperial power of the Ming Dynasty in Shu,inspiring awe.

From the day its construction began,its central axis formed the central axis of the city and established the urban layout of Chengdu for for 640 years, without being altered or abandoned.

Ultimately, a great fire burnt, turning it into a veritable inferno.

蜀王城：十三代皇族的楼起楼塌
Royal Residence of King of Shu: the rise and fall of thirteen generations of a royal family

橘井秋香
明·朱让栩

锦里清飔报素商，
内亭深院晚云凉。

Autumn Fragrance of the Tangerine Well
Zhu Rangxu, Ming Dynasty

On the streets af Chengdu, the breeze proclaims the fall,

鹤胎漫忆青天杳，
龙秘犹传玉井芳。
入镜灵漪江夏色，
御风神冽洞庭香。
翁源菊涧成虚语，
几度临风寿羽觞。

Within the courtyard, evening clouds cool in the deep hall.

A "crane-child", noble in its fledgling years, I recalls,

The days under the boundless sky.

In loong's dwelling place, the jade well, vague aromas still fly.

Like a mirror, the well reflects Jiangxia's beauty,

Through cool breeze, Dongting's sweet fragrances waft.

Seizing the day is now but empty words,

Raising my eared cup of wine,

I pray the scene will nevergo to waste.

蜀王府复原模型。蜀王府颇似故宫，是因为它们有同一个蓝本　何大江 摄

A restored model of the Royal Residence of the King of Shu, which resembles the Forbidden City due to shared architectural inspiration. (Photographer: He Dajiang)

秋高气爽的时节，晚风送来微凉，井中飘起幽香，眼前金橘井栏，正所谓“醉里乾坤，壶中日月”。

不过，这一处景观可不是普通人有缘一见的。它位于萧墙之内、深宫之中，是一处皇家景点；诗作者

In the crisp and refreshing autumn season, the evening breeze brings a slight chill, and a delicate fragrance wafts from the well. Before our eyes is a well adorned with golden tangerine, embodying the saying, "in inebriation, the heaven and earth, the sun and the moon are all in my flagon".

However, this particular sight was not something that ordinary people have the opportunity to see. This royal attraction was located within the palace walls, deep within the imperial court; the author of the poem, Zhu Rangxu, was not an ordinary person either:"Crane-child" and "Loong's dwelling place" in this poem reveal his identity—he was the ninth generation of the Kings of Shu,a direct descendant of the Ming Dynasty's imperial family. (Crane-child: ancient Chinese mistakenly thought that the crane was viviparous, unlike common birds which are oviparous, so the crane fetus is used as a metaphor for the nobleman's birth; Loong's dwelling place: According to the traditional Chinese culture, Loong, the imaginary creature like dragon, refers exclusively to matters related to the emperor.)

朱让栩也不是普通人，诗中的“鹤胎”“龙秘”透露了身份——他是第九代蜀王，朱明王朝的龙子龙孙。（鹤胎：古人误以为鹤是胎生，非同凡禽的卵生，故以鹤胎喻贵人后裔；龙秘：按照中国传统文化，龙这种虚构出来的物种，专用于跟帝王有关的事物。）

在十三代明蜀王中，朱让栩尤以贤明著称。除了政治上的作为，他还是一位儒雅之士。这首《菊井秋香》，无论从意蕴还是辞章，都算不得上乘之作，但繁复的用典，仍能体现出作者的文化素养。

其实，也不只是老百姓无福消受诗中的此情此景，这种有诗有酒的日子，对这些天潢贵胄来说也非永远。就在朱让栩离世后不到一百年，这处金橘飘香的景点便发生了极其惨烈的一幕——他的后代蜀王投井自尽，这个蜀中最显赫的家族就此灭绝。

这口井的位置，在今日的天府广场至后子门一带。自明代以来，成都人都把这里称作“皇城”。“皇城”得名缘由是：明朝初年，朱元璋分封第十一子朱椿为蜀王，并下令为其修建王府。

皇城，其实是蜀王府。

Among the thirteen generations of Kings of Shu, Zhu Rangxu was especially known for his sagacity. In addition to his political endeavors, he was also a man of refinement. This poem, *Autumn Fragrance of the Chrysanthemum Well,* is not considered a masterpiece in terms of implication or rhetoric, but the intricate use of allusions still reflect the author's cultural literacy.

In fact, not only were ordinary people unable to enjoy the scenes and emotions depicted in the poem, but such idyllic days filled with poetry and wine, were also not eternal for these high-born nobles. In less than a hundred years after the death of Zhu Rangxu, this golden tangerine scented attraction devolved into an extremely tragic scene—his descendants, the last King of Shu, threw himself into a well, marking the extinction of the most illustrious family in Shu.

The location of this well is in the area from Tianfu Square to Houzimen today. Since the Ming Dynasty, the people of Chengdu have called this area the "Imperial City", for at the beginning of the Ming Dynasty, Zhu Yuanzhang appointed his eleventh son, Zhu Chun, as the King of Shu and ordered the construction of a royal residence for him.

Imperial City, as a matter of fact, is the Royal Residence of the King of Shu.

分封藩王
爵位与忠诚的交换

元末至正十二年（1352年），25岁的朱元璋在濠州加入郭子兴的红巾军，开始了推翻蒙元统治的南征北讨。十六年后，在建康（今南京）称帝，建立明王朝。吸取元朝覆灭时无旁支相助的教训，朱元璋决定加强宗室力量，遂三次分封诸王，使子孙遍布全国。洪武十一年（1378年），年仅七岁的第十一子朱椿被册封为蜀王。

朱元璋分封诸子，有两个目的：一是让子子孙孙荣华永继；二是拱卫皇室，以便危难时有勤王之师。

第一个目标可以说基本达到了，至少藩王和郡王这两层过的都是人上人的生活。当然，明王朝覆灭时那些遭罪者除外，比如被李自成抓来跟鹿肉一起烹成“福禄宴”的福王朱常洵。

朱元璋很能生，共二十六个儿子。子又生子，子又生孙，这些有爵位的子孙也无不妻妾成群，后代数量就以几何级数增长。开国两百来年后，朱元璋的子孙已经多达几十万人。物以稀为贵，龙子龙孙也一样，

Enfeoffment of feudal kings in exchange for loyalty

In the 12th year of Zhizheng of Yuan Dynasty (1352), Zhu Yuanzhang, 25, joined Guo Zixing's Red Turbans Army in Haozhou, and began his campaign to overthrow the Mongol Yuan Dynasty. Sixteen years later, he was proclaimed emperor in Jiankang (present-day Nanjing) and established the Ming Dynasty. Learning the lesson from the destruction of the Yuan Dynasty (no support from other royal families when catastrophe befell), Zhu Yuanzhang decided to strengthen his clan, so he conferred the kings three times and spread his descendants all over the country. In the eleventh year of Hongwu (1378), Zhu Chun, the eleventh son of Zhu Yuanzhang, only seven years old then, was enthroned as the King of Shu.

Two purposes commanded Zhu Yuanzhang's decision of enfeoffment, one was to let the children and grandchildren enjoy the glory and wealth forever, the other was to defend the royal family, so that in times of crisis, reliable troops could be mobilized.

The first goal had practically achieved so to speak, at least in the two levels of the vassal king and county king, they lived a life far beyond the common people can imagine, except for those who suffered misery at the end of Ming Dynasty, when Li Zicheng captured the "King of Fortune" Zhu Changxun and cooked him with venison into "Feast of *Fu* and *Lu*". (福Fu means Fortune in Chinese, and 禄Lu shares the same phonetic attribute with deer鹿.)

Zhu Yuanzhang was very fertile and had 26 sons, who gave birth to sons and grandchildren, and all of them had wives and concubines, and the number of their descendants increased in a geometric

多了就不值钱。大明帝国纵然强盛，但财力毕竟有上限，要维护这几十万名不懂稼穑之徒的高标准生活也殊为不易。所以到了明末，经过一代又一代的降级，朱元璋的子孙穷得吃不上饭也不是稀奇事。

至于以地方拱卫中央，能否达到效果，看看朱元璋的前辈刘邦大致可以明白了。

成都潘家沟出土的彩釉陶将军俑　何大江 摄
A painted ceramic warrior figurine unearthed from Panjiagou, Chengdu. (Photographer: He Dajiang)

早先刘邦先为了笼络人，把最能打的韩信、彭越、英布等都封了异姓

progression. Two hundred years after the founding of the country, Zhu Yuanzhang's descendants have reached hundreds of thousands of people. Things are expensive when they are rare, and so are the descendants of the Son of Heaven (emperor), but the more the numbers, the less valuable they are. Even though the Ming Empire was strong, there was an upper limit to its financial strength, and it was not easy to maintain a high standard of living for these hundreds of thousands of people who did not know how to till and harvest. So by the end of the Ming Dynasty, after generations of downgrading, it was not strange that Zhu Yuanzhang's children and grandchildren were too poor to keep their heads above the water.

As to the question of whether the use of local forces to defend the central government can be effective, one can roughly understand this by looking at Liu Bang, the predecessor of Zhu Yuanzhang.

Earlier, in order to enlist people, Liu Bang first made the most capable fighters with different surnames vassal kings, such as Han Xin, Peng Yue and Ying Bu. After these people had fought for him to seize the throne, they were eradicated one by one. Liu Bang's second step was to enfeoff his own descendants to defend the imperial power.

He made a pledge with the civil officials and military generals by "killing a white horse", agreeing that "if the king is not from Liu's family, the whole world will fight against him together" — a phrase aimed at the kings of different surnames who had made great achievements. However, what Liu Bang did not expect was that only forty years after he died, it was his assigned kings of the Liu family who started the "Rebellion of Seven Kingdoms", which almost toppled the Han Dynasty to the ground.

Zhu Yuanzhang, no less a civilian founding

王。待这些人为他打下江山之后，又一一剪除。刘邦的第二步是，分封自己的子孙来保卫皇权。

他与文臣武将杀白马为盟，约定“非刘氏而王，天下共击之”——这句话针对的就是为曾立下过汗马功劳的异姓王。不过，刘邦没有想到的是，在他身后不过四十来年，正是他分封的刘姓诸王发动了“七国之乱”，差点将大汉王朝掀翻在地。

作为中国历史上为数极少的两个平民开国皇帝，朱元璋跟刘邦的权术之道极其相似，都是一得鼎就杀功臣，为接班人除荆棘。不过，朱元璋倒是吸取了刘邦封异姓王的教训，即使功劳大如徐达，也只封了公爵。

“七国之乱”旧事，朱元璋不可能不了解。但话分两头说，刘邦死后吕后掌权，她给自己的兄弟侄子都封了王。还是“白马之盟”起了作用，宗室、齐王刘襄起兵，开国之臣周勃、陈平里应外合铲除吕姓诸王，最终才保住刘氏江山。

处在朱元璋的位置，很容易想到的是：马皇后固然贤良，但难保之后不出现吕雉、武则天之类的女强人牝鸡司晨，果如此，怕是等不到“七国之乱”就会埋葬在“诸吕之乱”了。

明朝版的“七国之乱”，来得极

emperor in Chinese history than Liu Bang, was extremely similar to the latter in their approach to power, killing his meritorious ministers as soon as he gained the throne and removing thorns and thistles for his successor. However, Zhu Yuanzhang had learned the lesson of Liu Bang's practice of granting kings with different surnames, and even though Xu Da, whose contributions were enormous, was only granted the title of duke.

The old story of the "Rebellion of Seven Kingdoms" could not elude Zhu Yuanzhang's memory. However, there are two sides to the story. After the death of Liu Bang, Empress Lyu came to power, and she gave her brothers and nephews the title of king. It was the "White Horse Oath" that became a rally cry to arouse Liu Xiang, the King of Qi, a member of the royal family, to mobilise an army, and collaborated with Zhou Bo and Chen Ping, the founding ministers of the state, from within to eliminate the Kings of the Lyu family, which eventually saved Liu's kingdom.

In Zhu Yuanzhang's position, his wife, Queen Ma, was certainly a virtuous woman, but it is difficult to guarantee that strong women such as Lyu Zhi and Wu Zetian would not rise up to call the shots and to take the helm. If it is really the case, one could not wait until the break-out of the "Rebellion of Seven Kingdoms" before the "Rebellion of Lyus" would have buried him with the Dynasty.

The Ming Dynasty's version of the "Rebellion of Seven Kingdoms" came very quickly. The Battle of Jingnan, which broke out the year after Zhu Yuanzhang's death, followed the same path as the Han Dynasty's civil strife: the princes became powerful—the central government became uneasy—the central government tried to whittle down the power of the feudal lords—and the princes revolted. This time, Zhu Di, the King of Yan, seized the throne of

快。朱元璋死后第二年爆发的“靖难之役”，跟汉代内乱的路径一模一样：亲王坐大—中央不安—中央削藩—亲王造反。只是结局相反，这一次燕王朱棣夺取了建文帝的皇位。一百多年后，又发生了宁王朱宸濠叛乱。不过朱元璋若泉下有知，也许会庆幸：相较之下，江山落在同姓人的手里，再怎么也是自己的子孙，肉烂了还在锅里。

刘邦分封异姓王，其实是帝王与武将之间的一种约定：我给你荣华富贵，你帮我打天下。目的达到，就撕毁合同。朱元璋分封藩王，也是一种约定，是皇家与宗室的约定，是爵位与忠诚的交换。

蜀献王朱椿，是一名优秀的履约者。

Emperor Jianwen. More than a hundred years later, there was another rebellion by King Zhu Chenhao of Ning. However, if Zhu Yuanzhang were to know in his grave, he might still be glad for his kingdom was always in the hand of his descendants rather than being snatched by people with different surnames.

Liu Bang's enfeoffment of the kings to different surnames was actually a kind of covenant between the emperor and the military generals: I grant you glory and wealth, and you help me to seize the power. When the purpose is achieved, the contract is torn up. Zhu Yuanzhang's conferment of vassal kings were also a kind of covenant between the royal family and the clan, trading lordship for loyalty.

Zhu Chun, King of Shu Xian, was an excellent performer.

一代贤王
两百年蜀中无战事

明代开国之初周边未宁，大军还在云南征讨，蜀地西部更与辽阔的羁縻地区相接。无论从经济地位还是战略形势考虑，四川在大明版图上都处于特殊的位置。这种重要性，从朱元璋对茶马互市的高度警惕就可见一斑。

A Generation of Sage Kings
No war in Sichuan for 200 years

At the beginning of the Ming Dynasty, the neighboring areas were not yet pacified, the army was still in Yunnan, and the western part of Sichuan was bordered with the minority ethnic areas. Whether from the economic status or strategic situation, Sichuan in Ming's territory was in a special position and its importance was evident by Zhu Yuanzhang's high vigilance on the "tea and horse market".

The "tea and horse market" originated in the

茶马互市发端于唐宋，而兴盛于明代。对明朝来说，它绝不仅仅是边境贸易，更与国防军事、外交政治息息相关。

且看两个数据：一是汉中茶三百万斤，可换马三万匹，四川松潘、茂县一带的茶叶也是这个交换比例；二是从河州（甘肃临夏）、碉门（四川天全）两个通道出去的茶叶五十万余斤，换回了一万三千八百匹马。

运出去的是一箱箱边疆民族离不得的生活必需品，牵进来的是一匹匹军马。把控茶叶供给，是明王朝驾驭边疆民族的权术缰绳之一。

洪武五年（1372年），明朝在秦州（甘肃天水）建立了第一个茶马司，对边茶实施管控。二十五年之后，改置秦州茶马司于西宁。从天水到西宁，向西北方向迁移了近千里，这意味着明朝边贸疆界的扩展，以及对新增区域更加严格的控制。

果然，蜀王朱椿和秦王接到檄文，让他们派军队巡守关口，严禁私茶出境。边茶的垄断经营，对走私来说必然意味着暴利，也必然吸引着铤而走险者。然而，对边疆政策却会产生不利影响，军马的减少更是会削弱国防力量。朱元璋对茶马互市有多重

Tang and Song Dynasties, and flourished in the Ming Dynasty. For the Ming Dynasty, it is not just a border trade, but more related with the military defense and foreign affairs.

Take a look at two data: First, three million pounds of tea in Hanzhong can be exchanged for 30,000 horses. In Songpan and Mao County, Sichuan, such an exchange rate was also the same; the second, more than 500,000 pounds of tea was exported from the passage in Hezhou (Linxia, Gansu) and Diaomen (Tianquan, Sichuan) in exchange for 13,800 horses.

What shipped out were boxes of life necessities for the border people and what imported in were military horses. Controlling the tea supply was one of the reins to harness the frontier people by the Ming Dynasty.

In the fifth year of the Hongwu era (1372), the Ming Dynasty established the first tea horse division in Qinzhou (Tianshui, Gansu) to control border tea supply. Twenty years later, the division was relocated to Xining. From Tianshui to Xining, a move nearly a thousand miles to the northwest, meant an expansion of the Ming border trade frontier and stricter control over the additional area.

Sure enough, King Zhu Chun of Shu and King Qin received edicts telling them to send their troops to patrol the passes and strictly prohibit illicit tea from leaving the country. The monopolization of the border tea supply would inevitably mean huge profits for smuggling, and it would also ineluctably attract people who broke their necks for the benefits. However, the smuggling activities would have a negative impact on the frontier policy: the reduction of military horses would weaken the national defense force. The more emphasis Zhu Yuanzhang put on the tea and horse market, the angrier he became toward smuggling.

Ouyang Lun was a commandant, also Zhu Yuanzhang's son-in-law, husband of his daughter

视，对边茶走私就有多愤怒。

驸马都尉欧阳伦，是马皇后嫡出女儿安庆公主的夫婿。就在秦州茶马司改置于西宁这一年，他借着出使秦、蜀两地的机会，走私边茶牟取暴利。在朱元璋看来，这样的行为简直就是在断送国本，即便是自己的女婿，也一定活不成了。

用什么样的人来治理边陲，朱元璋是有考量的。他把悍勇善战的朱棣派到燕地，战北元；而将沉稳持重的朱椿封至蜀地，守西陲。

朱椿是朱元璋的第十一子，郭子兴之女郭惠妃所生，与谷王朱橞为同母兄弟。朱椿性格仁慈，博览笃学，气质儒雅，被朱元璋呼作“蜀秀才”。作为平民出身的开国皇帝，朱元璋可以是天纵奇才、韬略深远，也可以是阴狠毒辣、杀伐决断，但给朱椿取外号时的他，只是慈祥的父亲，就像一个摸着儿子的脑袋表达喜爱的老农民。

作为蜀王府的第一任主人，朱椿没有辜负朱元璋的厚望。他到蜀就藩之后，展现出与四哥朱棣完全不同的施政策略。

朱椿在蜀地时，番人（边疆民族）入侵，他经过观察，发现有一内一外两个原因。内因是，内地有人

Princess An Qin, the daughter of Empress Ma. In the year when the Qinzhou Tea Horse Division was re-located to Xining, he took the opportunity of his mission to Qin and Shu to smuggle border tea for profiteering. In Zhu Yuanzhang's eye, such behavior was simply destroying the country's foundation, and even his own son-in-law must not live.

With what kind of people to govern the borderlands,Zhu Yuanzhang had a consideration. He sent the brave and warlike Zhu Di to Yan territory to fight against the Northern Yuan; while Zhu Chun, who was calm and prudent, was appointed to Shu to guard the western frontier.

Zhu Chun was the eleventh son of Zhu Yuanzhang, brother of Zhu Hui (King of Gu)—both of them were born to Guo Zixing's daughter, Virtuous Consort Guo. Zhu Chun's character was kind, erudite and refined, and was called "Shu Xiu Cai"(Fine talent in Shu) by Zhu Yuanzhang. As the founding emperor rising from a commoner, Zhu Yuanzhang could be both brilliant and tactical, as well as ruthless and decisive, but when he nicknamed Zhu Chun, he was just a kind father, like an old farmer who caressed his son's head to express his love.

As the first master of the Royal Residence of King of Shu, Zhu Chun did not disappoint Zhu Yuanzhang's high expectations. After he arrived in Shu and assumed the throne, he showed a completely different governance strategy from that of his fourth elder brother, Zhu Di.

When Zhu Chun governed in Shu territory, the frontier people usually invaded. Through his observation, he summarized the causes of the invasion into internal and external aspects. The internal cause was that there were people in the territory to collude with frontier inhabitants; the external cause was that when the government officials privately did business with the frontier inhabitants, they, out of greed,

主动勾结、延揽；外因则是，衙门官员私自同番人做交易时，贪婪勒索引起不满。朱椿想了一个釜底抽薪的办法，他将进贡王府的精美丝织品和香扇等物品改为常贡，即每年只在正旦（正月初一）、万寿节（皇帝诞辰）、千秋节（朝贺皇后的节日）、冬至四个时节进贡，取消了临时性的别贡——这就大大减少了因借口采买贡品而骚扰民间的可能。

朱椿爱读书，也爱与读书人交往。一到蜀地，他就请来大学者方孝孺专门教授世子（亲王的嫡长子、王位继承人）。朱椿到郡学讲学，得知读书人贫困，就从自己的俸禄中给每人每月供米一石——后来成为定制。

宿儒陈南宾擅诗文，洪武二十九年与方孝孺同为四川考试官。朱椿将其提升为蜀王府长史（执管王府政令的幕僚长），送他适合老人乘坐的安车，并为他建造府第“安老堂”。

这种崇文重教的态度，影响了整个四川的风气。

对于普通百姓，朱椿也心怀悲悯。他设厂施粥，供给贫穷者。当时边境上不时有人被外族掳走，他下令用布匹赎回。每年救济的人数，多达上万人。

extorted the inhabitants, causing their dissatisfaction. Zhu Chun thought of a way to get rid of this problem by changing the tribute to the royal family of fine silk fabrics and incense fans and other items into a permanent tribute; that is, in each year only on the days of *Zheng Dan* (the first day of the first month), the *Wan Shou Festival* (the emperor's birthday), the *Qian Qiu Festival* (the festival of pilgrimage to congratulate the empress) and the winter solstice were the tributes offered, eliminating other temporary tributes— greatly reduced the possibility of harassing people when using purchase of tributes as an excuse.

Zhu Chun loved to read and socialized with readers. As soon as he arrived in Shu, he invited the great scholar Fang Xiaoru to teach his *Shizi* (the first-born son of the prince and heir to the throne). When Zhu Chun went to the county school to give lectures, he learned that the readers were poor, so he gave each of them one *Dan* (unit of measurement in ancient China) of rice per month from his own income—which later became a permanent practice.

Chen Nanbin, a Confucian scholar who excelled in poetry and literature, was an examiner in Sichuan with Fang Xiaoru in the 29th year of the Hongwu reign. Zhu Chun promoted him to be the Secretary General (chief of staff) in charge of the government decrees, sent him a sedan suitable for the elderly, and built for him the residence “Elderly Hall”.

This reverence for literature and education influenced the entire Sichuan ethos.

Zhu Chun also had compassion for the common people. He set up supply offices to give congee to the poor. At that time, people on the border were taken captive by ethnic people from time to time, and he ordered them to be ransomed with cloth. The number of people relieved each year amounted to tens of thousands.

Contrary to other feudal lords at that time who practiced military training to prepare for border

跟当时其他的藩王练兵以备边防相反，蜀王“以礼教守西陲”的方式取得了更为长远的效果。朱椿之后两百多年里，四川都没经历过战乱，这跟他轻兵戎、重文教的理政策略有很大的关系。

当然会有质疑：仅仅靠仁政好施就能抵御外敌、长治久安吗？史籍中的朱椿，给人留下的是谦谦君子、老好人的印象，但他对胞弟朱橞谋反一事的处理手法，却显示出了一个成熟政治家的稳重与老练。

谷王朱橞，曾深得明成祖朱棣的喜爱，只因他为朱棣即位立下了大功。靖难之役中燕兵渡江攻击南京时，朱橞正镇守金川门。他在城楼上远远见到朱棣的麾盖，就开门投降，让燕兵轻轻松松进了南京城。

恃宠而骄的朱橞，一步一步走向癫狂。除了强占民田、侵吞公税之外，他还滥杀无辜。长史虞廷纲，仅因劝其收敛，竟被诬为诽谤并施以割裂肢体的磔刑。跟朱椿对待长史的方式相比较，完全是两个极端。

导致朱橞走向灭亡的，是谋反。除了招纳亡命之徒、练兵习阵、制造武器战舰这些常规动作，朱橞还做了一些思路“清奇”之事：

一是伪造谶语，说自己当主神

defense, King of Shu’s way of “guarding the western frontier with culture and education” achieved a more long-term effect. More than two hundred years after his death, Sichuan experienced no war, which had a lot to do with his less on military and more on culture and education policy.

Obviously, people may question whether long-lasting peace and stability can be achieved and foreign enemies can be defended by merely relying on benevolent policies and good governance. In the historical records Zhu Chun left an impression of being a modest gentleman and a goody two-shoes, but his handling of the rebellion of his younger brother, Zhu Hui, showed the unflappability and sophistication of a mature politician.

Zhu Hui, the King of Gu, was once the favorite of Zhu Di, the Chengzu Emperor of Ming Dynasty, simply because he had made great achievements for Zhu Di’s accession to the throne. When the Yan soldiers (Zhu Di’s forces) crossed the river and attacked Nanjing during the Battle of Jingnan, Zhu Hui was guarding the Jinchuan Gate. When he saw Zhu Di’s banner from a distance on the citadel, he opened the door and surrendered, allowing the Yan soldiers to enter Nanjing with ease.

The bullying and arrogant Zhu Hui, however went to madness step by step. In addition to expropriating private land and embezzling public taxes, he also killed innocents indiscriminately. Yu Tinggang, the Secretary General, was slandered and punished by chopping off limbs simply because he advised Zhu Hui to restrain himself. Compared with the way Zhu Chun treated the Secretary General, it was literally two extremes.

What led to the demise of Zhu Hui was the plotting of rebellion. In addition to conventional actions such as recruiting outlaws, practicing military training, manufacturing weapons and warships, Zhu

器。朱橞所用的谶语，《明史》无明确记载，但反推过来，应当是“十八子，主神器”这句起源于晋代、南北朝的“十八子之谶”。朱橞原为朱元璋第十九子，但他借口九哥朱杞年仅一岁便早夭，自己当排序为第十八，应了此谶。到了明末，李自成也将此作为合法性证明的重要来源——“十八子”此处则被视为“李”字的拆分。

二是让上千僧人念诅咒之语。

三是与两个太监商议谋反之事，并将其尊称为“国老令公”。最后议定的主意是，利用元宵节献灯的机会，进宫刺杀朱棣。

朱橞还给哥哥朱椿写信，以寻求外援。而朱椿的反应是，回了一封信去责备弟弟。此时的朱椿不告发他，无外乎两个原因：一是念及同胞兄弟之情，不希望陷其于死地；二是证据尚不充分（朱橞的信是用隐语写的）。

另一件事发生了，朱椿的儿子朱悦燇犯了事害怕受到责罚，逃到了朱橞处，赶上朱橞正在加紧谋反的时节。朱悦燇与建文帝朱允炆为堂兄弟，也许相貌相似，又都有皇家气度，于是朱橞便寻思以朱悦燇冒充建文帝，对外宣称：当年是他打开城门

also did some other odd things:

First, he forged the prophecy that he would be the master of the kingdom. *History of Ming* has no clear records on prophecy used by Zhu Hui, but it can be inferred that it should be “the eighteenth son will lord over the kingdom” which originated in the period of Jin Dynasty and the North and South Dynasties. Zhu Hui was originally the nineteenth son of Zhu Yuanzhang, but he excused that his ninth brother, Zhu Qi, died young at the age of only one year so that he should be ranked as the eighteenth prince, which corresponded with this prophecy. At the end of the Ming Dynasty, Li Zicheng also used this prophecy as an important source of proof of legitimacy—“18th son” was interpreted here as a split of the Chinese character “Li”李.

Second, thousands of monks were called to recite words of curses.

Thirdly, he discussed with two eunuchs about plotting against Zhu Di and honored them as “Doyens of the State”. The final idea was to take advantage of the Lantern Festival to assassinate Zhu Di in the palace.

Zhu Hui also wrote a letter to his brother Zhu Chun in order to get his support. Zhu Chun’s reaction was to return a letter to reproach his brother. At this point, Zhu Chun did not inform on him for no more than two reasons: first, he was mindful of brotherhood and did not wish to set him up for death; second, the evidence was not yet sufficient (Zhu Hui’s letter was written in cryptic code).

In the meantime,Zhu Yuejun, Zhu Chun’s son committed a crime and was afraid of being punished. He then fled to seek the patronage from Zhu Hui who was stepping up his plot to rebel. Zhu Yuejun and Jianwen Emperor Zhu Yunwen were cousins, possibly similar in appearance, and both had a royal demeanor, so Zhu Hui sought to use Zhu Yuejun to impersonate Jianwen Emperor and conveniently proclaimed that

放走了建文帝，如今建文在他家中，他要伸张正义，帮建文把被夺走的皇位再夺回来。

天下竟有如此厚颜无耻之徒。当年正是朱橞打开城门放入燕兵，导致建文帝生死不明，如今在他口中却成了开门救了建文帝一命。如果建文帝知道了这话，恐怕会活则气死、死则气活。

朱椿得到朱悦燇传回的消息，知道拖不回这个蠢弟弟了，于是上书朱棣告发此事。

朱橞其人，算得上是又坏又蠢，但本质上依然是个银样镴枪头。尽管做了这么多准备，要了这么多花招，而朱棣派的宦官拿着一道敕谕就轻松将其带回了北京。

朱橞趴在地上请罪，众大臣纷纷要求处死他，朱棣说："他是我的弟弟，那么就把这件事交给兄弟们来议定吧。"包括朱椿在内的众藩王的意见是，"诛无赦"，核心理由有二：一是谋反大逆不道，二是证据确凿。朱橞至此再无生路。

回视朱椿对此事的处理，可以说是十分得体。往大里说，保全了国家；往小里说，保全了自己一家，尤其是逃到朱橞处的儿子。朱棣对这个弟弟十分激赏，将其夸赞为大明王朝的周公。

it was he who opened the city gates and let Emperor Jianwen escape, and now that Jianwen was at his home, he wanted to uphold justice and helped Jianwen take back the throne that had been taken from him.

Such a shameless person! Back then, it was Zhu Hui who opened the city gate and let in the Yan soldiers, rendering Emperor Jianwen's whereabouts unknown, but now he changed this story into another version that he opened the door and saved Emperor Jianwen's life. If Emperor Jianwen knew this, he probably would die of anger if he lived, and would come back to life after death.

When Zhu Chun got the message from Zhu Yuejun, he knew that he could not turn this stupid brother around, so he wrote to Zhu Di to tell on Zhu Hui.

Wicked and stupid as Zhu Hui was, he was nothing but a wimp, though prepped up and full of tricks, he ended up being taken back to Beijing by the eunuchs with Zhu Di's imperial edict.

On his knees, Zhu Hui begged for leniency. The ministers demanded for his death, but Zhu Di said, "Anyways, he is my younger brother, so let's leave this matter to my fellow brothers." After deliberation, all vassal kings, including Zhu Chun, reached unanimously to their verdict—"death without amnesty", with two core reasons: his insurrection was treasonous, and the evidence was conclusive. Zhu Hui reached to a point that had no return.

Looking back at how Zhu Chun handled this matter, it can be said to be very appropriate. Viewed from a wider perspective, he preserved the country; from a narrow perspective, he safeguarded his own family, especially his son who fled to Zhu Hui. Zhu Di was so impressed with his brother that he praised him as the Duke of Zhou (ancient Chinese King who was known for his sagacity) of the Ming Dynasty.

Going back to the previous question: is it possible to defend oneself against foreign enemies

回到前面的问题：仅仅靠仁政好施就能抵御外敌、长治久安吗？

黎州安抚司番人火烧黑崖关（位于今四川汉源县）那次入寇，朱椿向朝廷请来了名将蓝玉，在大渡河边击败了来敌。有菩萨之心，也有金刚之力，这是朱椿的两面。

其实，朱椿还有一个非常特殊的身份：他的正妃蓝妃是蓝玉的女儿。后来蓝玉案发，受牵连被屠戮者多达上万人，而朱椿以蓝玉女婿的身份独能幸免，可见其在复杂、严酷的政治斗争中的判断力与定力——虽说他是朱元璋亲儿子，但父子相残在帝王家从来不绝于书。

一直到明末张献忠大军到来之前，两百多年的时间里，四川都没有遭受过兵荒马乱的蹂躏，人民殷实富足，安居乐业。《明史》将其归功于朱椿，这个评价是得当的。

and achieve long-lasting peace and security simply by benevolent and good governance?

In the case of the invasion of the Heiyaguan Pass (located in present-day Hanyuan County, Sichuan Province), which was set ablaze by an ethnic group inhabited in the Lizhou Pacification Division, Zhu Chun invited the famous general Lan Yu from the imperial court and defeated the incoming enemy by the Dadu River. The heart of compassion of a Bodhisattva and the cruel strength of a vajra characterized the two sides of Zhu Chun.

In fact, Zhu Chun also had a very special identity: his main consort, Princess Lan, was the daughter of Lan Yu. Later on, up to tens of thousands of people were killed resulting from a conspiracy involved Lan Yu, and Zhu Chun, the son-in-law of Lan Yu was off the hook, mirroring his sound judgement and determination in the harsh political struggle—although he was Zhu Yuanzhang's own son, but cases of royal fratricide and patricide were never extinct in historic book.

Until the arrival of Zhang Xianzhong's army at the end of the Ming Dynasty, Sichuan had not suffered from the ravages of war for more than two hundred years, and the people were rich and prosperous and lived in peace and contentment. *History of Ming* attributes this to Zhu Chun, and this assessment is appropriate.

壮丽威仪
和故宫有同一个蓝本

1390年，朱椿就藩四川成都府，成为有明一朝第一代蜀王。在此之前，为了替他准备蜀王府，耗去了八年时光。

Magnificent and majestic
It has the same blueprint as the Forbidden City

In 1390, Zhu Chun became the first King of Shu in the Ming Dynasty when he took up residence in Chengdu Prefecture, Sichuan Province. Before that, it took eight years to prepare the King of Shu's residence for him.

明代三彩乐伎俑，从中可以想见当年王府排场　何大江摄

Ming Dynasty tri-colored musician figurines, showcasing the grandeur of the royal court. (Photographer: He Dajiang)

1382年，朱元璋下达诏令修筑蜀王府，还说“不要急，慢慢修。(徐图之，勿亟也。)”此时，明王朝已建立十五年。之所以拖了这么久，是因为朱元璋在等一件事和一个人——事是云南的安定，人是跟着蓝玉在云南远征的景川侯曹震。此人是跟着朱元璋起兵的安徽老乡，因军功而封侯。他在四川的时间也很长，修路架桥，多有德政，主建蜀王府是非常适合的人选。

洪武十五年初，云南平定，朱元璋任命曹震为蜀王府建设工程的总负责人，并叮嘱他：“非壮丽无以示威仪。”落成的蜀王府崔巍壮丽，其规模极其宏大。

在朱元璋看来，蜀王府不仅要具备实用功能，更应当是一个标志性建筑，是明朝在蜀地的皇权代表，能够让人一见就心生敬畏。

根据史料复原的蜀王府模型，像极了北京故宫。

In 1382, Zhu Yuanzhang ordered the construction of Royal Residence of King of Shu, demanding “do not rush, build it slowly”. At this time, the Ming Dynasty had been established for fifteen years. The reason why the progress delayed for so long was that Zhu Yuanzhang was waiting for one thing and one man—the thing is the pacification of Yunnan and the man was Cao Zhen, Marquis of Jinchuan who was following Lan Yu on his Yunnan expedition. Fellow-villager of Zhu Yuanzhang from Anhui, Cao Zhen joined Zhu Yuanzhang’s army, and was awarded a marquis for his military merits. He spent a lot of time in Sichuan, a very suitable candidate for the construction of the royal residence because he had built roads and bridges and governed there with many benevolent policies.

In the 15th year of Hongwu, Yunnan was initially pacified, and Zhu Yuanzhang appointed Cao Zhen as the general superintendent of the construction project, urging him “to show the majesty through magnificence”. Once completed, the Royal Residence of King of Shu exuded grandeur and splendor.

In Zhu Yuanzhang’s mind, the Royal Residence of King of Shu should not only have practical functions, but also should be a landmark building, representing the imperial power of the Ming Dynasty in Shu, and can make people feel awe at first sight.

The model of the Royal Residence of King of Shu restored according to historical data is very much

在整个亚洲，同样气势恢宏的宫殿建筑群还有韩国景福宫、越南顺化皇城等，它们也都有中轴线奠定整体格局、营建理念契合《周易》等特点。

景福宫，位于韩国首尔，是朝鲜半岛李氏王朝的正宫。它占地50公顷，呈正方形，正门、锦川桥、勤政门、勤政殿、思政殿、康宁殿等沿南北中轴线分布，殿阙命名都来自中国古籍。

顺化皇城，是越南阮朝的京城，也是东南亚最为完美的宫殿建筑。它的中轴线上面，分布着午门、太和殿、勤政宫、乾清宫、坤泰宫和建忠楼等。

单听这些建筑的名字，让人以为来到了北京故宫。其实，蜀王府、韩国景福宫的营建都早于北京故宫，之所以跟故宫如此相似，是因为它们都有同一个来源——明朝早期皇宫、被称作南京紫禁城的南京故宫。

越南顺化皇城，始建于1802年。

北京故宫，始建于1406年。

韩国景福宫，始建于1394年。

成都蜀王府，始建于1382年。

南京紫禁城，始建于1366年，二十六年后基本完工。它是亚洲宫殿

like the Forbidden City in Beijing.

Throughout Asia, the palace complex sharing the same majesty and magnificence include Gyeongbokgung Palace in South Korea and the Hue Imperial City in Vietnam, all possessing a central axis to lay the overall pattern, their building concepts basing on what *I Ching* stands for.

Gyeongbokgung Palace, located in Seoul, South Korea, is the main palace of the Lee Dynasty on the Korean Peninsula. It covers an area of 50 hectares and is square in shape, with the main gate, Gimcheon Bridge, Chinjeongmun, Chinjeongjeon, Sijeongjeon, and Kangnyeongjeon distributing along the north-south central axis, and the names of the halls were taken from ancient Chinese texts.

The Hue Imperial City, the capital of Vietnam's Nguyen Dynasty, is a perfect palace building in Southeast Asia. Above its central axis, it is dotted with the Noon Gate, the Hall of Supreme Harmony, the Palace of Qinzheng, the Palace of Qianqing, the Palace of Kun Tai, and the House of Jianzhong.

Those names alone would mislead people to think that they have come to the Forbidden City in Beijing. In fact, the Royal Residence of King of Shu and Gyeongbokgung Palace in South Korea were constructed earlier than the Forbidden City in Beijing. Their resemblance to the Forbidden City lies in the fact that they have the same source of inspiration—the early palace of Ming Dynasty, known as the Forbidden City of Nanjing or Nanjing Imperial Palace.

The Hue Imperial City was first built in 1802.

Beijing Imperial Palace was first built in 1406.

Gyeongbokgung Palace in South Korea was first built in 1382.

The Royal Residence of King of Shu in Chengdu was first built in 1382.

Nanjing Imperial Palace was first built in 1366

建筑群的母体，是蓝本中的蓝本。

南京紫禁城开创了城市中轴线与宫殿建筑中轴线相重合的先例，这一特点也被蜀王府继承。

可以说，成都几百年来的城市格局，从蜀王府开建的那一天就确定了。明代的成都城垣中，蜀王府几乎位于正中的位置，大致在今日天府广场—四川科技馆—成都体育中心一带。从1382年到今天，六百多年了，那条中轴线从来都没有更改或废弃，至今还在不断延长。

今日的地面上，见不到半分毫蜀王府建筑的痕迹。不过，翻开地图，当年王府的密码依然存留在街名中。

“御”字有个常见的意义，即跟帝王相关的事物。成都有几条含有“御”字的街——东御河沿街、西御河沿街，以及东御街、西御街。

东御街、西御街，是在明代即有的街道——当时就叫御街，它们处于蜀王城萧墙南垣脚下，是一条东西向的主干道。

东御河沿街、西御河沿街，街名得自御河。御河在哪儿？它位于蜀王府北端，是当年修筑王府时挖土筑墙形成的河道。御河是浩繁工程的第一步，它内连宫内的摩诃池，外接金水河。建造王宫时用于运送建筑材料，

and completed in 26 years later. It is the springhead and blueprint of the other Asian palace complex.

The Forbidden City in Nanjing set a precedent for the overlap of the city's central axis with that of the palace buildings, a feature that was also inherited by the Royal Residence of King of Shu.

It can be said that the urban pattern of Chengdu over the centuries was determined from the day the Royal Residence of King of Shu was first built. Within the Chengdu city walls in the Ming Dynasty, the Royal Residence of King of Shu was located almost right in the middle, roughly in the area of today's Tianfu Square-Sichuan Science and Technology Museum-Chengdu Sports Center. More than six hundreds years from 1382 to today past, that central axis has never been changed or abandoned, and is still being extended today.

No residues of the Royal Residence can be found on the ground now. However, turning over the map, one can still find the code of the then Royal Residence alive in the street names.

The Chinese character 御(Yu) denotes a usual meaning related to the emperor. Several streets in Chengdu embrace the character 御, such as East Yuhe Street, West Yuhe Street, East Yu Street and West Yu Street.

East Yu Street and West Yu Street are streets that have existed since the Ming Dynasty—at that time were called Yu Street or Royal Street, located at the foot of south screen wall of the Royal Residence, a main road with east-west orientation.

East Yuhe Street and West Yuhe Street get their names from the Yuhe River (the Royal River). Where is the Yuhe River? It is located in the north end of the Royal Residence, a channel formed by the excavation of the earth to build walls of the Royal Residence. Digging the Yuhe River was the first step of the massive project. Internally it was connected to

完工后则可运送生活物资——古代工匠的智慧由此可见。

东华门街、西华门街，分别是蜀王府东西两侧的过门——东华门、西华门之所在。这两道门听起来很熟悉？是的，北京故宫就有东华门和西华门。蜀王府是个小一号的“皇宫”，是降低规制的南京紫禁城，它跟北京故宫有着同一个母本，因此，这种相似一点都不奇怪。

要谈论古代建筑遗址，很重要的一个概念就是“四至”。换言之，它的东、西、南、北到底在哪里？对蜀王府这种方方正正呈矩形的建筑群来说，搞清楚了“四至”，就能够轻易确定其大小了。

蜀王府有两个“四至”。因为，它有两道城垣。

内城是宫城，城墙叫宫墙，宫墙之外则萧墙——两道墙之间，约有两百米的距离。

宫墙的四至，前文提及的东华门街、西华门街，分别是其东垣和西垣，东华门、西华门正是当年宫墙上东西两侧的过门。南垣即成都今日的东西主干道——人民东路和人民西路。北垣则是前文提及的东御河沿街和西御河沿街。

萧墙的四至，东至今日顺城大

the Maha Pond in the palace and externally, it was linked to the Jinshui River. It was used to transport building materials during the construction of the palace, and to transport living materials when it was completed—the ingenuity of ancient craftsmen can be witnessed here.

Donghuamen Street and Xihuamen Street, respectively, are the crossing gates on the east and west sides of the Royal Residence: Donghuamen Gate and Xihuamen Gate. The name of the two gates sounds familiar? Yes, the Forbidden City in Beijing has Donghuamen and Xihuamen as well. The Royal Residence of King of Shu is the “Palace” of a smaller size, a lower version of the Forbidden City, sharing the same motherboard, so the similarities are not surprising.

One of the most important concepts when talking about ancient architectural sites is the “four directions” (Peripheral boundaries). In other words, where is the boundary to its east, west, south and north direction? For the Royal Residence of King of Shu, which is a square and rectangular building complex, it is easy to figure out its size once you understand the “four directions”.

There are two “four boundaries” in the Royal Residence. Because it has two city walls.

The inner city was the palace city, the wall was called the palace wall, and beyond the palace wall was the screen wall— between the two walls, there was a distance of about nearly two hundred meters.

The east and west of the boundaries of the palace wall are the Donghuamen Gate and Xihuamen Gate which were mentioned earlier and were exactly the crossing gates of the palace wall on the east and west sides. In the south direction is the main east-west road—East People’s Road and West People’s Road in today’s Chengdu. In the north direction is the previously mentioned East Yuhe Street and West Yuhe Street.

街，西至东城根街。北垣在羊市街、玉龙街一线，南垣则是前文所言之明代御街、今日的东御街—西御街一线。

牌坊背后是明蜀王府遗迹红照壁，这或许是它留在世间唯一的影像 （德）恩斯特·柏石曼 摄

Behind the memorial arch lies the remains of the Ming Shu Kings' Palace, marked by the iconic Red Screen Wall, possibly its last surviving trace. (Photographer: Ernst Boerschmann, GER)

The "four boundaries" of the screen wall starts from current Shuncheng Ave in the east and to Dongchenggen Street in the west; stretches to the Yangshi Street and Yulong Street in the north and reaches Royal Street of Ming Dynasty and today's East Yu Street and West Yu Street in the south.

The "four boundaries" of the Royal Residence is relatively clear, with the only controversy being its south direction. Some says it lies in the Red Screen Wall Street—back then, there was a red screen wall of more than 20 feet long and four feet high red wall; hence the street was so named.Hong Zhao Bi (Red Screen Wall) was dismantled in 1927, a year before the City of Chengdu was founded, but the name has been preserved.

蜀王府的四至是比较清晰的，唯一有些争议的是其南垣，有说在红照壁街——当年，此处曾立有一堵长二十余丈、高四丈五尺的红色照壁，街即因此而得名。红照壁拆除于1927年，即成都建市的前一年，但名字一直保留了下来。

说蜀王府萧墙在红照壁一带，是一种认知上的错误，以为照壁就一定在王府之内。其实照壁是一种附属建筑，它主要有两种作用：一是装饰性，用于王府则是“示威仪”，展现皇家气派；二是风水上的挡煞气（也

It is a cognitive error to proclaim that the screen wall of the Royal Residence of King of Shu was in the Hong Zhao Bi area and to think the screen wall must be within the Royal Residence. In fact, a screen wall is an accessory building with two main roles: one is decorative, used for the royal family to exhibit the royal style; the second is for the *feng shui* purpose, such as blocking evil spirit (also has a certain practical function, i.e., fending off the wind blowing directly into the main gate). In fact, the location of the screen wall is outside the main building.

The East Yu Street and West Yu Street line are about 400 meters in a straight line from today's Red Screen Wall Street (the original site of Red Screen Wall). As an accessory building, the wall seems to be

具备一定的实用功能，可阻挡风直接刮进大门内）。实际上，照壁的位置是在主体建筑之外的。

东御街—西御街一线，距今日红照壁街（红照壁原址）的直线距离约400米。照壁作为附属建筑，相对于主体建筑来说，似乎是有些远了。但蜀王城的体量实在是太庞大了，将此因素考虑进去，从比例上来讲，这个距离是合适的。

a bit far away from the main building. However, the volume of Royal Residence is so huge that, taking this factor into consideration, this distance is appropriate in terms of proportion.

俯瞰蜀王城
大地上巨大的回字

如果回到明代，换成一种俯瞰的视角，那么会看到当年的蜀王府就是一个巨大的回字形。这个回字，最长的一竖（萧墙东、西垣）约有1200米，最短的那一横（宫墙南、北垣）也超过了六百米。其实，时至今日，那个回字依然存在。只是，车水马龙的街道取代了当年的两道围墙。

在回字的两个“口”之间，有些什么呢？

先看北面。最外面是萧墙，这道墙并不太高，只有一丈五尺（明代一尺为32厘米，跟现代极为接近）；向内，是一道壕沟，也可以视作护城河，即前文所言之御河（水道早已

Overlooking the Royal Residence of King of Shu: a Huge “Hui” 回 character on the ground

If we go back to the Ming Dynasty, looking from above, we would see that the Royal Residence of King of Shu is like a huge Chinese character 回. The longest vertical line (east and west side of the screen wall) is about 1,200 meters and shortest horizontal line (south and north side of the screen wall) is more than 600 meters. In fact, to this day, the form of the character still exists, only the hustle and bustle streets replaced the two walls back then.

What exists between the two 口 of the character 回？

Let’s look at the north side first. The outermost is the screen wall which is not too high, only one *zhang* (ancient Chinese measurement, 1 *Zhang* equals to 3.33 meters)and a half feet (a foot in the Ming Dynasty equals to 32 centimeters, pretty close to current standard); inward, there is a trench, which can also be regarded as a moat, namely, the Royal River mentioned earlier (the waterway has long been silted

淤塞而填平为街道）；再向内，回字的那个小“口”，却是一道高墙，高三丈九，是萧墙高度的2.6倍——它围起来的宫城，真是配得上深宫二字了。

萧墙与宫墙之间，在北面和东西两侧，是花红柳绿、姹紫嫣红的皇家园林。闽中才子曹学佺，万历末曾在蜀王府花园见识过“鱼血红”——当时四川最负盛名的牡丹——并留下了“水自龙池分处碧，花从鱼血染来红”的诗句。

萧墙、宫墙间的南面，即今日人民西路—人民东路一线、西御街—东御街一线之间，被称作天府广场的区域，分布着一组祭祀建筑群，从左至右分别是：山川坛、社稷坛和宗庙。

山川坛，祭祀先农（神农），也是行籍田礼之处。明代，在北京城的山川坛又被称为先农坛。

社稷坛，祭祀社（土地神）和稷（五谷神）。

宗庙，祭祀祖先的地方。

社稷坛和宗庙总会同时出现。据说，这是《周礼》传下来的祖制“左祖右社”（东为左，西为右——那是一种坐北朝南的视角）。南京故宫，社稷坛居西，太庙居东；北京故宫前方，也是同样的结构，社稷坛现在又

up and filled in for the street); and further inward to the small “口”, which is a high wall, three *Zhang*s and 9 feet high, 2.6 times as much as that of the screen wall—the palace surrounded by such a wall can really be called abyssal palace

On the north and east and west sides between the screen wall and the palace wall, there are royal gardens with beautiful flowers and willows. Cao Xuequan, a talented scholar from Min (Fujian Province), had seen “fish blood red”—the most famous peony in Sichuan at that time—in the garden of the Royal Residence at the end of the Wanli reign, and left the following poem: “water turns into deep green from the Dragon Pond, and the flowers are redder because of the fish blood red”.

The south side of the screen wall and the palace wall is the present-day West People’s Road - East People’s Road and West Yu Street- East Yu Street, the area today known as Tianfu Square was, back then, distributed with a group of ceremonial complexes, which were, from left to right: Shanchuan Altar, Sheji Altar and Zongmiao Temple (Temple of the Patriarchs).

The Shanchuan Altar is dedicated to the late farmer (Shennong, or God of Agriculture), and is also the place where the rites of the field were performed. During the Ming Dynasty, the Shanchuan Altar in Beijing was also known as the Xiannong Altar.

The Sheji Altar is a alter where the gods of *She* (God of Earth) and *Ji* (God of Grains) are enshrined.

Zongmiao Temple or Temple of the Patriarchs is where the ancestors are revered.

The Sheji Alter and Zongmiao Temple always appear at the same time. It is said that this is the ancestral system passed down from the *Zhou Rites*: On the left, ancestor, right, God of Earth (on the east means on the left, while west, right—that is a north-

叫中山公园。这种“左祖右社”的结构，同样在蜀王府得到了体现。不过，太庙是皇帝家的专用名称，在成都就只能叫宗庙了。

猎猎天风，刮走天上浮云与世间喧嚣。站在天府广场的位置，似乎回到1390年，脚下的位置是社稷坛，左手是蜀王宗庙，右手是山川坛——农神崇拜和祖先崇拜，是这个民族的遗传基因。

身后宫墙，端礼门内即宫殿区。从南向北，依次是承运殿、前宫、中宫、后宫、圜殿、存心殿，共有房屋八百多间。单说承运殿，共有柱子七十二根，分列两排，其壮丽若是。

身前萧墙，出了棂星门，河水潺潺流过。巧得很，故宫前的河叫金水河，而蜀王府前的也叫金水河（又称金河）。故宫的外金水桥总七座，为三孔拱券式；而蜀王府前的金水河上，也横跨着三座石桥，每座桥又有三个桥洞，桥南头有威严的石狮，这就是所谓的“三桥九洞石狮子”。

巧合之处，还有很多。北京有琉璃厂，是烧制琉璃瓦专供故宫建造的官窑；明代成都，城外东南也设有琉璃厂官窑（现琉璃场），为蜀王府和蜀王陵提供形形色色的琉璃瓷器、挂件。

south perspective). In Nanjing Imperial Palace, the Sheji altar locates in the west, the Imperial Ancestral Temple is seated in the east, while in front of Beijing Imperial Palace, the same structure is duplicated. The Sheji altar is now called Zhongshan Park. This “ancestor on the left and God of Earth on the right” structure was also embodied in the Royal Residence of King of Shu. However, the Imperial Ancestral Temple was the exclusive name of the emperor’s palace, and in Chengdu it could only be called the Clan Temple.

The strong winds of the sky blow away the floating clouds in the sky and the clamor of the world. Standing in the Tianfu Square, it seems to go back to the year 1390; the position under the feet was the Sheji Altar, with Clan Temple of the Shu family on the left and the Shanchuan Altar on the right—the worship of the god of agriculture and ancestors are the genetic heritage of this nation.

Behind the palace wall and the Duanli Gate, there were palace areas. From the south to the north, in turn, was the Cheng Yun Hall, Front Hall, Rear Hall, Huan Hall and Cun Xin Hall, a total of more than 800 houses. Magnificent as it was, Cheng Yun Hall alone had a total of 72 pillars, divided into two rows.

Passing the screen wall ahead and going out of the Lingxing Gate, one can see river gurgling through. Coincidentally, the river in front of the Royal Residence of King of Shu is also called the Jinshui River (aka the Jin River), the namesake of the Jinshui River girdling outside The Forbidden City in Beijing, which owns seven bridges, all being three-hole arch type. On the Jinshui River in front of the Royal Residence of King of Shu, there were three bridges sitting athwart, each bridge possessing three bridge holes; on the south end of the bridge there was a majestic stone lion, all together they were known as

这种偶然，背后藏着必然：蜀王府其实是小一号的皇宫，是明代皇权在四川地区的象征。

这种“小一号”，仅仅是从规制上来说。比如说故宫的太庙，到成都变成了宗庙；故宫有近万个房间，而蜀王府的房间不到其十分之一；故宫金水河上有七座桥，而蜀王府金河上只有三座……地理学家王士性在万历初年曾游历成都。在他的眼中，蜀王府的宫殿以及仪仗、乐舞、车马、保卫等卤簿仪制，不下于朝廷的一半。这种说法，也跟本文的“小号皇宫”比较模型是相吻合的。

若论规模，故宫占地面积为七十二万平方米，而蜀王府若以萧墙范围计算的话，占地达到一百二十万平方米，比北京故宫大上不少。

蜀王府宫墙之内的面积，李劼人先生说是三十八万平方米，占成都老城的五分之一，此数据也为许多文章所引用。但是，蜀王府虽然占地广阔，不管是萧墙还是宫墙，围起来的面积远远达不到成都城的五分之一——这一点在《天启成都府图》上也能得到直观的体现。

蜀王府并不仅仅存在于历史典籍中。

20世纪90年代开始的考古发掘，

“three bridges, nine holes and stone lions”.

The coincidence didn’t stop here. In Beijing, there was a Liulichang, an official kiln which was dedicated to burn glazed tiles exclusively for the Forbidden City; in Chengdu in the Ming Dynasty, there was also an official kiln (present Liulichang) in the southeast of the city to pursue the same undertaking for the King of Shu and its mausoleums, providing all kinds of glazed ceramics and pendants.

Behind this coincidence hid inevitability: Royal Residence of King of Shu was actually an Imperial Palace of smaller size, a symbol of the Ming Dynasty imperial power in the Sichuan region.

When we say “smaller size”, we mean a smaller one in terms of constraints and the structures. For example, the Imperial Ancestral Temple in the Forbidden City was replaced by the Clan Temple in Chengdu; the Imperial Palace had nearly 10,000 rooms, while the rooms in the Royal Residence of King of Shu were less than one-tenth of that number; over the Jinshui River of the Imperial Palace there were seven bridges, while over the Jin River of the King of Shu’s House stood only three… the Geographer Wang Shixing had traveled to Chengdu in the first year of the Wanli era. In his eyes, the palace of the King of Shu *per se*, the ceremonial band, the music and dance performance, the carriage, the security guards and other codes of conduct for major events were no less than half of the court’s. This statement was consistent with what we say “smaller size”.

When it comes to scale, the Forbidden City covers an area of 720,000 square meters, while the Royal Residence of the King of Shu covers an area of 1.2 million square meters if including the range within the screen walls, which is bigger than that of the Forbidden City in Beijing.

就陆陆续续发现了宫墙以及山川坛基址。2013年始，更是对东华门区域进行了连续五年的大规模考古发掘，清理出明代蜀王府左花园的建筑遗存以及大量的瓷器等物品。

考古发掘的建筑群主要分为南区和北区两部分，南区以水道为主，北区则发现了一个水池以及正中的台榭。

水道的修建方式非常讲究。首先是从挖出土圹至沙砾层，形成河床。其次，跟水体接触的部位，都建有护堤进行保护。

这种保护措施又分为四步：第一步，在沙砾层中楔入两排木桩；第二步，木桩之间铺青砖，并以石灰勾缝；第三步，青砖上铺大石板；第四步，石板上再垒红砂石条。红砂石条上刻有“左”或“右”，这是当年为确定施工位置而留下的痕迹。

北区的水池面积很大，将近1800平方米；中间的台榭超过六百平方米，残高两米。台榭与水池外缘之间并无桥梁，而是四周环以一条宽度为8.1米的水道。在台榭的南面，有一个小小的码头。可以想见，当年蜀王府里的贵族就是乘坐小船，从码头登上台榭，在此迎风吟赋或者欢歌达旦的。

The area within the Royal Residence walls was 380,000 square meters, one-fifth of scale of the old Chengdu city, according to Mr. Li Jieren, a famous scholar. This figure has also been cited by many articles. Although the Royal Residence covered a vast area, be it within the screen walls or the palace walls, the area enclosed was far less than one-fifth of the Chengdu city, which can also be visualized in the *Tianqi Chengdu Map*.

The Royal Residence of King of Shu does not just exist in historical texts.

Archaeological excavations began in the 1990s made the palace wall and the Shanchuan Altar site come to surface. Since 2013, five consecutive years of large-scale archaeological excavations have been underway to clean out the remains of the Left Garden in the Royal Residence and a large number of ceramics and other items.

The construction complex excavated from the archaeological activity was divided into two main sections—the southern section, which is dominated by the waterway, and the northern section, where a pond as well as a terrace in the center were found.

The waterway was constructed in a very elaborate manner. First, the riverbed was formed by digging out the earth from the gravelly layer. Secondly, the areas in contact with the water were protected by berms.

This protective measure involved four steps: first, driving two rows of wooden stakes in the gravel layer; second, spreading black bricks between the wooden stakes and adding lime among joints; third, covering the black bricks with big stone slabs; fourth, stacking red sandstone bars on those big stone slabs. The red sandstone bars were engraved with “left” or “right”, which were the traces left for determining the construction position back then.

成都出土的明代建筑构件——琉璃正脊　何大江摄

Ming-era glazed roof ridge components excavated in Chengdu. (Photographer: He Dajiang)

水道和水池的淤泥里，出土了大量瓷器和建筑构件。瓷器中，仅景德镇窑的釉色品类就可细分为青花、青白釉、白釉、仿哥釉、青釉、酱釉、蓝釉、红釉、绿釉、灰釉和红绿彩等多种，其纹饰则包括草叶、花卉、龙凤、瑞兽、人物、杂宝、祥云、水波等各类题材。其中一件青花碗的碗底，有“大明宣德年制”的楷书款识。

出土的建筑构件，可辨者有板瓦、筒瓦、瓦当、滴水、正脊筒、天马、垂兽、套兽等。部分表面覆以绿釉，造型古朴厚重。

水道、水池和台榭、码头，青花瓷器和绿釉瓦当，不仅以实物的方式证明了蜀王府的存在，也让皇权、王府这些宏大的辞藻变得可以触摸。手指叩在青花碗上，传来的是宣德年间的回响。

The pool in the north area was rather large, nearly 1,800 square meters; the central terrace was over 600 square meters and was two meters high. There was no bridge between the terrace and the outer edge of the pool, but a waterway of 8.1 meters in width around it. In the south of the terrace, there was a small dock. It can be imagined that in those years, the nobles in Royal Residence took a small boat and climbed up to the terrace from the dock, and chanted and sang day and night.

A large number of porcelains and architectural components were unearthed in the silt of waterways and pools. As far as porcelain concerned, those made in Jingdezhen kiln alone can be subdivided into blue and white glaze, white glaze, *Fangge* glaze, cyan glaze, brown glaze, blue glaze, red glaze, green glaze, gray glaze and red and green color and so on, and their patterns include grass and leaves, flowers, dragons and phoenixes, propitious beasts, figures, miscellaneous treasures, auspicious clouds, water waves and other kinds of subjects. One of the blue and white bowls was inscribed in regular script: “made in the year of Xuande of Da Ming Dynasty”.

Building components unearthed there can be recognizable as flat tile, tubular tile, eaves tile, water—dripping tile, ridge tube, heavenly horse (a decorative beast), pendant beast (a decorative beast), *taoshou* beast (a decorative beast), etc. Parts of the surface were covered with green glaze, simple, unadorned and dignified.

The waterways, pools, terraces, piers, the blue and white porcelain and green glazed tiles not only prove the existence of the Royal Residence in a physical way, but also make the grandiose rhetoric of royalty and kingship palpable. Knocking on the blue and white bowls with your fingers brings the reverberations of the Xuande period.

蜀多贤王
挡不住天灾异象

朱椿开了个好头。有明一代，蜀藩十世十三王（加上追封的悼庄王朱悦燫共十四王）以多贤王著称。从某种角度来看，与其说这是王族，毋宁说更像有传承的书香门第、学者家族。

第五代，蜀定王朱友垓，善草书，著有诗文辞赋集《定园睿制集》。（皇帝诗文称“御制”，亲王诗文称“睿制”。）

第六代，蜀怀王朱申鈫，著有诗文集《怀园睿制集》。

第七代，蜀惠王朱申凿，著有诗文集《惠园睿制集》。

第八代，蜀昭王朱宾瀚，为父亲编有《惠园睿制集》，并亲撰序言。

第九代，蜀成王朱让栩，著有诗文集《长春竞辰稿》，由大才子杨慎作序。朱让栩算得上是贤王中的贤王，他远离声色犬马，除了兴修水利、赈济灾荒，兴趣都在跟文化教育有关的事上。

朱让栩爱读书，敬重读书人，创办义学。他主持校勘编刻的《栾城集》九十六卷，收录了苏辙所有的诗

The Sage Kings of Shu
Can't stop the natural disasters and visions

Zhu Chun made a good start. Throughout Ming Dynasty, Shu clan turned out ten thirteen kings (plus the posthumous King of Daozhuang, Zhu Yeulian, a total of fourteen kings), most of whom were known for their sagacity. In a sense, this royal clan was not so much a royal family as a scholarly and literary family.

In the fifth generation, Zhu Yougai, King of Shu Ding, was good at cursive writing and wrote a collection of poems and essays called *Ruizhi of Dingyuan*. (The poems and writings written by emperors were called "written by the emperor", while those of princes were called "ruizhi or written by the prince".)

In the sixth generation, Zhu Shenyi, King of Shu Huai, was the author of a collection of poems and writings called *Ruizhi of Huaiyuan*.

In the seventh generation, Zhu Shenzao, the king of Shu Hui, wrote a collection of poems and writings called *Ruizhi of Huiyuan*.

In the eighth generation, Zhu Binhan, King of Shu Zhao, compiled the *Ruizhi of Huiyuan* for his father and wrote the preface himself.

In the ninth generation, Zhu Rangxu, the king of Shu Cheng, wrote a collection of poems and writings called *Manuscript of Changchun Jingchen*, which was prefaced by the great scholar Yang Shen. Zhu Janshu was considered the most virtuous of all the virtuous kings. He stayed away from licentious pleasure, and his interests were all related to culture and education, aside from water conservancy and disaster relief.

Zhu Rangxu loved reading, respected for the literati and founded school for poor and humble

赋文章。历代蜀王府都重视藏书，到了朱让栩这一代，更是将藏书楼开放，每日容纳上百读书人前去阅读、抄誊，其气宇格局可见。

饬守礼法，好学能文。蜀王府成功的家庭教育，也被皇帝看在眼里。明孝宗朱祐樘将蜀藩的治家规范在宗室中进行推广，嘉靖皇帝则将朱让栩树立楷模，题字赐建“忠孝贤良”石牌坊。

然而，世事无常，即便如明蜀王家族代代相传，即便有皇权与教育传承的加持，却依然避免不了最后结局的到来。

到了万历、崇祯年间，大明王朝阉宦当权，特务横行，江山风雨飘摇、千疮百孔。外有满清八旗虎视眈眈，内有李自成、张献忠及摇黄十三家等农民武装起于草莱。覆巢之下无完卵，作为明政权在蜀地象征的蜀王府，亦不能瓦全。

1628年，崇祯帝登大上位，随即除掉魏忠贤，试图扶大厦于将倾。

在此之前十二年，朱至澍已即蜀王位，过着太平王爷的好日子。巴蜀富饶自足，又为四塞之地，易守难攻，朱至澍因之心安，全然不知大难即将来临。

王朝兴衰似有定数。小冰河期带

families. He presided over the compilation and printing of the *Luancheng Set*, totally ninety-six volumes, including all the poems and articles of Su Zhe. Successive generations of Kings of Shu attached importance to the collection of books. In Zhu Rangxu's reign, he went further to open the library to public daily, allowing hundreds of readers to read and transcribe. This alone evidences his generosity and far-sightedness.

He was well-prepared to observe etiquette and law, and was good at learning and being able to write. The successful family education of the royal family of King of Shu also came to attention of the emperor. Emperor Xiaozong, Zhu Youtang, promoted Shu clan's family norms to other royal families; Emperor Jiajing set up Zhu Rangxu as a role model and granted a stone plaque inscribed "loyalty and filial piety, virtuous and good" to him.

However, things are unpredictable, even for the family of King of Shu, passing on from generation to generation, who was protected by imperial power and was equipped with education heritage, still cannot avoid the finale.

In the Wanli and Chongzhen eras of the Ming Dynasty, eunuchs were in power, the secret police were rampant and the regime were unstable and riddled with holes. Outside, there were Eight Banners Soldiers of Manchu coveting the sovereignty; inside, peasant rebel armies led by Li Zicheng, Zhang Xianzhong, Yao Huang and the other thirteen insurgents were in full swing. Once a nest was falling, nothing under it can remain intact. Royal Residence of King of Shu was not immune to the disaster.

In 1628, Emperor Chongzhen acceded to the throne, and he got rid of Wei Zhongxian, a powerful eunuch and tried to grasp the nettle to keep the mansion from falling down.

Twelve years prior to this change, Zhu Zhishu had assumed the throne of King of Shu and had been

来的灾荒直接导致了明王朝的巨大困窘，政权在内忧外患中左支右绌、力不从心。而在四川地区，同样是异兆频发，天灾人祸接踵而至。

崇祯登基第二年，四川大地震。

崇祯七年，叙州（宜宾）母猪洞突然发出铜鼓之鸣，并持续一整夜。这种金鼓之声，古人认为这是兵燹的先兆，实则是喀斯特溶洞地下水位上涨的声音，很可能将发大水。这一年，张献忠从湖北进攻四川。

崇祯十年闰四月，雅州（雅安）、叙州（宜宾）、建武（兴文）、泸州、越隽（治所在今西昌市）以及马湖四土司（宜宾、凉山州一带）发生地震。五月，李自成进入四川，攻陷南江、通江。

九月，龙安（平武）地震。十月，李自成军由汉中进攻广元，破昭化、剑州（剑阁）、梓潼、江油、绵竹，甚至焚烧、劫掠了成都附近的新都、郫县、金堂，围困成都二十余日。

崇祯十二年，保宁（阆中）天空中发出雷鸣之声，成都东岳庙的玉帝像无缘无故地摇动。

崇祯十三年春，全川地鸣（地震波能量形成的声音）。六月，安岳天降红雨。

living a peaceable life. Besides, the land of Sichuan is fertile and self-sufficient and the surrounding mountains renders it easy to defend and hard to attack. A peace of mind made Zhu Zhishu completely unaware of the impending catastrophe.

The rise and fall of the Dynasty seem to be predetermined. The disasters brought by Little Ice Age directly led to the Ming Dynasty's great plight and the regime trapped in the internal and external problems busied itself making ends meet. Likewise in the Sichuan area, anomalies were frequent and natural and man-made disasters came one after another.

The second year after Emperor Chongzhen ascended the throne, a huge earthquake befell on Sichuan.

In the seventh years of Chongzhen, a Sow Hole located in Xuzhou (Yibin) suddenly uttered a copper drum sound and lasted all night. This sound of drums, which the ancients believed to be the harbinger of war, was in fact the sound of rising groundwater levels in karst caves, which forebode possible great flood. In this year, Zhang Xianzhong attacked Sichuan from Hubei.

In leap April of the tenth year of Chongzhen, an earthquake raided Yazhou (Ya'an), Xuzhou (Yibin), Jianwu (Xingwen), Luzhou, Yue Jun (Xichang), and the four chieftain-governed areas of Mahu (Yibin and Liangshan area). In May, Li Zicheng charged into Sichuan and captured Nanjiang and Tongjiang.

In September, another earthquake attacked Long'an (Pingwu). In October, Li Zicheng's army aggressed Guangyuan from Hanzhong and penetrated Zhaohua, Jianzhou (Jiange), Zitong, Jiangyou, Mianzhu, and even burned and looted Xindu, Pixian and Jintang, the outskirt of Chengdu. What's more, they even besieged Chengdu for more than twenty days.

In the twelfth year of Chongzhen, sounds of thunder can be heard in the sky of Baoning (Langzhong), and the statue of the Jade Emperor

崇祯十五年，达州护城河之水变为血红，井里发出异响。

时间到了最后一年。崇祯十七年，彭县白鹿山崩裂（即今日彭州白鹿顶，在汶川大地震中也曾受到波及）。这一年，张献忠率部第五次入川，从夔门逆流而上，六月二十日攻陷重庆。此时，通往成都的门户已经洞开。

自崇祯帝登基十七年来，在四川地区类似的所谓凶兆、兵兆非常多，此处仅仅列举了一部分。古人对此的理解是“地震主兵”或者“地鸣者，伏尸流血”。以现在的观点来看，将自然现象视为凶兆、兵兆，当然是无稽之谈。但是，这些灾害造成的心理震慑却是实实在在的。

还有一些奇异现象很可能是并不存在的，比如川南的李树上长出了黄瓜（占云：李生黄瓜，民皆无家）；比如百姓家里的大米从米箕一粒粒跳出来，洒了一地——这其实是人在面临灾难时的一种集体癔症。然而，它们却真实反映出人心在此时受到的巨大震撼。

蜀中两百年无战事，固然是人民的福分。然而吊诡的是，蜀人却因此而不知兵事凶险。当灾难来临之际，上至蜀王下至普通市民，全部处于惊慌失措的状态。

at the Dongyue Temple in Chengdu shook for no apparent reason.

In the spring of the thirteenth year of, throughout Sichuan province, earth sound (sound formed by seismic wave energy) can be heard. In June, red rain fell from the sky in Anyue.

In the fifteenth year of Chongzhen, the moat of Dazhou City turned into blood red and strange sound can be heard.

In the seventeenth year of Chongzhen, the last year of Ming Dynasty, Bailu Mountain in Peng County (in today's Pengzhou, where the Wenchuan earthquake in 2008 also affected) collapsed. In this year, Zhang Xianzhong led his troops to storm Sichuan for the fifth time, beating upstream from Kui Men, and captured Chongqing on June 20th. At this time, the gateway to Chengdu was already wide open.

Seventeen years since Emperor Chongzhen ascended the throne, the so-called bad omens and military signs in the Sichuan area were very much and the above-mentioned were only a part of the long list. According to the ancient wisdom "earthquake bodes for war" or "when the earth rumbles, the bodies and bleedings are present". From the present point of view, it is, of course, nonsensical to regard natural phenomena as bad omens and military signs. However, the psychological shock caused by these disasters was real.

Some other strange phenomena probably didn't exist, e.g., the plum tree in southern Sichuan grew cucumbers (the result of divination: when cucumber grows out of a plum tree, people have no home to live); grain by grain, rice skip out of the rice basket and spill on the ground—this is actually a kind of collective hysteria in the face of disaster. However, they truly reflect the great shock to the human heart at this time.

The fact that there had been no war in Shu

这一年的农历三月十九，李自成部攻下北京城，崇祯已经上吊于煤山，整个大明王朝群龙无首。张献忠军队在四川摧枯拉朽，八月初五，献军抵达成都城下。

崇祯上吊一个月之后，有两个四川举人，一个叫杨锵一个叫刘道贞的，出面拥立蜀王朱至澍为监国。所谓监国，即帝国危急之际的临时皇帝。

这个时候，农民军虽然占领了北京，但仍然有相当大的地盘在各地藩王和地方政权的手中。只是没有了大明皇帝这个统一指挥者，他们只能各自为政，更是各怀心思。

平心而论，刘道贞的措施，不失为存亡之秋的应急之举。明代的藩王，虽然长期并不掌握地方治理的权力，但他们作为朱元璋的子孙，在当时是有着合法性和号召力的（类似虚君，平时不掌权，但一旦有社会动荡就能起到稳定人心的作用）。如果蜀王朱至澍具备雄才大略，此时振臂一呼，整合帝国残余力量，便能将乌合之众变成极富战斗能力的队伍。

但是，他能担当起这个重任吗？

territory for two hundred years was certainly a blessing for the people. However, paradoxically, the people of Shu were unaware of the danger of war. When disaster struck, all of them, from the King of Shu down to ordinary citizens, were in a state of panic.

In March 19 of the lunar calendar of 17th year of Chongzhen, Li Zicheng Department captured Beijing and Emperor Chongzhen hanged himself on the coal mountain; as a result, the entire regime was leaderless. Zhang Xianzhong's army devastated in Sichuan, and on the fifth day of that August, the army arrived at the city of Chengdu.

One month after Chongzhen's death, two Sichuan *Ju Ren*s(successful candidates in the provincial examination), one named Yang Qiang and the other Liu Daozhen, stepped forward to support Zhu Zhishu, the King of Shu, as the Supervisory State. The so-called Supervisory State is the temporary emperor of the empire in times of crisis.

At this time, although the peasant army occupied Beijing, there were still a considerable amount of territory in the hands of the feudal lords and local authorities. Without the Emperor of the Ming Dynasty as a unified commander, they could only go their own way and harbour their own agendas.

To do him a justice, Liu Daozhen's measure might be accepted as an emergency move at the time of crisis. Those vassal kings, not holding the local power for a long time, did have the legitimacy and appeal (similar to the virtual monarch, possessing no real power in peaceful times, but once there is a social upheaval, they are able to play a stabilizing effect) as they are grandchildren of Zhu Yuanzhang. If Zhu Zhishu, the King of Shu, had possessed great talents, he would have raised his arm and integrated the remnants of the empire and turned the disorganized troops into a team with great fighting ability.

But, could he live up to this heavy responsibility?

书生谋国
存亡之秋显本色

人的性格是复杂多面的，危难之际可见本色。先来看一段刘道贞的轶事，此文见于清人安士居士所著的《安士全书》。

那时刘道贞还是邛州一个没有功名的书生，有天准备杀鸡待客，鸡却忽然不见了，又欲杀鸭，鸭也躲了。刘生四处寻找，在暗处发现了那一对难兄难弟。此时，鸡正用脑袋推鸭，想让鸭出去受死，而鸭也正干着同样的事。它们为了不暴露于主人，都暗中用力较劲，却不敢发出声音。刘生见状，顿生同理之心，遂放下屠刀，并作文劝世人戒杀。

到了辛酉年（1621年）七月，刘道贞的朋友梦到文昌帝君拿着一张纸说："这是刘生所做的《戒杀文》，他今年高中了。"等到发榜，刘果然中举。

《安士全书》带有很强的佛教劝善色彩，其间也有很多历史故事，虽然不能当成信史，但也具有一定的参考价值。从中至少可以推断，刘道贞的心怀慈悲颇为人认同。

另一段史料见于清代翰林学士彭

the statecraft of a scholar can only be revealed when the state is hung by a thread

The human character is complex and multi-faceted, and in times of crisis the inherent qualities can be seen. First, let's look at an anecdote about Liu Daozhen, which is found in *The Complete Book of Anshi* written by Anshi, the householder, in the Qing Dynasty.

At that time Liu Daozhen was only a scholar without honor or achievement in Qiongzhou. One day, when he was ready to kill a chicken to entertain his guests. He found the chicken disappeared, and the he wanted to kill a duck instead, but the duck also hid. He looked around and found the pair in the dark. At that moment, the chicken was pushing the duck with its head, wanting the duck to go out and suffer death, while the duck was doing the same thing. In order not to be exposed to their masters, they both secretly exerted themselves harder and harder, but did not dare to make a sound. Seeing this, Liu Sheng was struck with empathy, so he put down his butcher's knife and wrote an essay to advise the world to abstain from killing.

In the seventh month of Xin You year (1621), Liu Daozhen's friend dreamed that Emperor Wen Chang (a god in ancient Chinese legend in charge of exam) was holding a piece of paper and said, "This is the *Abstention from Killing* written by Liu Daozhen, and he had successfully passed the exam." When the admission list was issued, Liu was indeed successful in the exam.

The *Complete Book of Anshi* has a very strong Buddhist coloring, and there are many historical stories in it, which cannot be regarded as credible history, but it has some reference value. It can at least be inferred from it that Liu Daozhen's compassionate

遵泗的《蜀碧》。说当时的邛州有旧例，凡是有人科举及第，就要为其建牌坊以作旌表，而主事者则借机骚扰民间，索取财物和劳力，让人苦不堪言。到了刘道贞登科要建旌坊时，他却因不愿让百姓受苦而决然推辞了。这跟作戒杀文的刘道贞，品性是相吻合的。

《安士全书》关于刘道贞那段文字之下，还有一段按语，阐述人与动物在面对死亡时具有同样的恐惧与哀伤："与人类当劫掠屠城之际，见父母血肉淋漓，妻孥节节支解，异乎不异？"

这段文字真是应景之极。此时的刘道贞，即将面对城破之际全成都人被屠宰的命运，不知他眼前是否浮现出了"父母血肉淋漓，妻孥节节支解"的惨状？数百年之后读史至此，很自然地就将救城救人视作刘道贞拥立朱至澍为监国的根本原因。其实在当时的成都城中，地位比他高、权力比他大的人数不胜数，而一个没有官职的读书人站出来，不可谓不是一种大担当。

一个连鸡鸭也舍不得杀的人，此时却变得如此杀伐决断，正所谓"霹雳手段，菩萨心肠"。

heart was quite recognized.

Another piece of historical material was evident in the *Shu Bi* written by Peng Zunsi, a Hanlin scholar (member of Imperial Academy who was employed as a secretary) in Qing Dynasty. It is said that in ancient Qiongzhou, a memorial gateway would be built for all who succeeded in the imperial exam. In building this gateway, the person in charge would avail himself of extracting money and manpower from the people. This harassment let the people suffer. When this entitlement was about to grant to Liu Daozhen, he summarily refused it because he didn't want to make the people suffer. The character of Liu Daozhen embodied in this anecdote was consistent with the one who wrote *Abstention from Killing*.

There is a remark under the passage about Liu Daozhen in the *Complete Book of Anshi*, which explains that human beings and animals share the same fear and sorrow when facing death, "Is there any difference between human beings and [animals] seeing their parents were drenched in blood and their wives and children were disintegrated when the looting and slaughtering a city began?"

This text is really appropriate. When Liu Daozhen was about to face the fate that all Chengdu people would be slaughtered once the city was captured, I do not know whether the daunting prospect of "their parents were drenched in blood and their wives and children were disintegrated" was floating in his mind. When we read the history, hundreds of years later, it is natural for us to understand that to save the city and the people, Liu Daozhen supported Zhu Zhishu as the Supervisory State. In fact, in the city of Chengdu at that time, there were a number of people whose social status higher than Liu Daozhen's and whose power greater than him, but none of them step up to the plate. His stepping forward was really larger than life.

A person who can't even kill a chicken and a duck had become so decisive, as the saying goes,

不过，刘道贞却没能成功，阻挠他的，也是一个好人。这个人叫刘之勃，是当时的四川巡按御史。他不仅是个好人，还是个好官。

刘之勃，陕西凤翔人，崇祯七年进士。在御史任上，曾上疏直言东厂的弊病，说一旦有刁民诬告，就会让人倾家荡产。人与人之间互相攻讦，正是东厂所喜闻乐见，可以从中取利的。以东厂的权势熏天，敢于捋虎须，足见其正直与勇气。

崇祯十五年，刘之勃巡按四川。巡按，在戏曲中有个著名的俗称——八府巡按。官不大，职位只是正七品，跟知县相当，权力却远在其上。上至藩王大臣，下至府州县官员，都要受其考察。巡按实际上是代替天子出巡，只对皇帝负责，可以直接举荐或弹劾人员。

刘道贞拥立蜀王朱至澍为监国的事发生在崇祯十七年四月，此时崇祯帝上吊殉国的消息已传至成都。一群四川官员和读书人在蜀王府中商议拥立一事时，刘之勃反应极其激烈，他跃入池中，以死反对。那么，刘之勃考虑的又是什么呢？

此时，虽然崇祯帝已死，但还有三个儿子藏在北京城（后均被多尔

apply the means “as quickly as a thunderbolt to exhibit Bodhisattva’s compassion”.

However, Liu Daozhen didn’t make it, and the one who stood in his way was also a good man whose name was Liu Zhibo, the Imperial Inspector of Sichuan at that time. He was not only a good man, but also a good official.

Liu Zhibo, a native of Fengxiang, Shaanxi Province, was a *Jin Shi* scholar, or the Imperial Examination Graduates in the seventh year of Chongzhen era. During his tenure as an imperial censor, he once submitted a petition to speak frankly about the shortcomings of the East Chamber(secrete police organization in Ming Dynasty), saying that once an unruly person falsely accuses a person, the accused will lose all his properties to defend himself. People attacking each other is exactly what the East Chamber is happy to see and can profit from. That Liu Zhibo had the nerve to challenge the powerful East Chamber was like to stroke the tiger’s whiskers, which shows his integrity and courage.

In the fifteenth year of Chongzhen, Liu Zhibo inspected in Sichuan. His position title, *Xun An* (inspector) is not eminent, only the seventh grade in the corridor of power, with the county equivalent. There is a famous popular name in the ancient Chinese drama—the eighth grade *Xun An*. However, the power of a *Xun An* is far superior over the county magistrate. Officials up to the ministers of the feudal lords or down to the prefecture-level are subject to his vetting and appraisal. This jobholder, actually a representative of the emperor and only responsible for the emperor himself, can directly recommend or impeach the personnel.

It was April of the seventeenth year that Liu Daozhen acclaimed the King of Shu, Zhu Zhishu, as the Supervisory State, and at this time the news of the death of the Emperor Chongzhen had been spread to Chengdu. A group of Sichuan officials and scholars

衮杀害）。本着忠于大明江山的立场，在崇祯的三个儿子尤其是太子还在世的情况下，刘之勃自然要反对蜀王另立江山。

藩王充作临时皇帝，固然可以凝聚人心，但是，处于此情此境，藩王想得更多的可能是登上大位，取得最高权力，而并非国家的安危、百姓的福祉（后来由诸多藩王建立的南明王朝的作为，正说明了这点）。况且，全国有那么多的藩王，他们声气不通、异心各存，一旦蜀王开了这个头，谁又会服他？大家都是朱元璋的龙子龙孙，谁也不鸟谁，到时不知几人称帝、几人称王？

作为明王朝的高级知识分子和有相当地位的官员，他考虑问题的角度自然跟刘道贞这样半官半绅的举人又有所不同。

在刘之勃的拼死反对之下，拥立监国一事搁浅了，剩下的选择只有死守，但此时人心溃散、军资匮乏，何堪再战？！

其实，不是没有人提醒过朱至澍要早做准备。这一年的正月，张献忠刚攻破夔门，华阳县令沈云祚就向蜀王奉上防御之策，却不被采纳。

沈云祚又劝说蜀王，将王府的

gathered in the Royal Residence of King of Shu to discuss the matter. Liu Zhibo’s disagreement was so fierce that he even jumped into the pool to make his case. So what was his consideration on this matter that he’d rather die in defending?

At this time, although Emperor Chongzhen died, his three sons were hiding in Beijing (all later were killed by Dorgon). In the spirit of loyalty to the the Ming Dynasty, Liu Zhibo naturally opposed to the King of Shu as the Supervisory State when Chongzhen’s three sons, especially the crown prince, were still alive.

With a vassal king acting as a temporary emperor, of course, can be a cohesive force, but, under this situation, the vassal king may think more than a temporary position, or the safety of the country and the well-being of the people but ascension to the throne to obtain the highest power. (The establishment of the southern Ming Dynasty, set up under the support of the vassal kings, illustrated this point). Moreover, there were so many feudal lords in the country, and they were not in harmony with each other. Who would be convinced by the King of Shu once he started to proclaim himself the Supervisory State? Everyone was Zhu Yuanzhang’s descendant and no one gave a damn about anyone. When one of them called himself emperor, how many others will follow suit?

As a senior intellectual of the Ming Dynasty and an official of considerable status, Liu Zhibo naturally considered issues from a different perspective than a *Ju Ren*, a half-official, half-squire like Liu Daozhen.

Under Liu Zhibo’s desperate opposition, the establishment of the Supervisory State was shelved. The only remaining option was to defend to death, but at this time the hearts and minds of the people were scattered and military funds were short of. How can they fight again?

In fact, it was not that no one had reminded Zhu Zhishu to make early preparations. In the first month of this year, when Zhang Xianzhong had just

财帛拿出来充作军饷，奖励士卒，也被朱至澍拒绝了。蜀王是没钱吗？早年间四川曾有传言，说蜀王府里藏有鸿宝之书，可以炼制黄金白银——此事非真，但反映了民间对于蜀王拥有财富的看法。蜀藩之富甲于诸藩，只是，朱至澍舍不得。

直到张献忠一路望风披靡，从重庆杀向成都，朱至澍这才慌了神。他能想到的就是跑，往云南跑，连刘之勃也挡不住。六月十三，朱至澍带着后宫与辎重开溜，却在城门被挡了下来。士兵们群情激愤，甚至抢掠财物、骚扰宫妇。

曾经高高在上的王，说话也不再管用，连守门的小卒子都可以不听从了。朱至澍不明白一个隐藏着的规则：权力越大，占有资源越多，则责任越大。这条规则不是总会起作用，但是，当社会被强制刷新、重回出厂设置时，它就显示出力量。

道义已失，规矩已无，这才是亡天下的先兆，比什么地震地鸣、李生黄瓜要紧太多。即便没有后来的屠城，成都城变成人间地狱也指日可待。

终于想起沈云祚的话了，朱至澍这时拿出钱财募兵守城，但接连三日无人响应。新上任的四川巡抚龙文光

broken through Kui Men Pass, and Shen Yunzuo, the magistrate of Huayang County, offered the King of Shu a defensive strategy, but it was not adopted.

Shen Yunzuo also persuaded the King of Shu to spend the royal family's wealth on soldier's pays and rewards and provisions. This suggestion was also refused by Zhu Zhishu. Had the King of Shu no money? In the early years, there were rumors in Sichuan that the Royal Residence of King of Shu hid a precious book, which can be refined into gold and silver—this was not true, but reflected the views of the people on the wealth of the King of Shu. Shu clan's wealth was more than any other royal family, and the only obstacle prevented it from being used was Zhu Zhishu's reluctance to let it be spent.

Until Zhang Xianzhong fought and killed all the way to Chengdu from Chongqing, Zhu Zhishu panicked. All he could think of was to run to Yunnan, even Liu Zhibo could not stop him. On June 13, Zhu Zhishu escaped with his harem and provisions, but was blocked at the city gate. The soldiers were furious and even looted the properties and harassed the palace women.

The once high and mighty king had no authority at this moment, and even the small-time gate guards disobeyed his command. Zhu Zhishu did not understand a hidden rule: the more power and the resources you possess, the more responsibility you have. This rule does not always work, but its effect can be revealed when society is forced to refresh and to reset.

That morality, justice and rules are no longer existed is the harbinger of the death of a regime, which matters more than the earthquake and earth sound or the "cucumber grows out of a plum tree". Even without the subsequent massacre, Chengdu would soon become hell on earth.

Finally remembering the words of Shen Yunzuo, Zhu Zhishu, until this time, decided to take out money to raise troops to defend the city, but three days in a row no one responded. The newly appointed Governor of Sichuan, Long Wenguang, relying on

靠着三千援兵，主持守城大局，而城中兵员不满一万。见到护城河水已干涸，龙文光紧急派人引都江堰之水。

three thousand reinforcements, presided over the defence of the city, while the total soldiers in the city were less than ten thousand. Seeing that the water in the moat had dried up, Long Wenguang urgently sent people to draw water from Dujiangyan.

宫阙作土 书生意气不死

The palace crumbled into earth, but a scholar's spirit will never die

八月初五，成都城已被六十万大军团团围住，攻防战开始了。

张献忠军取来数丈长的大木，从中剖开，放火药于其中，再用布帛缠裹，向城墙下运输。巡按刘之勃等官员身处一线，激励士兵，打退了进攻。

成都北、东、南三面被锦江环绕，这是唐代高骈筑罗城、改道郫江而形成的军事防御格局，最为薄弱的西面则成为张献忠军的进攻重点。献军强迫被俘的百姓抬着棺材，装着上万斤炸药，放进锦江楼下城墙边事先掘好的洞穴中，再放好引线，上面盖土敷平。

初九日黎明，突然一声巨响，建于唐代的锦江楼飞上半空，尘土迷了人眼，瓦木砖石天上乱飞。当漫天的尘埃落定时，城墙已塌，而引来充实护城河的都江堰之水刚刚到达。

大军涌入，屠城三日。

朱至澍无路可走，投入其五世

On the fifth day of August, the city of Chengdu had been surrounded by an army of 600,000 men, and the battle of attack and defense had begun.

Zhang Xianzhong's army took large logs several *zhang* long, split them open, put gunpowder in, wrapped them in cloth and silk, and transported them under the city wall. The Imperial Inspector Liu Zhibo and other officials were on the front line, motivating the soldiers and repelling the attack.

The north, east and south sides of Chengdu were encircled by the Jin River, a military defensive formation taken shape in Tang Dynasty when Gao Pian built Luo Cheng and diverted the Pi River, the west side being the weakest on which Zhang Xianzhong's army focused their attack. The captured people were forced to carry coffins loaded with tens of thousands of pounds of explosives and to put them into a cave which was dug in advance under the city wall by the Jin River. Next, they installed fuses and covered the cave by soil.

At dawn on the ninth day, a loud bang burst suddenly before the Jinjiang Tower which was built in the Tang Dynasty flew up into the air. Dust and dirt blindfolded people's eyes, while tiles and masonry splattered in the sky. When the dust settled, the city wall had collapsed, and the water from Dujiangyan which was induced to fill the moat had just arrived.

The army poured in and slaughtered the city for

祖朱让栩吟咏过的那口八角井中。而此际时维农历八月，簇拥在井边的菊花刚刚开放。追随他一同投井的，还有周贵妃等嫔妃、宫女，以及他的弟弟、太平王朱至渌。

“愿为五陵轻薄儿，生于贞观开元时。斗鸡走犬过一生，天地存亡两不知。”王安石的这首诗，不知是不是符合末代蜀王朱至澍投井之时的心态。如果生于太平年代，朱至澍最坏的际遇也不过是做一位爱吃爱玩还有点文艺情结的普通王爷，但身当乱世，他不仅没有朱元璋的神武，没有朱椿的持重，甚至也不明白：自己的锦衣玉食乃至身家性命，都跟守不守得住这座城息息相关。他用自己的短视与自私，为这出大剧画上一个悲凉又荒诞的句号。

蜀王之死让人叹惋，然而让人心生敬意的死国难者却不绝于书。

three days.

Zhu Zhishu had no way out and threw himself into the octagonal well that his fifth ancestor, Zhu Rangxu, had chanted a poem about. At this time in the eighth month of the lunar calendar, clusters of chrysanthemums around the well had just bloomed. Following him into the well were Noble Consort Zhou and other concubines, court ladies, as well as his younger brother, King Taiping, Zhu Zhilu.

“I would rather be a dandy of the eminences in the Five Tombs, born at the golden age of Zhen Guan and Kai Yuan. Spending my life in cockfight and dog-walking, not caring the ups and downs of the heaven and earth.”Whether the poem of Wang Anshi reflected the mindset of Zhu Zhishu, the last King of Shu, when he threw himself into the well, remained unknown. If born in the era of peace, Zhu Zhishu’s worst destination was just to be an ordinary king, fond of food, merrymaking and a bit of literary pursuit, but when in the chaotic times, he did not have Zhu Yuanzhang’s martial arts, nor Zhu Chun’s prudence, and even did not understand his wealth and prosperity and even his life were closely related with the city. His short-sightedness and selfishness signed a sad and absurd full stop to the grand drama.

The death of the King of Shu is lamentable, however, the other martyrs of the kingdom whose death wins people’s respect are recorded endless in the books.

《蜀难叙略》藏本　何大江 摄

A copy of *A Brief Account of the Shu Calamity*. (Photographer: He Dajiang)

曾经劝谕过蜀王毁家纾难的华阳县令沈云祚，在城破后被囚于大慈寺。张献忠派人送去食物，并以高官厚禄相诱。沈破口呵斥：“我恨不能咬下你们的肉，怎么会吃你们的东西？！”沈云祚是崇祯年间进士，本长身玉立、风雅非常，此时怒气充盈、须发皆张，令看守者大惊失色。张献忠知道劝降无用，才下令杀了他。为了保留其骨血，家人带着他五岁的儿子沈荀蔚在围城前逃入邛崃、洪雅一带山中。沈荀蔚成年后，一字一泪写下《蜀难叙略》，记录了十余年所见山河破碎、人民涂炭，也成为研究明末四川史最为宝贵的一手资料。

Shen Yunzuo, the magistrate of Huayang County who had once advised the King of Shu to take out his household property to provide financial relief, was imprisoned in Daci Temple after the city was broken down. Zhang Xianzhong sent people to give him food and lured him with offers of high-ranking posts and lucrative positions. Shen rained curses: “I hate to be unable to bite off your meat, how can I eat your stuff?!” Shen Yunzuo was a *Jin Shi* in Chongzhen era, slim and elegant, but at this time his anger was so immense that all his hairs and beards ruffled. The guards were shocked out of wit. Zhang Xianzhong knew it was futile to persuade him to surrender, so he ordered him to be killed. In order to preserve his progeny, his five-year-old son Shen Xunwei were secretly taken away and fled into the mountains around Qionglai and Hongya before the siege. After Shen Xunwei became of age, he wrote *Narration on Shu Disaster*, which recorded what he saw in more than ten years of the collapsed city, the suffering of the people, and it also became the most valuable first-hand information for the study of the history of Sichuan at the end of the Ming Dynasty.

刘之勃被抓捕之后，张献忠给了他两个选择：降，当宰相；不降，凌迟处死。刘之勃的答复是：“多剐我一刀，少杀我一个百姓。”直到绑在蜀王府端礼门前，被箭射成刺猬，头也没低下。

After Liu Zhibo was captured, Zhang Xianzhong gave him two options: surrender and become the prime minister; not surrender and the death of a thousand cuts. Liu Zhibo’s reply was: “Give me one more cut and kill one less people.” His head was never lowered even when he was tied up in front of the Duanli Gate and was shot into a hedgehog by arrows,

刘道贞更为传奇。当成都沦陷，张献忠部的一个参将带兵到了邛州时，刘道贞用计杀了他，再弃家逃到汉族跟少数民族杂居的沈黎（四川汉源县），激励黎州指挥使曹勋起兵。当张献忠的军队扫荡至此时，遭遇顽强抵抗。雅州小关山一战，刘道贞大

The whereabouts of Liu Daozhen was even more legendary. When the city of Chengdu fell, one of Zhang Xianzhong’s generals brought his troops to Qiongzhou and Liu Daozhen, by design, killed him and then abandoned his house and fled to Shenli (Hanyuan County, Sichuan Province), where Han Chinese and ethnic minorities lived together. He managed to rouse Cao Xun, the commander of Lizhou, to start an army. When Zhang Xianzhong’s army swept to this area, it was met with strong

获全胜，斩敌千余，献军从此再也不敢迈足严道（四川荥经县）以南。能想象吗，这就是二十多年前那个连鸡鸭也不忍心杀的书生做出的功业？

第二年正月，刘道贞派儿子刘睽度带兵向北推进，试图收复家乡邛州。献军抓了刘道贞的妻子王氏，刀架在脖子上让她劝降儿子，王氏大骂而惨被分尸，随后全家百余口遇害，睽度也死于兵马之中。刘道贞闻讯狂吐鲜血，在叮嘱同袍曹勋“无堕前功”之后，带着深切的遗恨辞世。

刘之勃愿以一刀剐换一人命，自然是与虎谋皮，典型的书呆子思维。以世俗之眼光来看，沈云祚、刘道贞又何尝不呆？然而，呆中自有意气，以上所举三人，皆自知必死而慨然以赴，以大义大勇成就了人格的终极完善。

1644年，在历史上是一个非常特殊的年份。这一年是大明王朝的最后一年，崇祯十七年；是南明弘光小朝廷建立的年份；是李自成大顺政权的永昌元年；是清军入关后第一个皇帝爱新觉罗·福临的顺治元年。

在各方势力的角逐中，张献忠锣鼓登场。1644年，也是大西政权的大顺元年。这一年冬十一月，张献忠在成都登基，建立大西国，以蜀王府为

resistance. In the battle of Xiaoguan Mountain in Yazhou, Liu Daozhen won a great victory, beheading more than a thousand enemies. Since then, Zhang Xianzhong's army never dared to step south of Yan Dao (Xingjing County, Sichuan) again. Can you imagine that this is the achievement of the scholar who could not even bear to kill chickens and ducks more than 20 years ago?

In the first month of the following year, Liu Daozhen sent his son, Liu Kuidu, to advance northward with his troops in an attempt to recover his hometown, Qiongzhou. Zhang Xianzhong's army captured Liu Daozhen's wife, Wang, and put a knife to her neck, forcing her to urge her son's surrender. Wang responded with curses and was brutally mutilated, and more than a hundred family members were killed later on, while Liu Kuidu also died in the battle. After Liu Daozhen heard the news, he vomited blood profusely. On his death bed, he exhorted his comrade Cao Xun "do not make our previous achievements for nothing", and then died with deep hatred.

Liu Zhibo would rather bear one more cut to save a life. Apparently, it is a Faustian bargain, typical of the nerd thinking. In the worldly-wise eyes, weren't Shen Yunzuo and Liu Daozhen nerds? However, there is a method to their madness. The three people, all knowing that they must die, achieved the ultimate perfection of their character with great virtue and courage.

The year 1644 was a very special year in history. It was the last year of the Ming Dynasty, namely the seventeenth year of Chongzhen era; the year of the establishment of the Hongguang regime, a small court of the Southern Ming Dynasty; the first year of Yongchang of Li Zicheng's Dashun Regime; and also the first year of Shunzhi, Aisin Gioro Fulin, the first emperor after the Qing army entered the Shanhaiguan Pass.

Zhang Xianzhong made his debut in 1644, the first year of Dashun under the Daxi Regime. In

王宫，改正殿承运殿为承天殿，意为其天下乃承天而得。

不过，他拥有蜀王府的时间也不过一年多。1646年初，清和硕肃亲王豪格偕吴三桂率满汉大军进剿四川。张见大势已去，决定放弃成都。

1630年张献忠在陕西起事，十六年的时间里辗转多省，他捣毁过朱元璋的祖坟，杀过襄王、贵阳王、楚王、瑞王等明代藩王，也多次被打得投降又反水。在成都建立政权，是他人生中最为高光的时刻，蜀王府便是这一刻最重要的象征。但是，现在有人要将它夺去，怎么办？

这是因绝望而产生的疯狂。烧吧，不能带走的都烧掉；得不到的，必须毁了它。撤离成都之前，张献忠杀了妻妾和幼子，捣毁国库，并将城内外的民居、寺庙和衙门付之一炬。但是，以砖石建成的蜀王府不好烧，尤其是那两根盘龙大柱不好烧。蜀王府旧址曾是后蜀皇宫，那两根石柱则是蜀宫旧物，名“擎天柱”，上有精美石雕。

不过，对于一个安心要摧毁一切的人，又有什么能阻挡他呢？张献忠让士兵在石柱上缠了数十层棉纱，并浸以油脂。三日之后，石柱已经吸饱了油，此时再点一把火，便有漫天的

November of this year, Zhang Xianzhong ascended the throne in Chengdu and established the Daxi Kingdom, taking the Royal Residence of King of Shu as his royal palace and changing the main hall, Cheng Yun Hall, to Cheng Tian Hall, which meant that his sovereign was obtained from the heavenly god.

However, he owned the Royal Residence for just over a year. In early 1646, Prince Haoge of Heshuo and Wu Sangui of the Qing Dynasty led armies of Manchu and Han Chinese to invade Sichuan. Seeing that the tide had turned against him, Zhang decided to abandon Chengdu.

In 1630, Zhang Xianzhong started a rebellion in Shaanxi, and over the course of 16 years he moved from province to province, destroying the ancestral tomb of Zhu Yuanzhang, killing feudal lords such as the King of Xiang, the King of Guiyang, the King of Chu, and the King of Rui of Ming Dynasty, and was also beaten to the point of surrendering and then turning back on himself on many occasions. Establishing power in Chengdu was the most glorious moment in his life, and the Royal Residence of King of Shu was the most important symbol of this moment. But now someone wanted to take it away, what would he do?

Out of despair, his insanity was born. All that cannot be taken away must be burned out; all that cannot be obtained must be destroyed. Before evacuating Chengdu, Zhang Xianzhong killed his wives, concubines and young sons, destroyed the treasury, and torched all the houses, temples and government offices inside and outside the city. However, the Royal Residence of King of Shu, which was built of stones, was not easy to burn, especially the two large pillars with dragons. The Royal Residence of King of Shu Palace was built on the old site of the Later Shu and the two stone pillars, whose name were “Pillars Buttressing the Sky”, belonged to the Later Shu’s Palace, with beautiful stone carvings.

However, for a man who had his mind set up to destroy everything, what could stop him? Zhang

烟焰。

大火烧了整整一天一夜，这两根有着七百年历史的盘龙柱终于断裂了，宫殿化为灰烬。经过大浩劫的蜀王府，仅仅剩下金水河上的三座石桥，以及桥南的石狮子、红照壁部分残垣等少量遗物，时为1646年阴历八月。

在蜀王府灰飞烟灭之前，它的主人们也大多已变成了灰与泥。蜀王投井了，但张献忠并没有放过这个家族的残存者。追杀极为严酷，深山老林也绝不放过。大慈寺因为收容、藏匿逃亡的宗室，千余寺僧被屠。蜀王世子被抓捕后，张献忠本想利用他，先封了个太平公，过了几个月又杀掉。

经过一系列的收捕，自朱椿就藩始至朱至澍投井至，在蜀地延续了二百五十四年的这一支明代皇室绝嗣，共历十世十三王。

朱元璋日理万机，却也在子孙如何取名一事上花了不少心思。他为儿子们的后代世系亲拟了字辈，各20字，甚至连子孙后代名字最后一个字所用的偏旁都做了规定。蜀王一系自朱椿以下，字辈为：悦友申宾让，承宣奉至平，懋进深滋益，端居务穆清。然而，这个字辈仅传了九

Xianzhong had his soldiers wrap dozens of layers of cotton gauze fabric around the stone pillars and soak them in grease. Three days later, the stone pillars had already absorbed the oil, and when a fire was lit at this time, there were roaring flames of smoke.

The fire burned for a whole day and night, and finally the two 700-year-old dragon pillars broke, and the palace turned into ashes. After the catastrophe of the Royal Residence, only the three stone bridges over the Jinshui River, as well as the stone lions by the south side of the bridge and the small number of remnants of the Red Screen Wall were left. It was the lunar August of 1646.

Before the Royal Residence went up in smoke, most of its masters had also been turned into ashes and mud. The King of Shu threw himself into a well, but Zhang Xianzhong did not spare the remnants of this family. The pursuit was extremely harsh, and no stone unturned. More than a thousand monks of Daci Temple were slaughtered for sheltering and hiding the fleeing clan members. After the capture of the son of the King of Shu, Zhang Xianzhong had wanted to utilize him, and first conferred him as Lord of Peace, and killed him after a few months.

After a series of arrests, since Zhu Chun started the clan to Zhu Zhishu threw himself to the well, in the course of 254 years, this branch of the Ming Dynasty royal heir, a total of ten generations of thirteen kings, came to an end.

Zhu Yuanzhang had his hands full with day-to-day business, but also found time in naming his children and grandchildren. He prepared 20 Chinese characters for his descendants, and even decided the *Pian Pang* (the left and right side of a split Chinese character, often the key [radical] and phonetic) of the last word of their first name. From the first King of Shu, Zhu Chun on, the following words were to be used generation by generation sequentially: 悦(Yue) 友(You) 申(Shen) 宾(Bin) 让(Rang), 承(Cheng) 宣(Xuan) 奉(Feng) 至(Zhi) 平(Ping), 懋(Mao) 进(Jin) 深(Shen) 滋(Zi) 益(Yi), 端(Duan) 居(Ju) 务(Wu)

代就戛然而止，连字辈谱的一半都不到。

当年的成都城中，还有永川王府、内江王府、德阳王府、石泉王府、汶川王府、庆符王府和南川王府等七座郡王府。它们的命运跟蜀王府一样，皆化为土。

“陋室空堂，当年笏满床；衰草枯杨，曾为歌舞场。”《红楼梦》里甄士隐的唱词，似乎是为人世间所有繁华家族所作的注解。

穆(Mu)清(Qing). However, this lineage was only passed on for nine generations and then came to an abrupt end, less than half of the words being used.

In the city of Chengdu, there were seven County Royal Residences, including the Royal Residence of Yongchuan, Neijiang, Deyang, Shiquan, Wenchuan, Qingfu and Nanchuan. Their fates, same as that of the Royal Residence of King of Shu, turned into dirt.

“The empty room used to be full of *Hu*s (in ancient China, when ministers had an audience with the emperor, a piece of flat wood or jade or ivory was used to write down what they were going to say, and at the same time record what the emperor commanded. This flat wood or jade or ivory was called *Hu*, symbolizing here as power)in those days; the decaying grass and withered poplars were once an arena of performance of song and dance.” In *Dream of the Red Chamber*, Zhen Shiyin’s lyrics seemed to be a commentary on all the prosperous families in the world.

石龙石虎
The Stone Dragon and Stone Tiger

彭山江口镇，曾经是万军厮杀的古战场。

江面光滑如缎，却暗藏杀机。1646年秋季的一天，从成都出发的数千艘战舰顺着府河来到这里，刚刚汇入岷江，就被一支带火的箭扎在木船上，然后是无数支箭。火，遮住了天空。不可一世的八大王张献忠，在这里遭遇了人生最大的败仗——战船尽毁，船上无数的金银珠贝也沉入江底。

而在岷江东面一千米外的山上，一条石龙和一头石虎，正冷眼看着这一切。

Jiangkou Town, Pengshan, was once an ancient battlefield where thousands of soldiers fought.

The river's surface smooth as satin, yet deadly dangers hide beneath it. One day in the autumn of 1646, thousands of warships set out from Chengdu, following the Fu River to this spot. As they merged into the Min River, a fire arrow struck one of the wooden ships, followed by countless more. Fire covered the sky. The invincible Zhang Xianzhong, the self-proclaimed "the king of scoundrels", met his greatest defeat here—his warships were destroyed, and countless treasures of gold, silver, and jewels sank to the river's bottom.

Meanwhile, on a mountain one kilometer east of the Min River, a stone dragon and a stone tiger looked coldly upon the scene, witnessing everything.

江口沉银：阻击八大王全能自恋梦

The Legend of the Jiangkou Sunken Treasure:Thwarting the Omnipotent Narcissistic Dream of the Eight big King

明末童谣

石龙对石虎，金银万万五。
谁人识得破，买尽成都府。

A Nursery Rhyme of the late Ming Dynasty

A stone dragon marks the ancient battlefield with A stone tiger,
Where countless taels of gold and silver buried in the river.
Whoever see through this riddle,
can extract enough wealth to buy every mansions in Chengdu,
That is foretold and to bestow.

江口古战场遗址，江底是当年张献忠丢下的巨大宝藏　何建军 摄
The Jiangkou ancient battlefield site lies beneath the river, hiding the enormous treasure discarded by Zhang Xianzhong. (Photographer: He Jianjun)

这首关于“江口沉银”传说的童谣，在四川彭山一带流传了数百年。童谣涉及一笔巨大的财富，而附着其上的文物价值与研究价值则更是难以估量。

石龙、石虎起到的是一个标识的作用——是破解藏宝图的关键。在这类藏宝和寻宝的故事里，不穿凿附会才是异事，然而神奇的是，这个世界上居然真的有着“石龙对石虎”。尤为神奇的是，在“石龙对石虎”不远处的岷江水底，竟然真的埋藏着数量巨大的金银。江口沉银这台牵动人心数百年的历史大戏，主人公是明末风云

For hundreds of years, the nursery rhyme of great fortune known as “The Sunken Silver at Jiangkou” spread throughout the Pengshan region of Sichuan province. It involved a vast treasure with priceless artifacts and research value attached to it.

The rhyme revolves around two iconic symbols: the Stone Dragon and the Stone Tiger. They hold the key to unlocking the fabled treasure map. In a world filled with tales of hidden riches and daring adventurers, the existence of these myth makings seems probable. Yet, against all odds, a wondrous truth emerges—the Stone Dragon and the Stone Tiger are real. Not far from the sight of these mythical creatures, lies the flowing waters of the Min River, and submerged beneath its surface lies a trove of untold gold and silver. The Jiangkou Sunken

人物张献忠以及他的对手、明参将杨展。关于张献忠，正史、野史中的记载浩若烟海，而杨展却多不为人所知。

Silver, a historical epic that has captivated hearts for centuries, centers around two main characters: Zhang Xianzhong, a big gun of the late Ming Dynasty, and his nemesis, Yang Zhan, a lesser-known Ming General. Zhang Xianzhong's story is like an ocean of records, found in both official historical accounts and wild tales spun by the masses. On the other hand, Yang Zhan, a brave and loyal general, played a vital but overlooked role.

阻击张献忠
火烧江口

府河绕过老成都城北垣，在合江亭会合南河之后，南行六七十千米，便遇到了同样北来而江面更为宽阔的岷江。与岷江合流，继续南行二百余千米，在宜宾汇入金沙河，折而向东，成为长江主干道。对于四面环山的成都平原，乃至更为广阔的四川盆地来说，这是突破崇山峻岭的阻隔，进入广阔的长江中下游地区的一条便捷通道。

当年的张献忠，也希望通过这条水路去往江汉地区。但是，他的想法在刚进入岷江干流时就破灭了。府河汇入岷江之处，便是已有两千多年历史的江口古镇（今日行政区划为眉山市彭山区江口街道）。古蜀国灭亡之际，末代开明王便在此地陨首。江口

Intercepting Zhang Xianzhong
Setting Jiangkou ablaze

The Fu River, winding its way around the northern walls of the old city of Chengdu, joined forces with the Nan River at Hejiangting. Continuing south for about sixty to seventy kilometers, it encountered the mighty Min River, which flowed wider than any other river in the region. Joined by the Min River, it continued its southern journey for over 200 kilometers, merging with the Jinsha River in Yibin before turning eastward to become the main artery of the Yangtze River. For the Chengdu Plain, surrounded by mountains on all sides, and even for the wider Sichuan Basin, this river system acted as a breakthrough, allowing a convenient passage through the towering peaks and into the vast regions of the middle and lower reaches of the Yangtze River.

Back in those days, Zhang Xianzhong also desired to travel to the Jianghan region through this waterway. However, his aspirations were shattered as soon as he entered the main stream of the Min River. It was at the confluence of the Fu River with the Min River that he encountered Jiangkou, an ancient town with a history of over two thousand years (now located in the Jiangkou Street of Pengshan District in Meishan City). During the downfall of the ancient

古镇地势狭长，一条五里长的街道贯穿全镇。因为地处要津，历来便是岷江上的重要集散码头。1646年的秋天，数千艘战舰出现在江口水面上。大船上的张献忠惴惴不安。这几年一路攻城拔寨，顺风顺水，先是在凤阳刨了朱元璋的祖坟，又在武昌府长江里淹死楚王朱华奎，再沿长江逆流而上攻克重庆、杀了瑞王朱常浩，在成都逼得蜀王朱至澍跳井，自己做了大西王，立着名目、变着花样杀人，过足了瘾。

然而，一个曾是俘虏的明朝参将杨展，却跟自己过不去，不仅收复了川南诸府县，兵锋还直指成都，当初为什么不抓住他时就一刀杀了呢？祸不单行的是，皇太极长子、清和硕肃亲王豪格正带着纵横天下的八旗兵逼进四川。曾有算命者告诉张献忠，从今年开始要走三年的背运，唯有躲入深山方可避免。那就走吧，到武当山当道士去，过几年出山，老子又是一条好汉。当然，这些年在成都捞的钱要统统裹走，大不了还可以当个富翁吧。

宁静的江面上，突然传来杀声震天。不知从哪儿冒出来的战船，堵住了岷江与府河合流后刚刚变宽的江

Shu Kingdom, its last ruler Kaiming met his tragic end in this very place. Jiangkou was a narrow and elongated town, with a five-Li long street running through its entirety. Due to its strategic location, it had always been an important hub for transportation and trade along the Min River. In the autumn of 1646, thousands of warships appeared on the surface of Jiangkou's waters. Zhang Xianzhong felt a sense of unease aboard his large vessel. Over the past few years, he had conquered cities and strongholds one after another, enjoying a string of successes. He desecrated the ancestral tomb of Zhu Yuanzhang in Fengyang, drowned Prince Zhu Huakui of Chu in the Yangtze River in Wuchang. He stormed upstream along the Yangtze River, conquering Chongqing and killing the Prince of Rui, Zhu Changhao. In Chengdu, he pushed the King of Shu, Zhu Zhishu, to his breaking point, forcing him to jump into a well. Zhang Xianzhong proclaimed himself the Great King of the West, indulging in a spree of killings, finding delight in creative and brutal methods of execution. His thirst for power and bloodshed knew no bounds.

However, there was one Ming general, Yang Zhan, who had once been a captive by Zhang Xianzhong's army. He held a deep grudge and not only managed to reclaim the various provinces and counties in southern Sichuan but also directed his forces towards Chengdu. Why didn't Zhang Xianzhong seize the opportunity to kill him outright when he had the chance? To make matters worse, Heshuo Su Prince Hao Ge, the eldest son of Emperor Taizong of Qing, was leading the mighty Eight Banners troops, approaching Sichuan with an iron grip. An oracle had warned Zhang Xianzhong that he would face three years of misfortune starting from this year and that the only way to avoid it was by hiding deep in the mountains. "So be it," he thought, "I'll become a Taoist on Wudang Mountain, lay low for a few years, and then emerge as a heroic figure

面。一支箭，尾部带火，射在木舷上，一支接着一支。很快，整艘大船烧了起来。烟火中，无数小舸蜂拥而至，最前面是一座铁塔一般的剪影，那正是让人心惊胆战的杨展。只听得火铳响起一声，自己这边的前锋就倒下一名。只见那座铁塔跳上江岸，手一挥，无数支箭镞飞来，无数道火焰飞来。舰队撤退不及，前面燃烧着的船又点燃了后面的船，整个舰队都燃起来了。宽阔的岷江水面变成了一片火海，将江口镇的天空烧得滚烫。

完了，船烧了，破了，沉了。这么多年搜刮的金银，牵连无数人丧身的金银，统统掉入了江底，几乎算得上是一无所有了。这应该是自行军凤阳、武昌、夔州、重庆、成都以来，遭遇的最大败仗吧。从江口败回成都的张献忠，变得更为疯狂。毁灭，毁灭，还是毁灭。只有毁灭，才能平息心中的怒火；只有毁灭，才能昭示存在的意义。看懂了这一点，就不难明白，张献忠在放弃成都之时，为什么要烧焚蜀王宫，为什么要花那么大的力气来做损人不利己的事。

once again." Of course, he planned to take all the wealth he had accumulated in Chengdu with him. At worst, he could live as a wealthy man.

The serene surface of the river suddenly erupted with the thunderous sound of battle cries. Out of nowhere, a fleet of warships emerged, blocking the widened junction of the Min River and the Fu River. Arrows, engulfed in flames, soared through the air, striking the wooden hulls. One after another, the ships caught fire, consumed by the spreading flames. Amidst the smoke and fire, countless smaller boats swarmed towards the scene. Leading the charge was the silhouette of a towering figure that resembled an iron tower—none other than the fearsome Yang Zhan. The sound of a musket echoed, and a vanguard soldier by Zhang Xianzhong's side fell to the deck. The iron tower figure leapt onto the riverbank, waving his hand. Arrows and spear-tipped projectiles filled the sky, accompanied by a barrage of flaming arrows. The fleet had no time to react. The burning ships in the front ignited those behind them, engulfing the entire fleet in a raging inferno. The once broad surface of the Min River transformed into a sea of fire, turning the sky above Jiangkou town scorching hot.

The flames wrecked the ship, shattering it to pieces, sinking everything aboard. Years of plundered gold and silver, wealth that claimed countless lives, all lost to the depths of the river. This was perhaps the biggest defeat since Zhang Xianzhong's military campaign from Fengyang, Wuchang, Kuizhou, Chongqing, to Chengdu. Returning from his defeat at Jiangkou to Chengdu, Zhang Xianzhong descended into even greater madness. Destruction, destruction, and more destruction. Only through destruction could he quench the fire raging in his heart; only through destruction could he find meaning in his existence. Understanding this, it becomes clear why Zhang Xianzhong, upon abandoning Chengdu, chose to burn down the Shu Palace and expend so much effort in actions that were good to none but worse to himself.

川南一柱
武探花杨展

张献忠的对手杨展，在历史上没有十分显赫的名声，但实在是一个传奇人物。

杨展是四川嘉定（今乐山）人，身材魁伟，长于骑射。进京应试武科的途中，遇到拦路的强盗，他一点也不惊惶，而是笑谈着约箭。百步之外，杨展一箭射破树干，强人大惊失色，拜别而去。

到了考场，题目是驯服一匹悍马。这匹马是挽马，归一权宦所有。挽马身高、肩宽、力大，军中往往用于牵引辎重、运送物质，而不适于骑乘，此马更是因凶狠倔强而挽以铁索。此时，主持考试的太监说，谁能骑此马就点其及第。众考生面面相觑，不敢上前。唯杨展持弓拨开众人，翻身跃上马背，拉弓搭箭，九发九中。狂马疾驰卷起的迷尘中，传来雄壮的喝声："四川杨展也。"

此时风姿去评书中的常山赵子龙亦不远。武艺过人，胆气豪迈，既成就了杨展，也最终断送了他。当武大定、袁韬请杨展前去赴宴而施以暗杀

The Pillar of Southern Sichuan
Yang Zhan, the runner-up in the military examination

Yang Zhan, the adversary of Zhang Xianzhong, may not have had a remarkable reputation in history, but he was truly a legendary figure.

Born in Jiading, Sichuan (now known as Leshan), Yang Zhan was a tall and robust man, skilled in horseback riding and archery. While on his way to the imperial capital to take the martial examinations, he encountered bandits blocking his path. Fearless, he simply smiled and challenged them to a contest of archery. Standing a hundred paces away, Yang Zhan shattered a tree trunk with a single arrow, leaving the bandits in awe before they bid their farewells and left.

When Yang Zhan arrived at the examination hall, the assigned task was to tame a fierce horse belonging to a top official. This horse was a draft horse, tall, broad-shouldered, and incredibly strong, often used in the military for hauling heavy loads and transporting supplies, but not suitable for riding. This particular horse was even more vicious and stubborn, requiring an iron chain to restrain it. At that moment, the eunuch overseeing the examination declared that whoever could ride this horse would be granted the highest honor. The aspiring examinee exchanged uncertain glances, none daring to step forward. Only Yang Zhan pushed through the crowd with his bow, leapt onto the horse's back, drew his bowstring, and shot nine arrows in quick succession, hitting their targets with precision. In the midst of the dust kicked up by the galloping horse, a resounding voice declared, "Yang Zhan from Sichuan!"

At this moment, his demeanor wasn't far off from that of Zhao Zilong in the famous Chinese epic *Romance of the Three Kingdoms*. Yang Zhan possessed extraordinary martial skills and a bold

时，杨展之子曾经加以劝阻，杨展却厉声喝道："我连张献忠也不怕，难道还怕谁吗？"坐下白马被牵出来时，似乎有所预感，曾多次用嘴去咬啮他的衣服，却仍旧不能阻挡。杨展遇害之后，南明兵部尚书吕大器对他有个评价："志大而疏。"疏，不是志大才疏的疏，而是指他粗疏、疏于防范。其实杨展是有过死里逃生的经历的。

当年以制服悍马、九射九中而名震京师之后，杨震被点为武进士第三名，授游击将军之职，不久就升为参将，成为正三品的高级武官。后来因为长辈去世而回乡服丁忧之际，正赶上乱世来临。

成都被张献忠大军围困时，杨展也在城中协助防御，他还带兵出去厮杀了一场，杀死与擒获敌兵二十多人。不过，个人的勇武在大军面前是不当事的，成都城破，披一身五彩锦甲的杨展被俘。因为不愿意投降，张献忠让人把他拉到河边砍了。押送杨展的士兵心爱其锦甲，向他讨要，杨展说："我命都不要了，还要这玩意儿干吗？等会儿请把我砍入河中，不要将尸体乱扔在地上，就是你的功德了。"

spirit. However, these qualities both brought Yang Zhan success and ultimately led to his downfall. When Wu Dading and Yuan Tao invited Yang Zhan to a feast with the intention of assassinating him, Yang Zhan's son tried to dissuade him. But Yang Zhan sternly shouted, "I fear not even Zhang Xianzhong, how could I fear anyone else?" As his white horse was led out and he mounted it, there seemed to be a premonition. The horse repeatedly bit and gnawed at his clothes, as if trying to stop him, to no avail. After Yang Zhan was killed, lü Daqi, the Minister of War of the Southern Ming Dynasty, had this evaluation of him: "Ambitious but negligent." "Negligent" does not mean he has grandiose aims but puny abilities; rather, it refers to his rough and careless nature when it came to taking precautions. In reality, Yang Zhan had experienced near-death encounters and narrowly escaped on previous occasions.

After gaining fame in the imperial capital for taming the fierce horse and hitting all the targets with nine arrows, Yang Zhan was awarded the third place in the martial examination and appointed as the staff officer of the mobile unit. It didn't take long for him to be promoted to the deputy general, a senior officer of the third rank. Later, on his return to his hometown to observe mourning for the passing of his elder, he found himself caught in the midst of tumultuous times.

During the siege of Chengdu by Zhang Xianzhong's army, Yang Zhan was also in the city assisting with the defense. He led troops out for a fierce battle, killing and capturing over twenty enemy soldiers. However, individual bravery meant little in the face of a massive army. When Chengdu fell, Yang Zhan, adorned in a vibrant and colorful brocade armor, was captured. Refusing to surrender, Yang Zhan was taken to the riverside to be beheaded by Zhang Xianzhong's order. The soldiers escorting him coveted his brocade armor and requested it from him. Yang Zhan replied, "I don't care about my life anymore, why would I need this thing? When you carry out the execution, please throw my body into

到了河边，士兵放下刀，正小心翼翼地解开锦甲，说时迟那时快，杨展一把拾起了地上的刀，砍翻两个士兵，一头扎入河水，消失得无影无踪。杨展再一次出现在历史的视线里，已经是来年。1645年三月，明朝留在四川的残余力量在南明朝廷派遣官员的整合下，集结三万溃散之兵攻下了川南重镇叙州（今宜宾），杀敌上千，杨展的军队即在其中。

因为缺乏粮草，杨展在打了胜仗之后率军顺长江东下，驻守江津。1646年三月，养精蓄锐的杨展开始卷土重来。嘉定的老百姓听说杨展军队杀了张献忠派的犍为县令，就打开城门争相迎接杨展进入。从此，嘉定成为杨展的根据地。杨展攻取嘉定后，联手游击将军马应试，收复了眉州（今眉山）、邛州（今邛崃）、雅州（今雅安）等多地。

此时的杨展，有一呼百应之势，资州、简州、泸州、洪雅、松州、茂州、夔州、万州也纷纷落入前明诸将手中。更有南明朝廷派出的督师、川陕总督居中调度，兵锋直指成都。张献忠正是因为感受到这种巨大的军事压力而不得不离开成都，欲顺江放舟

the river. That would be your act of merit."

At the riverside, as the soldiers put down the sword and carefully removed the brocade armor, an unexpected turn of events took place. Without warning, Yang Zhan swiftly grabbed the sword and struck down two soldiers, then plunged into the river, disappearing without a trace. Yang Zhan once again disappeared from the historical records, only to reemerge the following year. In March 1645, under the coordination of officials dispatched by the Southern Ming court, the remaining forces of the Ming Dynasty in Sichuan, consisting of a scattered army of thirty thousand, successfully captured the strategic town of Xuzhou (now known as Yibin) in southern Sichuan. They killed thousands of enemies, and Yang Zhan's troops were among them.

Due to a shortage of food and supplies, Yang Zhan led his army down the Yangtze River after winning a battle and stationed in Jiangjin. In March of 1646, with his troops well-rested and prepared, Yang Zhan began his comeback. The people of Jiading heard that Yang Zhan's army had killed the county magistrate of Qianwei, who was appointed by Zhang Xianzhong. They eagerly opened the city gates to welcome Yang Zhan's entry. From then on, Jiading became Yang Zhan's base of operations. After capturing Jiading, Yang Zhan joined forces with the staff officer of the mobile unit, Ma Yingshi and successfully reclaimed several areas, including Meishan, Qionglai, and Ya'an.

At this time, Yang Zhan had gained tremendous support, and the cities of Zizhou, Jianzhou, Luzhou, Hongya, Songzhou, Maozhou, Kuizhou, and Wanzhou all fell into the hands of the former Ming generals. Furthermore, the South Ming court dispatched the superintendent, the Governor-General of Chuanshan to oversee operations, with their forces directly aiming for Chengdu. It was because of the immense military pressure that Zhang Xianzhong had no choice but to leave Chengdu and intended to travel down the river. However, unexpectedly, his resources were depleted at

东下的，谁曾想在江口蚀光了老本而不得不退回成都。

话说杨展在江口击败张献忠，也得到了巨大的收益。光是所缴获的金银，就让他成了川南诸军阀中的首富。刘景伯因此在《蜀龟鉴》中批评他急于捞金，而错过了追击张献忠的时机，又容其在成都多了些时日作恶，包括烧毁蜀王府。根据史料，来捋清杨展在击败张献忠之后的行动，可以得出以下几个推论。

其一，杨展江口大胜之后，所取得的金银，是从岷江中打捞起来的，不然不至于耽误那么长的时间。

其二，杨展从南往北追击，一直追到了汉州（今广汉市），而成都则位于江口和汉州之间。实际上，张献忠是被杨展赶出成都的。不少史料和文章说，张献忠离开成都，继续逃向川北，是因为八旗兵入川——这种判断显而易见是错误的。

清军入关是南下，张献忠逃离成都是北上，这种路线不是要避清军，简直就是要寻清军而去的——事实上二者后来也的确是相遇于西充凤凰山。当然，张献忠北窜并不是为了去找八旗兵决斗，是被杨展封住了南逃之途而慌不择路。

Jiangkou, forcing him to retreat back to Chengdu.

Now, when Yang Zhan defeated Zhang Xianzhong at Jiangkou, he also reaped great benefits. Just the gold and silver he seized alone made him the wealthiest among the warlords in southern Sichuan. Liu Jingbo, in his *Shu Gui Jian* 蜀龟鉴 “the Yearbook on a Shu Turtle’s shell”, criticized him for being too focused on seizing wealth, which caused him to miss the opportunity to pursue Zhang Xianzhong and allowed him to cause trouble in Chengdu for some time, including the burning of the Shu King’s Residence. Based on historical records, we can deduce several conclusions regarding Yang Zhan’s actions after defeating Zhang Xianzhong.

First, the gold and silver that Yang Zhan obtained after the victory at Jiangkou were salvaged from the Min River. Otherwise, it wouldn’t have taken so long to acquire them.

Second, Yang Zhan pursued Zhang Xianzhong from south to north, continuing until he reached Hanzhou (now Guanghan City), with Chengdu situated between Jiangkou and Hanzhou. In reality, it was Yang Zhan who drove Zhang Xianzhong out of Chengdu. Many historical records and articles claim that Zhang Xianzhong left Chengdu and continued to escape towards northern Sichuan due to the entry of the Eight Banners troops. However, it is evident that this judgment is incorrect.

The Qing army entered China from the north, while Zhang Xianzhong’s escape from Chengdu was in the northern direction. This route was not to avoid the Qing army but rather to seek them out. In fact, the two eventually met at Fenghuang Mountain in Xichong. Of course, Zhang Xianzhong’s retreat to the north was not to engage in a duel with the Eight Banners troops but because Yang Zhan had blocked his escape route to the south and he was forced to flee in desperation.

Thirdly, after Yang Zhan killed the soldiers who would executed him and sneaked into the Jin River to escape for life, he reappeared with a new army after a gap of over six months. During this time, his

其三，杨展砍翻对他行刑的士兵潜入锦江逃生，到拉起一支军队再次出现，间隔超过半年。这段时间里，他主要干的事是募兵，而所招募的对象，无非是溃散的明军和流离失所的青壮年农民。

这支短时间拼凑起的民间部队展现出了强大的战斗力，面对献军完全是碾压之势，而回顾张献忠的行军线路，从凤阳、武昌、重庆到成都，完全是横行数省几千里，全然没有对手，充分说明当时明朝正规军的腐败和无能。杨展将张献忠赶出成都，一直追到成都东北方向近百里之外的汉州，因为献军远去而不得不放弃。

一路上，骸骨遍野，杨展心中不忍，将之一一埋葬，其上覆以黄土。从这件事情，还是能够看出慈悲。不过，生于乱世且拥兵自重，杨展的军队也难避免军阀骄矜的一面。当时各方势力不满驻扎遵义的总兵王祥，唆使杨展发兵讨伐。

杨展派儿子杨璟新率兵，诈取泸州卫，杀掉了曾经合作过的游击将军马应试。在攻打永宁（今泸州）不利、败给王祥之后，回程中竟然又将泸州卫屠了一遍。此事完全是将战事

main focus was recruiting soldiers, primarily from disbanded Ming troops and displaced young farmers.

This hastily assembled civilian army demonstrated formidable combat strength, overpowering the Xian (Zhang Xianzhong's) Army with ease. Looking back at Zhang Xianzhong's march route from Fengyang, Wuchang, Chongqing to Chengdu, he traveled thousands of miles across multiple provinces without encountering any substantial opposition, which clearly indicated the corruption and incompetence of the Ming Dynasty's regular army at that time. Yang Zhan drove Zhang Xianzhong out of Chengdu, pursued him until Hanzhou, nearly a hundred Lis northeast of Chengdu, and had no choice but to give up the chase when the Xian Army went further away.

As they advanced, the fields were strewn with bones, and Yang Zhan couldn't bear to see this. He and his soldiers buried the remains one by one, covering them with earth. This act reveals his compassion. However, being born in a chaotic era and commanding a powerful army, Yang Zhan's forces were not immune to being imperious and arrogant often associated with warlords. At the time, various factions were dissatisfied with the garrison commander Wang Xiang stationed in Zunyi and instigated Yang Zhan to launch a campaign against him.

Yang Zhan dispatched his son, Yang Jingxin, to lead the troops and deceitfully take control of the Luzhou Wei. During this operation, Yang Jingxin killed Ma Yingshi, who had previously collaborated with them. After facing defeat in the attack on Yongning (now Luzhou) and losing to Wang Xiang, they shockingly ravaged the Luzhou Wei once again on their way back. This was simply a manifestation of anger and frustration over their military failures inflicted upon the ordinary soldiers and civilians. Not to mention that the Luzhou Wei (Luzhou Garrison) had already come under Yang Zhan's control, killing those who surrendered was an act of cruelty. Moreover, considering that the Wei also housed

失利的愤怒发泄到普通军民身上。且不说当时泸州卫已经归杨展部所有，杀降本身就是残暴之举，再以卫所作为屯田军事编制的性质而言，除了拥有军籍的士兵，还有大量手无寸铁的军人家属——对其屠杀就显得尤为令人发指。

此次暴行即便不能直接归于杨展，但其教子无方、束军无能的责任是逃不掉的。人无完人。总体评价杨展，他仍然是有大志且有大才者。个人勇武及军功不说，其大志大才主要体现在两个方面。

一是杨展在江口击败张献忠之后，获取了大量金银，他并没有因之而挥霍，而是将这些钱财用于赈济贫苦、发展生产。

杨展派人至贵州、湖广一带买来大米，至川西土司处买来耕牛。命其子杨璟新屯田于峨眉，每年收获的谷物有数千石。杨展采取的措施还有：对县学学生予以资助；对穷苦无依者颁发口粮；对于耕种荒田的农民，则发放种子和耕牛；愿意跟随他打仗的，补充进队伍；有手艺的，则可以靠手艺养活自己。

他还在河边停靠有上千艘竹筏，以便将荣县、富顺和威远的百姓接到

unarmed military families and farming soldiers, the massacre carried out by Yang Zhan's troops becomes even more abhorrent.

Although this atrocity may not be directly attributed to Yang Zhan, he cannot escape his responsibility for his incompetent son and the lack of discipline within his army. No one is perfect. In an overall assessment of Yang Zhan, he is still regarded as an ambitious and talented individual. Aside from his personal valor and military achievements, his ambition and talent are primarily reflected in two aspects.

One aspect is that after defeating Zhang Xianzhong at Jiangkou, Yang Zhan acquired a large amount of gold and silver. Instead of squandering it, he used these resources for alleviating poverty and promoting economic development.

Yang Zhan dispatched people to buy rice from Guizhou and Hubei, and purchased farming cattle from the local chieftains in western Sichuan. He ordered his son, Yang Jingxin, to reclaim farmland in Emei, resulting in an annual harvest of thousands of Dan (one Dan is 60 kilograms) of grains. Other measures implemented by Yang Zhan included providing assistance to students in county schools, distributing food rations to the impoverished and destitute, distributing seeds and cattle to farmers cultivating barren land, recruiting those willing to join his army, and allowing skilled individuals to sustain themselves through their respective trades.

He also docked over a thousand bamboo rafts at the riverbank to transport the people from Rong County, Fushun, and Weiyuan to seek refuge in Tianquan and Wawu Mountain areas. The areas under Yang Zhan's control were self-sufficient and became rare havens of tranquility amidst the chaos of war. At that time, the military forces resisting Zhang Xianzhong in Sichuan regarded him as an important pillar of stability. With this reputation, Yang Zhan truly deserved the title of "the pillar of southern Sichuan". After Wu Dading and Yuan Tao plotted against Yang Zhan, believing that he had amassed a significant

天全、瓦屋山一带避难。杨展所经营之地自给自足，成为乱世硝烟中难得的宁静之地。当时四川一带抵抗张献忠的军事力量，都将其视作“定海针”。凭此，杨展担得起“川南一柱”的称号。武大定、袁韬谋害杨展之后，认为他在江口捞有大量金银，家中必定珠贝山积，于是拷问其夫人、丫鬟、仆僮，并发掘其窖穴，结果毫无所得。这也说明，杨展并非敛财之徒。

说杨展有大志大才，第二个理由是他对待收编袁韬、武大定的态度。

武大定原为明末农民武装小红狼别部，别号黄巢，后来降明，跟随贺人龙征战；袁韬则是摇黄十三家之一，号称“争天王”，隆武二年（1646年）归顺南明小朝廷。

因为兵败缺粮，二人率部走川南投奔杨展。对此，杨展一口回绝，理由是：自己数万部众都是家乡子弟，大家患难与共，哪怕是赴汤蹈火也皆无二心；如今掺入武大定和袁韬的外地队伍，可能会产生隔阂，引来灾祸。后来虽然经不住再三游说，答应为其供给军粮，但面对武、袁送上来的兵员花名册，杨展还是断然拒绝了。

amount of gold and silver at Jiangkou and that his house must be hiding a mountain of treasures, they interrogated his wife, maidservants, and servants, and even dug up his cellars, but found nothing. This also demonstrates that Yang Zhan was not a hungry hoarder of wealth.

The second reason why Yang Zhan was a man with great ambition and talent is his attitude towards incorporating Yuan Tao and Wu Dading.

Wu Dading was originally a leader of the peasant armed group called the Little Red Wolves during the late Ming Dynasty. He was also nicknamed Huang Chao, originally the rebel leader in the late Tang Dynasty. Later, he surrendered to the Ming Dynasty and followed He Renlong in battle. Yuan Tao, on the other hand, was one of the leaders of the thirteen Yao and Huang family rebel groups. He was known as the “Striving Heavenly King” and pledged allegiance to the Southern Ming Dynasty in the second year of the Longwu era (1646).

Due to their defeat in battle and lack of supplies, Wu Dading and Yuan Tao led their respective troops to seek refuge with Yang Zhan in Southern Sichuan. However, Yang Zhan flatly refused their request, stating that his tens of thousands of soldiers were all fellow countrymen from his hometown, who had stood together through thick and thin. He believed that they had unwavering loyalty and would go through fire and water for him. He expressed concerns that incorporating Wu Da Ding and Yuan Tao’s outside forces into his army might create divisions and cause trouble. Despite repeated persuasion, Yang Zhan remained steadfast in his decision. He eventually agreed to provide them with military provisions, but when faced with the rosters of troops submitted by Wu Dading and Yuan Tao, he firmly refused to accept them.

Based on this, Yang Zhan displayed remarkable prudence and resoluteness in his overall judgement. The instinct for aggressive expansion of troops and territory was deeply ingrained in the nature of warlords, particularly when provisions and fodder

据此，杨展在大局的判断上，是相当谨慎、有定力的。疯狂扩张部队、地盘，是割据力量刻在骨子里的基因（尤其是在粮草充足的情况下），但杨展能战胜这种诱惑，说明其见识远超普通军阀。南明之所以不能成事，很大程度在于文臣的勾心斗角、武将的互相攻杀。

在大明王朝灭亡之后，四川境内有三股力量保家护民，如三根柱石撑起乱世中的天空：一为川南之杨展，一为遵义（时属四川）之王祥，一为川东之女杰秦良玉。不过总体来说，这些力量仍不能拧成一股绳——杨展就攻打过同为明朝猛将的王祥——实在是让人叹惜。定下在酒宴上除掉杨展的计策后，武大定的妻子曾经加以劝阻，并派人报信，可惜杨展最终失之于疏，依然豪迈前往。杨展被害之后，武大定妻不愿承负背信忘恩的恶名，自尽而亡，也算得上是女中丈夫。

杨展如果不死，最后必然与清军遭遇。平心而论，以其军事实力，未必能挡得住八旗兵的锋锐。那么他实际上只有两条路：一是败亡，二是降清——这几乎是明末抗清诸将的唯二结局。倘如此，倒不如跟在现实世界一样死于遭遇战之前，倒能成就千古美名。

were abundant. However, Yang Zhan's ability to resist this temptation demonstrated his exceptional foresight and intelligence to rise above the self-serving ambitions that hindered many other factions during that chaotic period. The failure of the Southern Ming Dynasty to achieve success can be largely attributed to the power struggles among civil officials and the infighting between military commanders.

After the downfall of the Ming Dynasty, there were three forces in Sichuan that stood as protection for the people, like three pillars holding up the sky in turbulent times: Yang Zhan in Southern Sichuan, Wang Xiang in Zunyi (which was then part of Sichuan), and the remarkable woman Qin Liangyu in Eastern Sichuan. However, despite their efforts, these forces were unable to unite as one cohesive force. It is regrettable that Yang Zhan even launched attacks against Wang Xiang, who was also a valiant general of the Ming Dynasty. The plan to eliminate Yang Zhan during a banquet was conceived by Wu Dading, but his wife tried to dissuade him and sent a message to warn Yang Zhan. Unfortunately, due to some negligence on Yang Zhan's part, he still proceeded with his boldness. After Yang Zhan was assassinated, Wu Dading's wife, unwilling to bear the reputation of betrayal and ingratitude, took her own life. Her actions demonstrated the qualities of a virtuous and honorable woman in a time of crisis.

If Yang Zhan had not died, he would inevitably have faced the Qing army. In all fairness, considering his military strength, he might not have been able to withstand the fierce attacks of the Eight Banners. In that case, he would have had only two options: immortalized as a martyr or remembered as a surrendering general to the Qing Dynasty. These were essentially the only two eventualities for most of the Ming generals who resisted the Qing. In hindsight, it might be argued that his death before a decisive battle, mirroring the events of the real world, has resulted in a lasting heroic reputation.

全能自恋八大王
梦碎凤凰山

张献忠逃离成都，来到汉州之后，面临两个选择：一是沿金牛道继续往东北方向前行，回到陕西老家，但这样会跟八旗大军直接遭遇；二是转折向东，经中江、三台、盐亭、南充，由嘉陵江入长江，最终到达江汉平原，去武当山当道士以待时机东山再起。他选择了后者，不过依然在南充西北方向的西充凤凰山碰上了清兵。

相遇并非偶然，而是清军主动找上门来的。大西政权在保宁（今阆中）的守将叫刘进忠，但这个人并不得张献忠喜欢，后者曾经下过诏书，用陕西粗话骂他。此外，刘进忠的部下多蜀人，这也让张献忠不放心，密谋要尽数坑杀。从宫中守门人那儿听到消息的刘进忠又怕又气，于是跑到汉中投降了肃亲王豪格。得知距张献忠所在地疾驰五昼夜可至，豪格命鳌拜为先锋急行军征讨。

谍报人员不是没有报告清军的动向，但张献忠说，有刘进忠守着朝天关（位于今四川省广元市北，是蜀道上由陕入川的险关），哪儿能进

The self-obsessed King of the Eight Dreams shattered on Mount Phoenix.

After escaping from Chengdu, Zhang Xianzhong arrived in Hanzhou and faced two options: the first was to continue northeast along the Jinniu Road, returning to his hometown in Shaanxi. However, this would have led him to a direct encounter with the formidable Eight Banners army. The second option was to change direction and head east, passing through Zhongjiang, Santai, Yanting, and Nanchong, and then entering the Yangtze River via the Jialing River. Ultimately, he would reach the Jianghan Plain and become a Taoist priest in the Wudang Mountains, patiently waiting for the right moment to make a comeback. Zhang Xianzhong chose the latter option, but unfortunately, he unexpectedly encountered Qing soldiers on Mount Phoenix, northwest of Xichong.

This encounter was not coincidental but rather a deliberate move by the Qing army. Liu Jinzhong was the defender of Baoning (now Langzhong) under the Daxi regime, but Zhang Xianzhong did not favor him. Zhang once issued a decree using vulgar language from Shaanxi to insult Liu. Moreover, Liu Jinzhong's subordinates were mostly from Sichuan, which made Zhang Xianzhong distrustful and plan to eliminate them all. When Liu Jinzhong heard about Zhang's plot from a gatekeeper in the palace, he became both frightened and angry. He then fled to Hanzhong and surrendered to Heshuo Su Prince Hao Ge. Upon learning that they could reach Zhang Xianzhong's location after a strenuous journey of five days and nights, Hao Ge ordered Aobai to lead an expedition as the vanguard. They moved swiftly with an urgent march, ready to subdue Zhang Xianzhong.

得来？——他还不知道刘进忠此时已降——所谓清军，不过是花面狸觅食而闹出了些响动罢了。张献忠不仅不相信，还命人杀了报信者，如是者三。

梓潼七曲山大庙里的张献忠塑像　何大江 摄

A statue of Zhang Xianzhong in the Qiqu Mountain Great Temple of Zitong. (Photographer: He Dajiang)

这又是一个"花剌子模信使"的故事：传说花剌子模的国王，听到信使带来的好消息会予以嘉奖，若是坏消息则会杀之。张献忠肯定不知道杀信使的国外典故，他只是跟花喇子模国王有着同样的全能自恋心态，觉得

Although there were intelligence agents reporting the movements of the Qing army, Zhang Xianzhong dismissed their reports, stating that with Liu Jinzhong guarding the Chaotian Pass (located in present-day northern Guangyuan, Sichuan), how could the Qing forces make any advances? Little did he know that Liu Jinzhong had already surrendered. To Zhang Xianzhong, the so-called Qing army was merely creating disturbances like wandering bandits in search of prey. He not only refused to believe the reports but also ordered the execution of those who brought the news, a pattern that repeated three times.

Indeed, this story reflects a similar mindset to that of the "King of the Flatterers": according to the legend, this king of Chorasmia would reward messengers bringing good news and execute those bringing bad news. Zhang Xianzhong may not have been aware of this foreign anecdote about killing messengers, but he shared the same self-obsessed attitude as the King of Chorasmia. He believed that the sun, moon, and stars should revolve around him, and everything should be under his control. If he couldn't control something, he would destroy it if he had the power to do so.

Indeed, the harm caused by self-obsessed individuals is immeasurable, especially when they possess significant power. Zhang Xianzhong's actions in Sichuan serve as evidence of this. As the Qing army drew closer, Zhang Xianzhong finally came out of his tent with only a few dozen of his trusted generals to observe the situation. However, due to the haste, he had a mouthful of food, his clothes were not properly worn, and his bare arm was exposed. At the foot of Mount Phoenix in Xichong, the distance between the two armies was so close that it was visible to the naked eyes.

Liu Jinzhong pointed at Zhang Xianzhong and said to Yabulan, the sharpshooter in the Qing camp,

日月星辰都应该围绕自己旋转，一切都要在自己的把控中——如果不能把控，那就毁灭掉能够毁灭的。

全能自恋者如果只是普通人，不过带来小范围的烦忧苦痛，而如果是掌握极大权力的人，那带来的伤害就是罄竹难书，张献忠以他在四川的所作所为证明了这一点。清兵已至近处，张献忠才带着几十名牙将出帐察看。因为走得匆忙，此时他嘴里包着一口饭，衣服也没穿好，还露着一只膀臂在外。西充凤凰山下，两军的距离如此之近，以至于肉眼可见。

刘进忠指着张献忠对清营里的神射手雅布兰说："就是穿蟒衣那个。"（蟒衣为大臣所穿，上面蟒的形状似龙，但只有四爪，龙为五爪。至于张献忠为何穿蟒衣而非龙袍、为何称王而不称帝，似可与他为何用李自成政权名"大顺"为年号、借大顺政权年号"永昌"作永昌大元帅印等系列问题合并起来探讨。）雅布兰手起箭发，一箭射在其咽喉。张献忠此时倒显出了一些气魄，他用手拔出箭来，看了看道："果然是清兵。"

张献忠躲在柴堆下被清兵搜捕后，送到了豪格处。豪格以为民复仇之名向天祷告后，亲自用刀断其肢

"It's the one in the python robe." (The python robe was worn by the ministers, with the python shape resembling a dragon, but with only four claws on its feet, as dragons are five-clawed. As for why Zhang Xianzhong wore a python robe instead of a dragon robe, and why he proclaimed himself a king instead of an emperor, it seems that it can be discussed in combination with other questions, such as why he used Li Zicheng's reign title Dashun for his regime, borrowed Yongchang from the Dashun regime to make the seal of Grand Marshal, etc.) Yabulan swiftly raised his bow and shot an arrow, hitting Zhang Xianzhong's throat. At this moment, Zhang Xianzhong revealed some boldness. He pulled out the arrow with his hand and examined it, saying,"Indeed, it belongs to the Qing soldier."

After Zhang Xianzhong was discovered hiding under a stack of firewood and captured by the Qing soldiers, he was taken to Hao Ge. Believing it was an opportunity for vengeance on behalf of the people, Hao Ge offered a prayer to the heavens before personally using a knife to sever Zhang Xianzhong's limbs and cut his throat. The corpse was then displayed outside the barrack gate. When the local people heard the news, they quickly gathered with axes and knives, even fighting over the flesh and leaving nothing behind, not even leftover scraps. There is another version regarding the death of Zhang Xianzhong, claiming that he was executed by Aobai, the top warrior of the Manchu. So, in the end, did he die by the hands of the skilled archer Yabulan or the first brave warrior of the Manchu, Aobai?

The former version is found in unofficial historical accounts such as *Shu Bi* 蜀碧 (A Jasper Coagulated by the Blood of Shu People) and *Huang Shu* 荒书 (*the Book of Desolation: Records of Zhang Xianzhong's Army in Sichuan*) while the latter is mentioned in the *Shi Zu Zhang Huangdi Shilu* 世祖章皇帝实录 *Veritable*

体、割其咽喉，再把尸体陈于军门之外。当地百姓闻之，东一斧西一刀，甚至争肉而食，连残渣都不剩。张献忠之死，另有说法是为鳌拜所斩。那么，到底是死于神射手雅布兰，还是满洲第一勇士鳌拜？

前者见于《蜀碧》《荒书》等野史，后者见于《世祖章皇帝实录》。实录是修史的重要依据，似乎更为可信，然而明末清初四川一系列野史的价值绝不可小觑——称为私家史乘或非官方历史应当更为合适。比如《蜀难叙略》的作者沈荀蔚是成都城陷时就义的华阳县令之子；《荒书》作者费密曾做过杨展幕僚，二者都是那一段惨痛历史的亲历者。《蜀碧》作者彭遵泗是清代进士、学者，也担任过作为史官的翰林院编修一职，具有相当的学术水准；彭距离这段历史并不远，前辈的很多经历必然也亲耳听闻，比如他的祖父年轻时就曾救过被追杀的杨展之子杨璟新。

雅布兰后来当过管理翰林院的掌院学士，而曾与之共事的翰林院庶吉士刘如汉亲口告诉过费密：雅布兰正是因为射中张献忠而得到头等功牌。据此，这段史料的真实性相当可靠。那么，两种表述的矛盾之处如何解决？

Records of the Ancestral Emperors of Qing Empire, which is an official historical record and holds significant weight. However, the value of the series of unofficial historical accounts from the late Ming and early Qing periods in Sichuan should not be underestimated, as they were based on personal experiences and firsthand knowledge of individuals who lived through those turbulent times—they can be considered as private chronicles or unofficial histories. For example, Shen Xunwei, the author of *Shu Nan Xu Lüe* 蜀难叙略 (*A Brief Account of the Disasters in Sichuan*), was the son of Huayang County magistrate who was executed when Chengdu fell. The author of *Huang Shu*, Fei Mi, had served as a staff officer to Yang Zhan. Both lived through that painful period of history. The author of *Shu Bi*, Peng Zunsi, was a Jin Shi (Metropolitan Graduate) and a scholar who held the position of a compiler in the Imperial Hanlin Academy, the institution responsible for compiling historical records, during the Qing Dynasty. He had a considerable level of academic expertise. Peng was not far removed from that period of history, so he must have heard many firsthand accounts from his predecessors. For instance, when grandfather was young, he personally rescued Yang Jingxin, the son of Yang Zhan, who was hunted down.

Indeed, Yabulan later served as the Chief Academician in charge of managing the Hanlin Academy and Liu Ruhan, a meritorious candidate of the Hanlin Academy who had worked closely with Yabulan, personally told Fei Mi that Yabulan received a first-class merit plaque for shooting Zhang Xianzhong. Based on this, the authenticity of this historical account holds a considerable degree of reliability. So, how can we reconcile the contradiction between the two different accounts?

The original passage from the *Veritable Records of the Ancestral Emperors of Qing Empire* says: "(Hao

《世祖章皇帝实录》原话为："（豪格）随令护军统领鳌拜巴图鲁等分领八旗护军先发……次日黎明抵西充。献忠尽率马步贼兵拒师。鳌拜等奋击，大破之，斩献忠于阵。"

不要被那个"斩"字误导了，斩指杀，但并不一定只是用刀砍杀。古汉语简略，往往省掉主语，斩的动作发出者并不一定是鳌拜。且鳌拜作为战场上的最高指挥者，不管是谁杀了张献忠，都可以归功于他的名下。所以，可以得出结论：《世祖章皇帝实录》是粗线条的轮廓，而《蜀碧》等有着更多的细节描述，二者并不矛盾。

Ge) ordered the General of the Guard, Aobai Batu lu (Manchu title conferred on performer of great deeds, meaning Hero, Warrior) and others to lead the Eight Banners troops in advance... At dawn on the next day, they arrived at Xichong. Xianzhong personally led his rebel troops to resist the invasion. Aobai and others launched a fierce attack, resulting in a great victory. Xianzhong was executed on the battlefield."

It is important to note that the term "executed" does not necessarily mean it was done by beheading with a sword. In ancient Chinese language, it was common for the subject of an action to be omitted, so the act of "executing" does not necessarily imply that Aobai himself carried out the action. Furthermore, whoever killed Zhang Xianzhong, the merit could be ascribed to Aobai, the highest commander on the battlefield. Therefore, we can conclude that the *Veritable Records of the Ancestral Emperors of Qing Empire* provides a broad outline, while works like *Shu Bi* offer more detailed descriptions. These accounts are not necessarily contradictory and can complement each other.

岷江之上 几多寻宝人

江口沉银一事，其实一直见于史料。

除了上文提及杨展用所取得金银屯垦之外，乾隆五十九年（1794年）从江口镇的岷江之中也发现了大量金银。那一年冬天，有打鱼人在江中"获鞘一具"（李调元《新搜神记》），内藏大量银锭，转报给署理四川总督孙士毅。孙士毅派人打捞，耗时数

Above the Min River, Treasure seekers abound

The incident of sunken silver at Jiangkou has indeed been documented.

In addition to the earlier mention of Yang Zhan's acquisition of gold and silver for farming, in the 59th year of the Qianlong Emperor's reign (1794), a large amount of gold and silver was discovered in the Min River at Jiangkou Town. In the winter of that year, a fisherman in the river "found a scabbard" (Li Tiaoyuan, *Xin Sou Shen Ji* 新搜神记 *A New Search of the Supernatural*), which contained a large number of silver ingots. The news was reported to Acting

月，收获也不小，挖出了银锭上万枚，另有珠宝金花。不过因为打捞难度太大，而并未持续下去。

乾隆五十九年这场打捞的肇始，有很多文章称转引《彭山县志》句：“渔者于江口河中获刀鞘一具，转报总督孙士毅，派员赴江口打捞数日。”其实稍微动脑想一想就知道，刀鞘之中是不可能藏有银锭的；再者，仅凭一具刀鞘就开展大规模打捞，也不符合情理。

经查嘉庆《彭山县志》，原文实为：“乾隆五十九年冬，渔人获鞘一具，报县，转禀治军孙相国补山，饬令派官往捞，数月获银万两有奇。”其实，鞘乃木鞘，根据想象将之填补、解释为刀鞘，实为望文生义、以讹传讹。为什么要用木鞘来藏银？还是因为方便。一段圆木，将之对剖，中间掏空，藏银于其中，再合拢、箍牢，便可以装运了，甚至还具有一定的伪装作用。

跟将木材刨成板、锯成条，再钉成箱相比，显然木鞘更适合于军旅。1644年农历八月，张献忠军围攻成都城之时，也是取来大圆木剖开，置火药于其中，再合拢缠以布帛运送，图的也就是一个方便、快捷。想想人类

Governor-General of Sichuan, Sun Shiyi, who dispatched people to take several months to salvage it. The harvest was substantial, with tens of thousands of silver ingots and various pieces of jewelry being excavated. However, due to the difficulty of the salvage operation, it was not pursued further.

The salvage operation in the 59th year of the Qianlong Emperor's reign has been referenced in many articles, citing the *Pengshan Xianzhi* (彭山县志 *Pengshan County Annals*), which state, "A fisherman in the Jiangkou River caught a scabbard, which was reported to the Governor-General Sun Shiyi. He dispatched personnel to Jiangkou for several days of salvage." However, with a little logical thinking, it becomes apparent that a scabbard would not contain silver ingots. Furthermore, it does not seem reasonable to initiate a large-scale salvage operation based solely on the discovery of a single scabbard.

In the *Pengshan County Annals* of the Jiaqing period, the original text indeed reads, "In the winter of the 59th year of the Qianlong Emperor's reign, a fisherman discovered a sheath and reported it to the county. The report was then forwarded to Sun Bushan, the Military Affairs Officer, who ordered officials to conduct salvage operations. After several months, a remarkable amount of silver, totaling over 10,000 taels, was obtained." Indeed, the term "sheath" here refers to a wooden sheath. The interpretation of it as a "scabbard" through literal translation is a misinterpretation and an error that has been perpetuated. But why would silver be hidden inside a wooden sheath? The reason is likely for convenience. A large wooden log could be split open, hollowed out in the middle, and filled with silver. It could then be sealed and securely fastened, making it easier to transport. Additionally, it might have served as a form of disguise, making it less likely for the valuable cargo to be identified.

In contrast to the laborious process of planing

最先造船，是独木舟；早期的棺材，是船棺——都是将圆木掏空即可——道理就不难明白了。

其实，《蜀难叙略》和《蜀碧》对此有非常明确的记载。《蜀难叙略》称，杨展命人用长枪在江中探刺，将碰上的木鞘拖出水面，摆在军营之外。数日之间，已堆得跟城墙一般高。而这样的打捞支持了一年多。《蜀碧》则称，在江口一战发生上百年之后、他写作此书的年代里，还时常有居民从江底捞起大木鞘，上面的金锭、银锭还刻有各州邑的名号。只是，主流观点对此并不愿意轻易认同。然而，江口古战场考古发掘却一而再再而三地证实明末这一类非官方历史的价值。

孙士毅主持的这次打捞，很快传到乾隆耳中，竟然受到一通训斥。最主要的理由，竟然是要给贫困者留一线生机，这实在是跟世人眼中乾隆好大喜功的刻板印象大相径庭。“附近贫民或在彼捞拣，亦不过沙里淘金，藉资糊口，又何值派官打捞，与细民争利？”1795年的那道上谕，隔着两百多年的时空，勿与民争利的言辞依然能够温暖人心。

乾隆一朝国库丰盈，而与太平

wood into planks, sawing them into strips, and nailing them into boxes, it is clear that wooden sheaths are more suitable for military needs. In the eighth month of the lunar calendar in 1644, when Zhang Xianzhong's army besieged the city of Chengdu, they also used large logs, splitting them open, filling them with gunpowder, wrapping them with cloth, and transporting them. The purpose was to achieve convenience and speed. When one thinks of the earliest boats made by humans, they were dugout canoes. And the early coffins were boat-shaped - both were hollowed out from round logs. The reasoning behind this is not difficult to understand.

In fact, *Shu Nan Xu Lüe* and *Shu Bi* have very clear records on this matter. According to *Shu Nan Xu Lüe*, Yang Zhan ordered people to use long spears to probe the river, pulling out the wooden sheaths they encountered and piling them outside the military camp. Within a few days, they had piled up to a height equivalent to the city walls. Such salvaging efforts continued for over a year. *Shu Bi* also mentions that even centuries after the battle at Jiangkou, during the time when the author wrote the book, residents would often retrieve large wooden sheaths from the riverbed, with gold and silver ingots engraved with the names of various towns and cities. However, the mainstream opinion is not willing to easily accept this. Nevertheless, archaeological excavations at the ancient battlefield of Jiangkou have repeatedly confirmed the value of this kind of unofficial history during the late Ming Dynasty.

The salvage operation led by Sun Shiyi quickly reached the ears of Emperor Qianlong, who surprisingly gave it a stern rebuke. The main reason cited was the need to leave a glimmer of hope for the impoverished, which went against the stereotypical impression of Qianlong as someone who craved glory and achievements. "The nearby poor people may engage in salvaging and picking, just like

天国运动伴随始终的咸丰朝，则时刻因为军费的巨大开支而感到捉襟见肘了。1853年，翰林院编修陈泰初上条呈称，史载张献忠“窖有金银数千万于锦江之下”，自己也亲眼见到过彭山、眉山一带的居民捞得遗银。对于这一笔可能存在于河床上的巨大财富，咸丰显然上心了，于是他命令清廷在西南地区的最高官员、成都将军裕瑞，“悉心访察是否能知其处，设法捞掘”。

很多文章将此事演绎为时值太平天国运动爆发，清廷财政困难，因此希望借此筹措军费。陈泰初上条呈是在咸丰三年，这一年三月，太平军攻下了江宁，清廷军费欠缺实属正常，但纵览全文，并无一字述其意图。文史类的文章，合理的推测是可以容许的，但行文之间，一定得将推断与事实进行区分，这才是应有的态度。事实上，上谕叮嘱裕瑞“博采舆论，酌情筹办”，可见咸丰对此的态度是非常谨慎的，并不愿轻易劳师动众而落下话柄。而到了民国年间，以锦江为舞台背景，上演了一出轰轰烈烈的掘宝大剧，与咸丰的谨慎倒是可以形成对比。

上条呈的陈泰初，出生于广东番

panning for gold in the sand, to make a living. Why should officials be dispatched to salvage, competing for profit with common people?” This edict from 1795, spanning over two hundred years, still warms the hearts with its words of not competing with the common people for profit.

During the reign of Emperor Qianlong, the imperial treasury was abundant, while the subsequent Xianfeng reign, which was accompanied by the Taiping Heavenly Kingdom movement, constantly struggled with the enormous expenses of military funding. In 1853, Chen Taichu, a compiler of the Hanlin Academy, submitted a report stating that historical records mentioned Zhang Xianzhong’s “treasure of gold and silver worth millions of taels buried beneath the Jin River.” He personally witnessed the local residents in Pengshan and Meishan areas salvaging lost silver. This enormous wealth that potentially existed on the riverbed clearly caught Xianfeng’s attention. He ordered the highest-ranking official in the southwest region, the Chengdu general, Yurui, to “thoroughly investigate whether the location of the treasure could be known and make efforts to salvage it”.

Many articles interpret this event as occurring during the outbreak of the Taiping Heavenly Kingdom movement, when the Qing Dynasty was facing financial difficulties and thus hoped to use this treasure as military funding. Chen Taichu’s report was submitted in the third year of the Xianfeng reign, during March of that year when the Taiping army captured Jiangning. It is indeed normal for the Qing treasury to face shortages of military funds during this time. However, upon a close examination of the full text, there is no mention of any specific intent. In articles of a literary and historical nature, it is reasonable to make educated guesses, but it is crucial to distinguish between inference and fact in the writing. In fact, the edict instructed Yurui to “gather

禺一书香世家，咸丰二年以二甲庶吉士授翰林院编修。不过，陈泰初虽然亲眼见到过江口捞银，却也把江口之银与锦江之银混为一谈了。后文将对此加以辨析。

转眼到2005年4月20日，江口镇的岷江河道内，彭山县引水工程正在施工。在距地表2.5米之处，挖掘机挖出了一件木筒，内藏七枚银锭。这件木筒，便是《蜀碧》等记载，用来贮银的木鞘。该木鞘长118厘米、外径18厘米，内藏的七枚银锭中，六枚都有阴刻铭文。其中一枚全文为："沅陵县征完解司裁充兵饷银五十两 崇祯十年八月 日 银匠姜国太。"上面包含的信息非常丰富，有时间、地点、用途、重量，还落有制作银匠之名，这显然是为了事后追溯，以防粗制滥造、成色不足。

此枚银锭重一千八百二十五克。另外标明"五十两"的银锭，两枚重一千八百克、一枚重一千七百七十五克。明代一斤合596.8克，一斤16两，每两合37.3克，五十两当合一千八百六十五克。以最轻银锭的一千七百七十五克计，距标准重量约有4.8%的差距。不知这是当时的惯例，还是数百年来江水的冲蚀所致？

various opinions and make preparations accordingly", indicating that Xianfeng approached this matter with great caution and was not willing to easily mobilize the needed manpower, expose his vulnerabilities and make himself become the subject of ridicule. In contrast, during the Republican era, a grand treasure excavation drama unfolded on the stage set by the Jin River, which can be seen as a stark contrast to Xianfeng's cautious approach.

Chen Taichu, the minister presenting the report, was born into a scholarly family in Panyu, Guangdong. In the second year of the Xianfeng reign, he was awarded the position of Compiler in the Hanlin Academy for having achieved the second-tier distinction in the annual civil service examination. Although Chen Taichu personally witnessed the retrieval of silver at Jiangkou, he mistakenly mixed up the silver from Jiangkou with that from the Jin River. This will be further clarified in the subsequent text.s

In a blink of an eye, on April 20, 2005, during the construction of the Pengshan County water diversion project in the Min River channel in Jiangkou Town, a wooden tube was dug out by an excavator at a depth of 2.5 meters from the surface. Inside the wooden tube were seven silver ingots. This wooden tube corresponds to the descriptions found in *Shu Bi* and other records, which mention the use of wooden sheaths for storing silver. The wooden sheath measures 118 centimeters in length and 18 centimeters in outer diameter. Of the seven silver ingots found inside, six of them bear engraved inscriptions. One of the inscriptions reads, "Fifty taels of silver for replenishing the soldiers' pay from the Collection and Delivery Division of Yuanling County, made by silver artisan Jiang Guotai on the eighth month of the tenth year of the Chongzhen reign." This inscription contains rich information, including the date, location, purpose, weight, and the name of

将七枚银锭所涉及的五个地名连成一条线，黄冈—京山—巴陵（今岳阳）—湘潭—沅陵，从东向西，从北向南，正与张献忠由鄂、湘入川的路线高度吻合。

其中在黄冈至京山的路上，正是有“九州通衢”之称的重镇武昌府——当年张献忠正是在这里劫掠并淹死了楚王朱华奎。这些银锭都是崇祯年间由地方征解的饷银，吃粮打仗的大明官军连自己的粮饷都保不住，张献忠后来能从民间搜刮来那么多的耳环钗饰，也就不足为奇了。回过头去，与明末清初的私家史乘相印证，就会十分惊奇，《蜀碧》上的那句“至今居民时于江底获大鞘，其金银镌有各州邑名号”，该是何等的准确了。

当这七枚银锭现身江口时，笔者正在写作一本叫作《太平巷里》的书，其中涉及张献忠遗银，遂以新闻报道为据引用最新材料，提及这七枚银锭。不过，这一次的江口沉银现身并未引起时人的普遍兴趣。时间又过了六年，日子不多不少还是那一天，江口再次出现在新闻中。2011年4月20日彭山县金裕砂石厂在岷江河道挖取沙石，出土了包括金册、西王赏功

the silver artisan involved. It is clear that this was done for future verification to prevent counterfeit or substandard production.

This silver ingot weighs 1,825 grams. Additionally, there are other ingots marked as “fifty taels”, two weighing 1800 grams, and one weighing 1,775 grams. In the Ming Dynasty, one Jin (Chinese pound) was equal to 596.8 grams, with one Jin consisting of 16 taels, making each taels approximately 37.3 grams. Fifty taels should amount to 1,865 grams. Based on the weight of the lightest silver ingot at 1,775 grams, there is approximately a 4.8% discrepancy from the standard weight. It is unclear if this variation was a common practice at the time or if it resulted from erosion caused by the river over hundreds of years. The five place names engraved in the seven silver ingots form a line, connecting Huanggang, Jingshan, Baling (modern Yueyang), Xiangtan, and Yuanling, from east to west and north to south. This alignment perfectly matches the route Zhang Xianzhong took when he entered Sichuan from Hubei and Hunan provinces.

It is on the road from Huanggang to Jingshan that we find the important city of Wuchang Prefecture, known as the “thoroughfare of the Nine Provinces”. It was in Wuchang that Zhang Xianzhong plundered and drowned the Chu King Zhu Huakui. These silver ingots were all soldiers’ allowance levied locally during the Chongzhen reign. Even the Ming official army, who relied on this fund for food and warfare, could not safeguard their own provisions. It is not surprising that Zhang Xianzhong was able to confiscate so many earrings and ornaments from the common people. When we look back at the private historical records from the late Ming and early Qing Dynasties, we will be amazed at how accurately the statement in *Shu Bi* aligns: “Even in present times, residents often retrieve large sheaths from the riverbed, with gold and silver ingots engraved with

金币在内的文物。

当地文物部门反应十分及时，当天就发出通告，要求在次日下午六点前，主动将流失的出土文物上交国家。这一次沉银现身，终于引起了世人注目，不过，很多人感兴趣的不是其上承载的历史，而是文物或金银可以兑换的价格。随之而来的，是数年之间疯狂盗掘。2011年4月20日之后，江口出现了一种古老而又全新的职业——寻宝人。与早先挥舞着洛阳铲书写盗墓笔记的同行相比，他们更为专业，其设备不仅有马达动力木船，更配备了金属探测仪、潜水服等现代化设置，甚至有曾经从事过潜水的专业人员参与其中。

在一份一审判决书上，可以看到公安机关关于2015年4月26日对某犯罪嫌疑人住处搜查，发现的部分打捞设施：氧气瓶十七瓶、潜水服十八件、充氧机三台、金属探测仪五套、铅块三十二块、防水电筒四支、潜水眼镜三个、潜水指套三盒、铁锹五个、竹篼十四个、潜水鞋四双、潜水袜二十四只、潜水头套五个、潜水呼吸器三个、潜水背心三件、潜水背架二个、铁器六个、金属探测仪主机二个……

the names of various towns and cities."

When the seven silver ingots appeared in Jiangkou, I was in the midst of writing a book called *The Taiping Lane* 太平巷里, which involves the legacy of Zhang Xianzhong's silver. So, I used the latest news reports as a reference to cite this discovery of the seven silver ingots. However, this time the appearance of the sunken silver in Jiangkou did not generate widespread interest among the public. Six years passed, and on that very day, the news of Jiangkou resurfaced once again. On April 20, 2011, at the Jinyu Sand and Stone Factory in Pengshan County, relics including golden records and gold coins awarded by the Western King were unearthed during sand excavation in the Min River.

The local cultural relics department responded promptly and issued a notice on the same day, requiring the proactive submission of the recovered cultural relics to the state before 6 p.m. on the following day. This time, the resurfacing of the sunken silver finally caught the world's attention. However, many people were more interested in the value of the relics or the gold and silver that could be exchanged for money, rather than the history they carried. As a result, there was a frenzy of looting over the next few years. After April 20, 2011, a new and ancient profession emerged in Jiangkou - treasure hunters. Compared to their predecessors who wielded Luoyang shovels (A symbol of Chinese archaeological drilling tools, first widely used for grave robbing, later becoming an archaeological tool.) to record their tomb-raiding adventures, these treasure hunters were far more professional. They not only had motorized wooden boats but also modern equipment such as metal detectors and diving suits. Some even included former professional divers.

In a first-instance court verdict, it can be seen that on April 26, 2015, the public security authorities conducted a search at the residence of a certain

澎湃新闻的一篇稿件称："从2011年开始，大量'寻宝人'开始在这一片江水中反复搜寻，一个又一个'财富神话'从这里诞生。"

2012年底至2013年，彭山人徐某某团伙从水下淤泥中搜出国家级文物永昌大元帅印，被其中一名成员以八百万元的价格卖给一文物商。

2013年4月至2013年底，何某某、谢某等人组成团伙，盗得西王赏功币、银锭、碎银等物，其中多有二级文物和三级文物。庭审中辩护人提出：如果对何某某等几十名挖宝的青壮年予以重处，可能会出现影响社会稳定的情形。2013年夏天至2015年3月，邬某某、郭某团伙多次在江口沉银遗址进行盗掘。2013年六七月份，共挖出六张金册；2015年3月盗得的一张金册为一级文物。七张金册共卖出了五百六十万元。

2016年10月13日，由公安部挂牌督办的"四川特大盗掘古文化遗址"倒卖文物案告破，追回文物千余件。系列案件共涉及犯罪嫌疑人七十名，涉案文物交易额3亿元。实际上，将这种行为视作"财富神话"，实在有些勉强。人类就是如此短视，当他们在水下摸索时，只恨找到的文物不

criminal suspect, where they discovered the following salvage facilities: 17 oxygen cylinders, 18 diving suits, 3 oxygen filling machines, 5 sets of metal detectors, 32 lead weights, 4 waterproof flashlights, 3 diving goggles, 3 boxes of diving finger covers, 5 iron shovels, 14 bamboo baskets, 4 pairs of diving shoes, 24 diving socks, 5 diving hoods, 3 aqualungs, 3 diving vests, 2 diving backpacks, 6 iron tools, and 2 main units of metal detectors...

A news article from Pengpai News stated, "Starting from 2011, a large number of 'treasure hunters' began repeatedly searching in this stretch of river water, giving birth to one 'wealth myth' after another."

In late 2012 to 2013, a gang led by Xu, a resident of Pengshan, retrieved the national-level cultural relic, the Marshal Seal of Yongchang, from the underwater sediment. One of the gang members sold it to a cultural relic dealer for a price of 8 million RMB.

From April to the end of 2013, a gang led by He and Xie stole Western King's reward coins, silver ingots, and broken silver, many of which were secondary and tertiary level cultural relics. During the trial, the defense lawyer argued that if heavy penalties were imposed on He and others, who were in their youth and engaged in treasure hunting, it could potentially lead to a destabilization of social order. From summer 2013 to March 2015, a gang led by Wu and Guo carried out multiple thefts at the Jiangkou sunken silver site. In June and July 2013, they unearthed a total of six golden records, and in March 2015, they stole one golden record classified as a first-grade cultural relic. The seven golden records were sold for a total of 5.6 million RMB.

On October 13, 2016, the "Sichuan Major Theft of Cultural Heritage Sites" case, which was under the direct supervision of the Ministry of Public Security, was solved, and over a thousand cultural relics were recovered. The series of cases involved a total of 70 criminal suspects, with a total transaction value of

够多；倒手转卖时，只恨到手的金额不够大。但是，他们很快就会后悔，巴不得那些数额越小越好。

江口的重要文物相继出水现世，让文物管理部门进行抢救性发掘的想法越来越迫切。2017年1月5日，江口沉银遗址水下考古发掘正式启动。围堰围成的考古区域约两万平方米，而这大约只占遗址面积的百分之一。2010年10月，眉山市政府发布的将江口沉银遗址列为市级重点文物保护单位的通知称，“保护范围以岷江大桥为中心上、下约二千米，面积约二百五十万平方米”。

300 million RMB. In reality, it is quite far-fetched to view this behavior as a “wealth myth”. Humans are shortsighted in this manner—when they were searching underwater, they always lamented that they hadn’t found enough relics; but when they tried to sell them, they complained that the amount they receive was not large enough. However, they soon regretted it and wished that the amounts were even smaller.

The emergence of important cultural relics from the Jiangkou site one after another made the idea of salvage excavation by cultural heritage management agencies increasingly pressing. On January 5, 2017, the underwater archaeological excavation of the Jiangkou sunken silver site officially commenced. The archaeological area, enclosed by a cofferdam, covers an approximate area of 20,000 square meters, which is only about one percent of the total site area. In October 2010, the Meishan Municipal Government announced the inclusion of the Jiangkou sunken silver site as a key cultural heritage protection unit at the city level. According to the official notice, the protected area is centered around the Minjiang Bridge and extends approximately 2,000 meters upstream and downstream, covering an area of around 2,500,000 square meters.

两枚金宝
诠释色即是空

始于2017年1月的江口沉银遗址考古发掘，共进行了三期，出水五万余件文物，其中不乏国家级文物。分别于第二、三期出水的蜀王金宝和蜀世子宝，尤值一提。

蜀王金宝，是蜀王在藩地的印信，是明朝廷在蜀地最高级别的权力代表，它就是小一号的传国玉玺，

Two Golden Treasures:
Interpreting “Color is Emptiness”

The archaeological excavation of the Jiangkou sunken silver site, which began in January 2017, was conducted in three phases and yielded over 50,000 recovered artifacts, including several national-level cultural relics. Two treasures, in particular, are worth mentioning: the Golden Treasure of the Shu King and the Golden Treasure of the Shu Crown Prince, which were recovered in the second and third phases, respectively.

The Golden Treasure of the Shu Prince is the

跟皇太子册宝同一个档次。准确地说，它应该称作“蜀王之宝”，这也是其印面上的四个字。《明史·卷六十八·志第四十四·舆服四》对此有非常明确的记载：“亲王册宝：册制与皇太子同。其宝用金，龟纽，依周尺方五寸二分，厚一寸五分，文曰‘某王之宝’。”

明代规制，藩王之宝边长五寸二分，厚度为一寸五分，按现代度量衡换算，这是一枚印面为10.4厘米见方、高度为三厘米的方印。

蜀王金宝，残存的“蜀”字依然可见　高泓 摄
The royal seal of Shu, with the partial “Shu” character still visible. (Photographer: Gao Hong)

出水的蜀王之宝，主体部分只剩下四分之一，残存一个篆文“蜀”字，印面上还有两道呈钝角的斫痕。乱世中的军队，自然没有文物意识，砍斫这方代表蜀地最高权力的印信，其心理大致跟项羽火烧阿房宫相类。当然，金印的货币属性依旧是被看重

royal seal of authority used by the Shu King in his fiefdom. It represents the highest level of power of the Ming Dynasty in the Shu region, comparable to the smaller version of the Imperial Jade Seal, on the same level as the Prince's Official Conferring Record. In fact, it should be called the “Treasure of the Shu King”, as the four characters engraved on its seal face indicate. *Ming Shi*, the “Imperial Vehicles and Attire Four-Chronicle 44-Volume 68-Ming History” records this distinctly: “The Prince's Official Conferring Record: The format and regulations are the same as that of the Crown Prince. The treasure is made of gold, with a turtle-shaped knob, measured at five Cuns and two fens, with a thickness of one Cun and five fens. It is inscribed with the words ‘Treasure of Prince [Name]’”.

According to the regulations of the Ming Dynasty, the dimensions of the treasure of a prince were five cuns and two fens in length, and one cun and five fens in thickness. Converted to modern measurements, this would be a square seal with a surface area of 10.4 square centimeters and a height of 3 centimeters.

The main part of the Treasure of the Shu Prince that resurfaced out of the water is only one-fourth left, with a single seal script character “Shu”(蜀) remaining, and two hacking marks at an obtuse angle on the face of the seal. In turbulent times, military forces naturally lacked awareness of cultural artifacts protection. The psychology of hacking and damaging this seal, which represented the highest power in the Shu region, can be compared to Xiang Yu's burning of Epang Palace. However, the monetary value of the gold seal was still highly regarded. Dividing the gold into smaller pieces made it easier to carry and distribute. It is highly likely that the missing parts were melted down and became part of the multiple

的。分成小块的黄金，更便于携带、分配。那些消失的部分，很有可能回炉，成了张献忠为赏赐部下而制作的多枚西王赏功金币的一部分——2011年嘉德士春季拍卖会上，单枚金币曾拍出230万元的价格。蜀王之宝被毁，不幸之幸是，剩下的是一个“蜀”字，这就让确认其身份成为可能。

与之相比，第三期发掘出水的蜀世子宝，则相对幸运。世子宝被斫为四块，但能够还原为一个整体。《明史》没有记载其规制，然而对于世子正妻世子妃的印信，却有较为详细的描述：“洪武二十三年铸世子妃印，制视王妃，金印，龟纽，篆文曰‘某世子妃印’。”将实物与此互相参照，可确认世子宝亦为金印龟钮。蜀世子宝的印纽之上，龟的壳、裙边、爪、尾，甚至于爪尾上的鳞片皆清晰可见。已经缺失的则是被斫下的金龟头。

出水的蜀世子宝，重达十六斤，根据实物测量，其大小规制与蜀王之王相同，而黄金成色更好，纯度达到百分之九十五。

世子，是藩王的继承人，通常也是其嫡长子。《明史》中关于世子金宝的使用，有一句记载：“亲王世子金册金宝，承袭止授金册，传用金宝。”也就是说，朝廷册封亲王继承人时，使

gold coins known as the Western King's rewards, which were made by Zhang Xianzhong as rewards for his subordinates. In 2011, in Christie's spring auction, a single gold coin was sold for 2.3 million. Although the treasure of the Shu Prince was destroyed, the fortunate aspect is that the remaining "Shu" character allows for the possibility of confirming its identity.

In comparison, the treasure of the Shu Crown Prince, which was discovered in the third excavation, was relatively fortunate. Although it was hacked into four pieces, it could be restored as a whole. The Ming History does not record its regulations. However, there is a more detailed description of the seal of the Crown Prince's legitimate wife, the Crown Princess: "In the twenty-third year of the Hongwu reign, the seal of the Crown Princess was cast, following the same pattern as that of the Royal Concubine. It is a gold seal with a turtle-shaped knob, inscribed with the seal characters 'Crown Princess [Name]'." By comparing the physical objects and this description, it can be confirmed that the Crown Prince's treasure is also a gold seal with a turtle-shaped knob. On the knob of the Shu Crown Prince's treasure, the shell of the turtle, the edges of the turtle skirt, the claws, and even the scales on the claws and tail are clearly visible. The part that is already missing is the golden turtle head that was hacked off.

The treasure of the Shu Crown Prince, which resurfaced, weighs 16 Jin (Jin, a unit of weight, equals 1/2 kilogram). According to measurements of the physical object, its size and regulations are the same as those of the treasure of the Shu Prince. However, the gold used in the Crown Prince's treasure has a higher purity level, reaching 95%.

The Crown Prince, usually the eldest legitimate son, is the designated heir to the vassal king. The

用的是金册，所以明代有十四位蜀世子，就有十四张金册；而世子宝却只有一枚，它是蜀王继承权转移的象征。

江口沉银遗址出水的印 高泓 摄
Seals unearthed at the Jiangkou sunken silver site. (Photographer: Gao Hong)

蜀世子宝的首个拥有者，应当是朱椿之子、第一代蜀世子朱悦燫。他不幸早夭，并没有等到坐上王位的那一天。不过，埋葬他的陵墓，却比历代的蜀王陵要大、规格要高。于此，也可见明代蜀地对于世子的重视。那么，蜀世子宝的黄金成色高于蜀王之宝，似乎也就可以理解了。蜀王金宝的最后一位、世子宝的倒数第二位拥有者，是末代蜀王朱至澍。他因不愿拿出王府金银充作军费，而导致了成都城的沦陷。

如果他能得知这两枚金宝的最终结局，当于蜀王府的井下悔之莫及。面对出资犒军的呼吁，朱至澍曾指着蜀王府正殿承运殿，说了一句十分无赖的

usage of the gold treasure of the Crown Prince is mentioned in the Ming History: "The Crown Prince of the Prince's lineage receives gold records in inheritance, and the throne is passed on with the Golden Treasure." In other words, when the imperial court enthroned the heir of a prince, a gold record is given, hence there were fourteen gold records for the fourteen Shu Crown Princes in the Ming Dynasty. However, there is only one treasure of the Crown Prince, which symbolizes the transfer of the succession from the Shu Prince.

The first owner of the treasure of the Shu Crown Prince was likely Zhu Yuelian, the son of Zhu Chun, who was the first Shu Crown Prince. Unfortunately, Zhu Yuelian passed away at a young age before ascending to the throne. However, his tomb, where he was buried, had a larger size and higher specifications compared to the tombs of the other Shu Princes. This indicates the importance placed on the Crown Princes in the Shu region during the Ming Dynasty. Therefore, it can be understood why the gold purity of the treasure of the Shu Crown Prince is higher than that of the Shu Prince. The last owner of the treasure of the Shu Prince and the second-to-last owner of the treasure of the Shu Crown Prince was Zhu Zhishu, the last Shu Prince. He refused to use the gold and silver from the royal treasury for military expenses, which eventually led to the fall of Chengdu city.

If he could know the final fate of these two golden treasures, he would deeply regret his decisions in the depths of the well in the Shu Prince's Mansion. Faced with appeals to contribute funds to reward the army, Zhu Zhishu once pointed at the main hall of the Shu Prince's Mansion, the Chengyun Hall, and uttered a contemptible remark:

话："王府并没有多余金银，只剩下这一个大殿了，各位需要尽管拿去。"于此，后来殉国的巡按刘之勃愤然道，"这大殿恐怕只有李自成、张献忠之流敢拿去享用了"，果然一语成谶。

《般若波罗蜜多心经》说，"色不异空，空不异色，色即是空，空即是色"，就是对这两枚金宝命运的印证。

"In my palace there is no extra gold and silver, only this grand hall remains. You are welcome to take it if you need it." In response to this, Liu Zhibo, the provincial governor who later sacrificed himself for the country, angrily remarked, "Perhaps only Li Zicheng, Zhang Xianzhong and others would dare to take and enjoy this grand hall." As it turned out, his words proved to be prophetic.

The Prajna Paramita Heart Sutra states, "Color is not different from emptiness, emptiness is not different from color, color is emptiness, emptiness is color." This can be seen as a confirmation of the destiny of these two golden treasures.

石龙石虎
至今犹在

寻宝故事中，穿凿自是常事，但童谣中的石龙与石虎，却是真实的存在。

江口沉银第三期考古现场，此时已经淹没在江面之下。岷江南流，水面平静如一匹巨大的丝绸，看不出一年前考古的忙碌，更看不出375年前的战火硝烟。

石龙、石虎位于彭山江口街道石龙村石龙沟。如果没有当地村民带路，要找到它们几乎是不可能的事。

江口镇距成都不到八十千米的车程，但口音相差很大。虽然说的都是四川话，但作为"湖广填四川"移民的后裔，说湖广话的笔者跟操

The Tale of Stone Dragon and Stone Tiger Still Prevailing Today

In the quest for treasures, drawing far-fetched analogies is commonplace, but the legends surrounding the Stone Dragon and Stone Tiger have a basis in reality.

The third phase of the archaeological site at Jiangkou, where the sunken silver lies, now lies submerged beneath the surface of the river. As the Min River flows south, the water surface remains as calm as a colossal silk fabric, betraying no trace of the archaeological frenzy that took place a year ago, nor the echoes of the battles that roared 375 years ago.

The Stone Dragon and Stone Tiger are located in Stone Dragon Gully, within the village of Shilong in the Jiangkou Street of Pengshan. Locating them would be nearly impossible without the guidance of local villagers.

Jiangkou Town is located less than 80 kilometers away from Chengdu, but the dialects spoken here differ significantly. While both dialects

南路话的当地居民沟通得非常不畅顺，有时甚至完全听不懂彼此在说些什么。造成这种语言隔阂，也跟张献忠有关。

四川话大体可以分为湖广话、南路话两类——按学术语言，前者属于西南方言成渝片，后者为灌赤片。从成都往东到宜昌超过八百千米车程，差别极小；甚至再往东数百千米，同讲武汉话的人都完全沟通无碍，因为都是湖广话。但是，从成都主城区往南、往西仅仅二十来千米，如郫都区、大邑县和新津县，以及更远的邛崃、眉山、乐山、泸州等，交流就非常困难。因为，这些区域讲的是南路话——明代的四川话——保留有大量古汉语的特点，比如入声字等。

究其原因，是因为张献忠的势力限于成都城及以东，上述讲南路话的区域受到的“蹂躏”较少。也可以粗略地理解为，讲南路话的是明代原住民后裔，而说湖广话的主要是移民后裔。

几经打听，终于找到了去石龙沟的路。从江口小学旁，沿着一条水泥铺的山路斜着向上，路面很窄，只容得下一辆车，好在对面都没有来车。

面临岔道时非常紧张，山上找不到人问路，也没有任何标识，一旦走

are Sichuanese, the communication between the writer, who speaks the dialects of Huguang, and the local residents who speak the dialect of Nanlu, is not smooth or seamless. At times, we may even have difficulty understanding each other. This language barrier can be attributed to the historical influence of Zhang Xianzhong.

Sichuanese dialect can generally be divided into two categories: Huguang dialect and Nanlu dialect. From an academic perspective, the former belongs to the Southwest Mandarin branch of the Chengyu dialect, while the latter belongs to the Guanchi branch. When traveling from Chengdu to Yichang, which is over 800 kilometers to the east, one finds that the differences between the dialects are minimal. Further eastward for hundreds of kilometers, one's communicating with those in Wuhan dialect (which is also a form of Huguang dialect) poses no barriers because they belongs to the same linguistic family. However, when one traveling just 20 kilometers south or west of Chengdu's main urban area to places such as Pidu District, Dayi County, and Xinjin County, as well as more distant regions like Qionglai, Meishan, Leshan, and Luzhou, communication becomes challenging. This is because in these areas people speak Nanlu dialect, which is essentially the Sichuanese dialect of the Ming Dynasty, and it retains many characteristics of Old Chinese, such as the distinction of entering tones (入声字).

Indeed, the reason behind this linguistic divide can be traced back to the limited influence of Zhang Xianzhong's forces, which were primarily confined to Chengdu and its eastern regions. As a result, the areas where the Nanlu dialect was in use suffered less devastation. In a broad sense, those who speak the Nanlu dialect are descendants of the Ming Dynasty's original inhabitants, while those who speak the Huguang dialect are mainly descendants of

岔，当日就绝无可能再找到石龙、石虎。开车走了三四千米，终于被晒在路上的农作物挡住了去路，主人是位七十岁的奶奶，向她问路，说是走错了。在她的指挥下，倒车几百米才得以调头。几乎听不懂老奶奶的话，她似乎对左和右也并没有概念，讲不清楚该从哪儿分路。好在，她主动提出带笔者前去。

车往回开，拐一个锐角弯，再下一段陡坡，停在一家农户门前的坝子里。老奶奶说自己走回去，笔者也就沿着狭窄的石梯迈向密林深处。

一路向下近千步石梯，终于来了一小片修竹林中的平地。一抬头，只见黑黝黝的石虎蹲在一块巨石上，虽然连头带颈都已经被砍断，却依然威风凛凛。

石虎蹲着的巨石下面，撑满了小树枝。这是一种祈福的风俗，据说可以让撑树枝的人或其亲人免受腰痛之苦。从树枝的数量看，来过这儿的人并不算少。

再往前一二十米，峭壁之上，一条龙从天而降。石龙怒目圆睁，身形曲折盘旋，呈3字形，肢体粗壮，旁斜逸出。龙头朝下，贴近池面，似如渴龙取水。龙身约10米，身径半米，身上的龙鳞一片片清晰可见。

immigrants.

After much inquiry, the path to reach Shilong Gully was finally discovered. Starting from beside Jiangkou Elementary School, I followed a narrow, cemented mountain road that ascends at an incline. The road was so narrow that it could only accommodate one vehicle, but fortunately, there were no oncoming cars along the way.

Feeling anxious when faced with a fork in the road, I found no people to ask for directions on the mountain, nor were there any signs. Taking a wrong turn would mean the impossibility of finding the Stone Dragon and Stone Tiger on that day. After driving for about three or four kilometers, the path was finally blocked by sun-dried crops, and the owner happened to be a 70-year-old grandmother. She informed me that I had taken the wrong route. Under her guidance, I had to reverse for several hundred meters before being able to turn around. Understanding the grandmother's words was nearly impossible, as she seemed to have no concept of left and right and could not clearly explain the correct fork in the road. Fortunately, she graciously offered to accompany me to the destination.

As the car reversed, I made a sharp turn and descended a steep slope, ultimately stopping in front of a house in a small courtyard. The elderly grandmother offered to walk back, leaving me to traverse through the dense forest along a narrow stone staircase.

Descending the stone staircase for nearly a thousand steps, I finally arrived at a small clearing amidst a grove of bamboo. Looking up, I saw a darkened stone tiger perched atop a massive rock. Although its head and neck had been severed, it still exuded an awe-inspiring presence.

Beneath the massive rock on which the stone tiger crouched, were countless small branches

石龙从山壁上盘旋而下　何大江 摄
The stone dragon spiraling down from a mountain wall. (Photographer: He Dajiang)

石龙、石虎开凿于宋代，守护在伏虎寺山门之外。石虎头颈残损。因为年代久远，绝壁上的石龙长时间被泥沙掩没。1970年代，因修水渠时沙石滑落，巨龙重见天日。原籍彭山的媒体人邓晓洪告诉笔者，他在幼年时就对“石龙对石虎”的民谣耳熟能详，小学时春游还曾在老师的带领下去看过石龙。

石龙沟的一头是绝壁，即石龙、石虎所在位置，另一头可通至江口沉银古战场望江台，二者的直线距离大

propping it up. It is a testament to the belief in the power of this ritual, believed to protect the individual or their loved ones from the suffering of back pain. Judging from the number of branches, it was evident that many visitors had been to this spot.

Continuing forward for another twenty meters or so, a dragon descended from the cliff above. The Stone Dragon had piercing eyes, its body coiled and winding in a shape resembling the Chinese character“3”. It possessed robust limbs, slightly inclined to the side. With its head facing downwards, it was in close proximity to the surface of the pool, as if it were a thirsty dragon seeking water. The dragon’s body stretched approximately 10 meters in length, with a diameter of half a meter. The scales on its body were distinctly visible, each one clearly defined.

The Stone Dragon and Stone Tiger were carved during the Song Dynasty and guarded the entrance of Fuhu Temple. The Stone Tiger’s head and neck were damaged. Due to the passage of time, the Stone Dragon on the precipice remained buried under sediment for a long period. It was only in the 1970s, during the construction of a water channel, that the massive dragon was once again exposed to the sunlight as sand and stones slid down. Deng Xiaohong, a media professional originally from Pengshan, shared with me that he was familiar with the folk rhyme about the “Stone Dragon and Stone Tiger” since childhood. He even visited the site during a school outing, led by his teacher, when he was in elementary school.

As I ventured to explore the site of the Stone Dragon, I discovered that one end of Shilong Gully is marked by a sheer cliff, where the Stone Dragon and Stone Tiger reside. The other end leads to the Wanjiang Terrace, overlooking the Jiangkou Sunken Silver ancient battlefield. The straight-line distance

约一千米。而望江台，正是古战场遗址发现文物最密集之处。

毫无疑问，巨大的石龙与石虎相对于沉没于江底的无数金银器来说，具有非常明确的标识作用，这也是“石龙对石虎”能进民谣并广泛流传的原因。

石龙和石虎屹立千年，曾冷眼看过一千米外江面上的战火，以及数百年后忙忙碌碌的盗宝人，却不动声色。

between the two locations is approximately one kilometer. Wanjiang Terrace is known to be the area with the densest concentration of discovered relics from the ancient battlefield.

Without a doubt, the immense stone dragon and stone tiger, in contrast to the countless gold and silver artifacts that sank to the riverbed, has a very distinct identity. This is also the reason why the tale of “the Stone Dragon and the Stone Tiger” became part of folklore and widely circulated.

For centuries, the stone dragon and stone tiger stood tall, coldly witnessing battles fought a kilometer away on the river surface and the busy antics of treasure hunters hundreds of years later, yet they remained silent.

石牛石鼓
The Stone Ox And Stone Drum

石牛与石鼓，是石龙、石虎之外的另一对CP，二者都跟张献忠遗留的巨大宝藏有关。不过前者所在的地点为成都锦江，并非彭山江口；所涉及的事件叫锢金或锦江淘宝，这是介于正剧与闹剧之间的另一出大戏。

神奇的是，跟石龙与石虎一样，石牛、石鼓也都是真实的存在。

The Stone Ox and the Stone Drum are another coupling besides the Stone Dragon and the Stone Tiger, both of which are related to the huge treasure left behind by Zhang Xianzhong. However, the former pair is located in the Jin River in Chengdu, not in Jiangkou, Penshan, and the event involved is called Gujin, the Concealment of Gold or Jinjiang Treasure Hunt, which is just a tableau between a high drama and a farce.

Miraculously, like the Stone Dragon and the Stone Tiger, the Stone Ox and the Stone Drum are also real.

寻找张献忠锢金：锦江上的淘宝大戏
Searching for Zhang Xianzhong's stashed gold: The Treasure Hunt Drama on Jin River

明末童谣

石牛对石鼓，金银万万五。
有人识得破，买个成都府。

A Nursery Rhyme at the End of Ming Dynasty

The Stone Ox to the Stone Drum it faces,
Gold and silver, in hundreds of thousands.
One who can break the code, traces,
Buys for himself, Chengdu's graces.

这首童谣跟“石龙对石虎”极为相似，流传于成都地区。除了主体由石龙对、石虎变成了石牛、石鼓之外，几乎毫无差别。准确地说，它不是寻银诀的另一个版本，而是另一种寻银诀——对应的地点不是彭山江口，而是成都锦江；对应的事件，也不是江口沉银，而是跟张献忠遗银有关的另一个故事——锢金。

This nursery rhyme is strikingly similar to "the Stone Dragon and the Stone Tiger sitting face to face", which was widely circulated in the Chengdu area. There is almost no difference except that the main subjects have changed from "the Stone Dragon and the Stone Tiger" to "the Stone Ox and the Stone Drum". To be more precise, it is not another version of the Silver Hunt Clue, but a different story of Treasure Hunt—the corresponding location is not the Jiangkou (estuary), Pengshan, but the Jin River of Chengdu; and the corresponding event is not the sunken silver at the river mouth, but the Stash of Gold by Zhang Xianzhong.

设窖于江，匪夷所思的锢金

何谓锢金？它和江口沉银到底有何关联？

锢金，又叫江藏，《明史》则称之为水藏。锢者，隔绝也，幽闭也；江藏者，藏于江水之中也。

按照《明史》《蜀碧》等史料的记载，张献忠在撤离成都时，将锦江河水通过支流排干，在河床上挖出数丈深坑，将大量金银珠贝埋藏于其中，然后再掘开堤坝，恢复河流，使外人不能发现金银藏在何处。

锢金之法，显示了张献忠的思维异于常人之处。

人之藏金，多藏于窖，埋于地。且看权倾一时、富可敌国的和珅是如

Setting up a cellar in the river, and the unthinkable stash of gold

What is called the stashed gold? How is it related to the sunken silver in the Jiangkou?

Known as "Stashed Gold" (锢金), this concealment method is also referred to as "River Cache" (江藏) or "Hiding in the water" in *Ming History.* The character 锢 denotes sealing through isolation, while 江藏 means hiding in the river or river cache.

According to the historical records of *Ming History* and *Shu Bi*, when Zhang Xianzhong evacuated Chengdu, he first drained the Jin River through its tributaries, dug a few deep pits on the riverbed, buried a large amount of gold, silver, beads and shells therein, and then dug up the embankment to restore the river, so that outsiders could not find out where the gold and silver were hidden.

The method of hoarding golds shows where Zhang Xianzhong's thinking is different from normal people.

When hiding golds, most people stash them

何操作的："夹墙藏金二万六千余两，私库藏金六千余两，地窖内并有埋藏银二百余万两"（《清实录》）。和珅之思虑不可谓不缜密，但查抄之下，依然无处遁形。

张献忠册封后宫的金册，正面阴刻楷书　高泓摄

A golden record incised in regular script, used by Zhang Xianzhong to confer titles upon his concubines. (Photographer: Gao Hong)

in the cellar and bury them in the ground. Look at how Heshen, a powerful and rich official in Qing Dynasty, historical archieves document his operation: "between the walls more than twenty-six thousand taels of gold were hidden, in his private coffers another six thousand taels of gold were stashed, and in the cellar, more than two million taels of gold were buried." (*Qing History Archive*). Heshen's thinking cannot be said not meticulous, but under the raid, those golds were still nowhere to hide.

However, Zhang Xianzhong set up a cellar in the river and buried gold, silver and jade in it, which is really unbelievable. To locate this treasure, the posterity also racked their brains and staged one after the other dramas.

然而，张献忠却设窖于江，囚埋金银美玉于其中，这样的创意实在令人匪夷所思。后人为找到这笔宝藏也是耗尽心思，上演了一出出大戏。

锢金之地点，在锦江望江楼段，也就是童谣里的"石牛对石鼓"之处。最为神奇的是，跟彭山江口的石龙、石虎一样，锦江的石牛、石鼓也是真实的存在。

The place where the golds were stashed is in the Wangjianglou section of the Jin River, which is also known as the place of the "Stone Ox and Stone Drum sitting face to face" in the nursery rhyme. The most amazing thing is that, just like the stone dragon and tiger at Jiangkou of Pengshan River, the stone ox and stone drum of the Jin River also exist in real life.

石佛寺街的石牛

石牛曾经的位置，位于九眼桥下游、望江楼公园濯锦楼对岸，一条叫

The Stone Ox on Shifoshi Street

The Stone ox was seated on Shifosi Street, a small street located at the downstream of the Nine-

作石佛寺街的小街，也距顺江路、三官堂街和龙舟路的交会点很近。如今这条街已消失，成为顺江路的一部分。

林子女士（化名）1952年出生在石佛寺街27号的民房里。街正面对着空军医院的围墙，背靠锦江。因为对面没有民房，门牌号码并非单号、双号分别标识两侧，27号往下游方向依序是26号、25号……跟林子家相隔数间房子的22号是一处公房，住着一户卢姓人家，从卢家再往前十来米就是石牛所在。

在林子记忆中，她很小的时候石牛就在那里了。上小学时的她，做完家庭作业之后，时常会去石牛处玩上一会儿。红砂石雕的石牛，风化严重，以致表面变得很粗糙，不小心擦了一下，会让皮肤生痛。林子记得，石牛很宽大，应该有两米来长，几个小孩子骑在上面都没问题。

石牛后来消失不见了，只有在枯水的季节，才从河床上显露出来。石牛倾覆于江，大致是在1958年老成渝公路拓宽时。林子猜测，是因为石牛在道路工程中碍事，被修路工人掀到了河里。

就这样，在锦江枯水期与丰水期的交替中，石牛也时隐时现。大约是1976年夏天，在新繁当知青的林子已经回城了，她在河里清洗衣服时非

Eye-Bridge, opposite to the Zhuojin Tower of Wangjianglou Park, close to the crossing point of Shunjiang Road, Sanguantang Street and Longzhou Road. Nowadays this street has disappeared and become part of Shunjiang Road.

Ms. Lin Zi (a pseudonym) was born in 1952 in a private house at 27 Shifosi Street. The street is fronted by the wall of the Air Force Hospital and backed by the Jin River. Because there is no private house across the street, the door number is not marked by odd and even numbers respectively on both sides, No. 27 downwards are No. 26, No. 25 … and a few houses away from Lin Zi's house is No. 22, a public house, living in a family surnamed Lu, ten meters from whose house is where the stone ox was located.

Linzi remembered that the stone ox had been there when she was very young. When she was in elementary school, after doing her homework, she would often go to the stone ox to play for a while. The stone ox carved in red sandstone was so weathered that the surface became so rough that it would make her skin ache if she accidentally grazed it. In her memory the stone ox was very wide, about two meters long, big enough for a few small children to ride on.

The stone ox later disappeared, only to be revealed from the riverbed during the dry season. Roughly in 1958 when the old Chengdu-Chongqing Highway was widened, the stone ox was toppled into the river. Lin Zi guessed that it was because the stone ox stood in the way during the road project and was dumped into the river by the road construction workers.

In this way, the stone ox also appeared and disappeared in the Jin River, alternating between the dry season and the wet season. About in the summer of 1976, when Lin Zi, an "Educated Youth" who went to the countryside in Xinfan came back to the city, washed clothes in the river, she was very surprised to find that the stone ox moved upstream from its

常惊奇地发现，石牛从原来的十九中（现田家炳中学）附近向上游移到了空军医院一带，移动距离有一两百米。

不是向下游而是向上游移动，观察到的现象有悖于人们的常识。其实，类似的故事在纪昀《阅微草堂笔记·姑妄听之二》中早有记载。笔记中，沧州南一寺庙山门倒塌，门前两石兽沉于河中。重修时在原址和下游打捞，却皆未能发现。一老兵说，当于上游寻之。依照他的话，果然在上游数里之外找到石兽。

究其原因，老兵解释道：流水冲激石兽下方的沙石，形成一个坑，石兽便向下倾斜，再继续冲则会翻一个身；如是反复，一次接着一次，就会向上游翻滚。

后世也有人结合物理学上的伯努利原理解释：石兽迎水处流速快、压强小，背水处流速慢、压强大，能产生向上游的推动力。无论何种原理，林子见到的石牛向上游移动，也为《阅微草堂笔记》的记载提供了现实证据。

就如同“石龙对石虎”的传说在江口流传一样，那个年代生活在锦江边的成都人也没有不知道“石牛对石鼓”的。而由这首寻银诀引发的锦江寻银，林子就曾亲眼见到。而且，那是由考古人员主持的。

original position near No.19th Middle School (now Tian Jiabing Middle School) to the Air Force Hospital area, a distance about one or two hundred meters.

Instead of moving downstream, it moved upstream, and the observed phenomenon defied common sense. In fact, a similar story has long been recorded in Ji Yun's *Notes on Reading the Thatched Cottage-Giving the Benefit of the Doubt II*. In the notes, the gate of a temple in the south of Cangzhou collapsed, and the two stone beasts in front of the gate sank in the river. People tried to dredge out them around original site and downstream when repairing the temple, but their efforts were to no avail. A veteran said, "Search in the upper reaches." According to his words, the stone beasts were found several Li upstream.

The reason for this, the veteran explained, was that the running water rushes the sand and gravel below the stone beast, forming a pit; the stone beast will tilt downward, and then turns over after being rushed repeatedly. Finally, it will roll upstream after turning over and over again.

In later times, some people also combined the Bernoulli's principle in physics to explain: the part of the stone beasts facing the water experiences fast flow speed and low pressure, and the opposite part bears slow flow speed and high pressure, which can produce a push force upstream. Regardless of the principle, the stone ox that Lin Zi saw moving upstream also provided realistic evidence for the account in the *Notes on Reading the Thatched Cottage*.

Just as the legend of "Stone Dragon and Stone Tiger sitting face to face" spreads in Jiangkou, there was no one in Chengdu who lived along the Jin River in those days did not know about "Stone Ox and Stone Drum sitting face to face". The search for silver in the Jin River, which was triggered by this *Silver Hunt Song*, was witnessed by Lin Zi. Moreover, it was conducted by archaeologists.

白光，集体无意识里的真实

时间是在1972年，地点是在与她家相隔四户的石佛寺街22号卢姓人家。缘由是：这处公房的原主人，一位老太婆，为了立功而提供了宝藏位置，称多年前她还住在此处时，曾经在天井里看到过白光，她根据“石牛对石鼓，银子万万五”的口诀，判断地下有金银。

那道亮光，就有些玄学的意味了。从物理学的角度来说，即便地下埋有金银，也不可能透过地层将光射至地表。然而在中国传统文化的认知里，埋于地下的宝藏跟白光却是有着近乎必然的联系的，所谓“精金内含，宝光外灼”。

这种神秘的光芒，其实也出现在文学作品中。鲁迅发表于1922年的小说《白光》，写一读书人在第十六次落第后变得疯癫，在院子里见到一道白光，遂逐光掘银而最后淹死的故事。

小说中最诡谲的意象就是那道白光，后世多解读为科举制度以功名利禄对读书人的引诱和戕害。然而，解读者全然没有意识到，在小说主人公的认知中，白光即意味着银藏，那

White light, a truth among collective unconsciousness

The time was in 1972, and the place was in the house of Lu, No. 22, Shifosi Street, which is four households away from her house. The reason is that the original owner of this public house, an old woman, provided the location of the treasure in order to gain credit, saying that many years ago, when she was still living here, she had seen white light in the patio, and she had judged that there was gold and silver underground according to the mnemonic chant “A stone ox and a stone drum sitting face to face is worth hundreds of thousands taels in gold and silver”.

That bright light would be somewhat metaphysical. From a physical point of view, even if there is gold and silver buried in the ground, it is not possible to shoot the light through the ground to the surface. However, in the perception of traditional Chinese culture, treasure buried in the underground and white light must have almost inevitable connection, the so-called “fine gold has light inside, while treasure’s light burns outside”.

This mysterious light actually appears in literature. Lu Xun’s novel *White Light*, published in 1922, is a story about a scholar who, after losing his 16th challenge for the imperial examine and becoming insane, sees a white light in his yard and digs for silver by the light and eventually drowns.

The most treacherous imagery in the novel is the white light, which is interpreted as the seduction and killing of the scholar by the imperial examination system with the merit and fame. However, the readers do not realize that in the main character’s cognition, the white light means silver, which is completely

完全是真实的存在——“白光如一柄白团扇，摇摇摆摆地闪起在他房里了”“然而白光却分明地又起来了，这回更广大，比硫黄火更白净，比朝雾更霏微，而且便在靠东墙的一张书桌下。”

在很多年以前笔者就读过《白光》，但开始研究锦江淘宝之后，我才明白以前根本没有读懂。

据称，古时的大户人家为家业长久计，会在地下埋一笔财富供子孙落拓时取用。为了便于挖掘，还会留下口诀指引——小说里主人公祖母留下的口诀是：“左弯右弯，前走后走，量金量银不用斗。”

据周作人的说法，《白光》中主人公陈士成的原型为鲁迅本族叔祖周子京，他也是因历次科举失利而癫狂，并听信仆妇屋内有白光之言而掘藏。周家先人留下的口诀是“离井一纤，离檐一线”，周作人说：“本宅中确有两口井……只有子京试过，试了不止一二次。”

石佛寺街那名老太婆见到的白光，以及与之对应的藏银诀“石牛对石鼓”，让她对地下的宝藏深信不疑。她的说法惊动了文管部门，便有了那次小型考古发掘。据林子回忆，围观的居民挤满了半条街，现场还来了

real—“The white light, like a white fan, shook and flashed up in his room”.“However, the white light was clearly up again, this time being wider, whiter than the sulfur fire, foggier than the morning mist, and under a desk against the east wall.”

I read *White Light* many years ago, but after I started researching Jinjiang Treasure Hunt, I realized that I hadn't understand it at all.

It is said that in ancient times, for the sake of the longevity of their families, wealthy families would bury a fortune in the ground for their children and grandchildren to use in case that they came down. In order to facilitate the excavation, they would also leave a mnemonic chant to guide them—the one left by the grandmother of the main character in the novel is “Turn left and then right, walk forward and then backward, the treasures overflowed measure.”

According to Zhou Zuoren (the elder brother of Lu Xun), the prototype of the protagonist in *White Light*, Chen Shicheng, was Lu Xun's native uncle Zhou Zijing, who also became insane due to the successive failure of the imperial examinations and believing the white light story told by her servant, dug his house for buried treasure. The mnemonic chant left by Zhou's ancestor was “one rope-long distance away from the well and the eave”. Zhou Zuoren said, “this house does have two wells… only Zijing tried more than one or two times.”

The white light seen by the old woman in Shifosi Street, and the corresponding silver secret “Stone Ox and Stone Drum sitting face to face”, convinced her of the underground treasure. Her statement alarmed the cultural management department, and a small-scale archaeological excavation ensued. According to Lin Zi's recollection, the onlookers filled half of the street, and even the public security officers came to the spot to maintain order. The stone slabs under the patio were uncovered

公安人员维持秩序。天井下面的石板被一一揭开，发掘从早上一直持续到晚上，但结果是一无所获。挖得很仔细，林子回忆道："再挖下去，差不多房子都要塌下来了。"

四十九年以后，林子联系上了当年的卢家人。经过核对，二人对1972年天井里那场发掘的记忆是一致的。

潜意识或集体无意识会造成幻觉。如果深信白光即银藏，那么鲁迅的叔祖周子京和1972年的那名老太婆能见到白光，也就不那么难于理解了。但是，民国二十八年四月八日深夜十一点半，锦江淘江工程现场，监工员、司机及四位车水工人见到的白光突涌，言之凿凿，载之于档，则让人十分费解了。

跟张献忠宝藏相关的挖掘，除了江口沉银遗址考古，规模最大的就要算1939年的锦江淘江了。不过，锦江淘江算不上考古，其初衷依然是为了掘宝。四川历史上首次现代意义的考古，还要等到数年之后的永陵发掘。

八十多年前曾经轰轰烈烈的锦江淘江，涉及民国四川史上众多重要人物，甚至蒋介石也以"（四川省政府）兼理主席 蒋中正"之名签署了训令，准允开掘江藏，并下令加以保护。这一事件，有相当数量的材料存于成都

one by one, and the excavation lasted from the morning until the evening, resulting in nothing. The excavation was very carefully, Lin Zi recalled, "If they kept digging, the house would collapse."

Forty-nine years later, Linzi contacted the Lu's family. After comparing notes, they found their memories of the 1972 excavation on the patio consistent.

The subconsciousness or collective unconsciousness can cause hallucinations. If one is convinced that white light is where the silver is stashed, then it is not so difficult to understand that Lu Xun's uncle Zhou Zijing and the old woman in 1972 could see white light. However, what happened on April 8 of 28 year of the Republic of China (1939), late at night at 11:30, at the Jin River Dredging Project site, really puzzled people as the on-site supervisors, drivers and four car water workers saw in their naked eyes the sudden surge of white light, their words convincing and being recorded in files.

In addition to the archeological research on the sinking of the silver in Jiangkou, the largest scale excavation related with Zhang Xianzhong's treasure should be the Jin River Dredging Project in 1939. However, the dredging project is not considered archaeological one, and its original purpose is still to dig for treasure. The first modern sense of archaeological research in Sichuan history would wait a few years till the Yongling excavation.

More than eighty years ago, the Jin River Dredging Project involved many important figures in the history of Sichuan in the Republic of China era, and even Chiang Kai-shek got into the act by signing a decree in the name of "Chiang Chung-cheng, the concurrent chairman of the Sichuan Provincial Government", allowing the excavation of a river cache and ordering its protection. This event, which a considerable amount of material exists in the Chengdu

市档案馆，其肇始是一份申请挖掘江藏以资助抗日战争的意见书。

Municipal Archives, began with an application for permission to excavate the river cache in order to finance the war against Japan.

前清贡生二十七年的等待

意见书的呈请人是前清贡生杨白鹿、前川军师长马昆山二人，其中真正的发起者是杨白鹿。所呈交的对象是国民革命军第八十八军军长范绍增（四川方言电视剧《傻儿师长》主角樊傻儿原型）、国民政府行政院院长孔祥熙。按理说，范绍增作为军人，跟此事并无直接关联。应该是杨白鹿自忖跟孔祥熙身份地位相差太大说不上话，因此把四川老乡范军长拉来背书。

这份提交于民国二十七年（1938年）十二月的意见书概要为：当年张献忠锦江窖金载于史乘，经多年查方相信非虚，欲采用开矿之法乘枯水期挖掘锦江，其费用自筹；若真能挖掘出财富，则百分之八十交于国家，仅提留百分之二十归以总办杨白鹿、会办马昆山为首的开办者。

史料跟张献忠锦江藏银相关者，除了杨白鹿呈文所提及的《鹃碧录》《蜀碧》两书之外，《明史》《蜀难叙略》等也有记载。

《蜀难叙略》称，张献忠动用了

27 years waiting for a tribute scholar of the former Qing Dynasty

The petitioners of the application were the former Qing Tribute Scholar Yang Bailu and former Sichuan army division commander Ma Kunshan, of which the real initiator was Yang Bailu. The objects of the submission were Fan Shaozeng (the prototype of the protagonist, Fan, the fool, of the Sichuan dialect TV series *Silly Division Commander*) the 88th Army Commander of the National Revolutionary Army, and Kong Xiangxi, the Premier of the Executive Yuan of the National Government. In theory, Fan Shaozeng, as an army commander, was not directly related to this matter. It is supposed to be that Yang Bailu thought that his status difference with Kong Xiangxi was so wide that he had to rope in his fellow-townsman Fan Shaozeng as an endorsement.

The summary of the application submitted in December 1938 was that the record of Zhang Xianzhong's stashed gold in Jin River, after many years of verifying, was not false; the mining method would be adopted, in the dry season, to excavate the Jin River, and the related expenses would be self-financed; should the treasure be dug out, 80% of it would be handed over to the state, and only 20% of it would go to the start-ups such as the chief officer, Yang Bailu, and the assistant officer, Ma Kunshan.

Historical materials related to Zhang Xianzhong's Jin river cache, in addition to *Green Cuckoo Records* and *Shu Bi*, which were mentioned by Yang Bailu's application, also recorded in *The History of Ming* and

上千人的力量，将聚敛的金银运往锦江，前后花了三个月的时间。在水浅处挖掘支流放水，待得河枯则在河床上挖穴填以金银。

《蜀碧》所提及的锢金（或江藏），大同小异。二者也都提及，张献忠将搬运、挖凿之人尽数杀死在工地。不同的是，《蜀难叙略》称，将金银装入木鞘带到江口，是在江藏之后；而《蜀碧》则将锢金的时间，确定在败走江口、逃往川北之间。

淘掘江藏的源起，有人称，当年张献忠杀死江藏民工时，有一石匠侥幸得逃后，画下藏宝图传之后人，经历数百年辗转到了杨白鹿手中。

成都的锦江淘宝之后数年，重庆也发生过一起类似事件。一位黄姓长寿县民向政府献上藏宝图，称当年张献忠在嘉陵江埋宝后杀死数万民工，其先祖亦是漏网者，临死之际将地图传于子孙。

这类过于传奇的说法，带有非常强烈的藏宝小说痕迹，不足以采信。其实，成都档案馆馆藏资料，存有杨白鹿对此事由来之自叙。辛亥革命之后当月，一位名叫江希曾的前清官员（光绪十二年进士）在公馆单独宴请杨白鹿。席毕，突然向晚辈杨白鹿跪下，委托其发掘江藏、贡献国家。

Narrative on the Catastrophe of Shu.

According to *Narrative on the Catastrophe of Shu*, Zhang Xianzhong mobilized thousands of people to transport the gold and silver he amassed to the Jin River, which took three months. Tributaries were dug at shallow places to release water, and when the river dried up, holes were dug in the riverbed to be filled with gold and silver.

The stashed gold (or river cache) mentioned in Shu Bi is more or less the same. Both mention that Zhang Xianzhong killed all the people who were transporting and digging at the construction site. The difference is that the *Narrative on the Catastrophe of Shu* states that bringing the gold and silver in wooden sheaths to the river mouth happened after being stashed in the Jin river, while *Shu Bi* determines the time of concealment of the gold to be between the defeat at the river mouth and the escape to the north of Sichuan.

It was proclaimed that when Zhang Xianzhong killed the civilian workers, there was a stonemason luckily escaped and painted the treasure map to be passed on to the descendants. Hundreds of years later, this map ended up in the hands of Yang Bailu.

A similar incident occurred in Chongqing a few years after Chengdu's Jinjiang treasure hunt. A Huang resident living in Changshou County offered a treasure map to the government, saying that Zhang Xianzhong had killed tens of thousands of workers after burying the treasure in the Jialing River, and that his ancestor, who had a narrow escape, had passed the map on to his children and grandchildren on his deathbed.

This kind of sayings lean too much on legendary stories, tainted with very strong traces of the treasure-hunt novel, not enough to be believed. In fact, in the Chengdu Archives, there is a self-report of Yang Bailu's account of the origins of the incident. In the month after the 1911 Revolution, a former Qing official named Jiang Xizeng (a *Jin Shi*, or the Imperial

此说之所以具有可信度，在于江希曾跟前文咸丰年间上条呈发掘江口沉银的陈泰初相同，都是知识分子，有条件接触朝廷文档及史料，并有分析辨别能力；二者也皆多地为官，历练丰富，曾亲见遗银或多次实地调查。

受此委托后，杨白鹿处处留心。二十七年后正值抗战进入相持阶段，觉得时机成熟，故有此议。

杨白鹿其人，早年受的是旧式教育，考中过前清贡生，但绝非腐儒。实际上，光绪三十一年（1905年）杨白鹿在三十三岁时，就参加过反清的彭县起义。后来也多次起兵、逃亡、坐监，清王朝覆灭之后，还曾短暂担任过四川都督。

他的发掘江藏意见书开篇第一句话，就以哥伦布（文中作“科仑布”）为例，称其先后游说葡萄牙国王约翰二世、英国国王亨利七世，皆被视为妄诞，唯有西班牙王后给予支持，方才成就不世功业。仅此一例，亦可见杨白鹿之视野开阔。

大概是因为抗战的确需要钱，国民政府对此事还是很上心，算得上是一路绿灯。翻年之后，节奏明显加快。

民国二十八年（1939年）二月五

Examination Graduates, in the 12th year of the Guangxu reign) invited Yang Bailu alone to a banquet in his house. After the banquet, he suddenly knelt down Yang Bailu, who was his junior and entrusted him with the task of discovering the river cache and contributing to the country.

The credibility of this statement lies in the facts that both Jiang Xizeng and Chen Taichu, who submitted to Emperor Xianfeng to excavate the sunken silver in Jiangkou, were intellectuals. They had access to court documents and historical materials and the ability to analyze and discriminate; both of them were officials working in many places with rich experiences; both had personally seen the remains of the silver or conducted a number of field investigations.

After being entrusted with this task, Yang Bailu paid close attention to every aspect of it. Twenty-seven years later, when the Chinese People's War of Resistance Against Japanese Aggression entered a stalemate phase, he felt that the time was ripe for making his petition.

In his early years, Yang Bailu received the old-style education and qualified as a “tribute scholar” of the former Qing Dynasty. But by no means was he a pedantry. In fact, in the thirty-first year of Guangxu (1905), when Yang Bailu was 33 years old, he participated in the anti-Qing Peng County Uprising. Later on, he repeatedly took up arms, fled and was imprisoned, and after the collapse of the Qing Dynasty, he was briefly the Governor of Sichuan.

The first sentence in his excavation application cites Columbus as an example, saying he successively lobbied King John II of Portugal and King Henry VII of England, both attempts regarded as delusion. Only through the support of the Queen of Spain did he accomplish unprecedented exploit. This example alone shows the broad vision of Yang Bailu.

日，杨白鹿、马昆山再上呈文，提出施工地点为“东门外兵工厂湾内以华里计共三里”。所谓兵工厂，即成都人耳熟能详的南光厂。其位置与望江楼隔锦江相对，前身为四川总督丁宝桢创于清光绪三年的四川机器总局，宣统元年更名为四川兵工厂，1961年3月再度更名为国营南光机器厂。

仅仅在第二天，二月六日，四川省建设厅技正（总工程师）潘钟秀、技士（专业人员）徐煜就交出了查勘报告。而这份报告，还是在会同杨白鹿实地考察之后做出来的。足见这一次有了精心准备。

查勘报告确定了发掘地点，“仅在望江楼南约一华里处，大河与支流交叉口之河中如岛形大土墩上一处”。大河即锦江，支流即石牛堰，岛形大土墩即望江楼附近的江心岛。锦江南流遇上岛尖，石牛堰即从此分出，流绕近两千米后又回到锦江。两条河流环抱的土地上，今日有楼盘河滨印象及东湖公园。

报告交上去之后一路绿灯。

当年三月十八日，四川省会警察局即发出训令，命外东分局对淘江工程进行保护。三月二十日，成都市政府派出特务队驻扎郊外公园（现望江

Probably because the Resistance War against Japanese Aggression did need money, the National Government put great stock on this matter. After the turn of the year, the pace of execution picked up significantly.

On February 5 of the twenty-eighth year of the Republic of China (1939), Yang Bailu and Ma Kunshan submitted their petition again, and suggested “the East Gate outside the Arsenal, total of three Li” as the construction site. The so-called Arsenal was the Nanguang factory, a household name for Chengdu residents. Its location was opposite to Wangjianglou Park across the Jin River, and was formerly known as Sichuan General Administration of Machinery, which was created by the Governor-General of Sichuan, Ding Baozhen, in the third year of Guangxu. In the first year of the Xuantong, it was renamed as the Sichuan Arsenal, and in March 1961 was renamed once again as the state-owned Nanguang Machinery Factory.

Only on the next day, February 6, Pan Zhongxiu (Chief Engineer) and Xu Yu, a professional technician, from the Sichuan Provincial Department of Construction Technology handed over a survey report. And this report was completed on the basis of Yang Bailu’s field visit. It was clear that careful preparation was made this time.

This survey report identified the excavation site: “only about a mile south of Wangjianglou Park, a large island-shaped mound where the big river and the tributary intersect”. The “big river” here is the Jin River, the tributary is Shiniuyan and the island-shaped mound is the Jiangxin Island near Wangjianglou Park. The Jin River meets the tip of the island when it runs south; thus, Shiniuyan is bifurcated from this point; flowing around nearly two kilometers, it winds its way back to the Jin River. Today, on the land surrounded by the two rivers, there are Riverside Impression

楼公园）维持秩序。

民国二十九年三月十八日，财政部咨请四川省政府予以协助保护。四月十月日，四川省兼理主席蒋中正、建设厅长陈筑山签发训令，批准办理江藏事宜，令成都市政府予以保护。可以说，对此事的关注已经上升到了国家层面。

事实上，真正的发掘在此之前一年就开始了。

查勘报告交上去不到一个月，民国二十八年三月一日，杨白鹿任董事长、马昆山任总经理的锦江淘江公司就招集同人，谋划开工。公司分工明晰，除经理、外务、设计、工程等管理人员之外，另外招有工人九十六名。

淘掘轰轰烈烈。在上文所述江心岛岛尖，挖了一个长十丈、宽一丈的条形大坑。到了三月六日已挖有丈余之深，开始出现积水，于是拉来四架龙骨车排水。地下水越来越多，又加之下了两天雨，杨白鹿心中焦灼，担心在汛期前无收获，于是又弄来汽油吸水机排水，以图加快进度。

民国二十八年三月十二日，挖出东西来了：四具骷髅头及枯骨无数，同时还有五六寸厚的血浸砂石。这无法让人不想起《明史》《蜀碧》《蜀难

residence compounds and the Donghu Park.

The report was handed in and given the green light all the way through.

On March 18th of that year, the Sichuan Provincial Capital Police Department issued a directive ordering its Waidong Branch to protect the Jin River Dredging Project site. On March 20, the Chengdu Municipal Government sent a special squad stationed in the suburbs of the park (now the Wangjianglou Park) to maintain order.

On March 18, 29th year of the Republic of China, the Ministry of Finance requested the Sichuan Provincial Government to assist in its protection. On April 10, Chiang Chung-cheng, Chairman of Sichuan Province and Chen Zhushan, the Construction Director of Sichuan Province issued a directive, approving the proposal of excavation of river cache and entrusting Chengdu Municipal Government to protect. It can be said that this matter has risen to the national level.

In fact, the real excavation began a year before that.

Less than a month after the survey report was submitted, on March 1, 1928, Jinjiang Dredging Company, with Yang Bailu as chairman and Ma Kunshan as general manager, started to recruit and prepared for construction. The company's division of labor was clear—in addition to the manager, field operators, designer, engineers, there were ninety-six workers.

The panning and digging went on with great vigor. At the tip of the Jiangxin Island mentioned above, a large bar-shaped pit ten feet long and one foot wide was dug. By March 6, the excavation had gone more than ten feet deep, and water began to accumulate. Four keel-shaped vehicles were called to drain water. More and more groundwater came out, coupled with two days of rain. Yang Bailu was very anxious about nothing could pan out before the flood season, therefore, gasoline suction machines were

叙略》上张献忠杀尽运夫、凿工的记载。存于成都市档案馆的《锦江淘江股份有限公司工程经过记略》称，那一层血浸砂石，经多数专家研究判定，的确为人血浸渍而成。

整个三月份，在血砂层之下共挖出九十二根石条，上刻“张”字等字迹，连接处抹有桐油灰；石条之下两尺又有三合层；其下又有朽木——种种迹象表明，此处确进行过大规模的施工。

神奇之事发生在四月八日。当夜无月，到了深夜十一点半，监工员谢光前见到施工现场周围涌现出一大圈类似月色的白光。于是叫醒司机李忠义，又有四名抽水工人共同见证，均大为惊骇。

见白光，地下必有宝藏，这样的认知在传统文化中可谓沦肌浃髓，受过现代科学教育也不尽能免疫。《工程经过记略》中竟然有这样的记载：按照考古家的看法，“若中无金银宝物，外面决不能放光”。

对于前文提及的石佛寺街老太婆和周子京仆妇见到的白光，是集体无意识反射出的幻光。但是，民国二十八年四月八日深夜，锦江淘江工地上出现的白光，几乎不可能解释为六个见证者同时出现了幻觉；也很难

summoned to speed up the progress.

On March 12, 28th year of the Republic of China, something was dug out: four skeletons and countless dead bones, along with five or six inches thick blood-soaked gravel. It was impossible not to be reminded of the account of Zhang Xianzhong killing all the carriers and chiselers in the *The History of Ming*, *Shu Bi* and *Narrative on the Catastrophe of Shu*. In the *Project Log of Jinjiang Dredging Company Limited* (hereafter this text will be abbreviated as *Project Log)*which is stored in the Chengdu Municipal Archives of, the layer of blood-soaked gravel, judged by most of the experts, is indeed imbued with human blood.

Throughout the month of March, under the blood sand layer a total of ninety-two stone strips were dug out, all engraved with the word “Zhang”, and the joints were smeared with tung oil ash; two feet below the stone strips, there were triple layers under which rotten wood can be found—all indicated that a large-scale construction had been carried out here.

The magic happened on April 8th. That night there was no moon. Late at night at 11:30, the supervisor Xie Guangqian saw a large circle of white light similar to the moonlight around the construction site. He woke up the driver Li Zhongyi, with four pumping workers as witnesses; all of them are greatly shocked.

When white light is present, treasure must lie underground. Such cognition in traditional culture is deep-seated and even modern scientific education doesn’t render people immune. Such a record can be found in the *Project Log* that according to archaeologists,“if there are no gold and silver treasures inside, light shall not be overflown outside”.

The white lights seen by the old woman on Shifosi Street and Zhou Zijing mentioned earlier were phantom lights under the influence of collective unconscious. However, the white light that appeared

找到他们需要作假，编造出这样一个故事的动机。

那么，是否只能以神秘现象一言以蔽之呢？不！

细索档案，发现有这样一句话："当放光之前二时，掘壕发出河岸崩溃声。"岸崩与放光先后出现，指向一种并不太常见的自然现象——地震光，一种伴随地震或在其前后出现于地震区域上空的光芒。（对地震光的解释，目前还处于假说阶段，简言之可理解为：地震时岩石受到巨大压力产生电荷，在空气中产生发光现象。）很可能，当时曾经有过一次不为记载的小型地震。

on the Jin River dredging construction site late at night on April 8, 1928 was hardly explained away by a hallucination of the six witnesses at the same time; and it is also difficult to find the motivation for them to fake and fabricate such a story.

So, is it only possible to summarize it as a mystical phenomenon in a nutshell? No.

Perusal of the archives reveals the such a phrase "two hours before the release of the light, sound of collapsing of riverbank opposite to the construction site can be heard." The successive appearance of the riverbank collapse and the release of light point to a less common natural phenomenon: seismic light, a kind of light that accompanies earthquakes or appears in the air over the earthquake area around the time of the earthquakes. (The explanation for seismic light, which is still in the hypothesis stage, can be understood briefly as the phenomenon of luminescence in the air caused by the electric charge generated by the enormous pressure on rocks during earthquakes.) Most likely there was a small-scale unrecorded earthquake at that time.

石牛石鼓，现身江心岛

淘江现场江心岛西北方近处，与锦江一江之隔的是著名的望江楼园林区。此地有文物遗迹薛涛井，万历年间夔州通判何宇度《益部谈资》称"水极清澈，石栏周环"，蜀王府取此井水仿薛涛旧法制笺。嘉庆十九年（1814年）在此处建吟诗楼、濯锦楼，咸丰九年（1859年）建崇丽阁，民国十七年（1928年）以相关建筑群为基

The stone ox and drum showed themselves at Jiangxin Island

Near the northwest of the Jiangxin Island where the river dredging construction was underway was the famous Wangjianglou garden area, separated by the Jin River from the opposite riverbank. In this garden, there has a cultural relic Xue Tao Well, and in the years of Wanli of Ming Dynasty, He Yudu, the Controller-General of Kui Zhou described in his *Chatting Topics of Yizhou* "water here is extremely clear, dotted by stone fences", The Mansion of King of Shu used to take water from this well to make paper basing on a paper-making method created by

础建成“成都市第一郊外公园”。

江面淘宝，本身就极富戏剧色彩，成都的《新新新闻》《大公报》《宇宙风》和《现世报》几家报刊捕捉到机会，累牍连篇报道进度、重构现场，撩拨着市民的八卦之心。第一郊外公园，在当年就是踏青的好去处。锦江开挖之后，正值修竹万竿、春光无限，游人以凭吊薛涛为序曲，逛完望江楼后，正好隔江观看掘宝大戏。

民国时期成都发行量最大、影响面最广的民营性报纸《新新新闻》记者张善，得宪兵许可登岛，写出的报道中有不少有趣细节，比如章加活佛与一喇嘛在人群中一面观望一面高谈阔论，两名穿高跟鞋的时髦女郎不慎落水；等等。

为了尽快有所收获，淘江公司不惜投巨资使用先进技术。除了汽油吸水机之外，还聘请无线电专家抓紧制作金属探测仪。

锦江淘江投入巨大，据当时媒体测算，即便工人日工资仅有四角，但随着项目推进到四月下旬，工地上员工已达一百七十余人，加上汽油消耗，每日开支已达三百元大洋之巨——民国大洋的购买力，可以鲁迅三千五百大洋在北京购买四合院为参

Xu Tao herself. In the 19th year of Jiaqing (1814), the Yinshi Building and Zhuojin Building were built here; in the 9th year of Xianfeng (1859), the Chongli Pavilion was built; and in the 17th year of the Republic of China (1928), the First Suburban Park of Chengdu was built on the basis of the relevant architectural complex.

Treasure hunt in the river was itself imbued with dramatic hue, which caught the attention of several local newspapers, such as *Xinxin News, Ta Kung Pao, Cosmic Winds* and *Nowadays* to report the progress. Their series of articles reconstructed the scene and teased the public for gossiping. the First Suburban Park of Chengdu in those days was a good place for going for walk in the spring. When the excavation of the Jin River was underway, the ten thousand bamboo trees were in full swing and spring colors filled the garden. As a result, tourists, starting to pay visit to the Xue Tao Well as a prelude, then strolling through the Wangjiang Tower, came to the riverside to watch the excavation of the treasure hunt tableau.

Zhang Shan, a reporter from *Xinxin News*, the most widely circulated and influential private newspaper in Chengdu during the Republic of China period, boarded the island with the permission of the gendarmerie, and wrote a report with many interesting details, such as Zhangjia Living Buddha and a lama talking to each other while they watched in the crowd, and two fashionable women in high heels falling into the water, and so on.

In order to pan out as soon as possible, the River Dredging Company spared no expense in using advanced technology. In addition to gasoline suction machines, metal detectors were made by the hired experts.

The input of the Jin River dredging project was enormous. According to estimation by the media at the time, even if the daily wage of workers was only 40 cents, as the project advanced to the end of April, the site staff reached more than 170, plus

考。此数字尚不包括在工地上尽义务的公司职员（其实是有固定的薪水支出的），以及前期在设备上的巨大投入，而这些钱全部由公司股东筹集而来——他们对于回报的期待，必然对牵头者杨白鹿构成巨大压力，其焦灼可想而知，《工程经过记略》的"抱百折不挠之志"等话语，可视作自勉之语。

在漫长的焦虑和失望之中，也有提振信心之时。最让人兴奋的，莫过于在工地上挖出了石牛。

石牛是一头睡卧的水牛，其角朝向东北。在牛头对着的地方继续挖，居然又挖出了一块奇石。这块石头上圆下方，圆者如鼓，左右两侧凸出、中间凹陷。天哪，石鼓也挖到了！

确实，根据形状判断，这就是一块尚未完工的石鼓。石鼓又称抱鼓石，是传统建筑的宅门构件，以标识宅主的身份地位。无论如何，寻银诀中石牛、石鼓等要素都齐全了，这难道不是对四月八日深夜那道白光最好的印证吗？

gasoline consumption, the daily expenditure reached a stunning 300 Silver Yuan—the purchasing power of Silver Yuan in the Republic of China can be pondered by the fact that Lu Xun, a famous Chinese author, bought a four-roomed house in Beijing with 3500 Silver Yuan. This figure did not include the company's regular staff who did their duty on the construction site (in fact, they had a fixed salary), as well as the huge investment in equipment in the early stage. All of this money was raised by the company's shareholders—their expectation of return, as a huge pressure, inevitably fell on the shoulder of Yang Bailu; thus, his anxiety can be imagined. Words like "embracing an indomitable spirit" in *Project Log* can be regarded as words of self-encouragement.

Amidst the long hours of anxiety and disappointment, there have been moments of boosted confidence. There is nothing more exciting than digging up stone ox on a construction site.

The stone ox is a sleeping buffalo with its horns facing northeast. Continuing to dig where the ox's head was facing, people unearthed another strange stone. This stone is rounded on the top and square on the bottom, like a drum, with the left and right sides protruding and the center concave. Alas, the stone drum was also dug up!

Indeed, judged by the shape, this is an unfinished stone drum. The stone drum is a house door component of traditional architecture, to identify the status of the house owner. In any case, the elements of the *Silver Hunt Song* such as the stone ox and the stone drum are complete, and isn't this the best proof of the white light late at night on April 8th?

石牛堰上镇水兽

石牛从何而来？

挖出石牛的江心岛东岸，锦江向

The Water-Supressing Beast on the Shiniuyan

Where did the ox come from?

东南方向分出了一道支流，其状颇似都江堰之内、外江分流。这道支流，即前文提及的石牛堰。当年张献忠在锦江锢金，以支流排干锦江之水，即是此堰。

石牛堰在清代被称作洗瓦堰，其堤在明代叫万年堤。沿着河堰，堤坝上以石人、石牛间隔而立的方式，共置有石人九具、石牛九头——这在明正德《四川志》、天启《成都府志》，清雍正《四川通志》、嘉庆《华阳县志》中皆可印证。

其中，雍正《四川通志》的记载为：万年堤，在华阳县东河岸，长三百余丈，置石人、石牛各九，盖前人以之镇水患者。

On the east bank of the Jiangxin island, Jin River divided into a tributary to the southeast direction, its shape quite similar to the inner and outer river division of Dujiangyan Irrigation Project. This tributary is the aforementioned Shiniuyan and also the one used as a tributary by Zhang Xianzhong to drain the water of the Jin River when he buried the gold in it.

Shiniuyan was called Xiwayan in the Qing Dynasty, and its dike was called Wannian Dike in the Ming Dynasty. Along the river weir, stone figures such as people and ox were erected alternately, a total of nine stone people and stone oxen—which can be verified in *The Record of Sichuan* in the Zhengde reign of Ming Dynasty, *The Record of Chengdu Prefecture* in the Tianqi reign of Ming Dynasty, *The General Note of Sichuan* in the Yongzheng reign of Qing Dynasty and, *The Record of Huayang County* in the Jiaqing reign of Qing Dynasty.

It is recorded in *The General Note of Sichuan* in the Yongzheng reign of Qing Dynasty as "Wannian Dike is located on the east bank of the river in Huayang County, more than 3000 feet long, with nine stone people and nine stone oxen erected for the purpose of supressing floods by the former people."

出土于天府广场北侧建筑工地的镇水兽石犀牛。作为镇水兽，石犀外形后来演化为水牛　何大江 摄

A stone water-control rhinoceros unearthed at a construction site north of Tianfu Square. Its design later influenced the depiction of water buffalo. (Photographer: He Dajiang)

说得很明白了，这些石牛就是镇水兽——这是秦蜀郡守李冰制石犀镇水之风俗的流传，只是石犀后来演变为水牛的形状了。

民国二十八年淘江挖出的石牛，

It is obvious that these stone oxen were the Water-Supressing Beast— stone rhinoceros employed by Li Bing, the county chief of Shu in Qin Dynasty, to suppress floods. The only difference the stone rhinoceros later evolved into the shape of the buffalo.

The stone ox dug out by the Jin River dredging project in the 28th year of the Republic of China was

就是明代置于万年堤上的九头牛之一，也是20世纪50年代幼年林子在石牛堰东岸石佛寺街上见到的石牛。

如今，在锦江的西岸，即望江楼公园的河滩上，摆放着两头石牛。两头石牛呈卧姿，材质为红砂石，皆以圆雕手法雕成，大小相近，为1.4米长、0.8米宽（因为记忆的误差，林子童年眼中的石牛更大一些），不带底座0.8米高。

北边的那一头，两前肢皆作跪卧状；南边的石牛，则左前肢跪卧，右前肢伸向前方，意态似更闲适。北边的石牛，保存得更为完整，头上的角、耳、嘴缝皆清晰可见；南面的则风蚀损害严重得多，颈部以上已十分模糊，只剩下两个鼻孔还隐约可见。

那么，民国年间挖出的到底是哪一头呢？林子女士根据民国年间石牛出水老照片断定，是置放于南面、面目更加模糊的那一头，因为她小时候见到的石牛，头部结构较为简单。

考古界有句行话："干万年，湿千年，不干不湿就半年。"先出水的，接受的风蚀、雨淋、日晒更多——毕竟民国年间挖出的石牛在河滩上多摆放了若干年。此说不悖。

one of the nine oxen placed on the Wannian Dyke in the Ming Dynasty, and was also the stone ox seen by the young Linzi in the 1950s on the street of Shifosi Street on the east bank of Shiniuyan.

Today, on the west bank of the Jin River, that is, on the river bank of Wangjianglou Park, there are two stone oxen, both in reclining position, made of the red sandstone and carved in the round and similar size, 1.4 meters long, 0.8 meters wide (because of memory errors, in Lin Zi's childhood eyes, the stone ox was bigger), and 0.8 meters high without base.

The one on the north side kneels down both front limbs while the one on the south goes down on the left front leg and stretches out its right front leg, looking more leisure. The north one is preserved more completely, with its horns, ears, mouth slit clearly visible, but the one on the south, experiencing severe wind erosion, looks very vague above its neck, only two nostrils still vaguely identifiable.

Which one was dug up during the Republic of China? Ms. Lin Zi, basing on the old photos of the stone oxen that came out of the water during the Republic of China, concluded that it was the one placed on the south side, with a more blurred face, for the one she saw when she was a child had a simpler head structure.

There is a jargon in the archaeological community, "in a dry environment it can be stored for a thousand years, in a moist environment it can be stored for ten thousand years, while in an unstable environment where dryness and wetness alternate, it can only be stored for half a year." The one out of the water first received more wind erosion, rain cleansing and sun shining and was exposed on the river bank for more years; therefore, it experiences more wear and tear. Indeed, the finding corresponds with what the jargon says.

1997年府南河工程挖出的石牛　何大江 摄
A stone ox excavated in 1997 during the Funan River project. (Photographer: He Dajiang)

北面那头，是1997年10月修建府南河望江楼段生态河堤（府南河整治工程中的一段）时挖出的。南面的那头即林子在石佛寺街上所见，前文提及，在1958年修路时又回到了锦江之中，它啥时候重见天光未见记载——会不会也是在1997年修堤之时呢？

The one on the northern end was dug out in October 1997 during the construction of the ecological embankment of the Wangjianglou section of the Funan River (a section of the Funan River Improvement Project). The one on the southern end mentioned earlier, which Lin Zi saw on Shifosi Street, was returned to the Jin River in 1958 when a road was being repaired, and it has not been documented when it was exposed under the daylight—could it have been when the embankment was repaired in 1997 as well?

在激情与绝望中反复

Repeatedly in passion and despair

《工程经过记略》的记载止于1939年五月初。因为汛期来临、江水上涨，不得不停工。

到了第二年的二月中下旬，挖掘再次启动。这一次，施工方对金属探测仪寄予了厚望。《新新新闻》记者张善再一次登岛，并戴上耳筒亲身体验了金属探矿仪的效用。在普通的地面，耳筒中并无异响；然而到了施工点，工人将机器由高处往低移动，张善开始听到由小到大“质——质——

The record in the *Project Log* ends in early May 1939 when the work had to be stopped because of the onset of the flood season and the rise of the river.

In late February of the following year, the excavation had started again. This time, the construction team had high hopes for the metal detector. Once again, *Xinxin News* reporter Zhang Shan went to the island and put on earphones to experience the metal detector's effectiveness firsthand. On the ground, there was no sound in the earphones; however, when the construction site was reached, the workers moved the machine from higher place to lower place, and Zhang Shan began to hear

质”的声响。

按照此种方式探得的潜在埋宝地，最大一块有一百平方丈，换算出来即九百平方米。不过按照工程师的说法，探矿仪只能探得下方有金属，至于埋得有多深则无能为力。

然而，探矿仪、大规模排水、开掘机等先进技术及设备的使用，也并未带来想象中的财富。工程已经进入第三个年头，收获的仅有那数十枚张献忠时铸造的大顺通宝——跟投入的巨大花费相比，完全可以忽略不计。

据当时的官方通讯社中央社消息，到了1941年三月，在两丈八尺的深度发现了一层碎石块，由铁水及三合土凝成——这是否是张献忠埋宝时所加的盖子，令人揣想。

此时，金属探测仪发出了更为响亮的鸣叫。碎石层的深度在地下两丈八尺，而探测仪的有效深度为四丈左右——如果再向下挖掘一丈二，是否就可以找到宝藏，应该说很让人期待。但为什么没有继续再挖下去，颇让人疑惑。

1941年三月二十日，《大公报》刊载了一条名为《成都淘金记 张献忠藏金处发掘似获眉目》的短消息——跟中央社之文相比，却并无新意——这是最后的绝唱，从此再无有消息见

the sizzling sound from strength to strength.

The largest piece of potential buried treasure land explored in this way is 100 square feet, which amounts to 900 square meters. However, according to the engineer's statement, the prospector can only detect that there is metal underneath, incapable of knowing how deep it is buried.

However, the use of advanced technology and equipment, such as prospectors, large-scale drainage and excavators, did not bring the imagined wealth either. The project had entered its third year, and the only thing that had been harvested were the dozens of *Dashun Tongbao* minted during the time of Zhang Xianzhong—completely negligible compared to the huge expenses invested.

According to the *Central News Agency*, the official news agency at the time, by March 1941, a layer of crushed stone was found at a depth of 2.8 Zhang (roughly 28 feet), congealed by liquid iron and tabia—it was speculative whether this was the lid that Zhang Xianzhong put on when he buried the treasure.

At this point, the metal detector chirped even louder. The depth of the rubble layer was two Zhangs and eight Chi(Chinese unit of length; 1 Zhang equals to 10 Chi) underground, and the effective depth of the detector was about four Chis—it was very much to be expected that the treasure could be landed if one Zhang and two Chis were dug down. But why the digging did not continue any further was rather puzzling.

On March 20, 1941, *Ta Kung Pao* published a news nugget titled *Chengdu Gold Rush: Excavation of Zhang Xianzhong's Gold Cache Seems to Have Gained Promise*—nothing new compared to the article in the *Central News Agency*—and this was the last news report of the treasure hunt, no more appearing on the archives since then.

于档案。

结果可想而知：传说中的宝藏最终没有现身，杨白鹿、马昆山等始作俑者，在激情与绝望两种极端情绪的反复交错中，不得不承认现实、偃旗息鼓；而一众股东三年来只有投入未见回报，锦江淘江公司在耗光资金之后也不得不悄然关张了。

杨白鹿倡议开挖江藏，其初衷是在为国还是在为己，这类心理活动是无法推测的，抑或兼而有之也未可知，二者并不矛盾。

锦江淘宝动议之初，杨白鹿以哥伦布为例游说当局，也以哥氏自勉。然而吊诡的是，集冒险、欺骗等品性于一身的哥伦布开创了不朽功业，而劳心劳力的杨白鹿却毫无所获，其名亦埋葬于泛黄的故纸，几乎不为人寻得。

人事已尽，奈天命何？

锦江河床上的巨额财富，牵动着世人的心，甚至在彭山江口和成都之外，也有着类似的歌谣。诸如，“金鸡对石鼓，值银十万五。有人来识破，买个夔州府”“石人对石鼓，黄金五万五。谁能猜得着，买下重庆府”。而在重庆的嘉陵江上，更是发生过类似的淘宝大剧，即前文所述长寿县民贡献藏宝图一事。

The result is predictable: the legendary treasure eventually did not appear, Yang Bai Lu, Ma Kunshan and other initiators, running the gamut of human emotions from passion to despair, had to recognize the reality and called it quit and a group of shareholders, investing over three years only to find they have nothing in return, and the Jin River Dredging Company, depleting all of its funds, had to be quietly closed down.

It was Yang Bailu who initiated to dig the river cache, and it was impossible to speculate whether his initial intention was for the interest of his country or for his own or both. But the two were not contradictory.

At the beginning of this treasure hunt, Yang Bailu used Columbus's expedition as an example to lobby the authorities and encouraged himself accordingly. Paradoxically, however, Columbus's adventure, by hook or by crook, created a monumental achievement, while the labor of Yang Bailu had nothing to gain, and his name, buried in the abandoned papers, was long forgotten.

He's done what he should have done. What can he do about his destiny?

The huge wealth on the bed of the Jin River touched the heart string of the contemporaries, and there were similar songs even outside areas of Jiangkou, Penshan and Chengdu, i.e., “The golden rooster and the stone drum are worth one hundred and fifty thousand silver. If someone can solve the mystery, he can buy the Kui Zhou Prefecture”; “A stone man and a stone drum are worth fifty-five thousand gold. Whoever can riddle it out, can buy the Chongqing Prefecture”. And on the Jialingjiang River in Chongqing, a similar treasure hunt drama, the aforementioned Changshou County people contributing the treasure map to local government, was also on stage.

与锦江淘宝相比，嘉陵江上的发掘并无翔实的史料和可靠的探测支撑，却估计可以捞得白银、黄金共计二百五十吨。凭着发财的狂热，以一份来历不明的藏宝图为指南就开工，结果就可想而知了。根据1946年的报道，重庆嘉陵江上的淘宝，仅是抽水与测量就耗资六千万元，最后却连一枚小钱也未能发现。几乎是一场不折不扣的闹剧。

Compared with what happened on the Jin River, the treasure hunt on the Jialingjiang River were not supported by informative historical data and reliable detective findings, but it was estimated that a total of two hundred and fifty tons of silver and gold can be excavated. With the fervor of oil-striking and using a treasure map whose origin was suspicious as a guide, the results were predictable. According to a report in 1946, the treasure hunt on the Jialing River in Chongqing cost 60 million silver yuan in pumping and surveying alone, but in the end not even a single penny was found. It was almost an outright farce.

桥如弯弓塔似箭

从锦江淘宝现场施工情况来看，发现了刻有“张”字的条石、铁水及三合土凝成的盖子，甚至还有骷髅、枯骨及鲜血浸透的砂石，一切都符合史乘的记载——锢金之事，确乎发生过。

但为什么江口有金银，锦江中却没有呢？

同样是民谣，为什么一个版本应验了，而另一个却没有应验，虽然后者更便于打捞——毕竟锦江望江楼段比岷江江口段浅得多？

不妨从张献忠锢金的时间入手分析。

以江口沉银为时间原点，锢金或在其之后，如《蜀难叙略》之述；或

The bridge is like a bow and the tower is like an arrow.

From the Jinjiang treasure hunt construction site, the inscription of the word “Zhang” on stone strips, the liquid iron and lid congealed by tabia, and even skulls, bones and blood-soaked gravel were discovered, all in line with the historical record—the incident of gold stash indeed happened.

Why gold and silver were discovered at Jiangkou, but not at the Jin River?

Also a ballad, why was one version fulfilled while the other was not, even though the latter was easier to salvage—after all, the Wangjianglou section of the Jin River is much shallower than the Jiangkou section of the Min River?

It may be worthwhile to analyze the time of Zhang Xianzhong’s concealment of the gold.

If we consider the time Jiangkou silver-sinking happened as the origin, then the concealment of gold could be after it, as what the *Narrative on the Catastrophe of Shu* proclaims; or before it, as what

在其之前，如《蜀碧》所言。

在前在后，对应着不同的因果关系。

如果是在沉银之后，那么锢金则发生在张献忠江口大败逃回成都，又从成都逃往川北这两个时间点之内。既然还要储备金银，说明他还是有打算再回到成都的。杨白鹿必然是此说的坚定拥趸，因为只有这样，锦江河床上才可能找到那些财富。

如果是锢金在前，则又有两种情况。而不管哪种情况，江底都是没有金银的，再怎么挖都是白忙活。

一是从江口败回成都，因军资匮乏而不得不挖出储备于江中的金银。

二是走水路之前就捞出来了，没想到全部损失在江口。此时回到成都的张献忠，像一个丧失了所有本钱的赌徒，已经因为绝望而疯狂。他知道再也回不到成都了，能做的只有失心疯一般泄愤——再次逃离成都时，焚烧宫阙、民居的行为也证实了这种心态。笔者个人是持这种观点的。

江心岛发掘工地上游一千米左右处西岸，曾经耸立着一座名为回澜塔的九层高塔，旁边还有一座名为洪济桥的古桥，后来又被称作“九眼桥”。

Shu Bi claims.

Who comes first and who comes after correspond with different causes and effects.

If the silver-sinking happened after, then the concealment of the gold took place somewhere between Zhang Xianzhong's rout at Jiangkou, and then his fleeing from Chengdu to the north of Sichuan. To conceal gold and silver meant that he still had the intention to return to Chengdu again. Yang Bailu must have been a staunch supporter of this theory, because only in that case could the wealth be found on the bed of the Jin River.

If the concealment of the gold occurred prior to his fleeing, then there are two more scenarios to be considered. And in either case, there is no gold or silver at the bottom of the river, and any further digging is a waste of time.

One is that his defeat in Jiangkou and back to Chengdu forced him to dig out the reserves of gold and silver in the river due to the lack of military funds.

The second scenario is that the concealed gold and silver were fished out before his army taking the waterway to Jiangkou and never imagined they would lose all of treasures there. Zhang Xianzhong rushed back to Chengdu like a gambler who had lost all his capital, and had gone mad with despair. He knew that he could never have a chance to be here again, and all he could do was to vent his anger—his act of burning the palace and the people's houses also confirmed this mentality. The author personally holds this view.

On the west bank of about one kilometer upstream of the excavation site on Jiangxin Island, there used to be a nine-story tower called the Huilan Tower, and next to it, there was an ancient bridge called the Hongji Bridge, which was later called the Nine-Eye-Bridge.

The bridge and tower were constructed in the

桥与塔皆建于明万历年中，主建者为余一龙。

余氏是江西婺源人，进士出身，于明万历十九年（1591年）出任主管一省民政的四川布政使，多有德政。据雍正版《四川通志》，有风水师称锦江口宜筑塔以镇压狂澜，建长桥以截断江势——此即九眼桥和回澜塔的来历。据说，余一龙修桥建塔之后，官也越做越大。

建九眼桥和回澜塔，是不是余一龙为了升官所为，后来仕途顺畅是不是因为修塔建桥，未必如《四川通志》所言。其实，叫回澜塔的建筑不少，也都建于江边，以塔镇水是古人的理念，非独余一龙如此。

张献忠很可能就是在巡视回澜塔时，发现了江心岛是适合锢金之地——两侧有江，普通人不易登临；东侧有石牛堰分流，便于排水。不过，他却因为一句不吉利的谣谶，毁了此塔。

谶言道："桥是弓，塔是箭，弯弓射到承天殿。"

桥，锦江上的九眼桥；塔，桥西南侧的回澜塔；承天殿，则是原蜀王府正殿承运殿，张献忠建立大西政权后改为此名。

拱桥如弯弓，高塔似利箭，再

Wanli Reign of Ming Dynasty, whose constructor was Yu Yilong.

Born in Wuyuan, Jiangxi, Yu Yilong had risen from as a *Jin Shi* (Imperial exam graduate). In the nineteenth year of Wanli of Ming Dynasty (1591), he took up as Finance Commissioner of Sichuan and achieved many virtuous administrative accomplishments. According to *The General Note of Sichuan* published in Yongzheng era, some Feng Shui Masters or Geomancers, claimed that a tower should be erected at the mouth of the Jin River to suppress the torrential waves and a long bridge should be built to cut off the power of the river—that is the origins of the Nine-Eye-Bridge and the tower. It is said that after the completion of the bridge and tower, Yu Yilong ascended to higher positions.

Whether for his personal ambitions to be promoted or his later prosperity in career was ascribed to his early construction of the bridge and tower, to build the Nine-Eye-Bridge and the Huilan Tower in the first place may not have anything to do with what *The General Note of Sichuan* proclaims. In fact, towers named Huilan are not in short supply and all of them are built around the riverside because this is a concept carried along from antiquity and Yu Yilong was not the only official to do so.

It is likely that Zhang Xianzhong discovered that the Jiangxin Island was a suitable place for gold concealment when he inspected the Huilan Tower—with river on both sides, not easy for ordinary people to ascend; and on the east side, there was a diversion of Shiniuyan, making it easy to drain the water. Unfortunately, he destroyed the tower because of an inauspicious prophecy.

The prophecy said, "The bridge is the bow, the tower is the arrow, and the bent bow shoots to the Hall of Chengtian."

The bridge here referred to the Nine-Eye-

加上“射到承天殿”的预言，让张献忠心惊胆战。他最自然而然的反应就是：把箭折了，让它射不成。于是，下令拆毁回澜塔，并将就拆塔所得之砖，在原址上修筑将台。

又过了一百多年，在原回澜塔旧址上建起了三层高的同庆阁，亦称白塔。锦江边再一次呈现出“桥如弯弓塔似箭”的奇景，虽然这一支箭要短上很多。1945年，同庆阁毁于一场大火。

拆毁回澜塔，还有一个传说，见于《滟滪囊》和《蜀碧》。话说拆塔之际，挖出了一块古碑，上面的篆文不仅预言了回澜塔的建与毁，还预言了张献忠命运的终局。其文曰：

“修塔余一龙，拆塔张献忠。岁逢甲乙丙，此地血流红。妖运终川北，毒气播川东。吹箫不用竹，一箭贯当胸。炎兴元年诸葛孔明记。”

文中“吹箫不用竹”，实为一字谜，“箫”去竹字头，即和硕肃亲王豪格的“肃”。直至豪格率军于西充凤凰山射杀张献忠之际，世人才明白这些谶语的含义。

对张献忠命运的预言，竟是在一千四百多年前由诸葛亮做出的，这一看就是文人编出来的故事，自然荒

Bridge, the tower the Huilan Tower and the Hall of Chengtian the main hall of Chengyun Hall of the former mansion of King of Shu, whose name changed into Hall of Chengtian after Zhang Xianzhong established the Daxi Regime.

The arched bridge was like a bow, the tower was like a sharp arrow, and the prophecy of “shoots to the Hall of Chengtian” made Zhang Xianzhong’s blood run cold. His most natural reaction was to break the arrow so that it could not be shot. Therefore, he ordered the demolition of the Huilan Tower and used the bricks from the demolition of the tower to build a command post on the original site.

After another hundred years past, a three-story Tongqing Tower, also known as the White Tower, was built on the site of the former Huilan Tower. Once again, the Jin River showcased the spectacle of “a bridge is like a bow and a tower is like an arrow”. In 1945, the Tongqing Tower was destroyed by a fire.

There is another legend about the demolition of the Huilan Tower, which can be found in *Rippling Bag* and *Shu Bi*. It is said that when the tower was being demolished, an ancient stele was unearthed. The seal script on it not only predicted the construction and destruction of the Huilan Tower, but also the destiny of Zhang Xianzhong. The text reads:

“It was Yu Yilong who erected the tower and Zhang Xianzhong who demolished it. In the year A, B, C, the place would be tained by blood. The luck of the demon would end up in the north of Sichuan, and its poisonous gas would spread to the east of Sichuan. Bamboo is not needed to blow a bamboo flute, and an arrow can pierce chest. Noted by Zhuge Kongming in the first year of Yanxing.”

In the text, “Bamboo is not needed to blow a bamboo flute” is actually a crossword puzzle. If the classifier (relates to bamboo) of the Chinese character 箫 (bamboo flute) is removed, then the word changes into

诞不经，却也表明了四川人对张献忠的态度——是他，将两百多年无战事的天府之国变为了血火大地。

肃 (*Su*, also the name of the Prince Haoge of Heshuo). It was not until Haoge's army defeated and killed Zhang Xianzhong at Phoenix Hill, Xichong did the common people understand the meaning of this prophecy.

The prophecy of Zhang Xianzhong's fate was made by Zhuge Liang more than 1,400 years ago. This is a story fabricated by the literati, which is naturally absurd, but it also shows the attitude of Sichuan people towards Zhang Xianzhong—it is him who turned the land of heaven without war for more than two hundred years into a land of blood and fire.

明蜀王陵
Mausoleums of King of Shu

空中俯瞰，青龙湖如一条张牙舞爪的巨龙。龙背和龙爪附近，则分布着十数座明代皇室陵墓，其中心为第三代蜀王僖王之陵。

那是一座富丽堂皇的宫殿，跟蜀僖王生前居住的蜀王府相比较，有一种几乎可算严丝合缝的对应关系。甚而至于，蜀王府的运作模式也在地下以一种抽象的方式得到了体现。

地上的蜀王府被烧毁了，而地下的蜀王陵，则是它依然存留于世的镜像。

From a bird's-eye view, the Qinglong Lake resembles a ferocious dragon with its teeth bared and claws extended. Scattered around the dragon's back and near its claws are more than ten Ming Dynasty royal tombs, with the center being the mausoleum of the third generation Shu King, Prince Xi.

It is a magnificent palace that almost mirror the grandeur of the Shu King's residence during his lifetime. Interestingly, the operating model of the Shu King's residence is abstractly reflected underground.

Above the ground, the King of Shu's Mansion was burned down, while his underground Mausoleum survives as its enduring mirror image.

蜀王陵：红尘锦绣的地宫镜像
Mausoleums of King of Shu: an underground palace as well as a mirror image of a mortal world

蜀藩陵

清·王澹秋

铁券金符久寂寥，
景山园寝莽萧萧。

Mausoleum of King of Shu

Wang Danqiu, Qing Dynasty

The token granted by the emperor lies in long neglect,
Jing Shan Mausoleum stands desolate and quiet.
Surrounding hills devoid of royal spirit,

天生玉垒无王气，
地近沙河有怒飙。
杜宇声中残劫换，
棠梨影外故宫遥。
苍凉数亩成僧舍，
细读寒碑认旧桥。

Raging winds rake the Sha River nearby.
Cries of the cuckoos intermingle with remnants of disaster,
The shadows of the birchleaf pear blossoms cast outside the ancient palace afar.In the bleakness, a few Mu become monk's quarters,
Poring over the cold steles, making out the old bridge.

清人王澹秋之诗所咏，为成都东门外的一座明代蜀藩王陵，即《华阳县志》中的草皇坟。他在这儿看到陵园凋敝、林木萧瑟，听到河风怒号，感怀的是蜀王身后的萧条——纵然身为天潢贵胄，手执象征王权的金印，怀揣传说中可以免死的铁券丹书，却免不了在乱世中合族被灭的悲惨命运。

这是一座南向的寝陵，南北方向约三百米，东西方向约一百八十米。它北靠青龙湖，南邻成渝高速公路，所在区域今为大面街道。

诗中称此处为景山，是东景山的简称。明人喻茂坚所撰《重修观音桥碑记》称：“成都去城七里有沙河，近东景山，之寝园，车马经由通。”

《四库全书·四川通志》则有记载：“蜀怀王墓【在华阳县东二十里东景山】。”此说不仅可与王澹秋诗、喻茂坚文互相印证，也明确了这座陵园的主人是蜀怀王朱申鈘。

The poem by Wang Danqiu from the Qing Dynasty laments the desolation of the tomb of a Ming Dynasty Shu royal prince located outside the eastern gate of Chengdu, known as Caohuang Tomb in the *Huayang County Records*. Wang Danqiu observed the decay of the tomb grounds, the desolation of the trees, and heard the angry roar of the river wind. He reflected on the melancholy fate of the Shu prince - despite being born into nobility, wielding the gold seal symbolizing royal power, and carrying the legendary iron deed for escaping death, he could not escape the tragic destiny of his clan being exterminated in chaotic times.

This is a south-facing mausoleum, about 300 meters in the north-south direction and 180 meters in the east-west direction. It is close to Qinglong Lake in the north and the Chengdu-Chongqing Expressway in the south, and the area where it is located is now Damian Street.

The place Jingshan in this poem is a short for East Jingshan. In the *Repair the Guanyin Bridge Stele Record* compiled by Yu Maojian in Ming Dynasty, it is recorded that: “Seven *Li*s outside the City of Chengdu, there is a sand river near East Jingshan, passing the graveyard, which can be reached by carriages and horses.”

The Sichuan General History in *Complete Book Collection in Four Sections* records that “the tomb of King Huai was located at East Jingshan, twenty *Li*s east of Huayang County.” This record not only corroborates with Wang Danqiu's poem and

Yu Maojian's article, but also makes it clear that the owner of this mausoleum was Zhu Shenyi, the King of Shu.

传承十四世
王陵散落湖光山色间

实际上，蜀怀王陵只是成都龙泉驿西面低丘上散布着的上百座明代皇族成员墓葬之一，是这些工造精美、富丽堂皇的地下宫殿中的一座。此明代皇室墓葬群，被统称为“明蜀王陵”。

可是，哪儿来的这么多蜀王呢？明代的蜀王世系，由蜀献王朱椿至末代蜀王朱至澍共十三王，这一数字与上百座皇家陵墓有着很大的差距。要回答这一问题，需要先简单了解一下明朝的分封制度。

1368年，朱元璋建立明朝之后，将自己二十六个儿子中的二十四个都封为亲王（作为王储的太子朱标和早夭的幼子除外）。这类王爵属于一等王，以古国名为号，“王”之前只有一个字，如燕王之“燕”、蜀王之“蜀”，故又称“一字王”（即评书中常称的“并肩一字王”）。

这些亲王离开京城，到自己的封地就藩，又称藩王。藩王的嫡长

pass on for fourteen generations
The royal tombs are scattered among the lakes and mountains

In fact, the Mausoleum of King Huai is just one of the hundreds of tombs of Ming Dynasty royalty scattered across the low hills, west of Longquanyi, Chengdu, and is one of these beautifully crafted and magnificent underground palaces. This cluster of Ming Dynasty royal tombs, collectively known as the "Royal Mausoleums of Kings of Shu".

But where did so many kings of Shu come from? The lineage of the kings of Shu in the Ming Dynasty, from Zhu Chun, King Xian of Shu, to Zhu Zhishu, the last king of Shu, totaled thirteen kings, a number that is a far cry from the hundreds of royal tombs. To answer this question, we first need to briefly understand the enfeoffment system of the Ming Dynasty.

In 1368, after Zhu Yuanzhang established the Ming Dynasty, he made twenty-four of his twenty-six sons princes (except for Zhu Biao, the crown prince, and his youngest son, who died young). This type of kingship belonged to the first class of kings, with the ancient name of the country, and only one word linked with "king", such as "Yan" (燕) of the King of Yan, "Shu" (蜀) of the King of Shu, so it was also called"One Character King" (i.e.,"One Character Kings who are entitled to stand shoulder to shoulder with the emperor" frequently mentioned in the folk storytelling).

These princes left the capital to take up vassalage in their own fiefs, also known as vassal kings. The first-born son of the vassal king is the

子为世子，是爵位的继承者，余者降一等，封为郡王。郡王之号以郡县为名，如蜀王一系有“华阳郡王”“崇庆郡王”“崇宁郡王”等。“王”之前有两个字，故又称“二字王”。

可以看出，藩王的传承是一个同样以嫡长子为中心的、小号的皇位传承翻版，而郡王的则更小一号。

郡王往下，嫡长子继承王位，余者不再称王，封镇国将军。再往下，明代皇室爵位还有辅国将军、奉国将军、镇国中尉、辅国中尉、奉国中尉等，共计八等。八等及以下，皆称奉国中尉。

这个权力的金字塔的塔底是奉国中尉，塔顶则是君临天下的明朝皇帝。

视线拉回蜀地，明蜀王一共传承十三王，而各系支宗传世的郡王则有六十之多。这两项加起来，再算上王妃，跟那上百座皇室墓葬就数字基本相符了。

明蜀王墓葬群，大抵分布在龙泉驿区十陵街道青龙湖周围。

十陵在清代属成都府华阳县；1952年定名为青龙乡；1962年更名为石灵人民公社，其得名于辖区内的石灵寺（今十陵街道内有石灵社区）；

successor to the title, and the rest of the descendants are the county kings, to a lesser degree. The appellation of the county king named after the name of the county, i.e., “County King of Hua Yang”, “County King of Chong qing” “County King of Chong ning”and so on. There are two words associated with“king”, so it is also called “Two Characters King”.

As we can see, the vassal king’s lineage is a similarly first-born-centered, smaller-sized replica of the throne of emperor lineage, while the county king’s is even smaller.

From county King downwards, the eldest legitimate son inherits the throne, while the rests no longer claim the title of king, and are appointed as Zhenguo General. Further down the hierarchy, the Ming Dynasty royal titles also have Auxiliary General, Feng Guo General, Protector-Commandant of the State, Auxiliary-Commandant of the State and Supporter-Commandant of the State, etc., a total of eight classes. The eight ranks and below were called Supporter-Commandant of the State.

At the base of this pyramid of power is the Supporter-Commandant of the State, and at the summit reigns the emperor of the Ming Dynasty, ruler of all under heaven.

Back to the Shu, there were thirteen kings of Shu in Ming Dynasty, while the county kings of the various lineages of the clan were as many as sixty. These two items add up, plus the princesses, the total number matches the hundreds of royal tombs.

The cluster of Ming Dynasty royal tombs roughly distributed around Qinglong Lake, Shiling Street, Longquanyi District.

Shiling belonged to Huayang County, Chengdu Prefecture in the Qing Dynasty; it was named Qinglong Township in 1952 and renamed Shiling People’s Commune in 1962, which got its name from the Shiling Temple in the precincts (there is a Shiling

1994年建十陵镇，十陵这一名字首次出现。

“十陵”之由来，可以追溯到石灵寺，而辖区内有十座蜀王陵墓也是得名由来的说法之一——这类似于北京十三陵的得名。这十座陵墓，通常认为是：僖王陵、昭王陵、成王陵、怀王陵、南川安靖王陵、黔江悼怀王陵等六座藩王陵与郡王陵，以及成王次妃墓、僖王次妃墓、僖王赵妃墓和定王次妃墓等四座王妃墓。当然，现在探明的蜀王、郡王和王妃的墓葬，已不止于此。“十”，只是个概数。

原本叫石灵，取其音；后来又发现了十座陵墓，取其意——可从两层意义来阐释“十陵”。

大梁子山明代叫正觉山，从名字看，取自佛教的“无上正等正觉”。它其实算不上山，仅仅是高于湖平面数米的低丘。就是这座低丘，像一双张开的手臂，护抱着清澈的青龙湖。这些陵墓，大多分布于湖光与山色之间。

蜀王陵所在范围为蜀王大道以东、绕城高速以西、成洛大道之南、成渝高速之北。在这四条大道围成的区域内，青龙湖的水域形状正像一条由东南腾向西北的巨龙。龙头与成都

community in the present Shiling Street); Shiling Township was built in 1994, and the name of Shiling (ten tombs 十陵) appeared for the first time.

The origin of the “Ten Tombs” can be traced back to the Shiling Temple, and that there are ten tombs of the kings of Shu within the jurisdiction is also one of the claims of the origin of the name—similar to the name of the Thirteen Mausoleums in Beijing. These ten tombs are: the tomb of King Xi, the tomb of King Zhao, the tomb of King Cheng, the tomb of King Huai, the tomb of King Anjing of Nanchuan, the tomb of King Daohuai of Qianjiang, and the tombs of six vassal and county kings, as well as the tomb of King Cheng’s second consort, the tomb of King Xi’s second consort, the tomb of King Xi’s consort Zhao, and the tomb of King Ding’s second consort. Certainly, the tombs of kings of Shu, county kings and royal consorts which have been explored now, have been more than that. “Ten” is just a number in general sense.

Originally, it was called Shiling 石灵 because of its sound; later, ten tombs 十陵 were discovered, thus its name changed because of its meaning—the “Ten Tombs” can be interpreted from two levels of meaning. (In Chinese, the character 石 and 十 share the same pronunciation.)

Daliangzi Mountain was called Zhengjue Mountain in the Ming Dynasty, and the name is taken from the Buddhist phrase “Supremely upright amounts to enlightenment”. It is not really a mountain, but a hill that is only a few meters above the lake level. This low hill, like a pair of open arms, embraces the crystally clear Qinglong Lake. Most of these tombs are located between the lake and the mountains.

King of Shu Mausoleums is located in the scope of the Shuwang Avenue to the east, west of the Roundabout Expressway, Cheng Luo Avenue to the south, Chengdu-Chongqing Expressway to the north. In the area surrounded by these four avenues,

大学隔成洛大道相望，两只前爪环抱着成王陵，瞰视着西面的成王次妃陵和西南方的南川安靖王陵；其背部则是紧紧相邻的僖王陵和昭王陵，以及更远处的黔江悼怀王陵、定王次妃陵等；两只后爪斜伸入东南；龙尾则甩向东方。

“北有十三陵，南有蜀王陵。”北京郊区昌平天寿山麓埋葬着明代的成祖朱棣等十三位皇帝和二十三位皇后，而成都的明蜀王陵是否能与其媲美呢？

the waters of Qinglong Lake are shaped like a huge dragon that rises from the southeast to the northwest. The head of the dragon is face-to-face with Chengdu University across the Chengluo Avenue, its two front paws embracing the tomb of King Cheng, overlooking the west of tomb of King Cheng's second consort and the tomb of King Anjing of Nanchuan; its back is close to the neighboring tomb of King Xi and the tomb of King Zhao, as well as more distant King Daohuai of Qianjiang and the tomb of King Ding's second consort, etc.; its two rear paws extend diagonally into the southeast and its tail flings over to the east.

“There are Thirteen Mausoleums in the north, and the Mausoleums of the King of Shu in the south.” Thirteen emperors and twenty-three empresses, including the Emperor Zhu Di of Ming Dynasty, are buried at the foot of Tianshoushan Mountain in Changping, a suburb of Beijing, and are the Mausoleums of the Kings of Shu of Ming Dynasty in Chengdu comparable to it?

昭王陵龙盘
长得像朱元璋的龙

两条龙上下相望，中间一颗硕大的珠子；睛、须、额、嘴、角细致入微，惟妙惟肖；唯独不见龙身，只在云纹中显露一鳞半爪。传统图案中，“二龙戏珠”司空见惯，不足为奇——奇的是，那龙脸又瘦又长，额头高隆，下吻突起，倒像一张被称作“地包天”的人脸。没错，它正是模仿明代开国皇帝朱元璋那张两端凸

The dragon disk at Mausoleum of King Zhao
The dragon that looks like Zhu Yuanzhang

Two dragons, above and below, look at each other, with a large bead in the middle; their eyes, beards, foreheads, mouths and horns carved meticulously and exquisitely; the part that is missing is the body of the dragon, only a scale and a half claw revealing in the cloud. In traditional patterns, “two dragons playing pearls” is very common—what is strange is that the dragon's face is thin and long, bulging forehead, prognathous jaw, like the so-called “the lower part engulfs the higher part” of the human face. Make no mistake, it is exactly fashioned by imitating the face of the founder of Ming Dynasty,

出、下巴奇长的凹脸雕琢而成。谁有这么大的胆子，敢拿朱元璋来开玩笑呢？

这件造型繁复、雕饰精美的圆盘雕饰，是明蜀昭王陵石碑上的一个建筑构件——人头龙盘。这座王陵的主人蜀昭王朱宾瀚，明朝第八代蜀王，明弘治七年（1494年）袭封蜀王，正德三年（1508年）去世。

朱宾瀚的贤王称号，是经过明朝皇帝认证的。对蜀献王朱椿以来形成的擅约束、守礼法、尚人文的家风，弘治帝（明孝宗朱祐樘）大为激赏。对于这种家风熏陶出来的朱宾瀚，弘治帝将他比作西汉河间王刘德、唐代江夏王李道宗（皆为历史上有名的贤王），专门写了一首诗来称赞："异代岂能专美事，我宗亦自有贤王。"

明朝历代蜀王，共留下了五本文集。朱宾瀚没有自己的文集，却为父亲编纂了《惠王睿制集》，并亲自撰序。在序言里，朱宾瀚回顾了蜀王府爱书的传统、对民众的教化，也显示了自身文才："盖家教师承，惟书以为宝。是故嗣位多博雅之贤，通国被文明之化，九重眷西土之光，奕世拜褒扬之典，有由然哉。"

Emperor Zhu Yuanzhang: two protruding ends of the face, strangely long face. But who would have the audacity to make fun of Zhu Yuanzhang?

This complicated shaped and beautifully carved disk carving is the human head dragon disk on a building component of King Zhao of Shu of Ming Dynasty. The master of the mausoleum is Zhu Binhan, King Zhao of Shu, the eighth generation of the King of Shu of Ming Dynasty. In the seventh year of Hongzhi of Ming Dynasty (1494) he was crowned as the king of Shu, and he died in the third year of Zhengde of Ming Dynasty (1508).

Zhu Binhan's title, Wise King, was certified by the emperor of the Ming Dynasty. Emperor Hongzhi (Zhu Youcheng, Emperor Xiaozong of the Ming Dynasty) greatly appreciated the family style of discipline, observance of the law and humanism that had been developed since Zhu Chun, King Xian of Shu. For Zhu Binhan, who was nurtured by this family style, Emperor Hongzhi compared him to Liu De, the King of Hetian in Western Han Dynasty, and Li Daozong, the King of Jiangxia in Tang Dynasty (both are famous as wise kings in history), and wrote a poem to praise him: "How can beautiful things be dominated by other dynasties? In my clan, there also has a wise king."

The successive kings of Shu in the Ming Dynasty left behind a total of five collections. Zhu Binhan did not have his own anthology, but he compiled a collection for his father, *Collection of King Hui's Sagacious Governance*, and wrote the preface himself. In the preface, Zhu Binhan recalled the tradition of book-loving in the mansion of the King of Shu, the indoctrination of the people, and also showed his own literary talent: "What we hold high esteem and our family inheritance is to treat books as a treasure. Therefore, it is natural that the heirs to the family are full of elegant sages, all the kingdom is

遗憾的是，蜀昭王朱宾瀚的寿数不长，只活了二十八岁，留下九岁的嫡长子朱让栩。朱宾瀚跟王妃刘氏琴瑟和谐，良好的家庭关系对后代的成长很有好处，他们的儿子朱让栩长大之后，成为贤王中的贤王。朱让栩不喜欢声色犬马，而是崇尚文教，从事诸如创办义学、兴修水利、赈灾济贫等公益事业，《明史》评价为“让栩尤贤明”。

昭王陵是合葬墓。朱宾瀚生前跟刘妃鸾凤和鸣，离世十一年后刘妃也来到地下与他相会。墓室中央，昭王和刘妃棺床并排而放。也许是设计者被二人的恩爱激发出了灵感，产生了一个奇巧的构思。

两张石棺床被一道厚石墙隔开，石墙一角，雕刻出了一道精巧的大门，房檐、门柱、柱础、门扇俱备，檐上的瓦筒和螭吻清晰可见。石墙两面的大门，利用的是共同的门扇，昭王和刘妃从各自长眠之处，都能“看”到它。

最奇的是，其中的一张门扇是半开的。昭王与刘妃其实并没有被石墙完全隔开，其魂魄可缥缈于石门上凿开的空间，再凝聚成形，如生前一般促膝并肩、喁喁低语。

civilized, the light from the ninth heaven graces this west land, and the revered classics are shrined age after age.”

Unfortunately, Zhu Binhan, King Zhao did not live long and died only at the age of twenty-eight, leaving behind his eldest son Zhu Rangxu, who was nine years old then. Zhu Binhan was in harmony with his consort Liu, and the good family relationship was good for the growth of their offspring. When he came of age, Zhu Rangxu grew into a virtuous king among all the virtuous kings. He didn’t like licentious life, but advocated culture and education, engaged in public welfare such as the founding of charity schools, water conservancy, disaster relief and poverty alleviation. In *Ming History*, he was evaluated as “particularly virtuous”.

The mausoleum of King Zhao is a joint tomb. Zhu Binhan and Consort Liu were in harmony during his lifetime, and eleven years after his death, Consort Liu came to meet him underground. In the center of the tomb, the coffins of King Zhao and Consort Liu are placed side by side. Perhaps the designer was inspired by their love for each other and came up with an ingenious idea.

The two sarcophagus beds were separated by a thick stone wall, and in one corner of the stone wall, an elaborate gate was carved out, with eaves, pillars, column bases, folded doors, and the tile cylinders and the image of *Chi Wen* (the legendary ninth son of dragon) on the eaves were clearly visible. The gates on both sides of the stone wall utilize a common folded door, which can be seen by both King Zhao and Concubine Liu from their respective long-sleeping places.

The most amazing thing is that one of the doors is half open. King Zhao and Consort Liu were not completely parted by the stone wall, and their souls, flying over the carved open space, can take shape

昭王陵发现于1990年代初修建成渝高速公路。它原本在成渝高速北侧的洪河镇白鹤村，早年曾遭捣毁，1991年考古发掘后进行保护性搬迁，迁到了十陵正觉山麓的僖王陵左侧。

夫妻合葬，尚能通过隔墙上的小门交流，已足见巧思。人头龙盘，模仿朱元璋那张崛鼻突额的地包天脸，则让后人有些惊疑：敢于开这样的玩笑，不怕杀头吗？

again, and whisper to each other side by side as they did in life.

可供昭王夫妻在阴世交流的小门　何大江 摄

A small door allows King Zhao and his wife to communicate in the afterlife. (Photographer: He Dajiang)

The mausoleum of King Zhao was discovered in the early 1990s during the construction of the Chengdu-Chongqing Expressway. It was originally located at Baihe Village, Honghe Town, to the north of the Chengdu-Chongqing Expressway and had been destroyed in the early years. After the archaeological excavation in 1991, it was relocated to the left side of the tomb of King Xi at the foot of Zhengjue Mountain, Shiling.

It is a design ingenuous enough that husband and wife can still communicate through a small door on the partition wall after being buried. It is more surprising that a human head with a dragon disk was carved in the tomb, imitating Zhu Yuanzhang's bulging forehead and prognathous jaw, the so-called "the lower part engulfs the higher part" of the human face. Who dares to crack such a joke, not afraid of having his head chopped?

昭王陵的人头龙盘，酷似传说中朱元璋的地包天长相　余茂智 摄

The human-headed dragon carving in King Zhao's tomb resembles the rumored underbite feature of Zhu Yuanzhang, the founder of the Ming Dynasty. (Photographer: Yu Maozhi)

数年之前，笔者曾经写过蜀王陵，把雕刻这种人首龙盘的行为，归结为成都人的幽默、豁达。得出这样的结论是容易的，也是讨喜的，却是轻率的，没有太多依据，也经不起推敲。

也有另一条思维路径，把雕刻人首龙身这种行为艺术放入朱元璋相貌流变之中考察，真相就呼之欲出。

朱元璋流传下来的画像有十余幅，简言之，可分为两类：一是正像，相貌堂堂；二是丑像，所谓鞋拔子脸——昭王陵的中石刻龙盘，就是依照这个样子雕成的。

明清两代，收藏于宫廷的朱元璋画像共计十三幅，其中面颊丰圆、相貌端庄者有二。这两幅一为全身坐像，一为半身像。半身像除了脸上肌肉变松弛、皱纹平添、髭须由黑转白之外，外形极其相似，简言之，坐像为壮年版，半身像者为老年版。

剩下的十一幅也高度类似，如出一辙的丑脸。按照明景泰年间相书《古今识鉴》的描述是："天地相朝，五岳俱附，日月丽天，辅骨插鬓……"

额头和下巴相对，离得很近；鼻

Several years ago, the author once wrote about the mausoleums of the King of Shu, attributing the carving of such a human head and dragon disk to the humor and open-mindedness of the people of Chengdu. It is easy and pleasing to draw such a conclusion, yet it is rash, without much basis, and does not stand up to scrutiny.

There is also another explanation that relates the carving of the human head with a dragon body, a sort of behavioral art, to the variations of Zhu Yuanzhang's appearance. The truth will come to light.

More than ten portraits of Zhu Yuanzhang remained today which can be simply divided into two categories: ones are his front image, rather good-looking; the others are quite ugly, the so-called shoehorn face, the origin from which the stone carving of the dragon disk in King Zhao's mausoleum copies.

During Ming and Qing dynasties, there are total thirteen Zhu Yuanzhang's portraits collected in the palace, among which two portraits exhibit his round cheeks and dignified appearance. One is a full-body sitting statue, the other is a half-body image. The half-body image, in addition to the flaccid face muscles, added wrinkles and white moustache, is extremely similar to the previous one. Simply put, the sitting image reflects his robust years and the half-body one represents his elderly times.

The remaining eleven are also highly similar, with the same ugly faces. According to *Ancient and Modern Knowledge*, a physiognomic book published in Jing Tai period in Ming Dynasty, such a facial feature is: "Heaven(forehead) and earth(jaw) are facing each other, the five mountains (forehead, two cheekbones, nose and jaw) are close to the center, the sun and the moon (the upper part of two eyebrows) are high on the forehead, and the brow bones thrust diagonally to the temples ... "

The forehead and jaw are opposite but close to

子、额头、下巴、左右颧骨五处耸起，导致眉眼与嘴挤拢；左额日角、右额月角高悬；眉外侧的辅骨突起，插入两鬓。这是一种奇特又丑陋的相貌，从侧面看，脸型是所谓的“鞋拔子脸”，五官皱巴巴地挤在一起，额头却异常宽大、舒展。

朱元璋是否真的长成这样子，其实已经不重要了，在上百年的民间认知中，这就是他的相貌，甚至《明史》和《明太祖实录》两种正史都采用了类似的说法。《明太祖实录》成书于明成祖朱棣永乐年间，《明史》成书更晚，有意思的是，包括朱元璋自述在内的早期史料，并未提及其长相奇特、有异于常人。

对中国历史稍有熟悉，便会认识到，统治者的相貌绝不仅仅是生物学问题或者美学问题，更涉及心理学、社会学和政治学。朱元璋被长成这副丑像，其理论依据是传统文化中，将人的面相跟秉性、命运密切关联的相术。这种“异人必有异相”的集体无意识，也往往为帝王权术所利用，成为构建意识形态的一块基石。

中国数千年农耕社会，平民皇帝屈指可数。他们没有高贵的出身，需要通过异象、异相、异人的神化为合法性加持。

each other; the nose, forehead, jaw, and left and right cheekbones are raised, resulting in the eyebrows, eyes and mouth being crowded together; the upper part of two eyebrows are high on the forehead; and the auxiliary bones on the outer side of the eyebrows protrude and insert into the temples. This is a strange and ugly appearance, which, looked from the side, is the so-called “shoehorn face”, featuring wrinkled facial appearance, but the forehead is unusually wide and stretching.

Whether Zhu Yuanzhang really looked like this is actually no longer important. In the hundreds of years of folk cognition, this is his appearance, and even the two official history books, *Ming History* and *The Factual Records of Emperor Taizu of Ming*, adopt similar statements. *The Factual Records of Emperor Taizu of Ming* was written during the Yong Le period of Zhu Di, the Chengzu of Ming and *Ming History* was written much later. Interestingly, the early historical sources, including Zhu Yuanzhang’s own account, did not mention his peculiar and unusual appearance.

Anyone who is familiar with Chinese history will realize that the appearance of a ruler is not just a matter relating biology or aesthetics, but also involves psychology, sociology and political science. The theory behind Zhu Yuanzhang’s ugly appearance is based on the traditional cultural practice of physiognomy, which closely relates a person’s face to his nature and fate. This collective unconscious of “peculiar people must have peculiar faces” is often utilized by imperial ruling class, and becomes a cornerstone of ideological construction.

Thousands of years of agrarian society in China churned out only a handful of commoner emperors. They did not have noble origins and needed to add deification, such as unusual appearance, uncommon incidents and peculiar person, to their legitimacy.

《南史》称宋高祖刘裕降生时，神光照得室内彻明，当夜有甘露降于墓上之树。《史记》和《汉书》里，汉高祖刘邦左大腿有七十二颗黑痣（部分朱元璋的画像中，脸上也布满黑痣），他出生的故事更为传奇：其母歇息于大湖岸边，梦与神龙交而孕，当时雷电交加穿透昏暗夜空。

胡丹《相术、符号与传播："朱元璋相貌之谜"的考析与解读》一文，梳理、考据朱元璋相貌传播流变，得出的结论是：朱元璋"变丑"，其子朱棣是始作俑者、首任"整容师"。

那么，朱棣为什么要"丑化"自己的父亲呢？其实，当"异人之相"作为一种设定，承担着更重要的任务时，美与丑已经不重要了。

《隋书》描绘隋文帝杨坚的相貌，称"五柱入顶"。额头上有五根柱状突起，若说这模样好看，连他的母亲都不会同意。杨坚年幼之时，一次他的母亲抱着他，突然见到他头上长角、遍体生鳞，惊骇之下失手将其坠落于地。

可见，皇帝的相貌关键不在于美丑，而在于像不像龙。朱棣给他父亲相貌动手术，不是美化，也不是丑

According to *The Southern History*, when Liu Yu, the Gaozu of Song, was born, a divine light shone brightly in the room, and nectar descended on the tree over the tomb that night. In *The Records of the Grand Historian* and *The Book of Han*, Liu Bang, Gaozu of the Han Dynasty, had seventy-two black moles on his left thigh (some of Zhu Yuanzhang's portraits show his face covered with moles as well), and the story of his birth is even more legendary: his mother, resting on the shore of a large lake, dreamed of having intercourse with a divine dragon and conceiving him, when lightning and thunder penetrated the darkness of the night sky.

In his essay *Physiognomy, Symbols and Communication: Analysis and Interpretation of the Mystery of Zhu Yuanzhang's Appearance*, Hu Dan teases out and examines the variations of Zhu Yuanzhang appearance, and his conclusion is that Zhu Di, the son of Zhu Yuanzhang was the main culprit and chief "plastic surgeon" of Zhu Yuanzhang's "uglification".

So, why did Zhu Di uglify his father? In fact, when "peculiar people must have peculiar faces" is used as a presumption to take on a more important task, the beauty and ugliness are no longer important.

The Book of Sui describes the appearance of Yang Jian, Wendi of the Sui Dynasty, claiming "five pillars on top". With five pillars protruding from his forehead, even his mother would not agree that this was a good look. When Yang Jian was young, his mother was holding him in her arms when she suddenly saw that he had horns on his head and scales all over his body, and was so shocked that she dropped him to the ground.

It can be concluded that the key to the emperor's appearance does not lie in the beauty and ugliness, but in whether he bears resemblance to dragon or not. Zhu Di performed surgery on his father's appearance, not to beautify nor to uglify, but to deify.

化，而是神化。

1413年，朱棣为朱元璋孝陵建神功圣德碑，称“（朱元璋）项上奇骨隐起至顶”——以现代医学观之，很可能是颈椎骨质增生一类疾病；1451年，描绘朱元璋“天地相朝”鞋拔子脸的《古今识鉴》由相术家编纂成书；1509年，明昭王陵开建——从时间线就看得出来，昭王陵里的人首龙盘敢刻一张朱元璋的丑脸，也只是其外貌神化过程中的一个节点，跟成都人的幽默、豁达并没有太直接的关系。

In 1413, Zhu Di ordered to build Shen Gong Sheng De Monument for Zhu Yuanzhang's mausoleum, proclaiming "on Zhu Yuanzhang's neck, there is an odd bone bulging up to the top"—from the perspective of modern medical science, it is likely to be a disease relating to the cervical vertebrae osteoarthritis; in 1451, *Ancient and Modern Knowledge*, a physiognomic book, in which Zhu Yuanzhang's shoehorn face was described, was compiled and published by physiognomists. In 1509, King Zhao's mausoleum began construction—we can see from these time lines that those who dared to carve an ugly face of Zhu Yuanzhang in King Zhao's mausoleum had no direct relation to do with Chengdu's people's humor and open-mindedness; this is but a node in the process of deification of his physical appearance.

朱氏子孙姓名中的化学元素周期表

成都东郊的十陵那时还叫石灵。1978年初，推土机刚刚铲平了大梁子上一座宽7米、长30米的大土包，民工们已挖好石灰池，开始向里面放水。然而水一进去就很快渗掉，多次重复皆如此，以致无法搅拌灰浆。有何蹊跷？民工决定一探究竟。继续深挖，一层一层由青砖构成的弧形拱券石出现在眼前，再往下，则是数米深的积水。

由成都博物馆主持的发掘始于1979年。当积水被抽干之后，蜀僖王

Periodic Table of Chemical Elements In the name of Zhu's descendants

In early 1978, when Shiling 十陵, located at Chengdu's eastern suburb, was still called Shiling 石灵, bulldozers just shoveled and leveled a large hump that was 7-meter-wide and 30-meter-long. The workers dug a lime pool and began to put water into it. However, once the water went in, it quickly seeped away, which repeated many times, making it impossible to mix the mortar. What's wrong? The workers decided to find out and continued to dig deeper. Gradually, layer by layer of, arch structure stones composed of green bricks appeared in front of their eyes, and further down, there was water accumulation which was a few meters deep.

The excavation under the auspices of the Chengdu Museum began in 1979. When the water was drained away, King Xi of Shu was revealed to

呈现于世人眼前——这就是第三代蜀王朱友壎之墓。

朱友壎，生于永乐七年（1409年），十五岁时被册封为罗江王，宣德七年(1432年)，袭封为蜀王。朱友壎寿命不长，死时仅二十六岁，在位不过两年，死后谥号“僖王”。从谥号，可以大致想见其生前作为。

“僖”同“釐”，喜乐也，吉祥也。据苏洵《谥法》，“质渊受谏曰釐，小心畏忌曰釐”。小心谨慎，不犯过错，便是喜乐吉祥。检点历史上那些以僖或釐为谥的王公贵族：周僖王，周王朝东迁洛阳之后第一位被诸侯所尊的天王；鲁僖公，在三桓的跋扈中稳掌政权、有所作为的国君；晋僖公，多次与他国会盟的“春秋小三霸”之一。

总之，僖绝非贬义之谥。《大明蜀僖王圹志》竖立在僖王陵的正殿之中，这篇以五爪金龙为饰的墓志铭，对朱友壎的评价是：“王淳厚端淑，言动率礼，未尝有过。”看来，守规矩、不犯错，是他最大的特点。

朱友壎死于风疾，这种病类似于现代医学中的心脑血管疾病，有一定的遗传关系。朱友壎只活了二十六岁，跟他的哥哥蜀靖王朱友垓寿数相同，而他们的父亲朱悦燫只活了

the world—the tomb of the third king of Shu, Zhu Youxun.

Zhu Youxun was born in the seventh year of Yongle's reign (1409). At the age of 15, he was enthroned as King of Luojiang, and in the seventh year of Xuande's reign (1432), he inherited King of Shu. Zhu Youxun did not live long, and died at the age of 26, having reigned for only two years, and was posthumously named King Xi. From his posthumous name, one can roughly imagine what he did during his lifetime.

"Xi"僖, synonymous with 釐, means joyfulness and auspiciousness. According to *Posthumous Law* written by Su Xun, "Using caution in dealing with the political matters is called 釐". Carefulness, cautiousness and making no mistakes amount to joyfulness and auspiciousness. Surveying the historical records of the princes and nobles with Xi 僖 or 釐 as their posthumous names, we have King Xi of Zhou, the first heavenly king hailed by the vassals after Zhou Dynasty moved east Luoyang; Lord Xi of Lu, a king who reined firmly his sovereignty and achieved a lot while being surrounded by three powerful vassals; Lord Xi of Jin, one of "Three Little Hegemons in Spring and Autumn Periods" who allied many times with other countries.

In short, Xi was by no means a derogatory posthumous title. "Epitaph of King Xi of Shu of Ming Dynasty", which was erected in the main hall of Xi Wang's tomb and decorated with five-clawed golden dragons, evaluates Zhu Youxun as: "The king was sincere and generous, and his words and gestures were courteous, and he never made any mistakes." It seems that being disciplined and not making mistakes are his greatest characteristics.

Zhu Youxun died of "wind disease", which is similar to cardiovascular disease in modern medical term and this disease has a certain hereditary trait.

二十二岁。随着朱友壎离世，第一任蜀世子朱悦爑一系绝嗣。

不少文章称：圹志纠正了《明史》和《四川通志》的错误，在这两部书中，"友壎"皆被记作"友攩"。

其实，记作"友攩"这种说法也是错误的。朱元璋为各藩的后代子孙定下字辈，并规定了皆用"木—火—土—金—水"为最后一个字的偏旁，按五行相生的顺序循环使用。蜀藩第三代"友"字辈的偏旁为"土"，第二代蜀王为朱友堉，第五代蜀王为朱友垓，与之同辈的蜀僖王，姓名最后一字的偏旁不可能为"扌"。朱元璋定下的规矩，《明史》编撰者不可能不知道。

事实上，所谓的"攩"，在《明史》中本为一个由左"土"右"黨"构成的字。但这个字实在太生僻了，电脑打不出来，于是以"攩"替代，然后辗转相抄，以讹传讹。这便是"友攩"一说的来历。

朱元璋可能不会想到，他的子孙后来会繁衍到如此巨大的数量，以"金木水火土"为偏旁的常用字远远不够用，必须大量使用生僻字，甚至为了给朱家人取名而不得不自创用字。

这也产生了一种奇特的效果。把

Zhu Youxun only lived to be 26 years old, the same as his elder brother, Zhu Yougai, King Jing of Shu, while their father, Zhu Yuelian, only lived to be 22 years old. With the death of Zhu Youxun, the first primogeniture of King of Shu, Zhu Yuelian's clan, ended.

According to many essays, "Epitaph of King Xi of Shu of Ming Dynasty"corrected the errors in *Ming History* and *The General History of Sichuan*, in which "Youxun" 友壎 was recorded as "友攩".

In fact, it is also wrong to use 友攩. Zhu Yuanzhang had already set the nomenclature rules for his descendants and stipulated that their last name must contain Chinese character radical "wood-fire-earth-gold–water"—the auspicious sequence of five elements that one generates the other. Now that all kings of Shu in the same generation, such as Zhu Youyu朱友堉 and Zhu Yougai朱友垓, have "earth" 土 radical in their last name, how could King Xi of Shu, who was their peer, have a "gold" radical 扌 in his last name? The compiler of *The Ming History* could not be unaware of Zhu Yuanzhang's regulation.

As a matter of fact, the so-called "攩" was originally a character consisting of "土" on the left and "黨" on the right in *Ming History*. However, this character "壎" was too rare for the Microsoft Word to record, much less to represent, so it was replaced by 攩, which was then copied from one to the other and the mistake was repeated. This is the origin of the expression "友攩".

Zhu Yuanzhang might not have thought that his descendants would later multiply to such a huge number that the commonly used characters with "wood-fire-earth-gold–water" as the radicals were far from enough, so a large number of rare characters would be used, and some nonexistent characters would have to be created in order to name the Zhu family members.

This also produces an odd effect. Listing the

朱家子孙姓名以“金”为偏旁字的字列出来，如同见到了一份化学元素周期表：镭、铬、铌、钴、钯、铈、镧、钋、铍、镉、钒、铕……

names of Zhu's descendants with "gold" as the radical is like seeing a periodic table of chemical elements: 镭 radium, 铬 chromium, 铌 niobium, 钴 cobalt, 钯 palladium, 铈 cerium, 镧 lanthanum, 钋 polonium, 铍 beryllium, 镉 cadmium, 钒 vanadium, 铕 europium …

地下僖王陵
地上蜀王府

僖王陵是一座富丽堂皇的宫殿。是的，宫殿，不过深埋在地下。深，很深，从地宫底部到地表，距离为8.91米。

富丽堂皇的僖王陵地宫，述说着皇家气派　余茂智 摄

The magnificent underground palace of King Xi Mausoleum showcases royal grandeur. (Photographer: Yu Maozhi)

地宫通长二十八米，宽九米，高近七米，可分为前、中、后三部分：前部为大门、前庭、前殿；中部为主体，包括正庭、正殿和中殿；后部为后殿，又分为左侧室、中室和右侧室。

跟蜀僖王生前起居的蜀王府相

King Xi's mausoleum underground and his mansion on earth

The Mausoleum of King Xi is an opulent palace. Indeed, a palace, but buried deep underground. Deep, very deep, from the bottom of the palace to the surface, the distance is 8.91 meters.

With a length of 28 meters, a width of 9 meters and a height of nearly 7 meters, the underground palace can be divided into three parts: the front part includes the Entrance Door, the Forecourt and the Front Hall; the middle part contains the main body, such as the Main Court, Main Hall and Middle Hall; and the rear part is the Back Hall, which is further divided into the Left Side Room, the Middle Room and the Right Side Room.

Compared with King Xi's Mansion, where he lived during his lifetime, his Mausoleum has a corresponding relationship. The mausoleum was the king's palace for eternity, and he would spend much more time here than in his mansion on the ground.

When we open the floor plan of the King Xi's Mansion, there will be a surprising discovery that it is also be divided into the front, middle and rear parts, structurally strikingly similar to his mausoleum: the Duan Li Gate and Cheng Yun Gate in the front; the Cheng Yun Hall, Huan Hall and Cun Xin Hall in the middle; the Back Hall and Atrium of the Back Hall at the rear.

In this way, the correspondence is clear.

比，僖王陵存有一种相呼应的关系。陵是王永世的宫殿，蜀僖王在这里的时间要比在地上蜀王府多得多。

再打开蜀王府的平面图，会有一个惊奇的发现，它也可以分为前、中、后三部分，在结构上与地宫惊人地相似：前部端礼门、承运门；中部承运殿、圜殿、存心殿；后部为后殿、后殿中室。

如此一来，对应关系就一清二楚了。

端礼门对应地宫大门。

承运门对应前庭、前殿。

承运殿、圜殿、存心殿对应正庭、正殿、中庭，这是主体部分的唱和。

宫门对应后殿。

前寝、后寝对应后殿中室，分别是蜀王在地上与地下的歇息之处。

甚至，在中轴线两侧也可以找到对应物。比如：蜀王府有东西殿、地宫有左右厢房；蜀王府有东三所、东六宫，地宫有后殿左侧室；蜀王府有西三所、西六宫，地宫有后殿右侧室。

顺着墓道而下，最先看到的是两扇青砖砌成的八字墙，如两面影壁分列左右。八字墙是大门的附属建筑，主体则是两扇厚重的青石门。“厚重”二字，是写实的描述，石门厚度为十四厘米，单扇重量为两吨。尽管两扇门共计重达八千斤，但依然是可以

The Duan Li Gate corresponds to the Entrance Door in the mausoleum.

The Cheng Yun Gate matches the Forecourt and Front Hall.

The Cheng Yun Hall, Huan Hall and Cun Xin Hall parallel the Main Court, Main Hall and Middle Hall, which is the resemblance of the major parts of the two buildings.

The Palace Gate echoes the Rear Hall.

The Front Bedchamber and the Rear Bedchamber equate to the Back Hall and Atrium of the Back Hall, which are the resting places of the King of Shu on the ground and underground respectively.

The counterparts can be found even on both sides of the central axis. For example: In the Mansion of King of Shu there are East and West halls, while in his Mausoleum, there are Left and Right compartments; in his mansion, there are Three Houses to the East and Six Palaces to the East, while in his mausoleum, there are Left Side Room of Rear Hall; in his mansion, there are Three Houses to the West and Six Palaces to the West, while in his mausoleum, there are Right Side Room of Rear Hall.

The first thing you see when you go down the tomb passage are two Bazi Walls (the shape of the wall is like the Chinese 八, or eight) made of green bricks, like two walls on the left and right casting respective shadows on each other. The Bazi Walls is an accessory building of the gate, and the main body is two heavy green stone doors. The word “heavy” is a realistic description of the stone door, which is 14 centimeters thick and weighs two tons. Although the two doors weigh a total of 8,000 pounds, they are still movable. The square bars inside the doors should be a mechanism that holds the bars against the doors when they are closed and locked from the outside.

On each door, there carved eighty-one papillary

活动的。门内的方形条石应当是一种机关，当石门关闭、从外面锁上时，条石会抵住大门。

每扇门上，九横九纵刻着八十一颗乳钉，端的是皇家气派。“皇家”二字，也是实写，门钉九横九纵是皇宫的大门，藩王规制本是七横九纵。

青石大门的上方，是高度超过一米的门楼。十朵五重斗拱托起一个庑殿式的顶。斗拱的材质为石，仿照地面世界的木制斗拱，并按比例缩小。石仿木，不朽仿易朽，是一种高度抽象，也是一种带反讽性质的行为艺术。它所模仿的对象，蜀王府的大门，已在1646年的末日之火中化为浓烟，而地下的石雕斗拱依然完好无损。

明代的蜀王府，曾经有着规模庞大的左、中、右三支护卫军。即便经过建文帝和永乐帝两朝削藩，到了蜀僖王的时代，也仍然保留着左护卫军，兵士4900人。

地底下的蜀王陵，也以一种概括且抽象的方式，保留了地上蜀王城的运作模式。六具彩釉陶将军俑守卫在大门内的前庭厢房，以及墓室中部的正殿大门口——这两个位置，分别对应的是地上王府的宫门和主殿。

六名将军皆粗短壮实，皆身高57.8厘米，将军肚微微挺起。将军俑

nail, nine horizontal rows and nine vertical columns, a typical royal style. The word “royal” indicates that this kind arrangement is entitled otherwise only to the gate of the royal palace, while on the feudal king’s door, there should be seven horizontal rows and nine vertical columns.

Above the green stone gate is the gatehouse, which is more than one meter in height. Ten five-fold arches held up a hipped roof. The arches are made of stone, modeled after the wooden arches of the mortal world and scaled down. The stone imitates wood, and the imperishable imitates the easily perishable, a highly abstract and a performance art with irony. The object it imitates, the gate of the King of Shu’s Mansion, was reduced to smoke in the apocalyptic fire of 1646, while the stone arch on the ground floor remains intact.

In the Ming Dynasty, the Mansion of King of Shu used to have a large scale of left, center and right guards. Even after Emperor Jian Wen and Emperor Yong Le diminished the feudal powers, during the time of King Xi, he still retained the left guard army, totally 4900 soldiers.

The underground mausoleum also preserves the mode of operation of the aboveground mansion in a generalized and abstract manner. Six color-glazed ceramic figurines of generals guard the vestibule compartments inside the gate, as well as the main hall entrance in the middle of the tomb—two locations that respectively correspond to the Palace Gate and the Main Hall of the aboveground king’s residence.

Six generals are short and sturdy, all 57.8 centimeters tall, their bellies slightly raised. All general figurines are wearing phoenix-wing helmet. Phoenix wings exaggeratedly raised on both sides of the helmet, vividly and awe-inspiring. Their shoulder covered with shawls whose folds are clearly visible.

皆头戴凤翅盔，头盔两侧耳部的凤翅夸张地扬起，真如凤凰展翅，平添几分威风。肩上系着披巾，其上褶皱清晰可见。腰束缠腰，迎风摇摆。脚蹬长靴，八字分开。尽管时光褪去了陶俑身上的色彩，但仔细辨认，仍旧能看得出他们身上的战袍是绿色的，战袍下露出的甲片是赭石色的。

将军分为两组，一组颌下无须，手执板斧；另一组都蓄着一部大胡子，手持方天画戟。如将军、兵士护卫蜀王府中的王爷一般，地下的将军俑也守卫着地宫里的蜀僖王。

四合院于中国人，是身体栖息之所，也是灵魂安放之处。即便皇宫、王府，也不过是大号的、升级版本的四合院，无非多了些盘龙大柱、硕大斗拱、汉白玉台阶、天花藻井等。朱友壎的僖王陵，便是一座建在地下的四进四合院。

传统庭院式建筑中，庭是两个院落之间的过渡地带，它往往是一个大院子，或者说是一块两侧带着厢房的空地——如果建得小一些，就成了采光的天井。

地宫正庭，则是踏入核心地带正殿之前最后的序曲，在这里，仪式感必不可少。

僖王陵共出土陶俑四百二十六

Their waists are wrapped around with belts, swaying in the wind. Their boots splay out. Although wear and tear by time, the color of the terracotta figurines has been fading away, close observation can still reveal the colour of their robe is green and the armor is ochre-colored.

Generals are divided into two groups, one is beardless, with hand-held axe; the other wears beard, each holding a halberd. As the generals and soldiers guarded the king in his mansion, the underground general figurines also guarded King Xi in underground palace.

For Chinese people, *Siheyuan*, or the courtyard house, a type of Chinese residence, is the habitat for their bodies, as well as a resting place for their souls. Imperial palaces and royal residences are just larger and upgraded versions of *Siheyuan*, with more dragon pillars, big arches, alabaster steps and coloured ceiling. The mausoleum of Zhu Youxun, King Xi, is a four-room *Siheyuan*.

In traditional courtyard-style architecture, the court is a transitional area between two courtyards, and it is often a large yard, or an open space with compartments on either side—if built smaller, it becomes a light-filled patio.

The Main Court of the underground palace, on the other hand, is the final prelude before stepping into the main hall of the core, where ritual is essential.

Of all 426 terracotta figurines excavated from the mausoleum of King Xi, as many as 398 were placed in the Main Court. Surely, they are ceremonial figurines, divided into six major categories, with different styles and colors of clothes and hats. The warrior figurines carry long swords at their waists, and hold either round or rectangular shields, with animal heads carved on the round shields, while others hold spears in their hands, or hold double swords.

This underground honor guard is displayed in

件，其中就有三百九十八件摆放在这里。是的，它们是仪仗俑，分为六个大类，衣帽的样式与色彩各异。武士俑腰别长刀，手里拿着或圆形或长方形的盾牌，圆形盾牌上还刻着兽首，也有的手执长矛，或者持着双刀。

这支地下仪仗队陈列于前庭，牵着三十八匹或黄或绿或黑或白的陶马，多配有鞍或镫，还有些背上驮着箱子、布匹。似乎远来的商客还未洗去疲惫的尘土，庄重的文官刚刚致完欢迎辞，而杂立于仪仗俑之间的吹鼓俑和执事俑已拿起放在一旁的乐器，盛大的欢迎仪式即将开始。

殿，相当于四合院中的正房。

蜀王府里的承运殿、圜殿和存心殿，是蜀王处理政务、召见官员之处，尤为宏伟，其中的承运殿有七十二根大柱分布两侧。不过在蜀王陵，正殿仅仅是修了一道门（前殿、后殿也一样），采用了一种象征的表达方式。尽管是简化，却绝不简单——十二朵五铺作琉璃斗拱托起琉璃瓦庑殿顶，硕大的螭吻端坐在屋脊两头。

即便是尊贵如王侯之家，也一样免不了人间烟火。正殿之后的中庭，则站立着十四名男女侍俑，伴随着他们的，自然是椅柜几案、箱笼函匣。更具烟火气的盘、碗和瓶，则放在

the vestibule, leading 38 yellow or green or black or white ceramic horses, mostly equipped with saddles or stirrups, and some of them are carrying boxes and cloths on their backs. It seems that the merchants from afar have not washed off the dust of fatigue, the solemn civil officials have just finished the welcome speech, and the ceremonial figurines have picked up the musical instruments—a grand welcoming ceremony is about to begin.

The Hall, equivalent to the main room in a *Siheyuan*.

The Cheng Yun Hall, Huan Hall and Cun Xin Hall in the King of Shu's Mansion, where the king dealt with government affairs and summoned officials, are particularly grand, with seventy-two large pillars flanking each side of the Cheng Yun Hall. In his mausoleum, however, the Main Hall is simply a doorway (as are the Front and Back Halls), adopting a symbolic expression. Although simplified, it is by no means humble—twelve five-paved as glazed arches hold up the glazed tile hipped roof, and large *Chi Wen* (the legendary ninth son of dragon) sits at the ends of the roof ridge.

Even in a house as honorable as a prince's, the daily necessities are inevitable. In the Atrium after the Main Hall, fourteen male and female figurines stood, accompanied by chairs, cabinets and cases, boxes and cages. Dish plates, rice bowls and bottles, the most down-to-earth items, are placed in the two side rooms. There are five pieces of bowls, including the blue and white porcelain bowl, decorated with lotus pattern, the bottom of it stamped with "Xiping Good Ware", a common mark indicating the origin of the product, Jingdezhen folk kiln. It can be inferred that the bowls used in the mansion of King of Shu were bought from public market. Perhaps, this bowl was used by King Xi during his lifetime.

These terracotta figurines, as *Ming Qis* (burial objects), were not very finely made. For

两侧的厢房内。碗共五件，其中的青花瓷碗，饰青花缠枝莲荷纹，外底有“西平佳器”的字款。这种款识是景德镇民窑生产青花瓷的常用款识，可以推断，当时蜀王府用碗也通过民间购买。或许，这只碗就是蜀僖王生前所用。

这些陶俑作为明器（随葬器物，又称冥器），制作并不算精细。比如因为烧制温度不高，镇墓将军俑出土之时釉彩剥落严重，只能从其残余处探寻其本来面貌。但不可否认的是，这些地下将军都面目生动、不怒自威。而那些仪仗俑，则排列成阵，展示了一个井然有序的地下王权世界。

地宫的正庭、后庭也模仿四合院，建有厢房。不过这厢房也跟三大殿一样，无进深，仅有一道门，却依然精美。门窗栏额及室顶雕有莲荷、牡丹、菱花、菊花、蕉叶、海螺、双鱼、火轮、云朵等多种图案纹饰。

地上的蜀王府烧毁了，从地下的蜀王陵可想象其些许风采。

穿过中庭，则入后殿。后殿由左右两侧室及中室三部分构成，它对应着地上王府的后宫，那是历代蜀王生活、歇息之处。后殿中室，置一巨大的须弥座石棺床，蜀僖王朱友壎则长眠于此。不知是哪个年代的盗墓者

example, because of the low firing temperature, the glaze of the figurines of the tomb generals flaked off seriously when they were unearthed, and their original appearance could only be explored from their remnants. However, it is undeniable that these underground generals have vivid facial appearance, not angry but august. And those ceremonial figurines are arranged in formation, showing a well-organized underground world of kingship.

The Main Court and Back Court of the underground palace also imitated a *Siheyuan*, built with compartments. But this room, like the three halls, has no depth but a door only, exquisite nonetheless. The lintels and the ceilings of the room are carved with lotus, peonies, water chestnut flowers, chrysanthemums, canna leaves, conch, double fish, fire wheel, clouds and other patterns and decorations.

Above the ground, the Mansion of King of Shu was burned down, yet its elegance can still be imagined from its the underground counterpart.

Passing through the Atrium, one enters the Rear Hall. The Rear Hall consists of three parts: the side rooms on the left and right and the middle room, which corresponds to the chambers of imperial concubines on the ground, where the kings of Shu lived and rested. In the middle room of the Rear Hall, there is a huge sarcophagus on a heavy base, where King Xi, Zhu Youxun sleeps. It is not known when the grave robbers disturbed his good dream: when the mausoleum was opened by the archaeologists, his red-painted nanmu-carved coffin had already been destroyed, bones scattered all over the place, only a complete skull remains.

So far, the mausoleum of King Xi has been filled with Chinese cultural elements, but when you look up at the sarcophagus, the door to another world opens.

The “tianhua” in traditional architecture refers

惊扰了他的好梦：文物考古打开地宫时，只见楠木朱漆棺椁已被毁坏，尸骨散落一地，唯余一具完整头骨。

至此，在蜀僖王陵里所见皆为汉式文化意蕴，然而抬起头望向石棺上方，便打开了另一个世界的大门。

天花，是传统建筑中用于遮挡架梁的构件，可以理解为顶棚或天花板。庙宇或宫廷里的天花又称藻井，其下正对着佛像和皇帝、王爷的宝座。蜀僖王石棺上方的天花，由巨石拼接而成，薄薄地刻着一层纹饰，却是藏式的天花曼陀罗。

这方巨大的藏式石刻，最显眼的是三个红色的同心圆。最大的圆圈之外，曼陀罗花线装饰四周。曼陀罗是佛教中的天界之花，“天花乱坠”，坠的就有这种花。《法华经》称：“佛说此经已，结跏趺坐，入于无量义处三昧，身心不动。是时，天雨曼陀罗华、摩诃曼陀罗华、曼殊沙华、摩诃曼殊沙华……”

同心圆分为三层，外层与中层都刻有八瓣莲花，象征佛教的八种心识。外层莲花瓣内，分别刻着宝伞（清净吉祥）、宝瓶（福智吉祥）、金鱼（自在吉祥）、妙莲（妙舌吉祥）、右旋海螺（妙音吉祥）、经幢（事业吉祥）、吉祥结（不变吉祥）、金轮

to the component used to cover the beams, akin to a ceiling or canopy. In temples or palaces, this tianhua is also known as a “zaojing”, situated directly above Buddha statues, emperors, or princes’ thrones. The tianhua above Shu Xi Wang’s stone coffin is assembled from giant stones, delicately carved with motifs resembling Tibetan mandalas.

The most striking feature of this large Tibetan stone carving is the three concentric red circles. Outside the largest circle, mandala flower patterns adorn the surroundings. Mandalas are considered heavenly flowers in Buddhism, symbolizing the celestial realm where the flowers drift down. The *Lotus Sutra* states: “The Buddha spoke this sutra, assumed the cross-legged posture, and entered the samadhi of the immeasurable meanings without any stir of body or mind. At that time, heavenly rains of Mandarava flowers, Maha Mandarava flowers, Manjusara flowers, and Maha Manjusara flowers fell.”

The concentric circles are divided into three layers, with each outer and middle layer carved with eight-petal lotus flowers, symbolizing the eight consciousnesses in Buddhism. Inside the petals of the outer layer lotus flowers are eight precious symbols: the precious umbrella (symbolizing purity and auspiciousness), the treasure vase (symbolizing abundance and wisdom), the golden fish (symbolizing freedom and auspiciousness), the auspicious lotus (symbolizing the auspiciousness of eloquence), the right-coiled conch shell (symbolizing the auspiciousness of melodious sound), the victory banner (symbolizing the auspiciousness of success), the auspicious knot (symbolizing unchanging auspiciousness), and the golden wheel (symbolizing the auspiciousness of the Dharma), collectively known as the “Eight Auspicious Symbols”.

Within the middle layer lotus flowers, each petal contains three lotus blooms arranged in a Chinese

（佛法吉祥）等八宝，又称“八吉祥徽”。中层八瓣莲花，每瓣内都有三朵莲花垒成品字形。最中央的梵文图案，藏语中称为“星祥”。藏学家任新建先生曾考察过僖王陵的藏式石刻，他著文称，“星祥”相当于汉族丧葬中的灵牌，可以判断僖王生前接受过密宗灌顶。

僖王是如假包换的汉地藩王，为何生前身后带有如此多的藏文化痕迹呢？蜀地作为西陲，在汉与藏频繁的文化、贸易交流中作用巨大。以此视角观之，蜀僖王石棺上方的藏式石刻，也就不难理解了。

character “品” shape. The central Vajrayana Tibetan script design, known as “starry auspiciousness” in Tibetan, was studied by the Tibetologist Mr. Ren Xinjian during their exploration of the Shu Xi Wang Mausoleum’s Tibetan stone carvings. He claimed that “starry auspiciousness” corresponds to the spirit tablet in Chinese Han funeral customs, indicating that Xi Wang likely received initiation into tantric teachings of Vajrayana Buddhism during his lifetime.

Why did King Xi, who was a Han Chinese vassal king, carry so many traces of Tibetan culture in his life? As the western frontier, Sichuan province (the territory of Shu) played a huge role in the frequent cultural and trade exchanges between Han and Tibet. Viewed from this perspective, it is not difficult to understand that on King Xi’s sarcophagus, there are Tibetan stone carvings.

物产丰盈的世俗社会

陶、瓷、琉璃，是相似而又有差别的三种物什。

陶器外表粗粝，质地疏松；瓷器紧致细密，色泽均匀；琉璃则晶莹璀璨，流光溢彩。简言之，陶类瓦，瓷似玉，而琉璃如水晶。

陶、瓷、琉璃皆炼制于窑。陶的烧结温度最低，在八百摄氏度以下，而烧制琉璃，则需要达到一千五百度。更高的温度和更复杂的工艺，淬炼出了更绚丽的品质。

实际的操作中也有变通。蜀王陵

A secular society with an abundance of goods

Pottery, porcelain and glaze are three similar but different objects.

Pottery has coarse appearance and loose texture; porcelain possesses tight and dense shape and uniform color; glaze is characterizes by crystal brightness and colorful luster. In short, pottery is similar to tile, porcelain is like jade, and glaze is akin to crystal.

Pottery, porcelain and glaze are all refined in kilns. Pottery is sintered at the lowest temperature, below 800 degrees Celsius, while glaze is fired at 1,500 degrees Celsius. Higher temperatures and more complex processes result in more brilliant qualities.

There are alterations in the actual operation. The

的琉璃瓦等构件原由陶土烧结，与以二氧化硅为主要成分的琉璃器有本质区别，但因其上施彩釉而泽如琉璃，故有此名。

而出土于朱悦燫墓、以象辂（大车）为中心的庞大仪仗俑群，以及大量的椅、屏、案等模型，则品质更高。其釉面用色已超过"宋三彩"的绿、黄、褐，多了黑色。烧结温度则在一千二百摄氏度以上，敲之铿然有声。

僖王陵后殿棺椁背后的照壁上，镶嵌着一块镂空描金蟠龙雕盘。两条四爪金龙怒目相对，一条龙身先朝上再n字形盘曲而下，另一条则先朝下再u字形反转向上，造型生动的两具龙身围成了一个圆盘。圆盘外接一个方框，内四角镶以如意云纹，繁复而精细。

这些器物，均炼制于琉璃厂窑。

僖王陵照壁上的蟠龙雕盘　余茂智 摄

The coiled dragon carving on the screen wall of King Xi Mausoleum. (Photographer: Yu Maozhi)

glazed tiles and other components in the Mausoleum of King of Shu originally sintered from clay, differing fundamental with the glazed wares that use silica as the main component. Yet its application of colored glaze takes credit for its name.

A huge group of ceremonial figurines, mostly *Xianglu* (big chariot) and a large number of chairs, screens, desks and other models unearthed in Zhu Yuelian's tomb proclaim higher quality. Their glaze colors have exceeded the "Three Colors of Song Dynasty": green, yellow, brown, with black added. The sintering temperature is above 1,200 degrees Celsius, and the sound is resounding.

On the screen wall behind King Xi's sarcophagus, a hollowed-out gold coiled dragon carving plate was inlaid. Two four-clawed gold dragon eyes opposite each other, one of which first faces up and then coils down in a n-shaped fashion and the other first faces down and then reversely turns up in the u-shape way. The shape of the two vivid dragon body forms a disk. The disk is connected with an outside box, which was inlaid with *Ruyi* (a furnishing that symbolizes good luck) cloud pattern in the four corners, complex and fine.

These wares were all refined in the *Liulichang* kiln.

In Ming Dynasty, Chengdu Glaze Factory (*Liulichang* kiln) was an official kiln for firing glaze, porcelain and pottery. In addition to providing architectural components, daily utensils, and burial objects for the King of Shu's Palace and Mausoleums, it also supplied to temples and shrines.

Located east of the Xiaoshahe River and north of the southern third section of the Third Ring Road, *Liulichang* got its name from a kiln-fired factory. For more than seven hundred years, from the Sui and Tang dynasties to the early Ming Dynasty, there were a large number of kilns scattered here, from which a variety of ceramics were turned out. During the

在明代，成都琉璃厂是烧制琉璃、瓷器、陶器等的官窑。除了为蜀王府、蜀王陵提供建筑构件、日用器具、冥器外，也向寺观祠庙供应。

琉璃场位于小沙河以东、三环路南三段以北，它得名于以烧窑为业的琉璃厂。从隋唐到明初的七百多年时间里，这里曾散布着数量众多的窑包，它们烧制了品类丰富的陶瓷器。在隋唐时代，其品质可与中原陶瓷媲美。到了明代，这些民窑被收归官府，专为蜀王府服务。

随着明蜀藩的覆灭，琉璃厂也沦为废墟，无数的陶瓷器残片，伴随着它们身上光彩亮丽的色釉和精美绚丽的纹饰被埋入地下。直到20世纪20年代，这一片区域才重见人烟，逐渐形成场镇。新的场镇借用了琉璃厂之名，称作“琉璃场”。

沿着老成仁路由北向南，过了沙河大桥，是一块类似于三角形的拆迁待建区域。三角形的斜边是沙河绿化带，两条直角边分别是琉璃路与中环路锦绣大道段。从琉璃路1366号往东，是一条水泥小路，两边的围墙挡住了拆迁区，形成一条幽深的巷道。

行数十米，向左又是一条土路，破旧的墙后一个土坝，摆着数十张竹椅，是一个简易的露天茶馆。城中村

Sui and Tang dynasties, the quality of their ceramics was comparable to that of the Central Plains. During the Ming Dynasty, these kilns were taken by the government and were used exclusively for the service of the King of Shu.

With the collapse of the kingdom of Shu, *Liulichang* also fell into ruins; thus, countless pieces of ceramics, along with their glittering color glaze and exquisite and gorgeous decorations were buried in the ground. It was not until the 1920s that this area saw the return of people and the gradual formation of the town. The new town borrowed the name of *Liulichang* (琉璃厂) and called it *Liulichang* (琉璃场).

Along the old Chengren Road from north to south, after crossing the Shahe River Bridge, is an area similar to a triangle set aside for demolition and pending construction. The diagonal side of the triangle is the Shahe Green Belt, and the two right-angled sides are Liuli Road and the Jinxiu Avenue section of Middle Ring Road. East from 1366 Liuli Road is a concrete path with fences on both sides blocking the demolition area, creating a deep alleyway.

Walking dozens of meters, to the left is another dirt road. An earth dam behind a dilapidated wall can be found, with dozens of bamboo chairs: a simple open-air teahouse. Inside the urban village, there are still a few old houses with people still living inside, and the land is instead all utilized to grow vegetables, demonstrating the strong genes of the farming nation. The stars of pottery pieces here and there are set on the ridge, visible to the naked eye.

"On the slope, there are more tiles." Under the guidance of the tea guest, I climbed the not-so-high hill. Looking up and around, I found myself standing in the bottom of the valley, only because all around are tall buildings. Looking down, a bed of red-skinned radishes is all around my feet. This kind of radish is an important material for Sichuan pickles.

内，仍然有少许老旧房子里面还住着人，土地倒是全部被利用起来种了蔬菜，展示出强大的农耕民族基因。星星点点的陶片镶嵌在田埂上，肉眼可见。

"坡坡上，瓦片儿更多。"在茶客的指点下，笔者登上了并不高的小山坡。抬头四下环望，如处谷底，只缘四周尽是高楼。俯视脚下，一畦畦的红皮萝卜，正是制作四川泡菜的重要材料。茶客口中的瓦片随处可见，如天空里的漫天星斗。而这些瓦片，正是明代琉璃厂窑历年的废弃品。它们经历了一次又一次犁锄翻耕，在数百年的时间里，见证了一茬又一茬作物的播种与收割。

产于琉璃厂、出土自蜀王陵的琉璃瓷器，如管中豹之斑纹，透露出明代成都的信息：货物充陈、商业昌盛。

明代的成都府，辖六州二十五县。到了嘉靖年间，由成都县和华阳县构成的成都城人口已达数十万人。嘉靖年间进士张瀚，曾任四川按察副使，他在《松窗梦语》里说："城中为蜀王府，其富厚甲于诸王""（太原）富厚亦不及较蜀远矣。"他说，陕西人善经商，他们向西到陇、蜀贸易，都能达成赚钱的心愿；晋商南下

The tiles mentioned by the tea drinkers can be seen everywhere, like the stars in the sky. These tiles are the discarded products of the *Liulichang* kiln in Ming Dynasty over the years. They have been plowed over and over again, witnessing the sowing and harvesting of crop after crop over the centuries.

Produced in *Liulichang* and unearthed from the Mausoleums of the King of Shu, these glazed porcelains are like seeing a leopard through a narrow tube—what you see is only small part of a larger body. However, the livelihood of Chengdu could be partly revealed from this: full of goods and commercial prosperity.

During the Ming Dynasty, the Chengdu Prefecture governed six prefectures and twenty-five counties. By the Jiajing period, the population of Chengdu City, which consisted of Chengdu County and Huayang County, had reached hundreds of thousands. At that time, Zhang Han, a *Ju Ren* (a successful candidate in the provincial examination) who was the deputy inspect-general of Sichuan, said in his *Dream Words beside Pine Windows* that "the city was the residence of the King of Shu, whose wealth was greater than that of his peers" and that "the wealth (of Taiyuan) was not as great as that of Shu". According to him, Shaanxi people were good at business and they went west to Long and Shu to ply their trade and their desires to make a killing can always be achieved; Jin merchants went south to Sichuan, where is not only rich and affluent, but also convenient to going downstream to the east, through the Three Gorges and reaching the Jing of Chu territory, and Chengdu is the logistics intersection; the merchants along the southeastern coastline had only two choices: to the west into the Sichuan, or to south to Guangzhou if they wanted to earn more than ten times as much as the high profits.

Although the remarkable book *The Plum in the*

就到了巴蜀，这里不仅丰饶、富庶，而且可顺流东下，经三峡而达荆楚，成都则是其物流交汇之处；而东南沿海一带的商人，若图赚取十倍以上的高额利润，只有两个选择：向西入川，或南下广州。

奇书《金瓶梅》虽假托故事发生于宋代，但反映的其实是明代发达的商业社会和城市生活。主人公西门庆家的财富很大一部分来自在四川所做的生意："他父亲西门达，原走川广贩药材，就在这清河县前开着一个大大的生药铺。"

书中也多次提到"川扇"，有"真金川扇儿""洒金川扇儿""红骨细洒金、金钉铰川扇儿"等种种。"洒金川扇儿"是指扇面上贴金箔或洒金，是引领时尚的名贵品，仅此一项，永乐年间成都的年产量就达约两万把。

商品经济的发达，必催生市民意识的觉醒。明代出现了如此之多的世情小说，其实就是世俗社会的文化体现。

为什么要越制？

明朝对于帝后陵寝乃至大臣丧葬仪轨，都有非常严格的规定，但僖王陵里有两处已经明显地违规越制了：一处是九纵九横共有八十一枚石钉的

Golden Vase pretends that the story takes place in the Song Dynasty, it actually reflects the developed commercial society and city life in the Ming Dynasty. A large part of the wealth of the main character, Ximen Qing and his family, came from the business done in Sichuan, "His father, Ximen Da, originally traveled to Sichuan and Canton to sell medicinal herbs, and right here in front of the Qinghe County opened a large raw medicine store".

In several parts of the book a "Chuan fan" (fan made in Sichuan) was mentioned: "real gold Chuan fan", "sprinkled gold Chuan fan", "red-bone fine sprinkled-gold and gold-nail-hinge Chuan fan" and so on. "Sprinkled-gold Chuan fan" refers to the fan surface with gold foil or sprinkled gold, and is an expensive and fashionable product. In the Yongle period, Chengdu churned out this one alone about 20,000 annually.

The development of the commodity economy will give rise to the awakening of civic consciousness. The emergence of so many worldly novels in the Ming Dynasty was in fact the cultural embodiment of a secular society.

Why go over the top?

In Ming Dynasty, very strict regulations were enlisted for the funeral rituals and construction of mausoleum of emperor and queen and even ministers, but two places in the mausoleum of King Xi have been obvious in violation of those regulations: one is nine vertical and nine horizontal stone nails, a total of eighty-one, are installed on the door of his underground palace; the other is the epitaph monument engraved with a five-clawed golden dragon.

In traditional Chinese culture, the number "nine" signifies the ultimate number and is often reserved for use by emperors. When it comes to doors, only imperial palace gates are permitted to have 9 vertical rows and 9 horizontal rows of studs, symbolizing that all comes to one. For example, both the gates of the

地宫大门，另一处是刻着五爪金龙的圹志碑。

在传统文化中，“九”为数之极，多为皇帝专用。单就门而言，皇宫大门乳钉才能九纵九横，寓九九归一。比如紫禁城大门、明神宗定陵地宫的两扇汉白玉大门，上面都是九九八十一颗门钉。而蜀僖王为藩王，其陵墓大门上的石钉，按制当为六十三枚，以纵九横七的方式排列。

正殿之中的圹志碑，上方两端各饰一条五爪金龙。按制，五爪龙纹只能用于皇帝；四爪又称蟒，用于藩王；而三爪金龙则出现在太监墓内。

同样，昭王陵中的人首龙身石盘也来历不凡。在华夏民族的上古神话中，伏羲、女娲的形象皆为人首蛇身，这其实就是人首龙身的来源。虽然昭王陵中石盘上的两条龙皆为四爪龙，已经发掘的万历帝定陵中却并无此类构件。奉友湘、李后强《蜀王全传》引野史称，明代帝王墓穴中只有朱元璋孝陵中有此龙盘，显示昭王陵人首龙身石盘是据此仿制的。

蜀藩墓葬的越制，其实从第一代世子朱悦燫的墓葬就开始了。朱悦燫是朱元璋的孙子、首代蜀王朱椿的继承人，但是，他还没来得及继承王位就去世了。按理，其墓葬规模是不能

Forbidden City and the two Han white jade gates of the underground tomb of Ming Emperor Shenzong are adorned with 81 studs. As Shu Xi Wang held the title of a royal prince, the stone studs on the gate of his mausoleum were traditionally arranged in sets of 63, following a pattern of 9 vertical rows and 7 horizontal rows.

Over the epitaph monument in the main hall, two five-clawed golden dragons were decorated at the upper ends and the lower ends respectively. According to the regulation, five-clawed dragon pattern can only be used for the emperor; four-clawed pattern, also known as python pattern, was used for the feudal kings; and three-clawed golden dragon was found in the tomb of the eunuch.

Similarly, the stone disk with human head and dragon body in the mausoleum of King Zhao also has an extraordinary origin. In the ancient myths of the Chinese people, *Fuxi* and *Nuwa* are portrayed as human-headed and snake-bodied, which is actually the origin of the human-headed dragon body. Although the two dragons on the stone disk in the mausoleum of King Zhao are all four-clawed dragons, there are no such components in the Dingling Mausoleum of Emperor Wanli that has been excavated. In *King of Shu Biography*, Feng Youxiang and Li Houqiang, citing in the unofficial history, wrote that of all the mausoleums of Ming Dynasty emperors, only in Xiaoling, Zhu Yuanzhang's Mausoleum, a dragon disk can be found, showing that the disk in King Zhao's Mausoleum was an imitation.

The transgression actually began with the burial of Zhu Yuelian, the eldest son of first King of Shu. Zhu Yuelian was the grandson of Zhu Yuanzhang and the successor of Zhu Chun, the first King of Shu, but he died before he could inherit the throne. According to the rules, the scale of his tomb could not be compared with the tomb of a feudal king. However, in

跟藩王陵相比的。但事实上，成都凤凰山南麓朱悦燫墓的豪华却超过了昭王陵和以精美著称的僖王陵。

单就长度而论，朱悦燫墓长34米，而僖王陵长27.8米。而建于其中庭的圜殿，更是已发掘的蜀王陵寝所独有。圜殿四四方方如坛，前后各有梯步上下，上设供桌，下置几座。《明史·舆服四》论及亲王府制称："（洪武）七年定亲王所居殿，前曰承运，中曰圜殿，后曰存心。"若论与蜀王府之呼应，此陵中圜殿可直接映射府之圜殿。因此，也有人推测，朱悦燫墓的规格如此之高，是因为朱椿哀痛白发人送黑发人，将事先为自己准备的陵墓给了早逝的儿子。

蜀藩陵墓的屡屡越制，是其擅自所为吗？实际上，藩王的丧葬全程都处于朝廷的关切或者说是监视之下。亲王有丧，皇帝会辍朝三日，相关重要部门则全数调动：钦天监选择下葬吉日与坟地，工部遣官建造坟茔，礼部派员主持葬礼，翰林院撰写祭文，国子监则派出监生向其他藩王府报丧。

可以说，没有皇帝的允许，蜀王陵的越制（包括朱椿将自己的陵墓给儿子）是万万不可能的。那么，为什么明朝廷会给予蜀藩如此优待呢？这

fact, the luxury of Zhu Yuelian's tomb at the southern foot of Fenghuang Mountain in Chengdu exceeds that of the mausoleum of King Zhao and the mausoleum of King Xi, which is famous for its exquisite beauty.

In terms of length alone, Zhu Yuelian's tomb is 34 meters long, while Xi Wang's tomb is 27.8 meters long. The Huan Hall, built in the atrium was unique among all the excavated mausoleums of the kings of Shu. Huan Hall is as square as an altar, with steps up and down in front and behind, with an offering table on top and several seats underneath. According to *History of Ming—On Yufu No.4* (Yufu concerns rules of etiquette on carriage and dress codes) when it comes to the systems of the princes, "In the seventh years of Hong Wu, the rules of residential palace for the prince were established. The front part is called Cheng Yun Temple, the middle part is called Huan Hall and the rear part is called Cun Xin Temple." According to the correspondence mentioned earlier, the Huan Hall in Zhu Yuelian's mausoleum can be directly corresponded to the Huan Hall in the place of King of Shu. Therefore, it is also speculated that Zhu Chun, the father of Zhu Yuelian was so grievous for his son's early death that he yielded the mausoleum that was prepared for him to be granted to his son; thus the standards of Zhu Yuelian's tomb are set so high.

The deviation from traditional customs in the construction of the Shu royal mausoleum was not done autonomously but rather under the careful scrutiny and oversight of the imperial court. Upon the death of a prince, the Emperor would suspend court proceedings for three days, and all relevant government departments would be mobilized: the Bureau of Astronomy selected an auspicious day for interment and the burial site; the Ministry of Works dispatched officials to construct the tomb; the Ministry of Rites oversaw the funeral ceremonies; the Hanlin Academy composed the funeral orations; the

与首代蜀王朱椿治理西陲的功绩以及朱元璋、朱棣两代皇帝的偏爱是密切相关的。

在明初的政治斗争中，朱椿坚定地站在明成祖朱棣一边。他不仅向朱棣告发了同胞兄弟、谷王朱橞的谋反，更在朱棣同诸弟商量对此事的处理时，坚持要杀掉朱橞——这让朱棣不仅根除了后患，也堵住了天下悠悠之口，没有亲自背上杀弟的恶名。

所谓投桃报李，朱棣对蜀王朱椿的行为评价为"周公安王室之心也"，并在朱椿入朝时赏赐给他巨量的金银缯彩。对于朱悦燫这个侄儿的早逝，朱棣也像死了自己儿子一样痛心疾首，在木制谥册中称："尔蜀世子悦燫，为朕犹子，端谨重厚，孝友谦和……"

此后的历代蜀王，也与中央政权保持了良好的关系。自朱椿以下，蜀藩以家风好、多贤王著称，昭王朱宾瀚曾得弘治皇帝著诗称扬，而成王朱让栩则被《明史》认证为"尤贤明"。嘉靖二十年，朝廷建太庙，朱让栩奉上黄金六十斤、白银六百斤，而皇帝则回赐以玉带币帛。

蜀王陵突破丧葬规格，一方面说明蜀藩深受皇帝信任，恩宠有加；另一方面，其实也是自身的需求。

Imperial Academy sent students to inform other royal households of the funeral arrangements.

It can be said that without the emperor's permission, the transgression of the etiquette of the King of Shu's mausoleums (including Zhu Chun giving his own tomb to his son) was never possible. So why did the Ming court give such favorable treatment to the Shu clan? This is closely related to the achievements of Zhu Chun, the first king of Shu, who governed the western frontier, as well as the favoritism of the emperors Zhu Yuanzhang and Zhu Di.

During the political struggle in the early Ming Dynasty, Zhu Chun stood firmly on the side of Zhu Di, Chengzu of Ming. He not only denounced and informed on the rebellion of his compatriot brother, Zhu Hui, King Gu, but also insisted on killing Zhu Hui when Zhu Di was discussing the handling of the matter with his brothers—which allowed Zhu Di not only to eradicate the future problems, but also to gag the public opinion, without personally bearing the bad reputation of killing his younger brother.

In the so-called "return the favor", Zhu Di evaluated Zhu Chun's behavior as "Lord Zhou reassured the royal family", and when Zhu Chun had an audience with the emperor, Zhu Di rewarded him a huge amount of gold, silver, coloured silk and fabrics. For the early death of this nephew, Zhu Di was also as painful as the loss of his own son. In the wooden posthumous register, Zhu Di mourned: "Zhu Yuelian, my nephew, was like my own son. He was dignified, honest, sincere, filial and humble ... "

The subsequent generations of kings of Shu also maintained good relations with the central government. From Zhu Chun onwards, Shu clan had been preserving good family tradition and wise kings had been constantly emerging. Zhu Binhan, King Zhao obtained praising in a poem from Emperor Hongzhi, and Zhu Rangxu, King Cheng was certified

在全世界的范畴里，古埃及和华夏两个民族对待死亡最郑重其事。古埃及人修建金字塔，制作木乃伊，相信法老的身体会在未来复活，再一次君临人世。而中国人的生死观却更为复杂：道家有仙界；佛家相信轮回；儒家注重现世，称“未知生，焉知死”，却又“事死如生”。蜀王陵则是释道儒思想杂糅的产物，其间还杂有现实考量与利益算计。毕竟，皇帝的破例能够带给王府更大的荣耀，逝者已矣，活着的人却能得到更多的荫护。

有明一朝二百六十七年，蜀地共历十世十三王，此外还传袭郡王十六系计六十余人。早期蜀王如朱椿和早夭的世子朱悦燫、第二代蜀王靖王朱友堉都埋葬在城北凤凰山、天回山一带。而后期的蜀王、王妃以及若干郡王、镇国将军等，则分别葬于东郊的十陵、洪河、三圣乡、琉璃场一带，如已发掘的僖王陵和昭王陵。

僖王陵和昭王陵中，那些恢宏的布局、精美的石作，以及“星祥”图案、供亡灵沟通的石门，既有蜀藩对权势与财富的炫耀，也有对死者的怀念与祈福，盼望其魂魄能够极乐往生，并护佑家族永远的荣华富贵。

“北有十三陵，南有蜀王陵。”这

by *History of Ming* as “particularly wise and bright”. In the 20th year of Jiajing, when the court built a temple, Zhu Rangxu presented 60 pounds of gold and 600 pounds of silver, and in return, the emperor bestowed him the jade belt and other presents.

The transgression of etiquettes of the Mausoleums of King of Shu was acquiesced on account of two reasons: on the one hand, Shu clan was deeply trusted by the emperor and the favors were multiplied; on the other hand, it was the political calculation by the kings themselves.

Throughout the world, ancient Egypt and China treated death with the most solemnity. The ancient Egyptians built pyramids and made mummies, believing that the pharaoh’s body would be resurrected in the future to reign over the world once again. The Chinese concept of life and death is more complex: Taoism has a world of immortality; Buddhism believes in reincarnation; Confucianism focuses on the present world, saying that “without knowing life, how is it possible to know death”, and treating“the dead as they are alive”. The Mausoleums of the King of Shu is the product of a mixture of Buddhism, Taoism and Confucianism, which is also mingled with practical considerations and calculations of interest. After all, the emperor’s making an exception to the transgression can bring greater honor to the vassal king’s family—the dead are gone and the living can get more protection.

In 267 years of Ming Dynasty, ten generations of thirteen kings and sixteen lineages of county kings, a total of sixty people, were generated in the territory of Shu. Early kings such as Zhu Chun and his prematurely died son Zhu Yuelian, the second-generation king of Shu, Zhu Youyu, King Jing, were buried in Phoenix Hill and Tianhui Mountain area to the north of the city. While the late kings of Shu and their consorts as well as a number of county kings, Zhenguo Generals, etc., were buried in the eastern

样的说法固然存在，但无论规模、气派和知名度，蜀王陵其实是远不能跟北京十三陵相比的，这是由明代陵寝建制所决定的，是由皇帝和藩王之间的等级差决定的。比如按制帝陵有宝城（地宫之上的封土堆）和明楼（帝陵正前的高楼），藩王陵则二者皆无。《明史》载，最大的长陵宝城“径一百一丈八尺”，这实在是一个恐怖的数字。

又比如，僖王陵通长不到二十八米，朱悦燫墓亦不过三十四米，定陵仅中殿就长达三十二米，出土的文物珍品更是不可以道里计。

总言之，十三陵的确气派十足，也带有北国的粗犷豪迈，若论精工细作或其艺术性带给人心的震撼，则位居西南一隅的蜀王陵又胜过一筹。

suburbs of the Shiling, Honghe, Sanshengxiang and Liulichang areas, as were witnessed by the excavated the Mausoleums of King Xi and Zhao.

In the Mausoleums of King Xi and Zhao, those magnificent layout, exquisite stone work, the “Xingxiang 星祥” pattern, and the stone door for the dead to communicate with one another, show off the power and wealth of the Shu clan, but also long for the dead and pray for their souls to be able to go to the afterlife, and forever bless the glory and wealth of the family.

“There are Thirteen Mausoleums in the north, and the Mausoleums of the King of Shu in the south.” Such a statement certainly exists, but with regard to the scale, style and popularity, Mausoleums of King of Shu are actually far from matching the Thirteen Mausoleums. This is determined by the system in which the emperor and the feudal lords are of different hierarchs. For example, according to the regulations, the emperor’s mausoleum has a *Bao Cheng* (the earth mound above the underground palace) and a *Ming Lou* (a high-rise building in front of the emperor’s mausoleum), but none of the two can be found in a vassal king’s mausoleum. According to The *History of Ming*, the largest *Changling Bao Cheng* has a “diameter of one hundred and eleven *Zhang*s and eight *Chi*s”, which is really a horrible figure.

Another case in point: King Xi’s mausoleum is less than 28 meters, and Zhu Yuelian’s is only 34 meters, Dingling, however, only the Middle Hall is 32 meters long, and the unearthed treasures are countless.

In short, The Thirteen Mausoleums are indeed full of grandeur, tainted with the North’s rugged and heroic character. In term of the fine craftsmanship or the impact to the human heart due to its artistry, the mausoleums located in the southwest corner of the kingdom is a cut above the former.

贡院
The Examination Hall

上万名书生聚集于此，拎着食物和考具，背着被盖，各自走进一个宽三尺、深四尺的格子间。在这种蜂巢般的房间里，他们将待上九天，参加三场考试，顿顿吃干粮。这里是四川士子漫长应试之路中的一站，也是科举考试的正式起点——乡试。

这里就是四川贡院，它兴建于明蜀王城经火焚烧的废墟之上，因此被成都人称作皇城坝。

Tens of thousands of scholars gathered here, carrying sustenance, examination tools and quilts, each going into a cubicle three feet wide and four feet deep. In this beehive-like chambers, they would abide for nine days, partaking in three exams, sustaining themselves on dry rations. Here is one of the stops on these Sichuan scholars' arduous exam march, and serves as the official starting point for the imperial examinations—the provincial examination.

This is the Sichuan Examination Hall, which was built on the ruins of the Mansion of King of Shu (Ming Dynasty), burned by fire, and was therefore called the *Huangchengba*, or Prince's Mansion by the people of Chengdu.

贡院：皇城坝的浴火重生

The Examination Hall: A prince's mansion rises like a phoenix from ashes

贡院

清 · 杨揆

万瓦鱼鳞压短檐，
安排令甲最森严。

The Examination Hall

Yang Kui, Qing Dynasty

Myriad tiles, resembling fish scales, press upon the short eaves,

地名尚判东西院，
人望从分内外帘。
丛桂飘香风力峭，
疏槐脱叶露痕粘。
吟声消尽三条烛，
花样谁知蜀锦添。

Draconian examination act is issued, and this hall meticulously arranged is so grave.

Dividing the land, the halls bear names of East and West courtyards,

By their qualifications, there are examiners of inner curtain officials and outer curtain officials.

Amidst the fragrant breeze, osmanthus waft, their scent potent,

Sparse locust trees shed leaves, revealing dew-dropped imprints.

Chirping of autumn insects fade away; candle wouldn't stop burning till midnight when the exam ends.

Choosing talents for the country, is like embroidering a flower on the beautiful Shu brocade.

诗作者杨揆幼年聪慧，二十岁时逢乾隆南巡时召试，得赐举人，授内阁中书。四十四岁时因积劳成疾逝于四川布政使任上。

召试，即皇帝召见面试。它并非常规性的考试，而是科举制度的一种补充。清康熙、乾隆、嘉庆等巡幸全国时，屡有召试。清代由召试而位居高官者，也不乏其人。

杨揆以召试而进入仕途，是极其幸运的。清代的科举，是一条极其漫长而艰难的道路，县试、府试、岁试、科试、乡试、会试，殿试，每一场考试都有数不清的竞争者，每一关都有不测风云。

县试，在考生籍贯所在县举行，由知县主持。参加县试，算是迈进

The author of the poem, Yang Kui, was intelligent at an early age. At the age of twenty, he was summoned to take the examination during the southern tour of the Emperor Qianlong, and was awarded the title of Ju Ren and earned the position of the Cabinet Secretariate. He died at the age of forty-four at the post of the Administrator of Sichuan due to illness from hard work.

To be summoned to take an exam is so called because this is an unusual exam which is interviewed by the emperor himself. It's a supplement to the imperial examination system. During Kangxi, Qianlong and Jiaqing era of the Qing Dynasty when the emperors made a tour to the country, this kind of exams were repeatedly called upon. The Qing Dynasty witnessed no shortage of people to be exalted to high ranks through such an exam.

Yang Kui was extremely lucky to be selected by this way to enter civil service. The road of imperial examination is excruciatingly long and difficult. Examinees must challenge county exam (Xianshi), prefectural exam (Fushi), yearly exam (Suishi), pre-

了科举的第一道大门，获得参考资格者被称作童生。童生之童，并非儿童，考生中也有胡须全白者，童是指未获取功名，如同打麻将没有开胡。

通过了县试，方有资格参加由知府主持的府试。清代成都府试的考场在学道街。

岁试和科试通称院试，由主管一省教育的学政主持。通过岁试者，即获得功名，成为生员，即通俗所说之秀才。秀才还不具备当官的资格，但已被称作士，算是进入了士绅阶层，拥有减免部分赋税、见官不跪、革去功名之前不能用刑等特权。科试则是岁试之后，对乡试者的资格遴选。成都的院试考场称作成都府试院，从光绪二十年（1894年）吴绍伯所绘《四川省城街道图》可以看出，成都府试院在四川贡院东侧，也可视作其附属建筑。

严格地说，自乡试始，才算正式的科举考试。县试、府试、岁试、科试，合称童试，只能算作科举的预备考试，这跟1977年高考恢复后实行的预考制度非常相似——1980年至1989年，考生必须首先参加由各中学自行举办的预选考试，获得资格后才能进入正式的高考考场。究其原因，无非

provincial exam (Keshi), provincial exam (Xiangshi), national exam (Huishi) and court exam (Dianshi), each exam having countless competitors and each level full of unpredictable scenarios.

County examination is held in the candidate's home county, presided over by the county magistrate. Only through this exam is one considered to enter the first door of the imperial examinations. The qualified candidates are *Tong Sheng*, or candidates who have not yet passed the county exam. The "*Tong*" here doesn't mean "*child*", though the same word has several meanings. It is not unusual to pick up candidates wearing white beards. "*Tong*" here means the candidate who has yet obtained the title, as in playing *mahjong*, one is still waiting for the one necessary tile to win.

Only those who passed the county exams are eligible to take the prefectural exams, which are conducted by the prefectural magistrate. In the Qing Dynasty, the examination hall for the Chengdu Prefectural Examination is located at the Xuedao Street.

The yearly exam and pre-provincial exam, commonly known as the Academy Examination, are overseen by the provincial officer in charge of education. Those who passed the yearly exams are awarded the title of scholar, commonly known as *Xiu Cai*, or candidates qualified for local-level imperial examinations. While *Xiu Cai* does not yet have the qualifications to be an official, but is already called a scholar, and is considered to have entered the scholar-gentry class, with privileges such as exemption from part of the taxes, not kneeling before an official, and not being punishable unless being removed from their attained recognition. After the pre-provincial exam, there is provincial exam waiting for the candidates. The examination center of Chengdu is called Chengdu Prefectural Examination Hall, which can be seen from the *Street Map of Sichuan Province* drawn by Wu

是以国家当时的能力，尚无力组织如此大型的考试。

参加乡试，就正式踏上了科举之路，中试者被称作举人，已经具备了做官的资格。童试的考场叫考棚，乡试考场则有一个专门的名称，叫作贡院。贡者，为国家贡献人才也。清代时，全国共有十七座贡院，在明蜀王城废墟上修建的四川贡院，便是这十七分之一。

位于京城的顺天贡院，既是乡试考场，也是全国举子参加会试的考场。

至于由皇帝亲自主持的殿试，清代最初是在举行皇帝登基、大婚等重大典礼的太和殿，自乾隆五十四年始，则改在“故宫三大殿”之一的保和殿举行。

参加完保和殿的殿试，对于一个清代士子而言，算是走上了应试之路的巅峰——只是成功率太低，绝大多数读书人是无缘于此的——他的仕宦之途，也将从这里起步。

本文卷首诗的作者杨揆没受那些折磨，跨过了县试、府试、岁试、科试、乡试、会试，直接由皇帝面试，享受殿试待遇，极大减少了不确定性。说他跟普通士子相比节约了十数年的人生，也毫不为过。

Shaobo in the twentieth year of Guangxu reign (1894) locating to the east of the Sichuan Examination Hall, as an annex to it.

Strictly speaking, it is only after the provincial exam that the formal imperial examinations commence. The county exam, prefectural exam, yearly exam and pre-provincial exam, collectively known as the *Tong Shi*, or qualification exams, can only be considered as preparatory exams for the imperial examinations, which are very similar to the pre-screening system that was implemented after the resumption of the university entrance examination in 1977—between 1980 and 1989, candidates had to take the pre-screening exams organized by secondary schools first, and could not enter the official university entrance examination until they had qualified. The reason for this was that the state was not yet able to organize such a large-scale examination given its capacity at that time.

Participants of the provincial examination officially embark on the road of the imperial examinations. The successful candidates, known as “*Ju Ren*”, already have the qualification to be officials. The examination room of *Tong Shi* is called the examination shed, meanwhile the provincial examination hall has a special name called the *Gong Yuan*, or The Examination Hall. “Gong” here means “Tribute or contribute, that is, to contribute talents for the country”. During the Qing Dynasty, there were seventeen *Gong Yuan*s throughout the country, and Sichuan Examination Hall, completed on the ruins of the Mansion of King of Shu, was among them.

Shuntian Examination Hall in the capital is both the examination center for the provincial exam and the national exam for *Ju Ren*s coming from all over the country.

The court exam, presided over by the emperor himself of the Qing Dynasty, is initially held in the

然而也有遗憾。一是读书人孜孜以求，无非十年寒窗之后的金榜题名、普天同庆，召试者则缺失了一生中最重要的仪式感；正式的科举考试，会给登榜者提供一张广泛的人际关系网——同科中举或中进士者互称同年，相互往往声气相求，甚至共进共退，对于绝大多数士子们来说，这是他们初入官场的第一批同盟者，而召试者则在这张大网上少了些可呼应的节点。

无论如何，杨揆以召试出身，一步步成为主管四川行政和财赋的大员，此时深度参与乡试考场管理的他，或许少了一分共鸣，而多了一分超然。他的诗就是四川贡院里乡试场景的白描。

丛桂飘香，疏槐脱叶，点明的是乡试的时间——每三年一次，阴历的八月举行，故称秋闱。其实，"丛桂飘香"在传统文化中还有特别的含义。"犹桂林之一枝，昆山之片玉"，《晋书》中以桂花林中的一根枝条、昆仑山上的一片玉，来比喻出类拔萃之才。到了唐宋科举盛行，再结合"吴刚伐桂"的神话，"蟾宫折桂"便专指科举及第，而诗词中的桂花意象也多象征登科。

万瓦鱼鳞，是从空中俯瞰的场

Hall of *Tai He*, or the Hall of Supreme Harmony, where the emperor's enthronement, wedding and other major ceremonies are conducted. Since the 54th year of the Qianlong era, its name was changed to the Hall of *Bao He*, or the Hall of Preserving Harmony, one of the "Three Halls in the Forbidden City".

For a scholar in the Qing Dynasty, after participating in the court exam, he is considered to be on the pinnacle of imperial exam long march—the success rate is too low for the vast majority of scholars—his career path, therefore, starts from here.

Yang Kui, the author of the poem mentioned earlier in this paper, did not suffer from those tortures, and he, skipping over the county exam, prefectural exam, yearly exam, pre-provincial exam, provincial exam and national exam, was directly interviewed by the emperor, a privilege greatly reduced the uncertainty. It would not be an exaggeration to say that he saved more than a decade or so of his life compared with those ordinary scholars.

However, there are also regrets. First, what the scholars diligently seek is nothing less than the sense of achievement when, after ten years' toiling at studies, you find your name is eminent on the honor roll. This is the most ceremonial rite of passage in your life. Second, the official imperial examinations provide a wide interpersonal network for the participants—the successful candidates are called *Tong Nian*, or the co-participants in the imperial exam in that year—the same fate which they've shared bonds them together so that they can be of avail for one another and they may even advance and retreat together. For the vast majority of scholars, these co-participants are their first allies into the world of bureaucracy, while for the "summoned" candidate like Yang Kui, these important net lacks such a node for resonating with others.

Despite this shortcoming, Yang Kui, starting

面，那像鱼鳞一样密密地铺满眼前的，是号舍的瓦片。号舍是一个小格子间，深四尺、宽三尺、高六尺，面积一平方米多一点。像蜂巢一样，一个号舍纳容一名考生，他白天在里面答卷，晚上则睡在里面。号舍墙壁左右各有两道砖托，以铺放木板。白天，上面的木板作考桌，下面的木板为座椅；到了晚上，两张木板都铺在下方，作为考生睡觉用的床——当然得自带被子。这张床是非常简陋的，四尺的进深，连脚也伸不直，只能蜷曲着将就。

考生自带物品除了被子，还有这几天的食粮。当日若不能完成答卷，可延伸至夜间，以点完三根蜡烛为限，这也是唐人诗文中“三条烛”典故的来历。明清两代的乡试，都是考三场，每场考三天。九天时间里顿顿吃干粮、夜夜睡格子间，没有强大的意志力或者说出人头地的强烈欲望来支撑，怕是极度难熬的。

as a summoned exam participant, became a key provincial official in charge of the administration and finance of Sichuan stepwise. Thus, deeply involved in the management of the provincial exam, he may feel less empathy but more detachment. His poem is a straight line-drawing of what is in front of him in Sichuan Examination Hall.

When the scent of osmanthus flowers could be smelled and the leaves of locust tree start to shed, it is the provincial exam time: once every three years, in August of the lunar calendar, so it is also called the autumn exams. In fact, “fragrant osmanthus” has a special meaning in traditional Chinese culture. In *The History of Jin*, a twig of an osmanthus tree and a piece of jade from the Kunlun Mountain were used as metaphors for outstanding talents. In the Tang and Song dynasties, when the imperial examinations became popular, idioms such as *Wu Gang Fa Gui* or Wu Gang Cutting down Osmanthus Tree and the *Chan Gong Zhe Gui* refer specifically to the top three places in the imperial examinations, and the imagery of the osmanthus flowers in poems and lyrics symbolize pass in such examinations.

From a bird’s-eye view, the panorama resembles the intricate pattern of fish scales, in reality, it is the sea of tiles adorning the examination huts. Each hut, known as a *Hao She,* is a small cubicle measuring four feet in depth, three feet in width, and six feet in height, covering an area just over a square meter. Resembling beehives, each *Hao She* accommodates a single examinee who spends their days writing answers within and nights sleeping therein. The walls of the *Hao She* are supported on each side by two rows of bricks, providing a foundation for wooden boards. During the day, the upper board serves as a writing desk, while the lower one functions as a seat. When night falls, both boards are laid down below, forming a rudimentary bed for the examinee to rest—

of course, they must bring their own bedding. This bed is exceptionally plain, with a depth of four feet, leaving little room to stretch one's legs, forcing the occupant to curl up and make do.

In addition to their bedding, examinees bring with them provisions for the duration of these days. If one cannot complete the answer sheets on the same day, they may extend their efforts into the night, with the constraint being the burning of three candles—this limitation gives origin to the allusion of "three candles" found in Tang-era poetry and literature. During the provincial examination of the Ming and Qing dynasties, candidates faced three rounds of testing, each lasting three days. Over the course of nine days, they sustained themselves on dry rations, sleeping nightly in their small cubicles. Without a profound strength of will or an intense desire to excel, one could not endure the crucible of the extremely difficult cubicle days.

浴火重生

明末的战乱，将四川变成了人间地狱。

1646年，张献忠攻取成都之后仅仅两年，便因感受到八旗兵南下的压力，以及遭遇明将杨展的伏击而不得不撤离。在逃窜之前，他发了个狠，放火烧毁了成都城的民居、衙门，有着两百多年历史、繁华奢丽堪比紫禁城的蜀王府也在浓密的火焰中尽化为灰——真个是"宫阙万间都作了土"。

那场大火两年之前，张献忠攻

Resurrection from the Ashes

The war at the end of the Ming Dynasty turned Sichuan into a hell on earth.

In 1646, only two years after Zhang Xianzhong captured Chengdu, he had to withdraw because he felt the pressure of the Eight Banners soldiers coming south and encountered an ambush by the Ming general Yang Zhan. Before he decamped, he set fire to the houses and government offices in Chengdu. The Mansion of King of Shu, a history of more than two hundred years and as prosperous and luxurious as the Forbidden City, was also reduced to ashes in the dense flames—it was really a case of "all the palaces have bitten the dust".

Two years before that conflagration, when Zhang Xianzhong attacked Chengdu, Shen Yunzuo,

入成都时，华阳县令沈云祚死于国难，他五岁的儿子沈荀蔚跟随家人逃出城，在邛崃、洪雅躲避多年。顺治十六年（1659年），已经长大成人的沈荀蔚回到成都，破碎山河入眼，惨不忍睹。

在沈荀蔚的笔下，被火舌舔舐过的城市，从残垣断壁根本不能分辨其旧貌。城中已十五六年不见人迹，唯有麋鹿等野生动物奔跑跳跃，甚至还能见到虎熊等大型猛兽。

人到哪里去了？除了逃亡的，都已化作尸骨。成都城里曾有多口水井，但沈荀蔚见到的井大多填埋了，里面除了人的尸体就是藏匿的金银——可惜他们已永无机会消受。

大自然的再生能力是惊人的。没有人类的活动，三千年名城十数年间就可以变成野生动物乐园。人类的再生能力也足以让大自然惊奇。没有战乱的肆虐，他们在十数年的时间也能够修复一座名城。

文首的《贡院》一诗，描绘的便是在明蜀王城废墟上重新修建的四川贡院。清贡院的规模与富丽，固然不能与明蜀王城相比，但依然是新成都城的头等标志性建筑。而就其文化意义而言，或许更胜一筹。

城市地标的浴火重生，便象征着

the Huayang County Magistrate, died as a martyr. His five-year-old son, Shen Xunwei, followed his family to escape from the city, hiding in Qionglai and Hongya for many years. In the sixteenth year of Shunzhi (1659), he returned to Chengdu as a grown-up, the misery of the broken city was horrible.

In Shen Xunwei's writing, the city, licked by the tongue of fire, cannot be recognized from the broken walls. For fifteen or sixteen years, there were not even a single soul could be found in the city but wild animals such as running and jumping elk and deer, and even large beasts such as tigers and bears!

Where had all the people gone? Except for those who fled, they had all been turned into corpses. There had been many wells in the city of Chengdu, but most of the ones Shen Xunwei found had been filled in and contained nothing but corpses and caches of gold and silver—which, unfortunately, they would never have the chance to enjoy.

Nature's ability to regenerate is amazing. Without human activity, a 3,000-year-old city can be transformed into a wildlife paradise in a few decades. Meanwhile, the regenerative capacity of human beings is also enough to amaze the nature. Without ravages of wars, people were able to restore a famous city in a matter of ten years.

The poem *The Examination Hall* at the beginning of this paper depicts the Sichuan Examination Hall rebuilt on the ruins of the Mansion of the King of Shu. The scale and splendor of this rebuilt examination hall is certainly not comparable to that of the Mansion of the King of Shu, but it is still a first-class landmark of the new Chengdu City, perhaps even more so in terms of its cultural significance.

The rebirth of a city landmark symbolizes the rebirth of the city.

After the war, the population of Sichuan was only 500,000 to 600,000, and in some counties, there

城市的浴火重生。

战后四川，人口不过五六十万人，有些县甚至只剩数百人。

时任四川巡抚张德地忧心于地旷人稀、税赋难齐，遂于康熙七年上疏请求：请各省地方官员查报没有恒产、佣工度日的百姓，招其来四川垦田，并给予盘缠。同时建议，官员招民百家以上、垦田十顷以上者得以升迁。而他自己也是相关政策的受惠者，康熙九年，张德地因召674户流民回川安置，加工部尚书衔。

为吸引移民，清政府给出了优厚的土地政策，诸如对于移民垦荒地亩，五年起才征税；每户发给十二两白银以用于购买生活生产资料等。于是，一场被称作“湖广填四川”的大移民轰轰烈烈地开始了。移民历时百年，前后有数百万名湖广、两广、江南等地的百姓来到四川扎根。

“戚友初逢若相问，现无十世老成都。”清代的竹枝词，说的是成都人的籍贯结构，追溯的是那一段大移民的历史。其实，对人口来源的这种描述，地理界限可从成都扩展至四川大部分地区，时间范畴则可延伸至今。2010年左右，笔者所在文化公司六名工作人员，除一外省人外，其余五人皆自述，祖上是那次大移民时来

were even only a few hundred people left.

Zhang Dedi, the then Grand Coordinator of Sichuan, worried that the empty lands and sparse population were not enough to sustain the tax base, so in the seventh year of Kangxi (reign name),he proposed to the emperor: make a national survey on those who don’t have permanent properties and have to serve as day labourers. Then, conscript such labour forces, granting them with travel allowances so as they would relocate and cultivate in Sichuan. At the same time, he suggested that officials who successfully recruit more than a hundred households and cultivate more than ten hectares of reclaimed land can be promoted. He himself was a beneficiary of such policies. In the ninth year of Kangxi, Zhang Dedi was promoted to hold concurrent position as the Royal Secretary of Ministry of Construction, for recruiting and relocating 674 households of displaced persons to Sichuan.

In a bid to attract immigrants, the Qing government implemented generous land policies. For instance, those cultivating uncultivated land would only be subject to taxation after five years; each household would be granted twelve taels for purchasing necessities and production materials. Thus, a so-called“Huguang fills Sichuan”, or immigrants from Hunan and Hubei provinces filled up the population shortage of Sichuan, commenced in full swing. This large-scale immigration had been lasting for a hundred years and millions of people from Hunan, Hubei, Guangdong, Guangxi, and regions south of the Yangtz River undertook the journey to take root in Sichuan.

“If relatives and friends meet for the first time and ask each other, there is no native Chengduese within ten generations.” One of the Qing Dynasty’s Bamboo Branch Lyrics,a kind of poem originating from folk songs, gives account of the structure of Chengduese origins, which can be traced to the

到四川的，而祖籍地竟然也都是麻城县孝感乡。

如此多的四川人都从孝感这一个乡迁来，这可能吗？地图上是找不到麻城孝感乡的，此孝感也并不是现今的湖北省孝感市。更为神奇的是，历史上麻城确实有个孝感乡，但这个孝感乡已于明成化八年（1472年）并于仙居乡。也就是说，清初开始的"湖广填四川"，来自一个已经并不存在的地名？

笔者曾见到过外祖父于1959年写下的家谱，称"吾祖籍湖南省麻城县高阶檐人也"。湖北被误作湖南，高阶檐也称高阶堰，又称高坎堰。据考证，其地现为麻城市龙池桥街道办下辖的五脑山林场，已建为国家森林公园。

其实，在此之前的元末明初就有过一次"湖广填四川"，麻城孝感乡不仅迁来了众多人口，而且是一个巨大的移民中转站。在岁月的磨砺中，人们也许忘记了自己真正的祖籍地，却记住了祖先们曾经停留的地方。于是，麻城孝感乡便成为一个图腾，被写入"湖广填四川"的族群记忆之中。

清初的成都残破至此，自然不适合驻跸巡抚、布政司、按察司等官

Great Migration period. In fact, geographically, this description of the origin of the population can be extended from Chengdu to most parts of Sichuan, and chronologically, it runs the gamut from the Great Migration till today. In 2010, five out of six of my colleagues in a company that engaged in cultural communication acknowledged that their ancestors came to Sichuan at the Great Migration period, and all their ancestral hometown is Xiaogan of Macheng.

Is it possible that so many Sichuanese moved from one township, Xiaogan? In fact, it is impossible to find Xiaogan of Macheng on the map, and that Xiaogan is not the present Xiaogan City in Hubei Province. What is even more amazing is that there was indeed a Xiaogan Township in the history of Macheng, but that one was merged with Xianju Township in the eighth year of Chenghua (1472). Chenghua is a reign name of Ming Dynasty. In other words, the "Huguang fills Sichuan" that began in the early Qing Dynasty came from a place name that no longer exists.

I have seen the family tree written by my grandfather in 1959, which says, "My ancestry is from Gaojieyan, Macheng County, Hunan Province". Here, Hubei was mistaken for Hunan; Gaojieyan was also known as Gaojieyan (the two Chinese character *yan*s pronounce the same, but write differently), or Gaokanyan. According to the research evidence, this region is now under the jurisdiction of Wunaoshan Forest Farm under supervision of the Longchiqiao Street Office of Macheng City, which has been built into a national forest park.

In fact, before the end of the Yuan and early Ming Dynasty there was another "Huguang fills Sichuan". Xiaogan of Macheng not only mobilized a lot of people, but also served as a huge migrant transit center. In the wear and tear of the years, people may have forgotten their true ancestral home, but

署衙门，因此有十多年的时间里，四川省省垣被临时放置到保宁府（今阆中）。顺治八年（1651年）辛卯科四川乡试，也随着省垣的临时迁移，改在保宁府举行。此科由四川巡抚李国英充当监考官，参考士子约五百余人，取士七十二人。

此后，顺治十一年的甲午科、十四年的丁酉科、十七年的庚子科，康熙三年的甲辰科，都在保宁府举办。到了顺治十七年的庚子科乡试，考生已达两千人，是顺治八年的四倍，显示社会的活力在逐渐恢复。

remembered the place where their ancestors used to stay. Thus, Xiaogan of Macheng has become a totem, written into the memory of the ethnic groups of "Huguang fills Sichuan".

In the early Qing Dynasty, Chengdu was so dilapidated that it was naturally unsuitable for the Grand Coordinator Office, the Provincial Administration and the Ministry of Justice to be stationed there, so for more than ten years, the provincial capital of Sichuan was temporarily relocated to Baoningfu (present-day Langzhong). In the eighth year of Shunzhi (1651), the Sichuan provincial exam was, also with the temporary relocation of the provincial capital, held in Baoningfu. This examination was supervised by Li Guoying, the Grand Coordinator of Sichuan, and seventy-two people was selected out of about 500 participants.

Thereafter, all of the examinations in eleventh year, fourteenth year, and seventeenth year of Shunzhi(Chinese Lunar Year of Jiawu, Dingyou and Gengzi respectively)as well as the one in the third year of Kangxi (Chinese Lunar Year of Jiachen), were held in Baoningfu. By the seventeenth year of Shunzhi, the candidates had reached 2,000, four times as many as the one in the eighth year of Shunzhi, showing that the vitality of the community was gradually restored.

士子龙门

康熙三年（1664年），重建成都工程启动，明蜀王府的旧基改建亦在其中。因为怕被视作僭越，四川巡抚张德地不敢将巡抚官署建于皇城旧址，而是在此地修建了贡院，作为四川士子参加乡试的场所。

Scholars jump over the"Dragon Gate"

In the third year of Kangxi (1664), the reconstruction of Chengdu started, and the renovation of the Mansion of the King of Shu was also among the project. For fear of being regarded as a usurper's behavior, Zhang Dedi, the Grand Coordinator of Sichuan, did not dare to build his office on the old site of the Imperial City, instead he built the Examination

康熙四年，四川贡院落成。康熙五年，丙午科乡试在阔别十五年后，终于回到成都。

清代四川贡院的至公堂 （美）西德尼·大卫·甘博 摄

Zhigong Hall of the Sichuan Imperial Examination Hall during the Qing Dynasty. (Photographer: Sidney David Gamble, USA)

在清代的科举考试中，一直到道光年间，八十多科考试中，四川曾有七科未中进士，而这七科都在战乱年代。说乡试回归是成都乃至整个四川省的政治、文化、社会活动走向正轨的重要标志，一点也不夸张。

成千上万的四川读书人走进贡院，其出类拔萃者在这里考中举人，然后又走向北京参加会试，成为“天子门生”。有清一朝两百多年里，四川共产生进士八百名，其中著名者有“戊戌六君子”之一的刘光第、状元骆成骧、经学大师廖平等。

Hall there as a place for Sichuan scholars to participate in the provincial exams.

In the fourth year of the Kangxi, the Sichuan Examination Hall was completed. In the fifth year of the Kangxi, the provincial examination, after an absence of fifteen years, returned to Chengdu eventually.

In Qing Dynasty, as long as eighty years before the Daoguang reign, Sichuan failed to turn out any *Jin Shis*, or the Imperial Examination Graduates in seven years, and these seven years were full wars. It is not an exaggeration to say that the return of the provincial examination was an important symbol of the political, cultural and social activities in Chengdu and even in the whole Sichuan Province being put on the right track.

Thousands upon thousands of scholars from Sichuan entered the Examination Hall, with the most outstanding among them attaining the title of *Ju Ren* and proceeding to Beijing to participate in the imperial examination, becoming *Tianzi Mensheng* or the Emperor's protégés. Over the course of more than two hundred years in the Qing Dynasty, Sichuan churned out a total of eight hundred Jin Shis, among whom notable figures include Liu Guangdi, one of the "Six martyrs of the Hundred Days' Reform", the top scholar Luo Chengxiang (*Zhuang Yuan*, or The Number One Scholar), and the master of classical studies, Liao Ping.

As the society stabilized, the economy prospered and the number of scholars and *Hao She*s increased as well.

The Sichuan Examination Hall which was completed in the fourth year of Kangxi possessed about 1,000 *Hao She*. 111 years later, in the fifty-first year of the Qianlong, after large-scale additions, the total number of *Hao She* reached 5306. Since then and after more additions, till the ninth year of Tongzhi (1870), the total number of *Hao She* reached 13,935.

随着社会稳定、经济繁荣和读书人的增加，号舍也在不断增建。

康熙四年修建的四川贡院，号舍一千余间。一百一十一年后的乾隆五十一年，经大规模添建，号舍总数达到五千三百零六间。此后又经多次添修，至同治九年（1870年），四川贡院的号舍总数达到一万三千九百三十五间，同中国古代最大规模科举考场江南贡院的二万零六百四十四间相比，差距并不大。

同治元年（1862年），四川贡院在使用了近两百年后，变破变旧了，多处出现倒塌，于是四川各大政要部门通力筹得白银七万两余以启重修。此次培修，因为款项充足，共建堂院五百余间，均宽大敞阔。除建有主考、监临、提调、帘官等主考人员的住所，以及弥封所、誊录房、受卷所、劝科所等考试用房外，从现今成都人口中仍不时可听到的明远楼、至公堂，也于此次建成。

贡院内重要建筑沿南北中轴线布局，由南往北分别是候考区和考试区。

最南端为一大型石牌坊，上刻“为国求贤”，点明了贡院的宗旨。牌坊之北，是在原蜀王府端礼门的旧址上修建的贡院正门，其匾额上是“天

Even compared with the largest one in ancient China, The Jiangnan Examination Hall with 20,644 *Hao She*, the gap is not that wide.

In the first year of Tongzhi (1862), after nearly two centuries of use, the Sichuan Examination Hall had deteriorated, showing signs of aging with multiple areas in a state of collapse. In response, various prominent departments in Sichuan collaborated to raise over seventy thousand taels of silver for extensive renovations. Thanks to the ample funds available, this refurbishment project resulted in the construction of over five hundred spacious and grand halls and courtyards. Apart from residences for key examination officials such as examiners, invigilators, the supervisors and the coordinators, as well as examination rooms like the sealing room, re-transcription room, test paper reception room, and advisory room, this renovation also gave rise to enduring structures like Mingyuan Tower and Zhigong Hall, whose names are still occasionally heard in the mouths of Chengdu residents today.

The important buildings in the Tribute Academy are laid out along the north-south central axis, with the waiting areas and examination areas from south to north.

At the southernmost end was a large stone memorial arch, on which “Seeking Talents for the Country” was engraved, succinctly expressing the purpose of the Examination Hall. At the north of the stone memorial arch was the main gate, which used to be the original Duanli Gate of the Mansion of the King of Shu, on the ruins of which the examination hall was built. At the main gate there was a plaque inscribed“Heaven Opens the Path to Culture”. To the north of the main gate was the Dragon Gate whose name suggests “Carps Leaping over Dragon Gate” (According to Chinese tradition, that the candidates

开文运”四个字。正门之北为龙门，当有“鲤鱼跃龙门”之意，考生将在此处接受主考、监临、提调的点名，并领取考卷；龙门一共三进，点一次名进一道门，极为郑重其事。上万名考生提着食粮和考具，背着被盖，听到自己的名便走上前去，接受兵士的搜身，那场面也是蔚为壮观。

龙门再往北，便是考试区域，其中最主要的建筑是明远楼和至公堂。从南向北分布着龙门、明远楼和至公堂，几乎是所有贡院的共同格局。

明远楼建在原蜀王府前殿旧址上，为三重殿宇式建筑。明远者，远望而明察，这也跟该楼的实际功能相吻合——官员登楼巡察，严防作弊。在所有的贡院里，明远楼都是最高的建筑。

至公堂是贡院的主体建筑，其体量也是最大的。至公者，极度公正也，为国而无私心也。发榜的前一日，所有参与乡试的官员会齐聚至公堂，对录取名单的最后核对并填榜。四川贡院的至公堂，利用了原蜀王府正殿承运殿的殿基，修成一座气势宏大的大殿。不过，同当年的承运殿相比，还是有很大的差距，这一点从至公堂的柱础和承运殿残留柱础的对比

challenge the exam is like a carp jumps over a dragon gate. If you overcome the obstacle, you'll have a bright future.) It was here that candidates waited for the roll-call, receiving their examination papers. The Dragon Gate includes three entrances, each requiring a roll-call, extremely serious indeed. What a tableau when tens of thousands of candidates carried their provisions, examination tools and bedding, waiting for their names to be called and their bodies to be patted down by the soldiers!

Further north of the Dragon Gate is the examination area, in which the most prominent buildings are the Mingyuan Tower and the Zhigong Building. Distributed from south to north, the Dragon Gate, Mingyuan Building and Zhigong Hall are the common pattern of almost all examination halls.

The Mingyuan Tower, a three-tiered temple-style building, was built on the former Mansion of King of Shu. *Mingyuan* means "looking into the distance", which also corresponds with the actual function of the building—officials climbed the building for inspections and for preventing cheating. In all the examination halls, the Mingyuan Tower is the highest building.

The Zhigong Hall is the main building of the examination hall, and its volume is also the largest. *Zhigong* means "extremely fair", for selection talents for the country bears no selfishness. On the day before the release of the list, all the officials who participated in the provincial examination would gather in the Zhigong Hall to make the final check of the admission list and fill the names of the successful candidates in the list. The Zhigong Hall of Sichuan Examination Hall inherited the base of the Chengyun Palace of the original Mansion of King of Shu and built it into a magnificent hall. However, compared with its predecessor, there is still a big gap, which is evident from the comparison between the plinths of the Zhigong

就看得出来。

至公堂前的石柱牌坊，上有乾隆九年皇帝所赐“旁求俊乂”匾额。“俊乂”二字出自《尚书》，有才德者过千人为俊，过百人为乂。匾上四字，意与“为国求贤”同，又多了几分文气。

主轴线上由至公堂再向北，则是由清白堂、严肃堂、衡文堂和文昌宫组成的建筑群。中轴线两侧，分别是提调、监试和内帘等办公场所。

管理考试者，有一种重要的临时职务，称作帘官。帘官皆从省内各地抽调知县担任，其中，书读得好、会写文章的充内帘官，批阅考卷；精明强干、会办事的，充外帘官，巡察考场纪律。成都现在还有一条帘官公所街，当年就是帘官住宿之地——此处管理甚严，不得有宾客往来。

除此之外，考试管理机构还有弥封所、誊录所等。弥封所的主要工作是糊去考生姓名，再编号、盖印，要到阅卷结束填榜之后方能拆封；东誊录所，考卷在此处誊抄以呈阅卷官，以避免识出笔迹。

而鳞次栉比的上百万考生号舍，则分布于这些管理机构四周。

Hall and the ones of the Chengyun Palace.

In front of the Zhigong Hall, there is a stone memorial arch with a plaque entitled “Seek *Jun Yi*” granted by the emperor in the ninth year of the Qianlong. The words *Jun Yi* come from *The Book of Documents,* which mean talents whose capability and virtue are higher than what a thousand people and a hundred people respectively possess. This inscription shares the same meaning of the above-mentioned “Seeking Talents for the Country”, but with a little more literary flavor.

Along the central axis to further north from the Zhigong Hall, there is a complex of buildings consisting of the Qingbai Hall, Yansu Hall, Hengwen Hall and Wenchang Hall. Dotted around both sides of the central axis are examination related office spaces.

There is an important temporary position called *Lian Guan* that implements exam management. *Lian Guan*s are magistrates drafted from all over the province. Those who are good at writing and reading serve as *Inner Lian Guan,* i.e., to mark the papers; those who are well-versed in various routine works serve as *Outer Lian Guan*, i.e., to patrol the exam rooms and to execute disciplines. There is still a street in Chengdu called “Lian Guan Office Street”—once a strictly regulated official residence where no guests were allowed to enter.

In addition, the examination administration organization also set up the *Mifeng* Office and the *Tenglu* Office. The main work of the *Mifeng* Office is to attach paste on the name of the candidate, to mark with numbers and to affix seals. The paste can only be unsealed at the end of the marking. In the *Tenglu* Office, the examination papers are transcribed to present to the marking officer in order that the handwriting shall not be recognized.

Rows upon rows of *Hao She*s are scattered around those governing bodies.

号舍千字文

Thousand Character Classic in the Hao She

号舍上的千字文 （英）罗伯特 · 陶维新 摄

The inscription of Thousand Character Classic on Hao She, the examination huts. (Photographer: Robert John Davidson)

这是一张清代成都贡院老照片，由传教士陶维新拍摄于1905年。号舍的粉白墙壁上，写着“成律调云露丽”几个字。

这几个字连不成句，但粗通中国传统文化的，便会直觉到它们可能跟传统启蒙读物《千字文》有关。

研史如破案。不妨试着在《千字文》中选取一段跟这些字有关的文字，来探寻其中的规律。

闰余成岁，律吕调阳。

云腾致雨，露结为霜。

金生丽水，玉出昆冈。

然后，把这段文字按顺序每两个字排成一排：

闰余

成岁

律吕

调阳

This is an old photo of the Chengdu Examination Hall in the Qing Dynasty, taken by missionary Robert Davidson in 1905. On the powder-white wall of the *Hao She*, the words “Cheng, Lü, Tiao, Yun, Lu, Li” are written.

These words do not form a coherent sentence, but those who have rough idea of traditional Chinese culture will intuit those characters may be related to the traditional primer *Thousand Character Classic*.

Studying history is like solving an unsolved case. We might as well select a passage in the *Thousand Character Classic* that relates to these characters to find out the pattern.

Using one leap month in three years so that the calendar does not deviate from the seasons of heaven and earth. The ancients also used the Six lǜ and Six lǚ (ancient Chinese phonological system) to determine the twenty-four seasons of the year.

When clouds rise, they get cold and form rain, and when dew gets cold at night, it condenses into frost.

Gold comes from the bottom of the Jinsha River, jade from the Kunlun Mountains.

Then, put the passage above in order every two

云腾
致雨
露结
为霜
金生
丽水
玉出
昆冈

接下来，竖着读左边的粗体字，正是“成律调云”。那么也可以推断出，在它们对面的号舍墙壁上，写的是“岁吕阳腾”几个字。

这些字，表示的是考棚的顺序，而它们正是按《千字文》的内容左右分序排序，也可以简单地理解为：左边是一、三、五、七、九；右边是二、四、六、八、十。这些考生，对于《千字文》是无比熟悉的，如果自己的号舍在“律”这一排，那么可以根据上下文“闰余成岁，律吕调阳”轻易找到。

在陶维新拍摄的另一张照片上，至公堂前，号舍呈左右排列。可以看到，最前方的墙上正是《千字文》上的“玉出崑岗”这句话。

words:

Next, read the bold letters on the left vertically, which are “成(Cheng)律(Lü)调(Tiao)云(Yun)”. It can also be deduced that on the wall of the house opposite to them were the words “岁(Sui)吕(Lü)阳(Yang)腾(Teng)”.

These characters indicate the order of the examination halls, and they are sorted according to the left-right sequence of the *Thousand Character Classic*, which can be simply understood as follows: on the left, one, three, five, seven, nine; on the right, two, four, six, eight, ten. These candidates, who are very familiar with the *Thousand Character Classic*, can easily find their *Hao She*s. If one’s *Hao She* belongs to the row of “Lü”, it is easy to find it by reading the context: “闰(Run)余(Yü)成(Cheng)岁(Sui), 律(Lü)吕(Lü)调(Tiao)阳(Yang)”.

In another photo taken by Robert Davidson, in front of the Zhigong Hall, the *Hao She*s are arranged on the left and right. As can be seen, on the wall in the forefront are the words “玉(Yu)出(Chu)崑(Kun)岗(Gang)” from the *Thousand Character Classic*.

英雄风口

光绪三十一年（1905年），清廷诏准自次年始全国乡试会试一律停

The moment of truth for heroes

In the thirty-first year of Guangxu (1905), the Qing court issued an edict that since the following

止，各地开始兴办新式学堂。随着上千年科举制度的废止，贡院的历史也走到了尽头。

今人看科举，以诟病之辞居多。其实，究其本质，科举乃是以考试选拔文官，对于打破贵族世袭政治的特权，其意义再如何高估也不为过。现代中西方的文官考试制度，往前追溯，也一定会来到中国科举制这个源头。

四川贡院成片成片的号舍被拆除得干干净净。保留下来的房间，被新式学堂用作讲堂、校舍等。所办学堂有如四川通省优级师范学堂、绅班法政学堂、中等工业学堂、游学预备学校等。

作为科举考试场所的贡院不存在了，其承担教育的功能却被保留了下来。

号舍拆除之后，龙门、明远楼和至公堂之间，都露出了一大片青砖铺地的空坝子。龙门和明远楼之间的坝子，又扁又长，而明远楼和至公堂之间的坝子则是四四方方的形状。

有殿堂，有广场，又值波澜壮阔的保路运动期间，再加上还有这么多热血学子，曾经的贡院、成都人口中的皇城坝作为重大政治事件的集会场合再也适合不过了。比如1911年

year, the provincial examination would be stopped and new style of schools would be established. With the abolition of the imperial examination system which lasted for thousands of years, the history of the Examination Hall also came to an end.

Nowadays, people lean toward criticizing the imperial examination system. However, at its core, this system was to select civil officials through standardized tests. Its significance lies in breaking the privileges of aristocratic hereditary politics and the essence of the imperial examination system is undeniable. When tracing the roots of modern civil service examination systems in both Eastern and Western societies, one inevitably arrives at the source of the Chinese imperial examination system.

Pieces by pieces, the *Hao She*s in Sichuan Examination Hall were demolished thoroughly. The rooms that remained were used as lecture halls and school buildings of the new-style schools,such as the Sichuan Superior Provincial Normal School, Squire Class School of Law and Politics, Secondary Industrial School, Preparatory School for Studying Abroad, and so on.

The examination hall, which served as a place for imperial examinations, no longer exists, but its function of undertaking education has been preserved.

After the demolition of the *Hao She*s, a large empty open space with green brick pavement was revealed between the Dragon Gate, the Mingyuan Tower and the Zhigong Hall. The space between the Dragon Gate and the Mingyuan Tower was flat and long, while the one between the Mingyuan Tower and the Zhigong Hall was of a four-square shape.

With a hall, a square, and so many hot-blooded students gathering at the former Examination Hall, or the *Huangchengba* (Prince's Mansion), during the dramatic Railway Protection Movement, could not have been a more appropriate venue for a major

11月27日（辛亥年十月初七），大汉四川军政府的成立典礼就在至公堂举行。

“大汉四川军政府之宗旨，基于世界之公理，人道主义组织共和宪法，以巩固我大汉联邦之帝国而与世罔极，所当与吾川七千万人子子孙孙共守之。”成立仪式上，保路运动领袖、立宪派人士蒲殿俊，陆军第十七镇统制（师长）朱庆澜分别出任正副都督；27岁的陆军小学堂总办尹昌衡出任军政部长。

大汉四川军政府的成立，标志着清朝廷在四川统治的崩溃，但是革故鼎新的大波中仍有暗流涌动，以前清署理四川总督赵尔丰为首的残余力量仍在暗中策划，试图召边军入省城夺权。军政府成立不过十一天，巡防军即在阅操时发生兵变，驱逐正副都督，沿街放火劫掠。

事发仓促，军政部长尹昌衡单枪匹马出城，急奔凤凰山，从陆军新军六十五标借得两营士兵，回城平叛。次日凌晨，尹昌衡率兵进军皇城坝，在设于此地的军政府帅府中找到了招抚局长罗纶，二人同至皇城南边的金河桥上，安抚市民。当日，尹昌衡和罗纶即被推选为新的正副都督。

尹昌衡果敢刚毅，杀伐决断。他

political event. For example, on November 27, 1911 (the seventh day of the tenth month of the Lunar year of Xinhai), the founding ceremony of the Great Han of Sichuan Military Government was held in the Zhigong Hall.

"The purpose of the Great Han of Sichuan Military Government, based on the axioms of the world, humanitarian principles and the Republican Constitution, is to consolidate and perpetuate the empire of this Great Han Confederation so that our 70 million people in Sichuan and our future generations will hold on to it." At the founding ceremony, the leaders of Railway Protection Movement, Pu Dianjun, a constitutionalist, and the commander of the Seventeenth Division Zhu Qinglan were appointed as governor and deputy governor; Yin Changheng, 27, the headmaster of Army Primary School, assumed the Minister of Military Affairs.

The establishment of the Military Government of Sichuan, marking the collapse of the Qing Dynasty in Sichuan, but in this revolutionary big wave, undercurrent of violence was still seething. As a ringleader, Zhao Erfeng, the former acting Viceroy of Sichuan was secretly planning to call the border army into the provincial capital to seize power. Only eleven days after the Military Government established, a mutiny happened when a parade was being conducted, resulting in the expulsion of the governor and deputy governor. The rebel army set fire and looted along the streets.

The incident happened in such a hurry that Yin Changheng, the Minister of Military Affairs only escaped out of the city single-handedly. He rushed to Phoenix Hill, borrowed two battalions of soldiers from the 65th Regiment of New Sixth Army and thrusted back to the city to quell the rebellion. In the early morning of the next day, Yin Changheng led troops into the *Huangchengba* and found Luo Lun, Director of the Pacification at the military

亲执军刀，在大街上处决乱兵，数天内兵变终得以平息。尹昌衡一不做二不休，设计抓获了赵尔丰。12月22日黎明，公审赵尔丰的大会在明远楼前举行。

该年9月7日，赵尔丰在保路风潮中一手制造了“成都血案”，导致数十百姓被杀，因此成都人民对他恨得咬牙切齿，送他一个“赵屠夫”的尊号。得知赵被捕，数万人都在这一天涌到皇城坝来，要看他最后的下场。尹昌衡一身戎装，立于明远楼前，历数赵尔丰之恶，而台下万口同声，齐齐喊杀。在群情激愤中，赵尔丰的头颅被砍了下来。

尹昌衡出生于彭县（彭州），幼年聪颖，熟读诗书。1903年十九岁时入四川武备学堂，次年赴日本学习日文。1907年底，进入日本陆军士官学校中国留日士官生第六期学习。1910年，尹昌衡在回国的第二年出任四川陆军小学堂总办，这是一所为培养新式陆军军官而成立的军校，招收十五岁至十八岁的青年，尹昌衡二十六岁就当上军校校长，应该说是前途无量，不过他依然觉得黄钟毁弃，材大难用。

尹昌衡相貌英俊，长身玉立，时称“尹长子”。他早年恃才傲物，好

government’s office. The two went to the Jinhe Bridge that was near the *Huangchengba* to pacify the public. On the same day, Yin Changheng and Luo Lun were elected as the new Governor and Vice Governor.

Bold and resolute, Yin Changheng personally executed the rebel soldiers on the street with his saber, and the mutiny was finally quelled within a few days. Over shoes, over boots, he made a move to capture Zhao Erfeng. On 22th of December, at dawn, the public trial of Zhao Erfeng was held in front of the Mingyuan Tower.

On September 7 of that year, Zhao Erfeng created the *Chengdu Bloodshed* during the Railway Protection Movement, which led to the killing of dozens of people, and therefore the people of Chengdu hated him so much that they gave him the honorific name of “Zhao, the Butcher”. Upon learning of Zhao’s arrest, tens of thousands of people flocked to the *Huangchengba* on this day to see what would happen to him. Yin Changheng, dressed in military attire, stood in front of the Mingyuan Tower and counted the evils of Zhao Erfeng, while 10,000 people shouted in unison to kill him. In the crowd’s indignation, Zhao Erfeng’s head was cut off.

Yin Changheng was born in Peng County (Pengzhou), a bright young man who was well versed in poetry and classic books, enrolled in the Sichuan Military Academy in 1903 at the age of nineteen, and then went to Japan the following year to study Japanese, and at the end of 1907 entered the Class Six of the Chinese Cadet Studying in Japanese Army Cadet School. In 1910, the year after he returned to China, Yin became the headmaster of Army Primary School, which was set up for the purpose of cultivating new types of army officers and enrolled youths between the ages of fifteen and eighteen. At the age of only twenty-six, Yin Changheng became the headmaster, a career with a promising future, but

勇斗狠，被视为新军中四川籍军人的精神领袖，又常因觉得怀才不遇而酗酒，打架，顶撞上司。

清末保路风潮，给了这条蛟龙腾飞上天的机会。尹昌衡借兵平息成都兵变，诛杀赵尔丰之后，又创立“大汉公”袍哥公口，出任四川军政府都督，同时成为庙堂和江湖的大哥，时年不过二十七岁。随之带兵西征巴塘，平定西藏分裂势力发动的叛乱——可谓文治武功盛于一时。

与四川总督赵尔丰的争斗，更是精彩绝伦。赵尔丰何等枭雄，他平定西康土司叛乱，改土归流，收复西藏，称得上是晚清最后的名将——但尹昌衡单刀赴会拜见赵尔丰，约定互相保全，让赵安心地撤去三千护卫，然后派兵突袭，斩首号令天下。

远在北京的中华民国总统袁世凯，极为忌惮西南的两股力量，一为蔡锷，一为尹昌衡。1913年下半年，袁世凯先后将二人诱至京城。后来蔡锷借小凤仙之力，经日本辗转回滇，发起护国运动。尹昌衡却被罗织罪名，判处有期徒刑九年。

1916年7月，袁世凯死后的第二个月，尹昌衡蒙特赦出狱，并被黎元洪聘为总统府军事顾问。实际上，黎仍然对尹心有忌惮。当年11月，尹昌

he still felt that his talent cannot be fully utilized, any more than the yellow bell (one of ancient Chinese musical instruments) was discarded.

Yin Changheng was a handsome, long-limbed man known as“Yin Changzi (tall man)”. He was regarded as the spiritual leader of the Sichuanese soldiers in the new army, and often drank, fought and contradicted his superiors because he felt that his talents were not recognized.

In the late Qing Dynasty, Yin Changheng, the latent dragon, was given the opportunity to take off to the sky. He borrowed troops to quell the Chengdu mutiny, killed Zhao Erfeng, and then founded the “Da Han Gong”, a public brotherhood organization. He served both as the Governor of the Military Government of Sichuan and the chief of a gang-hood at the age of only 27 years old. Then he led an expedition troop westward to Batang to pacify a rebellion launched by the Tibetan separatist—his political and military achievements were brilliant at that time.

The fight with Zhao Erfeng, the Viceroy of Sichuan, was nothing short of a spectacular. A fierce, shrew and formidable general, Zhao Erfeng quelled the rebellion of the chieftains in Xikang, bureaucratizing the chiefdoms, and pacified Tibet by integrating it back into the imperial domain. He deserved the appellation of “The Last Famous General of the Late Qing”. Yin Changheng, in an audacious move, personally visited Zhao Erfeng. They reached an agreement to mutually ensure each other’s safety, convincing Zhao to dismiss his 3,000 guards. It turned out that Yin made a drastic turn and staged a sudden attack which finally led to Zhao’s beheading.

Yuan Shikai, the President of the Republic of China in Beijing, was extremely jealous and fearful of two forces in the southwest, one of them was Cai E and the other one was Yin Changheng, and in the second half of 1913, Yuan Shikai lured the two of

衡请假回乡省亲，不待批复即自行离京，却在武汉被挡下，送回京城。

半年后，尹昌衡借道上海返川，走到宜昌后再次被截。这一次，他被送到南京，成为冯国璋的顾问。北洋军阀对其始终放不下心来，段祺瑞就曾明言："倘令其赴川，不啻放虎归山。"尹昌衡纵然一时枭雄，但此时犹如虎在笼中，无法施展。

笔者曾见到过一段资料，说被软禁的尹昌衡为了发泄心中愤懑，同时羞辱北洋政府，在南京表演了一场行为艺术。他手持竹篙，在大街上吆喝着一群鸭子，背后则跟着负责看守他的特务。

放鸭子一说，笔者只在一处见到，孤证之可信度尚存疑。记于此，是因为这个场景确实让人对尹那种有力无处使感同身受。

等到1920年，尹昌衡终于回到重庆，却是时移世易，新一代川军军阀已然崛起，历史舞台上已经没有了前主角的位置。三十多岁的尹昌衡，开始念佛作诗，闭门不出，顶着"五老七贤"的标签度过了后半年。

尹昌衡一生自负非常，他曾在宴会中自矜："乃公诚东亚一怪杰矣。"乃公者，你爹也，亦即"家祭无忘告乃翁"之乃翁，其傲慢可知。当

them to the capital successively. Later on, Cai E was able to return to Yunnan through Japan with the help of Xiao Fengxian, and initiated the Defending-state Movement. Yin Changheng, however, was sentenced to nine years' imprisonment on trumped-up charges.

In July 1916, the second month after Yuan Shikai's death, Yin was pardoned and released from prison, and was hired by Li Yuanhong as a Military Advisor to the presidential administration. In fact, Li was still afraid of Yin. In November of that year, Yin Changheng asked for leave to go back to his hometown to visit his relatives and left the capital on his own without waiting for approval, but he was stopped in Wuhan and sent back to the capital.

Half a year later, Yin Changheng returned to Sichuan via Shanghai and was intercepted again after making his way to Yichang. This time, he was sent to Nanjing and became Feng Guozhang's advisor. The Northern Warlords could not let go of him, and Duan Qirui once said, "If we let him go to Sichuan, it's like letting the tiger return to the mountain." Yin Changheng was a great man for a while, but at this time it was like a tiger in a cage, unable to exert itself.

The author has seen a piece of information that Yin Changheng, who was under house arrest, staged a performance art in Nanjing in order to vent his anger and humiliate the Beiyang government at the same time. Holding a bamboo pole in his hand, he yelled at a group of ducks on the street, followed by the secret agents who were responsible for guarding him.

I have only seen the "duck story" in one place, and the credibility of the single evidence alone is still doubtful. This scene is mentioned here because it really makes people empathize with Yin that he had no place to put his power to use.

By the time Yin Changheng finally returned to Chongqing in 1920, the times had changed, and a new generation of Sichuan warlords had already risen to

然，这样的自我评价，其他人也未必赞同。曾经接任过尹权柄的胡景伊其时在座，就摇头晃脑道："见怪不怪，其怪自绝"，满座随即哄笑。果然，解构是消除严肃的利器。

尹昌衡前半生勇略无双，又站在时势之风口，因此以成都皇城坝为舞台，唱了一台英雄盖世的好戏。然而，时势也把一幕荒谬、乖张又悲情的大剧强加到了他的身上。

power, leaving the former protagonist without a place on the stage of history. Yin Changheng, in his thirties, began to recite Buddhism and compose poetry, and spent the latter half of his life with the label of "Five Old Men and Seven Sages"—those legendary recluses.

A very conceited man throughout his life, Yin Changheng once boasted in a banquet: "*Nai Gong* is truly an exceptional figure in East Asia" *Nai Gong* means your father, which is the *Nai Weng* in the famous poem "Family members shall not forget to tell *Nai Weng* at sacrifices". His arrogance is evident as such. Of course, such self-praise might not have garnered unanimous agreement from others. Hu Jingyi, a Yin's successor, was present at the time, shaking his head and saying, "Seeing a monster but not fearing the monstrous, and the oddity disappears." A laughter erupted in the audience. Sure enough, deconstruction is a potent tool for dispelling solemnity.

In the first half of his life, Yin Changheng was a man of unparalleled courage and guile, and stood on the cusp of the times, so he used the *Huangchengba* as a stage and put on a heroic show. However, the time and tide also imposed an absurd, perverse and tragic drama on him.

城头变幻大王旗

大局初定，学校迁出，军政府长官公署入驻。辛亥革命之中，皇城坝见证了一系列重大的历史事件。

1915年12月25日，反对袁世凯称帝的护国运动爆发，蔡锷率滇军北进四川。护国运动胜利后，蔡锷前往日本治病，滇军将领罗佩金暂署四川

Banners changed on the city wall

When the dust settled, the school moved out and the office of the chief of the military government moved in. In the midst of the Xinhai Revolution, the *Huangchengba* witnessed a series of significant historical events.

On December 25th, 1915, the Defending-state Movement against Yuan Shikai's claim to the throne broke out, and Cai E led the Yunnan army northward into Sichuan. After the victory of the Defending-state

督军，黔军将领戴戡暂署四川省长。因撤裁川军等问题，1917年4月18日，川军二师师长刘存厚率军队围攻罗佩金部。罗的军队驻扎在皇城，这里在明末清初之后再一次成为血火之地。刘部以大炮轰击，罗部则用煤油喷烧民房，以防川军借房屋掩护进行巷战。

滇军败退后，黔军坐收渔利，接管其防区，戴戡更是集省长、督军两职于一身，刘存厚大为不满。7月5日，刘戴两军发生冲突。黔军将军队集中于皇城，川军则用大炮猛轰击，随后又招募两百名敢死队员，利用云梯攻城。川军久攻不下，又学起了当年张献忠破城之法，在一口棺材里填满炸药，挖隧道通到皇城根下，然后点火引爆，炸出一个大缺口。刘戴之战持续了13天，黔军在突围过程中溃败，戴戡死于乱军，刘存厚随即接管了四川。

军阀巷战皇城，激起了成都百姓的痛恨。物议汹汹之下，官署迁出，明蜀王府旧址再一次成为学校集中地。民国前期，此地举办的学校有高师附中学校、明远中学、成城中学、成都大学、国立师范大学、高等师范学校和美术学校等。1931年11月9日，国立成都大学、国立成都师范大学和

Movement, Cai E left for Japan to take his medical treatment, and Luo Peijin, a general of the Yunnan Army, temporarily acted as the Military Chief of Sichuan, whereas Dai Kan, a general of the Guizhou Army, temporarily acted as the Governor of Sichuan. On April 18, 1917, Liu Cunhou, Commander of the Second Division of the Sichuan Army, due to the disarmament issue, led an army to besiege the *Huangchengba* where Luo Peijin's troops was stationed. Once again after the late Ming and early Qing Dynasty, this place was bathed in blood and fire. Liu's troops bombarded he *Huangchengba* with artillery, while Luo's troops sprayed kerosene on civilian houses with fire to prevent the Sichuan Army from using the cover of the houses to engage in alley battles.

After the defeat of the Yunnan Army, the Guizhou Army benefited from its failure and took over the defense area, and Dai Kan simultaneously wore two hats: the Military Chief and the Governor of Sichuan, which made Liu Cunhou very dissatisfied. On July 5, Liu and Dai's armies clashed. The Guizhou Army assembled in the *Huangchengba*, while the Sichuan Army bombarded them with artillery. Besides, the Sichuan Army recruited two hundred people as a death squad, deploying ladders to attack the city. However, this assault lasted for a long time without success, and the Sichuan Army decided to copy the method what Zhang Xianzhong used to break the city: filled in a coffin with explosives and dug tunnels to the root of the *Huangchengba* before igniting the detonation. A large gap was blown out. Liu and Dai's battle lasted 13 days, and the Guizhou Army was routed during the breakout. Dai Kan died in the chaos and Liu Cunhou took over Sichuan.

The alley battle in the *Huangchengba* among warlords provoked the hatred of the people of Chengdu. Amid the groundswell, the government

公立四川大学合并，成立国立四川大学，其文学院和法学院即在皇城。

然而，时处乱世，天下之大难于容下一张书桌。1932年11月16日，二十四军刘文辉与二十九军田颂尧为争地盘大打出手，开启民国史上第三次成都巷战。而此次巷战中，最为出名的煤山争夺战，就发生在国立四川大学的围墙内外。

清代贡院，并没有占去明蜀王府的全部，其东北角一带为宝川局所占用。宝川局是铸造铜钱的机构，烧炉过程中产生的煤渣堆积在皇城空地上，久而久之，便成了一座四五丈高，占地数亩的小山。

民国年间经历军阀混战后残破的皇城坝 （美）西德尼·大卫·甘博 摄

The remains of Huangchengba after the warlord turmoil in the Republic of China. (Photographer: Sidney David Gamble, USA)

office was moved out of there, and the former Mansion of King of Shu once again became a place where schools flocked in. In the early years of the Republic of China, schools such as Higher Normal Secondary School, Mingyuan Middle School, Chengcheng Middle School, Chengdu University, National Normal University, Higher Normal School and Fine Arts School swarmed here. On November 9, 1931, National Chengdu University, National Chengdu Normal University, and Public Sichuan University were merged to establish National Sichuan University, whose Faculty of Letters and Faculty of Law were located in the *Huangchengba*.

However, in the chaotic times, big as the world is, a single classroom table cannot be accommodated. On November 16, 1932, Liu Wenhui's 24th Army and Tian Songyao's 29th Army fought for the territory, ushering in the third Chengdu alley battle in the history of the Republic of China. The most famous battle of this alley war, the battle for Coal Hill, took place inside and outside the walls of the National Sichuan University.

The Examination Hall in Qing Dynasty did not cover all of the Mansion of the King of Shu, its northeast corner being taken up by Baochuan Bureau, an institution where copper money was cast. During the burning process, cinders were produced and piled up in the open space of the *Huangchengba*. Over time, it became a hill that was four or five feet high, covering several Mu.

Chengdu is located in the western Sichuan plain; therefore, even such a small artificial slope drew much of public attention. Climbing Coal Hill, surprisingly, had also become a New Year's custom. However, it is true that on Coal Mountain you can see Longquan Mountain in the east and Yulei Mountain in the west, if the weather is fine.

What makes people unknown whether to laugh

成都地处川西坝子，即便是这样一个人工小坡，也为市民稀罕。爬煤山，竟然也成为新年习俗。不过，的确在煤山上可以东眺龙泉山、西望玉垒山，如果天气晴好的话。

让人哭笑不得的是，刘田之间的战事一开，这个在地质学上根本不能称为山的煤山，便成为兵家必争之地。双方都想占领这个制高点，以架起大炮，轰击对方要塞。

为了夺取二十九军控制的煤山，二十四军派出一个团在夜半时分进入国立四川大学，破毁围墙，发动进攻。田颂尧部则在后子门一带撬起街面石板，垒筑工事进行防御。煤山失守之后，负责守卫的孙团长被枪决。二十九军师长王铭章组织敢死队，亲自督战，又夺回煤山。而刘文辉部如法炮制，同样组织敢死队，还用日常拉货的架架车制成土坦克，既可冲击，又可作活动掩体。

短短的十数年内，军阀们为了私利，在皇城这么小一块土地上进行过三次巷战，死伤士兵、平民数以万计——仅第一次巷战时，欲逃往川军控制区而被滇军刺死的平民，就有一千二百余人。对人命尚且轻贱若此，遑论历史文化古迹的保存和校园清静了。

or cry is that as soon as the war between Liu and Tian started, this Coal Hill, which could not even be called a mountain geologically, became a place where soldiers had to fight. Both sides wanted to occupy this high point in order to drive up the cannons and bombard the other side's fortress.

To seize Coal Hill, which was under the control of the 29th Army, the 24th Army sent a regiment to enter the National Sichuan University in the middle of the night, broke down the fence and launched an attack. Tian Songyao's troops, on the other hand, pried up the stone slabs on the street and built fortifications in the Houzimen area for defense. After the loss of Coal Hill, the Regiment Commander, Sun, who was in charge of the defense, was executed. The commander of the 29th Army, Wang Mingzhang, organized a death squad, supervised the battle in person, and reclaimed Coal Hill. By the same token, Liu Wenhui's troops also organized death squad and made "earth tanks" out of cargo-hauling-trolleys, which could be used as both assault vehicles and movable bunkers.

In just a few decades, the warlords, for their self-interests, engaged in three alley battles in the *Huangchengba*, such a small piece of land, incurring tens of thousands death of soldiers and civilians — the first alley battle alone claimed more than 1,200 people who tried to flee to the Sichuan Army-controlled area and was stabbed to death by the Yunna Army. With human life destroyed like this, there is nothing to be said about the preservation of historical and cultural sites and campus tranquility.

Until 1949, the *Huangchengba* was reduced to a bustling, chaotic hub of diverse activities; in addition to the food and drink stalls, it hosted gambling setups, fortune-telling booths, and peddlers of dubious elixirs, creating a lively mix of trades. The so-called "Eight Sects of the Underworld": fortune-teller,

到1949年之前，皇城坝沦落为一个百业繁生、龙蛇混杂之地，除了吃吃喝喝的摊子，赌博摊子、算命摊子、跑江湖卖打药的也都杂行其间。所谓江湖八大门，惊、疲、飘、册、风、火、爵、要，可谓门门尽有。成都人也给皇城坝取了个绰号，叫“撒谎坝儿”。到了今天“撒谎坝儿”一词还在流行，不过已不用于地名，而专指那些说话做事不靠谱的人。

1951年，皇城城门洞以南，开始修建人民南路，成都的南北中轴线初显。1969年，为修筑“毛泽东思想胜利万岁展览馆”（今四川科技馆），皇城门楼、明远楼和至公堂等被拆除殆尽，古建筑荡然无存。

quack doctor, vaudeville, antique dealer, alchemist, geomancer, strategist and beggar were all present, soup to nuts. Chengduese also gave *Huangchengba* a nickname “Liars’ den”—to this day, the moniker is still popular, referring not to the geographical location, but rather to unreliable people.

In 1951, the South People’s Road,lying to the south gate of the *Huangchengba*, was under construction and the central axis of Chengdu from the north to the south started to reveal itself. In 1969, for the construction of the “Exhibition Hall of Long Live the Victory of Mao Zedong Thought” (now the Sichuan Museum of Science and Technology), the gate tower of the *Huangchengba*, the Mingyuan Tower and the Zhigong Hall were dismantled, marking the end of this complex of ancient buildings.

第七卷

Volume 7

贲园
The Bi Garden

一座由盐商父子接力以继创建的藏书楼，极盛之时有三十万卷藏书。清末和民国，宋育仁、廖平、陈寅恪、吴宓等大儒曾受过它的滋养，林思进、龚道耕、向楚等学者曾在此编书。

严氏父子不只是藏书家，贲园也不只是藏书楼。

The Bi Garden, a private library, established through the successive efforts of the father and his son in the salt trade, at its zenith, housed a collection of over 300,000 volumes. Around the end of the Qing Dynasty and the Republic of China era, erudite scholars such as Song Yuren, Liao Ping, Chen Yinque and Wumi nourished their minds here; besides, other learned men, such as Lin Sijin, Gong Daogen and Xiangchu also compiled and collated books at this library.

The Yans, father and son, were not just book-collectors and Bi Garden was more than a library.

贲园：枣梨精刻饫群儒

The Bi Garden: Jujube and pear-block-printing books nourish the gathering of scholars

重九贲园赏月

清 · 李景复

晓霜晴日菊花篱，
倚槛临风触旧思。
率尔方停江上酒，

Enjoying the moon in The Bi Garden at the Double-Ninth Festival

Li Jingfu, Qing Dynasty

A clear day when the morning frost still hanging on the chrysanthemum fence,

Leaning on the railing, braving the wind, I

翻然又见案头诗。
八方多难今何日，
三径重来有远期。
但恐开迟复开尽，
故应强醉未开时。

found my mind in reminiscence,

Spontaneously stopped drinking on a river boat,

I instead saw the poems on the desk.

What the day is today when hardships are far and wide?

Back on the road to the recluse house, that is expected.

I fear the flowers are late to bloom or have already gone,

So better to be drunken before they are yet done.

民国时期，成都众多学者曾在贲园汲取精神养分　何大江 摄
During the Republic of China period, many scholars in Chengdu drew intellectual nourishment from Bi Garden. (Photographer: He Dajiang)

本文主人公严雁峰是个盐商。

说起盐商，你首先会想到什么？是富可敌国的商人，还是纵横乱世的枭雄？是弄到三万淮盐引的西门庆，《扬州画舫录》中那些炫富炫得千奇百怪的土豪，还是让唐王朝摇摇欲坠的黄巢，建立了前蜀的王建？那么，

Yan Yanfeng, the protagonist in this essay was a salt merchant.

Speaking of salt merchants, what comes to your mind at first? A merchant whose wealth was as much as that of a state? A fierce and ambitious hero whose footprints were all over the turbulent world? Perhaps, the likes of Ximen Qing, who controlled the permit for salt transportation on the Huai River? Those toffs portrayed in *Yangzhou Showboat* who conspicuously showcasing flamboyant extravagance? Or Huang Chao, who rocked the reign of Tang Dynasty? Or Wang Jian, who established the Former Shu Dynasty? What image did Yan Yanfeng leave in the annals of history?

We begin our story with aforementioned poem, which was written by Li Jingfu, one of the glitterati from Ya’an in late Qing and the Republic of China era. In this poem, no major factors contributing to a literati’s gathering are wanting—flowers, moon, poem and spirits—but it seems the banquet is not that jocund. There are thoughts of apprehension, sentiments of sorrow, a tinge of regret, and a sense of evading in solitude, nevertheless, they still strive for a forced inebriation.

The place to enjoy the moon at Double-Ninth Festival was in the Bi Garden, a well-known locale in

严雁峰在历史篇章中留下了什么形象呢?

先从这首诗说起。晚清、民国雅安名士李景复的这首诗，描绘的是一场文人雅集。有花有月，有诗有酒，不过酒喝得似乎并不开心。有愁思，有感伤，有惋惜，有归隐之意，但仍需勉力一醉……

重九赏月的地点在贲园。民国年间，那是成都文人中极有盛名的一处场所。它的首任主人严雁峰，跟诗作者李景复是尊经书院的同窗。贲园是花木掩映中的一座藏书楼，素有“蜀中天一阁”之称。其实，极盛之时它的藏书有三十万卷，已远超天一阁的十多万卷。

贲园所在附近，曾有一个占地近十亩的池塘。相传三国赵云曾在此洗马，故名子龙塘。同治时期建为芙蓉池馆，有亭台楼阁。

1867年，晚清重臣骆秉章离世后，芙蓉池馆改建为骆公祠以资纪念。骆秉章是左宗棠的伯乐，在四川总督任上曾大力整顿吏治，于民多有惠政。他离世之日，满城百姓缟素痛哭。骆公祠的石柱上，刻有他生前自撰的对联，记述了其为官之路及剿灭李蓝起事（清咸丰九年，李永和、蓝朝鼎起兵于云南昭通）和石达开的历

the era of the Republic of China. Its first owner, Yan Yanfeng, was a fellow student of Zun Jing Academy with the author of this poem Li Jingfu. Enveloped by flowers and trees, the Bi Garden was a family library, long been known as “The Tianyi Pavilion (one of the earliest family libraries in the world) in *Shu*”. As a matter of fact, in its heydays, the entire books in the Bi Garden were as many as 300,000 volumes, far exceeding the 100,000 volumes owned by Tianyi Pavilion.

In the vicinity of the Bi Garden, there used to be a pond covering an area near 10 *mu* (1 mu equals 0.16 acre). Legend has it that Zhaoyun, a general in Three-Kingdom era, used to wash his horse here, so it was called “Zilong Pond” as well. (Zilong is the courtesy name of Zhaoyun). During the Tongzhi period (Qing Dynasty), a “Hibiscus Pool house” was built here, with pavilions and terraces studded around.

In 1867, when Luo Bingzhang, an important minster died, the “Hibiscus Pool house” was renamed the “Lord Luo Memorial Temple” in his memory. It was Luo who discovered General Zuo Zongtang (a towering figure in the political arena of late Qing Dynasty) and entrusted with the job of recovering the lost land. Luo Bingzhang disciplined the corruptive officials when he was the Viceroy of Sichuan. When he died, many Sichuaneses, in white clothes, cried their hearts out. On the inscribed stele, he records the achievements he made in a couplet, accounting for how he became a government official and his suppression of “the Rebellion of Li and Lan” (in the ninth year of Xianfeng, Li Yonghe and Lan Chaoding uprose in Zhaotong, Yunnan Province) and Shi Dakai—“I’ve been in the civil service for 10 years, starting from being a member of the Imperial Academy, a supervisor, a section officer and an intendant to a central government official. Under emperor’s instructions, I traveled all over Qizhou,

程："十载忝清班，由翰、詹、科、道而转京卿，奉使遍齐州、汴州、吴州，回首宦途如梦幻；廿年膺外任，历鄂、黔、滇、湘以莅巴蜀，督师平李逆、石逆、蓝逆，殚心戎务识时艰。"

Bianzhou and Wuzhou. In retrospect, my journey to power was like a dream. Over 20 years, I worked outside the capital city and arrived Bashu (Sichuan Province) after holding offices in E (Hubei Province), Qian (Guizhou Province), Dian (Yunan Province) and Xiang (Hunan Province). Putting out all the stops, I commanded my troops to suppress rebels such as Li, Shi and Lan, and I knew how hard the situation and my struggle were."

因骆秉章之故，此处的街道被称为骆公祠街。

The street, accordingly, was called Lord Luo Street because of him.

清末民初，大盐商严雁峰在骆公祠街十八号（今和平街十六号）购产，将最后面的花园改建为藏书楼，用于收藏多年来搜寻的五万卷图书典籍。此即贲园之来历。

At the late of Qing Dynasty and early the Republic of China, Yan Yanfeng, the salt tycoon, bought the property at No.18 Lord Luo Memorial Temple Street (nowadays No. 16 Heping Street) and changed the garden at the rear part into a library to hoard his 50,000 books collected from everywhere for years. This is how The Bi Garden came into being.

贲园始建于1914年，十年后建成，开始成为众多四川知名学者的精神殿堂。

First constructed in 1914 and completed in ten years, the Bi Garden has become a spiritual sanctuary for a number of well-known scholars in Sichuan.

史学大家张森楷著《通史人表》《廿四史校勘记》和《四川省历代地理沿革表》，学者宋育仁主持纂修三百余册《重修四川通志》，大儒廖平考订《伤寒》古本、研究《公羊传》《穀梁传》，皆离不开贲园所藏之书。

The reference books in The Bi Garden had a strong stake for completing such works as the *General Historical Figures*, *Collation on the Twenty-Four History Books* and the *Geographic Evolution in Various Ages of Sichuan* by a great historian Zhang Senkai, *A Revised Sichuan History* (300 volumes as a whole set) compiled under the supervision of Song Yuren, the textual research of the ancient *Treatise on Cold-Induced Disorders* conducted by the learned scholar Liao Ping, and the research of *The Commentary of Gongyang* and *The commentary of Guliang*.

1940年代初，张大千去敦煌临摹壁画前后，曾长时间在贲园为客。

In the early 1940s, Zhang Daqian, one of the most famous contemporary Chinese painters, lived in The Bi Garden for quite a long time before he left for Dun Huang to copy the murals.

1943年，陈寅恪流寓华西坝，曾专程到访贲园，查阅刘咸炘所著《推十书》。

In 1943, Chen Yinque, another savant, when he sojourned in Huaxiba, paid a special visit to the

1945年，学者吴宓日记记载，他

曾经受赠贲园藏书《费氏遗书》一部三册、《贲园诗钞》一册。

余者如于右任、邵力子、章士钊、沈尹默、蒙文通、谢无量、顾颉刚等一流学者、艺术家，也都曾经是贲园的座上宾。如果说，一部贲园史，就是半部民国年间的成都文化史，似乎并不太夸张。

民国年间的教育家陶亮生有诗，“贲园三十万卷书，枣梨精刻饫群儒”，说的就是此事。所谓枣梨，是雕版的指代。枣与梨木质皆坚硬密实，适合制作雕版印书。饫，宴食也。这三十万卷藏书，其中还有无数珍本，正是众多成都学者的精神美食。

当然，严氏藏书并非对所有人开放。1905年，日本人山川早水任四川高等学堂日文教师，在成都盘桓数月，他对严雁峰也有所耳闻，“城里的某氏说有人藏书数万卷，说是不肯让人看，所以没去看。现在想来，也许对待我们外国人可能会网开一面。当时未能去试一试，甚为遗憾”。

题外话，从山川早水的自述中，可以看出当时的来到中国的外国人还是很有些心理优势的。

严雁峰去世之后，养子严谷声继承了贲园和他的藏书事业。父子俩

Bi Garden to consult the *Tuishi Books* written by Liu Xianxin.

In 1945, in his dairy, Wumi, a famous scholar, recorded how he was given books from the Bi Garden such as *Fei's Remaining Books* (3 volumes as a whole set) and an *Anthology of Poetry in Bi Garden*.

Other prestigious men of mark, such as Yu Youren, Shao Lizi, Zhang Shizhao, Shen Yinmo, Meng Wentong, Xie Wuliang and Gu Jiegang used to be guests of The Bi Garden. It doesn't seem too much of an exaggeration to say that the half part of the cultural history of Chengdu in the Republic of China was related to the history of The Bi Garden one way or another.

In his poem, Tao Liangsheng, an educator in the Republic of China era, mentioned that The Bi Garden possesses “300,000 volumes of books, printed with meticulously carved jujube and pear in the Bi Garden are nourishing the gathering of scholars”. The jujubes and pears refers to the woodblocks used for printing because these hard and dense materials are most suitable for crafting woodblocks. The books in Bi Garden, among which numerous rare editions can be found, were like pabulum for many scholars in Chengdu.

Certainly, Yan's book collection didn't open to all. In 1905, Yamakawa Sosui, a Japanese teaching Japanese at Sichuan Higher School, spent several months in Chengdu. He had heard of Yan Yanfeng's name—“a man told me that someone had a collection of tens of thousands of books, but he wouldn't let anyone see them, so I didn't make it. In retrospect, the owner might bend the rule a little bit toward us foreigners. It's a great regret that I didn't make an attempt.”

As a side note, from Yamakawa Sosui's account, we can infer that the foreigners in China may have quite a lot psychological advantage.

After Yan Yanfeng passed away, his adopted son, Yan Gusheng, inherited The Bi Garden and all

一个盐商，一个富二代，却一生都在做跟书相关的事业，读书、寻书、买书、藏书、刻书、印书。

何故？

the book-collection undertaking. Both the father, a salt merchant, and the son, a wealthy second generation dedicated their whole lives to everything about books: reading, searching, purchasing, collecting, engraving and printing.

Why?

耗尽一生为藏书

严雁峰，1855年生于陕西渭南孝义里。雁峰是学名，之前曾用过祖馨、岳莲等名，后又以“贲园居士”作别号。严雁峰七八岁时，陕甘地区发生了一场大动乱。这场动荡始于同治元年（1862年），持续十二年。在早期的冲突及后期左宗棠平定乱局的过程中，大量房屋、书院被烧毁，关中地区人口损失将近一半。

当是时，附近的三原、高陵和蒲城等地已被攻破，渭南危在旦夕，父老乡亲却不愿背井离乡，决意守土死战。关中承平日久，老百姓根本不懂如何打仗。因此，严雁峰力劝寡母到祖籍地蒲州（山西永济）避难。果然，在被围困三日之后，孝义里陷落，遭到的杀戮比其他地方更为惨重。严雁峰的远见，在幼年时已见端倪。

严家数代为官。从曾祖父开始，就拿到了盐引，拥有永川、涪陵一带

Devoting whole life for book-collection

Yan Yanfeng was born in Xiaoyili of Weinan, Shanxi in 1855. Yanfeng was his school-name and he also used other alias such as Zuxin and Yuelian. Later he adopted “Recluse in The Bi Garden” as his art name. When he was around 7 years old, there was a big upheaval erupted in Shan and Gan region, which started in the first year of Tong Zhi (1862) and lasted for 12 years. During the early ethnic conflict and later suppression on this revolt led by General Zuo zongtang, a great deal of houses and libraries were burnt down, almost half of the population in Guanzhong region being eliminated.

At that time, the fate of Weinan was at stake when the neighboring cities, such as Sanyuan, Gaolin and Pucheng were collapsed. However, the local people refused to desert their homes and determined to close ranks. However, the civilians didn’t know how to conduct a war since they had been enjoying a long period of peace. As such, Yan Yanfeng saved no efforts in persuading his widowed mother to take refuge in Puzhou (Yongji, Shanxi), her homeland. As he forecasted, after only three days of siege, Xiaoyili fell to the prey of the enemy; as a result, the casualties there was more desperate than other places. His foresight was manifested when he was only in his childhood.

Yan’s family kept turning out government officials in generations. From his great grandfather

的食盐特许经营权。为了避难，严雁峰跟着母亲，辗转河南、湖北入蜀。定居于成都，严雁峰开始发奋苦读。他博闻强记，能默诵儒家典籍十三经。这一点，连有“头号经学家”之称的廖平也自愧不如。光绪初年（1875年），学者吴大澂出任主管陕甘两省教育的官员。二十岁的严雁峰回到原籍陕西，递补成为府学生员。吴大澂素以识人闻名，颇想笼络严雁峰。有人放出风来，暗示其拜于吴门，而严不屑于此，只是遵照惯例与众生一同谒见，并不单独备礼求见。

就在那一年，在张之洞的支持下，尊经书院在文庙街落成，四川教育的近代史就此开端。尊经书院抛却了传统书院注重时文贴括的陈习，严禁八股，以研习儒家经典为本，更注重经世致用。1878年，著名经学家王闿运出任山长，开创新风尚，尊经书院由此成为清代末期蜀学复兴和维新运动的重镇，还培育出了经学大师廖平、四川历史上“睁眼看世界”第一人宋育仁、状元骆成骧，以及“戊戌六君子”中的杨锐、刘光第等大才。

王闿运早年曾在权臣肃顺家中任西席，又在曾国藩军中为幕僚。他主持尊经书院后，二十三岁的严雁峰

on, salt franchise in Yongchuan and Fulin region was obtained. To avoid war disaster, he followed his mother trudging all the way from Henan and Hubei and finally settled down in Chengdu where he began to toil at reading books. He had a strong memory so that he was able to recite the 13 classics of Confucianism, which even humbled Liao Ping, the “No. 1 Confucian”. In the first year of Guang Xu (1875), scholar official Wu Dacheng took the position in charge of education in Shan and Gan. Yan Yanfeng, who was 20, went back to his hometown where he became a candidate for prefectural school. Wu Dacheng was known for his discernment for talents and he tried to rope Yan Yanfeng in. Words on the street implied that Yan could fall back on Wu. Rather than seeking a private audience with gifts, Yan preferred instead to pay a formal visit to Wu, following the common practice with his fellow candidates.

It was in that year that Zun Jing Academy, through the patronage of Zhang Zhidong, established in Wenmiao Street, inaugurating the modern education in Sichuan Province. As oppose to sticking to the entrenched stereotypes, Zun Jing Academy prohibited the “eight-legged essay”, valued classics of Confucianism and highlighted on application of what was learnt to pragmatic purposes. In 1878, when Wang Kaiyun, a famous Confucian, took the rein of the academy, a fresh air lifted this academy into a bulwark of reinvigorating “the Study of Shu” and a rampart of The Movement of Reform, disgorging Liao Ping, a Confucian master, Song Yuren (who was claimed as “the first one opened his eyes to see the world” in the history of Sichuan), Luo Chengxiang (a *Zhuangyuan,* or The Number One Scholar), Yang Rui and Liu Guangdi (who were among Six Martyrs of the Hundred Days’ Reform).

Wang Kaiyun served first as a private tutor in Sushun’s family (a bigwig in the late Qing Dynasty)

自请入弟子列，却由于籍贯不在四川，不能成为书院正式学生。王闿运惜才，便在内院设一房间，留严雁峰为生。

上有名师，侧有嘉友。严雁峰在书院所交往者，除了上文提及的杨锐、廖平、宋育仁，还有后来的史学大家张森楷、学者吴伯英、教育家丁树诚、跟杨锐等并称“蜀中三杰”的陈纬元等，皆为一时之俊杰。

数年后，王闿运辞别尊经书院，于成都东门设置帐篷，与送行者千余人聚饮，盛况一时无两。宴饮中，王闿运拿出著作《湘军志》手稿和手写的古体诗长卷，单独送给严雁峰。王闿运何等身份，在一众俊彦中如此偏爱一个后辈，也证明严雁峰确有过人之处。

严雁峰的性格，立于出世与入世之间。

尽管看上去很有些孤标傲世，但实际上，严氏入世的事业非常顺畅，这或许是因为他对世事的深切洞察。其世事洞明，在一件事上可以得到反映。

严雁峰曾巡视家族产业中的盐仓，到了涪陵一带。那段时间，群山之中昼夜传来锣鼓之声，众人皆言将有战祸。严则认为这是水患的先兆，

and then a staff in Zeng Guofan’s military command. With him behind the wheel of Zun Jing Academy, Yan Yanfeng, 23 years old, spontaneously asked to be enlisted among Wang’s disciples. However, he could not be enrolled as a formal student owing to his native place, which was not Sichuan. Cherishing talents, Wang Kaiyun set apart a room in the academy for Yan to live and study.

Yan Yanfeng clustered himself around famous teachers and helpful friends: besides Yang Rui, Liao Ping and Song Yuren, there were Zhang Senkai, an illustrious historian, Wu Boying, a scholar, Ding Shucheng, an educator, Chen Weiyuan (who was jointly addressed as “Three Outstanding Figures in Shu” with Yang Rui *et al.*). All of them were elites at that time.

Years later when Wang Kaiyun resigned from Zun Jing Academy, his farewell party, hosted at the east gate of Chengdu, where a marquee was pitched, drew thousand people to attend, a pageantry nonpareil at that time. In this banquet, Wang Kaiyun took his manuscript of *The History of the Xiang Army* and a long scroll of ancient style poetry handwritten by himself to give Yan Yanfeng separately. Wang Kaiyun, prominent as his status was, revealed his preference to Yan Yanfeng among a phalanx of younger generation, speaking volumes about Yan Yanfeng having something special and distinctive.

Yan Yanfeng’s character stands between *Rushi*, or to enter the world to become a part of society and to gain achievement, and *Chushi*, or to leave the world, or to detach oneself from society in order to achieve spiritual enlightenment.

Solitary as he appeared, his enterprise, as a matter of fact, was very successful, which could be ascribed to his insightful observation on the worldly matters. Here is a case in point.

Once he inspected his salt inventory in Fulin

应该早做准备。乌江流域这一带，是典型的喀斯特地貌，所谓“金鼓之声”，很可能是地下河与溶洞之中发出的水声。

可惜，没有人把严雁峰的话放在心上。不久，大水突发，多处盐仓被淹，损失超过五万两白银。此时严雁峰做了两件事，态度都非常坚决。一是向有司上书请求补配，被多次拒绝后仍继续坚持；二是最终拿到补配之后，立即请辞，不再经营盐业。靠着这桩生意发财的舅子老表，力劝而不能阻止，都对严雁峰十分怨怼。不到一年，辛亥革命就爆发了，还在继续经营的盐商个个倾家荡产。这时候，大家又佩服起严雁峰的远见卓识了。

严雁峰早年也曾参加过科举，“三试乡闱一试京兆”，结果都落第了。他倒也胸怀旷达，不愿再作寻章摘句雕虫之事。

甲午战争前夕，严遵母命入京，以捐官所得候补知县身份赴吏部应选。京城所见，庙堂之上的鼠目寸光、夸夸其谈、谄媚求进，让严雁峰深感失望。战事中的惨败，更让他觉得国事已不可收拾。于是放弃了捐官的机会，收拾回乡。

接下来的几年里，又有几件大事发生。先是戊戌政变，“戊戌六君

region. At that time, the sound of gong and drum could be heard in the evening from mountains. While other believed it was a battle cry, Yan, however, made a prediction that a flood was upcoming and warned others to mend the fence in advance. According to his judgement, this region around the Wujiang River is a typical karst landform and the so-called “sound of gong and drum” was probably emitting from underground water and karst cave.

It was a pity that his words were like water of the duck’s back. Before long, there was a flood coming and as a result, a number of inventories was inundated, with total loss over 50,000 *Liang* (ancient Chinese measurement) silver ingot. Yan Yanfeng did two things with adamant attitude: first he asked for compensation from government agencies concerned, and he insisted so after repeated rejection; second, he immediately exited from this business when the compensation was finally obtained. His relatives, who made fortunes on this business, persuaded vigorously but failed to convince him, and were livid at his decision. Less than one year, Xinhai Revolution erupted, other salt merchants who kept on business all went bankrupt. It was until this moment that people started to admire Yan’s foresight.

Early in his life, he also challenged imperial exams, three times on provincial level and once on capital level and all his attempts were unsuccessful. He, however, was broad-minded and would not waste his time any more on trivialities such as those hair-splitting and logic-chopping matters.

On the eve of the First Sino-Japanese War, at behest of his mother, he went to the capital city, wait-listed as a candidate for a county magistrate to be selected by the Ministry of Personnel, because of his donation for such a position up for grabs. While in his stay in the capital city, all the high-ranking government officials he witnessed were blinkered,

子”之一、好友杨锐殉难。不到两年，又是“庚子国难”，山河表里惨遭八国联军蹂躏。经历山河破碎，严雁峰更加心灰意冷，他将自己的姓名改为了严遨。这个遨字，是向隐士郑遨致敬。郑遨是唐末五代人，人称“逍遥先生”，见天下将乱，便入少室山当了道士，曾拒绝过石敬瑭的邀请。

玉露金飙下九天，
此君高洁得秋先。
深岩绝壁无人到，
且赋淮南招隐篇。

这首《林山腴舍人嘱题岩桂图》收于严雁峰自选集《贲园诗钞》，其中“淮南招隐篇”一典，是指西汉淮南王刘安门客所作《招隐士》赋。此赋极写幽谷险峻，呼唤“王孙兮归来”。严雁峰之诗不算出众，但文学素养是过关的。以岩桂明志，有浊世清流之慕。

断绝登科之望的严雁峰，在经营家族的盐业生意之外，主要有两件爱好。一是纵情山水，登泰山以临东海，渡邗沟而观钱塘。二是搜罗天下奇书，而藏之读之。甲午年间来到京城，严雁峰就不计资财，大量收购图书。建书库藏书的念头，此时已经在他心中生发了。归途路过西安，听说

grandstanding and ingratiating, which disappointed him immensely. Besides, the ensuing fiasco in the war further added his frustration and made him believe the future of this country was hopeless. Giving up the opportunity in officialdom, he packed up and left.

In the following years, several incidents happened. First came the Hundred Days Reform during which Yan's good friend, Yang Rui (one of the Six Martyrs of the Hundred Days' Reform) was decapitated. In less than two years, the Boxer Rebellion and ensuing ravages led by the Eight-Nation Alliance smashed the whole country into pieces. Facing the devastation and ruins, Yan Yanfeng, depressed and disillusioned, changed his name into "Yan Ao". The word "Ao" was used to pay tribute to a recluse named "Zheng Ao", addressed by people as "Mr. Leisure", who lived around the end of Tang Dynasty and Five dynasties. Seeing the chaos throughout his country, Zheng Ao secluded into the Shao Shi mountain to be a Taoist priest and refused the invitation from Shi jingtang (one of the emperors in Five dynasties)to hold public office.

Jade dew and gold dusts descend from heaven's hall,
this noble gentleman's purity precedes him in the fall.
In deep caves and isolated cliffs where none ventures,
but he recites the *Huainanzhaoyin* scrolls.

This poem, *At the Request of Lin Shanyu, the Inn Master, to Inscribe on Painting Depicting Osmanthus*, was recorded in Yan Yanfeng's personal collection: *Anthology of Poetry in Bi Garden,* in which the allusion—*Huainanzhaoyin* or "King of Huainan recruiting recluse" refers to a poem written by one of retainers of Liu An, King of Huainan. This poem, mentioning "steep cliffs and precipices", practically invokes the return of noblemen. Yan's poem is not outstanding, but his literary quality is up

已故前东河总督（山东河道总督）张井的藏书要出售，共计有上千部。严雁峰于是联系上张井的孙子，全部买了下来。

后来，又听说清军提督唐友耕之孙有一批家族藏书要出售，便亲自登门求购。购得的这一批文献中，有胡林翼、曾国藩的信札、手稿，有顾炎武的《肇域志》手抄本，有刘永福（晚清将领，曾率黑旗军大败法军）的《使越日记》，都是极为难得的珍品。

to the scratch. Osmanthus reveals his aspiration to be the clear current in a muddy river.

While his political career was dim and his family salt business turned sour, he had another two hobbies to keep him busy. One was to indulge himself in mountains and rivers—he climbed Mountain Tai, surveying the East Sea and crossed the Hangou River (an ancient canal) to view the Qiantang River. The second was to collect rare books throughout China. During his stay in the capital city, he never grudged money on book-collecting. The idea to build a library burgeoned at that time. On route to home, passing the city of Xi'an, he heard the book collection of the late Donghe Viceroy (River Viceroy of Shandong) Zhang Jing was on sale. He contacted the grandson of Zhang Jing and bought all those books.

Upon hearing there were a batch of books for sale in the house of a late commander-in-chief, Tang Yougeng, he came in person to buy it. Among this purchase there were letters, manuscripts of Hu Linyi and Zeng Guofan, handwritten copy of Gu Yanwu's *History of Zhaoyu* and Liu Yongfu's *Diary on the Mission to Vietnam* (Liu was a general in the late Qing Dynasty who commanded "Black Banner Troops" and routed the French Army in Vietnam), all of which are rare treasures.

筑成名园藏奇书

得天下名书，当筑名园以贮之。清末民初，严雁峰开始策划修藏书楼，要做一番范钦当年建“天一阁”一般的事业。他的房产是三进院落，藏书楼就建在最后一进的花院里，四周修竹嘉木、绿荫蓊郁、丹

A garden built to hoard treasures

Once you have collected the famous books in the world, to build a famous garden to match is a proper thing. At the end of the Qing Dynasty, Yan Yanfeng began to plan the building of a library, taking the cue from Fan Qin, who built the "Tianyi Pavilion". Yan's property involves three entrances, with the library built in the last one, surrounded by bamboo and trees, dotted with green shade and

桂飘香。

藏书楼效仿明清两代的皇家档案馆、始建于明嘉靖十三年的皇史宬。皇史宬之宬，“屋所容受也”。三个字连起来，就是存放皇家史乘之屋。

皇史宬又有“石室金匮”之称。正殿皆以砖石建造，不用一钉一木，谓之石室；木材作柜，外包鎏金铜皮，谓之金匮。如此建制，一是显其尊贵，二是防火防潮。明清两朝，金匮置于正殿石台之上，内放皇帝实录、制诰等重要文件。明代的皇史宬，除了放置还保存过《永乐大典》副本。

号称仿皇史宬建成的严氏藏书楼，名为贲园。“贲”是个多音字，此处读作bì，意为装饰、修饰。贲园之名，来自周易六十四卦之卦二十二——贲卦，其爻辞曰：“贲于丘园，束帛戋戋，吝，终吉。”丘园为丘坂之园，非喧嚣市井，正适合藏书、读书；戋音jiān，意为少。用少量的帛，去装饰山丘园林，不必搞得富丽堂皇。文质彬彬，文不必胜质而已。

这幢两层高的青砖小楼，立在两棵银杏树金黄的落叶之上。整个外形是西式的，像一个方方正正的石头匣子。墙体足有半米厚，显得极为

suffused with osmanthus fragrance.

The library is modeled after *Huangshicheng*, or the royal archives which was built in the 13th year of the Jiajing (reign name of the Ming Dynasty) and continued its role to Qing Dynasty. The word *Huangshicheng* means “the house that stores the royal archives”.

Huangshicheng is also known as the “Golden Chamber in Stone Room”. The main hall was built of masonry without a single nail or piece of wood, hence its name “stone-room”. Wood was used as a cabinet, and the gilded copper skin outside was called the golden chamber. Such a configuration shows its honor and prevents fire and moisture. During Ming and Qing dynasties, the cabinet was placed in the main hall on the stone platform, inside it deposited the emperor’s record, edicts and other important documents. Other than that, the copy of *Yongle Daxian Canon* (an encyclopedia book) was also stored there.

Yan’s library, which is said to be modeled after *Huangshicheng*, is called The Bi Garden. “贲” is a polyphonic character, here pronounced as bì, meaning decoration. “贲” comes from the Bi hexagram, the No. 22nd of the 64 hexagrams (divinatory figures) of the *Zhou Yi* (*Zhou Yi* is also called *I Ching*, the oldest and most powerful Chinese oracle of wisdom), whose lines say, “When ‘Bi’ is present in a hill garden where a small amount of silk and cloth could be used to adorn, eventually, it is auspicious.” Such a garden is away from the hustle and bustle of the city, suitable for collecting and reading books. Besides, the garden simply possesses plain adornment—external appearance should not triumph over the content.

This is a two-story brick building, standing beside two ginkgo trees with their golden leaves. The whole shape is of the western style, like a square stone box. The walls, half a meter thick, appear extremely solid. On top of the façade an ochre-

牢固。正面的顶端镶嵌着一块赭色石板，上刻“书库”二字，为学者俞樾所题。

学者俞樾题写的匾额　何大江 摄

A plaque inscribed by scholar Yu Yue. (Photographer: He Dajiang)

外形厚重，又不乏生动活泼的细节。四条垂脊的外端，是翘得略微夸张的檐角。一楼和二楼之间的瓦檐，像是给石匣子加了一道腰线。这两道檐，能为楼面上的方形窗挡住斜飘的雨水。

基座饰有浮雕图案，似祥云又略显抽象。

进入楼内，沿着木楼梯可上二楼。两层书皆空空荡荡，那些由楠木、香樟制成，曾经贮有三十万册珍本、孤本、善本的书架、书柜和书箱已经不见。二楼的方形窗上端还加有弧形小气窗，以促进空气流通，避免潮湿。

基座的浮雕图案亦中亦西　何大江 摄

The base's relief pattern blends Chinese and Western influences. (Photographer: He Dajiang)

colored slate is inlaid, engraved with the word “Stack Room”, inscribed by the scholar Yu Yue.

The shape is heavy, yet not lacking in lively details. At the outer ends of the four hanging ridges are cocked cornices that are slightly exaggerated. The tiled eaves between the first and second floors seem to add a waistline to the stone box. These two eaves are able to shield the square windows on the floor from the slanting rainwater.

The base is decorated with relief patterns, like auspicious clouds although a bit abstract.

Entering the building, you get to the second floor by the wooden stairs. All the books are gone. The shelves, bookcases and boxes made of Nanmu and camphorwood, which used to contain 300,000 rare, the only extant or strictly edited books, have vanished into thin air. The square windows on the second floor have small curved transom to allow air circulation and avoid humidity.

To say that The Bi Garden is modeled after *Huangshicheng*, it only refers to the use of stone to prevent fire and that both of them ooze elegance. In fact, the two are not very similar in appearance. In terms of scale, *Huangshicheng* is a group of courtyard buildings, composed of the main hall, the east side of the hall, the west side of the hall, the imperial monument pavilion and the entrance door, dwarfing any private library like The Bi Garden.

说贲园效仿皇史宬，无非是指其多用石材以防火，且气象典雅而已。其实二者外形并不十分相似。就规模而言，皇史宬是一组庭院式建筑，由正殿、东配殿、西配殿、御碑亭和宬门构成，绝非贲园这样的私家藏书楼可以望其项背的。

若真要比较，贲园与宁波藏书楼天一阁倒是可以相提并论。天一阁建于明嘉靖四十年（1561年），其传承时间、声名远都胜于贲园。但若论数书数量，至1950年代初，天一阁存仅有原藏一万三千余册，以及乾隆所赐《古今图书集成》八千三百余册，但即便以全盛时期十万余册的藏书量，距贲园的三十万册还是有相当差距。

范钦建天一阁，为了防止藏书的散佚，制定了“书不出阁”的规矩。有一个故事，说嘉庆年间有爱书女钱绣芸，为一睹天一阁藏书而嫁入范家，却终未能如愿。直到1673年，黄宗羲首以外姓登阁而石破天惊，直到清末又是两百余年，也仅有十余名大学者、大文人有幸入阁阅书。书如水，可浸润人心，但若不流动，便为死水。相较之下，贲园自1924年建成至1951年移交藏书，仅二十多年的时间里，就接纳学者和传播文化而言，态度更为开放。

A proper reference for comparison is The Tianyi Pavilion. Located in Ningbo, it was built in forty years of Jiajing of the Ming Dynasty (1561), whose long history and reputation are far better than The Bi Garden. But in terms of the number of books, The Tianyi Pavilion only possesses 13,000 books of the original collection as well as 8,300 *Integration of Ancient and Modern Books* granted by the Emperor of Qianlong. Even taking into consideration the number at its height, 100,000, we find it still has a considerable gap from 300,000 books in The Bi Garden.

To prevent the collection of books from being dispersed, Fan Qin formulated an iron rule: books are not allowed to leave the pavilion. A story goes that during the Jiaqing (reign name) period, there was a woman Qian Xiuyun who loved books so much so that she even wanted to marry herself into the Fan family in order to get a glimpse of the collection of, but ultimately failed to fulfill her wish. Until 1673, Huang Zongxi, an outsider, broke the record and was allowed to enter the pavilion, a stunning news at that time. Only a little more than a dozen great scholars and writers had the honor to enter the pavilion to read books until the end of the Qing Dynasty (1911), another two hundred years after Huang Zongxi's first visit. Like water, books provide people with nourishment, but if not allowed to flow, books will be like stagnant water. In contrast, The Bi Garden, in merely 20 years, from its founding in 1924 to 1951 when its collection was handed over, assumed more open attitude when it comes to the acceptance of scholars and dissemination of culture.

Yan Yanfeng has no biological children. It was his adopted son Yan Gusheng who inherited his legacy. Yan Gusheng and his courtesy name Shihui come from a poem in the *Classic of Poetry*: Bollworm has a son, but it is the potter wasp who brings it up,

严雁峰没有亲生子女，继承其事业的，是他的养子严谷声。谷声，字式诲，其名与字出自《诗经》句："螟蛉有子，蜾蠃负之。教诲尔子，式谷似之。"古人以为蜾蠃不产子，收螟蛉为义子，以此诗取名，前一句表述严氏父子的收养关系；后一句，谷即善，似即嗣，继承先人之志，阐明对养子的期待。

谷声，又写作谷孙、谷荪。笔者曾查到过严氏于1955年售卖六册明弘治刻本《伤寒类证便览》六册的手迹，签名作"嚴穀聲"；而于右任书法条幅，上款则题作"穀孙"。严谷声表字为式诲，根据名与字含义相关的原则，取名之诗句中下句即为"载飞载鸣"，"声"和"诲"的相关性显然更强。孙、荪和声，在四川话里是一个音，故"孙""荪"应该是根据"声"读音的误写。

严谷声是个富二代，却不好声色犬马。更准确地说，他是个不折不扣的"书二代"。严雁峰去世后，严谷声接手了贲园的修筑。他跟养父一样勤学敏思、学识渊博，同样致力于收罗天下典籍。说他嗜书如命，毫不夸张，他甚至可能把书看得比命还重要。

严氏藏书，本是精神财富，但总有觊觎者以金钱衡量之，要干出些焚

teaching it so that it can carry on good tradition. According to ancient thoughts, the potter wasp does not give birth, but to adopt bollworm's son to bring up. The first part of the poem expresses the adoptive relationship between the father and son; the latter part consigns expectation for the adopted son to inherit the will of the father.

Gusheng, can also be written as Gusun. When thumbing through the engraved edition of the six volumes of the *Brief Guide of Typhoid Category*, published in Hongzhi (reign name) of Ming Dynasty,sold by Yan Gusheng in 1955, I came across his handwriting"Yan Gusheng"; meanwhile in a scroll written by Yu Youren, a famous politician and calligrapher in the Republic of China, "Gusun" was inscribed there. Yan Gusheng's courtesy name "Shihui" can be traced in the *Classic of Poetry* as well for the surname and courtesy name, according to the Chinese principle and tradition, shall have relevance to "sheng". We can also find in the context of the same poem, "(birds) fly and warble". The meaning of the word "Sheng" (meaning "sound") has a strong correlation with "warble". Although "Sheng" and "sun" pronounce similar in Sichuanese, we have good reason to say "sun" is a corruption or cacography.

As a rich second-generation, Yan Gusheng didn't live a pompous and sensual life. He was a typical second-generation of bookworm. After Yan Yanfeng's death, Yan Gusheng took over the construction of the Bi Garden. Like father, like son. He was as studious and knowledgeable as his adoptive father, and was equally devoted to collecting books from all over the world. It is not an exaggeration to say that he was addicted to books as if his life depended on it, and he might even have regarded books as more important than his life.

For Yan's father and son, to collect books was to seek pabulum, but there were always coveted eyes

琴煮鹤的事来。1931年，严谷声被成都城防司令囚于市政厅，理由居然是要替他保护藏书。严谷声不愿舍书，被关押达半年之久。多年后，严氏后人为严谷声写的墓志铭上，有“宁舍万金，不弃一卷”之语，可谓十分贴切。

1951年，严谷声将贲园书库及其全部收藏移交给四川省图书馆，书计三十万卷，经、史、子、集皆备，其中善本五万卷，地方志约两千余种，另有自刻书版三万余件。

当年，严雁峰在家族中挑选继承人时，有一个标准，“只求保我五万卷藏书”。而严谷声不仅做到了克绍箕裘，更可谓发扬光大。

严氏父子不仅搜书、买书、藏书、读书，更是编书、校书、刻书，以出版家的身份深度参与文化传播。

严雁峰留有诗集《贲园诗钞》，其中的《辟咡集》《既冠集》所收诗作，写作时间以古代男子行加冠礼的二十岁为界；另有《读晋书笔记》及四卷《随笔》。

20世纪初，严雁峰即创办镐乐堂书坊。镌刻并出售古籍之外，严雁峰还参与校勘，早年曾刻印出版有《关中金石记》《明四子诗集》《戴东原文集》等。

driven by money to grab and abuse them. In 1931, Yan Gusheng was imprisoned in the city hall of Chengdu by the Defense Commander for the reason of protection his book collection on his behalf. Yan Gusheng was unwilling to give up his books, and was henceforth incarcerated for half a year. Years later, on his epitaph, these sentences can be found written by Yan's descendants “would rather give up ten thousand gold than forsake a volume”. Appropriate indeed.

In 1951, Yan Gusheng donated all his collection in The Bi Garden to the Sichuan Provincial Library, totally 300,000 volumes, including all Confucian classics, history, philosophy and literature, among which three were 50,000 volumes of strictly edited books, more than 2,000 kinds of books on local history, and more than 30,000 self-engraved books.

Yan Yanfeng, selecting a heir within his family, set up a standard “All I wish is that my 50,000 volumes of books can be preserved”. And Yan Gusheng not only fulfilled the task of maintaining the family's cultural heritage but also can be said to have expanded and enriched it.

The Yans not only searched, bought, collected and read books, but also edited, proofread and engraved books. They involved deeply as publishers to the transmission of culture.

Yan Yanfeng left a collection of poems called *Anthology of Poetry in Bi Garden,* in which *Collection of Pi Er* and *Collection of Ji Guan* were written at the age of twenty when according to ancient custom, men came of age, rite of passage should be performed; he also wrote *Notes on Reading the Book of Jin* and four volumes of *Essays*.

At the beginning of the 20th century, Yan Yanfeng founded Hao Le Tang Bookstore. Engraving and sale of ancient books, Yan Yanfeng also involved in the proofreading. In his early years he published the engraved *Record on Guanzhong Inscriptions on*

严雁峰去世之后，严谷声继任镐乐堂经理。其时，书店开办于桂王桥西街，刻书则于贲园藏书楼外的厂房，有写字工、刻字工等数十名工人。20世纪20年代起，严谷声耗时十余年，编辑、刻印《音韵学丛书》三十二种，共计一百二十三卷。书成，章太炎先生为之作序。

严谷声除组织编校刊印之外，还著有《颜氏家训补校注》《切韵指掌图校记》等。

严氏出版古籍，有不少独特优势。首先是藏书丰富，在版本的选择与比较上，有充分的余地。再者，众多学者亲自参与编校，保证了出版的高质量，比如《音韵学丛书》之编辑，"发端于华阳林君山腴，编次雠校则成都龚君向农、巴县向君先翘"。严谷声在序言中提及的林思进、龚道耕、向楚，为蜀中一流学者，三人皆考中过清末举人，也都曾在朝廷担任过掌文墨的内阁中书。

镐乐堂之书，在20世纪前半叶即有盛名，后流布海外。牛津大学图书馆、大英博物馆皆陈列有其印本，美国国会图书馆则专门辟有"渭南严氏精刻善本书籍室"。

藏书，固然是文人雅事，但只是一味藏书并不可取，一味读书也不

Ancient Bronzes and Stone Tablets, Four Talents Poetry Collection of Ming Dynasty, Dai Dongyuan Anthology and so on.

After the death of Yan Yanfeng, Yan Gusheng succeeded as the manager of Hao Le Tang. At that time, the bookstore was located in Guiwangqiao West Street, while the engraving workshop situated beside The Bi Garden, with dozens of writers and engravers working there. Since the 1920s, Yan Gusheng spent more than ten years editing, engraving and printing *Series of Phonology*, totally 32 kinds and 123 volumes. When the book was completed, the well-known scholar Mr. Zhang Taiyan wrote a preface.

In addition to organizing the editing and printing, Yan Gusheng also wrote *Supplementary Notes on Yan's Family Motto* and *Proofreading Note on Finger and Palm Chart of Rhyme Dictionary.*

Yan's publication of ancient books enjoyed a number of unique advantages. First and foremost was the richness of their book collection, providing ample room for choices and comparisons in selecting editions. Furthermore, with many scholars personally involved in editing, the high quality of the publication was guaranteed. For instance, the editors of *Series on Phonology* included Lin Sijin, Gong Daogeng and Xiang Chu, all of whom were first-class scholars in Sichuan at late Qing Dynasty and were nominees who passed the imperial examinations and and all served in the imperial imperial responsible for literary and artistic matters.

The books published by Hao Le Tang have been enjoying a high reputation since the first half of the last century, and then spread overseas. Both The Oxford University Library and the British Museum display their printed books, and the Library of the U.S. Congress reserves a separate room for "Weinan Yans' delicately Engraved Books".

Collection of books is a hobby pursed by

值得称道，无非为世间添一“两脚书橱”而已。严氏父子，由藏书而至读书，由读书而至编书、著书，完成了由藏书家向出版家、学者的升华；而贲园，也不仅是一座藏书楼，实则是汇集了众多一流学者的学术场、编印了众多精品的出版机构。

严雁峰、严谷声父子与贲园的史实，在图书馆学史、出版史和文化史上，是极难复制的样本。古往今来，富商巨贾如过江之鲫，其间却少有对于文化事业存雅兴者——偶有者也多是附庸风雅之徒，很难有人愿意把白花花的银子投入筑园藏书这种看似虚无缥缈的事上。而学富五车者，多是靠专注于精神世界才能取得成就，往往不通人情世故，不懂得也不齿于攫取财富。

同时拥有巨额资产和极高文化素养，又能经世致用，且爱书胜命如严氏父子者，几稀。

the literati, but collection for collection's sake is not desirable, only to add some bookshelves to the world. Yan's father and son, starting from collecting to reading books, from reading to editing and writing books, consummated the sublimed shift from bibliophile and connoisseur to publishers and scholars. The Bi Garden is no longer a library only, but an academic sphere and publishing house where first-class scholars gathered to edit and publish a number of high-quality books.

Yan's father and son and the history of The Bi Garden are extremely hard to copy in the history of librarianship, publishing history and cultural history. Throughout the ages, rich merchants are as countless as the grains of sand in the Ganges, but few of them have real fancy for the cultural pursuits—a few exceptions only indulge in histrionics and are unwilling to put hard-earned money into the construction of a library whose prospect looks nebulous. On the other hand, real scholars, mainly focusing on their spiritual world and are not worldly wise, no knowing and even scorning to seize wealth.

Yan's father and son were one of a kind, possessing both huge amount of assets and very high cultural literacy, pursuing practical wisdom and loving books over life.

嵇中散集叙

贲园收藏的明代刊刻版《嵇中散集叙》，由收藏家彭雄保存　何大江 摄

The Ming Dynasty printed edition of *the Preface to the Collected Works of Ji Zhongsan*, housed in the Bi Garden, is preserved by the collector Peng Xiong. (Photographer: He Dajiang)

成都水系
The Water system in Chengdu

水，来自岷山，汇入长江。

成都平原上的水系，合而又分，分而又合，你中有我，我中有你。岷江一摊开手掌，从都江堰鱼嘴分出的五条河道就如五根手指，就伸展在川西坝子上；而这五条河道一收成拳头，又变回了岷江。

岷江，是一条黄金水道，它让成都平原突破了千山万壑的包围，让“蜀道难”只是事实上的刻板印象。但是，成都原本是没有这条水道的。一切改变，始于秦国蜀郡守李冰的天才构想。

Water in Chengdu rises from the Minshan Mountains and empties itself into the Yangtze River.

The water system on the Chengdu Plain converges and diverges, containing one another. Min River spreads like an open palm, its five channels bifurcating from Yu Zui, the fish-mouth-like dividing dyke of Dujiangyan, resembling five extended fingers over the Chuanxi Plain (alias the Chengdu Plain); yet, when these five channels clench into a fist, they transform back into the Min River.

Min River, a golden waterway, granted the Chengdu Plain escape from the encircling mountains and rendered “the treacherous road to Shu” merely a stereotyped notion. However, originally, Chengdu did not possess this water passage. All changes began with the visionary concept of Li Bing, the Qin Dynasty’s Governor of Shu County.

成都水系：一切始于一个天才构想
The Water system in Chengdu: all begins with a genius’s conception

登二王庙远眺

清·张凤翥

凭虚敞高殿，极目六江喷。
派自彭山合，源从灌口分。
烟波浴沙鸟，远树镇斜曛。
苍狗悲今事，悠然感白云。

Ascend to the Er Wang Temple and Gaze Afar

Zhang Fengzhu, Qing Dynasty

Upon this lofty and spacious hall I stand,
Beholding six rivers gushing to the land.
In River mouth of Pengshan County, they combine,
Origins at Guankou, they divide.
Mist and ripples embrace, where birds preen,
Distant trees stand aslant, with the sun's descent.
Clouds in the sky,change shape from time to time,
How uncertain, I sadly recall the ancient events.

金马河是岷江正流，也是都江堰鱼嘴分水后的外江。图为金马河双流段 冉玉杰 摄

The Jinma River is the main flow of the Min River, also the outer river after the diversion at the Yu Zui. This photo shows the Shuangliu section of the Jinma River. (Photographer: Ran Yujie)

凤翥意即凤凰高飞，在古代叫这个名字的人很多。明末清初，叫张凤翥的人也不少，文首诗的作者，应为乾隆年间的彭山县令，他曾参与通济堰修复查勘事宜。

张凤翥站在都江堰二王庙上，六条江水尽收眼底，场面极为壮观。哪六条江？从北到南，蒲阳河、柏条河、徐堰河、走马河、江安河、金马河。

金马河即岷江经都江堰鱼嘴分水后的外江，从都江堰外闸至新津岷江

"Fengzhu" means phoenix flying high, a common name in ancient China. Between the late Ming Dynasty and the early Qing Dynasty, a number of people were named Zhang Fengzhu. The author of the poem should be a county magistrate of Pengshan County in Qianlong era, who participated in the reparation and survey of the Tongji Irrigation Project.

Standing on the Erwang Temple over the Dujiangyan Irrigation Project, Zhang Fengzhu had a panoramic view of six rivers, namely the Puyang River, the Baitiao River, the Xuyan River, the Zouma River, the Jiang'an River and the Jinma River from *Yu Zui*.

Eighty kilometer long, spanning from the floodgate of Dujiangyan Irrigation Project to the Minjiang Bridge of Xinjin, the Jinma River is the outer river of the Min River after separating itself from Yu Zui.

大桥段，全长约八十千米。

剩下五江，皆来自鱼嘴分水之内江，经宝瓶口在成都平原上铺散开来。从空中俯瞰，蒲阳河、柏条河、徐堰河、走马河、江安河、金马河，又如川西坝子上的巨大手指，而江水的来处，万峰聚集的岷山，就是那只手掌的掌根。在成都平原这只巨掌上，掌纹密布，纵横交错，都是由这五条江生发出来的水道。《成都通览》上，列出了五十二条河流之名。

成都平原上的水系，合而又分，分而又合，你中有我，我中有你。即使是同一河流同一水道，往往也过一段距离又换一名，让人难辨头绪。

比如，蒲阳河下游为青白江，又汇入沱江，在泸州汇入长江。

柏条河，至石堤堰分为毗河、府河，毗河汇入沱江，而府河则与南河合流。

走马河，至两河口分出清水河、磨底河，二者至成都西郊又汇成南河。南河与府河合流并称锦江，最终在彭山江口汇入岷江。

派者，江河支流也。张凤翥诗“派自彭山合，源从灌口分”，仅十字，倒是对纷繁的成都水系进行了一个高度凝练。

All of the other five rivers come from the inner river after splitting from *Yu Zui*, spreading through the Chengdu Plain after flowing from the *Baopingkou*, or precious-bottle-neck. Seen from above, the Puyang River, the Baitiao River, the Xuyan River, the Zouma River, the Jiang'an River and the Jinma River look like giant fingers on the Chuanxi Plain, while the origin of these rivers, the Minshan Mountains, where thousands mountain peaks cluster, is the heel of the palm. On the palm-like Chengdu Plain, waterways crisscross, all springing from the 5 rivers. In *Chengdu Overview*, as many as 52 rivers are enumerated.

The river system in the Chengdu Plain converges and diverges, containing one another. Even the same river in the same river system, after passing through some distance, has its name changed and often get people confused.

For instance, the downstream of the Puyang River is called the Qingbaijiang River which flows into the Tuojiang River and merges into the Yangtze River at Luzhou.

The Baitiao River diverts from the Shidiyan weir into the Pihe River and the Fuhe River, with the Pihe River pouring into the Tuojiang River and the Fuhe River converging with the Nanhe River.

The Zouma River bifurcates into the Qingshui River and the Modi River, both of which join at the west outskirt of Chengdu and converge into the Nahe River. Jointly, the Nanhe River and the Fuhe River are called the Jin River, which discharges into the Min River at the estuary of Pengshan at length.

Pai, or flowing water, means the tributaries of a river. In his poem, "In Peng Mountain's realm, they combine; Origins at Guankou, they divide", Zhang Fengzhu summarized in concise words the river system in Chengdu.

岷江来自巍巍雪山，在鱼嘴分为内江和外江。内江又化作千百条水渠，泽润了整个成都平原　余茂智 摄
The Min River originates from the towering snow-capped mountains and is divided into the inner and outer rivers at Yu Zui. The inner river further splits into thousands of irrigation channels, nourishing the entire Chengdu Plain. (Photographer: Yu Maozhi)

一条无中生有的水道

蜀道难，人所共知，但千万别被刻板印象统摄了认知。

难是难，并非不与外交流。自古以来，向南有五尺道，往北有金牛道、米仓道，其实最便利的，还有一条冲破千山万壑的黄金水道——连接着长江的岷江。

有了这条向南，最终向东的水道，成都的一切便有了不同。

清初顾祖禹《读史方舆纪要》，以天下大势的视角，对四川地形有一个论述："夫江南之所以为固者，长江也。而四川据长江上游，下临吴楚，其势足以夺长江之险。"

长江天堑，不可飞渡。三国时孙吴据长江，与魏蜀抗衡；南北朝时，宋齐梁陈凭借它对抗北魏。拓跋焘饮

A river route starts from nowhere

It's well-known that the roads to Sichuan are tough and rough, but don't let this typecast impression dominate your perception.

Indeed, the difficulty is here to stay, but that doesn't mean the communication to the outside world is entirely blocked. Since the ancient times, there have been roads linking to the outside world: to the south there is the Wuchi Road and to the north there are the Jinniu Road and Micang Road. The most convenient one, the Min River, as a matter of fact, is a golden river route which breaks through mountains and valleys and connects with the Yangtze River.

Everything here in Chengdu is different when this river route, initially flowing to the south and finally winding its way to the east, was opened up.

In his book: *A Summary from Reading the Local History*, Gu Zuyu (Qing Dynasty) made a narrative on the topography of Sichuan from a macro-perspective, "That the solidity of the area south of the Yangtz River depends on the Yangtze River itself. Sichuan, seated on the upper reach of the Yangtze River and adjacent to the States of Wu and Chu downstream, is able to hold sway the precipitous spots on the Yangtze River."

马长江，兵锋直指金陵，而南岸战舰云集，严阵以待，一生征战天下的拓跋焘只能望江兴叹。

长江是不可逾越的吗？当然不是，但渡江需要船，运送大量士兵则需要大型战船。从北往南打的军队，没有大船便过不了河。如果战事不利，南方军队会将所有船只无论大小一律撤到南岸。

不能在长江北岸建船吗？不能。南军当然不会坐视对手造船渡江，而会不断派出船只对北岸的造船基地进行骚扰、破坏。在这样的情况下，在长江北岸造小船还行，但这对于战争没有什么用；要造出大船下水绝无可能。

唯一可行的办法，是在安全的地方造好大船，并训练好水军，再让它们进入长江。这样的地方有两个，一个是江淮之间有众多大型湖泊，中有水系与长江连通。在这些湖泊中造船练兵，再进入长江，就可以对南岸军队展开攻击。有句话叫"守江必守淮"，是因为守住了淮河流域，就能阻止敌方建造大船。另一个造船之地便在长江上游，最上可以上到成都。

再往前溯，回顾秦国朝堂上关于灭蜀的争论。群臣以为，蜀国是

The Yangtze River is a natural moat that cannot be crossed. In the Three Kingdoms era, the State of Wu occupied the area surrounding the Yangtze River so that it could compete with both the State of Wei and Shu. In the North and South Dynasties, the State of Song and Qi and Liang and Chen, relying on the Yangtze River, could hold against the Northern Wei. Tuoba-tao (the Emperor of the Northern Wei) used to water his horse in the Yangtze River and pointed his sword to Jinling. However, his opponent's warships gathered along the south bank of the Yangtze River to confront him. Tuoba-tao, who spent his entire life fighting here and there, could do nothing but sigh deeply at the sight of the broad river.

Is the Yangtze River really insurmountable? Certainly not. But to cross the river, ships are needed; furthermore, big size warships are indispensable to transport a great number of soldiers. Without such big warships, the troops from the north cannot be carried to the south. If the war situation is not favorable for the south, the troops will withdraw the ships, big or small, to the south bank.

Would it not possible to build ships on the north bank? No. The south troops certainly would not sit on their hands without sending their warships to harass and sabotage the ship-building base. Under such a circumstance, it could be possible to build small ships which are of little help for waging war. But it is absolutely out of the question to build big ships.

The only feasible way is to build large ships in a safe place and train the navy there before allowing them to enter the Yangtze River. There are two such places, one is that there are numerous large lakes between the Yangtze and Huaihe River, in which the water system is interconnected. By building ships and training troops in these lakes, and then entering the Yangtze River, they could launch a surprise attack on the south bank army. There is a saying that "to defend the River, one must

西僻之国，打蜀国不如攻楚国。但攻打楚国必然受到长江的阻挡，于是司马错、中尉田真黄说："（蜀）水通于楚，有巴之劲卒，浮大船舶以东向楚，楚地可得。"这确实是非常有见地的看法，理论上完美解决了长江天堑的问题。

不过，司马错"浮江伐楚"之策，实施起来更复杂一些。当时李冰还没有引岷江而至，成都并未通航。司马错灭掉巴国之后，随即顺江东下攻击楚国，其战船应该是在巴国首都江州（重庆）下水的。数次伐楚，虽然获得了取楚商於地建黔中郡的成效，但由于在峡口受阻，并未完全实现灭楚的目标。

西晋灭吴，同样采取这一策略。益州刺史王濬在成都造大船、练水军，顺流东下，终于突破长江天险，攻克石头城。"王濬楼船下益州，金陵王气黯然收。"可以说，司马错的策略具有很强的前瞻性，终于在几百年后完全发挥了功效。

到了东晋初年，占据成都的是成汉政权。后赵皇帝石虎给成汉皇帝李寿写信，邀约一起出兵瓜分东晋，李寿也是兴致勃勃地练兵补船。晋咸康六年（340年），李寿登楼检阅水师，

defend the Huai", because if one secures the Huai river area, one can stop the enemy from building big ships. The second of such a place to build ships is in the upper reaches of the Yangtze River, up to Chengdu.

In retrospect, when the discussion on whether to annihilate the State of Shu resonated in the court of the State of Qin, ministers preferred to attack the State of Chu first since Shu locates in the western hinterland. However, considering efforts to attack Chu would be obstructed by the Yangtze River, Sima-Cuo and Tian Zhenhuang said, "The river routes in Shu are interlocked with that in Chu. If we dispatch strong troops in the State of Ba (Shu and Ba are neighbors) by taking warships eastward, we can occupy the State of Chu with ease." Indeed, this was a very insightful scheme which theoretically and perfectly tackled the challenging issue put forward by the natural moat of the Yangtze River.

Sima-Cuo's scheme "crusading Chu by taking river route", however, was more than small effort when it was put to reality. At that time, navigation to Chengdu, before Li Bing channeled the water from the Min River, had yet to effect. After annihilating the State of Ba, Sima-Cuo led his army eastward to attack Chu. It is believed that his troops should have boarded at Jiangzhou (the city of Chongqing), the capital of the State of Ba. His repeated efforts to annihilate Chu, although achieved some effects, i.e., the establishment of Qianzhong County in the territory of Chu, had yet fully achieved because of the narrows' hindrance in the Yangtze River.

The same scheme was adopted when the Western Jin eliminated the State of Wu. Wang Jun, the prefectural governor of Yi Zhou (ancient name of Chengdu), built big ships and trained his marine troops in Chengdu. His troops finally charged downstream to the east and captured the City of Stone (ancient name of Nanjing) by penetrating the natural screen of the Yangtze River. This feat was embodied

战船逆流而上，擂鼓呐喊之声响彻锦江。虽然李寿最终听群臣劝谏，并未贸然伐晋，但再一次证明：成都是可以作为军港的。

这条水道，战时用于打仗，和平时期作用更大，于文化、经济交流如虎添翼。但是，成都原本是没有这条黄金水道的。

in a poem, "When Wang Jun's ships descended from Yi Zhou, the fate of Jinling was sealed."Sima-Cuo's scheme was so forward-looking that in hundreds of years later it finally exercised its function completely.

In early years of the Eastern Jin Dynasty, it was Chenghan regime that reigned in Chengdu. Shi Hu, the emperor of the Later Zhao, wrote to Li Shou, the emperor of Chenghan, inviting him to join forces to partition the Eastern Jin. Li Tao jumped at the offer and started to train his marine troops. The sixth year of Xiankang (the reign title of the Eastern Jin Dynasty),Li Shou inspected his troops, his fleet sailing against the current and the battle cry reverberating over the Jin River. Persuaded by his ministers, Li Shou eventually gave up this reckless idea. But again, it proved that Chengdu can serve as a naval port.

This river route can be used as a battle ground in wartime, while in peacetime, it can play a more important role when it comes to cultural and economic exchange. But, Chengdu should never have such a golden route.

蜀守李冰的表演天赋

早年的成都，倒不是缺水，而是浸泡在水中，以涝灾为患。

岷江发源于松潘县境内的岷山之中。两个源头，东为海拔三千七百米之弓杠岭，西为海拔四千六百米之朗架岭。东边的漳腊河与西边的霍隆沟，在川主寺合流后，继续向南，沿途招集支流涧溪，收纳高山融雪，穿行于崇山峻岭之中。

到了今都江堰一带，终于冲破龙门山脉的阻挡，扑向古地质年代上的

Li Bing, the county chief of Shu, and his performance talent

Chengdu in its early year was not wanting in water, but soaked in water, and often plagued by floods.

The Min River starts from the Minshan Mountains that locate in Song Pan Prefecture. The sources of water can be traced to the Gonggang Range (elevation of 3,700 meters) to the east and the Langjia Range (elevation of 4,600 meters) to the west. The Zhangla River to the east and the Huolong River to the west converge at the Chuanzhu Temple and keep flowing south, soliciting tributaries on its way, collecting melting snows from the high mountains and zigzagging among the lofty mountains and ranges.

巴蜀湖。亿万年来，岷江水在龙门山脚下冲积出土地肥沃的成都平原。然而，成都的地势西北高、东南低，大河东流却被龙泉山脉堤坝似的拦住了去路。河水只好向西南方向和东北方向找出路了。西南方河谷还好，可容岷江外江——金马河从容穿过，东北方的金堂峡峡口却非常狭窄，蜿蜒二十多里路的峡谷又细又长。河水灌漫，便潴滞在成都平原。

东侧的龙泉山阻断水的东流，西侧的龙门山却挡住季风的西去。来自东南方向的水汽便在龙门山东侧形成暴雨区。地上水加天上水，把成都平原变成了一个巨大的堰塞湖。

因此，古蜀时成都的建筑，以干栏为多。所谓干栏，底层是粗大的木柱子，浸在水中，木柱子上铺木板住人，可以理解为吊脚楼。

在成都平原上，第一个因治水而留名的是鳖灵，他是古蜀国杜宇王朝的相。鳖灵带领蜀民，首开宝瓶口，拓宽金堂峡口，解除了平原上的涝灾。

治水成功，给蜀民带来福利的鳖灵，取得了巨大的声望，这让他成功取代杜宇，开创了开明王朝。从此，治水成为蜀地政治传统，兴水利之名臣能吏不绝如缕，后继者如李冰、文翁、诸葛亮、韦皋、高骈、白敏中、赵汝愚

On arriving present-day Dujiangyan area, the Min River eventually breaks through the hindrance of the Longmen Mountains and swoops upon the lakes in Ba and Shu whose ages can be traced back to the paleogeologic era. Under the Longmen Mountains, after hundreds of millions of years' impacts by the Min River, Chengdu has been gradually shaped into a fertile alluvial plain. However, the terrain in Chengdu is high in the northwest and low in the southeast. Rivers flowing to the east, blocked off by dam-like Longquan Mountain, can only find their exits to the southwest and northeast. The valleys on the southwest allow the Jinma River, the outer river of the Min River, to pass through readily, while on the northeast, the Jintang Gorge, 20 Li long, elongated and thin, is so narrow and meandering that the river inundates the Chengdu Plain and is here to stay.

Longquan Mountain on the east side cuts off the east-flowing river whereas the Longmen Mountains on the west side hold off the monsoon heading west. Water vapor, coming from southwest, contributes to the formation of torrential rainfall zone on the east side of the Longmen Mountains. Water on the ground as well as water falling from the sky turn the Chengdu Plain into a massive "barrier lake".

Therefore, most of the buildings in ancient Chengdu were of "Gan Lan", a construction style that is characterized by erecting huge wooden pillars with the bases soaked in water, and people inhabit on the boards sustained by those pillars. This kind of building is a "stilted" or "hanging" one, so to speak.

On the Chengdu Plain, Bieling was the first person known for taming the rivers. As a chancellor of the Duyu Dynasty of ancient Shu, Bieling led the Shu people to carve into the *Baopingkou*, and expanded the Jintang Gorge, alleviating the flooding on the plain.

以及本章文首诗的作者张凤翥等。

尽管有这么多的水，然而早年的成都并不通航。在成都平原上，未经组织与管理的水，原本是一摊巨大的混乱与麻烦。

《道德经》言："水善利万物而不争，处众人之所恶……"鳖灵解决了水为人所恶的问题，而变水害为水利，则需等到秦国蜀郡守李冰的横空出世。

此时的成都平原，仍像一个半瘫的巨人，营养过剩，经脉混乱。李冰的治疗方案，从进口着手，控制输入量——修都江堰渠首工程；再打通七经八脉——建立了成都平原上密如蛛网的水道，再将其引导入岷江主干道中。

都江堰渠首工程是一个博大的体系，环环相扣，相互支撑。

内江，外江。

竹笼，杩槎。

水则，铁桩。

鱼嘴，金刚堤。

飞沙堰，人字堤。

离堆，宝瓶口。

立湃阙，留漏罐。

深淘滩，低作堰。

遇弯截角，逢正抽心。

乘势利导，因时制宜。

有硬件，有软件。有治理思想，也有管理制度。

The success of taming the rivers to benefit the Shu people won him great prestige. As a result, he substituted Duyu to establish the Kaiming Dynasty. Since then, river regulation has become a political tradition in the Shu region while the abled officials, such as Li Bing, Wen Weng, Zhuge Liang, Wei Gao, Gao Pian, Bai Minzhong, Zhao Ruyu and the author of the poem mentioned above, Zhang Fengzhu, emerged on end.

So much water didn't make Chengdu a navigable area. On this plain, water, without being tamed and regulated, should have been a colossal trouble and huge mess.

According to the *Tao Te Ching*, "Beneficial to everything, however, water is in a place where everybody detests." Bieling held the detestable flood issue at bay; however, to turn the disaster into benefit, history has to invoke Li Bing, the county chief, to come into the world.

In Li Bing's time, the Chengdu Plain was like a hemiplegic giant, over-nourished and with confused meridians. His treatment focused on the importing part: control the volume flowing in by building the Dujiangyan headwork project before breaking through other channels. Cobweb-like river routes were built up on the Chengdu Plain and then were channeled into the arterial traffic of the Min River.

The Dujiangyan headwork project is an enormous system. To ensure each and every link is interlocked and mutually supported, the following concepts were adopted.

the Inner River and the Outer River;

Bamboo Cages and *Ma Cha* or abatises;

Shui Ze or Water Level Measurements and *Tie Zhu* or Iron Pillars;

Yu Zui or the Fish Mouth Type Water Dividing Dyke and the Jin Gang Dyke;

the Feishayan Weir and the Herringbone Dyke;

最重要的管理制度为轮灌、岁修。轮灌，利益均沾，众享其利。岁修，每年保养，常修常新。

历史上的浩大工程数不胜数，今日能见到痕迹者少之又少，而都江堰历时二千二百七十年依然能发挥功效，使用如昨，跟持之以恒的管理是分不开的。

李冰不仅是水利专家，也是管理专家，更是懂得人心的民族学家、心理学家，甚至是一个表演大师。

勘探岷江到了两山对峙的天彭阙，李冰说，自己似乎见到了神灵。于是建三座神祠，以三牲隆重祭祀，并将玉璧、玉圭沉水以示敬意。这是做给当地的氐人看的，以示尊重其习俗。氐人与蜀人有着千丝万缕的联系，他们相信，人死之后魂魄会穿过天彭阙，回到远在岷山之上的老家。

刻五头石犀，以镇压兴风作浪的水精，是做给蜀人看的。其中的一头石犀，在二千多年后重见天日，出土于天府广场北侧电信大楼建筑工地。它长3.3米，高1.7米，重8.5吨，前肢与躯干交接处刻有古朴的卷云纹。现存于成都博物馆，成为镇馆之宝。

刻三座石人像于白沙邮，也是做给蜀人看的。李冰与江神要约："你要干旱可以，但水不能低于石人的脚背；要涨水也可以，但不能高过石人

Li Dui (the diverting clitter near *Yu Zui*) and the *Baopingkou*, or precious-bottle-neck;

Setting up weirs to release water and to arrange culverts to induce water for farm land irrigation without blocking the river route;

Excavating deeply in the inner river to eliminate sludge and not to make the dyke too high to avoid too much water being allowed into the inner river;

At the turning point, cutting off the right angle to reduce the erosion on the river bank; where the river runs smoothly, scooping the river bed deeply, allowing water to concentrate in the middle of the river in order that the river will not flood the farm land;

Making the better of the circumstances and taking measures according to the local resources and conditions;

Li Bing's river-taming strategy involved forward-thinking idea as well as management regulation.

The most important management regulations are *Lun Guan* or Rotational Irrigation, and *Sui Xiu* or Annual Maintenance. *Lun Guan* guaranteed the benefit of every stakeholder and *Sui Xiu* ensured the annual maintenance and renovation of the project.

Historically, huge projects are numerous; however, only a few can be preserved. After 2270 years, the Dujiangyan Irrigation Project can still function as before, a wonderous miracle which is impossible without its consistent management regulations.

Li Bing was not only an irrigation specialist, but also a management guru. More than that, he was an ethologist, psychologist and even a performance master.

When, in surveying the Min River, Li Bing came to Tianpengque (an ancient place name) that nestled among two face-off mountains on the bank of the Min River, he said he seemed to see gods. To showcase the local people, a *Di* ethnic group, how he respected the local custom, he built three shrines and

肩头。”李冰当然不能见到江神并与之签订协议，但这种信誓旦旦，是很容易让人津津乐道的。

东汉应劭《风俗通义》，为现知最早记录李冰为蜀守者，里面有一段李冰与江神打斗的文字，煞是好看。

江神每年要娶两名童女为妻，李冰便把自己的女儿嫁给了他，并来到江神祠庙给女婿敬酒。不过江神是个敬酒不吃吃罚酒的家伙，杯子里的酒总是下不去，李冰大怒，变脸厉声训斥。突然，两人都消失不见，过了很久，冒出了两头牛在江边打架。

百姓在伏龙观里为李冰塑制了神像，以纪念他的功绩　（德）恩斯特 · 柏石曼 摄

People constructed a statue of Li Bing at Fulong Guan to commemorate his accomplishments. (Photographer: Ernst Boerschmann, GER)

killed three sacrifices (pig, sheep and cow). Besides, he dropped jade discs and *Yu Gui*s, or jade bars for ritual service into river to pay his tribute to the gods. The *Di* people, having inextricable linkage to the *Shu* people, believed that after persons died, their souls would pass through Tianpengque and reside at their native place far beyond the Minshan Mountains.

To exhibit to the *Shu* people, he ordered to carve five stone rhinoceros to be used to suppress those evil spirits that made waves. One of the stone rhinoceros was excavated after two thousand years in Chengdu when a construction job to erect a telecommunication building was being done to the north of Tianfu Square. 3.3 meters long, 1.7 meters high and 8.5 tons weight, with primitive cirrus-pattern engraved on where the fore limbs meet the torso, this stone rhino is preserved in The Chengdu Museum as the most prominent centerpiece.

Besides, he had three stone statues carved at Baishayou, a show performed for the Shu people. He made a covenant with the god of the river: Do what you desire to bring drought, but the water cannot be allowed to go below the arch of the stone statues; do what you desire to flood, but the water cannot be allowed to overpass the shoulders of the stone statues. It goes without saying such a covenant shall not be revealed to the public, but such a vow, solemn as it was, never failed to fascinate the local people to talk it again and again.

In his *Historical Romance on Customs* where Li Bing's position as county chief of Shu was first documented, Ying Shao, an author in the Eastern Han Dynasty, depicted a fighting between Li Bing and the river god, which is indeed intriguing.

It was said that the river god took two young girls as his wives every year. Li Bing married his daughter to the Devil and proposed a toast to his son-in-law at the river-god-temple. Rather than taking the toast,

一会儿，李冰满头大汗地跑回来，对下属说："这架打得激烈，你们要帮我的忙。南面那头牛是我，腰间还绑了根白带子。"于是，属官主簿通过方位和绶带辨别，刺杀了江神。

今日大可以把这段记载看作神话故事，但它更应该是李冰主持的一场祭祀、一场表演。郡守大人能够亲自下场演戏、与民同乐，还是非常够意思。百来年后，同为蜀郡守的文翁把这招学了去，也在江边跟江神打了一架。

总之，李郡守就靠着这些虚虚实实的表演以及实实在在的福利征服了老百姓。大堰岁修，农户们不仅得出力，还要自带口粮、自带工具。不过倒是干得心甘情愿、高高兴兴，谁叫大家都得到了好处呢？

the river god refused to drink it out so the spirit in his cup was not drunk to the bottom. Outraged and full of curses, Li Bing suddenly turned hostile. In two shakes, both of them disappeared. Only after a long while, two oxen were found at loggerhead on the river bank.

Before long, Li Bing ran back, forehead drenched with sweats, demanding his subordinates, "This fight is fierce. Come to my help. The ox standing on the south is me, with a white band tied on its loin." His adjutant, by differentiating the position and the band, killed the River Devil accordingly.

Nowadays, people might as well only view this record as a myth. Inasmuch as this, it should be seen, most probably, as a sacrifice or a play put on the stage masterminded and performed by Li Bing *per se* to amuse the common people so that they can mingle together happily. It was so inviting that, after hundreds of years, Wen Weng, also a county chief of Shu, learned this trick and fought with a river god as well.

By dint of these artificial performances and the down-to-earth benefits, Li Bing convinced the civilians. The annual maintenance required manpower, rations and tools; all were provided by the civilians themselves. Tough as the job was, people did it willingly and cheerfully. All got benefit, didn't they?

把岷江搬到成都来

下一步便是整理经络，疏通被堵住的动脉血管。

漫水归流，好处不仅仅是百姓脚下有了一块踏实的土地（《华阳国志》：民得陆处）。

岷江经都江堰工程鱼嘴分流，内江通过宝瓶口，化为蒲阳河、柏条

Introduce the Min River to Chengdu

His next move was to straighten out the river channels and to dredge the clogged "arterial vessels".

The benefit of bring the flood into line is not merely giving people a solid piece of land (*Records of the States South of Mount Hua:* people obtain land).

The Min River, bifurcates from the *Yu Zui* of the Dujiangyan Irrigation Project, with its inner river running through the *Baopingkou* and evolving into the Puyang River, the Baitiao River, the Xuyan River,

河、徐堰河、走马河、江安河五条河流，再向下分为干渠、支渠、斗渠、农渠、毛渠。时至今日，五级渠道总共近二千五百条，灌溉着川西坝子上七地市三十七县上千万亩良田。

河道带来的另一大便利是运输。单说一种特殊的运输——放排。

放排的特点在于，利用河道的流动性，以及起点与目的地的地势高差，自行运输，无需付出别的成本。木材不怕水浸泡，也不会沉于水，捆绑起来就是木筏。木筏入水后会自行漂流，除了雇用放排人，再没有别的运输费用。放排人固然栉风沐雨，甚至有生命危险，但好歹是一份职业，可以养家糊口。无数的原木便通过李冰时就建起的河道，从岷山上的原始森林来到成都的码头，再进入各细分市场。

作为一个规划专家，李冰是个天才。这样说只因为一点，他能够想出“把岷江搬到成都”来这样的创意。

the Zouma River and the Jiang'an River, further divided into the main canal, the branch canal, the later canal, field ditch and sublateral ditch. Up to this date, there are nearly 2,500 canals like these five-level categories in total, irrigating thousands of Mu of fertile farmlands covering seven cities and thirty-seven counties all over the Chuanxi Plain.

Another benefit brought by the river channel is transportation. *Fang Pai*, or timber conveyance by raft, a special means of transportation, is worth mentioning.

Fang Pai is characterized by taking advantage of the drop height between the point of commencement and point of arrival, utilizing mobility of the river and transporting on itself without generating extra costs. Timbers, bound into rafts, will not be soaked or sunk into water. Rafts will run its own course and incur no transporting expenses except for some labour costs. As a vocation, steering the raft sometimes associated with life-threatening risk, let alone suffering wind and rain; notwithstanding, it was a vocation that can support a family. Innumerable logs passed through the river channels already completed at Li Bing's time, traveled from the primeval forests on the Minshan Mountains to the Wharfs of Chengdu and then entered respective market segments.

Li Bing was a genius in terms of planning only because he can come up with the brainchild as "introducing the Min River to Chengdu".

都江堰放水节重现了砍倒杩槎，让岷江水奔流的场景　何勃 摄

The Dujiangyan Water Release Festival reenacts the scene of cutting down the Ma Cha to allow the Minjiang water to flow. (Photographer: He Bo)

成都人引以为自豪的锦江，其实是都江堰水利工程的副产品。曾经被视作灾害的水，李冰没有一排了事，而是把它变成了环绕成都的两条河——郫江和流江，即后来合称锦江的府河、南河。锦江来自岷江，在成都绕了一圈，又在下游归入岷江。

有了锦江，成都便大不一样了。

从微观角度来说，无数成都人能够回忆起幼年时在锦江里游泳、捞鱼的乐趣。

甚至饮用，也独爱锦江之水。成都地下水丰沛，井当然很多，但成都人认为井水含卤质重，最多只能煮饭烧菜，而饮茶这等讲究之事，万万不可。锦江水来自高山融雪，清澈甘洌，不必再经沙滤，实为泡茶上等用水。李劼人笔下，成都每条街上的茶铺，都在纱灯上用宋体字写着“河水香茶”，以招徕生意。

清末的成都城，生活着三十万人，有着近千的挑水夫。他们靠一根扁担赚取营生，码头阶梯下到河边，把木桶放入水中，荡开表面的落叶，再取出清亮的河水，送进家家户户的石水缸中。每一挑水收费二十个铜钱，水是免费的，挑水夫赚取的是劳力钱。

自汉代起，锦工便在江里濯锦，

The Jin River, which is the pride of the Chengduese, turns out to be the by-product of the Dujiangyan Irrigation Project. Rivers flowing through Chengdu, used to be banes for some people, were turned into two rivers by Li Bing—the Pi River and the Liu River—later called the Fuhe River and the Nanhe River. The Jin River starts from the Min River and finally empties into the Min River after circling all the way around Chengdu.

Chengdu is no longer the same having the Jin River.

From personal perspective, a number of Chengdueses could recall the zest of swimming and fishing in the Jin River in their childhood.

They even have preference in drinking water from the Jin River. Although Chengdu possesses abundant underground water, so do a variety of wells, they refuse to use well water to infuse tea because they suppose the halogen composes the significant parts of the well water, to be used only for cooking, not for activity such as tea-drinking that sets high demands on ingredients. Water drawn from the Jin River comes from melting snow of high mountains and tastes fresh and sweet. Unnecessary to be filtered, it is indeed first-class water to make tea. In Li Jieren's works, on every street of Chengdu, the tea house solicited its business by hanging a gauze lantern, written in Song font, “fragrant tea, river water”.

Chengdu was inhabited by around 300,000 people by the end of Qing Dynasty, thousands among whom were water-bearers, making their living by shoulder poles. Descending from the flight of Wharf stairs, they ran to and fro between different households and river banks: sinking wooden barrels into the river, brushing aside the falling leaves, scooping out the pellucid river water and delivering into the stone-water-tanks in thousands of households. Water was free and the charge, 20 copper coins per

据说这条江里洗涤出来的锦缎色泽特别鲜明，由此催生出蜀锦这样一个庞大的产业，和锦官这样的职位，以及成都“锦官城”的别称。

从宏观角度讲，成都原本并不通航，但自有了锦江这条人工河道，便突破了盆地四周高岸丘陵的包围，纳入了长江航运，与近两百万平方千米的长江流域有了广泛的政治、经济和文化沟通。

锦江通航，为沿江港口、集市的形成提供了先决条件。舟楫往来，客商如云。没有锦江，可能很难在唐代产生“扬一益二”这样的品牌美誉度。不妨再来回忆一遍马可·罗波《东方见闻录》里的那段话：“在这条江的两旁和邻近的地方有许多市镇与要塞。江中的船舶川流不息，运载着大批的商品，来往于这些城市。”

没有锦江，三国时诸葛亮送费祎出使吴国，便只能走陆路出川了。世人不会听到费祎的那一句“万里之行，今始于此”，长星桥也不会改名万里桥。世间会少了很多吟咏万里桥的诗句，课本里也不会有杜甫那句“门泊东吴万里船”。

李冰引岷江入成都，为什么会分成两条河？原因很多，但最重要的理由应当是：将一条河的风险由两条

barrel, was only for the labour costs.

Since the Han Dynasty, weavers had been rinsing fabrics in the Jin River. It was said that the brocades washed in this river presented with lustrous and bright colour. As a result of this, a large-scale industry spawned: *Shu Jin* or Brocade Made in Shu. Besides, *Jin Guan*, a job title granted for official in charge of brocade-spinning, ensued. The alias of Chengdu, *Jin Guan Cheng*, also owes its origin to this industry.

Seen from a broad view, Chengdu is not supposed to have the navigation channels. A man-made river route like the Jin River made it possible for the basin to push the envelope made by high mountains and hills encircled on its borders to be accepted into the Yangtze River waterways. Subsequently, the extensive political, economic and cultural connection to the Yangtze River valley which covers millions square meters can be established.

The Jin River's navigation creates prerequisite for the formation of the ports and markets along the river. As a results, business men flock to here and various ships come and go. Without the Jin River, it's hard to imagine that Chengdu garners such a "brand reputation"—"(All cities considered,) Yangzhou comes first and Yizhou (ancient name of Chengdu) the second". Let's revisit what Marco Polo wrote in his *The Travels of Marco Polo*: "on the two sides and in the vicinity of this river, there are many counties, cities and fortresses. Ships streams across the river, carrying a large number of merchandises and shuttles back and forth among those cities."

In the Three Kingdoms epoch, when Zhuge Liang saw off Fei Yi, the envoy to the State of Wu, they would choose land route instead river route if there weren't the Jin River. People would not remember Fei Yi's saying, "the thousands of miles' journey starts here" and the Changxing Bridge would not change its name into *the Wanli Bridge*

河分担，而把一条河的益处由两条河共享。

不知李冰有没有想到，锦江还可以具有军事防御功能？不过，不管他想到没有，他在千年后的同行，同为蜀地最高长官的高骈将此变为了现实。

(the Thousand-Mile-Bridge). Many famous poems chanted *for the Wanli Bridge* would no longer exist and the poet Du Fu's famous verse "moored in front of my house are the ships sailing for the East Wu" would vanish out of the text book.

Why did Li Bing separate the Min River into two when he diverted it into Chengdu? Among all possible reasons, this one stands out prominently: To spread the risk burdened by one river to two rivers and to share the benefit of one river also with two rivers.

Did he think of or not that the Jin River can be used in militarily defensive purpose? No matter, his counterpart in thousands of years later, Gao Pian, the highest ranking official in Shu, turned this idea into reality.

开新辟渠的节度使们

高骈的官职是唐代剑南西川节度使。

唐太宗贞观元年（627年），依山川形势将全国分为十道，形成以道统领州府、以州府统领县的三级行政格局。以成都为中心的剑南道即十道之一，所辖区域大致相当于今日嘉陵江以西的四川中部地区。统辖剑南道军民两政的官员为剑南节度使。安史之乱后，剑南节度使之职一分为二，所辖分别由剑南西川节度使和剑南东川节度使承担。从这两个称呼，大致也能推想其管领领域。

唐乾符元年（874年），同中书门下平章事、天平军节度使高骈紧

The ground-breaking military governors

Gao Pian's official position was the Jiannan/Xichuan Military Governor in Tang Dynasty.

In the first year of Zhenguan (reign name) of Emperor Taizong of Tang (627 AD), the whole country was divided, according to the location of the mountains and rivers, into ten *Dao*s (provinces), with the *Dao* governing the county and the county governing the prefecture, a three-level administrative structure. Jiannan Dao, with Chengdu as its center, was among the ten *Dao*s and its jurisdictions amounted proximately to the central region of today's Sichuan Province locating to the west of Jialingjiang River. Jiannan Military Governor was the officer presiding over the military and civil issues in the Jiannan Dao. After the *Anshi Rebellion*, its job demarcation was split into two parts—Jiannan/Xichuan Military Governor and Jiannan/Dongchuan Military Governor. People can roughly guess their jurisdictions according to what their names implied.

In the first year of Qianfu (reign name) of Tang

急调任成都尹、剑南西川节度使。之所以有此项任命，是因为南诏国再次进犯，而高骈曾在十年前同南诏打过交道，从其手中收复了安南都护府辖地。

南诏军队一路破黎州（汉源），入邛崃关，兵锋直指成都。百姓惊恐万分，俱躲入成都城内。几万户人挤在湫隘之地，缺少水源，又热又潮，痛苦不堪。高骈果真是声名远播，而他对此也是极为自信，一入剑门关就派人先至成都，打开城门，放百姓出城。

虽然凭声名就吓退了南诏大军，但高骈并不满足于此。他到任不满一个月，就点起精锐骑兵五千，在大渡河击败南诏，缴获铠甲马匹，俘虏并斩首其酋长多达五十人。

高骈武功显于外，于内其实是深谋远虑。自己能打，但未必所有的节度使都能打。太和三年（829年），南诏就曾攻入成都外城，而节度使杜元颖只能闭门死守内城。南诏兵大肆剽掠财宝、工匠、女人，并烧毁了外城。高骈明白，只有重建城防，才是万世之计。

核心工程是，抽调成都府所辖十县之民工，及剑南道所统八州之兵丁，在以前矮小狭窄的子城之外，重

Dynasty (874 AD), on an urgent order, Gao Pian, the Joint Staff of Affairs with the Secretariat-Chancellery as well as the Tianping Army Military Governor, was transferred to take the Jiannan/Xichuan Military Governor because the Nanzhao Kingdom made another invasion. Ten years ago, when the Nanzhao Kingdom made it first move, it was Gao Pian who set his face against it; furthermore, he regained those lost grounds that used to be under jurisdiction of Annan (ancient name of Vietnam) Protectorate.

Making it inroad into Tang's territory, the Nanzhao troops first conquered Li Zhou (Han Yuan) and then penetrated into the Qiong Lai Pass, their swords pointing directly to Chengdu. Terrified, ordinary people took refuge in the Chengdu city; thousands upon thousands of people jammed in this packing, hot and humid place short of water. What a miserable situation! Gao Pian was very confident with his well-known name. No sooner did his troop enter the Jianmen Pass than he dispatched his advance force to Chengdu to open the city gate and to let the populaces out.

His ambition didn't stop here although his fame alone scared off the Nanzhao troops. Less than one month after he assumed office, he ordered his elite cavalry, 5,000 in total, defeated the Nanzhao troops at the Daduhe River, capturing a number of armours and horses and decapitating their chiefs as much as 50.

He knew better than to believe military accomplishment alone can achieve the goal. Forward-thinking was the only key. Indeed, he was good at fighting, but that didn't mean other military governors can fight as excellently as he did. In the third year of Taihe (829 AD), the Nanzhao troops had already infringed on the outer city of Chengdu while the then military governor, Duyuanying, did nothing but to close the city gate and defended to the last. In the end, the Nanzhao troops plundered, pillaged and raped all

新建设墙体高大坚固的罗城。每天参与的民夫多达十万，费时三个月，共计九百六十万个工，耗钱一百五十万贯。新建成的罗城，周长四十三里，同以前周长八里的子城相比，已不可同日而语。更何况其墙高二丈六尺，墙厚一丈，垛高四尺，城墙上的瞭望台和廊屋多达五千六百零八间。

作为军事防御工程，城砖厚、城墙高、望楼多并非全部，古代大城还有一个标准配置——护城河。高骈建罗城，倒是有一个便利之处，即至少有南面的护城河是现成的——流江。李冰引两条河到成都，形成二江珥市。也许高骈觉得两条河都从城南流过，还是有些浪费水资源，于是让郫江在成都城的西北角改道，从城墙外的北面和东面流过，并在东南角与流江合流。新的郫江，固然要在城北、城东重新开掘河道，但挖的土正好填充于城墙的内、外墙之间，可谓一举两得。以前流江、郫江两条河在成都南门城墙外并行，如今城市扩展，郫江改道，那么郫江故道便成为城内的一条渠，因为缺少水源，也就慢慢湮没、填埋了。

有些城市的护城河是死水，而成都的则是具有通航、生态功能的活水。而且因为是河道，它比普通的护

the way in the outer city to the point of burning it up. To reconstruct the city defensive works, Gao Pian understood, was the lifetime solution.

The essence of his strategy was to draft labour forces from ten prefectures within the jurisdiction of Chengdu as well as soldiers from eight counties under the Jiannan Dao to reconstruct a high and solid outer city outside the small and short inner city. Every day, around 100,000 labour forces participated in the construction. After three months, with the total cost as high as 9.6 million *Guans* (ancient Chinese currency), a new outer city was completed; its perimeter was 43 Li,dwarfing the previous inner city (8 Li perimeter), let alone its 2.6 *Zhangs* height (ancient Chinese measure, 1 *Zhang* equals to 3 and 1/3 meters),its 1 *Zhang* depth, 4 feet high battlement and its watchtowers and porch houses up to 5,608.

As a defensive work, its features were more than thick bricks, high city walls and watchtowers. An ancient big city must have a moat to complete its standard configuration. In constructing the outer city, Gao Pian had a convenient advantage to avail—at least the moat on the south side was already there—the Liu Jiang River. The two rivers diverted by Li Bing to Chengdu forms two ear-rings. Perhaps Gao Pian thought it was a waste on water resources with both two rivers running through the south city. His idea was to change the Pi River courses from the northwest of Chengdu and to let it flow from the north and east and converge with the Liu River on the southeast of the city. To form a new Pi River, a new river route had to be dug at the north and east of the city. It would be killing two birds with one stone: the earth excavated can be used to fill the gap between the inner and outer city. Previously, the Pi River and the Liu River ran shoulder to shoulder outside the south gate of Chengdu. After the new route was created, the old river route turned out to be a ditch, landfilled and

城河要宽很多，从防御功能上讲，也要强很多。

如此，成都三面都有护城河了，唯剩西面防线。这个弱点，久经沙场的高骈自然想到了。于是顺着西城墙的边沿另开凿了一条西濠。濠者，护城之河也。名字一目了然，就是西边的护城河。

西濠北接郫江，南连流江，沟通两大河道。如此，流江、郫江加上西濠，又形成了一个闭环。补齐了阿喀琉斯踵的成都城，算得上是固若金汤了。

西濠故道上，今日流淌着两条河：北边饮马河，清代的八旗兵在此河中饮马，故得名；南河西郊河，俗称洗脚河。奇的是，两条河流向相反，饮马河向北，在五丁桥处注入府河（原郫江）；西郊河向南，在百花潭公园北面注入南河（流江）。

饮马河与西郊河有一个共同的上游，叫桃花江，又称笕槽河。笕槽，本指将竹筒一剖为二做成的小型引水槽，可以推断，早年成都人或在此河引水，用于灌溉或生活。

笕槽河流至马家花园处，一分为二，饮马河向北注入府河，西郊河向南汇入南河。而早年，整个西濠都是从北向南，由郫江分水到流江之中，

lost to oblivion given no more water pouring into.

Some city moats were dead water, but the one in Chengdu was running water, of navigational and ecological function. What's more, it was wider than regular moats as it was a river route. Defense-wise, it was much stronger.

Now Chengdu possessed three moats on three sides, with only the west side open to attack. This Achilles' heel was not a blind spot for a seasoned general like Gao Pian, but right in his crosshairs. Along the edge of west city, the *Xihao*, or the West Moat, was canalized. The name *Hao* spoke for itself.

Collecting the Pi River on the north and reaching out to the Liu River, the *Xihao* linked the two rivers. A close circus has thus taken shape and the Chengdu city, leaving nothing to chance, became impregnable.

On the old course of the Xihao, two rivers are still running today: the Yinmahe River (the Horse-watering River) on the north; the Eight-Banners-Soldiers in Qing Dynasty used to water their horses there, hence the name. The Xijiao River, commonly known as the Feet-washing River, lies on the south. Strangely enough, the flowing directions of the two rivers are just opposite——the Yinmahe River runs north, emptying itself into the Fuhe River (the previous Pi River) at the Wuding Bridge——the Xijiao River flows south, pouring into the Nanhe River (the Liujiang) at today's Hundred-flower-pool Park.

The two rivers have a common waterhead: the Taohua River, or the Jiancao River. Originally, Jiancao was a small-scale water channel made of split bamboos. It is inferred that at early times, the Chengduese used to bring water here to irrigate or to make a living.

At the Majia Garden, the Jiancao River divides into two where the Yinmahe River empties into the Fuhe River on the north and the Xijiao River pours

这也是由成都北高南低的地势决定的。饮马河为什么改变流向，袁庭栋在《成都街巷志》里推断，可能是由于饮马河泥沙淤积抬高河床所致。总之，如今的饮马河、西郊河水量都不大，跟当年的西濠不可同日而语。

古时要在成都当一个好官，必须懂水利。治水，在很大程度上就是成都几千年来最大的民生。水治理得好，多能成为一代名臣，甚或政治家。成都历代治水者，自古蜀开明以降，除了李冰建都江堰、文翁穿湔江、诸葛亮修九里堤，仅在唐代就有章仇兼琼筑硬堰、软堰，韦皋开解玉溪，白敏中开金水河，高骈改郫江道、凿西濠等。

章仇兼琼的官职也是剑南西川节度使。开元二十八年两败吐蕃，夺得安戎城（位于今红原县梭磨河谷）。他本来的官职为益州司马，因为上司不懂军事而得以上位。

章仇知兵，也懂得治水。

开元年间，他在成都城以北十八里的万岁池筑堤，引水灌田。在新津开通济堰，从南河（非成都城南的流江）与岷江汇合处引水向南，灌溉一千六百顷田，流过一百二十里后又在眉山汇入岷江。直到今天，通济堰

into the Nanhe River on the south. In early years, the whole the *Xihao* flew from the north to the south and separated at the Pi River before flowing to the Liu River, which was destined by Chengdu's terrain that it is high in the north and low in the south. Why did the Yinmahe River change it courses? Yuan Tingdong, in his *Chengdu History of Streets and Valleys*, inferred that the river bed of Yinmahe River was lifted because of sediment accumulation. Nowadays, the water flow of the two rivers is not enormous, hardly compared with that of the *Xihao* at its early years.

To be a qualified official in Chengdu, knowing how to tame the rivers was indispensable. For thousand years, river regulation has been the most important issue concerning people's well-being. Every Dynasty since Kaiming regime of ancient Shu witnessed skillful water regulators: Li Bing for his Dujiangyan Irrigation Project, Wen Weng for his boring the Qianjiang River, and Zhuge Liang for his repairing the Jiuli Dyke. Only in Tang Dynasty, there were Zhangchou Jianqiong building hard and soft weirs, Wei Gao canalizing the Jieyu Creek, or jade-cutting Creek, Bai Minzhong cutting the Jinhe River, and Gao Pian diverting the Pi River and boring the *Xihao*.

Zhangchou Jianqiong was also a Jiannan Military Governor. In 28 of Kaiyuan, he twice defeated Tubo regime (regime in ancient Tibet) and claimed Anrong City (locates at today's Suomo River Valley of Hongyuan Prefecture). He used to be a Chancellor of Wars, promoted because his supervisor knew little about military issues.

He knew not only how to command troops but also on how to regulate rivers.

During Kaiyuan era, he constructed a dyke at the Wansui Pool, 18 Li to the north of the Chengdu city, diverting water to irrigate the farmlands. Besides, he canalized the Tongji Weir at Xinjin, bringing water to the south from where the Nanhe River (not

仍在发挥作用。

章仇治水，深知因地制宜的道理。蜀州（今崇州、新津一带）因岷江宽阔平缓，便用粗木大石筑硬堰，以强力压制水势；而汉州（今德阳、广汉、什邡、绵竹一带）的绵远河、石亭江狭窄湍急，便不去跟它硬抗，而是以粗竹子编竹笼装小石子作堤，形成有缓冲作用的软堰。

到了北宋，以才识闻名的鲜于惟几在汉州当官时，把老家蜀州的那一套带过来，在沱江上筑硬堰，结果一夜之间木石被洪水冲得荡然无存。

《道德经》里描述水的特性，说“天下莫柔弱于水，而攻坚强者莫之能胜”。武将懂得的道理，而以识见称者未必懂。

唐代的蜀地治理者中，那些著名的剑南节度使们，都有一个共同特点，兼备两项特长：擅治水，能打仗。治论水，最具规模者，非高骈莫属；若论打仗，则无可与韦皋匹敌者。

剑南道与吐蕃、西南夷两个外番相接，韦皋对二者采取了不同的策略。早先吐蕃与西南夷通好，每入寇必以西南夷为先导。韦皋思忖，如果拿下西南夷就相当于斩断吐蕃的右

the Liu River on the south of Chengdu) and the Min River converge to irrigate 1,600 hectares farmland. Water from the Tongji Weir empties into the Min River at Mount Mei. Till today, the Tongji Weir is still functioning.

Zhangchou knew how to utilize the local resources and conditions. At Shuzhou (today's Chongzhou and Xinjin), to suppress the flow of water, he selected rough woods and boulders to build a hard weir, for at that stage, the Min River is wide and gentle. While at Hanzhou (today's Deyang, Guanghan, Shifang and Mianzhu), the Mianyuan River and the Shiting River are narrow and torrential, to meet them head-on is not desirable, but to build a soft weir made of bamboo-cage full of pebbles could provide a buffer against the river.

However, in Song Dynasty, Xianyu-weiji, who was known for his talents and insights, held a position in Hanzhou and applied mechanically what he practised when working at Shuzhou—building a hard weir on the Tuojiang River. It turned out that the weir was flushed out thoroughly overnight.

In depicting the character of water, *Tao Te Ching* maintains,“the weakest object in world is water; however, even those who can assault the strongest are not able to triumph over water.”

The well-known Jiannan Military Governors who regulated water in Shu territory shared a common characteristic: they were both skillful in battle and in taming water. Speaking of the most accomplished one in water-taming, Gao Pian was second to none, while in battlefield, Wei Gao was nonpareil.

The Jiannan Dao bordered on Tubo and Southwestern Barbarians, both vassal states of Tang. Wei Gao assumed different strategies toward them. Tubo used to be friendly with Southwestern Barbarians and whenever they launched an invasion, Southwestern Barbarians acted as the spearhead.

臂，于是暗中交好。

贞元五年，韦皋与西南夷中的东蛮部联手破吐蕃于台登（今冕宁、喜德一带），杀悍将、青海大酋乞臧遮遮，败退的吐蕃酋长们一路哭着逃回。

翻开史籍，凡有韦皋处，几乎就是他的战功簿。

贞元八年，与吐蕃战于维州，胜。

十年，再败吐蕃，克峨和城（茂县）。

十三年，收复巂州（西昌）。

十六年七月，克吐蕃末恭城（汶川）；八月克颙城。

十七年，与吐蕃战于鹿危山（理县东北），胜。

韦皋治蜀二十一年，与吐蕃多次交战，屡战屡胜。共擒杀各级将领一千五百余人，斩首兵士五万余，缴获牛羊二十五万头、兵械六百三十万件。

千万不要以为吐蕃是软柿子，大唐与吐蕃两百年间几乎都是拉锯战，后者甚至于763年攻破过长安城。韦皋战吐蕃不败，只是因为他个人能打——《新唐书》评价贞元八年吐蕃入寇的战事时说："当是时，韦皋功最多，破堡壁五十余所。"

It dawned on Wei Gao that to forge alliance with Southwestern Barbarians was tantamount to mutilating the right arm of Tubo. Toward this end, he, under the table, reconciliated with Southwestern Barbarians.

In the 5th year of Zhenyuan (reign name), Wei Gao combined Dongman tribe of Southwestern Barbarians to defeat Tubo utterly at Taideng (today's Mianning and Xide), killing its ferocious general—Qizangzhezhe, the great chief. The desperate Tubo chiefs cried and shouted all the way in retreat.

Wei Gao's battle achievements were everywhere whenever his name was mentioned in history books.

In the eighth year of Zhenyuan, he defeated Tubo at Weizhou.

In the tenth year of Zhenyuan, defeated Tubo again, taking Ehe City (Mao Prefecture).

In the thirteenth year of Zhenyuan, he recaptured Xizhou (Xichang).

In July of the sixteenth year of Zhenyuan, he overcame Mogong city of Tubo (Wenchuan); In August of the same year, he captured Yongcheng.

In the seventeenth year of Zhenyuan, he defeated Tubo at Luwei Mountain (northeast of Li Prefecture).

In the twenty-one years under Wei Gao's administration in Shu, he battled with Tubo many times and won every time. In total, he captured and killed 1500 generals in different levels, decapitated over 50,000 soldiers and captured over 250,000 herds and flocks as well as 6.3 million weaponries.

Don't be misled into believe that Tubo was a pushover. Over 200 years in Tang Dynasty, all its wars with Tubo were tug of war, and the latter even broke into the capital city, Chang'an in 763. Wei Gao's indefatigable records were attributed to his personal capabilities. According to the review on the war with Tubo in the eighth year of Zhenyuan documented in *the New Book of Tang*, "at that time, Wei Gao's achievements

韦皋喜欢结交读书人，有婚丧嫁娶皆重金资助，其幕府中即有“大历十才子”之一的司空曙等人。他还时常推荐一些有才学的读书人去做官，如表段文昌为校书郎，孙从为西山运务使，房式为云南安抚使、蜀州刺史等。

韦皋对百姓极好，每三年就免除一次各州租赋。而蜀人也报之以爱戴。韦皋去世之后，百姓见其遗像，必定下拜，石头上面有“皋”字也会铲除掉，以示避讳。

开解玉溪，则是韦皋为成都市政建设做的一件大好事。

解玉溪之所以得名，是因为河道中出产的沙子，可以解玉，即分割玉石。沙能解玉，是因为它的硬度比玉石高。古人分解玉石，主要工具是麻绳。但仅仅靠绳子不可能将玉石分开，因此要在锯玉时再加一些坚硬的沙子，同时加水以降温并增加沙子的附着度。其中，粗沙用于切割，细沙则纹饰打磨，所谓的“如切如磋，如琢如磨”。

解玉溪之水，来自成都城西北角的郫江。穿城之后，解玉溪在东南方向汇入郫江。从西北流向东南，是因为成都西北高、东南低的地势；而出于郫江，又归于郫江，唯一的原因是

were prominent. He broke through over 50 fortresses."

Wei Gao liked associating with scholars. Whoever these people engaged in ceremonies such as weddings and funerals, he generously assisted them with cash. Among his staffs, there included Sima-Shu, one of the "ten greatest talents in Dali period". From time to time, he recommended talented people for official posts: Duanwenchang as the Proof-reading Officer, Sun Congwei as the Xishan Transportation Representative, Fang Shi as the the Yunnan Pacification Officer and Shuzhou Inspector.

He was very kind to the common people and exempted them, once in every three years, from rents and taxes. In return for his kindness, the Shu people revered him by kowtowing to his portrait after he died. Wherever his given name was mentioned on steles, it was chiselled off as a naming taboo. (A naming taboo is a Chinese cultural taboo against calling out the given names of ruling emperors, former emperors of the ongoing Dynasty, one's own ancestors, or other exalted people.)

Canalizing the Jieyu Creek was a project that benefited the urban construction of Chengdu.

The name "Jieyu (Jade-cutting) Creek" comes from a legend that the sands in this river are hard enough to cut the jade. In ancient times, people used to use the hemp rope to cut the jade. But the hemp rope alone cannot have the jade cut off; hence, sands shall be added when sawing the jade, accompanied by watering to reduce the temperature and increasing the adhesion of sands. In this process, the rough sands were to be used to cut and fine ones were to be used to emblazon and polish so that this craftsmanship is called "cutting and grinding; carving and polishing".

The Jieyu Creek rises from the Pi River to the northwest of Chengdu. After running through the city, it empties into the Pi River again to the southeast. Flowing from the northwest to the southeast is

解决城内新兴区域的用水。这个新兴区域就是大慈寺。

大慈寺规建于757年，而韦皋于785年就任西川节度使，二三十年的时间，香火带来流量，流量造就繁荣。有上万和尚的大慈寺，也是各类集市汇聚地的大慈寺片区，的确是需要这样一条河来运送物资，并提供生活用水。

推测的解玉溪流向，起初与郫江北段大致平行，穿流于城北，到了今桂王桥南街一带，遽然折向南，并在镋钯街以南一线折向东，与大慈寺南沿并行。流向的变化，也能为解玉溪的功用作一个佐证。

解玉溪后来湮没无闻，典籍中绝少记载，估计跟佛教和大慈寺的荣辱起伏有些关系。

除了在成都治水，韦皋跟他的前任章仇兼琼还共有一件留传至今的大功德，那就是乐山大佛的开凿。唐开元（713—741年）初，和尚海通因慈悲而立志，要把整座凌云山凿为弥勒佛，既传佛法且填河谷除水害。海通有生之年，募款制作出了佛头及面容。海通法师去世之后四十年，章仇兼琼出任剑南西川节度使，他捐出俸禄二十万两银，使大佛得以向下雕刻至膝盖部分。贞元元年（785年），韦

decided by the terrain of this city, which was mentioned earlier in this article. The sole reason that the river is out of the Pi River and into it again lies in the fact that the drinking water issue facing a new district. This new district was the Daci Temple.

The construction of the Daci Temple was completed in 757 and Wei Gao assumed the Xichuan Military Governor in 785. In these years, people swarmed into this area to worship josses, making this area so prosperous that over thousands upon thousands of monks living here and a variety of markets flocking together, which called for a river to bring goods in and out and to provide drinking water.

We can infer the flowing direction of the Jieyu Creek: at the early stage, it parallels with the northern passage of the Pi River, then shuttled through the northern city to arrive at the area of today's South Guiwangqiao Street. In a sharp turn to the south, it zigzags to the east at the area of today's South Tangpa Street, and runs head-to-head along the south of the Daci Temple. The change of its direction is an example for its function.

The Jieyu Creek was consigned to oblivion and was seldom mentioned in books and records. Perhaps, its ups and downs were somewhat related to the fate of the Buddhism and the Daci Temple.

Saving for his river regulation in Chengdu, Wei Gao and his predecessor Zhangchou shared another great accomplishment that reverberates even today—the carving of Leshan Grand Buddha. At the early year of Kaiyuan (reign name, 713-741) of Tang Dynasty, a monk named Hai Tong set up his mind, out of compassion, to build a Buddha figure by carving the whole Linyun Mountain into a statue in the hope that Buddhism could be further promoted and the valley there could be filled to exterminate the bane of the river. He devoted his remaining years in fund-raising and completed a part of his job: the

皋治四川时，再捐俸银五十万两，又历时十九年方成。韦皋也因此成为乐山大佛的集大成者。

韦皋凿解玉溪六十年之后，又有了白敏中开金水河之举。

白敏中是白居易的堂弟，兄弟关系很好，少年时就是在年长二十岁的白居易训导之下成长的。唐武宗早就听说过白居易的大名，一登基就想征用他。宰相李德裕说，白居易年老多病，堂弟敏中的辞章才艺跟其相似，不妨试一下。这样，白敏中得以留在皇帝身边，入翰林、任学士，开启了五年十三升迁的开挂之路。

不过，白敏中后来在“牛李党争”中同令狐绹结盟，跟有知遇之恩的李德裕关系并不好。李被贬，他使劲下烂药。在宰相任上，李党一律不用，被李贬过的统统重用。因此，李德裕评价他：“惟以怨报德为不可测。”白敏中死后谥号为丑，典型的恶评，或与此类党争有关。

其实，白敏中在政治上非常有作为。卢求在《成都记序》里说，蜀人性子刚直，只能感化，不能凭借智力优势玩弄其于股掌之中。而白敏中治蜀五年，赏罚有度，颇有刘邦“约法三章”之风，蜀人多称颂之；府库充盈，财政上的余额多达三百万缗，其

engraving of the head and face of Buddha statue. Forty years after his death, Zhangchou Jianqiong became the Jiannan/Xichuan Military Governor and he donated 200,000 *Liang* (Chinese weight) silver ingots out of his own pocket so that the progress was able to be extended to the knee of Buddha figure. In the first year of Zhenyuan(reign name), Wei Gao, who then governed in Shu, donated his part: 500,000 *Liang* silver ingots. Another 19 years later, this project finally accomplished. We Gao thus became the synthesizer of Leshan Grand Buddha.

Sixty years after the canalization of the Jieyu Creek, Bai Minzhong realized another feat: cutting the Jinhe River.

Bai Minzhong was a cousin of Bai Juyi (a famous Chinese poet). They were on good terms. Bai Minzhong grew up under the tutelage of Bai Juyi who was 20 years his senior. Emperor Wuzong of Tang Dynasty heard the name of Bai Juyi so early that no sooner did he ascend the throne than he summoned Bai Juyi. According to the Chancellor Li Deyu, Bai Juyi was senile and susceptible to diseases, and his cousin, Bai Minzhong was on a par with him as regards knowledge and talents; hence, it was worth a try. As such, Bai Minzhong could stay at the side of the emperor, enrolling in Hanlin Academy (an organization in the central court with scholars who did drafting and editing works for the emperor) to become a secretariat.

However, in the “Factional Struggles between Niu and Li (Deyu) Parties”, Bai Minzhong made an alliance with Linghu Tao, a rival of Li Deyu. Rather than returning the favour Li Deyu showed to him, Bai Minzhong became his political enemy. When Li Deyu was banished, Bai Minzhong added more insults to the injury. In his incumbency, he abandoned all officials serving for Li’s party and reinstated all those discarded by Li. “The only thing unpredicted is

时一缗为一千文，三百万是一笔巨额财富。

开金水河，是白敏中任剑南西川节度使之时，在蜀德政之一。

金水河后称金河，它源于郫江，贯穿东西。

金河穿流于成都城南部，与未折向之前的解玉溪一南一北，大致平行。从这两条河流的分布，可以看出其功用，一在城北，一在城南，分别向流经区域提供水源：饮用、溉园、洗涤、防火。

如此，在成都城墙内外的范畴里，从北到南，郫江、解玉溪、金河、流江四河并行。而在解玉溪消失之后，金河则独自承担着城内供水的功能。

高骈改郫江道、建西濠之后，金河即改为从西濠引水，大致在今日西胜街西口与下同仁路的交会处进入城内。此处的城墙还特意开了一道口，供金河进入。这道只进水，不进人的城门，叫作水西门。

说“只进水，不进人”，其实有个时间限制，仅仅是指康熙五十七年至清王朝覆灭的这一百九十年里。

金河进入满城后，流经将军衙门南侧，再在满城东垣半边桥流出满城。半边桥下的水道上，同样设有铁

to pay back one's gratitude by ingratitude", Li Deyu commented afterward. Bai Minzhong's posthumous name was "Ugly", a typical odium, which could be associated with his role in such partisan contentions.

Inasmuch as this, Bai Minzhong was a high achiever in politics. In his *Foreword on the Record of Chengdu*, Lu Qiu pointed out the Shu people as a whole were straightforward in character; only by education and persuasion could they be influenced and twisting them around one's finger didn't work at all. In the 5 years of Bai Minzhong's reign in Shu, his reward and punishment were proportionate, much alike the "agreement on three chapters of law" (presented by Liu Bang, the first emperor of Western Han Dynasty when he started his rule), for which he took his credit. Besides, during his reign, the fiscal income of the government was abundant, with a surplus as much as 3 million *Min* (one *Min* equals to 1,000 *Wen* or 1 *Liang* silver ingot), a huge fortune.

To open up the Jinshui River was one of his benevolent governances when he held the Jiannan/Xichuan military governor.

The Jinshui River, aka the Jin River, rises from the Pi River and transverses east and west.

The Jin River flows along the south of Chengdu city and roughly parallels with the Jieyu Creek before its turning to the south. The function of the two river lies in their distribution: one in the north and the other in the south, providing water for drinking, irrigation, washing, and fire-proofing to the areas on their way.

In and out of the Chengdu city, from the north to the south, accordingly, there were four rivers running concurrently: the Pi River, the Jieyu Creek, the Jin River and the Liu River. After the disappearance of the Jieyu Creek, the Jin River alone holds the responsibility of providing water to the city.

After Gao Pian changed the courses of the Pi River and bored the Xihao, the Jin River drew its

栅栏，前文已述。因此，在清代金河上的通航是分段的，满城内为一段，半边桥到汇入郫江处为另一段。

金河流出满城后，流经明皇城旧址——那一段河流上横跨有三座三孔石桥，因此被称作“三桥九洞石狮子”——大致在镋钯街南面一带汇入解玉溪，随即出城墙东垣，在今东门大桥处归入郫江。此处所言满城、明皇城旧址，是就明清时期的历史视角而言，而那时解玉溪已经消亡。

金河通航，明确记载始于清雍正九年（1731年）的疏淘之后。从满城东垣半边桥到大城东门水关，航线是双向的，成都城所需的柴米油盐酱醋茶，都由小船逆流而上运送进城。

到了清末，因水量减少而停航，民国年间则渐至淤塞。

秦华祥先生幼年时就居住在金河边，那是20世纪50年代。他见到的金河，流经拱背桥后汇入府河，“就在二十二中背后”。桥当然早就不在了，二十二中也改为礼仪职业中学。而如今的礼仪职中，北面是镋钯街，南面正是一条叫作拱背桥街的小巷子，再往东三百来米则是大致呈南北走向的府河——这跟前文所叙述，金

water from the *Xihao* instead. Approximately, the river from the Jin River entered the city at where today's West Xisheng Street and Lower Tongren Road intersect. A water passage was specially left for the river, not for the people to enter. Consequently, it is called Shuixi Gate (West Gate for water).

The so-called "water only", as a matter of fact, only referred to the period from the 57th year of Kangxi (reign name) to the end of the Qing Dynasty, 190 years in total.

After entering the Manchu City, the Jin River ran through the south of the Jiangjunyamen (the General's Office) and flew out of the Manchu City to its east at the Banbian Bridge. The iron fence, which was mentioned earlier, could also be witnessed here. In Qing Dynasty, the navigation on the Jin River was divided into different passages, the one in the Manchu city was one and the one from the Banbian Bridge to the Pi River was another.

After flowing out of the Manchu City, the Jin River bypassed the former site of the Imperial City of Ming Dynasty where three "Three-Hole" stone bridges straddled, also known as "Three-Bridge-Nine-Hole-Stone-Lion". At South Tangpa Street, the Jin River merged into the Jieyu Creek and flew out the east gate of the city and allowed itself into the Pi River at today's East City Bridge. Here, the Manchu city and the former site of Imperial City of Ming Dynasty were seen from the perspective of Ming and Qing Dynasty when at that time, the Jieyu Creek was no longer there.

Navigation on the Jin River was definitely recorded in the ninth year of Yongzheng (reign year, 1731) of Qing Dynasty, after dredging. The navigation route, starting from the Banbian Bridge in the east of the Manchu city to the *Shuiguan* (Water-Pass-Way) in the east Chengdu city, was a two-way traffic. Wherewithal such as firewood, rice, oil, salt, soy sauce, vinegar and tea were transported upstream into the Chengdu city.

河于锐钯街以南一线汇入解玉溪，再归流郫江，正相符合。

金河存在的历史比解玉溪长很多，生于853年，亡于1971年。究其原因，大致是因为人口繁衍，城市无序扩张，而与河道争地。于是有些河段填埋了，有些则加了拱形顶盖改成了防空洞。总之，金河几经废兴，河中水在流淌了一千一百一十八年之后，终于彻底断流，仅仅在今人民公园内正门拱桥下留下一小段不能流动的水体——金河故道，以及“金河路”“金河宾馆”两个带有往事记忆的名称。

成都城里人工开凿的著名河流，还有御河，即明皇城北垣的护城河。御河跟金河的命运差不多，也于1970年12月加上了拱形顶盖，变成了防空洞。

To the end of Qing Dynasty, navigation came to an end on account of reduced river flow. During the Republic of China era, it was silted up.

It was in 1950s that Mr. Qin Huaxiang spent his childhood along the Jin River. The Jin River he saw, running from the Gongbei Bridge before charging into the Fuhe River, “was at the back of No. 22 Middle School”. Sure enough, the bridge was no longer there and the name of No.22 Middle School was changed into Protocol Vocational Middle School, to the north of which there is Tangpa Street, and to the south there is an alley called Gongbei Bridge Street; three hundred meters further to the east, the Fuhe River, flowing roughly from the south to the north, can be seen. This is corresponded to what narrated before: At South Tangpa Street, the Jin River merged into the Jieyu Creek and allowed itself into the Pi River.

The Jin River had a longer history (853-1971) than that of the Jieyu Creek. Overpopulation and urban sprawl resulted in land grubbing. Consequently, some river routes were filled up and some were morphed into air-raid shelters with vaulted ceiling. As a rule, after running for 1118 years, experiencing ups and downs, the Jin River was utterly shut off, leaving a small pool of stagnant water body under the arched decorating bridge at the front gate of People’s Park: the Jin River remnant. Only The Jin River Hotel and Jin River Street in the vicinity remind people of its past.

In the city of Chengdu, there was another man-made canal, the Yuhe River, a moat located at the north of the Imperial City of Ming Dynasty. The Yuhe River shared the similar fate with the Jin River. Covered by vaulted ceiling, this river was transformed into an air-raid shelter in Dec of 1970.

锦江上的老码头

李冰开辟郫江和检江，成都始成

Old Wharf over the Jin River

It’s only half right to say with the Pi and the

为港埠，这句话既对也不对。

说不对，是因为除了郫江和检江之外，成都其实还有一条沱江，沱江虽然时常为涝，但它通航之时，世间尚无郫、检二江；说对，是因为成都这个概念，在很长时期仅仅指那道城墙之内的城市——就此而言，倒的确是在李冰开堰之后才通航的。

李冰“将岷江搬到成都”之后，通航带来了巨大改变。有通航，就有人员流动和物质集散，就有码头和集市，再于人口密集处筑城设县，沿着岷江内江、外江新产生的城镇则星罗棋布于成都平原——其历史可以上溯至唐宋甚至秦汉——而秦灭蜀时，整个川西坝子上只筑有成都、郫、临邛三座城市。

还在秦代，即有放排，将岷山的竹木材漂运至成都。到了汉代，锦官城和车官城两大产业功能区都靠着检江而建，显然是为了利用水道带来的交通便利。

秦汉始而至唐宋元明清，成都两江航运都十分发达，成都平原形成了三大港区：成都港、新津港和金堂港。

单说成都港，到了清代末年，又分为三大码头区——北门府河码头区、东门府河码头区、南门南河码头

Jian River opened up by Li Bing, Chengdu has become a port city.

It is not entirely right because without adding the Tuojiang River, another river possessed by Chengdu, on top of the Pi and the Jian River, the river system in Chengdu is incomplete. The Tuojiang River usually incurs floodings. When it was rendered navigable, the Pi and Jian River were not yet born. It is partly right because the concept of “Chengdu”, for quite a long time, only referred to the city inside the city wall—for that matter, the navigation in Chengdu indeed started after Li Bing’s water conservancy project.

Navigation brought sea change for Chengdu after Li Bing “removing the Min River here” and made possible the mobility of population and material. For these reasons. Wharfs and market places ensued. Cities and counties emerged among the populated areas. Newly constructed cities, along the inner and outer of the Min River, dotted around the Chengdu plain whose long history can be stretched back to Tang and Song and even Qin and Han Dynasty—when Qin annihilated Shu, there were only three cities on the Chuanxi Plain: Chengdu, Pi and Linqiong.

As early as Qin Dynasty, *Fangpai*, or rafting, started. Timbers cut from Minshan Mountain floated by rafting to Chengdu. Until Han Dynasty, the construction of *Jin Guan Cheng* and *Che Guan Cheng* (military industry zone)—two major industrial zones built along the Jian River—was to utilize the transportation benefits of the river system.

From the Qin and Han dynasties to Tang, Song, Yuan, Ming and Qing dynasties, shipping industry on the above mentioned two rivers had been so prosperous that three big harbour zones emerged: Port of Chengdu, Port of Xinjin and Port of Jintang.

In Chengdu alone, till the end of Qing Dynasty,

区，而每一码头区又包括众多小码头或作业区。

北门府河码头区，位于今西北桥至北门大桥两岸，在成都港的三大码头区中，最靠近内江的来处——都江堰。近水楼台，北门码头区因此理所应当地接纳了漂流自岷山山区的木筏——毕竟，木筏在航道中会阻碍其他船只的航行，需要首先清理以腾出航道。

木筏有两种功用，首先是货物本身；其次也是运输工具，上面还载有其他货物。木筏到了北门码头，进行的第一步作业是起货，将上面的货物卸载上岸。

第二步是拆筏，将已经到达目的地的木筏拆散，变回木材，转运至专事销售的木行。木行多分布于不远处的上河坝，这也符合市场选点接近原材料产地的原则。同样符合此原则的，还有“木综厂”，建于1954年的四川省成都木材综合加工厂。该厂曾拥有五千余名职工，是西南最大的木材加工企业。

第三步是放筏。北门码头并未能消化掉所有的木筏，剩下的仍将顺河东流，到达东门和南门码头。

之所以被称为码头区，是因为码头一个接着一个，如大码头、二码

there were three Wharfs: Fuhe Wharf in the north and east (North and East Wharf), Nanhe Wharf in the south (South Wharf). Within each Wharf, there were number of wharfs or operation terminals.

The North Wharf located at the areas along today's Xibei Bridge to the North Gate Bridge. Among the three Wharfs, this one was the nearest to the Dujiangyan Irrigation Project, the source of the inner river. By dint of its favourable position, the North Wharf took the lead in taking the rafts floating down from the Minshan mountainous region - after all, rafts would obstruct other vessels in the channel and needed to be cleared first to free up the channel.

The raft served two purposes, firstly as the cargo itself, and secondly as a means of transportation, carrying other goods on board. When the rafts came to the North Wharf, the first assignment was to unload the goods ashore.

The second step was the dismantling of rafts, whereby rafts that had reached their destination were dismantled, turned back into timber and transported to the wood companies for sale. Most of the wood companies were located not far from Shangheba, the upper river dam, which was in line with the principle that the market should be located close to the origin of the raw materials. Also in line with this principle, there was the Chengdu Wood Comprehensive Processing Plant, built in 1954 in Chengdu, Sichuan Province. With more than 5,000 employees, it was the largest timber processing enterprise in Southwest China.

The third step was to release the rafts. The remaining rafts which were not absorbed in the North Wharf would flow east to East and South Wharf.

The Wharf zone was so named because there were rows upon rows of Wharfs, such as the Big Wharf, the Second Wharf, the Lichang Wharf, etc. In addition, warehouses and inns were pervasive, all

头、利昌码头等。此外，货栈、客栈鳞次栉比，皆为码头衍生。

东门府河码头，起自东门大桥，经两江交汇处的南河口，至石牛堰止。清末至民国年间，东门码头主要承接三项大宗货物：盐、柴、煤炭。

府河左岸，自东门大桥至南河口，为柴码头。

南河口至九眼桥，为盐码头。

其中的南河口，因为是府河与南河的交会处，而繁忙异常。

当然，此码头不只是起卸货物，也运送客人，望江楼码头就是重要的客人上下处。《成都通览》里讲述了清末招徕客人时的一个场景。船主大声喊叫："快上船，上来就开。"等到客人上来，却又去招呼新客，一早上船，常常要等到中午，甚至是第二天——跟20世纪90年代时中巴车揽客极为相似。

望江楼码一直存续到1970年代才被拆除，是成都中心城区最后的锦江码头。

南门码头区，位于南门大桥（万里桥）两岸，规模小于东门和北门码头，主要起卸粮食、煤炭等。

在前蒸汽机时代，同陆路相比，航运是具有相当大的优势的。有研究人员计算过：清代前期，就运输成本

derived from the Wharfs.

The East Wharf started from the Dongmen Bridge, passing through the Nanhe estuary at the confluence of two rivers, and ended at Shiniuyan. Between the late Qing Dynasty and the Republic of China, three bulk cargos constituted the majority of East Wharf's workloads: salt, firewood and coal.

The east bank of the Fuhe River, from the Dongmen Bridge to estuary of the Nanhe River, located the Firewood Wharf.

From the estuary of the Nanhe River to the Nine-Eye-Bridge was the Salt Wharf.

The estuary of the Nahe River, marking the confluence of the Fuhe and Nanhe River, was exceptionally busy.

It goes without saying that the Wharfs served the purpose not only for loading and unloading goods, but also for ferrying guests; *Wangjianglou Wharf* (River view gazebo Wharf) was such an important station for guests to get on and off. In *Chengdu Overview*, the following scene at the end era of Qing Dynasty was recounted: a boat owner shouted: "Come on board quickly. It's about to set out." When the guests came on board, the owner, however, went on to solicit other guests. If you came early in the morning, the chances were you might wait till noon, even the second day before the boat would depart. This scenario was very much similar to the minibus drivers drumming up business in the 1990s.

Wangjianglou Wharf survived until the end of 1970s when it was dismantled, and was the last Jinjiang Wharf in the center of Chengdu.

The South Wharf, located on both sides of the Nanmen Bridge (*the Wanli Bridge* or the Thousands-Mile-Bridge), was smaller than those in the East and the North, and mainly handled cargos like grain and coal.

In the pre-steam engine era, shipping had

而言，陆路超过水运的百分之八十，这也是大宗货物往往走水路的主要原因。无数的货物在成都集中上船，在宜宾汇入长江主流，转销至长江中下游各地，甚至国外；在相反的方向上，也有无数地区的货物来到成都卸载——所谓“填不满的成都府”。

1950年代初，是成都水运最为繁荣的时节，当时大成都范围内的通航里程上千千米。至1953年起，通航里程和航运能力逐渐减弱。到了1984年，全成都的货运周转量仅相当于1952年的八分之一。这个数据表明，运送相同重量的货物，其运输距离大幅缩短。

船运衰退，除了时代更替，陆上交通高度发达之外，还因为岷山山区——成都水系源头——的原始森林在一个时间段被大量砍伐，水土流失致水量减少；另外，筑坝拦水也是航道中断的重要原因。

如今的锦江上，已经见不到舟楫如云、迎来送往的景象。附着于其上的民风民俗，也风流云散于时代的江水之中。

considerable advantages over land transportation. Some researchers have calculated that in the early Qing Dynasty, in terms of transportation costs, land transportation exceeded water transportation by 80%, which is the main reason why large quantities of goods tend to go by water. Countless goods were put together in Chengdu for shipping. At Yibin, they merged into the mainstream of the Yangtze River before being distributed to the middle and lower reaches of Yangtze River, and even to overseas. In the opposite direction, innumerable goods from various areas were brought to Chengdu for unloading. No wonder “Chengdu shall never be up to ears”.

At the early 1950s, shipping in Chengdu was at its heydays and the shipping mileage was at thousand kilometers’ level within the big Chengdu area. From 1953 onwards, both shipping mileage and capacity gradually dwindled. By 1984, the total freight turnover was only 1/8 of what it was in 1952. This figure indicated that to transport the same weight of goods, the distance was significantly curtailed.

The decline of shipping industry, aside from the vicissitude of times, such as the advancement of land transportation, can also be ascribed to water and soil loss. At some time, the primeval forests in Minshan Mountain, the water source of Chengdu’s water system, were subject to largescale and uncontrolled chopping down. Other than that, the construction of dams to block waterflow was also an important reason for the waterway navigation.

At today’s Jin River, sailing boats coming and going are no longer to be seen. Customs attached to those rivers and ships are also carried away with wind and cloud and thrown into the rivers in our time.